VIETNAM

JOSHUA ZUKAS

www.bradtguides.com

Bradt Guides Ltd, UK
The Globe Pequot Press Inc, USA

Bradt GUIDES
TRAVEL TAKEN SERIOUSLY

Cao Bằng: With mountains that nurtured a world-shaking revolution, this province contains multitudes, including the magnum opus of Vietnam's waterfalls
page 178
Hanoi: Vietnam's magnetic capital exudes a cluttered charisma, with absorbing museums and epochal landmarks that contextualise the country
page 80
Đà Nẵng and Hội An: Twin settlements that are chalk and cheese, Đà Nẵng's skyscrapers reflect a shimmering sea while Hội An safeguards centuries-old houses
pages 227 and 299
Phong Nha: This karst-encircled riverside town is the gateway to the biggest caves – and most wide-ranging caving experiences – on the planet
page 235
Huế: Flaunting Southeast Asia's grandest walled fortress, this scandalously overlooked monarchical city harbours the gaudy palaces and weatherworn tombs of a doomed dynasty
page 244
Bradt
N
0 100km
0 100 miles
CHINA
MYANMAR
LAOS
Hainan
East Sea
Hoàng Sa (Paracel Islands)
Cao Bằng
Hà Giang
Lào Cai border crossing
Lào Cai
Hữu Nghị border crossing
Lạng Sơn
Móng Cái border crossing
Thái Nguyên
Fansipan 3,143m
Red
Yên Bái
The Northwest
Hạ Long
The Northeast
HANOI
Hải Phòng
Sơn La
Điện Biên Phủ
Tây Trang border crossing
Hòa Bình
Nam Định
Cúc Phương National Park
Ninh Bình
The Red River Delta
Nậm Cắn border crossing
Vinh
Pù Mát National Park
The Northern Central Coast
Phong Nha
Đồng Hới
Mekong
DMZ
Lao Bảo border crossing
Huế
Bạch Mã National Park
Đà Nẵng
Hội An

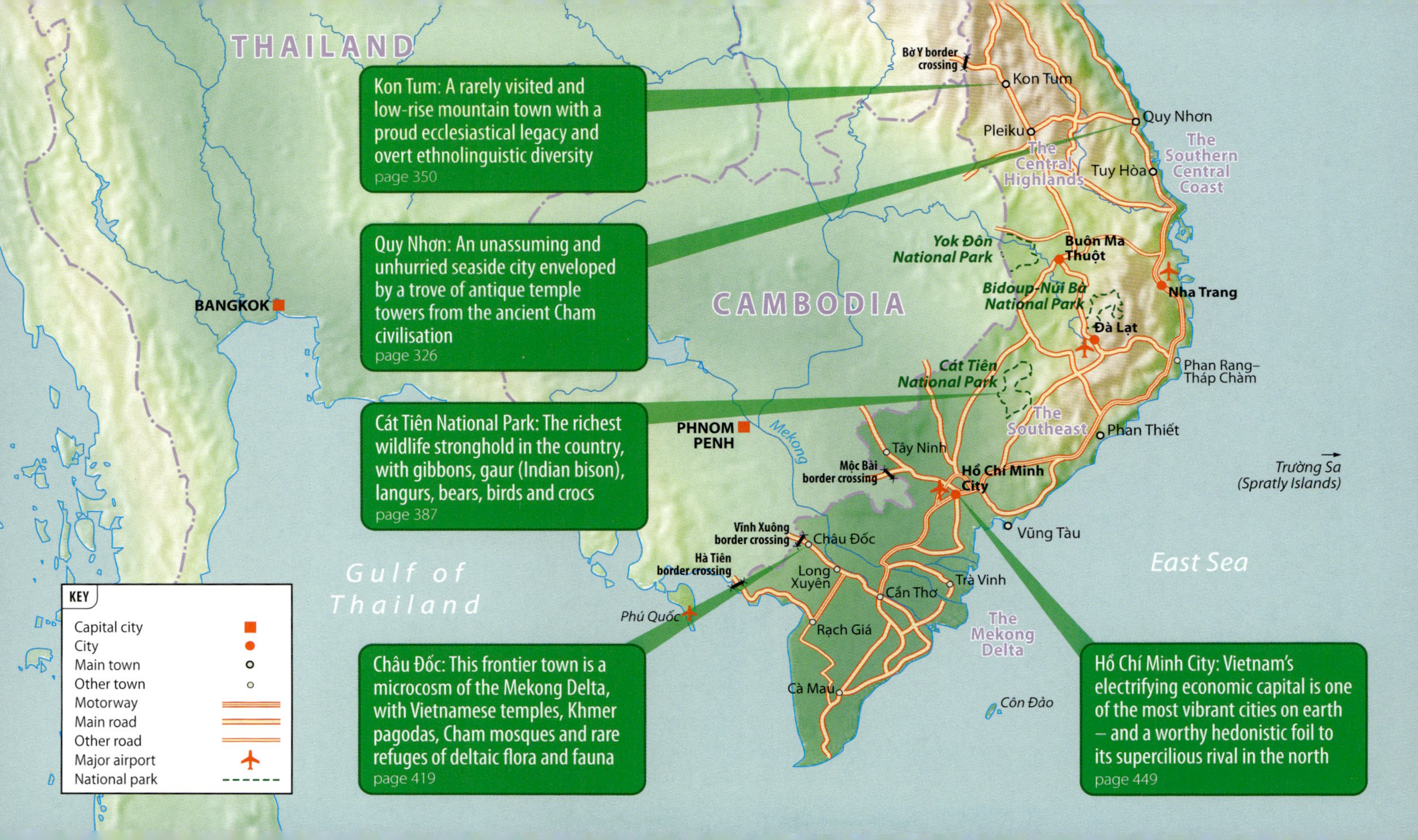

THAILAND
CAMBODIA
BANGKOK
PHNOM PENH
Mekong
Gulf of Thailand
East Sea
Bờ Y border crossing
Kon Tum
Pleiku
Quy Nhơn
Tuy Hòa
The Central Highlands
The Southern Central Coast
Yok Đôn National Park
Buôn Ma Thuột
Nha Trang
Bidoup-Núi Bà National Park
Đà Lạt
Phan Rang–Tháp Chàm
Cát Tiên National Park
The Southeast
Phan Thiết
Tây Ninh
Mộc Bài border crossing
Hồ Chí Minh City
Trường Sa (Spratly Islands)
Vũng Tàu
Vĩnh Xương border crossing
Châu Đốc
Hà Tiên border crossing
Long Xuyên
Trà Vinh
Cần Thơ
Phú Quốc
Rạch Giá
The Mekong Delta
Cà Mau
Côn Đảo
Kon Tum: A rarely visited and low-rise mountain town with a proud ecclesiastical legacy and overt ethnolinguistic diversity
page 350
Quy Nhơn: An unassuming and unhurried seaside city enveloped by a trove of antique temple towers from the ancient Cham civilisation
page 326
Cát Tiên National Park: The richest wildlife stronghold in the country, with gibbons, gaur (Indian bison), langurs, bears, birds and crocs
page 387
Châu Đốc: This frontier town is a microcosm of the Mekong Delta, with Vietnamese temples, Khmer pagodas, Cham mosques and rare refuges of deltaic flora and fauna
page 419
Hồ Chí Minh City: Vietnam's electrifying economic capital is one of the most vibrant cities on earth – and a worthy hedonistic foil to its supercilious rival in the north
page 449
KEY
Capital city
City
Main town
Other town
Motorway
Main road
Other road
Major airport
National park

VIETNAM
DON'T MISS...

THE HERITAGE

Vietnam is modernising fast, but that doesn't detract from the heritage neighbourhoods in cities and towns like Hanoi, Huế, Hội An, Đà Lạt and Hồ Chí Minh City. Pictured: Minh Mạng Tomb in Huế PAGE 267
(O/S)

THE MOUNTAINS

Vietnam's mountains – such as those in Hà Giang (pictured) – are the stuff of legend, sometimes quite literally. The Vietnamese, after all, are the children of a mountain fairy and a sea dragon PAGE 169
(BW/S)

THE CAVES

Caves speckle the Vietnamese countryside, but the most cavernous are in and around Phong Nha, which has quickly become one of the world's most coveted caving spots, thanks to caves such as Hang Én PAGE 235

(C/A)

THE RUINS

Ruins manifest in many forms in Vietnam, from the near-millennium-old Cham towers near Quy Nhơn to the 19th-century dynastic tombs in Huế. Pictured: the Bánh Ít Towers PAGE 330

(H/S)

THE FOOD

Vietnam has a food culture that could rival just about anywhere, with regions, provinces, cities and sometimes even individual neighbourhoods rustling up their own speciality dishes PAGE 64

(V/S)

VIETNAM
IN COLOUR

above left (S/D) Hồ Chí Minh City's meta-modern skyline is becoming increasingly psychedelic PAGE 449

above right (EIG/S) Colourful textile traditions are alive and well in the northern mountains, especially among Hmong communities, such as in Bắc Hà PAGES 160 & 161

below (BN) In August and September, just before the harvest, the terraced rice paddies of Mù Cang Chải turn burnt yellow PAGE 152

Phú Quốc has seen unprecedented development in recent years, but it's still possible to find long stretches of aquamarine coastline PAGE 427

above (HT/S)

Hội An's so-called Japanese Bridge was probably built in the 17th century, but its wooden frame and carmine walls were restored in 2024 PAGE 306

right (RC/S)

Đà Lạt's kaleidoscopic Linh Phước Pagoda was pieced together from millions of shards of broken glass, pottery and porcelain PAGE 377

below (E/S)

AUTHOR

Prioritising depth over breadth, **Joshua Zukas** (**w** joshuazukas.com) writes almost exclusively about Vietnam, a country he first visited in 2007 and has called home since 2013. In addition to writing this brand-new Bradt guide, he has co-authored more than half a dozen titles for other publishers, and his travel and culture stories have appeared in various global publications, including *The Economist, National Geographic Traveller* and *Michelin Guide*. His architecture stories can be found in the world's top design magazines, including *Interior Design Magazine, Wallpaper, Icon* and *Frame*. Joshua holds a BA in Linguistics and Southeast Asian Studies from SOAS, University of London, where he specialised in Vietnam and Indonesia; and an MSc in Sustainable Tourism from the University of Glasgow, where he wrote his thesis on shifting attitudes to sustainability and travel.

CONTRIBUTOR

Tom Divers is the author and creator of Vietnam Coracle (**w** vietnamcoracle.com), an independent online travel resource for Vietnam, a decade-long project providing travellers with hundreds of free guides. He quit coaching tennis in 2005 and moved from his native London to Vietnam, where he has been living, working and travelling ever since. Although Hồ Chí Minh City is home, he's on the road more often than not. He's ridden his motorbike over a quarter of a million kilometres across the length and breadth of Vietnam, researching and producing travel guides to the farthest-flung corners for his website. When he's not in the saddle, you'll find him on a beach with a margarita, in a tent on a pine-studded mountainside or at a streetside noodle house. In other words, he's at the office. Tom wrote *Chapter 12* on Phú Quốc and Côn Đảo.

AUTHOR'S STORY

Since ariving in Huế almost two decades ago, I've spent much of the time since getting to grips with an intricately layered country that has the extraordinary ability to inspire. After all these years, I remain most excited about Vietnam's vast chronicles of unsung stories, from just-so tales and wartime legends to modern heroes and trailblazing solutionists. I especially enjoy writing stories and guides that challenge preconceptions about a country awash with stereotypes. This has led me to cover tourism projects that are preserving landscapes and generating employment, ancient ateliers who are innovating with the times, and the biophilic headquarters of architects who are spearheading Vietnam's green architecture movement. To research this guidebook, I travelled the length of Vietnam more times than I can remember by foot, bicycle, scooter, motorbike, car, bus, coach, train, sampan and ferry (not one domestic flight was taken). Although I first lived in Huế, a city I still love dearly, I'm now based in Hanoi with my partner (though I'm usually elsewhere). Track me down online at **w** joshuazukas.com, Instagram (@joshuazukas) or LinkedIn (Joshua Zukas). I'm always keen to connect.

First edition published August 2025
Bradt Travel Guides Ltd
31a High Street, Chesham, Buckinghamshire, HP5 1BW, England
www.bradtguides.com
Print edition published in the USA by The Globe Pequot Press Inc,
PO Box 480, Guilford, Connecticut 06437-0480

Project Manager: Samantha Fletcher
Cover research: Pepi Bluck, Perfect Picture

ISBN: 9781804692035

British Library Cataloguing in Publication Data
A catalogue record for this book is available from the British Library

Photographs Alamy Stock Photo: Cavan Images (C/A), Hemis (H/A), RooM the Agency (R/A); Bao Khanh (BK); Bien Nguyen (BN); Dreamstime.com: Aoshivn (A/D), Duc Hong (DH/D), Efired (E/D), Luca Roggero (LR/D), Rodrigolab (R/D), saiko3p (S/D), Sonha95 (SO/D), Thi Kim Nhung Tran (T/D), Yen Mai Kim (Y/D); Samantha Fletcher (SF); Shutterstock.com: aindigo (A/S), Balate.Dorin (BD/S), BenWassink (BW/S), Dong Nhat Huy (DN/S), Duc Huy Nguyen (DH/S), Dzung Vu (DV/S), Efired (E/S), ELENA INFANTE GUERRERO (EIG/S), FrentaN (F/S), Gonzalo Buzonni (GB/S), Hien Phung Thu (H/S), Huy Thoai (HT/S), mridulablog (M/S), naytoong (N/S), Oleskaus (O/S), Pansim (P/S), Richie Chan (RC/S), saiko3p (S/S), TH Media (TH/S), Tiep.Nguyen (TN/S), Vietnam Stock Images (V/S), Wim Hoek (WH/S), Xita (X/S); SuperStock (SS); Vietnam Travel: Aaron Joel Santos (AJS/VT)

Front cover Bản Giốc Waterfall (R/A)
Back cover, clockwise from top left Côn Đảo (TN/S), Tết celebrations (Y/D), Tự Đức Tomb in Huế (BD/S)
Title page, clockwise from top left Fujian Assembly Hall, Hội An (S/S), Mỹ Sơn Sanctuary (H/S), Bắc Hà Market, Lào Cai (BK), a boat in the Mekong Delta (F/S)
Part openers Page 77: Bích Động Pagoda in Ninh Bình Province (E/D); page 223: the Marble Mountains in Đà Nẵng (S/D); page 379: the Mekong Delta (HT/S)

Maps David McCutcheon FBCart.S. FRGS, assisted by Simonetta Giori

Typeset by Ian Spick, Bradt Travel Guides
Production managed by Imprint Press; printed in India
Digital conversion by www.dataworks.co.in

Acknowledgements

First and foremost, I'd like to thank my aunt, Professor Miriam Zukas, a discerning devourer of guidebooks and an impassioned Bradt advocate. She volunteered her time liberally to scrutinise the bulk of this book, offer astute suggestions and entertain frivolous debates (always initiated by me) about writing style and word choice. I'd also like to thank my research assistant, Vietnamese journalist Lam Nguyễn, who offered crucial local insight, which I believe to be a foundational building block of any guidebook for a more sensitive and discerning world. For her contribution on Vietnam's bamboo diplomacy, see page 24.

On the topic of local input, I'd like to thank my multi-talented partner Biên Nguyễn, an activist, entrepreneur, educator, photographer and, more recently, a rival travel writer. This guidebook would lack much of its depth without his extemporaneous, insightful and irreverent commentary on Vietnamese linguistics, literature, customs, politics and folklore. For his contribution on The Song of Đăm Săn, see page 363. He's also generously contributed one or two photos for the colour section.

Other Vietnamese friends to whom I will forever be indebted include Trần Thúy Hải, Đặng Đình Sĩ, Lê Thị Phương Dung, Hương Nguyễn, Liên Hoàng Lê, Hoàng Liễu, Bảo Khánh and many others. It's sometimes said that backpackers are the first to discover a place. This is Western-centric nonsense. It's always local people that uncover a place's visitor appeal, and it is a true privilege that this patient and hospitable subgeneration of intrepid adventurers shared their discoveries with this ceaselessly curious and mildly annoying Brit.

From the immigrant community in Vietnam, of which I myself am a member, I'd like to thank Graham Buckley, Ian Paynton, Sheereen Amran, John Sylvan and others who, usually unwittingly, joined me on research trips and fed me useful titbits that I squirrelled away before finding space for them in this book.

I'd also like to spare some words to acknowledge the spaces where much of this book was written: Oriberry Xuân Diệu in Hanoi (now Oriberry Quảng An), The Cocoa Project in Hồ Chí Minh City, One Workspace in Chiangmai, Neilson Hays Library in Bangkok, Tring Library in Hertfordshire, the Design Museum in Kensington, Venture X in Shepherd's Bush and Sølvberget Library in Stavanger. These makeshift offices serve as reminders that access to quiet spaces in which to write, read and reflect is a privilege that one shouldn't take for granted.

At Bradt, I'd like to thank Claire Strange, Sam Fletcher and the rest of the team, who accepted the left-field idea to revisit Vietnam after a 25-year hiatus and skilfully shepherded the guidebook from inception to publication. Their decades of experience meant that when presented with an idea, no matter how trivial or wacky, they had the patience to listen, the courage to say yes and the wisdom to say no.

I'd also like to acknowledge fellow Vietphiles John R Jones, who authored the last *Bradt Guide to Vietnam* (published in 1998!), and David M Lloyd and Claire Boobbyer, authors of Footprint's *Vietnam* (2015), and Tim Doling, author of

Exploring Huế (2018), *Exploring Quảng Nam* (2020) and *Exploring Saigon–Chợ Lớn* (2019), all of which were core sources for this guide. Special thanks also to everyone who contributed sections and photos to this book: Tom Divers, Bảo Khánh, Liên Hoàng Lê, Mai Thanh Hoa and Phil Hoolihan, Lý Thị Mỷ and Hoàng Hương Duyên.

Last but far from least, I'd like to thank my mum, Kezzie Zukas, for being my most earnest cheerleader.

DEDICATION

This book is for my niblings: Dexter, Lando, Zadie and those who are yet to come. May your lives be forever filled with adventures that inspire the spirit and stories that nourish the soul.

FEEDBACK REQUEST

At Bradt Guides we're aware that guidebooks start to go out of date on the day they're published – and that you, our readers, are out there in the field doing research of your own. You'll find out before us when a fine new family-run hotel opens or a favourite restaurant changes hands and goes downhill. So why not tell us about your experiences? Contact the author at **w** joshuazukas.com. Alternatively, you can add a review of the book to Amazon, or share your adventures with us on social:

f BradtGuides
X BradtGuides
Instagram BradtGuides & joshuazukas

Contents

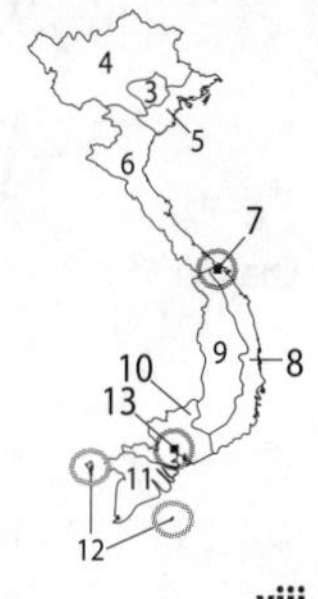

LIST OF MAPS

Introduction

Vietnam has many faces, some of which seem to contradict one another. Hanoi and Hồ Chí Minh City, the two major gateways and thus the likely first impression, are a far cry from the bastions of tradition perpetuated by travel media. Instead, these megalopolises are increasingly cosmopolitan and meta-modern: swirling helter-skelters of hedonistic urban life and haphazard construction. Heritage may not be immediately discernible for the uninitiated, but that doesn't mean that history is forgotten. In Hanoi, Vietnam's millennium-old capital, tear your gaze away from the hypnotic motorcycle brawl to absorb a city of pre-colonial temples, French façades and socialist realism. The creative classes in Hồ Chí Minh City, the country's impetus of progress, seem disinterested by derivative ideas imported from abroad, and instead ponder their own past to innovate in the present and shape the future.

Escape either city in any direction and Vietnam's diverse landscapes await. Extolling the nation's countryside treasures is almost too easy for loquacious travel writers keen to peddle their craft. As such, there is no shortage of effusive accounts glorifying the flower-fringed rivers that amble past conical peaks, ethereal caves ensconced in jungle, gently dimpled crescents of sand lapped by the surf and neon-green rice paddies scythed by bicycle lanes. While these words are written without exaggeration, Vietnam is not merely a pastoral Arcadia. Linking Hanoi and Hồ Chí Minh City is a chain of diverse municipalities, including the subtropical Soviet city of Vinh, the erstwhile imperial capital of Huế, the future-forward miniature metropolis of Đà Nẵng, the heritage riverside port of Hội An, the overlooked beach town of Quy Nhơn and the eccentric mountain retreat of Đà Lạt.

Where there are cities, there are people, and where there are people, there is extraordinary food. Vietnam's chequered history and dramatic geography provide the ingredients for a truly titanic food culture, and as the country has grown more prosperous, it has become increasingly difficult to suffer a bad meal. Centuries of strained contact and prolonged domination have left Vietnam with remnants from many of the world's other great culinary cultures, including China, India, France, Japan and Thailand. At the same time, pounding rains, relentless floods, intense sun and topographical diversity mean that few corners of the world can compete with Vietnam's abundance and viridity of ingredients. The result is a rich hotpot of dishes that are – perhaps inexplicably – hearty but delicate, simple yet nuanced.

While the cityscapes, landscapes and cuisine pull visitors to the country, many find that it's the human connections that leave the greatest impression. An hour spent sidestepping boisterous street kitchens and strolling past overflowing cafés in any town or city will reveal that the Vietnamese are perpetually sociable. There is a keenness to connect and the confidence to be curious, including with foreigners. Playful banter flows quickly and freely, fast-tracking friendships. Hospitality and generosity is heartfelt and widespread. Vietnam is a constellation of connections and amenable newcomers can quickly become a cog in its vast social infrastructure.

There is much to love about Vietnam, but it is not an airbrushed holiday destination where the issues are hidden from view; it is a country where people live, work, play and face very real, everyday challenges. It's taken decades of peace for the country to shake off its reputation as war-ridden and destitute. But replacing those outdated misconceptions are a slew of new oversimplifications: the cities are polluted, the countryside is degraded and the people are unscrupulous. The pragmatic Vietnamese will be the first to tell you that there is truth to this: the war did leave its mark, the cities do face tremendous challenges, the countryside is at the forefront of the environmental crisis – and everyone gets scammed from time to time. But accepting these realities is key to comprehending Vietnam's ongoing story.

The best approach to understanding (and enjoying!) Vietnam is to accept the bad with the good and forget most of what you think you know about the country – perhaps including what you've read in this introduction. Instead, do as the Vietnamese do. Expose yourself to risk, oblige your sense of humour, indulge your inner hedonist, allow your curiosity to run wild and be open to meeting a montage of new faces.

KEY TO SYMBOLS

—·—	International boundary	✝	Church
- - - -	Regional boundary		Tomb/mausoleum
✈	Airport		Ancient city gate
	Bus station		Cave
M	Metro station		Waterfall
	Ferry		Beach
	Historic/important building		Gardens
	Museum/gallery		Viewpoint
	Theatre		Historic (archaeological) site
	Statue/monument		Border crossing
	Hospital/clinic	▲	Summit (height in metres)
	Hotel/guesthouse	•	Other point of interest
✕	Restaurant		Sports facility/stadium
	Bar		Urban market
	Pagoda		Urban park
	Cham tower		National park
☸	Buddhist temple		

HOW TO USE THIS GUIDE

STRUCTURE This guide's primary organisation is based on Vietnam's regions: Northern Vietnam in Part 2, Central Vietnam in Part 3 and Southern Vietnam in Part 4. Where logical, the chapters map on to the subregions, with some exceptions: the major cities of Hanoi, Đà Nẵng and Hồ Chí Minh City deserve their own chapters (*chapters 3, 7* and *13*); the mountainous zones of Northeast Vietnam and Northwest Vietnam combine as the 'northern mountains' in *Chapter 4*; the coastal zones of Northeast Vietnam and the Red River Delta also constitute a single chapter (*Chapter 5*); though Côn Đảo and Phú Quốc are parts of the Southeast and Mekong Delta respectively, they have been allocated their own chapter (*Chapter 12*). In 2025, just as this book was going to print, the government was on the verge of announcing measures to combine various provinces and subregions. In this guide, mentions of provinces and subregions refer to the administrative structure before this overhaul.

When referring to an official region or subregion, the area is capitalised (eg: Northern Vietnam, the Central Highlands, the Southeast, etc). When referring to an unofficial zone delineated for convenience, such as carving out a chapter in this book, the area is not capitalised (eg: northern mountains, central lowlands, the islands, etc). Any reference to North Vietnam or South Vietnam refers to the countries that existed between the French withdrawal in 1954 and reunification in 1976.

DIACRITICS This book uses *quốc ngữ* diacritics for Vietnamese words and places. For more information, see page 29.

AUTHOR'S FAVOURITES Finding genuinely characterful accommodation or that unmissable off-the-beaten-track café can be difficult, so the author has chosen a few of his favourite places throughout the country to point you in the right direction. These 'author's favourites' are marked with a ✷.

PRICE CODES Throughout this guide we have used price codes to indicate the cost of those places to stay and eat listed in the guide. For a key to these price codes, see page 63 for accommodation and page 64 for restaurants. Note that these codes are only an indication as prices fluctuate wildly.

MAPS

Keys and symbols Maps include alphabetical keys covering the locations of those places to stay, eat or drink that are featured in the book. Note that regional maps may not show all hotels and restaurants in the area: other establishments may be located in towns shown on the map. On occasion, hotels or restaurants that are not listed in the guide (but which might serve as alternative options if required or serve as useful landmarks to aid navigation) are also included on the maps; these are marked with accommodation (⌂), café (☕) or restaurant (✕) symbols.

Grids and grid references Several maps use gridlines to allow easy location of sites. Map grid references are listed in square brackets after the name of the place or site of interest in the text, with page number followed by grid number, eg: [90 C3].

Part One

GENERAL INFORMATION

VIETNAM AT A GLANCE

Country The Socialist Republic of Vietnam, the official name since the reunification of North Vietnam and South Vietnam in 1976; Việt Nam in Vietnamese
Location Eastern edge of mainland Southeast Asia, with China to the north, Laos and Cambodia to the west and the South China Sea, known in Vietnam (and this guide) as the East Sea, to the east
Size 331,345km²
Regions Five municipalities and 58 provinces across three regions: Northern, Central and Southern
Climate Subtropical temperate in the north, tropical savannah in the south and a mix of both in the centre; the entire length of the country is affected by the annual monsoon (see opposite)
Capital Hanoi (Hà Nội); population 5.4 million (source: UN)
Other main cities Hồ Chí Minh City (Saigon/Sài Gòn; 9.3 million), Cần Thơ (1.9 million), Hải Phòng (1.5 million), Đà Nẵng (1.3 million)
Population 101,403,000 (2024 estimate) across 54 officially recognised ethnolinguistic groups; 85% are Kinh, the ethnolinguistic majority
Life expectancy 77 years for women, 71 years for men
Economy Agriculture, industry (including manufacturing) and services (including tourism) are the key sectors
GDP US$505 billion (2025 estimate)
Currency Vietnamese Đồng (VND)
Exchange rate £1 = 34,427VND, US$1 = 25,922VND, €1 = 28,940VND (May 2025)
Language Tiếng Việt (Vietnamese), spoken natively by more than 85% of the population
Religion No state religion, but belief systems based on a blend of Buddhism, Confucianism and Taoism are widely practised; Christianity, Hinduism and Islam are also represented
National airline Vietnam Airlines
International telephone code +84
Time GMT+7 (no daylight savings)
Electricity 220V/50Hz; both European and American sockets
Weights and measures Metric
Flag Red background with a five-point yellow star
National anthem 'Tiến Quân Ca', or 'The Song of the Marching Troops'
National flower Lotus
Public holidays See page 68

1

Background Information

GEOGRAPHY AND CLIMATE

Vietnam is in the shape of a severely deformed S, covering a land area of 331,345km^2, with a coastline 3,000km long. Due in part to its unusual shape, topographical diversity and circumferential geography, Vietnam offers a miraculous assortment of landscapes, seascapes and climates. The most important economic zones, containing the main concentrations of population, are focused on two large deltaic areas. In the north lie the ancient rice fields and settlements of the Red River Delta and, in the south, sits the fertile alluvial plain of the Mekong Delta. In between, the country narrows to less than 50km wide in parts, with only a thin ribbon of fertile lowland suited to intensive agriculture. Much of the interior, away from the coastal belt and the deltas, is mountainous.

The French subdivided Vietnam into three regions, administering each separately: Tonkin or Bắc Kỳ (the north region), Annam or Trung Kỳ (the central region) and Cochinchina or Nam Kỳ (the south region). Although these administrative terms are no longer used, the Vietnamese authorities recognise the country as consisting of three official regions: Northern Vietnam, Central Vietnam and Southern Vietnam. At least until 2025, these were further divided into eight subregions: Northeast Vietnam, Northwest Vietnam, the Red River Delta, the Northern Central Coast, the Southern Central Coast, the Central Highlands, Southeast Vietnam and the Mekong Delta. Spread between these regions and subregions are five major geographical zones: the northern highlands, the Red River Delta, the central lowlands, the central highlands (not all of which are in the Central Highlands subregion) and the Mekong Delta. For information on when to visit each geographical zone, see page 40. For an explanation of how this guide organises the regions and subregions into parts and chapters, see page x.

NORTHERN HIGHLANDS In the far north are the northern highlands, which ring the Red River Delta and form a natural barrier with China. The rugged mountains on the west border of this region – the Hoàng Liên Sơn – exceed 3,000m in places. The tributaries of the Red River have cut deep, steep-sided gorges through the mountain range, which are navigable by boat. The eastern part of this region, bordering the Gulf of Tonkin, is far less imposing. The provinces in the northern mountains experience a subtropical monsoonal temperate climate, with four seasons that map more or less to the seasons of temperate Europe and North America, but also with the heavy rains of the rest of Southeast Asia. Spring (March–May) temperatures range from 15°C to 25°C; summer (June–August) temperatures range from 20°C to 35°C; autumn (September–November) temperatures range from 15°C to 30°C; in winter (December–February) temperatures can plunge to below freezing at the highest peaks, but mostly hover around 10°C to 20°C in inhabited areas.

RED RIVER DELTA The second zone lies in the embrace of the hills of the north. The Red River Delta can legitimately claim to be the cultural and historical heart of the Việt nation, with Hanoi at its centre. The delta covers almost 15,000km^2 and extends 240km inland from the coast. Rice has been grown on the alluvial soils of the Red River for thousands of years, yet despite the intricate web of canals, dykes and embankments, the Vietnamese have never been able to tame the river into submission, and the delta is the victim of frequent and sometimes devastating floods. The area is very low-lying, rarely more than 3m above sea level. During the monsoon season (May–October), the tributaries of the Red River can quickly become torrents rushing through the narrow gorges of the Hoàng Liên Sơn, before emptying into the main channel, which then bursts its banks. Like the northern highlands, the Red River Delta also experiences a subtropical monsoonal temperate climate with four seasons, though summers are longer and winters are milder. Spring (March–April) temperatures range from 20°C to 30°C; summer (May–August) temperatures range from 30°C to 40°C; autumn (September–November) temperatures range from 20°C to 35°C; and winter (December–February) temperatures are around 15°C to 25°C, though cold gusts from the north occasionally bring the temperature down to single digits.

CENTRAL LOWLANDS South of the Red River Delta zone lie the central lowlands. To the east, the Annamite Range falls off steeply, leaving only a narrow and fragmented band of lowland suitable for agriculture. In places the mountains advance all the way to the coast, plunging into the sea as rock faces. The soils are often rocky or saline, and irrigation is seldom possible. Nonetheless, the inhabitants have a history of sophisticated rice cultivation and it was here that Champa was established perhaps 2,000 years ago. These lowlands have also formed a conduit along which people have immigrated. Even today, the main north–south road and rail routes cut through the coastal lowlands. Central Vietnam, including the central lowlands region, is largely tropical and monsoonal, though whether there are four seasons (spring, summer, autumn and winter) or two (wet and dry) depends on where you are in the region. In March and April temperatures range from 20°C to 30°C; from May to September temperatures range from 25°C to 40°C; in October and November temperatures range from 20°C to 30°C. December to February is particularly complicated in the central lowlands; temperatures can plunge into single digits in the northernmost provinces, but can reach 30°C in the southernmost ones.

CENTRAL HIGHLANDS South of the Red River Delta zone and west of the central lowlands lie the central highlands and the mountains of the Annamite Range. The central highlands, also known as the Trường Sơn mountain range, form an important historical and cultural divide between the regions influenced by India to the west and those influenced by China to the north. The northern rugged extremity is in Thanh Hóa Province. From here the Trường Sơn stretches over 1,200km south, to peter out 80km north of Hồ Chí Minh City. In its southern zone, the Central Highlands subregion is an upland plateau on which plantation agriculture and hill farms are interspersed with stands of bamboo and tropical forest. Once rich in wildlife, the plateau was a popular hunting ground during the colonial period. Central Vietnam, including the central highlands zone, is tropical and monsoonal, but like elsewhere in the region, it can feel like this large swathe of land experiences all six seasons: spring, summer, autumn, winter, wet and dry. Temperatures generally hover between 20°C and 30°C throughout the year, though

ZOMIA

In *The Art of Not Being Governed: An Anarchist History of Upland Southeast Asia* (2009), political scientist James C Scott refers to a highland region in Southeast Asia that spans several countries, including parts of Vietnam, Laos, Thailand, Myanmar, Yunnan, India and Bangladesh, as 'Zomia', a term previously popularised by anthropologist Willem van Schendel in 2002. Van Schendel coined the term from the roots *zo*, meaning 'hill', and *mi*, meaning 'person', from Tibeto-Burman languages. This enormous region is home to various ethnolinguistic groups, many of which have historically resisted incorporation into centralised state structures. The tenet behind Zomia is that the highland peoples have consciously chosen to live in ways that make them less vulnerable to state control, including remote living, subsistence farming, oral traditions and shifting cultivation. This makes Zomia a symbol of autonomy and resistance to state power, particularly in the context of Southeast Asia's historically authoritarian governments. In the context of Vietnam, Zomia can refer to the vast highlands regions in Northern and Central Vietnam, where dozens of ethnolinguistic groups reside.

they can plunge to single digits in the highland city of Đà Lạt in December and January. April to November is generally considered the wet season and December to March the dry season.

SOUTHERN VIETNAM AND THE MEKONG DELTA Unlike the Red River Delta, the Mekong Delta is not so prone to flooding because of the Tonlé Sap, a lake in Cambodia, and so rice production is more stable. During the rainy season (May–October), when the water flowing into the Mekong becomes too great for even this mighty river to absorb, rather than overflowing its banks, the water backs up into the Tonlé Sap, which can quadruple in size. The Mekong Delta covers 67,000km^2 and the river divides and drains into five major branches as it flows towards the sea. The vast delta is one of the great rice bowls of Asia, producing nearly half of the country's rice. Although the area had been forested, in the late 19th century the French supported its settlement by Vietnamese peasants, recognising that it could become enormously productive. Over the years a patchwork of canals has expanded irrigation and rice cultivation. The deposition of silt by the rivers that cut through the delta means that the shoreline is continually advancing – up to 80m each year in some places.

Whenever a study or report is published detailing the countries most likely to be affected by the **climate crisis**, Vietnam usually makes an appearance – and, perhaps more than anywhere else in the country, the Mekong Delta is under considerable threat. By some estimates, large swathes of the Mekong Delta and Hồ Chí Minh City north of it could be under water by 2050 unless drastic action is taken.

Southern Vietnam is more typical of a tropical and monsoonal climate, with a wet season from May to October, a dry season from November to April and consistent temperatures of 25°C to 35°C throughout the year. The climate here is similar to that of Cambodia and central Thailand.

GEOLOGY

Vietnam is situated on the southeastern zone of the Eurasian Plate. Northern Vietnam is dominated by the Red River Delta and mountain ranges like the Hoàng

Liên Sơn, which contain metamorphic rocks, granites and sedimentary basins. In Central Vietnam, the Trường Sơn range comprises complex formations, including gneiss metamorphic rocks and volcanic rocks. Southern Vietnam, primarily made up of the Mekong Delta, features sedimentary deposits. Vietnam's most visually iconic rock type is limestone, the medium of the dramatic karst landscapes of the north. The country is also rich in mineral resources, including bauxite, gold, iron ore, lead, zinc, coal and phosphate. Vietnam's oil and gas reserves in the East Sea are significant. Earthquakes are uncommon, but the country is prone to landslides and flooding during storms and to coastal erosion, especially in the deltas. For a very dry account (both literally and figuratively) of the geology of Vietnam, visit the geology museums in Hanoi and Hồ Chí Minh City.

NATURAL HISTORY AND CONSERVATION

Together with overseas conservation agencies, Vietnamese institutions have recently paid more attention to accounting for and protecting their fauna and flora. The establishment of nature reserves began in 1962 with the gazetting of the Cúc Phương National Park and today there are almost 100 protected areas. However, many parks also house humans and some are so small that they cannot sustain sufficiently large breeding populations of endangered species. Given the difficulty of getting to Vietnam's more remote areas, the country is hardly a haven for amateur naturalists. Professional photographers and scientists have been escorted to the country's wildest areas but this is not an option for the average visitor. A wander around the markets of more far-flung cities in Vietnam reveals the variety and number of animals that end up in the cooking pot, including deer, snakes and turtles.

FAUNA

Mammals Among the larger mammals, there are small numbers of clouded leopard (*Neofelis nebulosa*), Asian elephant (*Elephas maximus*), Malayan sun bear (*Helarctos malayanus*), Himalayan black bear (*Ursus thibetanus laniger*), sambar deer (*Rusa unicolor*), langurs (*Trachypithecus* genus), gibbons (*Hylobatidae* family) and gaur, or Indian bison (*Bos gaurus*). With the exception of gibbons, gaurs and langurs, these are rarely seen, except in rehabilitation centres and zoos. Many large, rare mammals are confined to isolated pockets, where the government goes to some effort to protect them from hunters. On Cát Bà island (page 205), the national park is home to the world's last wild troops of white-headed langur (*Trachypithecus poliocephalus*). In Cúc Phương (page 218) and Cát Tiên (page 387), gibbons rescued from captivity are being carefully rehabilitated. Semi-wild elephants can be tracked and spotted in Yok Đôn (page 365). Further south, territorial battles rage between elephants and farmers, often resulting in government compensation.

Reptiles The larger reptiles include two species of crocodile, the estuarine (*Crocodylus porosus*) and Siamese (*C. siamensis*). The former grows to a length of 5m and has been reported to have killed and eaten humans. Among the larger snakes are the reticulated python (*Python reticulatus*) and the smaller Indian python (*P. molurus*), both non-venomous constrictors. Venomous snakes include two species of cobra (the king cobra and common cobra), two species of krait and six species of pit viper. Reptiles are found across Vietnam, but in particular in the national parks of Cúc Phương (page 218) and Cát Tiên (page 387).

Birds Birds have, in general, suffered rather less than mammals from hunting and the effects of the American War. There have been some casualties, however: the eastern sarus crane (*Grus Antigone*) of the Mekong Delta – a symbol of fidelity, longevity and good luck – disappeared entirely during the war, though may finally be returning. In waterlogged areas across the country, it is common to see various types of storks (*Ciconiidae*), herons (*Ardea*) and kingfishers (*Alcedinidae*). The common kingfisher is especially striking, with a turquoise back and wings and orange breast. Among the more unusual birds are the snake bird (*Anhinga anhinga*), named after its habit of swimming with its body submerged and only its snake-like neck and head above the surface; the argus pheasant (*Argusianus argus*), which some believe resembles the mythical phoenix; and a quail of which the male hatches and rears the young. Prime bird-spotting areas include Ba Bể (page 165), Cúc Phương (page 218), Bạch Mã (page 271), Bidoup-Núi Bà (page 378), Trà Sư (page 424) and Tràm Chim (page 416).

Butterflies A dazzling kaleidoscope of butterflies reside in Vietnam, including tigers (*Parantica*), swallowtails (*Papilionidae*), the brilliant common birdwing (*Troides helena*) and the rare Vietnamese Catopsilia (*Catopsilia scylla*). These butterflies are most abundant in Vietnam's tropical forests. In Cúc Phương (page 218), Ba Bể (page 165) and Phong Nha-Kẻ Bàng (page 240) national parks, populations flourish during the spring and summer months. Conservation programmes, though still developing, aim to protect these vital pollinators from threats such as habitat loss and climate change.

FLORA Vietnam is home to vivid rice terraces, lush forests and an array of colourful flowers depending on the season. In the north, from January to March, peach (*Prunus persica*) and apricot (*P. mume*) blossoms burst in pink and white, while flame trees (*Delonix regia*) and golden shower trees (*Cassia fistula*) conjure yellow and red glows in late spring and summer. In the south, the wetlands of the Mekong Delta hold vast swathes of mangroves (*Rhizophora*), nipa palms (*Nypa fruticans*) and water lilies (*Nymphaea*). Vietnam's lowland rainforests are rich with dipterocarps (*Dipterocarpaceae*), strangler figs (*Ficus*), and bamboo (*Poaceae*) species, while montane forests feature pines (*Pinus*) and rhododendrons (*Rhododendron*). In protected areas like Cúc Phương and Bạch Mã national parks, visitors might spot creeping lianas and orchids clinging to towering trees. Growing on the limestone karst formations in Hạ Long Bay, Ninh Bình and Phong Nha-Kẻ Bàng is unique vegetation adapted to rocky environments. The roadside verges and trails often feature wild gingers (*Zingiberaceae*), heliconias (*Heliconia*) and grasses (*Gramineae*), while water spinach (*Ipomoea aquatica*) and lotus (*Nelumbo nucifera*) grow abundantly in rice paddies and ponds.

HISTORY

*This section has been written with input from Hồ Chí Minh City-based historian Tim Doling (**w** historicvietnam.com), who has written a number of books and guides to Vietnam (page 489).*

ARCHAEOLOGY, PREHISTORY AND LEGENDS The earliest record of humans in Vietnam is from an archaeological site in Thanh Hóa Province. The remains discovered here have been dated to the Lower Palaeolithic (early Stone Age). So far, the earliest human remains have been unearthed in Northern Vietnam, invariably in association with limestone cliff dwellings. Unusually, tools are made of basalt rather than flint, the more common material found at similar sites in other parts of the world.

Archaeological excavations have shown that between 5000BCE and 3000BCE, two important Mesolithic cultures occupied Northern Vietnam: these are referred to as the Hòa Bình and Bắc Sơn cultures after the principal excavation sites. Refined stone implements and distinctive hand axes with polished edges (known as Bắcsonian axes) are characteristic of the two cultures. These early inhabitants of Vietnam were probably of Melanesian or Austronesian stock.

There are 2,000 years of recorded Vietnamese history and another 2,000 years of legend. The Vietnamese people trace their origins back to the Lạc Việt, who settled in what is now Northern Vietnam at the beginning of the Bronze Age, around 1000BCE. They established the agrarian kingdom of Văn Lang, ruled by the Hùng kings, who some believe were direct descendants of ethereal beings (page 10). The artistically prolific Đông Sơn culture followed and proliferated; of the artefacts associated with this civilisation, none is more technologically or artistically impressive than the huge bronze drums unearthed in Northern Vietnam (see below).

CHINESE RULE Văn Lang seemed to have vanished by the 3rd century BCE, and from 111BCE to CE938, Vietnamese territory, which extended south only as far as present-day Thanh Hóa Province, was assimilated by the powerful Chinese Han

THE ĐÔNG SƠN DRUMS, PAST AND PRESENT

The squat, bronze Đông Sơn drums show their makers to have been master casters. They can measure over 1m in height and width and consist of a decorated tympanum, a convex upper section, waisted middle and expanding lower section. Decoration is both geometric and naturalistic, most notably on the finely incised drumhead. Debate about the function of the drums continues. They have usually been found alongside human remains and other precious items, leading archaeologists to argue that they symbolised power and prestige and were treasured objects in the community.

Also known as rain drums, they are sometimes surmounted by bronze figures of frogs (or toads). It is thought that perhaps the drums were used as magical instruments to summon rain, since tailless amphibians are associated with water. Other decorative motifs include dancers (again, possibly part of rain-making rites) and boats with feather-crowned passengers (perhaps taking the deceased to the Kingdom of the Dead) and warriors. Other Đông Sơn drums have been found as far east as the island of Alor in Nusa Tenggara, Indonesia, indicating possible trade links between Vietnam and the archipelago. As if to stress the nationalist symbolism of the drum, an image of an ornate tympanum is used as an icon by Vietnamese television, and Vietnam Airlines prints the motif on its tickets.

Understandably, Vietnamese archaeologists have been keen to stress the 'Vietnamese-ness' of these objects, rejecting many of the suggestions made by Western scholars that they are of Chinese or Indian inspiration. As Professor Phạm Huy Thông of the Academy of Sciences wrote, Western studies are 'marked by insufficient source material, prejudices and mere deductions', and that their 'achievements [in understanding the drums] remain insignificant'.

FUNAN AND ÓC EO (CE100–600)

According to Chinese sources, Funan was a Hindu kingdom founded in the 1st century CE, with its capital, Vyadhapura, close to the Mekong River near the border with Cambodia. A local legend records that Kaundinya, a great Indian Brahmin, acting on a dream, sailed to the coast of Vietnam carrying with him a bow and arrow. When he arrived, Kaundinya shot the arrow and, where it landed, he established the capital of Funan. Following this act, Kaundinya married the princess Soma, daughter of the local king of the Nagas, giant water serpents that feature regularly in Thai and Cambodian religious architecture. The legend symbolised the union between Indian and local cultural traditions: the Naga represented indigenous fertility rites and customs, and the arrow the potency of the Hindu religion.

Funan built its wealth and power on its strategic location on the sea route between China, the islands of Southeast Asia and India. Seafarers were forced to stop here and wait for the winds to change before they could continue on their way. This sometimes meant a stay of up to five months. The large port city of Óc Eo in present-day Kiên Giang Province (page 418) offered a safe harbour for merchant vessels and the revenues generated enabled the kings of the empire to expand rice cultivation, dominate a host of surrounding vassal states as far away as the Malay coast and South Burma, and build a series of impressive temples, cities and irrigation works.

Funan reached the peak of its powers in the 4th century and went into decline during the 5th century, when improving maritime technology made Óc Eo redundant as a haven for sailing vessels. By the mid 6th century, Funan, having suffered from a drawn-out leadership crisis, was severely weakened. Champa (page 12) ultimately conquered the state. What is particularly interesting about Funan is the degree to which it provided a model for future states in Southeast Asia. Funan's wealth was built on its links with the sea, and with its ability to exploit maritime trade. The later rulers of Champa, Langkasuka (Malaya), Srivijaya (Sumatra), and Malacca (Malaya) repeated this formula.

feudal empire. They left behind a rich cultural legacy but, during their rule – known as the Bắc Thuộc Period – they were constantly harassed by insurrection. Revolutionaries from this period include the women warriors of Hai Bà Trưng (the Trưng sisters; page 118) in CE40 and Bà Triệu (Lady Triệu; page 221) in 248, Mai Thúc Loan in 722 and Ngô Quyền, who masterminded the victory at the battle of the Bạch Đằng River (page 203) in 938. This battle, which occurred 32 years after the fall of the Han Dynasty, proved to be the end of more than 1,000 years of Chinese domination.

THE DYNASTIC ERA A tumultuous period followed the Chinese defeat. Ngô Quyền took control in 939, but by 968 he had been replaced by the short-lived Đinh Dynasty, who ruled from their capital at Hoa Lư. They were overthrown by the first **Lê Dynasty**, also short-lived, though they gained victories against Champa (page 12), which ruled over much of present-day Central and Southern Vietnam. A series of short dynasties followed, each overthrowing the previous.

Stability was established by the **Lý Dynasty** (1010–1225), when the country, then named Đại Việt, stretched only as far as the southern border of Hà Tĩnh

LEGEND HAS IT: MYTHOLOGICAL BEGINNINGS

Despite the archaeological evidence, the Vietnamese might tell you a different story about how their country came into being. According to legend, Âu Cơ was an ethereal mountain fairy who lived in the highlands and Lạc Long Quân was a powerful dragon lord that resided in the ocean. Their union resulted in the birth of a sacral clutch of 100 eggs, and from these eggs emerged not dragons or fairies but human children. However, as they grew, they began to diverge, displaying the traits of either their terrestrial mother or aquatic father.

Knowing that the union couldn't last, Lạc Long Quân called off the relationship, taking 49 kids with him to the coast. Only one remained, and he became Hùng Vương I, the first king of Vietnam's first dynasty. The remaining 50 followed Âu Cơ into the mountains. The descendants of Lạc Long Quân and Âu Cơ's children became the subjects of the Hùng Dynasty, the people of modern-day Vietnam. This is why the Vietnamese sometimes boast that they are the descendants of dragons and fairies.

A controversial extension of this myth tells that the 49 children who followed Lạc Long Quân are the first ancestors of the Kinh (page 189), Vietnam's ethnolinguistic majority who historically live near the coast. The 50 that followed Âu Cơ are the forebearers of Vietnam's various mountain-dwelling ethnolinguistic groups.

Vietnam's creation myth isn't lost on today's city planners. All big cities have streets named after Lạc Long Quân and Âu Cơ – and they always meet. In fact, myths – from just-so stories to legendary patriots – continue to play an important role in contemporary Vietnamese society. Look out for these stories in the various 'Legend has it' boxes speckled throughout this guide.

Province today. It's important to note that a millennium ago, the southern half of present-day Vietnam was separate from Đại Việt. Champa occupied the coastal belt (present-day Central Vietnam), while the entire Mekong Delta region (present-day Southern Vietnam) was part of the Cambodian kingdom. Meanwhile, Champa and Cambodia were separated by the southern Annamite range, which was settled by various Zomian (page 5) groups. Lý Thái Tổ, the founder of the Lý Dynasty, made Thăng Long (now Hanoi) Đại Việt's capital. With a growing population, Đại Việt pushed further south into Champa under the command of the general Lý Thường Kiệt. During the reign of Lý Thánh Tông, Lý Thái Tổ's grandson, Confucianism became the dominant religion, and its central temple – the Temple of Literature, which still stands in Hanoi – was the centre of learning.

During the **Trần Dynasty** (1225–1400), considerable unrest raged throughout the country. Mongol-Yuan forces attempted to invade in 1258, 1282–84 and 1285. At times of crisis, a congress was convened in Thăng Long, still the capital, to discuss and assess troop strength and tactics. This was the nation's salvation because elders arrived from throughout the country to report on village production, training of peasant troops and general morale of the people. They would then return to their various localities and present the people with royal demands. Very quickly the royal troops would be considerably reinforced and ready to fight any invasion. The climactic battle came in 1287–88, when Trần Hưng Đạo, a prince and military commander, won a magnificent victory (page 203) against the mighty armies of Kublai Khan, putting an end to the Mongol ambitions to push south. The Trần

Dynasty was also a period when handicrafts such as cotton and silk weaving and the manufacture of porcelain and ceramics developed. Buddhism became the dominant religion, sacred texts were written, pagodas built and bells cast.

The Trần Dynasty fell slowly from grace throughout the 1300s, leading to an overthrow in 1400 that ushered in the **Hồ Dynasty** (1400–06) – but China then regained control of Vietnamese territory, lasting until 1427. The Ming burned priceless artistic treasures, destroyed Vietnamese scripts, stole the people's wealth and forced tradesmen to work for the Chinese court. The people of Đại Việt became despondent and resentful of their overlords. Women who refused to dress in a Chinese fashion or wouldn't put their hair up in a bun were punished by death. Salvation came when Lê Lợi, a spirited tactician, skilfully and perhaps divinely expelled the Chinese (page 104).

Lê Lợi became king, and the second **Lê Dynasty** (1428–1776) is known as one of the golden ages of Vietnamese history. Much of the credit for Lê Lợi's success must go to Nguyễn Trãi (1380–1442), a brilliant scholar and astute military strategist. Releasing the full brunt of their military in a single battle at Thanh Hóa, Lê Lợi and Nguyễn Trãi put an end to the occupation. Nguyễn Trãi, as well as being a liberator, was a statesman, poet, writer and geographer. The expansion of the Vietnamese state under the Lê followed the decline of Champa at the end of the 15th century.

By the early 18th century Champa was extinct as an identifiable political and military force and the Vietnamese advanced still further south. This geographical over-extension and the logistical impracticability of ruling from distant Thăng Long, disseminating edicts and collecting taxes, led to the disintegration of the imperial rule. Empowered by southern expansion, noble families, locally dominant, challenged the emperor's authority and the Lê Dynasty took a back seat to regional dynastic fiefdoms. The **Trịnh** lords dominated the north while the breakaway **Nguyễn** lords gradually subjugated the Cham and then exploited dynastic divisions within the Cambodian court to wrest control of the Mekong Delta. By the middle of the 18th century, the Việt nation was essentially divided in two: Đại Việt in the north and Đàng Trong in the centre and south. While the Trịnh and Nguyễn overlords appeared powerful, the people were mired in poverty.

Widespread discontent, coupled with the rivalry between the Trịnh and the Nguyễn, gave three ambitious brothers from present-day Bình Định Province an opportunity to seize power. Leading the 1771 so-called Tây Sơn Rebellion (see page 332 for the full story) were Nguyễn Nhạc (the oldest), Nguyễn Huệ (the youngest), and Nguyễn Lữ, supported by an army of dissatisfied peasants. The brothers achieved considerable military success, redistributing to the peasants any land they captured from the gentry and defeating the opportunistic forces of Siam, which supported the Nguyễn lord Nguyễn Ánh in the south, and the Chinese army that had taken Thăng Long in the north. After reunifying the country in January 1789, Nguyễn Huệ became Emperor Quang Trung, who began implementing reforms that were to improve the lives of the peasant class. Lands were confiscated from the feudal lords and their regime was terminated. Quang Trung proved to be better at conquering than ruling, and after his death in 1792, his dynasty quickly crumbled.

Nguyễn Ánh returned from exile and mustered a mercenary army, which successfully took the southern wetlands. With the help of the French government, who had colonial ambitions, the rest of Vietnam soon fell, marking the start of the **Nguyễn emperors** (1802–1945). Nguyễn Ánh proclaimed himself Emperor Gia Long and moved the capital to Huế. From here he ruled over the new kingdom of Vietnam (he coined the name Việt Nam) which now extended from its northern

CHAMPA: AN ALTERNATIVE HISTORY OF VIETNAM

This section was written with considerable input from Dr Nguyễn H H Duyên, curator at Đà Nẵng Museum of Cham Sculpture (page 289) and managing editor of Pratu Journal (w pratujournal.org)

In present-day Central and Southern Vietnam, the dynastic Việt lords achieved hegemony only in the 18th century. During the preceding centuries, the Mekong Delta came under the Khmer empire while Champa was the most significant power in the central coastal belt. Champa evolved in the 2nd century CE, possibly from the ancient Sa Huỳnh civilisation (1000BCE–CE200), and was focused on the narrow ribbon of lowland that runs north–south down the Annamite coast, with its various capitals south of the present-day city of Đà Nẵng. Chinese sources record that in CE192 a local official, Khu Liên, rejected Chinese authority and established an independent kingdom. From then on, Champa's history was one of conflict with its neighbour: when imperial China was powerful, Champa was subservient and sent ambassadors and tributes in homage to the Chinese court; when it was weak, the rulers of Champa extended their own influence and ignored the Chinese.

Champa consisted of five states that took names from areas of India: Indrapura, Amaravati (page 318), Vijaya (page 329), Kauthara (page 339) and Panduranga (page 341). The difficulty for scholars is to decide whether Champa had a single identity or whether it consisted of numerous powers with no dominant centre. One prominent perspective is that Champa was more diffuse than previously thought and that only rarely during its history is it possible to talk of Champa in singular terms. The endless mobility of the capital of Champa is considered to reflect the shifting centres of power that characterised the country.

Like Funan (page 9), Champa built its power on its position on the maritime trading route through Southeast Asia. During the 4th century, as Champa expanded into formerly Funan-controlled lands, they came under the influence

border with China to the southern tip of the Mekong Delta. During his reign, Huế was transformed into a sumptuous city with palaces, pagodas, mausoleums and temples.

Negotiations with the French government continued long after Louis XVI was guillotined in 1793 and French merchants and missionaries were given free access to Vietnamese territory. Gia Long's son, Prince Nguyễn Phúc Cảnh, was sent to be educated in a Catholic missionary school in Malacca. Many had thought that he would become the next emperor and would be able to put his newly gained international skills to good use; this was not to be as he died at the age of 21, possibly from poisoning. His brother, Prince Nguyễn Miên Tông, became Emperor Minh Mạng, much to the disappointment of the imperial court's French supporters. Minh Mạng's anti-French policy was more and more apparent and his execution of French Catholic missionaries provoked anger and disgust among high-ranking officials in France. Soon, the protests of French Catholics in Vietnam echoed loudly through the country; this in turn sparked riots, which continued after Minh Mạng's death in 1841. Throughout Emperor Thiệu Trị's short rule (1841–47) matters worsened.

FRENCH COLONIAL RULE France's first naval action against Vietnam came in 1847, when they attacked Đà Nẵng harbour; 11 years later, during the reign of Emperor

of the Indian cultural traditions of the Funanese. Champa's rulers embraced these traditions enthusiastically, tacking the suffix '-varman' on to their names (for example, Bhadravarman) and adopting the Hindu-Buddhist cosmology.

Though a powerful trading kingdom, Champa was geographically poorly endowed. The coastal strip between the Annamite highlands to the west and the sea to the east is narrow and the potential for extensive rice cultivation limited. This may explain why Champa was never more than a moderate power: it was unable to produce the agricultural surplus necessary to support an extensive court and army, and therefore could not compete with either the Khmers to the south nor with the Việt to the north. But the Cham were able to carve out a niche for themselves between the two, and to some art historians, their art and architecture represent the finest that Vietnam has ever produced.

For over 1,000 years the Cham resisted the Chinese and the Vietnamese. But by the time Marco Polo wrote of the Cham in 1285, their power and prestige were much reduced. Champa saw a late flowering under King Chế Bồng Nga, who led numerous successful campaigns against the Việt, culminating in the sack of Hanoi in 1371. Subsequently, the treachery of a low-ranking officer led to Chế Bồng Nga's death in 1390 and the military eclipse of the Cham by the Vietnamese. The demographic and economic superiority of the Việt, coupled with their gradual drift south, contributed most to the waning of the Champa Kingdom, and finally, in 1471, the Cham suffered a terrible defeat at the hands of the Vietnamese. Some 60,000 of their soldiers were killed and another 36,000 captured and carried into captivity, including the king and 50 members of the royal family. The kingdom shrank to a small territory in the vicinity of Nha Trang (page 335), which existed until 1720 when surviving members of the royal family and many subjects fled to Cambodia to escape from the advancing Vietnamese, who finally brought about Champa's end. Though the kingdom is defunct, various pockets of Cham people remain throughout Vietnam (page 343).

Tự Đức (1848–83), a large French naval fleet attempted to invade the city again, which was well defended by two citadels, four castles and eight fortresses, as well as an extensive defensive city wall system. The French were gradually overwhelmed and pushed back by General Nguyễn Tri Phương's superior army, so they refocused their efforts on Gia Định (now Hồ Chí Minh City) in the south. Emperor Tự Đức, like Thiệu Trị and Minh Mạng before him, had become so immersed in Confucian doctrine and hatred of the Catholics that he had given little consideration to military improvements. When the French attacked, they met with little resistance and soon a French Consulate barged into the city. By 1861, Gia Định had been taken and, in 1867, the southern part of Vietnam was rechristened Cochinchina after total annexation by the French.

By 1883, most of Vietnam was under French control. The central part of the country became known as Annam. The northern provinces, which had become French protectorates too, were renamed Tonkin. Tự Đức was dead and the emperors Dục Đức (1883), Hiệp Hòa (1883) and Kiến Phúc (1883–84), who followed, were powerless to free the country from the colonial yoke. The next in line to the Nguyễn Dynasty, the Emperor Hàm Nghi (1883–85), set up resistance movements, which were unsuccessful. Đồng Khánh (1885–89) chose to capitulate and collaborate with his conquerors.

VIỆT NAM QUỐC DÂN ĐẢNG

Though dwarfed in the annals of history by the seismic significance of the Việt Minh (see below), Quốc Dân Đảng, formed in 1927, was Vietnam's first nationalistic party. It began as an attempt to alleviate the great strain put on the people through increased French taxation and oppression. A republican democratic government was established and Nguyễn Thái Học, the organisation's founder and leader, garnered support from large swathes of society, including young intellectuals and military leaders. Sensing the threat, the French never allowed him to participate in Vietnam's electoral process, compelling the group to take more assertive and aggressive actions. In 1930, the Quốc Dân Đảng orchestrated an uprising of soldiers in Yên Bái Province, but the rebellion was swiftly quashed and Nguyễn Thái Học was put to death. Today, many of Vietnam's most important streets and schools carry his name.

Emperor Thành Thái (1889–1907) 'ruled' during a period when the French were tightening their grip on the whole of Indochina. By 1896, the entire continent had fallen. Duy Tân (1907–16) made some attempt to liberate his country and was soon replaced by Khải Định (1916–25), who did not. Right from the days of early French occupation, Vietnamese literary critics such as Phan Châu Trinh and Phan Bội Châu had kept Vietnamese nationalism alive. The belief that their country would one day be free of colonial rule was impossible to crush.

During Bảo Đại's rule (1925–45), Nguyễn Ái Quốc (later Hồ Chí Minh), who had been inspired by the triumph of the Bolshevik Revolution, applied Marxist-Leninist dogma to the colonial problem: he established the Indochina Communist Party in 1930, a turning point in a political and armed struggle that would ultimately lead to independence.

Soon after the start of World War II in September 1939, the French were overrun in Europe by Nazi Germany and, in 1940, the Japanese invasion of Indochina began. The Japanese were even more brutal than the French, forcing peasants to work inhumane hours and many collapsed from fatigue and malnutrition. The only people to resist the Japanese occupation were the members of the Revolutionary League for the Independence of Vietnam, the **Việt Minh**, which was formed by Nguyễn Ái Quốc in May 1941. Under his new name, **Hồ Chí Minh**, he and Việt Minh military commander Võ Nguyên Giáp set up communist cells throughout the country in 1944. They all had one aim: independence for Vietnam. On 22 December 1944, the Armed Propaganda Brigade for the Liberation of Vietnam, the forerunner of the Vietnam People's Army, was formed.

By 8 August 1945, the Soviet Union had declared war on Japan. Hồ Chí Minh felt that independence was close, founded the National Committee for Insurrection on 13 August and issued a mandate ordering nationwide insurrection (the August 1945 Revolution). On 15 August, Japan unconditionally surrendered. By 19 August, over 1 million people seized power in Hanoi; less than a fortnight later, the insurrection was nationwide. Emperor Bảo Đại abdicated a week later, officially ending the Vietnamese monarchy (though he retained some political relevance until 1955). On 2 September 1945, President Hồ Chí Minh read the Declaration of Independence, which signalled the birth of the Democratic Republic of Vietnam (DRV):

> 'A people who has courageously opposed French domination for more than 80 years, a people to have fought side by side with the Allies against the fascists during these later

> years, such a people must be free and independent. For these reasons, we...solemnly declare to the world that Vietnam has the right to be a free and independent country... The entire Vietnamese nation is determined to mobilise all their physical and mental strength, to sacrifice lives and property in order to safeguard their independence and liberty.'

In front of hundreds of thousands of people gathered in Ba Đình Square in Hanoi, Hồ Chí Minh solemnly took the oath of 'leading the people, safeguarding resolutely the independence of the fatherland, carrying out a programme for the people's freedom and happiness'. The next step was to obtain US recognition for the new republic. When Hồ Chí Minh tried, American President Truman refused and sided with the French. It was a decision that was to change the course of history.

THE FIRST INDOCHINA WAR (1945–54) On 23 September 1945, under cover of the British, French troops landed in Saigon. It signalled a new war of resistance – the First Indochina War – that was to last nine dreadful years. The French, although they had always insisted that Vietnam be returned to French rule, were in no position to force the issue. Instead, in the south, it was British troops (mainly Gurkhas) who helped the small French force against the Việt Minh. When 35,000 French reinforcements arrived, the issue in the south – at least superficially – was all but settled, with Cà Mau at the southern extremity of the country falling on 21 October. From that point, the war in the south became an underground battle of attrition, with the north providing support to their southern comrades.

In the north, the Việt Minh had to deal with 180,000 rampaging Nationalist Chinese troops, while preparing for the imminent arrival of a French force. Unable to confront both at the same time, and deciding that the French were probably the lesser evil, Hồ Chí Minh decided to negotiate. To make the DRV government more acceptable to the French, Hồ Chí Minh proceeded cautiously, bringing only moderates into the government and dissolving the Indochina Communist Party (at least on paper) in November 1945. But in the same month, he also prophetically said: 'The French colonialists should know that the Vietnamese people do not wish to spill blood, that it loves peace. But if it must sacrifice millions of combatants, lead a resistance for long years to defend the independence of the country, and preserve its children from slavery, it will do so. It is certain the resistance will win.'

In February 1946, the French and Chinese signed a treaty leading to the withdrawal of Chinese forces, and shortly afterwards Hồ Chí Minh concluded a treaty with French President Charles de Gaulle's special emissary to Vietnam, Jean Sainteny, in which Vietnam was acknowledged as a 'free' state (the Vietnamese word *độc lập* being translated as free, but not yet independent) that was within the French Union and the Indochinese Federation.

It is interesting to note that in negotiating with the French, Hồ Chí Minh was going against most of his supporters, who argued for confrontation. But Hồ Chí Minh, ever a pragmatist, believed at this stage that the Việt Minh were ill-trained and poorly armed and he appreciated the need for time to consolidate their position. The episode usually highlighted as the flashpoint that led to the resumption of hostilities was the French government's decision to open a customs house in Hải Phòng at the end of 1946. The Việt Minh forces resisted and the rest, as they say, is history. It seems that during the course of 1946 Hồ Chí Minh changed his view of the best path to independence. The French claimed that five Frenchmen and 5,000 Vietnamese were killed during the customs house episode; the Vietnamese put the toll at 20,000.

In a pattern that was to become characteristic of the next 25 years, the French (and later the Americans) controlled the cities, but the Việt Minh were dominant in the countryside. By the end of 1949, with the success of the Chinese Revolution and the establishment of the Democratic People's Republic of Korea (North Korea) the year before, the US began to offer support to the French in an attempt to stem the 'Red Tide' that seemed to be sweeping across Asia. At this stage, the odds appeared stacked against the Việt Minh, but Hồ Chí Minh was confident that time was on their side. As he remarked to Sainteny, 'If we have to fight, we will fight. You can kill ten of my men for every one I kill of yours, but even at those odds, I will win and you will lose.' It also became increasingly clear that the French were not committed to negotiating a route to independence.

The decisive battle of the First Indochina War was at Điện Biên Phủ in the hills of the northwest, close to the border with Laos. At the end of 1953 the French, with American support, parachuted 16,000 men into the area in an attempt to protect Laos from Việt Minh incursions and to tempt them into open battle. The French in fact found themselves trapped, surrounded by Việt Minh and overlooked by artillery. There was some suggestion that the US might become involved, and even use tactical nuclear weapons, but this was not to be. In May 1954 the French surrendered – the most humiliating of French colonial defeats – effectively marking the end of the French presence in Indochina and beyond (for a fuller account, see page 144).

In July 1954, in Geneva, the French and Vietnamese agreed to divide the country along the 17th parallel, so creating two states – the communists occupying the north and the non-communists occupying the south. The border was kept open for 300 days and over that period about 900,000 Vietnamese travelled south. At the same time nearly 90,000 Việt Minh troops along with 43,000 civilians went north, although many Việt Minh remained in the south to continue the fight, now for reunification.

THE SECOND INDOCHINA WAR (1954–75) From July 1954, **Ngô Đình Diệm**, a non-communist nationalist elite from a Catholic background, took over as premier of South Vietnam. Together with his brother Ngô Đình Nhu, who was appointed head of security, he faced many formidable problems. To many it seemed unlikely that a man who had led an unsophisticated, unworldly life, boxed away in various Catholic monasteries, could possibly succeed. After almost a decade of self-imposed exile following Hồ Chí Minh's failed attempt to win Ngô Đình Diệm's support for the Việt Minh, he was completely out of touch; even his military commanders and senior administrators thought that he faced an insoluble dilemma. In the countryside surrounding Saigon, trouble was already brewing from Cao Đài (page 33) and Hòa Hảo (page 34) militia. In the city itself, a criminal gang called Bình Xuyên was terrorising the people and unscrupulous opponents were waiting for him to make his first big mistake. The only support he had was from his family and the Americans, who had their eye on South Vietnam as an American protectorate. Despite all this, he managed to defeat the Bình Xuyên and suppress the Cao Đài and Hòa Hảo militia all within a year.

In October 1955, the monarchy was abolished and Bảo Đại retired to France. Ngô Đình Diệm became the first President of the Republic of Vietnam and his next move was to challenge the communists. The Việt Minh that remained in the south and their sympathisers were arrested, tortured, imprisoned and killed. Acting under orders from Hanoi, those that escaped capture carried out hundreds of brutal murders during 1957; many victims were government officials. In retaliation, Diệm increased his anti-communist campaign.

Many more were rounded up and put to death, sometimes without a trial. It had been the policy of the Communist Party Central Committee that official armed retaliation was not the way forward. When repression against their dwindling numbers in South Vietnam increased, they decided in May 1959 to start guerrilla strikes. Cold-blooded resistance fighters were recruited, including some sent down from North Vietnam. Cao Đài and Hòa Hảo militia joined the struggle and the establishment of the National Liberation Front of Vietnam in 1960, in direct opposition to Diệm, heightened the crisis.

Already, arms were pouring into the South via a route called the Hồ Chí Minh Trail (page 275) and, between 1959 and 1964, the People's Liberation Army in the North sent over 44,000 **Việt Cộng** (the Việt Minh's southern military arm) to join another 100,000 communists who had been amassing in the South. Meanwhile, John F Kennedy, who had been inaugurated as the US president in January 1961, had already sent 400 troops and 1,200 military advisers to Vietnam. By 1962 their total number had increased to 11,000. Many of these were experts, trained in combat techniques that could be used to coach the army of the Republic of Vietnam. It wasn't long before American military involvement intensified, and US helicopters bombed, napalmed and machine-gunned suspected Việt Cộng hideouts.

Diệm adopted a strategic hamlet policy, rounding up villagers and resettling them into areas where they could be observed. A bloody repression campaign against the Buddhists followed because of their opposition to the Diệm regime. The public suicide by self-immolation of Thích Quảng Đức (page 472), a well-loved 66-year-old monk, in Saigon on 11 June 1963 provoked worldwide public outrage. Diệm's brother, Ngô Đình Nhu, worsened the crisis by ordering attacks on Buddhist pagodas.

Clearly, through their unpopularity, Diệm and his brother were becoming a threat to the American anti-communist war effort and, when a coup d'état led by General Dương Văn Minh rocked the presidential palace on 1 November 1963, the Americans paid no attention. Diệm and Nhu escaped but were later found brutally murdered.

Wanting to accelerate the downfall of the Saigon regime, the North stepped up their efforts to improve their supply line via the Hồ Chí Minh Trail. Infantry troops were sent to the South, where the government, following another successful coup d'état to unseat Dương Văn Minh, had been thrown into turmoil. Further periods of unrest were the order of the day for more than a year. Quarrels among the military and the general disarray caused by power struggles and discontentment led US officials to the conclusion that American intervention was quickly becoming necessary.

The American War After Diệm's brutal murder and Kennedy's assassination in Dallas in 1963, the new American president, Lyndon Johnson, at first took a cautious approach. He was forced to act when the US destroyers USS *Maddox* and USS *C Turner Joy* were shelled during the 'Gulf of Tonkin incident' of 2–4 August 1964. In retaliation, the president ordered air strikes on North Vietnamese installations on shore. On 8 February 1965, communists bombed US installations in South Vietnam. A White House directive was issued to bomb North Vietnam. In March this escalated into 'Operation Rolling Thunder', which lasted until October 1968.

During 1967 alone, 108,000 sorties were flown; it was as if 'a sledgehammer was being used to sink a floating cork', commented war journalist Malcolm Browne. No matter how heavy the bombardment, massive supplies for the communist war effort in the South continued to get through, as well as thousands of reinforcement troops. The attempt to 'bomb them back into the Stone Age', the threat made by US Air Force General Curtis LeMay, was certainly not working, but industrial facilities were badly affected, communication channels were disrupted and cities flattened. Thousands of lives were lost, economic growth was stunted and agricultural productivity was greatly reduced.

As the war progressed, every year well over 30,000 civilians were killed and over 60,000 wounded in the South alone. By the end of 1967 over 500,000 US troops, together with 90,000 Australian, Thai, New Zealand, Philippine and South Korean troops, fought alongside an estimated South Vietnamese force (ARVN) of around 1.5 million.

Anti-war demonstrations in the West were in full swing. US General William Westmoreland's directive to use any means possible to increase the communist body count, including the use of chemicals and defoliants, provoked public outrage. Just as the sun came over the horizon on 31 January 1968, the communists hit back, hard and furious. The truce that had been imposed for Tết, the new-year holiday, was broken by guerrilla attacks on cities and towns throughout the South.

Việt Cộng throughout the region, however, failed to win the massive support they expected from ordinary people. The American counter-offensive that followed was successful, but the loss of over 2,000 American lives spurred further anti-war demonstrations, which made Lyndon Johnson think again about his Vietnam policy. His trusted advisers, secretary of defence Clark Clifford and former secretary of state Dean Acheson, advised him to withdraw. His first step was to refuse a request for an extra 200,000 soldiers to be drafted into the area. He then spoke on national television on 31 March 1968 saying that the bombing of North Vietnam was stopping so that peace negotiations could take place with the Hanoi government. The bombing actually ceased on 31 October 1968. For the first time in well over three years, the people of Hanoi could sleep somewhat soundly in their beds.

When Richard Nixon took over the American presidency, it was his policy to withdraw as many Americans as possible from Vietnam while supplying the ARVN with money and weapons. The so-called 'Vietnamisation' policy was a term coined by US secretary of defence Melvin Laird. After talks on 8 June with Nguyễn Văn Thiệu, who had taken over as leader of South Vietnam in 1965, Nixon decided to withdraw 25,000 troops as a starter. By December, 60,000 had been recalled. As 1970 ended, only 280,000 American combat troops were left in the country. The same year it became evident that Nixon had given the order for the secret bombing of Cambodia in March 1969. This resulted in a new wave of anti-war demonstrations.

In February 1971, ARVN forces began attacking key installations along the Hồ Chí Minh Trail in Laos. The 'Phoenix Programme', which was nearing completion, had successfully removed much of the Việt Cộng guerrilla threat from the southern wetlands. Peace had returned to the delta and everyday life was becoming happier. More and more American troops were leaving the country and it seemed to the general population that the worst was over. On 15 March 1972, North Vietnamese military incursions occurred across the Demilitarised Zone around the 17th parallel, and 16 days later Nixon ordered bombing of an area close to Hanoi. This intensified during May and many important strategic sites in the north, such as Hanoi and Hải Phòng harbour, were hit. Nixon ordered further bombing of the North, the so-called 'Christmas Campaign', which came into effect on 18 December and lasted for 11 days.

A ceasefire treaty was signed on 27 January 1973, negotiated by US national security adviser Henry Kissinger and Communist Party representative Lê Đức Thọ. That year the Nobel Peace Prize was awarded to them jointly: Lê Đức Thọ turned it down; Kissinger did not. By 30 March the last American troops had left Vietnam.

During the eight years of war, over 2 million Vietnamese (from both sides) died. Some 3.3 million Americans served in Vietnam; 57,505 were killed and 303,700 wounded. As much as 7 million tonnes of ordinance was dropped on Vietnam, twice as much as the total tonnage used during World War II. Laos was also badly affected, due mainly to bombing of the Hồ Chí Minh Trail supply route. In all, 2.2 million hectares were sprayed with defoliants.

By mid-1973, the South Vietnam government was in a sorry state: rife corruption and the worst recession ever experienced, together with the increasing political discord, were making matters worse. For the South Vietnamese, the ceasefire treaty had served no purpose. In October, it was abandoned by North Vietnam and by the spring of 1975 they were ready to make their final move. Buôn Ma That was taken by 10 March, Quảng Trị Province by 19 March, Đà Nẵng by 30 March, and the major cities along the Southern Central Coast fell in quick succession. Everywhere along the route to Saigon there were scenes of devastation and terror. As the North Vietnamese tanks headed for their final destination on 30 April, a massive evacuation of the city was under way.

Around 7,000 evacuees were transported by helicopter to ships waiting offshore. Although hampered by storms, the operation succeeded. The last flight to leave the embassy roof was at 07.53, only 4 hours before the first North Vietnamese tank crashed through the gates of the Presidential Palace. The mounting of the Liberation flag on the palace balcony symbolised that the Second Indochina War had ended and the country was finally one, although this was not made official until July 1976 when it received its new (and current) name: the Socialist Republic of Vietnam. Saigon was renamed Hồ Chí Minh City the same year.

REUNIFIED VIETNAM When US ambassador Graham Martin flew out of Saigon on 30 April 1975, over a century had elapsed since the city had first been occupied by French troops. For the first time in 20 years, it was possible to send letters between the north and south, and thousands of people became reunited with their loved ones. There was obviously great joy but also great anxiety about the future. The war had left an appalling legacy.

The countryside was littered with an estimated 20 million bomb craters; there were 362,000 people with disabilities and 800,000 orphans (including those abandoned by GI fathers); over 3 million people were unemployed; over 1 million had tuberculosis; there were 2 million widows. Saigon crawled with gangsters. Rehabilitation programmes required the rebuilding of cities, towns and villages, roads, railroads and railway bridges, state farms, water conservation projects, schools, hospitals and health centres. Thousands of tonnes of unexploded bombs had to be cleared and millions of hectares of soil impregnated with deadly carcinogens had somehow to be treated.

The war had bitten very deeply into the fabric of the economy and the post-war government also faced social problems on an unprecedented scale. The consolidation policy of the new government created numerous problems for southerners, many of whom failed to come to terms with Marxist-Leninist dogma and were politically repressed; many were imprisoned and an unknown number found themselves in re-education camps. Thousands joined the increasing numbers

VIETNAM'S BOAT PEOPLE

One of the most potent images of Vietnam during the 1970s and 80s was of foundering, overloaded vessels carrying 'boat people' to Hong Kong, Thailand, Malaysia and the Philippines. Beginning in 1976, these boat people initially fled political persecution. Later, most were economic migrants in search of a better life.

Escaping the country was not easy. Many prospective boat people were caught by the authorities, often having already paid their life savings to secure a place on a boat, and sent to prison or a re-education camp. Of those who embarked, it has been estimated that at least a third died at sea, from drowning, dehydration or at the hands of pirates. The boats were usually small and poorly maintained, hardly seaworthy for a voyage across the East Sea. Captains rarely had charts and most had never ventured further afield than the coastal fishing waters with which they were familiar.

By 1977, the exodus was so great that some freighters stopped picking up refugees – a sacrosanct habit among sailors. Malaysia instructed their coastal patrol vessels to force boats back out to sea – and in the first half of 1979 they did just that to 267 vessels carrying an estimated 40,000 refugees. One boat drifted for days off Malaysia, with the passengers drinking their own urine, until they were picked up – but not before two children had died of dehydration. The Singaporean and Malaysian governments adopted a policy of allowing boats to replenish their supplies, but not to land, forcing some vessels to sail all the way to Australia (more than 8,000km). Cannibalism is also reported to have taken place.

As numbers of refugees rose, so did the incidence of piracy. Pirates, mostly Thai, realising that the boats often carried families with all their possessions (usefully converted into portable gold), began to target the boats, sometimes raping the women and killing all passengers. Some commentators have estimated that by the late 1970s, 30% of boats were being boarded, and the United Nations High Commissioner for Refugees (UNHCR) in 1981 reported that 81% of women had been raped. Despite these risks, Vietnamese continued to leave in huge numbers: by 1980 there were 350,000 awaiting resettlement in refugee camps in Southeast Asia and in Hong Kong.

of 'boat people' (see above) prepared to risk everything, including their lives, to escape communist repression.

Just as the exodus was at its height in April 1977, border atrocities involving murderous Khmer Rouge communists in neighbouring Cambodia occurred with increasing frequency from Tây Ninh to Hà Tiên in the Mekong Delta. By December 1978, an estimated 30,000 Vietnamese soldiers had been killed by Khmer Rouge leader Pol Pot's troops. Countless innocent people had been maimed, eviscerated, decapitated and raped. By now perhaps as many as 300,000 boat people had left the country.

Early in 1979, Vietnamese troops entered Cambodia to remove Pol Pot from power. This had not received backing from Deng Xiaoping's communist government in China and, when word of the overthrow reached Peking, it intensified its military activity along the Chinese border with Vietnam. Chinese vice-premier Li Xiannian had issued a stern warning that an invasion would follow if Vietnam failed to withdraw from Cambodia. In February 1979 attacks came hard and furious across the borders of six northern provinces, a skirmish now referred to as the Sino-Vietnamese War. Official Vietnamese sources claimed that 600,000 troops

Initially, most boat people left from Southern Vietnam; identified with the former regime, they were systematically persecuted, particularly if they also happened to be Hoa (page 477; the Chinese 'invasion' of 1979 did not help matters). But as conditions worsened in the north, large numbers also began to sail from Hạ Long Bay and Hải Phòng. Soon the process became semi-official, as corrupt officials realised that fortunes could be made providing boats and escorts. Large freighters began to carry refugees; one 1,600-tonne ship, which eventually docked in Malaysia, was carrying 2,500 passengers who claimed they had left with the cognisance of the authorities.

The peak of the crisis spanned the years 1976–79, with 270,882 leaving the country in 1979 alone. The flow of refugees slowed during 1980 and 1981 to about 50,000 and until 1988 averaged about 10,000 each year. But in the late 1980s the numbers picked up once again, with most sailing for Hong Kong and leaving from the north, driven by economic pressures. Daily wage rates in Vietnam at that time were only 3,000VND (about 25 cents), so it is easy to see the attraction of leaving. With more than 40,000 refugees in camps in Hong Kong, the authorities there began to forcibly repatriate (euphemistically termed 'orderly return') those screened as economic migrants at the end of 1989. Such was the international outcry as critics highlighted fears of persecution that the programme was suspended. But in May 1992, an agreement was reached between the British and Vietnamese governments to repatriate those living in camps in Hong Kong and the orderly return programme was quietly restarted. As part of their deal to hand Hong Kong to China, the British government had agreed to empty the camps before the handover date in 1997 (a target they failed to meet).

Ironically, the evidence is that those repatriated have fared well – often better than those who never left – and there was no real evidence of systematic persecution, despite the fears of such groups as Amnesty International. With the European Community and the UN offering assistance to returnees, they have set up businesses, enrolled on training courses and become embroiled in Vietnam's thrust for economic growth.

were involved, a fact that remains unproven. The border conflict continued until March, but in the end there was no major Chinese invasion. Vietnam remained in Cambodia, and did not officially withdraw until 1989.

***ĐỔI MỚI*: RENOVATION** An attempt to revitalise the Vietnamese economy began in 1979, with plans for administrative decentralisation. However, rampant inflation, unemployment and lack of foreign investment considerably stunted socio-economic reform until 1986, when the *đổi mới* (renovation) policy was endorsed by the Sixth Congress of the Communist Party of Vietnam. Decentralisation of the national economy during the 1986–90 transition period resulted in an average growth of around 4% per year. The improvements were mainly due to relaxing foreign investment laws, offering greater tax incentives and less rigorous state control of collectives.

Despite the collapse of the Soviet Union and the closure of one investment door, others began to open, stimulating a big economic upsurge. By 1995 GDP was increasing, living conditions were improving and many parameters that had contributed to the socio-economic crisis had been brought under greater control.

Between 1989 and 1993 government figures showed that the number of poverty-stricken households fell from 55% to 19.9%. Agricultural production between 1990 and 1995 rose from 21.5 million tonnes to 27.5 million tonnes, and 2 million tonnes of rice could be exported annually.

The period of greatest economic upsurge followed the lifting of the American trade embargo in 1994, which helped in the restoration of diplomatic relations with the US the following year. Industrial output in 1995 was 14% higher than in 1994 and 88.5% higher than in 1990. Vietnam's popularity as a tourist destination started to increase dramatically after the 1990 'Visit Vietnam Year' worldwide advertising campaign. Figures rocketed from 250,000 tourists in 1990 to well over 1 million in 1994.

Vietnam's economic achievements astounded even financial institutions, including the World Bank. Foreign observers recorded a 774.7% hyperinflation rate in 1986. By 1989 it had slumped to 34.7%. The 1995 inflation figure of 12.7% was remarkable for a country still rated as one of the world's poorest. Vietnam's relationship with the countries of the Association of Southeast Asian Nations (ASEAN) warmed markedly following the dark days of the early and mid-1980s, and in mid-1995 Vietnam became the association's seventh (and first communist) member.

The delicious irony of Vietnam joining ASEAN was that it was becoming part of an organisation established to counteract the threat of communist Vietnam itself. After the fall of the Soviet Union, there was no longer a deep schism between the capitalist and communist countries of the region, either in terms of ideology or management. The main potential flashpoint concerned Vietnam's long-term historical enemy: China. The hostility and suspicion that underlies the relationship between these two communist powers stretches back over 2,000 years. Indeed, one of the great attractions to Vietnam of joining ASEAN was the bulwark that it created against a potentially aggressive and economically ascendant China. Many foreign investors did not have an easy run for their money, but tourism fared well.

The per capita GDP in 1996 was less than that seen in all other large ASEAN countries. During 1996–98 economists agree that the main handicaps affecting Vietnam's economic development were inadequate infrastructure, mismanagement on a macro scale, ambiguous and inconsistent policies, red tape bureaucracy, drastic cuts in government spending, corruption, smuggling, strikes, unemployment, archaic monetary management and legal back-up.

THE NEW MILLENNIUM The progress in relations with the US was slow because many Americans still harboured painful memories of the war. With large numbers of ordinary people continuing to believe that servicemen shot down and captured during the war and listed as MIAs were still languishing in jungle jails, presidents Bush and Clinton had to tread exceedingly carefully.

The normalisation of trade relations between the two countries was agreed in a meeting in July 1999, after three years of discussions. But conservatives in the Politburo prevented the agreement from being signed into law, worried, apparently, about the social and economic side effects of such reform. The signing did not happen until 28 November 2001, when Vietnam's National Assembly finally ratified the treaty. It led to a substantial increase in bilateral trade. In 2003 the USA imported US$4.5 billion worth of Vietnamese goods, roughly four times more than it exported to Vietnam. And not only goods: by 2004 the US consulate general in Hồ Chí Minh City handled more applications for American visas than any other US mission in the world.

More good news came for Vietnam when it became the 150th member of the World Trade Organization in January 2007. The immediate effect was the lifting of import quotas from foreign countries, thereby favouring Vietnamese exporters. In June 2007 President Nguyễn Minh Triết became the first president of Vietnam to visit the US. In 2009, the International Bank for Reconstruction and Development loaned the country US$500 million. From 2010 onwards, the Vietnamese economy grew 5.5–7.5% each year until the Covid pandemic of 2020, where this decreased to a still-respectable 2.9%, one of the highest rates of growth in the world at the time.

As this book was going to print, Vietnam was grappling with the prospect of 46% tariffs on goods entering the US as part of President Trump's bizarre so-called 'reciprocal tariffs'. At the time, the US was Vietnam's most important export destination, and these tariffs have the potential to cripple the economy.

GOVERNMENT AND POLITICS

Vietnam is a one-party communist state. The posts of president and prime minister were created when the constitution was revised in 1992. The president is head of state and the prime minister is head of the cabinet of ministries (including three deputies and 26 ministries), all nominated by the National Assembly, a body of 500 delegates elected for five-year terms. The president at the time of writing was Tô Lâm and the prime minister Phạm Minh Chính. Although the National Assembly is the highest instrument of state, it can still be directed by the Communist Party, and the vast majority of National Assembly members are also party members. The Communist Party is run by a Politburo of 15 members. The head is the general secretary; Tô Lâm (also the president) took over in 2024 from the deceased Nguyễn Phú Trọng, who held the position from 2013. While Nguyễn Phú Trọng's term was characterised by high-profile corruption clampdowns and so-called 'bamboo diplomacy' (ie: the art of balancing international interests and influence; page 24), Tô Lâm, who comes from a police background, has embarked on the daunting task of streamlining and consolidating Vietnam's bloated government institutions. The Politburo meets every five years and sets policy directions of the party and the government. There is a Central Committee made up of 161 members, who are also elected at the Party Congress.

In the country as a whole there is virtually no political debate, certainly not in the open. There seem to be two reasons for this: firstly, there is a genuine fear of discussing something that is absolutely taboo; secondly, and more importantly, is the booming economy. Since the 1990s, economic growth in Vietnam has been unprecedented. As every politician knows, the one thing that keeps people happy is rising incomes. Hence, with not much to complain about, most Vietnamese people are content with the political status quo.

ECONOMY

Vietnam's economy is resilient and growing, the population is increasingly well educated, and it has good access to world markets. Vietnam currently enjoys one of the highest rates of growth (around 6%) in one of the most economically dynamic regions in the world. This state of affairs is the product of a hard-working, underpaid labour force generating massive profits and of the switch from an agrarian economy to an industrial economy. In other words, 200 years after Britain, Vietnam is now undergoing its version of an industrial revolution. Indeed, industry and construction are a huge segment of Vietnam's economy. A China-style property bust is predicted but yet to take hold. Services, including tourism, also account for a large segment of

BAMBOO DIPLOMACY AND BEYOND

By Lam Nguyễn, freelance journalist, video producer at the Agence France-Presse (AFP) and research assistant for this guidebook.

Vietnam's so-called bamboo diplomacy is a political approach to foreign policy that pursues independence, national interests and non-alignment. The term was first mentioned publicly by Nguyễn Phú Trọng, General Secretary of the Communist Party, in 2016. As the nation's top-ranking politician, his speech popularised the concept nationwide and it was quickly picked up by international media. He has reaffirmed this approach several times since. Through bamboo diplomacy, Hanoi has diversified its network of strategic and comprehensive partnerships, taking measures not only to sustain economic development but also strengthen its international standing.

In Asia, the bamboo plant represents adaptability, pliability and perseverance. This is analogous with how Vietnamese diplomacy values flexibility while navigating great power rivalries. This growth-first attitude explains how Vietnam can simultaneously profit from commerce with China, enjoy access to the West's export markets and maintain close military connections with Russia.

In the midst of escalating international power struggles, the bamboo analogy still accurately describes Vietnam's position. For example, in reaction to Beijing's growing dominance in the East Sea, Hanoi has expanded its connections with the West. At the same time, Vietnam continues to adhere to the 'four nos' outlined in its 2019 Defence White Paper: no participation in military alliances; no siding with one country to act against another; no foreign military bases on Vietnamese soil or use of Vietnam as leverage against other countries; and no use of force in international relations. Formally embracing the bamboo diplomatic approach enables Vietnam to take a neutral stance. In other words, there is no impetus to choose between China, Russia and the United States.

However, after Nguyễn Phú Trọng's death in July 2024, Vietnamese politicians and the media have rarely mentioned bamboo diplomacy, perhaps paving the way for the 'new era' discourse of General Secretary Tô Lâm's major administrative reforms.

the economy, and this figure is rising fast. One of the driving forces behind Vietnam's growth has been the export of textiles, food and, more recently, manufactured goods. Vietnam is set to benefit from the West's decoupling (or derisking) from China, but may also suffer severely from the import tariffs imposed by US President Trump.

Vietnam's population now exceeds 100 million and, as the World Bank has pointed out, this means 'the country will have to develop on the basis of human resources rather than natural resources'. But, despite the rapid rise of the middle class, poverty in the countryside over large areas of the north and interior uplands remains the norm rather than the exception. Education and health facilities also require massive investment, not to mention physical infrastructure including roads and power. Though lucrative, the country's export base is also still fairly narrow: coffee, coal, oil, textiles, rice, footwear, clothing and marine products are the country's key exports.

Economic growth has also brought problems. Inequalities, both spatial and personal, are widening. Growth in agriculture is down, while industry is expanding.

So, while the economies of Hanoi, Hồ Chí Minh City and other large cities have been growing annually, the countryside is lagging behind. This is drawing people in from the countryside, creating a slew of urban problems, including poor living conditions and strained infrastructure. Inequalities will likely widen further in the short to medium term.

PEOPLE

ETHNOLINGUISTIC GROUPS The Vietnamese government recognises 54 ethnic groups, reflecting a complex tapestry of customs, beliefs, art, architecture and apparel. An encyclopaedic archive of this immense ethnolinguistic diversity is beyond the scope of this guide, but below is an alphabetised list of the official groups with a few unique or distinct practices put together by Mai Thanh Hoa and Phil Hoolihan, directors of ETHOS, a community-based tourism company that organises experiential tours and supports social programmes in Sa Pa, one of Vietnam's most diverse areas. There is more detailed information on the groups that you're likely to meet in the respective geographical chapters. For further reading, visit **w** special.nhandan.vn/alternate-name-vietnamese/index.html, which has comprehensive information on all 54 groups, and visit the Museum of Ethnology (page 120) in Hanoi. It is important to note that Vietnam has a history of misidentifying and collapsing ethnolinguistic groups that goes back hundreds of years and ill-judged received wisdom remains rife, including in government-sanctioned materials.

Bahnar Population: 300,000. Live in: Central Highlands. See page 354 for details.
Bo Y Population: 3,232. Live in Lào Cai & Hà Giang. They speak a Tai-Kadai language & believe in a 3-layered universe: humans, gods & an underground realm of diminutive people.
Brau Population: around 550. Live in: Đắk Mế village. They migrated to Vietnam from southern Laos & Cambodia & have no written language. The Brau practise ear stretching & construct circular village layouts.
Bru Van Kieu Population: 95,000. Live in: western mountains of Quảng Bình, Quảng Trị & Thừa Thiên Huế. They live in stilt houses, practise Animism & celebrate rice cultivation through various ceremonies.
Cham Population: 180,000. Live in: Ninh Thuận, Bình Thuận & An Giang. See page 343 for details.
Cho Ro Population: 30,000. Live in: Southern Vietnam. Mon-Khmer ethnic group; traditional matriarchal structures are declining, yet women retain special respect.
Chu Ru Population: 24,000. Live in: Lâm Đồng & Bình Thuận primarily. They speak Chru, follow a matrilineal family structure & engage in unique marriage customs involving match-making & family proposals.
Chut Population: 7,500. Live in: Quảng Bình & nearby areas. They are known for their cave dwellings & belief in nature spirits, along with musical traditions.
Co Lao Population: 4,000. Live in: Hà Giang. Their language belongs to the Tai-Kadai family, & they believe in 3 elements: heaven, earth & water.
Co Tu Population: 74,000. Live in: Thừa Thiên Huế & Quảng Nam mostly. Their famous dances are *tung tung* (performed by men) & *ya ya* (performed by women). Each village has a common house, which is the tallest & most ornate.
Co Population: 40,442. Live in: Quảng Ngãi & Quảng Nam. They have a chieftain-led society, spiritual belief in souls & celebrate New Year with rituals & music.
Cong Population: around 2,600. Live in: Lai Châu & Điện Biên. They follow clan-specific customs & hold annual ancestor worship ceremonies to protect their crops.
Dao Population: 900,000. Live in: northern provinces. See page 172 for details.
Ede Population: 400,000. Live in: Central Highlands. This group speaks a Malayo-Polynesian language. See page 362 for details.
Giay Population: 68,000. Live in: northern mountainous provinces. They wear cotton clothing & celebrate the Roóng Poọc Festival for

A NOTE ON TERMINOLOGY

While 'ethnic minority' (a direct translation of the Vietnamese *dân tộc thiểu số*) is commonly used to describe all ethnolinguistic groups other than the majority Kinh, this term is at best simplistic and inaccurate and at worst derogatory. For example, in some northern provinces, the so-called ethnic minorities are in fact the majority population. In other parts of Vietnam, the Kinh are the majority, but other ethnolinguistic groups settled in the area hundreds, sometimes thousands, of years before. The French referred to the mountain-dwelling groups in the Central Highlands as 'Montagnards', a colonial term that won't be used in this book. 'Tribe' and 'tribal' are also avoided. The term 'ethnolinguistic group' is the preferred term in this guide, reflecting the roles played by ethnicity and language in uniting peoples. English, not Vietnamese, is used to refer to the different ethnolinguistic groups in this guidebook (thus Bahnar, not Ba Na; Hmong, not H'mông), which is why the words carry no diacritics.

the rice season. They traditionally treat farmland as communal property.

Gie Trieng Population: 64,000. Live in: Central Highlands. They live in villages led by a knowledgeable elder & practise unique traditions, including hanging coffins in trees.

Ha Nhi Population: 12,500. Live in: Lai Châu & Lào Cai. Lo Lo-speaking group who live in earthen houses, perform rituals for water & forest gods & celebrate a significant harvest festival.

Hmong Population: 1.4 million members. Live in: the northern highlands (predominantly). See page 160 for details.

Hoa (Vietnamese Chinese) Population: up to 1 million. Live in: Hồ Chí Minh City & surrounding areas. See page 477 for details.

Hre Population: 149,460. Live in: Quảng Ngãi mainly. They speak a Mon-Khmer language, live in stilt houses & have distinct clothing. Their spirituality includes belief in souls & gods, which are celebrated through traditional gong performances.

Jarai Population: 500,000. Live in: Central Highlands. See page 355 for details.

K'Ho Population: 200,000. Live in: Central Highlands. They speak K'Ho, live in matriarchal villages & practise a folk religion honouring various deities. A subgroup, the Lạch, originates from Đà Lạt.

Khang Population: 16,180. Live in: Northwest. Austro-Asiatic group known for hot & sour cuisine & a tradition of burying the dead with personal items to prevent spirits from returning.

Khmer Population: 1.3 million. Live in: Mekong Delta. See page 411 for details.

Kho Mu Population: 90,000. Live in: Northern Vietnam. Austro-Asiatic society originally from Northern Laos. They grow crops communally & swap stories by firelight, often involving sharing silver pipes (originally opium, but now predominantly tobacco). Some Kho Mu are heavily tattooed.

Kinh Population: 85% of Vietnam's total. Live in: whole country. Vietnam's largest ethnolinguistic group. See page 189 for details.

La Chi Population: 15,126. Live in: Hà Giang & Lào Cai. The La Chi, who speak a Tai-Kadai language, live in groups where family patriarchs manage economic & social relations. They believe in 12 souls per person & practise sex-based child exchanges to balance their population.

La Ha Population: 10,000. Live in: Yên Bái & Sơn La. This patriarchal group has strict taboos regarding family interactions & burial practices, with deceased members buried in 'ghost forests' where certain activities are prohibited.

La Hu Population: 12,000. Live in: Lai Châu. They are 1 of the 1st ethnic groups to be chronicled in the Chinese historical record & speak a language similar to Lo Lo.

Lao Population: 20,000. Live in: the Northwest mostly. This group, which migrated from Laos, builds stilt houses & practise traditional customs like betel chewing. Their New Year festival (Apr) features rituals, dances, folklore & music.

Lo Lo Population: 5,000. Live in: Northern Vietnam. A Tibeto-Burman community known for their intricately crafted traditional garments. See page 175 for more.

Lu Population: 6,000. Live in: Lai Châu. They migrated to Vietnam from Yunnan, China, around 1,000 years ago & live in stilt houses. Their polytheistic beliefs emphasise ancestor worship & the existence of good & evil ghosts.

Ma Population: 50,000. Live in: Lâm Đồng & Đồng Nai provinces primarily. A Mon-Khmer group known for their vibrant attire, rich oral traditions & animal sacrifices like the buffalo ceremony.

Mang Population: 5,000. Live in: Lai Châu. Group known for their corn-based cuisine. Traditionally, face tattoos marked adulthood, allowing community recognition & ancestral connection after death.

Mnong Population: Fewer than 100,000. Live in: Central Highlands. The Mnong speak a Mon-Khmer language influenced by Ede. See page 366 for details.

Muong Population: More than 1 million. Live in: Hòa Bình mostly. See page 136 for details.

Ngai Population: Fewer than 2,000. Live in: Quảng Ninh. Hakka-speaking community descended from southern Chinese ancestors. They practise diverse worship rituals for various deities & celebrate traditional festivals, including Lunar New Year.

Nung Population: 1 million. Live in: Cao Bằng & Lạng Sơn. This group, which fled China in the 11th century, has a rich culture & practises polytheism, ancestor worship, Animism & shamanism.

O Du Population: Fewer than 500. Live in: Nghệ An mainly. Because of their small population, their culture is heavily influenced by the Kho Mu & Thai. The O Du have a patriarchal social structure where women have no inheritance rights.

Pa Then Population: More than 8,000. Live in: Hà Giang & Tuyên Quang primarily. They migrated here some 200–300 years ago from China. After harvests, they express gratitude through a fire dance festival.

Phu La Population: 12,500. Live in: Lào Cai. Their gender-specific costumes feature indigo dyes & natural colours, with unique decorative art influenced by other ethnicities.

Pu Peo Population: around 900. Live in: Hà Giang. Village heads, chosen for their experience & prestige, manage daily life & have spiritual roles. They enjoy herbal drinks & traditional corn wine.

Raglai Population: 145,000. Live in: Central Vietnam. Related to the Cham, they believe in a divine world, practise regular worship with sacrifices & express their culture through myths, songs & musical instruments such as bronze gongs.

Ro Mam Population: More than 500. Live in: Le village, Kon Tum, primarily. They speak a Bahnaric language & their traditional attire reflects cultural values, featuring white, undyed fabrics. Key celebrations include post-harvest festivals.

San Chay Population: 205,000. Live in: Tuyên Quang mainly, but also other northern provinces. They consist of 2 subgroups, Cao Lan & San Chi, each with distinct languages, which makes a case for them to be considered distinct official groups.

San Diu Population: 115,000. Live in: Northern Vietnam. Sinitic Cantonese group that likely migrated from Guangdong around 1600BCE. They celebrate festivals like Dong chi, focusing on fertility prayers & marriage renewal.

Sedang Population: More than 200,000. Live in: Kon Tum, Quảng Nam & Quảng Ngãi. Traditionally live in communal villages governed by elders, & maintain close-knit, multi-generational family structures.

Si La Population: around 600. Reside in: Lai Châu. Migrated from Yunnan about 150 years ago. Women collect fallen hair to gift to their daughters-in-law during marriages.

Stieng Population: More than 100,000. Live in: Bình Phước. They do not have a written language. Their culture includes distinctive clothing & jewellery that makes use of ivory. The Stieng worship the gods of thunder, heaven, earth, moon, sun, mountains & rivers.

Ta Oi Population: More than 50,000. Live in: Thừa Thiên Huế & Quảng Trị mainly. Mon-Khmer group whose traditional society features clan leaders & unique customs such as rituals honouring a water spirit believed to ensure plentiful fish & safe water.

Tay Population: 1.7 million. Live in: Northern Vietnam. Vietnam's 2nd largest ethnic group. See page 170 for details.

Thai Population: 1.8 million. Live in: Northwest subregion primarily. Known for their weaving, which is done on large looms. See page 138 for details.

Tho Population: 92,000. Live in: Nghệ An mostly. Practise Animism & unique customs include rooftop sleeping, where members of the opposite sex can spend a platonic evening together in public view.

Xinh Mun Population: 30,000. Live in: Sơn La & Lai Châu. Speaking a Mon–Khmer language, they have unique wedding & naming customs & specific burial traditions involving gunfire to signify that someone has passed.

Unofficial ethnic groups In addition to the aforementioned official ethnic groups, there are various other peoples that could be considered distinct, such as the Xa Phang, officially a Hoa subgroup in Điện Biên but with unique cultural traditions, such as shoemaking, a nationally celebrated craft. The Thuy community in Thượng Minh village, Tuyên Quang Province, with around 100 members, has preserved forest beliefs not shared with other groups. They classify forests into holy, watershed and ordinary types, emphasising sustainable practices. The Xa Pho, officially a subgroup of the Phu La, celebrates a unique 'village sweeping ritual' on the second day of the first lunar month to chase away evil spirits and ensure good fortune, emphasising their strong communal ties. The Pa Di in Mường Khương, Lào Cai, speak a Tai–Kadai language and identify as a distinct ethnic group despite the absence of official recognition.

LANGUAGE

Vietnamese has a reputation for being fiendishly difficult to master. Its origins, once the subject of dispute, are now somewhat settled. At one time it was thought to be a Sino-Tibetan language related to Chinese, because it is tonal (a type of language where the pitch can alter the semantic meaning of a word). But it is now believed to be Austro-Asiatic (a non-tonal language family) and related to Khmer. The theory is that the Vietnamese, who for thousands of years lived in close proximity to communities that spoke tonal languages, like Thai and Chinese, somehow absorbed tones into their language, a process linguists call tonogenesis. Standard Vietnamese has six tones, whereas some dialects have only five.

Sometime after the 10th century, when Vietnam was no longer under Chinese domination, Chinese ideograms were adapted for use with the Vietnamese language. This script – *chữ nho* – was used in all official correspondence and in literature right through to the early 20th century. Whether this replaced an earlier writing system is not known. As early Vietnamese nationalists tried to break away from Chinese cultural hegemony in the late 13th century, they devised their own script, based on Chinese ideograms but adapted to meet Vietnamese language needs. This became known as *chữ nôm*. So, while Chinese words formed the learned vocabulary of the intelligentsia (largely inaccessible to the man on the street or in the paddy field), non-Chinese words made up a parallel popular vocabulary. Much like English, which has words with similar meanings taken from both Latin and Germanic languages (eg: liberty and freedom), Vietnamese has both native words and words borrowed from Chinese (eg: *ngựa trắng* and *bạch mã* both mean 'white horse', with the latter derived from the Chinese 白马).

In the 17th century, European missionaries under the tutelage of Portuguese Jesuit Father Alexandre de Rhodes created a system of Romanised writing: *quốc ngữ* ('national language'). It is said that Rhodes initially thought Vietnamese sounded like the 'twittering of birds', a view interestingly echoed by Graham Greene in *The Quiet American* ('To take an Annamite to bed with you is like taking a bird: they twitter and sing on your pillow'), but he had mastered the language in six months. The first *quốc ngữ* dictionary (Vietnamese–Portuguese–Latin), *Dictionarium*

THE USE OF *QUỐC NGỮ* IN THIS GUIDEBOOK

You will have noticed by now that this guidebook uses *quốc ngữ*. This is to show respect for the richness of the Vietnamese language and the creativity of its written form, but it is also for practical reasons. It's sometimes said that writing Vietnamese without diacritics is like writing English without vowels: the Vietnamese will do their best to deduce the meaning, but it can lead to frustrating misunderstandings. For example, *sữa chua* means 'yoghurt' and *sửa chữa* is 'to fix', two very different words that would both be written *sua chua* without the diacritics. Write down or point at the word *sua chua* and the person you're talking to might think that you're trying to satisfy a dairy craving, when what you really want is to fix your motorbike. Diacritics have not been used for the words 'Vietnam', 'Hanoi' and 'Saigon' in part because they resonate across all languages that use the Latin alphabet, but also because using diacritics would result in some ugly-looking derivatives (eg: Hà Nộian, Sài Gònese, Việt Namese etc).

Annamiticum Lusitanum et Latinum, was published in 1651. *Quốc ngữ* uses marks – called diacritics – to indicate differences in vowel quality and tones. Initially it was ignored by the educated unless they were Roman Catholic and it was not until the early 20th century that its use became a mark of modernity among a broad spectrum of Vietnamese. Even then, engravings in the mausoleums and palaces of the royal family continued to use Chinese characters. It seems that the move from *chữ nôm* to *quốc ngữ*, despite the fact that it was created by a European, occurred as people realised that it could be mastered more quickly. The first *quốc ngữ* newspaper, *Gia Định Báo*, was published in 1865 and *quốc ngữ* was adopted as the national script in 1920. While native speakers of European languages may find speaking Vietnamese more difficult than other tonal languages in Asia like Chinese and Thai (both have fewer tones), the writing system provides some respite.

Standard Vietnamese (*tiếng chuẩn*) is based on the language spoken by an educated person living in the vicinity of Hanoi. This has become Vietnam's equivalent of BBC English to the British. There are also important regional dialects in the centre and south of the country and these differ from Standard Vietnamese in terms of tone and vocabulary, but use the same system of grammar. These regional differences can be huge and unidirectional; while all Vietnamese speakers understand those from Hanoi and Saigon, it's common for urbanites from these cities to have trouble understanding people from other parts of the country.

RELIGION AND BELIEFS

Many arrive in Vietnam surprised to find an extraordinary amount of spirituality for a communist country. Vietnam is home to a large number of followers of many of the major world religions, as well as belief systems that are peculiarly Vietnamese. This includes Theravada and Mahayana Buddhism, Protestant and Roman Catholic Christianity, Taoism, Confucianism, Cao Đài and Hòa Hảo.

There are also small communities of Muslims and Hindus among the Cham of the Southern Central Coast and Châu Đốc. The Cham of the Southern Central Coast have been Hindu for at least a thousand years; the Cham in Châu Đốc were converted to Islam more recently by Muslim traders. There are also several mosques and Hindu temples in Hồ Chí Minh City and Chợ Lớn, some of them built by Indians from Kerala. In addition, spirit and ancestor worship are also practised widely. Confucianism, more philosophy than religion, is probably the most pervasive doctrine of all. Nominal Christians and Buddhists will still pay attention to the moral and philosophic principles of Confucianism and it continues to play a central role in Vietnamese life.

Following the communist victory in 1975, the authorities moved quickly to curtail the influence of the various belief systems. Schools, hospitals and other institutions run by religious organisations were taken over by the state and many clergy either imprisoned or sent to re-education camps. The religious hierarchies were institutionalised and proselytising severely curtailed.

During the late 1980s and into the early 1990s some analysts identified an easing of the government's previously highly restrictive policies towards religious organisations. At the beginning of 1993, former general secretary of the Vietnamese Communist Party, Đỗ Mười, even went so far as to make official visits to a Buddhist monastery and a Roman Catholic church. However, the communist hierarchy remains highly suspicious of priests and monks. They are well aware of the prominent role they played in South Vietnamese political dissension and are quick to crack down on any religious leader or organisation that becomes involved in politics.

There is no question that many people today are attending Buddhist pagodas, Christian churches and Cao Đài temples. However, whether a rise in attendance actually means some sort of religious rebirth is questionable. Đặng Nghiêm Vạn, the former head of Hanoi's Institute of Religious Studies, poured scorn on the notion that young people are finding religion. They 'are not religious,' he said, 'just superstitious. This isn't religion. It's decadence.' Religious tourism, like pilgrimages for the modern age, has become enormously popular, especially during festivals, national holidays and the first few months of the lunar new year.

ANCESTOR WORSHIP For the Kinh, Vietnam's ethnolinguistic majority, ancestor worship is widespread and often takes place alongside the practices of Buddhism, Christianity and Islam. You'll notice that most family altars have pictures. On the deceased's birthday and on the anniversary of their death, Vietnamese will pay their respects at the family altar, believing that they are now protected by their spirit. If anyone in the family gets married or does especially well, they might also come to pay their respects. In many temples throughout Vietnam there are also small altars on which people can pin photographs or messages about sick relatives who need the help of their ancestors' spirits. Ancestor worship is also commonplace among Vietnam's other ethnolinguistic groups.

BUDDHISM Although there are both Theravada (also known as Hinayana) and Mahayana Buddhists in Vietnam, the latter are by far the more numerous. Buddhism was introduced into Vietnam in the 2nd century CE: Indian pilgrims came by boat and brought the teachings of Theravada Buddhism, while Chinese monks came by land and introduced Mahayana Buddhism. In particular, the Chinese monk Mau Tử is credited with being the first person to introduce Mahayana Buddhism in CE194–195.

Initially, Buddhism was very much the religion of the elite and did not impinge upon the common Vietnamese man or woman. It was not until the reign of Emperor Lý Anh Tông (1138–75) that Buddhism was promoted as the state religion, nearly 1,000 years after Mau Tử had arrived from China. By that time it had begun to filter down to the village level, but as it did so it became increasingly syncretic;

Buddhism became enmeshed with Confucianism, Taoism, spirituality, mysticism and Animism. In the 15th century it also began to lose its position to Confucianism as the dominant religion of the court.

There has been a resurgence of Buddhism since the 1920s. It was the self-immolation of Buddhist monks in the 1960s that provided a focus of discontent against the government in the south, and since the communist victory in 1975, monks have remained an important focus of dissent, hence the persecution of Buddhists during the early years following reunification. Mahayana Buddhists are concentrated in the centre and north of the country and the dominant sect is the Thiền (Zen) meditation sect. Of the relatively small numbers of Theravada Buddhists, the majority are Khmer and are concentrated in the Mekong Delta. In Vietnam, Buddhism is intertwined with Confucianism and Taoism to form a kind of religious trinity.

CONFUCIANISM Although Confucianism is not strictly a religion, the teachings of the Chinese sage and philosopher Confucius (551–479BCE) form the foundations on which Vietnamese life and government were based for much of the historical period. Even today, Confucianist perspectives are, possibly, more strongly in evidence than communist ones. Confucianism was introduced from China during their rule of Vietnam in the Bắc Thuộc Period (111BCE–CE938).

The 'religion' enshrined the concept of imperial rule by the mandate of heaven, constraining social and political change. In essence, Confucianism stresses the importance of family and lineage and the worship of ancestors. Men and women in positions of authority were required to provide role models for the 'ignorant', while the state, epitomised by the emperor, was likewise required to set an example and to provide conditions of stability and fairness for his people. Crucially, children had to observe filial piety. This set of norms, which were drawn from the experience of the human encounter at the practical level, were enshrined in the *Forty-Seven Rules for Teaching and Changing* first issued in 1663.

A key element of Confucianist thought is the Three Bonds: (1) the loyalty of ministers to the emperor; (2) obedience of children to their parents; and (3) submission of wives to their husbands. Added to these are mutual reciprocity among friends and benevolence towards strangers. Not surprisingly the communists are antipathetic to such a hierarchical view of society, although ironically Confucianism, which inculcates respect for the elderly and authority, unwittingly lends support to a Politburo occupied by old men. In an essay entitled 'Confucianism and Marxism', Vietnamese scholar Nguyễn Khắc Viện explains why Marxism proved an acceptable doctrine to those accustomed to Confucian values: 'Marxism was not baffling to Confucians in that it concentrated man's thoughts on political and social problems. By defining man as the total of his social relationships, Marxism hardly came as a shock to the Confucian scholar who had always considered the highest aim of man to be the fulfilment of his social obligations. Bourgeois individualism, which puts personal interests ahead of those of society and petty bourgeois anarchism, which allows no social discipline whatsoever, are alien to both Confucianism and Marxism.'

TAOISM Taoism was introduced from China into Vietnam at about the same time as Confucianism. It is based on the works of the Chinese philosophers Lao Tzu (c 6th–5th centuries BCE) and Chuang Tzu (4th century BCE). Although not strictly a formal religion, it has had a significant influence on Buddhism (as it is practised in Vietnam) and on Confucianism. In reality, Taoism and Confucianism can be

ĐỀN, ĐÌNH OR *CHÙA*?

You'll have worked out by now that it's not easy getting your head around Vietnam's belief systems, but a good place to start is establishing a loose understanding of the difference between the three main types of religious buildings: *đền*, *đình* and *chùa*. This guide translates *đền* as 'temple' and it denotes a traditional place of worship that is not Buddhist. Prayers here are typically directed towards a deity, like the Jade Emperor, also known as the King of Heaven, divine heroes, like Thánh Gióng (page 473), and historical heroes, like Trần Hưng Đạo. *Đình* is translated in this guide as 'communal house' and is like a town hall where meetings take place, important decisions are made and festivals are hosted. The *đình* is traditionally the central point of the community, and many will have at least one area where any number of gods, spirits and village ancestors are worshipped. *Chùa* is 'pagoda', or a place dedicated to the worship of Buddha and his various derivations. The Khmer (page 411), who are largely Buddhist, pray at *chùa*, and places of worship dedicated to Quan Âm (page 293), who was adopted by Buddhism to become the Goddess of Compassion, are also *chùa*. In practice, there is considerable overlap, and you'll find Buddha in *đình* and heroes in *chùa*, plus there are a whole host of other buildings, including *miếu* ('shrine'), *tháp* ('temple tower') and *nhà thờ* (church). If you find it confusing, it's best to take the information as it comes and remain open-minded, much like the general Vietnamese approach to spirituality.

seen as two sides of the same coin: the Taoist side is poetry and spirituality; the Confucianist side is social ethics and the order of the world. Together they form a unity. Like Confucianism, it is not possible to give a figure to the number of followers of Taoism in Vietnam. It functions in conjunction with Confucianism and Buddhism and also often with other belief systems.

Of all the world's major belief systems, Taoism is perhaps the hardest to pin down. It has no formal code, no teachings and no creed. It is cosmic by name and cosmic by nature. Even the word Tao is usually left untranslated or merely translated as 'The Way'. The inscrutability of it all is summed up in the writings of the Chinese poet Po Chü-i: 'Those who speak know nothing; those who know keep silence. These words, as I am told, were spoken by Lao Tzu. But if we are to believe that Lao Tzu was himself one who knew, how is it that he wrote a book of five thousand words?'

Central to Taoist belief is a world view based upon yin and yang, two primordial forces on which the creation and functioning of the world are based. The yin–yang is not specifically Taoist (or Confucianist), but predates both and is associated with the first recorded Chinese ruler, Fu-hsi (2852–2738BCE). The well-known yin–yang symbol demonstrates the balance and equality between the great dualistic forces in the universe: dark and light, negative and positive, male and female. J C Cooper explains in *Taoism: the Way of the Mystic* the symbolism of the black and white dots: 'There is a point, or embryo, of black in the white and white in the black. This is essential to the symbolism since there is no being which does not contain within itself the germ of its opposite. There is no male without feminine characteristics and no female without its masculine attributes.'

The dualism of the yin–yang is not absolute, but permeable. To maintain balance and harmony in life it is necessary that a proper balance be maintained between yin (female) and yang (male). This is believed to be true both at the scale of the world and the nation, and also for an individual, for the human body is the world in microcosm. The root cause of illness is imbalance between the forces of yin and yang. Even foods have characters: 'hot' foods are yang and 'cold' yin. Implicit in this is the belief that there is a natural law underpinning all of life, a law upon which harmony ultimately rests. Taoism attempts to maintain this balance and thereby harmony. In this way, Taoism is a force promoting inertia, maintaining the status quo. Traditional relationships between fathers and sons, between siblings, within villages, and between the rulers and the ruled, are all rationalised in terms of maintaining balance and harmony.

CHRISTIANITY Christianity was first introduced into Vietnam in the 16th century by Roman Catholic missionaries from Portugal, Spain and France. The first Bishop of Vietnam was appointed in 1659 and by 1685 there were estimated to be 800,000 Roman Catholics in the country. For several centuries Christianity was discouraged and, at times, outlawed. Many Christians were executed and one of the reasons the French gave for annexing the country in the late 19th century was religious persecution. Today, 8–10% of the population are thought to be Roman Catholic; less than 1% are Protestant. This Christian population is served by around 2,000 priests. Following reunification in 1975, many Roman Catholics in the former south were sent to re-education camps. They were perceived to be both staunchly pro-American and anti-communist and it was not until 1988 that many were returned to normal life.

Today, Roman Catholics are still viewed with suspicion by the state and priests felt to be drifting from purely religious concerns into any criticism of the state (seen as anti-government activity) are detained. And this is the key point: the Vietnamese remain tolerant and open in matters of religion and spirituality. It is the political overtones that come with any established religion that the authorities find impossible to accept. While memories of the role of the Roman Catholic Church in the downfall of Polish communism linger, relations between Hanoi and the Vatican are not warm and Rome finds it difficult to appoint bishops. However, in 2007 the prime minister at the time became the first head of government to be received at the Vatican to discuss relations. More generally, the authorities have been slow to permit Vietnamese men to become ordained, and they have limited the production and flow of religious literature. Nevertheless, centuries of existence in what for the Roman Catholic Church has been the hostile environment of Vietnam has enabled it to reach an accommodation and degree of acceptance.

CAO ĐÀI Cao Đài took root in Southern Vietnam during the 1920s after Ngô Văn Chiêu, a civil servant, was visited by 'Cao Đài' or the 'Supreme Being' and was given the tenets of a new religion. Ngô received this spiritual visitation in 1919 on Phú Quốc island. The Cao Đài later told Ngô in a seance that he was to be symbolised by a giant eye. The religion quickly gained the support of a large following of dispossessed peasants. It was both a religion and a nationalist movement. In terms of the former, it claimed to be a synthesis of Buddhism, Christianity, Taoism, Confucianism and Islam. Cao Đài 'saints' include Joan of Arc, the French writer Victor Hugo, Sir Winston Churchill, Sun Yat-sen, Moses and Brahma. Debates over doctrine are mediated through the spirits, who are contacted on a regular basis through a strange wooden contraption called a *corbeille-à-bec* or planchette.

The five Cao Đài commandments are: do not kill any living creature; do not covet; do not practise high living; do not be tempted; and do not slander by word.

But, as well as being a religion, the movement also claimed that it would restore traditional Vietnamese attitudes and was anti-colonial and modestly subversive. Opportunist to a fault, Cao Đài followers sought the aid of the Japanese against the French, the Americans against the Việt Minh and the Việt Minh against the South. Following reunification in 1975, all Cao Đài lands were confiscated and their leadership emasculated. The centre of Cao Đài is still Southern Vietnam where – despite communist efforts– there are thought to be perhaps 2.5 million adherents and 1,000 Cao Đài temples. The Cao Đài Great Temple (page 392) is in the town of Tây Ninh in the Southeast, 100km from Hồ Chí Minh City.

HÒA HẢO Hòa Hảo is another Vietnamese religion that emerged in the Mekong Delta. It was founded by Huỳnh Phú Sổ in 1939, a resident of Hòa Hảo village in the province of Châu Đốc. Effectively a schism of Buddhism, the sect discourages temple building and worship, maintaining that simplicity of worship is the key to better contact with God. Hòa Hảo is not a visitor-friendly religion, as it were, as there are no temples, sites or shrines, and curious travellers who seek out the village where it was founded will leave without any photos to show for it. For more on Hòa Hảo, see page 425.

EDUCATION

Vietnam enjoys near-universal literacy. Primary education is mandatory, beginning at age six and lasting five years. This is followed by lower secondary school, which lasts four years. Despite education being compulsory until the age of 14, many students in rural areas struggle with access and drop-out rates remain a concern in highland areas. Upper secondary education spans three years and culminates in a national high school exam, the results of which determine entry into higher education. Competition is intense, and the exam system, which emphasises rote memorisation, often draws criticism for not adequately preparing students with practical skills for the workforce or for further studies abroad. University education remains highly sought after, although overcrowded classrooms and a lack of resources often diminish the quality. Vocational education is also available and aims to provide students with skills tailored to Vietnam's growing industrial economy, yet it still lacks prestige compared with university degrees.

CULTURE

LITERATURE In ancient Vietnam, texts were reproduced laboriously, by scribes, on paper made from the bark of the mulberry tree. Printing technology was introduced in the late 13th century, but due to the hot and humid climate no early examples exist. Vietnam has a rich folk literature of fables, legends, proverbs and songs, most of which were transmitted by word of mouth. A number of these tales are in this guide in 'Legend has it' boxes. In the 17th and 18th centuries, satirical poems and, importantly, verse novels appeared. These were memorised and recited by itinerant storytellers as they travelled from village to village.

Like Vietnamese art, Vietnamese literature also owes a debt to China. Chinese characters and literary styles were duplicated and although a tradition of Nôm literature did evolve (*nôm* being a hybrid script developed in the 13th century; page 28), many Vietnamese efforts remained derivative. One exception was the scholarly Nguyễn Trãi, who bridged the gap: he excelled in classical Chinese, as well as producing some of the earliest surviving, and very fine, poetry and prose in the new *chữ nôm* script. An important distinction is between the literature of the intelligentsia (essentially Chinese) and that of the people. These later works, dating from the 15th century onwards, were simpler and concerned with immediate problems and grievances. They can be viewed as the most Vietnamese of literary works and include 'Chinh Phụ Ngâm' ('Lament of a Soldier's Wife'), an anti-war poem by Phan Huy Ích (1750–1822). The greatest Vietnamese literature was produced during the social and political upheavals of the 19th century: *Truyện Kiều* (*The Tale of Kiều*) written by Nguyễn Du (1765–1820) is a classic of the period. This 3,254-line story is regarded by most Vietnamese as their literary magnum opus. Nguyễn Du was one of the most skilled and learned mandarins of his time and was posted to China as Vietnam's ambassador.

French influence, and the spread of the Romanised Vietnamese script, led to the end of the Chinese literary tradition by the 1930s and its replacement by a far starker, freer, Western-derived style. Poetry of this period is known as Thơ Mới (New Poetry). The communist period saw restrictions on literary freedom and in recent years there have been numerous cases of authors and poets, as well as journalists, being imprisoned owing to the critical nature of their work. Much of Vietnam's literature is allegorical (which people readily understand); this reflects a centuries-old intolerance of criticism by the mandarin and royal family. Although the Communist Party might be expected to approve of anti-royal sentiment in literature it seldom does, fearing that the Party itself is the true object of the writer's scorn. Vietnamese writers after *đổi mới* (economic reform; page 21) with works that have been translated into English include Bảo Ninh, Nguyễn Huy Thiệp and Dương Thu Hương. Members of the Vietnamese diaspora who write in English, like Nguyễn Thanh Việt and Ocean Vương, have also achieved literary success. See page 488 for a reading list.

MUSIC AND THEATRE Traditional music has existed for millennia, evidenced by bamboo flutes dating back 2,300 years and Đông Sơn bronze drums (page 8) dating back 2,700 years. Lithophones made from sonorous rhyolite stones have been discovered in the Central Highlands and date back to 3,000–4,000 years ago. These days, traditional folk music and theatre or performance usually go hand in hand in Vietnam. Traditional royal chamber music known as ***ca trù***, which has its roots in 15th-century religious music, has enjoyed a revival since it was inscribed as an intangible cultural heritage by UNESCO in 2009. *Ca trù* is a poem which has been put to song and groups consist of three performers: a female singer and two instrumentalists. Many performances include some form of audience participation and some also include dance. Despite efforts from practitioners, *ca trù* had a tough time in the 2020s when the Covid-19 pandemic put a halt to performances, and groups have struggled to get things up and running again. UNESCO remarks that *ca trù* is 'in need of urgent safeguarding'.

While *ca trù* has received the greatest international recognition, other music and theatre styles include *tuồng*, *chèo*, *quan họ*, *hát xẩm*, *chầu văn* and, more recently, *cải lương*. It is possible that ***tuồng*** first appeared in Vietnam during the 10th and 11th centuries. The performance follows strictly set rules of facial expression and accented speech, and the story, which is mimed, is usually an epic taken from Vietnamese history. Performers wear colourful costumes and paint their faces in different colours depending on their rank. ***Chèo*** originated at around the same time in the Red River Delta and combines music, dance and acting, often using humour and satire to depict everyday life and teach moral lessons. Chèo is typically performed with live musicians, colourful costumes and archetypal characters. ***Quan họ*** also developed in the north, though probably after *chèo* and

WATER PUPPETRY

The most original theatrical art form in Vietnam is *múa rối nước*, or water puppet theatre. This seems to have originated in Northern Vietnam during the early years of the last millennium, when it was associated with the harvest festival. An inscription in Hà Nam Province mentions a show put on in honour of King Lý Nhân Tông in 1121. By the time the French had begun to colonise Vietnam in the late 19th century, it had spread to all major towns.

As the name suggests, this form of theatre uses the surface of the water as the stage. Puppeteers, concealed behind a bamboo screen symbolising an ancient village communal house, manipulate the characters while standing in a metre of water. The puppets – some over half a metre tall – are carved from water-resistant wood that is also very lightweight and then painted in bright colours. Most need one puppeteer to manipulate them, but some require three or four. Plays are based on historical and religious themes: the origins of the Việt nation, legends, village life and acts of heroism. Some include the use of fireworks – especially during battle scenes – while all performances are accompanied by folk opera singers and traditional instruments. Performances usually begin with a clown figure taking the stage and he acts as a linking character between the various scenes.

tuồng, and involves singing in pairs, exchanging verses in a call-and-response manner. ***Hát xẩm*** developed in the 13th or 14th century and was traditionally performed by blind street musicians, featuring improvised melodies accompanied by instruments like the *đàn nhị* (two-string fiddle) and *đàn bầu* (monochord). Performances often tell parables or deliver social commentary. ***Chầu văn***, which developed in the 16th century in Nam Định Province, is a form of spiritual singing often used in rituals to invoke spirits. The performances, often led by a young man dressed as a female divinity, are highly rhythmic and accompanied by traditional musical instruments. ***Cải lương*** is a modernised form of Vietnamese opera that developed during the French colonial period, blending traditional Vietnamese music with Western theatrical elements. Leon Lê's 2018 film *Song Lang* masterfully tells the story of two men, a gangster and a *cải lương* performer, set in 1980s Hồ Chí Minh City.

ART The first flourishing of Vietnamese art occurred with the emergence of the Đông Sơn culture between 500 and 200BCE. The inspiration for the magnificent bronzes produced by the artists of Đông Sơn may have originated from China: the decorative motifs have clear affinities with earlier Chinese bronzes. But at the same time, the exceptional skill of production and decoration argues that these pieces represent among the first, and finest, of Southeast Asian works of art. This is most evident in the huge and glorious bronze drums (page 8) that can be seen in museums in both Hanoi and Hồ Chí Minh City.

After Vietnam's independence from China in CE938, there was a flourishing of dynastic art and architecture, though some remark that it is derivative and draws heavily on Chinese prototypes. Much of the pre-European art and architecture you see today came about during Vietnam's last dynasty, the Nguyễn, represented in temples, pagodas and palaces in and around Huế and Hanoi. Art that preceded the Nguyễn is found in history museums across the country, as well as in the

Thăng Long Imperial Citadel in Hanoi. Some historians have made the interesting argument that dynastic era art is more like a craft, as it was mostly produced by artisans rather than artists, and their skill was judged by their ability to replicate rather than create.

The beginnings of modern Vietnamese art can be traced back to the creation of the École de Beaux-Arts Indochine in Hanoi in 1925. By this time there was an emerging Westernised intelligentsia in Vietnam who had been schooled in French ways and taught to identify, at least in part, with French culture. Much of the early painting produced by students taught at the École de Beaux-Arts Indochine was romantic, portraying an idyllic picture of Vietnamese life and landscape. However, by the 1930s a Vietnamese nationalist tone began to be expressed both in terms of subject matter and technique.

In 1945, with the Declaration of Independence, the École de Beaux-Arts Indochine closed, and art for art's sake came to an end. From this point, artists were strongly encouraged to join the revolutionary project and, for example, paint posters of heroic workers, stoic peasants and brave soldiers. Painting landscapes or pictures of rural life was no longer on the agenda. In 1950 a new School of Fine Art was established in the north with the sole remit of training revolutionary artists. Central control of art and artists became even more stringent after 1954 when many artists were sent away to re-education camps. Many established artists were no longer permitted either to exhibit or to teach, so lacking were they in revolutionary credentials.

THE GOLDEN AGE

This section was written with considerable input from Dr Nguyễn H H Duyên (page 12).

If there was ever a golden period in ancient Vietnamese art and architecture, it was that of the former Central Vietnamese kingdom of Champa (page 12), in modern-day Central Vietnam, which flowered in the 10th and 11th centuries. Tragically, however, many of the 250 sites noted in historical records have been pillaged or damaged and only 20 have survived the intervening centuries in a reasonable state of repair. Most famous are the sites in Mỹ Sơn (page 314). Many of the finest works have been spirited out of the country to private collections and foreign museums, while others were destroyed by bombing and artillery fire during the American War. Nonetheless, the world's finest collection – with some breathtakingly beautiful work – is to be found in Đà Nẵng's Museum of Cham Sculpture (page 289).

Cham art shows stylistic similarities with Indian Sanchi and Gupta works, although even at this early stage in its development Cham art incorporated distinctive indigenous elements, most clearly seen in the naturalistic interpretation of human form. By the 9th century, the Cham had developed a unique style of their own. Archaeologists recognise several periods of Cham art, including Mỹ Sơn (early 8th century), Hoa Lài (early 9th century), Đồng Dương (late 9th century), Late Trà Kiệu (late 10th century), Tháp Mẫm (12th–13th centuries) and Po Klong Garai (13th–16th centuries). The Cham Kingdom was ethnically and linguistically distinct, but was overrun by the Vietnamese in the 15th century. It might be argued, then, that their monuments and sculptures have little to do with Vietnam per se, but with a preceding dynasty.

In 1957 a new premier art school was created in the capital: the Hanoi School of Fine Arts. Students were taught the methods and meanings of socialist realism and Western art became, by definition, capitalist and decadent. But while the state saw to it that artists toed the revolutionary line, fine art in North Vietnam never became so harsh and uncompromising as in China or the Soviet Union. In addition, the first director of the Hanoi School of Fine Arts, Nguyễn Đỗ Cung, encouraged his students to search for inspiration in traditional Vietnamese arts and crafts, in simple village designs and in archaeological artefacts. Old woodblock prints, for example, strongly influenced the artists of this period.

Since *đổi mới* (page 21) there has come a greater degree of artistic freedom. The first exhibition of abstract art in Vietnam was held in 1992. Today Vietnam is experiencing a resurgent art scene. While limits set by the Communist Party have been considerably relaxed, art does not receive much state-sanctioned financial backing. A small network of passionate and diligent curators and wealthy benefactors have stepped in to fill the void, and there is a growing number of art galleries in Hanoi and Hồ Chí Minh City.

CRAFTS Vietnamese craft heritage dates back thousands of years, evidenced by the stone carved ruins of ancient cities, various archaeological excavation sites and the antique pottery and porcelain that is dredged up from riverbeds. Today the country is known internationally for its lacquerware, ceramics, bamboo, rattan and silk weaving.

The conical hat, an iconic symbol of Vietnamese culture, is a craft product associated with Chuông, a village outside of Hanoi. This arrangement, where one village focuses on a particular craft, is a remnant from feudal times, when rural guilds formed and developed links to specific streets in Hanoi's Old Quarter. Other centuries-old craft villages near the capital include Bát Tràng, known for its ceramics, and Vạn Phúc, famous for its silk. Many of these villages continue to be centres of traditional craftsmanship and some have become part of the global supply network. For an informative though rather out-of-date guide to some of the craft villages around Hanoi, look for *Discovering Craft Villages in Vietnam: Ten Itineraries Around Hanoi* by Nicholas Stedman and Sylvie Fanchette (2009). The mountain-dwelling ethnolinguistic groups, particularly the Thai, Hmong, Dao and Ta Oi, are known for their textiles, which are woven, embroidered and dyed. Some Vietnamese artists and artisans continue to innovate while preserving ancestral techniques. This is best seen in contemporary art galleries and shops in Hanoi and Hồ Chí Minh City.

SPORT

Despite Vietnam's size and rising economic standing, it tends to fare poorly in international sporting competitions. It took home no medals at the 2024 Paris Summer Olympics, a repeat of the performance at the 2020 Tokyo Summer Olympics. Vietnam has only qualified for the Football World Cup once – the women's team in 2023 – but football is the unofficial national sport and international competitions and football leagues are followed with great interest. Things may be looking up, however: in January 2025, the Vietnam men's football team beat regional rivals Thailand to win the ASEAN Championship. During major tournaments, those with the biggest televisions will lug them on to the street so that the whole neighbourhood can enjoy the matches. If you see this, hang around for long enough and you'll soon be invited to join. Despite Vietnam's performance on the international stage, the Vietnamese are very active, and parks often fill with joggers, walkers, badminton players, calisthenics practitioners and enthusiasts of jianzi (a kind of foot badminton known as *đá cầu* in Vietnamese) in the early morning and late afternoon. Sports such as wrestling, rowing and dragon-boat racing sometimes feature at festivals.

2

Practical Information

WHEN TO VISIT

In terms of good weather, it's notoriously difficult to identify the right month to visit Vietnam. There are two clashing climates (subtropical temperate and tropical savannah; page 3) across three regions (Northern, Central and Southern) and there are both lowland and highland zones. While typhoons pummel the centre, it's cheerfully cool in the north. When it's insidiously cold in the north, it's comfortably warm in the south. When the centre is sunny but not too sticky, the north can be depressingly drizzly and the south swelters. In short, when it comes to weather at least, there is no single best time to visit all three regions of Vietnam.

Added to the mix are air quality considerations in the big cities, the various festivals and national holidays – both highlights and hinderances – which speckle the solar and lunar calendars (Vietnam follows both) and divergent domestic and international high seasons. To help contend with these layers of complexity, all chapters in this guide have 'When to visit' sections. Below is a brief overview broken down by region.

NORTHERN VIETNAM Northern Vietnam is best to visit during autumn and early winter (October–December). Days tend to be sunny, dry and cool, and there are no major holidays to disrupt travel. The worst time to visit might be the summer (May–September), which is hot, humid and wet, and the occasional typhoon can cause major damage (as Typhoon Yagi did in September 2024). The winter (December–February) is cold, especially in the mountains, though temperatures are rarely sub-zero. Note that winter also tends to be the worst time for air quality in Hanoi. Spring (March–April) is unpredictable; a mixture of sun, rain, drizzle, high humidity and a couple of cool days.

CENTRAL VIETNAM The best time to visit Central Vietnam is spring (March–April). After many months of rain, the cities are bright and beautiful and the beaches are clean and calm. The worst time to visit the centre is the typhoon season (October–November), when, between the storms, much of the region hibernates to escape the seemingly endless grey days of rain. Summer (May–September) tends to be extremely hot, though fortunately a beach is never too far away in the lowlands. The beach resort cities of Đà Nẵng, Hội An and Nha Trang can get busy with domestic tourists. North of Đà Nẵng, winter (December–January) can be cold and rainy; south of Đà Nẵng it's often sunny and pleasant. The anomaly is the Central Highlands subregion – the uplands – which sees relatively cool and dry days from November to February.

SOUTHERN VIETNAM Southern Vietnam is best to visit at the beginning of the dry season (December–February), when days tend to be sunny and warm and evenings

TRAVELLING DURING TẾT (JANUARY OR FEBRUARY)

Is Tết a good time to visit? Depends on who you ask. While the energy of the lead-up to Lunar New Year (it takes place at the same time of year, but don't call it Chinese New Year here) can be fun, especially in the big cities, traffic is at its absolute worst. Once it begins, most have already *về quê* (returned to their hometown) and the cities are calm and peaceful, though those restaurants and cafés that remain open raise their prices to account for the increase in labour costs (300%). Smaller towns and villages can be quite lively, as childhood friends who haven't seen each other all year reunite in cafés and bars. The holiday usually lasts about a week, sometimes longer. If travelling during Tết, the best advice is to find somewhere you won't get bored – like a beach city – and switch off for the week. Book accommodation many weeks in advance and arrive at least two days before the start of the holiday.

are cool and breezy, though the beach resort island of Phú Quốc is at its busiest. The worst time to visit is the latter half of the dry season (March–April/May), when days can be extremely hot and Hồ Chí Minh City suffers from poor air quality. The rains usually arrive in the south in May or June, and last until November. The wet season is hot, though the rains, which are usually sudden, severe and brief, provide some respite.

HIGHLIGHTS

HANOI Vietnam's political and cultural capital safeguards heritage and exudes character, reflecting 1,000 years of history.

CAO BẰNG The northern province that has it all but hardly anyone visits, with ethnolinguistic intrigue, illustrious scenery and revolutionary significance.

NINH BÌNH A tiny province with much to offer, including iconic limestone outcrops, laid-back river cruises, an ancient capital and the overlooked wildlife refuges of Cúc Phương and Vân Long.

PHONG NHA Home to Vietnam's – and some of the world's – biggest caves, Phong Nha is also a karst-studded countryside retreat.

HUẾ Vietnam's former capital and Southeast Asia's greatest walled fortress, the criminally underappreciated city of Huế has palaces, tombs and a rich food culture.

ĐÀ NẴNG AND HỘI AN Twin settlements that couldn't be more different: Đà Nẵng is a shimmering modern city whereas Hội An guards one of Vietnam's largest collections of heritage architecture.

QUY NHƠN A seaside city with a trove of things to see, including fishing villages, hidden coves and ancient Cham towers.

KON TUM A rarely visited but completely captivating low-rise mountain town surrounded by Bahnar communal houses and Jarai cemeteries.

CÁT TIÊN NATIONAL PARK The richest wildlife refuge in the country, with gibbons, gaur (Indian bison), langurs, birds and crocodiles.

HỒ CHÍ MINH CITY Vietnam's electrifying economic capital and one of the most vibrant cities on earth, though with historical neighbourhoods that hide behind the neon.

CHÂU ĐỐC A microcosm of Mekong Delta life, with Khmer temples, spiritual diversity and river life. There are also hills to climb – a rarity in Vietnam's flattest subregion.

SUGGESTED ITINERARIES

Vietnam is a big, beautiful, complicated place, and covering the entire country in any kind of depth will take a minimum of three months. Although three-month tourist visas are available, most visitors only stay for a few weeks. There is scope to be extraordinarily creative with tour itineraries in Vietnam, basing the experience around themes and interests. Throughout the 1990s, many visitors stuck to the 'classic' places of Hanoi, Hạ Long Bay, Huế, Hội An and Hồ Chí Minh City (sometimes referred to as 5H by industry insiders). These days, virtually every corner of the country is visitable and there are no must-see provinces or cities. Indeed, the most memorable moments are likely to be enjoyed far away from the hotspots. Like this guide, the following itineraries are organised from north to south, though they can be done in any direction.

ARCHITECTURE AND HERITAGE (THREE TO FOUR WEEKS) After arriving in Hanoi and exploring the dynastic heritage of the Thăng Long Citadel, the Old Quarter and the French Quarter, head to Hải Phòng to see its well-preserved colonial buildings that boast Neoclassical and Art Deco motifs. Move on to Huế and tour the various Nguyễn Dynasty-era palaces, tombs, temples and pagodas. Make a quick stop in Đà Nẵng to get a sense of what Vietnam's cities of the future might look like before settling into Hội An, the country's best-preserved old town. Be sure to make a day trip to Mỹ Sơn, an extensive Cham religious sanctuary constructed between the 4th and 13th centuries. For more Cham heritage, make a stop in Quy Nhơn and temple-hop between the ancient towers that perch on the hills surrounding the city. From Quy Nhơn, head to the mountainous town of Đà Lạt, where the French constructed their largest hill station, with provincial villas and Art Deco hotels. Then descend to Hồ Chí Minh City and delve into districts 1 and 3 (the old French city) and Chợ Lớn, with its centenarian Chinese temples and pagodas. Finish in unassuming Trà Vinh and hunt out the province's diverse collection of Khmer pagodas.

WAR AND REVOLUTIONARY HISTORY (TWO WEEKS) In Hanoi, be sure to include the National Museum of History and the brand-new Military History Museum in your itinerary. After leaving the capital, first strike north to Pác Bó in Cao Bằng, where Hồ Chí Minh mustered a revolutionary force that would shake the world. Return to Hanoi before heading west to Điện Biên Phủ, where the French colonial project came to a grisly end. Moving south, make a stop in Vinh to see the birthplace of Hồ Chí Minh before moving on to Huế, which saw intense fighting during the Tết Offensive, and make a day trip to the Demilitarised Zone (DMZ) and its various sites related to the American War. In Hồ Chí Minh City, prioritise the War Remnants Museum and Củ Chi Tunnels.

LANDSCAPES AND SEASCAPES (TWO TO FOUR WEEKS) If it's nature you've come for, Vietnam won't disappoint. Take your pick of mountainous provinces based on the outdoor activities that appeal: motorbiking in Hà Giang, Mù Cang Chải or Cao Bằng; hiking in Sa Pa or Bắc Hà; boating in Ba Bể; rock climbing in Hữu Lũng; or simply relaxing in Mai Châu or Pù Luông. For Vietnam's iconic karst scenery, investigate Hạ Long Bay, Lan Hạ Bay or Ninh Bình. If you opt for the latter, spend some time in Cúc Phương National Park for some hikes through the jungle. Then head south and go underground to see one of Vietnam's great natural wonders: the caves of Phong Nha. Stay inland and drive, cycle or motorbike south along the Hồ Chí Minh Highway until dropping down to the coast at Huế. Consider a few days in Bạch Mã National Park, one of Vietnam's most unspoiled, before traversing the Hải Vân Pass to Đà Nẵng. Continuing south, the coast gets increasingly more dramatic until you reach Nha Trang. From here, ascend to Đà Lạt, surrounded by waterfalls.

ETHNOLINGUISTIC GROUPS (TWO TO FOUR WEEKS) In Hanoi, the Women's Museum and Museum of Ethnology are crucial starting points to begin understanding Vietnam's ethnolinguistic diversity. Spend some time exploring the rich cultural heritage of the Kinh through water puppetry and craft villages, and learn about some of the various myths and legends that are tied to the city. Choose a northern mountain destination based on the activities offered there: hiking in Sa Pa, markets in Bắc Hà or motorbiking in Hà Giang. All three places have significant communities of Hmong, Dao, Giay and many others. Consider tagging on some time west of Hanoi in Mai Châu or Pù Luông to spend time with Thai and Muong, or Ba Bể to stay in a Tay stilt house. In Central Vietnam, move through the Central Highlands slowly to learn about the Bahnar and Jarai in Kon Tum; Mnong and Ede in Buôn Ma Thuột; and the K'Ho in Đà Lạt. From there you can head south to explore pockets of ethnolinguistic diversity in Southern Vietnam, in particular the Khmer in Trà Vinh, Cham in Châu Đốc and Hoa (Han Chinese) in Hồ Chí Minh City.

NATIONAL PARKS AND WILDLIFE (TWO TO THREE WEEKS) Hunting, war and weak conservation programmes make Vietnam a disappointing place for wildlife enthusiasts, but there are several conservation centres that guarantee sightings. If they are accepting visitors, consider starting with a visit to the bear sanctuary in Tam Đảo, just outside Hanoi. Heading south from the capital, the first stop is Cúc Phương National Park. You probably won't see anything in the wild in the forests, but the excellent conservation centres – some of the most informative in the country – rehabilitate gibbons, lorises, pangolins and turtles. Nearby is the Vân Long Nature Reserve, which hosts a large troop of wild Delacour langurs. Continuing south, make a stop at Phong Nha, where animal track-spotting tours are beginning to develop off the back of successful conservation programmes. South of here is Đà Nẵng and the Sơn Trà Peninsula, where you'll find the red-shanked douc langur. Head to the highlands and stop at Yok Đôn National Park, home to wild elephants (which you won't see) and semi-wild elephants (which you can). The final stop is Cát Tiên National Park, home to the most diverse set of large animals in Vietnam, including crocodiles, gibbons and gaur (Indian bison).

BEACHES AND ISLANDS (TWO TO THREE WEEKS) Truth be told, beaches are cleaner in other Southeast Asian countries, like Thailand, but Vietnam still maintains some enviable metropolitan beaches, pretty coves and paradisical islands. Start in Đà Nẵng, the city's broadest city beach, before moving south to the more natural beaches around Hội An. Continue south and base yourselves in the beach cities of

Quy Nhơn, Tuy Hòa, Nha Trang and Phan Rang, while exploring a diverse set of nearby coves and bays. Once in Vũng Tàu, take the boat to the Côn Đảo archipelago to see out your trip.

COUNTRYWIDE ROAD TRIP (TWO TO THREE MONTHS) Vietnam was built for the motorbike, but this trip is almost as enjoyable by car. Spend three to four weeks in the northern mountains on a gigantic clockwise loop, encompassing (in order) Mai Châu, Sơn La, Điện Biên Phủ, Lai Châu, Sa Pa, Bắc Hà, Hà Giang, Ba Bể, Cao Bằng, Lạng Sơn and Hữu Lũng. Recover in Hanoi before heading southwest to Pù Luông, and keep far away from the busy coast as you move through the provinces of Hà Tĩnh, Quảng Bình, Quảng Trị and Thừa Thiên Huế on the Hồ Chí Minh Highway. Drop to the coast in Huế and drive over the Hải Vân Pass, continuing south all the way to Quảng Ngãi, where you can turn inland again and head to Kon Tum via Măng Đen. Continue south, this time through the Central Highlands, passing the inactive volcanoes near Pleiku, coffee plantations of Buôn Ma Thuột and waterfalls and national parks near Đà Lạt. In Đà Lạt, drop to the coast again and track south along the water all the way to Vũng Tàu. Spend a few days out of the saddle and stroll around central Hồ Chí Minh City before delving into the Mekong Delta. Stick to country lanes and circle through some of the delta's less industrial provinces: Bến Tre, Trà Vinh, Cà Mau and Kiên Giang. If time, put your motorbike on a ferry to Phú Quốc to enjoy some island life for the remainder of the trip.

TOURIST INFORMATION AND TOUR OPERATORS

Vietnam's official **tourism website** (w vietnam.travel) is funded by the country's major stakeholders and the information presented, though sometimes useful, should be taken with a pinch of salt. For features, guides and narrative stories written by the author of this guidebook, visit and subscribe to w joshuazukas.com. Vietnam Coracle (w vietnamcoracle.com) offers excellent advice for independent travellers, covering motorbike itineraries, hotel reviews and street-food guides. For other useful online resources, see page 492.

Armed with this guide, it's easy to travel independently in Vietnam, and booking a countrywide tour is not generally recommended, though it's worth looking at websites like **Get Your Guide** (w getyourguide.com) and **Airbnb** (which offers experiences as well as accommodation; w airbnb.com) for specialist tours, courses and classes that will help you get under the skin of a place. For localised tour companies offering **half- and full-day tours** in specific places, look under 'Tour operators' for bigger towns or cities, and 'Other practicalities' for smaller locations, in each section of the guidebook. Some **activity-specific tour operators** can be found under *Outdoor activities* (page 70).

That said, several tour companies offer excellent-value **tailor-made tours**, and sometimes this is the easiest way to experience some specialist activities, like a private *hát xẩm* (page 36) performance in Hanoi or cooking class in someone's home in Hội An. If taking this option, reach out to a few companies, be clear and specific about what you want and your budget and see which ones best meet the brief. Most will list various itineraries on their websites that make a good starting point, but almost everything is adjustable.

All Asia Vacation w allasiavacation.com. Formerly Sisters Tours, All Asia Vacation has a wide collection of in-depth, insightful experiences.

Amica Travel w amica-travel.com. Amica targets the French-speaking market (hence the French website), but they excel at crafting tailor-made hiking trips in remote areas of Northern Vietnam.

Aurora Travel w auroratravel.asia. Good-value tours put together by an award-winning team with decades of experience; they are highly responsive & go above & beyond.

Chôm Chôm Travel w chomchomtravel.com. Boutique, Hồ Chí Minh City-based travel company that works with local suppliers to organise in-depth family trips that dodge the more touristy places and experiences.

Exotic Voyages w exoticvoyages.com. Luxury tour company with a broad network of upmarket hotels & restaurants – & experienced tour guides.

Magnolia w magnoliatravel.vn. Run by a small team of travel enthusiasts with impressive sustainability credentials, Magnolia has an extensive network in more unknown provinces across Vietnam.

Mundo Asia Tours w mundoasiatours.com. Founded by 2 industry veterans, Mundo puts together personalised classic tours with skill &, if desired, flair. They have a network of multilingual tour guides.

TravelLocal w travellocal.com. A UK-based website where you can book direct with selected local travel companies, allowing you to communicate with a ground operator without having to go through a 3rd-party travel operator or agent. Your booking with the local company has full financial protection, but note that travel to the destination is not included. Member of ABTA, ASTA.

Vietnam in Focus w vietnaminfocus.com. Both group and tailor-made tours for amateur and professional photographers, which can adhere to a theme or special interest, like train travel or the harvest season.

RED TAPE

Since the end of the Covid-19 pandemic, when Vietnam's borders were effectively closed to tourists for almost two years, visa policies have been liberalising quickly. Barring another major global event, this is likely to continue. At the time of research, visitors from Belarus, Denmark, Finland, France, Germany, Italy, Japan, Norway, Republic of Korea, Russia, Spain, Sweden and the UK were visa-exempt for trips of up to 45 days, regardless of passport type and entry purpose. In addition, visitors from the Association of Southeast Asian Nations (ASEAN) countries are visa-exempt for trips of up to 30 days. Citizens of all countries – including the aforementioned – may also apply for 90-day single or multiple-entry E-visas for longer stays, at w evisa.xuatnhapcanh.gov.vn or w vietnamimmigration.org. Apply for visas at least two weeks before arriving to account for mistakes and national holidays, when the offices might be closed. It's also possible to pay extra for fast-track. Once you've received your E-visa (always by email), you must print it to present at immigration.

Vietnam has 13 international airports, 16 land border gates and 13 sea border gates. It's important to note that extending visas after arriving in the country is not usually possible. If you want to enjoy a longer stay, you may have to leave the country and re-enter. For up-to-date information on all of the above, visit w vietnam.travel/plan-your-trip/visa-requirements.

EMBASSIES Many countries have some form of diplomatic presence in Hanoi. There's a list of embassies, including addresses and opening times, at w vietnamimmigration.org/list-of-embassies-in-hanoi-capital-city, but always double check on the respective embassy's website.

GETTING THERE AND AWAY

BY AIR Vietnam is increasingly well connected by air. Although there are 13 international airports, most visitors will arrive at Nội Bài (Hanoi) or Tân Sơn Nhất (Hồ Chí Minh City), or to a lesser extent at Đà Nẵng (in Đà Nẵng City) or Phú Quốc (Kiên Giang Province). Over the years, only Vietnam Airlines has consistently operated direct 12-hour flights between Europe (Frankfurt, Paris and London) and Vietnam (Hanoi and Hồ Chí Minh City). Most of those travelling from European countries will transit in a regional hub in the Middle East or elsewhere in Southeast Asia. Those travelling from the United States will likely transit in East Asia or elsewhere in Southeast Asia. There are direct flights to Australia and New Zealand, though most will transit elsewhere in Australasia or Southeast Asia. As an increasingly globalised country, the best-value routes change from year to year. Use a flight-comparison website like Skyscanner (**w** skyscanner.com), Trip (**w** trip.com) or Kayak (**w** kayak.com) to find the best deals.

The two Vietnamese airlines are Vietnam Airlines (**w** vietnamairlines.com) and Vietjet Air (**w** vietjetair.com). A third, Bamboo Airways (**w** bambooairways.com), has been embroiled in a large corruption scandal, but at the time of research was still operating.

Nội Bài's international and domestic terminals are far enough away that a free transfer bus is available. The international and domestic terminals in Tân Sơn Nhất and Đà Nẵng are close enough to walk between.

Private companies offer so-called VIP services that enable passengers to skip the immigration queues at both Nội Bài and Tân Sơn Nhất airports, though they're not always necessary as queues can be quick and some customers have run into problems using them. At the time of research, there wasn't a company to recommend, but it's worth doing an online search if this service appeals.

BY LAND Vietnam has 16 land borders, but the ones most commonly used by foreigners to enter or exit the country are Móng Cái (Quảng Ninh), Hữu Nghị (Lạng Sơn) and Lào Cai (Lào Cai) on the Chinese border; Tây Trang (Điện Biên), Nam Cảnh (Nghệ An), Lao Bảo (Quảng Trị) and Bờ Y (Kon Tum) on the Laotian border; and Mộc Bài (Tây Ninh), Vĩnh Xuông (An Giang) and Hà Tiên (Kiên Giang) on the Cambodian border. If arriving to Vietnam from these countries, make sure you are either visa-exempt or you arrive with a pre-arranged E-visa (page 45). Note that you most likely need a pre-arranged visa to enter China, Laos or Cambodia, which you can apply for online or process at the embassies and consulates in Vietnam. Common international bus routes are between Hồ Chí Minh City and Phnom Penh (Cambodia) via Mộc Bài, Hà Tiên and Kep (Cambodia); Kon Tum and Pakse (Laos) via Bờ Y; and Huế and Savannakhet (Laos) via Lao Bảo. For many routes you need to switch buses at the border. Another popular border crossing is by river boat between Châu Đốc and Phnom Penh. There are currently no railways connecting Vietnam with Laos and Cambodia, and at the time of research passenger trains between China and Vietnam were not in operation.

HEALTH *with Dr Daniel Campion*

Vietnam is generally a healthy place to visit, but travellers should take some precautions, including taking out adequate **medical travel insurance** before leaving home. If you have an existing health condition, take sufficient medication for your trip. Vietnam restricts many medicines it classifies as 'addictive' or 'psychotropic'. The UK Foreign Office travel advice website for Vietnam (**w** gov.uk/foreign-travel-advice/Vietnam) has more details; check with the embassy before travel if you are in any doubt. Carry all medication in its original packaging in your hand luggage. Keep the prescription with your pills and a letter from your doctor stating how much of the medication you need during your trip.

IMMUNISATIONS It is wise to be up to date with standard vaccinations including **tetanus**, **polio** and **diphtheria** (usually available as an all-in-one vaccine), and also **measles**, **mumps** and **rubella**. If you are at higher risk, be up to date with vaccines against Covid-19 and influenza. Immunisation against **hepatitis A** and **typhoid** are also recommended. **Hepatitis B** vaccination may be recommended for those working in medical settings and with children, as well as for those playing contact sports. The **Japanese encephalitis** vaccine is recommended for those staying in rural parts of the country or for visits of a month or more, and consists of two doses ideally given one month apart, although a shorter schedule is possible if time is short. **Rabies** vaccine may also be recommended if you're a long-term visitor, working with animals or travelling to rural areas. No vaccination certificates are required.

MEDICAL CONCERNS

Rabies Rabies kills more than 70 people per year in Vietnam, mostly from dog bites. If you're bitten or scratched by any mammal, seek treatment as soon as possible. Firstly, scrub the wound with soap under a running tap, or while pouring water from a jug, then pour on a strong iodine or alcohol solution, which will guard against other infections and might reduce the risk of the rabies virus entering the body. Whether or not you underwent pre-exposure vaccination, it is vital to obtain post-exposure prophylaxis as soon as possible after the incident. Don't wait until you are back in your home country. Those who have not been immunised will need a full course of four vaccinations, as well as rabies immunoglobulin (RIG), which is expensive but usually available in cities. If you have been vaccinated before exposure, then you should not need the RIG, and just two further doses of vaccine in most cases. It is important to tell the doctor if you have had the pre-exposure vaccine – carry your vaccine record with you. Treatment may differ if your immune system is weakened eg: if you take immunosuppressant medication. Do take rabies seriously – death from rabies is probably one of the worst ways to go, and once you show symptoms it is too late to do anything. The mortality rate is close to 100%.

Mosquito-transmitted infections There is a low risk of **malaria** only in some border regions of Vietnam, and anti-malarials are not usually required. But outbreaks of **dengue fever** can happen anywhere in the country. Dengue fever is transmitted by day-biting mosquitoes and it is therefore important to **avoid mosquito bites** by covering up with trousers and a long-sleeved shirt, and applying insect repellent containing the chemical DEET (50% is the optimum strength); icaridin at 20% is an effective alternative. Symptoms include strong headaches, rashes, excruciating joint and muscle pains and high fever. Dengue fever only lasts for a week or so and is not usually fatal. Complete rest and paracetamol are the usual treatment. Plenty of fluids also help. It is especially important to protect yourself and consider vaccination if you have had dengue fever before: a second infection with a different strain can result in the potentially fatal dengue haemorrhagic fever. A dengue vaccine is now available in Europe, although it is used mainly in those who have had dengue once already, to prevent a severe second infection. **Chikungunya** is a virus carried by the same *Aedes* mosquitoes. It occurs in periodic outbreaks and the symptoms overlap with dengue, although joint pain is predominant and some patients may develop ongoing and sometimes disabling joint inflammation. Vaccines against Chikungunya are also on the horizon, and may be recommended for long-stay or high-risk travellers.

Zika virus Zika virus is a flavivirus similar to dengue, also spread by the day-biting *Aedes* mosquito. All travellers to countries where Zika virus is reported, including Vietnam, are at risk of infection. The longer you spend in the destination, the more at risk you will be. The infection is often asymptomatic, and in those with symptoms the disease is usually mild with an itchy rash, fever, joint pains and red, sore eyes. Severe disease is uncommon. Travellers are advised to use DEET- or icaridin-based repellents during the day on all exposed skin. In areas where mosquitoes are particularly prevalent, covering up and using a permethrin spray on clothing would also be advised.

Pregnant women need to discuss their travel plans with health-care professionals and should, wherever possible, cancel the trip. Women wishing to become pregnant who are travelling in moderate- to high-risk Zika virus areas should use barrier precautions while travelling and for two months after. If travelling with their partners, then barrier precautions need to be used during the trip and for three months after leaving. Zika vaccines are being developed.

Hepatitis B Hepatitis B is a liver infection that can lead to scarring and ultimately failure of the liver. It can only be passed on by exchange of bodily fluids; however, many people carry the disease without showing symptoms and it is 100 times more infectious than HIV – only small quantities of a wider range of bodily fluids are needed to transmit the virus. The prevalence of chronic hepatitis B in the Vietnamese population is relatively high. Realistically the main risks are through unprotected sex and through exposure to contaminated needles, or through blood-to-blood contact from accidents or through contact sports. Given its consequences, it makes sense to be vaccinated against the disease, especially if you are working in a health-care setting or with children, or if spending four weeks or more in Vietnam. The vaccine comprises a course of three injections and ideally these should be given over a six-month period. However, shorter courses are possible if time is limited, with a booster dose later. It is best to visit your doctor or travel clinic in plenty of time before you travel. The vaccination is also available locally eg: in private clinics.

Tick-borne diseases If you are walking in forested areas of Vietnam, it is wise to take precautions against tick bites. Surveillance data suggest that people in rural Vietnam have been exposed to various tick-borne infections, although data on human cases is limited and any risk to travellers is likely to be low. Smaller mites may transmit scrub typhus. Avoid ticks by wearing long clothes and repellent, especially if walking in scrubby countryside where you are brushing through vegetation. Use a repellent containing DEET on exposed skin. Ticks should ideally be removed complete, and as soon as possible, to reduce the chance of infection. You can use special tick tweezers, which can be bought in good travel shops; or failing this, with your fingernails, grasp the tick as close to your body as possible, and pull it away steadily and firmly at right angles to your skin without jerking or twisting. Applying irritants (eg: Olbas oil) or lit cigarettes is to be discouraged as a means of removal since they can cause the ticks to regurgitate and therefore increase the risk of disease. Once the tick is removed, if possible douse the wound with alcohol (any spirit will do), soap and water, or iodine. If you are travelling with small children, remember to check their heads, and particularly behind the ears, for ticks. Spreading redness around the bite and/or fever and/or aching joints after a tick bite imply that you have an infection that requires antibiotic treatment. In this case seek medical advice.

Leeches These bloodthirsty parasites hunt their victims in the jungle, either by dropping from vegetation or ascending from the ground. Sturdy footwear, long trousers tucked in to your socks and/or gaiters help to provide a physical barrier, although leeches can squeeze through small gaps. DEET insect repellent on exposed skin can also deter them. Leeches inject local anaesthetic as they bite, so you might not feel anything. If detected before attachment they can be flicked off. Trying to pull them off once attached may leave the mouthparts in place, leading to infection and bleeding. Instead, apply salt, vinegar, iodine, alcohol or other irritant to persuade them to release. On detachment they leave an open wound, so apply antiseptic and a dressing. Aquatic leeches can invade various body cavities or be swallowed. They attach for longer than land leeches and may need a medical procedure (endoscopy) to extricate them.

Leptospirosis This bacterial infection is caught by swimming in rivers contaminated with the urine of infected animals. It is relatively uncommon in Vietnam and human infection was last reported in 2017. Symptoms include a sudden fever, headache, jaundice and muscle aches, between two and 26 days after exposure. If you develop these symptoms, see a doctor. Leptospirosis can be treated with antibiotics, ideally at an early stage.

Liver flukes These unpleasant parasites can cause long-term liver disease. They are fortunately rare in travellers but were often detected in soldiers after the American War. Avoid raw or undercooked water plants (eg: watercress), meat or crustaceans, especially in the rural central region of the country.

Japanese encephalitis This viral infection is transmitted by the night-biting *Culex* mosquito, which picks up the virus from pigs and wading birds in and around rice-growing areas. Infection is rarely reported in travellers. There is no specific treatment for Japanese encephalitis and the mortality rate in those who develop symptoms is up to 30%. Vaccination may be advised (page 47).

Tuberculosis Vietnam is considered a high-burden country for TB but the BCG vaccination would only be recommended in certain circumstances (eg: some health workers, or unvaccinated children who are under 16 and will be staying for three months or more).

Deep-vein thrombosis Prolonged immobility on long-haul flights can result in deep-vein thrombosis (DVT), which can be dangerous if the clot travels to the lungs. The risk increases with age, and is higher in obese or pregnant travellers, heavy smokers, those taller than 6ft/1.8m, and anybody with a history of clots, recent major operation or varicose veins surgery, cancer, a stroke or heart disease. If any of these criteria apply, consult a doctor before you travel.

OTHER HEALTH ISSUES

Food preparation and drinking water Individuals with delicate stomachs should be OK if they exercise common sense. Night markets and roadside eateries aren't necessarily less sanitary than proper restaurants. If a place looks popular, that's usually a sign that the food is clean as well as tasty. Also, high turnover means food isn't left lying around. Even street food, if cooked in front of you and eaten then and there, can be perfectly safe. Drinking tap water is not recommended and almost every hotel and homestay provides bottled water, which is what most Vietnamese people drink.

Rule one in avoiding diarrhoea and other sanitation-related diseases is to wash your hands regularly, particularly before snacks and meals, and after handling money.

Bringing with you an antibacterial handwash to use before meals is recommended. As for what food you can safely eat, a useful maxim is: PEEL IT, BOIL IT, COOK IT OR FORGET IT. This means that fruit you have washed and peeled yourself should be safe, as should hot cooked foods. However, raw foods, cold cooked foods, salads and fruit salads prepared by others, ice cream and ice are all risky. In particular, avoid dishes containing uncooked blood or meat of pigs, wild boar or other animals because of the risk of trichinellosis (a parasitic worm) and bacterial infections.

If you do experience **diarrhoea**, the best advice is to drink plenty of clear fluids such as diluted soft drinks or water, to help stave off the worst effects of dehydration, and to stick to plain foods such as biscuits until the condition passes. Rehydration salts may also be helpful. Seek medical advice if symptoms do not improve within three days, or immediately if you develop a fever, notice blood or mucus in the stool or experience severe abdominal pain. Have a lower threshold for seeking help with young children, the elderly and other vulnerable travellers.

Environmental factors Because of the high population density, coughs and colds sometimes spread quickly; this is why many Vietnamese wear masks in crowded places. Regular handwashing and avoiding contact with ill children can reduce the risk of hand, foot and mouth disease (HFMD): this viral disease causes outbreaks among Vietnamese children and adolescents. If you visit during the hot season, always carry a long-sleeved shirt or cardigan. If you're sightseeing in a city you'll find yourself constantly entering and leaving air-conditioned areas and the temperature changes can be uncomfortable. In the mountains, be prepared for differences between midday and evening temperatures.

In regions with heavy industry and lots of motor vehicles, especially Hanoi and Hồ Chí Minh City, air quality is often an issue, especially in the dry months. Secondhand cigarette smoke may be an annoyance, though not a serious problem; smoking in restaurants, cafés, bars and other enclosed places is fairly common.

There is a fine art to crossing the road in Vietnamese cities and injures from scooters and motorcycles (including burns from making contact with an exhaust pipe) are not uncommon.

Public toilets It is not common to find public toilets in Vietnam, except for in some tourist areas. Many toilets don't have toilet paper, so carry your own or get comfortable using a bidet, which is what the Vietnamese use. It's also a good idea to bring soap. These days, squat toilets are rare. If there's a wastepaper basket next to the toilet, put used toilet paper and sanitary items in it, not in the toilet. In many older buildings the plumbing may get blocked if you toss paper down the toilet. Also, many guesthouses and hotels in the countryside have septic tanks instead of sewer connections, and these systems don't deal with paper well. Consider carrying alcohol swabs or some kind of sanitising gel for cleaning your hands if you come across a tap that's run dry (this sometimes happens on trains).

RECEIVING TREATMENT

Clinics and pharmacies In small towns and cities you'll find plenty of clinics. Many doctors and nurses speak basic English, and in major hospitals they'll probably assign an English speaker to see you to the right department. Prescription medicines are dispensed on site. Major hospitals also have commercial pharmacies where you can buy over-the-counter medicines, contraceptives and other items.

There are private clinics in major cities – eg: Family Medical Practice (**w** vietnammedicalpractice.com) and Raffles Medical (**w** rafflesmedical.vn) – geared towards foreign visitors and expatriate workers. Blood transfusion services, in-patient care and specialist services are generally of lower quality: seriously ill patients often need air evacuation to hospitals in Bangkok or Singapore. Mental health support for foreign nationals is very limited and some medication is restricted.

Paying for treatment At clinics and hospitals you may be expected to pay a registration fee before seeing the doctor, and for any medicines immediately afterwards. Bring your passport and cash in case they don't accept credit cards. Treatment is inexpensive by European standards and an absolute bargain compared with the US. You'll be given a receipt, but it might be entirely in Vietnamese. At major hospitals they'll be able to provide you with a document in English, which you can submit when making an insurance claim.

TRAVEL CLINICS AND HEALTH INFORMATION A list of current travel clinic websites worldwide is available on w istm.org. For journey preparation information, consult w travelhealthpro.org.uk (UK) or w wwwnc.cdc.gov/travel (USA). All advice found online should be used in conjunction with expert advice received prior to or during travel.

SAFETY

Vietnam is generally a safe country for travellers, with low levels of crime and a stable security situation. Violent incidents are rare, and most visitors feel secure while exploring both urban and rural areas. The biggest issues are related to petty crime, such as pickpocketing and bag snatching, especially in crowded areas or tourist hotspots. Always be mindful of your belongings while out and about, exercising the same caution and common sense that you would elsewhere in the world. Additionally, insect-borne diseases such as dengue fever (page 47) can pose health risks in some areas. Drug laws are enforced haphazardly, but involvement with illegal substances can lead to severe legal consequences. For up-to-date information, visit either the UK government website (w gov.uk/foreign-travel-advice/vietnam), or the US version (w travel.state.gov/content/travel/en/traveladvisories/traveladvisories/vietnam-travel-advisory.html).

TRAFFIC ACCIDENTS Given the chaotic nature of the roads and the heavy presence of motorbikes, traffic accidents are a concern. The most serious accidents can happen when petty crime and traffic accidents are combined: bag snatching from a moving motorbike. If riding pillion, hold on to a small bag with both hands and keep it in your lap between you and the driver. Wear larger backpacks as you would normally, using both straps. If you're travelling with a suitcase or single-strap large bag, take a taxi. After any accident in a populated area, the traffic police (dressed in blonde-yellow uniforms and usually holding batons) will arrive almost immediately to assess the situation. They have a poor reputation, but are unlikely

EMERGENCY PHONE NUMBERS

112	lifesaving (search and rescue)
113	police
114	fire brigade
115	ambulance and first aid

TYPHOON YAGI

In September 2024, Typhoon Yagi, one of the most powerful storms the country had seen in three decades, ripped through Hanoi before dissipating in the northern mountains. It caused widespread devastation, with 1.6 million people affected and at least 325 people dead. The storm triggered severe flooding, landslides and infrastructure damage. Due to the impacts of the climate crisis, typhoons such as these are likely to increase in number and intensity in the coming years.

to cause problems unless you've broken the law. For information on driving in Vietnam, see page 60.

WATER SAFETY Drowning is a leading cause of death in children in Vietnam, largely because most Vietnamese, particularly in rural areas, are not taught to swim at school. Those with basic swimming abilities should have no problems in Vietnam, but be careful with fast-flowing rivers inland and undertows and rip currents in coastal regions, particularly during rough weather. Metropolitan beaches are carefully monitored, with designated areas where people can swim. Swim outside these zones and you'll be whistled at and reprimanded, a minor annoyance rather than an all-out danger. For more information about drowning prevention efforts in Vietnam or to learn how to get involved, reach out to Huế Help (**w** huehelp.org).

NATURAL DISASTERS Typhoons (hurricanes but in the Northwest Pacific Ocean) wreak havoc in Vietnam every year, often leading to floods in the lowlands and landslides in the mountains. Typhoon season in Northern Vietnam is July–September; the season in Central Vietnam is September–November. Typhoons can be tracked up to a week in advance and it's usually possible to see where in the country they'll hit a few days beforehand. If you have the means and the flexibility, the best defence is to avoid them altogether and move to another part of the country. If you find yourself in a city or town that is going to be hit by a typhoon, prepare for power outages and flooding, plus landslides if you're in the mountains. It may take a few days before you can start moving again. In the wake of such disasters, charities such as Blue Dragon (**w** bluedragon.org) mobilise appeals quickly.

POLICE The police (usually dressed in army-green unforms and sporting large hats) are everywhere in Vietnam, including an unknown but not insignificant number of plain-clothes officers. Police stations, large and small, are dotted around cities and towns, but can also appear in unlikely places in the very remote countryside. During any kind of incident, the police are likely to appear quickly. They have substantial powers in Vietnam, but are adept at solving minor problems quickly without taking things further. If you do find yourself dealing with the police, remain respectful, calm and polite. In serious cases, request help from your embassy and insist on an interpreter. There are no tourist police in Vietnam.

WOMEN TRAVELLERS

Vietnam is generally a safe place for women, including solo female travellers. The biggest problem that women are likely to face is groping, which can happen suddenly and unexpectedly in quiet alleyways, around the dinner table, in busy areas or on motorbikes and in taxis, buses and trains. If this happens, remove yourself from the situation immediately. If it persists, consider drawing attention to what is happening or find a nearby older woman. Though it will not affect travellers, domestic violence is an issue in Vietnam. Perhaps as many as 60% of married Vietnamese women have suffered some form of sexual assault. You can learn more about the issue at Hagar International (**w** hagarinternational.org/vietnam).

TRAVELLING WITH A DISABILITY

A tragic legacy of the American War is the abnormally high number of people in Vietnam with disabilities, many of whom are hidden away at home. The Vietnamese are generally very considerate towards travellers with disabilities and will do what they can to help. However, Vietnam is a chaotic, cluttered place. It is not easy being a pedestrian in much of Vietnam, let alone someone who uses a wheelchair. Pavements are not just for walking, but also parking, eating and commerce. Many Vietnamese who use wheelchairs simply stick to the roads, which isn't as dangerous as it sounds considering the plethora of vehicle types and largely slow-moving traffic. Some cities and neighbourhoods are easier than others. Hanoi and Hồ Chí Minh City are generally terrible places to operate a wheelchair, though the broad boulevards of the French quarters are more or less navigable. It's easier in the less-congested cities of Huế, Đà Nẵng and Quy Nhơn. Hilly cities like Đà Lạt, with its steep slopes and stairs, and heritage towns like Hội An, with their pokey old buildings, will also present problems. Things may be improving, however, albeit very slowly. Most cities these days have pedestrianised zones on the weekends that are fairly accessible for those who use wheelchairs. Most new public buildings, such as museums, must be wheelchair-accessible. Those with hearing loss or visual impairment will face a unique set of challenges; museums, for example, are not yet set up for these visitors. Whatever the disability, airlines and airports will provide assistance if told in advance. Buses and trains will not.

The UK's gov.uk website (**w** gov.uk/government/publications/disabled-travellers) has a downloadable guide giving general advice and practical information for travellers with a disability (and their companions) preparing for overseas travel. The Society for Accessible Travel and Hospitality (**w** sath.org) also provides some general information. The website Wheelmap (**w** wheelmap.org) has an interactive global map showing accessible and partially accessible properties, including museums, hotels and restaurants.

Specialist UK-based tour operators that offer trips to Vietnam include: Enable Holidays (**w** enableholidays.com; including accessible holidays for children with specialist needs), Disabled Holidays (**w** disabledholidays.com) and Disabled Access Holidays (**w** disabledaccessholidays.com).

LGBTQIA+ TRAVELLERS

When it comes to the position of LGBTQIA+ communities, Vietnam somehow strikes a balance between conservatism and tolerance. Homosexuality is not illegal and the right to change genders was legalised in 2015. In 2013 the ban on same-sex weddings was lifted – not unimportant considering the community significance – although same-sex marriage is not yet legally recognised. The LGBTQIA+ community has become more visible in the big cities, and they are being represented more and more in the media. Increasingly ambitious Pride celebrations happen in both Hanoi and Hồ Chí Minh City, usually in September. Hanoi, Hồ Chí Minh City

QUEER VIETNAM

For those keen to explore non-heteronormative Vietnam, there is a rich repository of traditional and contemporary culture, as well as some notable historical figures. Chầu Văn, music that accompanies religious folk art that developed in the 16th century, involves trance singing and dancing where male performers present as feminine deities. Though it's hard to find his work translated into English, celebrated poet Ngô Xuân Diệu (1916–85), who has streets named after him, was probably gay, and it's generally believed that Khải Định, Vietnam's penultimate king, was too. Acclaimed Vietnamese-American author Ocean Vương, who wrote *On Earth We're Briefly Gorgeous*, identifies as queer, a theme reflected throughout the novel. While many members of the LGBTQIA+ community tend to be underrepresented in Vietnamese art and culture, this is not true for gay men, particularly in cinema. *Lost in Paradise* is a highly dramatised depiction of gay life in Hồ Chí Minh City, with openly gay actors who remain the subject of interest by voracious gossip columnists and bloggers. *Để Mai Tính 2*, which features a flamboyantly camp protagonist, broke box office records. Though not explicitly a gay film, the beautifully shot and emotionally engaging *Song Lang* has clear queer undertones. *Goodbye Mother* is the touching family drama that follows a young man returning to Vietnam with his boyfriend while he prepares to come out to his relatives. Non-heteronormative themes are explored at A Queer Museum (103 Ngọc Lâm; w linktr.ee/aqueermuseum), a new queer-friendly space in Hanoi that is still finding its feet. iSEE (w isee.org.vn) is a Hanoi-based organisation that fights for the rights of marginalised members of the queer community across the country.

and to some extent Đà Nẵng have queer scenes, and some bars are listed in their respective chapters (pages 100, 463 and 287). In urban areas, Gen Z and younger millennials are not too dissimilar to their counterparts in the Western world, and will for the most part see queer communities as a normal part of the social fabric. However, Vietnamese culture remains family-orientated, and if a Vietnamese person does have a problem with a queer person, it's often a family member whom they fear will have trouble finding a life partner to have children with.

Same-sex travellers are very unlikely to face any issues in Vietnam. Situations that may be problematic in other parts of the world – like a same-sex couple requesting a room with a double bed – are unlikely to be viewed as abnormal here. Same-sex parents travelling with children might be viewed with wonder and perhaps even awe, but they are very unlikely to experience any discrimination. Indeed, Vietnamese people can be curious, direct but also open-minded, so it's not unheard of for same-sex couples to receive blunt questions about their relationship status. If this happens, it's perfectly acceptable to be open about a same-sex relationship. Indeed, this can sometimes lead to heartwarming exchanges with tour guides and reception staff. Note that public displays of affection are not common regardless of sexual orientation.

TRAVELLING WITH KIDS

Vietnam's official tourism website (w vietnam.travel/things-to-do/family) has a reasonably helpful collection of articles offering tips and ideas for travelling with kids. **Chôm Chôm Travel** (page 45) also offers tours for families.

BABIES The Vietnamese adore babies as much as anyone else, but the difference is that they wear their enthusiasm on their sleeves. It's quite normal for strangers to approach babies and smaller children and attempt to provoke a reaction through clapping, singing, smiling, sniffing and kissing. In some instances, people might move to pick up smaller children without asking for permission first. Bathrooms can be cramped and unclean, and nappy-changing facilities are practically non-existent, so try to do this in your hotel room. The Vietnamese are unlikely to be irritated by a screaming baby.

YOUNG CHILDREN There's generally a higher tolerance for the disruption that young kids might cause than in Western countries. Staff at restaurants and cafés, for example, don't seem to have any qualms about children tearing around making a mess that they will inevitably have to clear up. There is a culture in Vietnam of large multi-generational families travelling together, which will make some things easier than expected. Asking for an extra bed in a hotel room, for example, is usually provided at little extra cost if it's for a child. Many entrance fees are lower for children, but you might need to ask. This is determined by either age or height, depending on the place. However, road safety may be of concern. Car seats and good children's helmets are difficult to come by, so consider bringing them from home.

TEENAGERS From riding on the backs of motorbikes and canyoning down waterfalls to luxuriating in coffee houses and shopping for streetwear, Vietnam has plenty to keep even the moodiest of teenagers entertained (or at least occupied). Many Vietnamese teenagers, especially in towns and cities, speak English and some might be keen to practise with their peers from abroad.

WHAT TO TAKE

What you pack for a trip to Vietnam is similar to what you'd take to other countries in the tropics. If you forget anything, there's a good chance that you can pick it up cheaply and quickly in Vietnam, which has large supermarkets, sprawling markets and well-stocked pharmacies. The exception is specialist gear such as walking boots and waterproofs, which tend to be of a lower quality in Vietnam. Some key things to remember include:

- **Electrical plugs**. Most sockets in Vietnam accept both American and European plugs. The standard voltage is 110/220 V at a frequency of 50 Hz.
- **A smartphone that accepts foreign SIM cards**. Having access to travel apps such as Google Maps, Airbnb and Grab will make travelling throughout Vietnam significantly easier, and often more enjoyable, and it's advisable to do this by buying a local SIM card (page 72). Alternatively, use an eSIM app like Airalo (**w** airalo.com).
- **A light raincoat, even if it's the dry season**. Some parts of Vietnam have a dry season, but that doesn't mean it won't rain. In reality, it can rain on any day anywhere in the country regardless of the season.
- **Comfortable, covered walking shoes**. Vietnamese cities can be grubby and the ground can be slippery. Wear shoes that will protect your feet for walking around, but bring flip-flops and sandals for beaches and villages. Removing shoes before entering temples, pagodas and people's homes is the norm, so slip-on shoes can be a good idea.

- **A waterproof sack.** These can be helpful for keeping valuables and a change of clothes dry in case your main bag gets drenched.
- **Helmets.** If spending significant amounts of time on a motorbike, consider bringing an internationally certified helmet from home. These are only available to buy in the bigger cities in Vietnam.
- **Triple check the weather of all the places you're visiting.** Even seasoned travellers get caught out by the rain in Huế in October or the chill in Sa Pa in January. See page 40 for a general overview of the weather in each region; specific notes are also included for individual places.
- **Don't bring too many clothes.** You'll want your bag to be as light as possible when jumping on and off trains and in and out of taxis. Washing clothes is cheap and easy anywhere in the country. Instead of packing enough clothes for your whole trip, pack for five to six days and wash regularly.
- **Ear plugs.** Vietnam is a noisy place, even in the countryside, where karaoke can continue late into the night (a phenomenon that urban Vietnamese playfully refer to as *quốc nạn*, meaning 'national disaster').
- **Passport photocopies.** You may need to leave a passport as a deposit when renting a motorbike, and some hotels hold on to them for you. It's always a good idea to have some form of identification on you.

MONEY AND BUDGETING

Though digitising quickly, Vietnam is still predominantly a cash-based society, especially in smaller towns or rural areas. In big cities and towns, credit and debit cards (mainly Visa and Mastercard) are widely accepted in hotels, restaurants and shops, but it is still essential to have **cash** on hand at all times. Note that some places might charge a small fee if you choose to pay with a card. Rather annoyingly, most **ATMs** have a withdrawal limit of 2,000,000–3,000,000VND per transaction, although this can vary depending on the bank and card used. If you need to take more out, reinsert your card and endure more fees. Some ATMs in big cities allow withdrawals of up to 5,000,000VND, but these can charge higher fees. ATMs are everywhere, including in small towns (look for Agribank in remote areas). At the time of research, TPBank and VPBank ATMs were not charging fees for withdrawals from foreign bank cards, so look for these to save a few dollars.

The Vietnamese currency is đồng (₫ or VND; this guide prefers the latter), with banknotes in denominations of 500,000VND, 200,000VND, 100,000VND, 50,000VND, 20,000VND, 10,000VND, 5,000VND, 2,000VND and 1,000VND. There are no coins. Note that the 500,000VND and 20,000VND notes and the 200,000VND and 10,000VND notes can look similar, so familiarise yourself with the difference as soon as you arrive. Most vendors won't have problems accepting any notes, but may not always have sufficient change if presented with 500,000VND. Break these at restaurants and in busy cafés.

The best option for exchanging foreign currency into VND is at gold shops, which offer extraordinarily good rates, especially in Hanoi and Hồ Chí Minh City. These are found everywhere, but especially near markets and in busy commercial areas. Bigger cities and towns have entire streets devoted to gold shops. They are identifiable by the red façades and glittering jewellery. Note that rumours abound as to how they can offer such competitive rates, including dodgy dealings. Airports, banks, currency exchange counters and large hotels all also change money, though rates are less competitive.

ENTRANCE FEES Entrance tickets are unlikely to exhaust a significant chunk of your travel budget. Most religious buildings, including pagodas, temples and churches, are free to enter. Those that charge an entrance fee do so to restrict the flow of visitors, and the price won't be more than US$1–2. Government museums and heritage sights such as ancient houses are similarly cheap, while entrance ticket prices to national parks may be US$2–4. A few major sights, like Mỹ Sơn Sanctuary and Huế's Imperial City, and some private museums can be as much as US$10. Unlike many other countries in Southeast Asia, Vietnam does not generally exercise dual pricing (ie: one price for the Vietnamese, another for everyone else). As so many sights are free to enter, if a price is not indicated in a listing in this guide, you can assume it's free.

BUDGETING Vietnam is a good-value travel destination regardless of your budget. Daily travel costs here are similar to those in Thailand and Malaysia. The price ranges listed here, in US$ for ease, assume you're travelling with another person and thus sharing the cost of a hotel room.

Shoestring (<US$35 per day) With dorm beds, entrance fees, street-food meals, motorbike Grab journeys, local bus tickets and short-distance train journeys on a hard wooden seat just a few dollars each, it's possible to survive on very little in Vietnam. Note that this amount does not cover tours, which are necessary to see some parts of the country, such as Hạ Long Bay.

Budget (US$35–75 per day) Spending around US$50 will afford you a basic but comfortable hotel room and some meals in restaurants, which cost US$5–10, to supplement the street eats. An increased budget will also enable you to choose softer seats or beds on trains, sleeper buses and some budget tours in select destinations, like hiking in Sa Pa and Phong Nha or a cruise in Hạ Long Bay or the Mekong Delta.

Mid-range (US$75–175 per day) Spending around US$125 a day will make for a very comfortable trip through Vietnam. Accommodation will always be more than satisfactory, if not spectacular, and you'll be able to spring for guides who will help you get under the skin of a destination. Mid-range travellers can also take opportunities to splurge for special experiences, like a fine-dining meal or a multi-day caving tour in Phong Nha.

Luxury (US$175+ per day) Budgeting at least US$175 a day just about affords a luxury experience in Vietnam, though double this if you plan on staying in the top hotel in each place you visit. You won't have to think twice about which restaurants to eat in and the activities you want to do. Bear in mind that some of the top experiences in Vietnam – like visiting Sơn Đoòng Cave or a luxury Hạ Long Bay cruise – can cost thousands of dollars.

WHAT COSTS WHAT

Large bottle of water	US$0.80	Quality T-shirt	US$15
Small bottle of beer	US$1.20	Litre of petrol	US$0.80
Cup of coffee	US$1.20	Overnight sleeper bus	US$25
Bowl of noodles	US$1.80	Bed on overnight train	US$50
Restaurant meal	US$5–10		

TIPPING In cafés and at street kitchens, tips are not expected. In restaurants, especially those catering to tourists, tips are appreciated but also not expected. Tour guides and drivers who are with you for more than a day will expect to be tipped, but there isn't a set amount, so offer what you feel is fair. Most visitors tip up to US$10 per person per day. Massage therapists also expect to be tipped as this might form the bulk of their income, especially if the massages themselves are cheap. If satisfied with the service, tip 50–100% of the price of the massage. If less than satisfied, perhaps just 30%.

GETTING AROUND

An overview of how to travel from place to place in Vietnam follows here, but specific information is given for each destination in the relevant chapters.

BY TRAIN Though more than a little rough around the edges and in dire need of an upgrade, Vietnam's threadbare, antiquated, colonial-era train network is a delight to travel on. The North–South line, also known as the Reunification Express, covers almost the entire length of the country, from Lào Cai on the Chinese border to

VIETNAM'S MOST SCENIC TRAIN JOURNEYS

The following journeys assume you're travelling from north to south, but are beautiful in either direction.

HANOI TO HẢI PHÒNG Connecting Northern Vietnam's two biggest and most historic cities via colonial-era train stations, this route passes over the Long Biên Bridge, a symbol of defiance during the American War.

VINH TO ĐỒNG HỚI This track moves inland to pass through rugged Hà Tĩnh Province, with church spires in villages punctuating the thick jungle that blankets the mountains.

HUẾ TO ĐÀ NẴNG Soon after leaving Huế, the train winds around lagoons bordered by jungled hills and fish farms before crawling over the bridge- and tunnel-studded Hải Vân Pass, offering elevated coastal views of the East Sea. Badly damaged during the war, it was quickly rebuilt after 1975 and remains one of the most extraordinary infrastructure projects of the colonial period. For more information, see page 251.

ĐÀ NẴNG TO DIÊU TRÌ (QUY NHƠN) This track passes through Quảng Nam, which emerged relatively unscathed from American bombs, evidenced by the modernist villages encircled by paddies and palm trees. The Vietage (see opposite) makes the route.

PHAN THIẾT TO HỒ CHÍ MINH CITY This route includes a spur from Phan Thiết to Ga Bình Thuận, where it meets the main north–south line. Departing the arid and gusty coast, the tracks pass wind and vegetable farms before entering the southern megalopolis. The highlight of the trip is arriving in and traversing Hồ Chí Minh City, where the meandering train seems to be the only creature that can hold back the wild traffic.

Hồ Chí Minh City in Southern Vietnam, and stops at most of the major coastal cities in between. There are also a few spur lines, including Hanoi to Hải Phòng, Hanoi to Lạng Sơn (not in use since 2020, but this may change) and Hồ Chí Minh City to Phan Thiết. The three subregions without train tracks are the Northeast, the Central Highlands and the Mekong Delta. Moving by rail is an opportunity to reflect on the changing landscapes and climates of this geographically remarkable country, but also form fleeting friendships with fellow passengers. Tourists do use the train, but the Vietnamese remain the majority of passengers. Most trains have four seat types. Hard-seat carriages are uncomfortable and not air-conditioned, but fine for short journeys. Soft-seat carriages are air-conditioned and the seats are comfortable, though quite often broken. Six-bed compartments are tight and larger passengers may struggle. Four-bed compartments are the most comfortable (and expensive); the ground-floor beds are the most desirable as you can sit on them comfortably while not sleeping and you don't have to haul yourself up to an upper bunk. Some trains, including one from Hanoi to Đà Nẵng, now also have two-bed compartments, which have proved popular. In terms of luggage, you can take what you can carry, but you're responsible for finding a place for it. If your bag doesn't fit under the bed or in the tight overhead compartments, it may have to share the bed or seat with you. In recent years, private companies have started taking over train carriages, elevating the standards (and prices) in the four-bed compartments. Targeted at foreign tourists, these tend to be cleaner and more comfortable and, crucially, it's usually easier to book tickets at short notice. Companies include Laman Express (w lamanexpress.com), Lotus Train (w lotustrain.com), Sapaly Express Train (w sapalyexpresstrain.com) and Family Express Train (w familyexpresstrain.com). At the time of research, these companies only operated in Northern and Central Vietnam. For an uber-luxury experience, there is **The Vietage** (w thevietagetrain.com), a carriage with two-person booths, a bar serving free-flowing drinks, a free massage service and three-course dining. At the time of research, The Vietage only connected Đà Nẵng with Diêu Trì (for Quy Nhơn) and Diêu Trì with Nha Trang, but they are looking to expand.

The best way to **book train tickets** online is on the official website for Vietnam Railways (or VNR/Đường sắt Việt Nam; w dsvn.vn), but it does not always accept foreign cards. If you're having trouble, try booking platform Bao Lau (w baolau.com). If travelling with one of the private companies, book on their website (see above). Failing that, there are ticket counters at train stations. Many travellers simply book trains through their hotels, which incurs a small additional fee. Try to book as far in advance as you can to reserve the seat type you want.

BY BUS Travelling by bus in Vietnam is cheap, fast, convenient, uncomfortable and only mildly terrifying. From the tiniest villages to the biggest cities, buses go just about everywhere. While there is an extensive national network of public buses (they look a little like enlarged VW campervans), they are slow and only travel short distances. Most of those travelling by bus will be taking long-distance private buses, which are competitively priced. There is a vast range of seat types, but the sleeper version seems to be taking over as lying horizontal appears to be more popular with Vietnamese travellers. But there is a large range even between sleeper bus types: some have hard beds that are narrow and short whereas others offer roomy and plush pleather mattresses with disco lights and televisions (that never work). In theory, these sleeper buses should be quite comfortable, but in a country where almost anything can happen on the roads, this is sadly not the case. Don't expect a good night's sleep, as drivers will break suddenly and beep constantly. If

HOW TO BOOK BUSES

The simplest way to book buses is through your accommodation. Hotel receptionists are used to dealing with transport requests from guests, and can be clear about where you need to be and when for pick-up. Try to book far in advance, though it's usually possible to get the bus you want at the last minute outside busy times. The best websites (and apps) for booking buses online are Ve Xe Re (w vexere.com) and Bao Lau (w baolau.com), or directly on the website of bus company Futa (w futabus.vn). Futa is especially good, but unfortunately their network only covers Southern Vietnam and a small part of Central Vietnam, and at the time of research it was not possible to pay with a foreign debit or credit card. Ve Xe Re and Bao Lau are countrywide and usually accept foreign cards, and some of the bus companies they list allow you to pay in cash after boarding. In larger cities and towns, it's usually possible to turn up at the city bus station and be on the bus you want within an hour, though there is no guarantee.

you find yourself getting irritated by this, try to remind yourself that the incessant beeping and breaking is keeping you safe(r). There is also a growing number of so-called limousine or VIP buses plying the roads between major cities. Something has got lost in translation here as these are not limousines, but minibus shells kitted out with comfy armchairs. These tend to be more expensive than other long-distance buses, but are often worth the extra few dollars. Most settlements have a bus station; big cities have dozens. However, many of the private bus companies opt not to use them, preferring instead to pick up and drop off passengers at their offices. In some cases, usually with the 'limousines' and VIP buses, you'll be picked up and dropped off at your hotel.

BY CAR Hiring a car without a driver is very unusual in Vietnam and a professional nationwide car hire company is yet to surface. Cars have only become commonplace within the last two decades, and it's taking time for the visitor infrastructure to catch up. As labour is cheap and the driving culture is unconventional, most people who wish to travel by car will also hire a driver. This costs US$100–150 per day, depending on the car. If travelling for multiple days, the driver will find their own accommodation, but it's polite to invite them to eat meals with you. If you do decide to drive yourself, you will need to arrange an international driving permit before you arrive. Present this with your original licence if pulled over. Note that it's quite easy to accidentally break the law while driving in Vietnam, as signs telling you what you can and can't do are in Vietnamese and sometimes hidden behind trees or wiring. If pulled over for doing something wrong, you'll be presented with a book that explains what you've done and what the fine is. Vietnamese drivers will usually attempt to negotiate this number down, and the money goes straight into the pockets of the traffic police. It's also worth bearing in mind that traffic accidents are a serious concern in Vietnam (page 51).

BY MOTORBIKE Given the landscape, travelling Vietnam by motorbike is extremely rewarding. Even a quick glance at the roads will reveal that driving here is not for the faint of heart, but it is probably easier than it looks. Nevertheless, Vietnam's roads are dangerous, and you should take all the precautions that you would at home, including wearing protective clothing and a good helmet. To ride a motorbike legally in Vietnam, you need a local licence or an international driving permit, but many foreign drivers don't bother. If you're caught driving in Vietnam without the right paperwork, you'll be fined, but arrests and vehicle confiscation are very unlikely if you remain polite. Much like Vietnamese motorists, Vietnamese motorbikers will usually attempt to negotiate this fine down. Note that your insurance may not cover you if you have an accident while riding without a licence. Renting a motorbike long-term is easy practically anywhere in the country: simply approach any secondhand motorbike shop and explain what you want (perhaps using Google Translate). You will need to leave a hefty cash deposit or identification, most likely your passport. If you do need to leave your passport, make sure you carry digital and paper copies, as it will always be requested at check-in at hotels.

WHY I DON'T FLY

By Joshua Zukas

When it comes to extreme heat, unpredictable weather and sea-level rise, Vietnam is experiencing the consequences of the climate crisis more acutely than many other countries. While the bulk of the responsibility for confronting the crisis must lie with governments and corporations, that doesn't give us licence to ignore our individual role in impacting the climate. Perhaps the single most important thing that a traveller to Vietnam can do to reduce their carbon footprint is to avoid taking domestic flights, which can cut the carbon emissions generated from a trip by more than half.

But this shouldn't be the only reason to avoid taking flights. Flying is an objectively unpleasant experience, and this might be especially true in Vietnam. Airports are rarely exactly where you want to be, leading to long transfers, often through heavy traffic. Check-in and security processes can be tedious, and the boredom of sitting around in an airport with nothing to look at only intensifies after the near-inevitable announcement of a delay. On the other hand, train stations are almost always central and long-distance buses often drop you in the middle of town. Travelling by train is especially enjoyable as it's the ticket to a front-row seat for observing Vietnam's shifting, cinematic landscapes away from road traffic. It's also an opportunity to contemplate a symbol of Vietnamese national identity, the so-called Reunification Express, an heirloom of early 20th-century infrastructure that survived two calamitous wars and was painstakingly rebuilt. Vietnam's decrepit, diesel-powered rail infrastructure is not without its problems and is in desperate need of an upgrade, but this won't happen if people stop using it.

The ethical dynamics of travel, the climate and personal decisions, are complex, which is why this guide does offer information on domestic flights. However, this information always appears at the end of the list because I believe that domestic flights should only be considered after exhausting the other options. In keeping with this philosophy, over the 18 months that I spent researching and writing this book, I didn't take any domestic flights. Not only did this keep my carbon footprint down, but it also led to meaningful and sometimes amusing experiences, like learning about local speciality dishes over a shared meal with fellow passengers, playing English-language games on an iPad with children and bantering with ticket inspectors about why I'm not married. All these experiences strengthened the connection I have with this country, and hopefully this guidebook has benefited as a result.

Another option, especially for longer trips, is to buy a secondhand motorbike – unsurprisingly, these are very affordable in a country full of motorbikes – and then sell it on when you're done. If starting and finishing in the same place, it's possible to agree a buy-back fee with the seller, though it's not uncommon for them to find reasons to negotiate this down. If renting or buying a motorbike in Hanoi, reach out to AZ Motorbikes (w azmotorbikes.com). For Hồ Chí Minh City, try Style Motorbikes (w stylemotorbikes.com). If renting a motorbike just for the day, you can usually do this through your hotel. Vietnam Coracle (w vietnamcoracle.com) is an excellent resource for motorcyclists, with dozens of itineraries that have been expertly researched and written.

BY BOAT A few places are accessible by boat, notably the islands in *Chapter 12* (page 427) and Vũng Tàu (page 382), plus some cities of the Mekong Delta (page 396), from Hồ Chí Minh City. See the relevant chapters for more information.

BY AIR If you must move quickly between places, flying is the fastest way – although do consider the impact of taking flights (page 61). Vietnam's domestic flight network is extensive and there are dozens of civilian airports scattered throughout the country, sometimes surprisingly close to one another. Most smaller airports only have flight connections with Hanoi and/or Hồ Chí Minh City. The domestic airlines are Vietnam Airlines (w vietnamairlines.com) and Vietjet Air (w vietjetair.com). Note that the former offers one checked bag included in the fee whereas the latter does not. It's usually simpler to use a price comparison website to see which airline offers the best times and prices (and to see if there are any new airlines). For more information about airports in Vietnam, see the official tourism website (w vietnam.travel/things-to-do/travellers-guide-vietnams-airports).

GETTING AROUND TOWNS AND CITIES Getting around urban areas in Vietnam is a combination of walking, bicycling, taxis, motorbike taxis and, for some travellers, motorbiking. Some cities – namely Hanoi, Huế and Hội An – have cyclos, tricycle contraptions powered by the leg muscles of middle-aged men. City buses, though cheap, are difficult for short-term visitors to get their head around and the ambitious metro projects are yet to be realised. An invaluable tool while travelling around Vietnam is Singaporean ride-hailing app Grab, to which you can link a credit or debit card and therefore use without cash (though you can also pay with cash if preferred). An interesting local competitor to Grab is Xanh SM, which only uses electric vehicles. Renting a motorbike for the day is usually possible through your hotel.

ACCOMMODATION

There is generally an oversupply of accommodation in Vietnam, facilitating both pre-planned itineraries and spontaneous travel with the freedom to book just a few days (or hours) in advance. In many cases, accommodation providers will even have space for you if you walk in on the day. In a country that changes quickly, with so many options to choose from, it is impossible to keep an evergreen list of hotels. Those recommended in this guide are all special in some way, whether that be in terms of value, location, history, architecture or service. Many locations in this guide have an introductory paragraph before the hotel listings recommending well-situated districts, neighbourhoods and streets to consider staying in. This should enable you to go online and find good deals for the right hotels in the best locations.

ACCOMMODATION PRICE CODES

Hotel prices are especially elastic in Vietnam, so the code indicators in this book should only be used as a rough guide. Prices are based on the cost of a double room per night.

$$$$$	3,000,000VND+
$$$$	1,500,000–3,000,000VND
$$$	750,000–1,500,000VND
$$	400,000–750,000VND
$	less than 400,000VND

The websites that offer the best deals tend to be Booking.com (**w** booking.com), Agoda (**w** agoda.com) and Airbnb (**w** airbnb.com), which lists both hotels and rooms in private houses. In Vietnam it is particularly important to check both ratings *and* reviews, as photos can be deceiving.

Accommodation comes in many forms, including hostels, homestays, guesthouses, lodges and hotels. If paying at the property, lodges and hotels usually accept cards; the rest do not. Words that refer to a specific characteristic or type of accommodation in Western countries are used loosely here: 'boutique' hotels can have more than a hundred rooms, a 'homestay' might be a set of garden bungalows with a pool, and somewhere called 'Luxury Hotel' might be very ordinary.

HOSTELS Hostels usually provide beds in both dorms and private rooms, and only really exist in places that are popular with young travellers. These are not usually cheaper than homestays or guesthouses, but do have communal spaces like rooftop bars and large lounge lobbies for meeting other people. They also arrange group activities.

HOMESTAYS Homestays come in all shapes and sizes. Some adhere to the original sense of the word and offer a private room or a mattress on the floor in a shared space in a family home. Others began like that, but have evolved into boutique hotels where the original family have hired staff and contact with them is limited. Regardless of the manifestation, all homestays should offer excellent, home-cooked meals that may or may not be eaten with the family. In very basic homestays the meal can cost twice as much as the room or bed for the night. Homestay meals take time and should always be booked at least 8 hours in advance, and preferably the day before.

GUESTHOUSES Known as *nhà nghỉ* in Vietnamese, guesthouses are the most ubiquitous type of accommodation in the country, existing just about everywhere, from Hanoi's Old Quarter to remote borderland villages. A Vietnamese guesthouse should be satisfyingly affordable and adequately clean, with a hard bed, hot water and, in most cases, air conditioning. In rural areas and small towns they are often extensions of peoples' homes, so it's quite normal to walk through a 'lobby' of playing children and television-watching parents. The term has a somewhat negative connotation, as cheap hotels that you can rent by the hour for sex are also called *nhà nghỉ*. To avoid these, check the entrance to the lobby. If it's separated from the outside world in some way, perhaps with a blind or beaded curtain, it's probably a hotel used for sex. (The screen exists to shield customers who may be engaging in extramarital activities.) Another giveaway are the signs outside advertising that rooms can be rented by the hour.

LODGES Lodge is a vague term used in this guidebook for a rural low-rise hotel that has made some effort to blend in with its surroundings. Rooms are often in thatched bungalows shaded by trees and encircled by gardens. Some lodges are like overgrown homestays and cost little more than a guesthouse, whereas others offer the most expensive rooms in the country. The northern mountains and the Mekong Delta have the best selection of lodges, and both chapters have sections devoted to this author's favourites.

HOTELS *Khách sạn* in Vietnamese, hotels are a step up from guesthouses in size but not necessarily in quality. Like hotel in English, the term is vague, and it can refer to both uber-luxury urban retreats and oversized and drab rural accommodation. In cities, many newer places simply use the word 'hotel', which is universally understood, but in remote towns and on roadsides *khách sạn* is still common. Most hotels these days are privately owned, but some are run by the government and are in a poor state of repair.

EATING AND DRINKING

Food is everything to the Vietnamese. Between family and close friends, a more common greeting than *khoẻ không?* ('how are you?') or even *xin chào* ('hello') is *ăn cơm chưa?* ('have you eaten yet?' or, more literally, 'have you eaten rice yet?'). The Vietnamese eat three meals a day: breakfast is typically 06.00–08.00, lunch is 11.00–13.00 and dinner is after 18.00. Between these meals are opportunities to snack extensively on simple sweets like fruit and biscuits and smaller meals like after-work noodles, wraps and rolls. Rice is eaten for lunch and/or dinner but never breakfast, unless it's the sticky variety. Other breakfast foods include noodle soups, dumplings and *bánh mì*. Traditionally, all rice-based meals would also be served with vegetables, a broth, a dipping sauce and perhaps a little meat or fish. As Vietnam has grown richer, meat and fish plates have taken up more space on the dinner table, but vegetables remain indispensable. Indeed, one reason for Vietnam's relatively low rates of obesity, even by East Asian standards, is the importance of vegetables. The dipping sauce is usually fish sauce-, soy sauce- or vinegar-based.

At its best, Vietnamese food is light, fresh, healthy and balanced. While some recipes are unfathomably complex and painstakingly difficult to execute, others require just a few simple ingredients. One of the most important ingredients

RESTAURANT PRICE CODES

Meal prices vary depending on what you order, so the code indicators in this book should only be used as a rough guide. Prices are based on the cost of enough dishes to constitute a full meal, without drinks.

$$$$$	600,000VND+
$$$$	300,000–600,000VND
$$$	150,000–300,000VND
$$	50,000–150,000VND
$	less than 50,000VND

VIETNAM'S SPECIALITY DISHES

Vietnam has an unknown number of regional speciality dishes. This guide attempts to feature as many as possible in the relevant chapters. Many of these specialities are noodle dishes, but some are wraps, rolls and dishes eaten with bread or rice.

Hanoi page 94
Northern mountains page 134
Hải Phòng page 201
Huế page 252
Đà Nẵng page 285
Hội An page 303
Central Highlands page 348
Vũng Tàu page 385
Mekong Delta page 406
Phú Quốc page 432
Côn Đảo page 442
Hồ Chí Minh City page 460

is, of course, fish sauce, which has the culinary wizardry to make a humdrum combination of basic ingredients taste delicious. Other flavour enhancers include salt, pepper, soy sauce, MSG and chilli.

Vietnamese food is different in the three different regions, and everyone thinks their region or city does it best. To get a taste for the major differences, try the most popular noodle soups and focus on the flavour of the broth. *Hủ tiếu* in Southern Vietnam tends to be sweet, perhaps because of culinary influence from Cambodia and Thailand. *Bún bò* in Central Vietnam is hot, sometimes uncomfortably so, due to the region's taste for chilli. *Phở* in Northern Vietnam is predominantly savoury, though never overwhelmingly so, as northerners prioritise balance. In other words, northerners complain that food in the centre is too hot, those from the centre might say that food in the south is too sweet and southerners joke that northern food is boring.

While food is superb across Vietnam, it's not superb everywhere. It's perfectly feasible to be served a bad meal, but avoiding this is usually down to timing. For example, arrive at a rice restaurant too long after the lunch rush and the remaining least popular dishes will be cold and congealed; if you arrive at a homestay in the evening and you haven't ordered dinner, you may have to settle for instant noodles. With a little planning and the recommendations in this guide, it should be easy enough to eat like royalty in Vietnam. In addition, the Michelin Guide (**w** guide.michelin.com) also lists a good directory of restaurants in Hanoi, Đà Nẵng and Hồ Chí Minh City, including street food. The best way to find good food in any given area in Vietnam, however, is to ask a Vietnamese person where they eat. This shouldn't be too much trouble in the big cities as receptionists in hotels and servers in cafés speak English, and they are often keen to show off their favourite spots. Alternatively, point at the name of a speciality dish (see above) in this book and whomever you're talking to should understand the message. If you're struggling with a menu that's only in Vietnamese, see page 484.

STREET KITCHENS You probably know that Vietnam has one of the best – if not *the* best – street-food scenes in the world. While street food in other Asian countries has moved into shopping centres and food courts, in Vietnam it is, for now at least, alive and kicking where it belongs. Some street-food restaurants serve just one type of dish and only operate at certain times of the day (eg: for breakfast; 06.00–10.00). Others seemingly never close. Street food is almost always served on Lilliputian tables and their accompanying stools, so sometimes requires some flexibility. It might at first glance appear unhygienic, but remember that street-food joints buy their ingredients fresh on the day, and when they sell out they close up shop. Compare this to a tourist restaurant that seeks to satisfy everyone by having Vietnamese food, pizza and curry all on the same menu. Street food is special for many reasons, one of which is that it transcends social boundaries. Some street-food restaurants in Hanoi are so well regarded that they have rows of luxury cars parked out front while their millionaire owners eat noodles for just a few dollars. Meals at street kitchens range from 20,000VND to 100,000VND.

MOM-AND-POP EATERIES These are somewhere between street food and fully fledged restaurants. Called *quán ăn* ('eating shop') in Vietnamese, these eateries are usually family owned and specialise in a few dishes based around a key ingredient. A *quán ăn* that specialises in eel might serve eel rice porridge, deep-fried eel cakes and eel with glass noodles. Choice is limited, but the food almost always tastes good and is good value, and tables and chairs are not diminutive. Sometimes that key ingredient is rice, in which case the eatery is called *cơm bình dân* ('people's rice'). At these simple rice eateries, popular at lunchtime, the dishes are pre-cooked and presented behind a glass counter for customers to peruse. These may be particularly appealing for non-Vietnamese speakers, as you can see the dishes on offer and point at what appeals. The server will load your plate with rice, top it with whatever you've pointed at – usually four or five dishes – and charge accordingly. *Cơm bình dân*

EAT STREET FOOD LIKE A PRO

Settling down for some street food can be intimidating the first few times, but once initiated, it will feel like second nature. Here are some tips to get you started:

- **Make friends.** If a street kitchen appeals, hover around and try to catch the eye of a diner. Many young Vietnamese people speak some English, and will be keen to introduce you to what they're eating and help you order.
- **Observe the other diners to decide what you want**. Street kitchens generally don't serve just one dish, but a few versions of the same dish. A street kitchen selling *phở*, for example, will serve the famous noodle soup dish, but perhaps also the same noodles without the soup and a kind of salad (ie: just the protein and the veggies). Many street-food restaurants also serve sides and accompaniments. If you observe what others are eating before you order, it will help you decide what you want. It's not particularly rude to look at other people's meals, as it is in some Western countries.
- **Ask the price before you sit down**. Getting ripped off is never fun, and unfortunately street-food sellers are principal offenders. Always ask the price first, and if it feels like too much, simply smile and move on. Some places might have the price of the dish written on a sign that hovers above the chef's head.
- **Don't be put off if you're ignored.** People eat street food for the food and the experience – not for the service. The best places are busy, and busy staff members will be more concerned with serving customers than making you feel comfortable. If you're being ignored, just keep trying to get someone's attention. They will serve you in the end. Besides, conversing with surly street-food sellers is all part of the theatre.

VEGANS AND VEGETARIANS

Vegetarianism is a relatively new phenomenon in Vietnam, but with the prevalence of Buddhism, veganism has existed for centuries. As such, the older generations don't tend to distinguish between the two. Due to its long history and the Vietnamese love for food, vegan cuisine is delicious, creative and ubiquitous. Even small towns will usually have some kind of vegan eatery. Vegan food here is very much like food everywhere else, but chefs have an armoury of meat and animal product alternatives for protein and flavour, like fake meat made from gluten or a fish sauce alternative made from tamarind extract. The issues that vegetarians and vegans may face is in non-vegan restaurants. It can be quite difficult to ask chefs not to use fish sauce in otherwise vegan dishes like tofu in tomato sauce or stir-fried vegetables. These days, eateries targeting tourists will always have vegan and vegetarian dishes on the menu.

are especially cheap, hence the name. If eating in a restaurant where the dishes are pre-prepared, come early when the food is hot. Meals at eateries such as these range from 60,000VND to 150,000VND.

RESTAURANTS There is considerable overlap between *quán ăn* and *nhà hàng* ('restaurant'), but the latter implies a more upmarket and expensive establishment with a bigger menu. Food is cooked to order and is usually served with rice in all its forms (steamed, sticky, porridge, fried), though other carbs include noodles, bread and sometimes potatoes. Menus tend to be huge, with meat, fish, vegetable and tofu dishes. Some *nhà hàng* have a particular food theme, like farmed salmon (popular in Sa Pa), goat (popular in Ninh Bình) or hotpot (popular everywhere). Hanoi, Hồ Chí Minh City and to a lesser extent Đà Nẵng also have burgeoning fine-dining scenes. Meals in standard restaurants range from 80,000VND to 300,000VND per person. Eating in fancier restaurants in the cities can cost up to 600,000VND. Fine-dining restaurants will cost a minimum of 2,000,000VND.

INTERNATIONAL CUISINE Non-Vietnamese food is found everywhere in Vietnam. Unsurprisingly, the best foreign restaurants are found in the big cities, where you can find world-class French, Italian, Russian, British, American, Indian, Japanese, Korean, Chinese and Thai cuisine (to name but a few). Should you really need it, a break from Vietnamese food is never too far away.

DRINKING AND NIGHTLIFE The Vietnamese are social, with large friendship networks, but nightlife remains relatively low-key. Most Vietnamese seem to prefer getting together for food or coffee rather than going to bars and nightclubs. However, along with the pubs, bars and clubs that you find in most parts of the world, there are a few nightlife categories to look out for.

Beer taverns *Bia* (beer) is big in Vietnam, and open-air spaces serving the stuff in bottles and cans are found across the country. Popular local beers include Bia Hà Nội and Trúc Bạch (in Hanoi), Bia Sài Gòn and 333 (in Hồ Chí Minh City), Huda (in Huế and around) and Larue (in Đà Nẵng and around). These are light lagers that, in all honesty, taste pretty much the same. In Hanoi and other parts of Northern Vietnam, *bia hơi* – fresh, light beer with a low alcohol content – is also popular and is the perfect refreshment during Hanoi's long, hot summers. Beer taverns are known as *quán nhậu* in Vietnamese, where *nhậu* is the verb 'to drink, eat and socialise', so food is also, inevitably, an important part of the experience. Menu styles tend to be similar to those in restaurants and it's perfectly acceptable to order a full meal in a tavern and not consume any beer at all. Meals at taverns range from 100,000VND to 500,000VND, depending on what you eat and how much beer you drink.

Craft beer Given Vietnam's love for beer and a growing middle class who are open to new ideas, it was only a matter of time before craft beer took off in the country. It did this with zeal in the 2010s, and has since gone from strength to strength. Some of the more well-known breweries include Pasteur Street Brewing in Hồ Chí Minh City, Heart of Darkness in Hanoi and 7 Bridges in Đà Nẵng. Craft-beer pubs are usually found in the more touristy areas of big cities and towns, but still attract many locals. Craft beer is also served in upmarket restaurants and bars.

Cocktail bars Perhaps because of the similarities they share with coffee houses, cocktail bars have taken off in Vietnam. Like craft-beer pubs, cocktail bars began in Hanoi and Hồ Chí Minh City in the 2010s, but they are now popping up everywhere, including in far-flung border cities. All the cocktail classics are there, most of which are executed with skill. Mixology tends to be creative and occasionally theatrical, incorporating tropical flavours such as lemongrass and tamarind. In a bid to appeal to a market that is always in search of something new, many cocktail-bar menus are becoming increasingly unusual, featuring drinks based on street-food dishes like *phở* and *bún chả*.

Coffee houses From big cities to remote roadsides, getting caffeinated in Vietnam is never a challenge. Though introduced by the French in the early 20th century, when it comes to the prevalence, importance and diversity of café culture, the Vietnamese have since outpaced their former colonial overlords. Vietnamese *cà phê* uses the Robusta bean, which grows better in the local climate and tends to be bitter rather than sour, unlike the Arabica beans used in espresso-based coffee. Rather than using fresh milk, the Vietnamese mix their coffee with condensed milk to concoct a bitter-sweet combination reminiscent of dark chocolate. Coffee shops are open early in the morning to late in the evening, and all of them serve coffee alternatives. The simpler cafés may offer just lemon juice, but many now have an expansive menu of smoothies, juices, soft drinks, tea and more. Some serve meals and snacks. Coffee shops are so popular and accessible in Vietnam that many are actually art galleries, artisan workshops and other creative hubs in disguise. Spending time in coffee shops is a highlight of any visit to Vietnam, which is why this guide has a designated coffee-house section in many places. While many coffee shops serve food, meals are almost always better in restaurants and on the street. Note that the coffee houses in this guide do not have price codes, as a cup of coffee is rarely more than US$2–3, even in big cities.

PUBLIC HOLIDAYS AND FESTIVALS

Vietnam follows the lunar and solar calendars, and celebrates public holidays and festivals from both. Domestic tourism is a big deal in Vietnam, but while the public holidays are worth considering, there's no need to avoid them completely or plan entire trips around them. Vietnam is a country where people work every day and supply usually exceeds demand, so it's possible to find hotels and book transport tickets even during busy times. That said, accommodation prices can increase during public holidays, and if you want to avoid traffic and booked-out trains and buses, don't travel immediately before or after them. Public holidays in Vietnam often mean that businesses and banks will close, and certain attractions, especially in cities, might be harder to access. If the holiday falls on a weekend, it is observed on the following Monday. For information on travelling during Lunar New Year, or Tết Nguyên Đán (or simply Tết), see page 41.

For details of local festivals, see the destination chapters. The following are national public holidays with paid leave from work:

New Year's Day 1 January. Celebrates the new (solar) year.

Tết Nguyên Đán (Lunar New Year) Usually between late January and mid-February; officially five days long, but usually longer. The biggest festival of the year.

Hùng Kings' Festival Tenth day of the third lunar month (usually in April). Commemorates the legendary Hùng kings, considered the founders of Vietnam.

Reunification Day (Liberation Day) 30 April. Celebrates the reunification of North and South Vietnam in 1976 after the taking of Saigon in 1975. Usually combines with Labour Day for an extra-long holiday weekend.

International Labour Day (May Day) 1 May. Honours the working classes.

National Day 2 September. Marks the declaration of independence from French colonial rule in 1945.

The following are important national festivals that do not involve any paid leave:

Tết Hàn Thực (Cold Food Festival) Third day of the third lunar month (March or April). A traditional festival where Vietnamese people eat cold dishes, particularly *bánh trôi* and *bánh chay* (glutinous rice balls), to honour ancestors.

Buddha's Birthday Eighth day of the fourth lunar month (usually May). Festival for Buddhists in Vietnam, celebrated with lanterns, prayers and offerings at pagodas across the country.

Tết Đoan Ngọ (Mid-Year Festival) Fifth day of the fifth lunar month (usually June). Festival to cleanse the body and spirit, with rituals that include eating fermented sticky rice and other specific foods.

Vu Lan (Hungry Ghost Festival) 15th day of the seventh lunar month (usually August). Day for honouring deceased ancestors and making offerings for wandering spirits.

Tết Trung Thu (Mid-Autumn Festival) 15th day of the eighth lunar month (usually September). Traditional harvest festival, especially popular with children, and one of the most visually interesting. Celebrations include lion dances, lantern processions and eating mooncakes.

Lễ Giáng Sinh (Christmas) 24–25 December. Christmas is widely celebrated in major cities and among the Christian population. Streets are often decorated with lights and ornaments, and churches hold midnight Mass.

SHOPPING

MARKETS Markets are extraordinary things in Vietnam, regardless of the location. Those in the big cities tend to specialise (eg: wholesale, food, fabric, etc) but elsewhere in the country they'll sell just about everything – including souvenirs for tourists. You'll quickly realise that quantity is prized over quality, but you may still find the clothing, food, household items and artisanal products like lacquerware, ceramics and embroidery you're looking for. Bargaining is customary, but that doesn't mean it's easy. It's a good idea to check different prices for the item across different stalls in a market, but do this discreetly to avoid irritating market sellers. When you're ready to bargain, try to identify a stall that has a few things you want. Ask for the price of just one thing, and then the more you add to your shopping basket, the more leverage you'll have to bring the price down.

TOURIST AREAS While not always the most interesting neighbourhoods, tourist enclaves in towns and cities tend to have the best selection of craft shops, fashion boutiques, art galleries and design shops. To generalise, markets tend to have more generic souvenirs, whereas shops in touristy areas are more likely to offer boutique items. The goodies available are vast, including fashion, lacquerware, silk products, hand-embroidered items, bamboo products, ceramics, paintings, calligraphy, wooden carvings, textiles, jewellery and food and drink items including alcohol, coffee and tea. Bargaining is generally not customary and many items have a price tag, but it's acceptable to ask politely, especially if purchasing more than one item.

TAILORING Vietnam is famous for its tailoring. While places like Hội An have a historic, competitive tailoring industry that has adeptly adapted to the tastes of foreigners, Hanoi and Hồ Chí Minh City also have some excellent tailors, especially for suits and dresses. If you decide to get something made, don't simply explain what you want, but leave photos, magazine clippings and website addresses as inspiration. Express tailoring, when you receive your item in 24 hours or less, exists in Vietnam, but it's always better to stay for a few days and build in a few return visits for adjustments. Before agreeing to the item, ask to see an example of the fabric so you can be confident with the colour, texture and quality. Some of the most successful tailoring experiences come from tailors being left an item and asked to replicate it across different colours and fabrics. So if you have a favourite dress, shirt or pair of trousers consider getting it copied. Leaving a deposit of at least half is standard. Some tailors will also mend clothes for you, though the more upmarket ones will usually politely refuse. For recommended tailors in Hội An, see page 305.

OUTDOOR ACTIVITIES

CAVING Since the rediscovery (page 238) of Sơn Đoòng Cave in Phong Nha-Kẻ Bàng National Park, by some measures the biggest cave on the planet, Vietnam has become one of the world's premier countries for commercial caving. Phong Nha-Kẻ Bàng remains the hub, with more than a dozen underground labyrinths, though the nearby Tú Làn cave system, which is outside the national park boundaries, is becoming an increasingly popular alternative. Other caves in Vietnam exist wherever there are karst mountains, namely the provinces of Hà Giang, Cao Bằng and Bắc Kạn in the northern mountains and Quảng Ninh and Ninh Bình and closer to the coast, as well as Cát Bà island. Most of Vietnam's caves are wet caves that fill with water during the annual monsoon and grow in width and height. Generally speaking, there are two types of caving experiences. The first is the relatively unadventurous type, where you turn up, pay an entrance fee and see several chambers illuminated by artificial lights. The second is more intrepid, and possible in and around Phong Nha. These are multi-day guided tours that need to be booked in advance, and most include hiking through jungles. See page 238 for details.

CYCLING Casual cyclists can explore lowland areas independently, with numerous villages and cafés offering convenient stops along the way. Meanwhile, more adventurous cyclists often book guided tours that tackle remote regions, complete with support vehicles and logistical arrangements. If seeing Vietnam on two unmotorised wheels appeals, reach out to **Velo Vietnam** (w velovietnam.cc) or **Oriental Sky Travel** (w orientalskytravel.com). The Mekong Delta, with its flat terrain and scenic waterways, is perfect for leisurely rides through coconut groves and skirting rice paddies. Northern provinces like Lào Cai and Hà Giang in the northern mountains deliver rugged, mountainous trails for seasoned cyclists.

HIKING Vietnam's dramatic landscapes make for ideal hiking, and this is perhaps the country's most common and accessible outdoor activity. In Vietnam, where there is nature, there is hiking. Sa Pa has long been the country's hiking hub, where a network of pathways plunge from terraced rice fields to misty valleys. Also in the north, Cát Bà island features hikes through dense jungle and up to panoramic viewpoints, while Cúc Phương National Park has trails through ancient forests. In Central Vietnam, the best hiking tends to be in Bạch Mã National Park and close to Đà Lạt, and in Southern Vietnam there is a limited trail network in Cát Tiên National Park. National park offices are getting better at providing maps and instructions for do-it-yourself half-day hikes, but for anything longer it's better to enlist a guide. This is particularly true in the northern mountains, and it's one way to give back to the local community (page 156).

MOTORBIKING It's no secret that Vietnam is an excellent place for motorbiking. Fabulous vistas and hairpin bends aside, renting motorbikes is easy anywhere in the country, mechanics are ubiquitous and, despite somewhat lawless roads, motorbike awareness is high. Especially good ribbons of road are found across the northern mountains, but especially those on the Chinese border, including Lai Châu, Lào Cai, Hà Giang and Cao Bằng. Meandering coastal roads run south from Huế, particularly on the Hải Vân Pass and the areas immediately north and south of Nha Trang.

ROCK CLIMBING Vietnam has two areas for rock climbing: Cát Bà island and Hữu Lũng in Lạng Sơn. **Langur's Adventures** (w langursadventures.com) has long been the most reputable tour company on Cát Bà, with several rock-climbing routes, including those over water which can be done without a harness (known as deep-water soloing or DWS). Just a few hours from Hanoi and sheltered by a tangle of karst mountains, Hữu Lũng is one of Northern Vietnam's best kept secrets and a burgeoning rock-climbing destination. Reach out to **VietClimb** (w vietclimb.vn), who have worked with a local family to set up a homestay.

TRAIL RUNNING The **Vietnam Trail Series** (w vietnamtrailseries.com) dominates the trail-running scene in Vietnam, with four races a year in Sa Pa, Mai Châu, Pù Luông and Mộc Châu. The dates change each year so check the website for details. Trail running has become extremely popular with Vietnam's middle classes in recent years, and more races are starting across the country's upland subregions.

WATERSPORTS Kayaking tends to be most available where the coastal scenery is the most dramatic, particularly around Cát Bà island and Lan Hạ Bay. Mỹ Hoà Beach in Ninh Thuận Province is cultivating a kitesurfing community, while windsurfing is popular and possible in Mũi Né. Most beaches will have water activities like kayaking and snorkelling, particularly the ones with sizeable visitor economies, like Nha Trang and the beaches in Phú Quốc.

OPENING HOURS

In Vietnam, general opening hours for businesses and institutions vary depending on the type of establishment, but most operate within a standard framework. Most businesses are open every day, including Sunday and public holidays, but may close unpredictably and for unknown reasons. **Retail shops and restaurants** typically open between 07.00 and 10.00 and close around 21.00–22.00. **Cafés** open between 06.00 and 08.00 and stay open late into the evening (many also serve alcohol). **Shopping malls, supermarkets and department stores** usually operate from 09.00, seven days a week, including public holidays. **Banks and government offices** generally open from 08.00 to 17.00 on weekdays, with a 1-hour lunch break around noon. Some banks may also offer limited services on Saturday mornings, but government offices are typically closed. **Hospitals** often operate around the clock. **Museums** are a mixed bag. Some open every day from 08.00 until 17.00. Some take a lunch break of up to 90 minutes in the middle of the day, but many don't. Some close on Mondays, others close on Sundays. As opening hours change regularly, the times in this book are only a rough guide. The information given online tends to be accurate.

MEDIA AND COMMUNICATIONS

INTERNET AND WI-FI Almost every hotel, guesthouse, homestay, coffee house, bar and even street kitchen offers Wi-Fi access to guests and customers for free. Generally, the more professional the business, the better the connection. For travellers who need a more reliable or constant connection, purchasing an eSIM app or local SIM card with a data plan is a good option (see below). Note that a few news websites – most notably BBC News – are blocked. Unlike in China, you should have no issues connecting to Google, Meta and other major websites and apps.

TELEPHONES, DATA AND SIM CARDS Aside from bigger businesses (like large hotels), landlines are seldom used in Vietnam. Regardless of length of stay, it's advisable to purchase a local SIM card (and bring an unlocked smartphone that supports them). Purchasing a SIM card is a quick and easy process that can be done at airports, convenience stores or mobile phone shops. It's common to hand your phone over to the shop seller and for them to set everything up for you: don't leave until you've sent or received a message to make sure it's working. For less than US$15, you can buy sufficient airtime for calls, texts and a data package that will last you for up to a month. Alternatively, consider an eSIM app like Airalo (w airalo.com). Vietnam's major mobile providers include Viettel, which has the most widespread network coverage, even in remote and rural areas, and Vinaphone and MobiFone, which also provide reliable service, particularly in urban centres. Reception in remote mountainous areas may vary, but in most regions, the coverage is solid and data speeds are fast. For emergency phone numbers, see page 51.

POST Posting letters and parcels domestically is cheap and fairly straightforward; ask your hotel receptionist for help as the slightly pricier services will pick up the letter or parcel from anywhere, including hotel reception desks. International post, however, is unreliable and slow, though cheap. To send anything internationally, use the post office headquarters in the major towns or cities.

MEDIA In the 2024 Press Freedom Index, Reporters Without Borders (RSF) ranked Vietnam 174 out of 180 countries, putting it behind Russia, China and Myanmar. For additional resources, including books to read, films and television shows to watch and podcasts to listen to, see page 488.

Newspapers and magazines The only English-language newspaper still in print is the government-run **Việt Nam News** (w vietnamnews.vn), which covers local and international news in a dry and tedious manner. This is available at major hotels and at airports. Between Vietnam Airlines and Vietjet Air there are three **in-flight magazines**: Heritage (w heritagevietnamairlines.com), Heritage Fashion and One2Fly (w one2fly.vn). All three print stories in English and Vietnamese. The writing is reliably drab, though the photography can sometimes provide some travel inspiration.

Websites Economic, political and societal issues are covered more critically, sometimes even controversially, by **VnExpress International** (w vnexpress.net) and **Tuổi Trẻ** (w tuoitrenews.vn), English versions of two of Vietnam's leading newspapers. **Saigoneer** (w saigoneer.com), though based out of Hồ Chí Minh City, covers cultural issues across Vietnam.

CULTURAL ETIQUETTE

Vietnam is relaxed and easy-going regarding cultural conventions. The people, especially in small towns and rural areas, can be traditional and conservative, but it is difficult to cause offence unwittingly. Most Vietnamese people value politeness, and behaviours considered courteous in other countries translate to Vietnam. If in doubt, simply smile and give a gentle nod of the head.

APPEARANCE The main complaint Vietnamese have of foreigners is their fondness for dirty and torn clothing. Backpackers come in for particularly severe criticism and the term *Tây ba lô* (literally 'Western backpacker') is a contemptuous one reflecting the low priority many budget travellers seem to allocate to personal hygiene and the antiquity and inadequacy of their shorts and vests. For men, going topless is only acceptable on a beach, or in close proximity to one. For women, topless sunbathing is never acceptable but bikinis are fine. Modesty should be preserved and excessive displays of bare flesh are not generally considered good form (even if you do see young Vietnamese breaking with convention). Shoes should be removed before entering many religious buildings and before going into people's houses.

EATING There are rules around eating and drinking, as there are anywhere in the world, but you won't cause offence by breaking them. The best piece of advice is simply to observe how the Vietnamese are acting and follow suit. When attending a meal at a restaurant or in someone's home, it's customary to allow elders to be seated and to begin eating first. Never stick chopsticks upright in a bowl of rice, as this mimics funeral rituals and is considered inauspicious. Passing food from one person's chopsticks to another's is also frowned upon. When not in use, chopsticks should be placed neatly on the rest or across your bowl. Vietnamese meals are often served family-style, with shared dishes placed in the centre. It's polite to offer food to those near you and to use communal utensils to serve food into your bowl. When taking food from shared dishes, it's important to take small portions and avoid overloading your bowl, always finishing what you take before getting more. Rice is a staple in Vietnamese cuisine, and it's considered polite to hold your rice bowl close to your mouth to avoid dropping food. Showing appreciation for the meal is important, and compliments to the host or the cook are always welcomed. When it comes to paying the bill at a restaurant, it's common for the organiser to cover the cost, especially in formal or business settings. Although it's polite to offer to pay or contribute, the host will often insist on handling the bill. Likewise, if you invite a Vietnamese person for a meal, they might expect you to pay for it. Meals in Vietnam are typically leisurely, with a focus on conversation, so eating slowly and enjoying the food is encouraged.

DRINKING Drinking is often a part of social gatherings, and it is polite to accept a drink if offered, even if you just take a small sip. Toasting is a common practice, and when participating, it is respectful to hold your glass lower than that of an elder. For additional respect, use both hands to lift the glass. Refilling others' glasses is a thoughtful gesture.

CONDUCT Kissing and canoodling in public are likely to draw attention, not much of it favourable. But walking hand in hand is now accepted, including for same-sex couples. Hand shaking among men is a standard greeting and although Vietnamese women will consent to the process, it is sometimes clear that they would prefer not to; a smile and slight bow of the head will often suffice instead. Never bring your hands together in prayer position and bow slightly like in Thailand – the Vietnamese do not do this.

TERMS OF ADDRESS Vietnamese names are written with the surname first, followed by the middle name, followed by the given name. Thus Nguyễn Văn Minh is not called Nguyễn as we would presume in the West, but Minh. Some include their middle names in the name they go by, so Trần Minh Phương may be called Minh Phương. The conventions around how to address people according to age, gender and status are quite complicated and visitors aren't expected to master them. Vietnamese has more than two dozen of these familial terms, including older sister, older brother, aunt, uncle and so on. Vietnamese people take great pleasure in teaching these terms to unsuspecting foreigners, who inevitably butcher the maddening pronunciation, so if this topic is of interest, simply ask someone.

TRAVELLING POSITIVELY

ENVIRONMENTAL CONSIDERATIONS Vietnam struggles with waste management and is, according to some studies, one of the world's biggest source countries of ocean plastic. Minimising your individual rubbish output can feel like a challenge in a country (and continent) that is obsessed with plastic packaging, but a few small things done consistently can make a difference. For example, it's sensible to bring a reusable bag of your own for your purchases. In Vietnam, your item is often bagged up before you notice, but it is never impolite to take your purchases out of the bag and return it to the shopkeeper or market trader. Learn how to pronounce '*không cần túi*' ('I don't need a bag') early on and use it liberally. It's also a good idea to develop the habit of saying '*không ông hút*' (no straw) for juices and cold drinks in restaurants and cafés (paper straws still have a carbon footprint). While drinking several plastic bottles of water a day may intuitively feel like a bad idea, the situation is actually quite complicated. Empty plastic bottles carry value in Vietnam, and their existence provides an income for thousands of trash pickers in big cities and towns.

Other environmental considerations may be related to where and how you travel. For example, though there are signs that the situation is improving, environmental regulations on Hạ Long Bay cruises are still loosely enforced and it's impossible to know that your luxury cruise ship isn't spewing waste into the ocean. On the other hand, the caving companies in Phong Nha take waste management extremely seriously, and the tours provide jobs for would-be loggers and hunters. This guide has tried wherever possible not to recommend hotels that have blemished the countryside or have an outsized impact on the climate through, for example, gigantic air-conditioned lobbies and the overuse of harmful materials during construction.

It is also worth trying to engage wherever possible in slow travel rather than taking domestic flights (page 61).

ECONOMIC CONSIDERATIONS Where and how you spend your money matters. Independent businesses in Vietnam come in many guises, and it can be a good idea to build the habit of giving them your custom. For example, when wandering around a city or town, it's just as easy to buy water and snacks from a family shophouse as it is a larger convenience store. *Bánh mì* can be just as good from the woman pushing a mobile cart around as they are from the big chain restaurant next door. Small guesthouses with only a handful of rooms are often family owned and run, whereas foreign conglomerates often own big hotels. Small businesses are an important part of any healthy economy, and giving them your custom also helps to land as much money as possible into the pockets of local people.

SOCIAL CONSIDERATIONS Perhaps the most important social consideration that a traveller can make is to remember that, first and foremost, Vietnam is not a destination that people travel to but a place that people live in. The way we think about a place can make a difference in how we interact with it, which is one reason this guide refrains from using the word 'destination'. The post-Covid world has seen a huge backlash against overtourism in many communities across the world, and while this movement has not reached Vietnam, that does not mean that overtourism isn't an issue. There are places in Vietnam that, at times, struggle with the number of visitors. Consider reducing your time in these inevitably touristy places and opt to spend more time elsewhere instead. For example, parts of Hội An and Hạ Long Bay suffer from overtourism; consider spending more time in Huế and the northern mountains instead. This lessens the strain on popular places, but can also bring incomes to people who are less likely to benefit from Vietnam's tourism boom.

It's not very difficult to move through Vietnam spending money to support marginalised communities. When looking for souvenirs, visiting markets instead of shopping centres can help to sustain Vietnam's vibrant market culture and small-business owners. Vietnam is full of artists and artisans, but most struggle to make ends meet. In the bigger towns and cities, look for shops that celebrate Vietnam's creative classes instead of importing cheap products from factories abroad. Handle and inspect a product before you buy it; if you suspect it's been mass-produced, it probably has. Throughout the country you'll find artisanal items produced not just by Vietnam's creatives but also by marginalised communities, such as remote ethnolinguistic groups and people with disabilities. Restaurants, cafés and some hotels double as social enterprises, offering employment and training opportunities for disadvantaged youngsters. Many of these are listed in this guide.

NGOS, CHARITIES AND VOLUNTEERING This guide does not endorse voluntary placement schemes unless the volunteer is in possession of a particular skill that is hard to come by in Vietnam, such as accessibility consultancy, English-language communications or climate change adaption. Vietnam has enough construction workers and child-care workers, so while volunteering time to build a nursery in a rural area or take care of kids in an orphanage may feel like a good idea, it's not usually what's best for the community – and it can take jobs away from local people. Cash and online donations to charities can have an outsized impact considering how far money can go in Vietnam. There is a temptation sometimes to donate something other than money, like clothes or books, but charities and NGOs will almost always tell you that money is preferred. If you're moved by an issue in Vietnam and looking for charities in Vietnam to donate to, here are some reputable organisations.

Blue Dragon w bluedragon.org. Provides care & support for Vietnamese children in crisis, including rescue from trafficking & street life.
Cristina Noble Children's Vietnam w cncf.org. Supports vulnerable children through health care, education & community development programmes.
CSAGA w csaga.org.vn. Advocates for gender equality, supports victims of gender-based violence & promotes LGBTQIA+ rights.
Dear Our Community w dearourcommunity.com. Specialises in helping disadvantaged young people to find meaningful employment, with an additional focus on environmental activities.
Education for Nature Vietnam w env4wildlife.org. Dedicated to wildlife conservation, with a focus on combating wildlife trafficking & illegal trade.
Huế Help w huehelp.org. Supports disadvantaged children & teaches water safety through swimming lessons & social programmes.
iSEE w isee.org.vn. Advocates for the rights of marginalised communities, including ethnic minorities & LGBTQIA+ individuals, through policy & social initiatives.
Keep Vietnam Clean w keepvietnamclean.org. Engages communities in waste management & environmental protection initiatives for a cleaner environment.
Lighthouse w lighthousevietnam.org. Provides HIV prevention, counselling & support services for the LGBTQIA+ community & others at risk of sexually transmitted diseases in Vietnam.
Mine Action Group w maginternational.org. Removes landmines & unexploded ordnance (UXO) in conflict-affected areas in Vietnam & elsewhere.
Newborns Vietnam w newbornsvietnam.org. Works to reduce neonatal mortality & improve newborn health care through training & medical support.
Saigon Children's Charity w saigonchildren.com. Gives disadvantaged children access to education & essential support for personal development.
Vietnet-ICT w vietnet-ict.org. Promotes information & communication technology (ICT) development in under-served communities to enhance education, economy & social inclusion.

Part Two

NORTHERN VIETNAM

Northern Vietnam: An Overview

Northern Vietnam is a region of landscapes and legends, from the Martian peaks that brush the Chinese border to the storied islets of the Gulf of Tonkin. The Red River, which slices the region in two, nourished the beginning of the Vietnamese civilisation and nurtured its earliest capitals: Cổ Loa, Hoa Lư and Thăng Long (Hanoi). After a tumultuous millennium, Hanoi, which sits at the heart of the region, is once again Vietnam's capital, the country's most intricately layered metropolis and a major gateway to the country.

HIGHLIGHTS

HANOI (page 80) Vietnam's charismatic capital and the grand old dame of Southeast Asia, Hanoi has weeks of sights to explore, including the ancient Imperial Citadel, the expansive Hồ Chí Minh Mausoleum Complex and the Old Quarter. Hanoi's museums – the Museum of Ethnology, the Women's Museum and Hỏa Lò Prison, to name but a few – are the most comprehensive in the country, and can provide context to the rest of your trip.

ĐIỆN BIÊN PHỦ (page 143) This distant settlement, nestled in the mountains, is the city where the French colonial project came to a cacophonous and catastrophic close. The Battle of Điện Biên Phủ is now commemorated through a well-funded museum, several combat sites and one or two triumphant victory statues.

CAO BẰNG (page 178) For a remote province that sees few visitors, Cao Bằng punches above its weight in terms of things to see and do, from Bản Giốc, the magnum opus of Vietnamese waterfalls, to Pác Bó, where the revolutionary movement gained its unstoppable momentum, and ancient villages such as Khuổi Kỵ.

HÀ GIANG (page 169) Hà Giang is home to Vietnam's most extraordinary landscapes, a constellation of connected valleys with hypnotising rice terraces, tumbling valleys and rocky conical karst mountains that disappear into nebulous skies. There's also historical and cultural intrigue, including the Chinese settlement of Phó Bảng, the ancient trading town of Đồng Văn and a cluster of French forts.

CÁT BÀ ISLAND AND LAN HẠ BAY (page 205) Fast becoming the go-to alternatives to overtouristed Hạ Long Bay, Lan Hạ Bay offers the karst islet seascapes that its neighbour is known for, but with only a fraction of the visitors. Cát Bà, the biggest island in the area by far, constitutes a vast national park for hiking, kayaking, swimming and rock climbing.

HẢI PHÒNG (page 198) A proud but overlooked city that exudes old-world charm, Hải Phòng's colonial core erupts in colour when the flame trees blossom in the intense summer heat. October and November, when the days are dry and the evenings are cool, are the ideal months to devour the city's acclaimed noodle soups.

NINH BÌNH (page 213) Ninh Bình offers a diverse set of activities, including cycling on countryside lanes, boating through river valleys, wildlife-spotting in nature reserves and uncovering Vietnam's ancient history in the former capital of Hoa Lư.

3

Hanoi (Hà Nội) and Around

Hanoi is a city of contrasts, a place where pre-20th-century traditions are coming to terms with 21st-century advancement. All those who come here have their own preconceptions and misconceptions. Journalists looking for extra hype to jazz up their headlines brand it the ultimate oxymoron, a place where capitalist extremism suffocates hard-line communism. Tourists prefer to view the capital through a rose-tinted, tunnel-visioned camera lens, capturing its seductive charms while blocking out the warts. Businesspeople see it as a city of opportunities, which after two decades of meteoric growth remain myriad but elusive. Architectural conservationists fear that the capital has become a distasteful salmagundi of old and new.

Hanoi may be Vietnam's political capital, but its economy trails that of its southern sibling. Despite efforts to expand and empower Hanoi, Hồ Chí Minh City remains Vietnam's flagship megacity, and it continues to hoover up the bulk of foreign investment and human talent. This is a mixed blessing for the capital. Many Vietnamese scoff that, in comparison, Hanoi is less open, less free, less fun, less cosmopolitan, less capable. But rather than dwell on Hanoi's perceived inferiorities, the city's irrepressible inhabitants call attention to its uniqueness: tree-festooned streets like Phan Đình Phùng, charismatic lakes like Hoàn Kiếm, premier cultural institutions such as the Museum of Ethnology, the heritage architecture of the French Quarter – and an unrivalled street-food scene. Unsurprisingly, these things are often what visitors to Hanoi are most taken with.

Today, Hanoi has more than 5 million inhabitants. Many of these are public servants trying to grease the wheels of a bloated and bureaucratic state. Many others are students that attend the country's leading universities. But most Hanoians are diligent, multi-skilled employees and entrepreneurs trying to harness the dynamism of the private sector for the betterment of their families and their social standing. Some Hanoians have become obscenely wealthy over the past few decades; others have remained precariously poor. Ask a southerner what people from Hanoi are like, and she'll likely tell you that they are direct, aggressive and unfriendly. Ask a Hanoian, however, and she might tell you that her city folk are discerning, traditional and don't suffer fools gladly. You'll be able to make up your own mind: these days many Hanoians speak English and are keen to connect with visitors.

Rich or poor, young or old, educated or not, all Hanoians grapple with the same problems as those of other Southeast Asian metropolises: horrendous traffic, worsening air quality, sprawling development and inadequate infrastructure. But you'll find that Hanoi is less of a grind than other regional capitals like Jakarta and Manila. Traffic is rarely at a standstill, at least in districts that are of interest to visitors. When you need a quiet spot to recover your energy and plot your

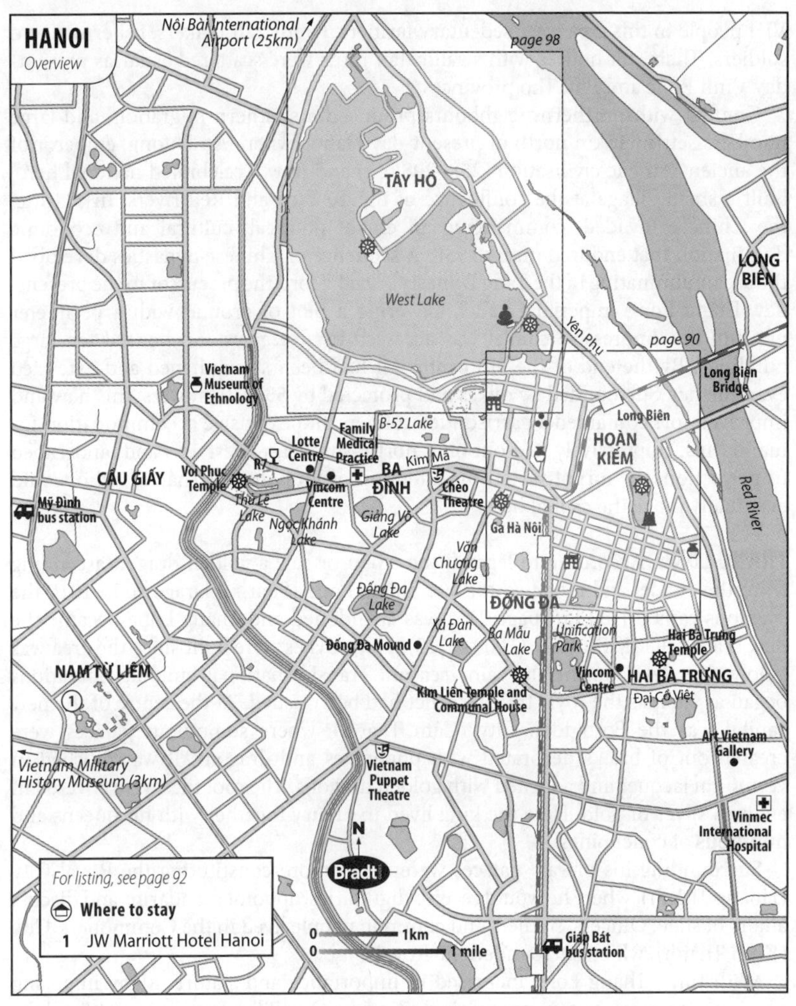

next move, calming coffee houses, parks and lakes are never far away. And many neighbourhoods are surprisingly walkable, once you accept that the pavements are a free-for-all.

Vietnam's capital isn't for everyone. But whatever your view, one thing is certain: Hanoi will leave an everlasting impression.

HISTORY

EARLY HISTORY The site of present-day Hanoi once lay in a deep depression which, over years, filled with erosion debris from the surrounding mountains and hills. Where the Red River (Sông Hồng) and Sông Đuống joined, a gulf was created which silted up after the sea receded, forming a swamp. Excavations over the years have revealed Stone Age artefacts that date back as far as 2000BCE. By studying engravings on bronze drums and motifs on fragments of pots, jars and vats, and piecing together other parts of the jigsaw from other finds, we know that the early

Việt people in this area were sedentary farmers, handicraft makers, fishermen and soldiers. Their stilt houses with swallowtail roofs were scattered as far as present-day Vĩnh Phúc and Phú Thọ provinces.

Conflict with northern neighbours produced a southern migration, and large numbers settled 15km north of present-day Hanoi, where An Dương, emperor of the ancient Âu Lạc civilisation (258–208BCE) and now a celebrated national hero, built a small village at the confluence of the Tô Lịch and Red rivers. In 111BCE, the Chinese invaded, commencing an era of political, cultural and economic domination that endured until CE938. A sequence of Chinese dynasties developed the area, culminating in the Tang Dynasty's Đại La fort, the precursor to the present-day Thăng Long Imperial Citadel. Covering a plot of ground with a perimeter of 6km, this impressive citadel was accessed by five gates and housed ten large buildings. By the end of the 9th century it had been strengthened and extended even further. Surrounded by dykes and protected by 55 watchtowers, this new and improved fort contained a garrison for soldiers and extensive accommodation for mandarins. Impressively laid out on a north–southeast–west axis and landscaped to perfection, the fort attracted the attention of Emperor Lý Thái Tổ, who would eventually move the capital here.

THĂNG LONG According to legend, the emperor saw a golden dragon ascending from the citadel and renamed the site Thăng Long (Soaring Dragon). In 1010 the previous capital Hoa Lư (page 215) was abandoned and Thăng Long became the new seat of the Lý Dynasty (1009–1225). Huge dykes were built since the area was below river level during the rainy season. Transformational building operations began as soon as the royal transfer edict had been issued. At the centre of the new capital was the Forbidden City (Cấm Thành), where sumptuous palaces were created out of bricks decorated with phoenixes and dragons. It was finished in vermilion lacquer and adorned with golden dragons. The roof tiles were covered in enamel, silver or gold. Here the king lived in luxury together with his queens and hundreds of concubines.

Surrounding his private palaces were many more constituting the Royal City (Hoàng Thành), where he would receive dignitaries, appoint mandarins and discuss affairs of state. Officers, soldiers and common people lived in the Commoners' City (Kinh Thành), which surrounded the Royal City.

With time, Thăng Long increased in importance and stature. Many imposing religious centres were constructed, including the One Pillar Pagoda in 1049 and the Temple of Literature (Văn Miếu) in 1070. In the 12th century, palaces built by the Lý emperors appeared along the right bank of the Red River and around West Lake.

Over the centuries, Thăng Long experienced more than its fair share of troubles. Constant peasant rebellions upset the peace of the city during the Lý Dynasty. During the Trần Dynasty (1225–1400), the Mongols attacked the country three times between 1257 and 1288. They devastated the city in 1258, then occupied it in 1285 and again in 1287, though they were expelled once and for all by the celebrated military tactician Trần Hưng Đạo.

Towards the latter part of the Trần Dynasty the capital's square became stained with the blood of court officials and many members of the royal family. The cold-blooded culprit, a Machiavellian official called Hồ Quý Ly, murdered three Trần emperors and pronounced himself emperor of the short-lived Ho Dynasty (1400–07). He set up his new capital in present-day Thanh Hóa Province, but was overthrown in 1407 by the Chinese Ming, who were in turn overthrown by Lê Lợi, a lord, in 1428. During the 16th century, many palaces were built and restored and the citadel was fortified to resist future invasions, but from then on, the city fell into a long period of neglect. By the time the Tây Sơn took control towards the end of the 18th century, palaces had started to crumble. When the Nguyễn defeated the Tây Sơn in 1802, they built a new capital in Huế and the city was stripped of its royal status, marking the beginning of the end of Thăng Long.

RENAMING THE CITY The official name Hà Nội ('inside the riverbend') was used for the first time in 1831. As the Royal City diminished in importance, improvements were made to the Commoners' City. The Báo Ân Pagoda was built near Hoàn Kiếm Lake, Ngọc Sơn Temple nearby was restored in 1865 and a wall was built around the Temple of Literature. Fortunes flipped in 1882 when Hanoi was taken over by the French, led by Captain Henri Rivière. They destroyed much of the ancient citadel, pulled down old houses and built a post office on the site of Báo Ân Pagoda. On the rubble of what was left around Hoàn Kiếm Lake, the French built a colonial capital. The Old Quarter, north of the lake, remained the city's commercial hub, though French architecture came to envelop it. The French Quarter, which still wraps around the Old Quarter, was transformed into leafy European-style neighbourhoods, with boulevards, gardens and oversized mansions.

In 1902 Hanoi became the capital of the French Indochinese Union, but by 1945 their rule was at an end (for a short period anyway), formalised by Hồ Chí Minh's reading of the Declaration of Independence in Ba Đình Square (now the site of his mausoleum). In 1946, France was back, and many parts of the city, including around Đồng Xuân Market, suffered as the French tried to recover their former colony. After the Battle of Điện Biên Phủ (page 144), they were finally ousted from the country in 1954, Vietnam was split into North and South and Hanoi was named the capital of an independent North Vietnam.

During 1955, many industrial establishments were set up in the city, including engineering factories in Gia Lâm and Đông Anh districts. By 1965, rubber, soap, tobacco, fertiliser and more engineering works had been added. The first American bombs fell on the city on 17 April 1966. This devastation continued until 1972. In 1976, after the end of the war, Hanoi became the capital of a newly reunified Vietnam.

***ĐỔI MỚI* TO THE PRESENT DAY** Reunification gave way to a deluge of economic problems that stunted Hanoi's development, including rampant inflation, unemployment, poor foreign investment, a US trade embargo and conflict with China and Cambodia. In 1986, the Sixth Congress of the Communist Party of Vietnam endorsed *đổi mới* (page 21), which decentralised the national economy, relaxed foreign investment laws, offered greater tax incentives and reduced state control of collectives. *Đổi mới* would change the face of Hanoi forever. Despite the collapse of the Soviet Union, Vietnam's strongest post-war ally, the reforms catalysed an economic surge throughout the 1990s. Though affected, the Asian Financial Crisis of 1997 did not strike Vietnam with the same intensity as its neighbours, and Vietnam's economy continued to roar into the next millennium.

Almost four decades later, the struggling Hanoi of 1986 has vanished and the population has quadrupled. An ongoing construction boom has expanded Hanoi upwards and outwards. The city absorbed neighbouring province Hà Tây, as well as several districts from neighbouring provinces, in 2008. In more recent years, Hanoi has faced challenges related to intense urbanisation, traffic congestion, environmental degradation, increasing social inequalities, heritage conservation concerns and the Covid-19 pandemic, which decimated the city's tourism economy. In September 2024, Typhoon Yagi, the biggest to hit Vietnam in decades, swept through the city, bringing winds of up to 150km/h that caused power outages and flash floods. But, as it has done throughout a thousand years, in the wake of a crisis Hanoi somehow manages to quickly rediscover its feet while simultaneously lurching into the future.

WHEN TO VISIT

Ask any Hanoian why their city is special and there's a fair chance they'll say it's because it has four seasons, a trait that sets the capital apart from Hồ Chí Minh City (and other Southeast Asian capitals). Spring (March–April) tends to be warm and wet (with a late cold snap, see below). Summer (May–September) can be brutally hot, with the occasional storm. Autumn (October–November) is cool and dry, though pollution can be a problem. And winter (December–February) tends to be grey, with a handful of very cold snaps. It's important to pack accordingly; too many travellers get caught out by this Southeast Asian meteorological anomaly, especially in the chilly winter months when the rest of the region is rather comfortable.

LEGEND HAS IT: THE PRINCESS AND THE PEA COAT

Hanoi heats up quickly during the spring months of March and April, but each year, just when Hanoians start thinking about packing away their winter coats, a sudden cold snap – known as *rét nàng Bân* – descends on the city. Bân, a princess of heaven, was loved dearly by her parents, but unlike her capable sisters, she was a rather useless homemaker. Her parents, wishing to see her happy, arranged for her to marry a young man in heaven, hoping marriage would help her become more adept at everyday household tasks.

Princess Bân adored her new husband, and to express her love she decided to make him a warm coat for the colder months of the year. As winter persisted, Princess Bân worked tirelessly to complete the coat, but her poor needlework hindered the process; she seemed to spend more time fixing mistakes than making progress. As winter approached, Princess Bân had only completed the sleeves of the coat. The laughter and teasing from her sisters didn't deter her, however, and she continued her work with unwavering dedication.

Tết (Lunar New Year; usually in January or February) came and went but she still hadn't finished the coat. She worked extra hard for the next month, but just as she finished the final few buttons, she could feel the sun's warmth on the back of her hands. Gazing at the completed work, she felt a deep sadness, wishing she had finished it sooner. Surely her husband would no longer have any need for such a thick, warm coat!

Her father, the king of heaven, watched the whole episode with great sadness, and when his daughter came to him filled with regret that she hadn't finished the coat in time, he commanded the cold to return for just a few more days. Overjoyed, Princess Bân presented her husband with the coat and watched as it kept him warm for this final cold snap. From that day on, each year a cold northern wind engulfs Hanoi for a few days, usually in April. *Rét* means 'chilly wind' in Vietnamese, and thus *rét nàng Bân* is 'lady Bân's chilly wind'.

GETTING THERE AND AWAY

BY RAIL Hanoi's central train station [91 B6] (Ga Hà Nội) is conveniently located close to Hoàn Kiếm, Hai Bà Trưng, Ba Đình and Đống Đa districts (see page 86 for orientation), with two entrances: one at 120 Lê Duẩn and another at 1 Trần Quý Cáp. Arriving at the station, especially when you're bleary-eyed after a rocky night train, can be an overwhelming experience, with dozens of taxi drivers jostling for your business. Top tip: instead of negotiating with a driver in the station or car park, go straight out to the road and find one there. The station has ATMs and snack stands, but no decent food. The vast majority of trains north (eg: to Sa Pa through Lào Cai) and south (eg: to Ninh Bình and beyond) go from here, but some northbound trains, like those to Hải Phòng, go from Long Biên station [90 E2] in the Old Quarter. For information on how to purchase train tickets, see page 59.

BY BUS You'd be hard pressed to find somewhere in the country that Vietnam's extensive and chaotic bus network doesn't access. But all of Hanoi's major bus stations are far from the city centre. Some of the bigger and more important bus stations include Mỹ Đình [map, page 81] in the east and Giáp Bát [map, page 81] in the south. If you arrive at any station, navigating onward travel in a taxi or Grab will be easy. In theory, buses from Mỹ Đình tend to go north and west, whereas buses from Giáp Bát go south and east. In reality, bus companies operating from either station (and many others) go all over. Adventurous travellers can turn up at a major station without a ticket and usually be on a bus within an hour since they are numerous and regular, but try to check with someone, for example the receptionist at your hotel, first. An easier option is to book the day before through your accommodation or in one of the travel agents in the Old Quarter. They will tell you where to be and when, and tickets often include shuttle-bus pick-up in the Old Quarter. For information on how to book buses online, see page 60.

BY CAR AND MOTORBIKE Driving in and out of Hanoi is almost as hair-raising as driving within it. If you have a driver, they will be responsible for dropping you off, picking you up and parking. If you're driving a car yourself and require parking, look for the more high-end hotels in Tây Hồ and Nam Từ Liêm districts. You'll need to call ahead to check and tell them you're coming, and parking may incur extra fees. Most hotels outside the Old Quarter, even budget ones, will have parking, but it's still a good idea to check.

BY AIR The terminus for international and domestic flights, Nội Bài International Airport [map, page 123], is 30km north of central Hanoi. Allow around 30 minutes to move between international and domestic terminals, which is possible on a free shuttle bus. Ask at the information desk how to find this. If arriving from abroad, there's a suite of handy services immediately after baggage reclaim, including kiosks where you can buy a local SIM card with data (highly recommended; page 72), money exchange desks and ATMs. Note that ATMs usually offer better rates than the exchange desks, even when you factor in the charges imposed by the local banks. The journey into the city takes 30–45 minutes by taxi, a line for which is always present outside arrivals, and shouldn't cost more than 450,000VND. It's sensible to ask taxi drivers to commit to using the meter before loading your luggage. You can also attempt Grab taxis (page 62) for a slightly cheaper price, though it usually means trying to locate your driver in the car park across from the terminals. Many hotels can arrange pick-ups at competitive prices. There's also the clean and air-conditioned orange 86 bus, which was 45,000VND at the time of research and passes by West Lake, Long Biên bus station, Hoàn Kiếm Lake and the Old Quarter, terminating at Hanoi train station. Buy your ticket on board from the conductor; if you show them where you're staying, they'll tell you where to disembark.

ORIENTATION

Hanoi, an assemblage of urban districts, rural districts and satellite towns, has a rather complicated layout. Of the 12 urban districts, five are of most interest to visitors: Hoàn Kiếm, Hai Bà Trưng, Ba Đình, Tây Hồ and Đống Đa.

Hoàn Kiếm is Hanoi's central downtown district and home to several intriguing neighbourhoods, including Hoàn Kiếm Lake, the Old Quarter and a large chunk of the French Quarter. Hoàn Kiếm Lake and its environs have several important sights, including Ngọc Sơn Temple and the Turtle Tower, many decent places to eat, and a handful of lakeside hotels. The Old Quarter's labyrinthine alleyway network begins on the lake's northern shore and fans out north and east. The Old Quarter is packed with boutique hotels, historical sights, atmospheric cafés and boisterous bars – and it's the epicentre of Hanoi's street-food scene. Hugging the southeastern section of Hoàn Kiếm Lake in a kind of tilted U-shape is Hoàn Kiếm District's share of the French Quarter, with more upmarket hotels (including the storied Metropole), Hanoi's grandest colonial buildings (like the Opera House) and broad boulevards with actual pavements.

The warped but elegant grid system of the French Quarter continues south into **Hai Bà Trưng**, leading to the neighbourhoods surrounding Thống Nhất (Unification) Park and Thiền Quang Lake. South of Đại Cồ Việt Street, a major thoroughfare in Hanoi, Hai Bà Trưng changes personality, as the grid system gives way to a warren of small streets that coil around some important universities, including Bách Khoa University and the National Economics University.

Ba Đình is a diverse district northwest of Hoàn Kiếm, with the Imperial Citadel, Hồ Chí Minh's Mausoleum and the tempting Trúc Bạch neighbourhood all within the area's eastern flank. This rather grand part of the city also holds some of the French Quarter's most photogenic *rues*, including Hoàng Diệu Street and Phan Đình Phùng Street, and Long Biên Market. Into the west, the district becomes a bizarre blend of tightly knit neighbourhoods, such as Ngọc Hà, and super-tall skyscrapers, like the Lotte Centre.

Immediately north of Ba Đình is **Tây Hồ**, which is home to the somewhat confusingly named Hồ Tây (West Lake) and its handful of lakeside neighbourhoods, including the cosmopolitan enclave of Quảng An, with its faux French villas, staid hotels and luxury apartment blocks.

Đống Đa sits west of Hoàn Kiếm, with Hanoi's train station, the Temple of Literature and several fascinating but sight-less neighbourhoods around the district's many lakes.

Most of your time will likely be spent in the aforementioned districts, but Hanoi's more far-flung zones also hold some intrigue. You'll pass through Long Biên, a large leafy district on the east side of the Red River, to reach Gia Lâm and the pottery craft village of Bát Tràng. The Museum of Ethnology, one of Vietnam's best museums, is out west in Cầu Giấy District. Hanoi's large national convention complex and the JW Marriott Hotel (page 92), one of the city's best accommodation options for business travellers, are in Nam Từ Liêm. Exploring Hanoi's rural districts reveal how far the capital has spread. For example, the Chùa Thầy and Chùa Tây Phương (page 123), two magnificent pagodas, and Thành Chương Palace (page 125), a glorious collection of ancient antiques, are technically in Hanoi, though they feel like the middle of the countryside.

GETTING AROUND

Rambling randomly around Hanoi is one of the highlights of a visit here, but be prepared for drizzle in the spring, heat and humidity in the summer and cold snaps in the winter. Many of the central neighbourhoods, including Hoàn Kiếm Lake and the Old Quarter (both in Hoàn Kiếm District), the French Quarter (which straddles Hoàn Kiếm, Hai Bà Trưng and Ba Đình districts), around Trúc Bạch Lake (in Ba Đình District) and Quảng An (in Tây Hồ District), are **walkable**. Getting between them, however, usually requires motorised transport.

Hanoi's confusing **bus** network (w tramoc.com.vn) traverses the whole city, but few travellers make the effort to familiarise themselves with it. Of all the **metro** lines (w hanoimetro.net.vn) planned for the city, only one (2A) had been completed at the time of writing but it was designed for commuters, not sightseers. You can flag down **taxis** (there are dozens of companies all offering similar prices) anywhere and journeying between the central neighbourhoods won't cost more than 100,000VND. Going further afield, to the Museum of Ethnology for example, will cost around 200,000VND. Always ask taxi drivers to use the meter. You'll find motorbike taxi drivers – which *never* use a meter – loitering on street corners, but they drive a hard bargain. Alternatively, book a motorbike with Grab (page 62), which tends to be half the price of a car or less. Another way to move around Hanoi is by **cyclo**, a three-wheel contraption with a driver who sits in an elevated position behind one or two passengers. They are slow-going, but the experience can be fun. Cyclo drivers are astute negotiators; flag one down in the Old Quarter, always agree the price before getting in and don't pay more at the other end (though tips are appreciated). If you're brave and feel confident behind the handlebars, you can rent a **motorbike** from a tour company in the Old Quarter or at your hotel. You can also **rent a car** (and driver) for the day at any tour agency at short notice, though you'll need to explain where you want to go for the agent to work out a price.

TOURIST INFORMATION AND TOUR OPERATORS

Hanoi is ideal for intrepid and spontaneous urban adventures, but there are a few notable boutique tour providers that can help get under the skin of the city. A little-known and useful resource is **Friends of Vietnam Heritage** (w fvheritage.org), a volunteer team of passionate heritage enthusiasts who organise walks and talks in the city, some of which are free. **Flavors of Hanoi** (w flavorsofhanoi.com) arranges tailor-made food tours and cooking classes with passionate and knowledgeable guides. **Hanoi Backstreet Tours** (w hanoibackstreettours.com) is one of a number of companies that organise tours by motorbike or open-air jeep through back alleys. In addition to countrywide tours, **Vietnam in Focus** (w vietnaminfocus.com), a photography tour company based in Hanoi, arranges a dozen or so day trips for shutterbugs in and around Hanoi. Queer and queer-friendly travellers can reach out to Tuấn and his team of gay and trans guides at **Gay Hanoi Tours** (w thevietnamconcierge.com/gay-hanoi-tours) for highly regarded bespoke tours around the city. For an audio tour of Hoàn Kiếm Lake designed and narrated by the author of this guidebook, download the **VoiceMap app** (w voicemap.me) and search 'Temples and Dragons'. Many of the Hanoi offerings on **Get Your Guide** (w getyourguide.com) are standard Hạ Long Bay cruises, but there are a few more interesting experiences available, including traditional music performances and food tours. **Vietlesson** (w vietlesson.com) offers a range of class types for learning Vietnamese, headed by academic and linguist Liên Hoàng Lê, who contributed the section on 'Worship of the Mother Goddess' in *Chapter 5* (page 188). **Hop-On Hop-Off Bus Tours** (w hop-on-hop-off-bus-tours.com) are in Hanoi, and although it may seem mad to tackle a city of alleyways in an oversized open-air double decker, it is one way to see some major landmarks and look down on the chaos of the streets from above. It might also appeal to those with restricted mobility.

WHERE TO STAY

With a little planning you'll have no trouble finding somewhere to stay in Hanoi. However, hotel names, prices, quality, service and virtually everything else that makes a good stay change so fast that it's impossible to keep an evergreen directory of recommended accommodation options. Here follows a list of hotels that are special in some way – usually because of the design, location or history – and are more likely than not to see out the decade.

Online booking platforms such as Agoda and Booking.com tend to list the best selection and prices for hotels in Hanoi, while Airbnb offers some more unique stays in apartment buildings and private homes. Occasionally, walk-in guests or those booking directly on a hotel website will secure better deals. However, due to the growing popularity of such platforms with up-to-date reviews, it's sometimes better to get a sense of where exactly you want to be in the city and then go online; with that in mind, there are specific streets and neighbourhoods that are recommended.

Though there are areas of interest across Hanoi, **Hoàn Kiếm District** is most likely where you'll stay. There is a broad range of choice, from the city's premier luxury heritage hotel (Sofitel Legend Metropole Hanoi) to budget beds in and around **Huyện Alley** [91 D5–E5]. If researching accommodation online, consider places on **Hàng Hành Alley** [90 E4], **Báo Khánh Street** [91 E5] and **Ấu Triệu Street** [91 D5]. These atmospheric lanes strike a balance between local charm, tourist facilities and choice.

If you don't want the boisterous Old Quarter right at your doorstep, **Ba Đình**'s broader streets are a good alternative – though don't expect your neighbourhood to be that much quieter. If you're looking online, especially charming spots to stay are near **Trúc Bạch Lake** [90 B1] and the zone between **Phan Đình Phùng** [90 C2] and **Yên Phụ** [90 D1] streets. As you move further west, the district begins to cater more to business travellers than tourists.

Though relatively central, **Tây Hồ District** is one of the few parts of Hanoi where you can step back from the chaos. Unfortunately, the neighbourhood is undergoing an overhaul that is unlikely to finish this decade, and dusty construction is a nuisance. That said, if you're close enough to West Lake, it shouldn't be too much of an issue. If you're looking for accommodation, there are fewer hotels in this part of the city, but you'll find sweet Airbnbs in charming locations on **Vũ Miên Street** [98 D3] and **Từ Hoa Street** [98 C3].

HOÀN KIẾM DISTRICT

Little Charm Hanoi Hostel [90 E4] 44 Hàng Bồ; w littlecharmhanoihostel.vn. Private rooms & dorms aimed at quieter backpackers, with a homey atmosphere & genuinely warm & inviting staff. There's a small indoor pool with a water feature that you'll either find delightful or disappointing. **$$**

The One Hostel Hanoi [90 D3] 70 Hàng Mã; w onehostels.com. Excellently run backpacker hostel with jovial staff, organised dorm rooms & regular events in the communal areas (which includes a swimming pool). This is the place to meet young travellers who prioritise socialising over privacy. Mere steps from some of the Old Quarter's most interesting streets. **$$**

Bespoke Trendy Hotel Hanoi [90 D4] 12–14 Nguyễn Quang Bích; **w** bespokehotels.vn/trendyhn. On a relatively calm Old Quarter street with some stunning tiled rooftops visible from the loftier rooms & close to the city's famous railway tracks. The room design is industrial chic meets Old Hanoi, which somehow works. **$$$**

M Village Hotel Hồ Gươm [91 F6] 38 Hai Bà Trưng; **w** mvillage.vn. Ideally located just south of Hoàn Kiếm Lake, this is the 1st property of a fast-growing local hotel group, whose target market skews young (M stands for millennial). Rooms are bright & minimalist & there's a shared kitchen & coworking space. **$$$**

Mia Casa by Satori [91 C6] 26 Nam Ngư; **w** miacasa.vn. A crisp & modern design that is ahead of the curve in Old Hanoi. For some the location will be ideal: it's outside Hanoi's main tourist zone, but still close to important sights – & the train station is in walking distance. **$$$**

Apricot Hotel [91 E5] 136 Hàng Trống; **w** apricothotels.com. This would be a fairly standard upmarket corporate-feeling hotel were it not for the fabulous (& valuable) art on display throughout the property, plus an enviable location overlooking the lake & a rooftop pool. **$$$$**

✷ **Silk Path Boutique** [91 F6] 21 Hàng Khay; **w** silkpathhotel.com/hanoiboutique. A special little hideaway squeezed into a tube house overlooking Hoàn Kiếm Lake, the Silk Path Boutique is the smallest branch of a Vietnamese hotel empire (there is a much larger Silk Path on Hàng Bông St, as well as branches in Huế & Sa Pa). The best & most expensive rooms look out over the lake, & there's a top-floor bar. **$$$$**

✷ **Sofitel Legend Metropole Hanoi** [91 F6] 15 Ngô Quyền; **w** sofitel-legend-metropole-hanoi.com; see also page 104. One of Southeast Asia's legendary heritage hotels, the Metropole has existed in 1 form or another for well over a century. The old wing, with its antique staircase & creaky floorboards, offers unrivalled charm, but

HANOI *Hoàn Kiếm and Ba Đình districts*

For listings, see opposite

Where to stay

1 Apricot ... E5
2 Bespoke Trendy Hotel Hanoi ... D4
3 The Flower Boutique ... D1
4 Little Charm Hanoi Hostel ... E4
5 M Village Hotel Hồ Gươm ... F6
6 Mia Casa by Satori ... C6
7 The One Hostel Hanoi ... D3
8 Silk Path Boutique ... F6
9 Sofitel Legend Metropole Hanoi ... F6

Where to eat and drink

10 Bancông Café & Restaurant ... E4
11 Bánh Cuốn Gia Truyền Thanh Vân ... D3
12 Bia Hà Nội Lan Chín ... F4
13 Bít Tết Ông Lợi ... E3
14 Bún Bò Nam Bộ Bách Phương ... D4
15 Bún Cá Sâm Cây Si ... F4
16 Bún Chả Hương Liên ... F8
17 Bún Đậu Cô Tuyến Mắm Tôm Hàng Khay ... E6
18 Café Đinh ... F4
19 Café Nuôi ... E4
20 Café Thái ... E8
21 Chả Cá Thăng Long ... E3
22 Chapter Dining ... D5
23 Cộng Cà Phê ... E5
24 The East ... C5
25 Etēsia ... F4
26 Gia ... A5
27 Habakuk Fine Coffee & Bistro ... G7
28 Loading T ... D5
29 Luk Lak ... G7
Manzi Art Space & Café (see Manzi Art Space & Café) ... D2
30 Muối Tiêu – Salt n' Pepper Kitchen ... C5
31 A New Day ... F3
32 Ngoặm ... D5
33 Nhà Hàng Thanh ... C5
34 Phở Bưng Hàng Trống ... E4
35 Phở Gà Châm ... C1
36 Phở Gà Tĩnh ... D2
37 Phở Gia Truyền Bát Đàn ... D4
38 Phở Huyền ... C1
39 Pizza Belga ... F4
40 Quán Bánh Cuốn Bảo Khánh ... E5
41 Quán Bia Hơi Bát Đàn ... D4
42 Quán Bún Bung Chân Giò Bún Thang ... F4
43 Quán Cũ ... C2
44 refined. ... A5
45 Tầm Vị ... B5
46 Tanh Tách ... C7
47 T.U.N.G Dining ... E6
48 Ưu Đàm Chay ... D8
49 Vege-ro ... D5

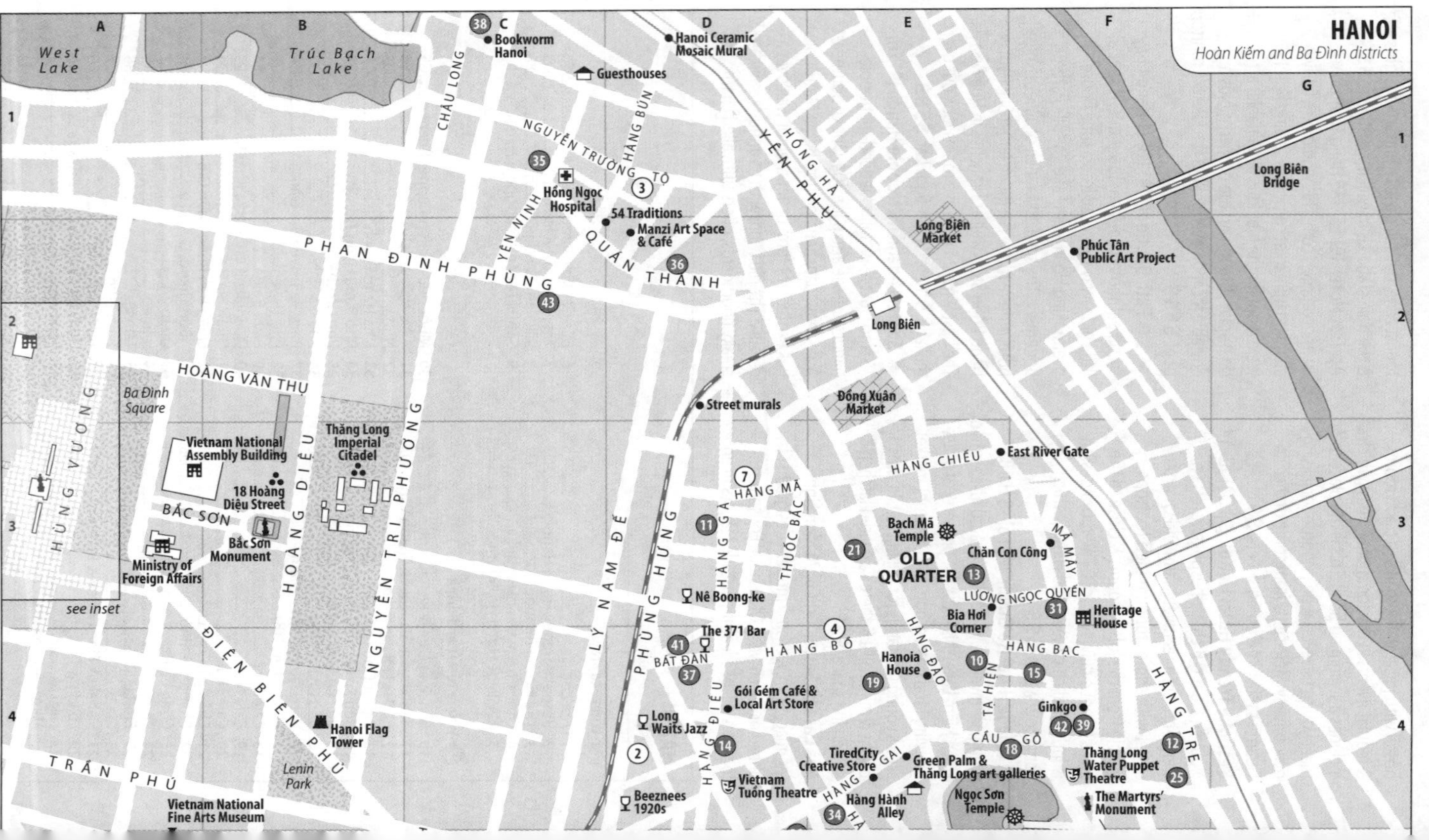
HANOI
Hoàn Kiếm and Ba Đình districts
A
B
C
D
E
F
G
1
2
3
4
West Lake
Trúc Bạch Lake
Bookworm Hanoi
Hanoi Ceramic Mosaic Mural
Guesthouses
CHÂU LONG
NGUYỄN TRƯỜNG TỘ
HÀNG BÚN
HỒNG HÀ
YÊN PHỤ
Hồng Ngọc Hospital
54 Traditions
Manzi Art Space & Café
YÊN NINH
QUÁN THÁNH
PHAN ĐÌNH PHÙNG
Long Biên Bridge
Long Biên Market
Phúc Tân Public Art Project
Long Biên
HOÀNG VĂN THỤ
Ba Đình Square
HÙNG VƯƠNG
Vietnam National Assembly Building
18 Hoàng Diệu Street
Thăng Long Imperial Citadel
HOÀNG DIỆU
NGUYỄN TRI PHƯƠNG
BẮC SƠN
Bắc Sơn Monument
Ministry of Foreign Affairs
see inset
Street murals
Đồng Xuân Market
HÀNG CHIẾU
East River Gate
HÀNG MÃ
THUỐC BẮC
HÀNG GÀ
LÝ NAM ĐẾ
PHÙNG HƯNG
Bạch Mã Temple
Chăn Con Công
MÃ MÂY
OLD QUARTER
LƯƠNG NGỌC QUYẾN
Heritage House
Nê Boong-ke
Bia Hơi Corner
The 371 Bar
BÁT ĐÀN
HÀNG BỒ
HÀNG ĐÀO
HÀNG BẠC
Hanoia House
TẠ HIỆN
HÀNG TRE
Gói Gém Café & Local Art Store
HÀNG ĐIẾU
ĐIỆN BIÊN PHỦ
Hanoi Flag Tower
Long Waits Jazz
Ginkgo
CẦU GỖ
TRẦN PHÚ
Lenin Park
TiredCity Creative Store
HÀNG GAI
Green Palm & Thăng Long art galleries
Thăng Long Water Puppet Theatre
Vietnam Tuồng Theatre
Ngọc Sơn Temple
The Martyrs' Monument
Vietnam National Fine Arts Museum
Beeznees 1920s
Hàng Hành Alley
1
2
3
4
7
10
11
12
13
14
15
18
19
21
25
31
34
35
36
37
38
39
41
42
43

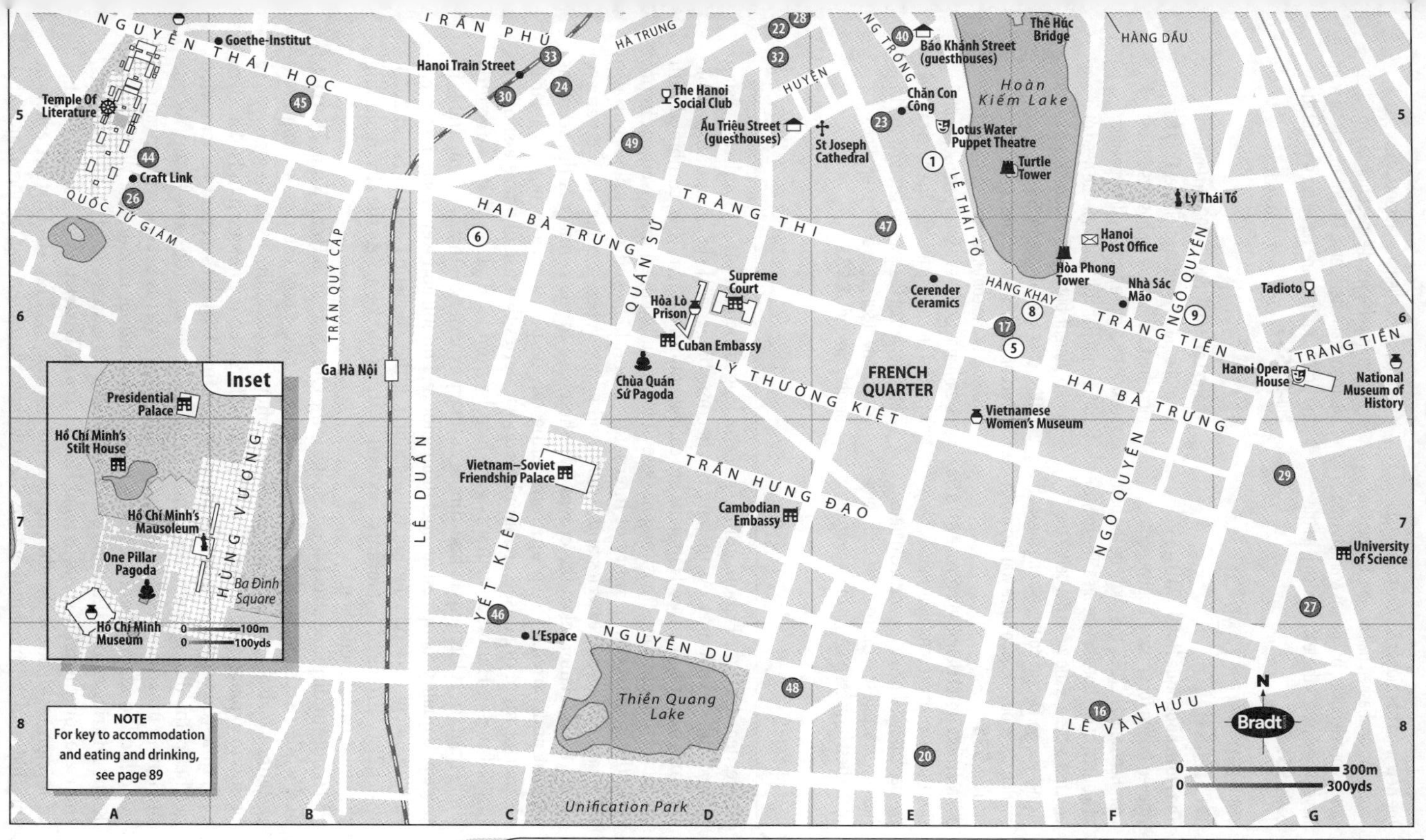
NGUYỄN THÁI HỌC
Goethe-Institut
TRẦN PHÚ
HÀ TRUNG
Hanoi Train Street
Temple Of Literature
Craft Link
QUỐC TỬ GIÁM
The Hanoi Social Club
HUYỆN
Ấu Triệu Street (guesthouses)
St Joseph Cathedral
Báo Khánh Street (guesthouses)
Chăn Con Công
Lotus Water Puppet Theatre
Hoàn Kiếm Lake
Thê Húc Bridge
HÀNG DẦU
Turtle Tower
LÊ THÁI TỔ
Lý Thái Tổ
Hanoi Post Office
Hòa Phong Tower
Nhà Sắc Mão
NGÔ QUYỀN
Tadioto
HÀNG KHAY
Cerender Ceramics
TRÀNG THI
HAI BÀ TRƯNG
QUÁN SỨ
Supreme Court
Hỏa Lò Prison
Cuban Embassy
Chùa Quán Sứ Pagoda
LÝ THƯỜNG KIỆT
FRENCH QUARTER
TRÀNG TIỀN
Hanoi Opera House
National Museum of History
Vietnamese Women's Museum
TRẦN HƯNG ĐẠO
Cambodian Embassy
University of Science
TRẦN QUÝ CÁP
Ga Hà Nội
LÊ DUẨN
Vietnam–Soviet Friendship Palace
YẾT KIÊU
L'Espace
NGUYỄN DU
Thiền Quang Lake
Unification Park
LÊ VĂN HƯU
Bradt
N
0 300m
0 300yds
Inset
Presidential Palace
Hồ Chí Minh's Stilt House
Hồ Chí Minh's Mausoleum
One Pillar Pagoda
Hồ Chí Minh Museum
HÙNG VƯƠNG
Ba Đình Square
0 100m
0 100yds
NOTE
For key to accommodation and eating and drinking, see page 89

the new wing has bigger & more comfortable rooms. An unabashed hall of fame flaunts the dozens of celebrities, politicians & artists who have stayed here & the leafy garden is a little oasis. **$$$$$**

BA ĐÌNH DISTRICT AND WESTERN HANOI

The Flower Boutique Hotel [90 D1] 55 Nguyễn Trường Tộ; **w** flowerboutiquehotel.com. Renovated in 2022, this might be the best of a bunch of city hotels in the area. The rooms are crisp & clean, & the views get better the higher you go. Decent double glazing means the roaring street outside won't give you too much trouble. **$$$**

JW Marriott Hotel Hanoi [map, page 81] 8 Đỗ Đức Dục; **w** marriott.com/en-us/hotels/hanjw-jw-marriott-hotel-hanoi/overview. Gigantic modern structure that can compete with some of the best business hotels in the region, with a handful of excellent restaurants, gym, spa & everything else you'd expect from a top international hotel brand. The location is far from the sights, but for some travellers it will fit the bill. **$$$$$**

TÂY HỒ DISTRICT

Thắng Lợi Hotel [98 C3] 200 Yên Phụ; **w** brghospitality.vn/thangloihotel. Only for Modernist architecture enthusiasts & those seeking to glimpse a quickly disappearing communist Hanoi. It's in desperate need of refurbishment, but the dated furniture & lakeside setting offer a certain charm. **$$$**

InterContinental Hanoi West Lake [98 C3] 5 Từ Hoa; **w** ihg.com/intercontinental/hotels/us/en/hanoi. Occupies a small peninsula with 3 arms that creep on to the lake. The hotel can feel a little sterile, but the lakeside setting is special, particularly at sunset, as are the surrounding neighbourhoods. **$$$$**

WHERE TO EAT AND DRINK

Three decades ago, Hanoi's culinary scene lagged behind other Southeast Asian capital cities. No longer. As the city has become bigger and richer, and disposable incomes have risen, more Hanoians are eating out more often. This, combined with an increasing number of visitors, has inevitably resulted in an improvement in not only the quality and quantity of international and high-end restaurants but also mid-range everyday eateries and street-food joints. When it comes to Vietnamese **street food**, Hanoi takes the crown. Nowhere else in the country is the scene as vibrant and varied. A step up from eating on the pavement but not necessarily cleaner or more organised are simple indoor eateries that usually have a similarly limited menu. Hanoi's restaurants vary hugely, from local places that charge little more than street kitchens to fine-dining culinary experiences that are comparable in price and quality to top restaurants in Singapore, London and New York. Testament to Hanoi's culinary reinvention is the launch of the Michelin Guide there in 2023, which lists dozens of restaurants – as well as street food – across the city, including three with a Michelin Star.

Hanoi's undisputed street-food capital is the Old Quarter in **Hoàn Kiếm District**, and while street food is the headliner, plenty of mid-range eateries and high-end restaurants also jostle for the limelight, often successfully. Even though you're bound to explore outside the district, you'd be forgiven if you return to Hoàn Kiếm each time you want to eat. In keeping with **Ba Đình District**'s elegant yet tempered aesthetic, the dining scene here tends to be a little less riotous and flashy. As one of Hanoi's inner-city residential hubs, Đống Đa District is packed with cheap and good local food, but there are also a handful of standout restaurants. While Hoàn Kiếm District enjoys the lion's share of Hanoi's best street food and restaurants, there are some notable spots in regal **Hai Bà Trưng District**. With its high number of foreign residents, it should come as no surprise that **Tây Hồ District** excels in international cuisine, but there are a few notable places serving the local fare.

Coffee houses are everywhere in Hanoi and hopping between them while exploring the sights is one of the highlights of visiting the city. You'll have no trouble finding your favourite, but in this guide are listed some standout examples. Cafés in Vietnam are open all day every day.

RESTAURANTS AND STREET FOOD

Hoàn Kiếm District

✷ **Bánh Cuốn Gia Truyền Thanh Vân** [90 D3] 14 Hàng Gà; 🕘 07.00–13.00 & 17.00–21.00 daily. Serving *bánh cuốn* but on higher tables & chairs than in streetside places, this is one of the rare places that has an option of fillings: chicken, pork or shrimp. $

Bún Cá Sâm Cây Si [90 F4] 5 Ngõ Trung Yên; 🕘 07.00–17.00 daily. Atmospheric & hidden street food with an alley that runs straight through the middle & overshadowed by a tree possessed by a spirit (look out for the small shrine next to the broth pot). They serve *bún cá* & *bánh đa*, as well as deliciously crunchy fish rolls (*cá cuốn*). $

✷ **Bún Đậu Cô Tuyến Mắm Tôm Hàng Khay** [91 E6] Ngõ 31 Hàng Khay; 🕘 09.00–21.00 daily. Hidden down an alleyway & hugely popular with lunching Hanoians, this humble *bún đậu* joint has an eclectic array of add-ons to go with the fried tofu & noodles base. Freshen your breath with complimentary checking gum after the meal & come before 11.30 or after 13.00 to avoid the lunch rush. $

Nhà Hàng Thanh [91 C5] 3 Trần Phú; 🕘 all day daily. Serving all things *ngan* (goose), this family-run establishment has been selling noodles next to the train tracks for generations. *Miến ngan* (glass noodles with goose) is the standout dish. You can ask for it as a noodle soup or with the broth served on the side. $

Phở Bưng Hàng Trống [90 E4] 8 Hàng Trống; 🕘 15.00–20.00 daily. The family team here used to jostle for customers on the pavement but grew weary of Old Quarter street politics so moved their operation inside. There's no sign, so head down the alleyway between 2 souvenir shops & up the stairs on the right. On a good day this might be the perfect *phở bò* broth. *Quẩy* is served on the side. $

Quán Bánh Cuốn Bảo Khánh [91 E5] 14B Báo Khánh; 🕘 06.30–13.30 & 16.30–21.00 daily. Specialising in *bánh cuốn* until lunchtime (in the afternoon they serve *phở*), this 2-room Old Quarter favourite makes rolls to order on 2 circular steaming pots on the street. The establishment has passed through 3 generations. $

Quán Bún Bung Chân Giò Bún Thang [90 F4] 32 Cầu Gỗ; 🕘 all day daily. One of only a handful of Old Quarter restaurants serving traditional *bún thang*, just steps from Hoàn Kiếm Lake. $

Bún Bò Nam Bộ Bách Phương [90 D4] 73–75 Hàng Điếu; f BachPhuongBBNB; 🕘 all day daily. This narrow local favourite, also popular with foreigners, serves up beef noodle salad on long, communal tables. The *bún bò nam bộ* is generously topped with stir-fried beef & served with a moreish sauce. $$

A New Day Restaurant [90 F3] 72 Mã Mây; 🕘 10.00–22.30 daily. Streetside dining gives way to a rabbit warren of rooms that go back through the restaurant & up the stairs. The menu, which has a slight Chinese twist, is decent, but the better dishes are cooked at lunchtime & displayed for all to see in a small room at the front of the restaurant. Find a table & then point at what you want. $$

Phở Gia Truyền Bát Đàn [90 D4] 49 Bát Đàn; 🕘 06.00–10.00 & 18.00–20.30 daily. Expect to queue at this Old Quarter institution, which many claim serves the best *phở bò* in the city. Waiting, squeezing on to a table & watching staff carve up huge chunks of beef is part of the experience. $$

Bia Hà Nội Lan Chín [90 F4] 22 Hàng Tre; 🕘 09.30–22.00 daily. Reliable *bia hơi* bar with an English menu. Though a bar, you can have a full meal here, from hotpot to stir-fried vegetables to grilled meat. $$$

Bít Tết Ông Lợi [90 E3] 51 Hàng Buồm; 🕘 08.00–21.00 daily. If you have a hankering for steak and chips but don't want to settle for a tourist restaurant, this decades-old establishment embedded in a covered alleyway serves *bít tết* (from the French *bifteck*). The food is just OK, but the location and atmosphere are classic Hanoi. $$$

✷ **Chả Cá Thăng Long** [90 E3] 6B Đường Thành; w chacathanglong.com.vn; 🕘 10.00–15.30 & 17.30–21.00 daily. One of the more established *chả cá* restaurants is set over 2 floors in a gorgeous French mansion with a bucolic garden. Aside from the *chả cá*, it also serves tasty fried spring rolls with fish (*nêm cá*). Booking recommended. $$$

HANOI'S SPECIALITY DISHES

This list of Hanoi's speciality dishes is by no means exhaustive. Many of these dishes are found not only in Hanoi, but across Northern Vietnam. The places to try them at are listed from page 92.

BÚN CHẢ Hanoi's number-one lunch dish is *bún chả*, consisting of grilled pork belly, meatballs, rice vermicelli and a green herb salad, dipped in a sweet-and-sour *nước mắm* (fish sauce) dipping sauce. The pork is best prepared over charcoal. Spring rolls, called *nem* in the north, usually accompany *bún chả*; traditional ingredients include minced pork, vermicelli, mushroom, eggs, onion, crab (if you're lucky) and *mộc nhĩ*, an edible fungus. Try it at **Bún Chả Hương Liên**.

PHỞ BÒ/PHỞ GÀ The quintessential Vietnamese noodle soup and the assumed national dish, *phở* in Hanoi is served with beef (*bò*) or chicken (*gà*) but never both. In Hanoi, unlike in Hồ Chí Minh City, *phở* is relatively simple, usually consisting of flat rice noodles, a clear broth, thin slices of meat, spring onions and coriander. You may be offered ***quẩy***, crunchy fried dough that soaks up the soup, and lime or vinegar, pickled garlic and fresh chilli. A good *phở* broth is cooked for at least 8 hours and is flavoured with fish sauce, star anise, ginger and various secret ingredients known only to the chef. Try it at **Phở Bưng Hàng Trống** (beef), **Phở Gà Tĩnh** (chicken), **Phở Gia Truyền Bát Đàn** (beef), **Phở Gà Châm** (chicken) and **Phở Huyền** (chicken and beef).

BÁNH CUỐN A hero of Hanoian cuisine, *bánh cuốn* are steamed wet rice paper rolls with minced pork and *mộc nhĩ*, though other variations exist. As a side you can order an egg, also rolled in wet rice paper, and some *chả* (a kind of square sausage, often flavoured with cinnamon or young green sticky rice). Hanoians eat *bánh cuốn* for breakfast, but they also make a delicious light lunch. Try it at **Bánh Cuốn Gia Truyền Thanh Vân** and **Quán Bánh Cuốn Bảo Khánh**.

BÚN CÁ A somewhat sour noodle soup with white vermicelli rice noodles, deep-fried fish, dill, spring onions and other greens. *Bún cá* is sometimes served with tempting sides, such as fish spring rolls (*nem cá*). Try it at **Bún Cá Sâm Cây**.

BÁNH ĐA Sometimes served alongside *bún cá*, this noodle dish is associated with Hải Phòng and usually served with deep-fried fish (*cá*) or crab (*cua*), green vegetables and fried shallots, and with (*nước*) or without (*trộn*) soup. *Bánh đa* noodles are flat, a little like *phở* noodles, but chewier and browned with a little sugar. Try it at **Bún Cá Sâm Cây Si**.

BÚN THANG This *phở gà* alternative – a mix of shredded fried egg, cured ham and dried shitake mushrooms – has an interesting back story. Some believe it was Vietnam's original cure-all: a mountain of medicinal herbs dumped into chicken bone broth, used to nurse bed-ridden patients. Over time, it evolved into the eclectic (and probably tastier) dish we have today. Try it at **Quán Bún Bung Chân Giò Bún Thang**.

MIẾN NGAN A dish that is hard to find outside Northern Vietnam, *miến ngan* is boiled goose, baby bamboo and glass noodles served with (*nước*) or without (*trộn*) soup. The broth is rich and something of an acquired taste. Try it at **Nhà Hàng Thanh**.

BÚN BÒ NAM BỘ The name translates to 'southern-style beef noodles', which is odd because *bún bò* in the south usually refers to beef noodle soup from Huế in Central Vietnam. This is essentially a beef noodle salad with a sweetened vinegar-based dressing. As the dressing usually doesn't use fish sauce, this dish is somewhat vegetarian- and vegan-friendly – just ask them not to add the beef. Try it at **Bún Bò Nam Bộ Bách Phương**.

PHỞ CUỐN Nothing like *phở* soup, this is a wet spring roll stuffed with stir-fried beef and coriander, to be dipped in a sweet-and-sour sauce flavoured with sliced pickled vegetables and chilli. It's a speciality of Ngũ Xã Islet near Trúc Bạch Lake and is hard to find elsewhere. Try it at **Phở Cuốn Chinh Thắng** and **Phở Cuốn 31**.

BÚN ĐẬU MẮM TÔM A fabulous dish, especially for those looking for unusual flavours, *bún đậu mắm tôm* is deep-fried tofu, a vermicelli noodle cake, herb salad and a pungent fermented-shrimp dipping sauce. If the sauce is too much to handle, fish sauce or soy sauce also work. Many *bún đậu mắm tôm* eateries also serve fried spring rolls, boiled pork and intestines on the side. Try it at **Bún Đậu Cô Tuyến Mắm Tôm Hàng Khay**.

BÁNH TÔM Deep-fried dough balls with shrimp, *bánh tôm* is more of a snack than a meal. This is a West Lake speciality, but it's also sold in and around Trúc Bạch Lake. Try it at any restaurant outside **Phủ Tây Hồ**.

CHẢ CÁ No longer a street-food dish, *chả cá* has become extremely popular with middle-class Hanoians. One of Hanoi's proudest culinary achievements, the dish has a street named after it in the Old Quarter. *Cá lăng*, a large, white freshwater fish, is seasoned with turmeric and stir-fried before you with dill and spring onion. It's served with vermicelli noodles, herbs, peanuts and a dipping sauce. If Hanoi had only one must-try dish, this might be it, and the theatre adds to the dining experience. Try it at **Chả Cá Thăng Long**.

BIA HƠI Not a dish but a drink, *bia hơi* (fresh beer) is hugely popular with locals and visitors alike. The best place to try this light beer is in a local streetside pub, which usually have a huge range of bar snacks. Irritatingly, many bars in so-called Bia Hơi Corner (where Tạ Hiện and Lương Ngọc Quyến streets intersect; page 108) actually serve bottled beer that they might try to pass off as fresh beer. Try *bia hơi* at **Quán Bia Hơi Bát Đàn** and **Bia Hà Nội Lan Chín**.

CÀ PHÊ TRỨNG Egg coffee is something of a legend in Hanoi. The story goes that when milk became scarce during the war years, Hanoians started using whisked egg white instead. They developed a taste for it, and the drink has since become a Hanoi must-try. It can be very sweet, so can double as a dessert or pick-me-up. Try it at most of the coffee houses listed from page 97, especially **Bancông Café & Restaurant** and **Loading T**.

The East [91 C5] 5B Tống Duy Tân; w theeast.vn; ⌚ 10.00–14.30 & 17.00–22.00 daily. Superb new restaurant serving elevated Vietnamese classics in dignified surroundings. The Vietnamese salads & fried spring rolls are freshly prepared & crunchy. Booking recommended. $$$

Muối Tiêu – Salt n' Pepper Kitchen [91 C5] 28 Tống Duy Tân; f muoitieusnp; ⌚ 09.00–20.30 Tue–Sun. Western comfort brunches at their very best, Muối Tiêu serves classics like an English b/fast, eggs benedict & fluffy American pancakes alongside fresh juices & excellent coffee. $$$

Ngoạm [91 D5] 19 Chân Cầm; f Ngoamhanoi; ⌚ 11.00–14.00 & 18.00–21.30 Wed–Mon. Probably serving the best burgers in town, Ngoạm is a hole-in-the-wall hipster paradise, with creative menus, funky staff & a handful of delicious drinks. $$$

✷ **Quán Bia Hơi Bát Đàn** [90 D4] 50 Bát Đàn; ⌚ 10.00–23.00 daily. This boisterous fresh beer bar is one of a cluster of places that provide a local alternative to the highly touristy Bia Hơi Corner (page 108). As with all *bia hơi* bars, there is a gigantic food menu covering all Vietnamese bases. $$$

Ưu Đàm Chay [91 D8] 55 Nguyễn Du; f Uudamchay; ⌚ 10.30–21.30 daily. Elegant vegan restaurant that leans wholeheartedly into the Asian chic interior design aesthetic. Credited with making vegan food trendy in Hanoi, the restaurant serves inspired vegan versions of some of Vietnam's best dishes. The pomelo salad & any of the tofu dishes are particularly good. Booking recommended. $$$

✷ **Vege-ro** [91 D5] 23 Ngõ Hội Vũ; f hanoivegetarianramen; ⌚ 17.00–22.00 Tue–Fri, 11.45–13.45 & 17.00–22.00 Sat–Sun. Tiny vegan & vegetarian ramen bar with a Japanese chef. The broth is suitably rich & salty, even without the use of a meaty broth, & the delicious vegan sides include tempeh & tofu skin. $$$

Etēsia [90 F4] 14B Lò Sũ; f etesiahanoi; ⌚ 10.30–14.00 & 17.00–midnight daily. Excellent European hideaway sat on an atmospheric Old Quarter street, Etēsia has a small & thoughtful menu showcasing some of the best contemporary Western cuisine in the city. It also boasts one of the city's best wine collections. Booking recommended. $$$$

Luk Lak [91 G7] 4A Lê Thánh Tông; w luklak.vn; ⌚ 07.30–22.00 daily. The dishes at Luk Lak are inspired by Vietnam's mountain cuisine but served with contemporary flair, so expect meat grilled to perfection with an array of herbs & spices & flavoured, colourful sticky rice. Booking recommended. $$$$

✷ **Chapter Dining** [91 D5] 12C Chân Cầm; w chaptergrill.vn; ⌚ 18.00–23.00 Mon–Sat. One of a handful of fine-dining restaurants in Hanoi, the tasting menus here have a rustic edge, with many recipes inspired by dishes from Vietnam's more far-flung hinterlands. Flash this guidebook & chef patron Quang Dũng, who studied in the UK, might come & say hello in his perfected British accent. $$$$$

T.U.N.G Dining [91 E6] 2C Quang Trung; w tungdining.com; ⌚ 18.00–23.00 Tue–Sun. Probably Michelin Star-worthy (though currently without), T.U.N.G Dining pioneered fine dining in the capital. Head chef Hoàng Tùng crafts a seasonal tasting menu with 20 or so dishes that explore a diverse flavour profile. One of Hanoi's best splurge options; bookings required. $$$$$

Ba Đình and Đống Đa districts

Phở Cuốn Chinh Thắng [98 D1] 7 Mạc Đĩnh Chi; f phocuonchinhthang; ⌚ 10.00–21.00 daily. The neighbourhood is packed with *phở cuốn*, a neighbourhood speciality, but this small establishment is still friendly & family-owned. $

Phở Gà Tĩnh [90 D2] 42 Quán Thánh; ⌚ all day daily. Local favourite serving a clear, hearty chicken broth. For something different, try the soup-less version (*phở gà trộn*) with the broth served on the side. $

✷ **Phở Gà Châm** [90 C1] 64–68 Yên Ninh; ⌚ 06.30–noon daily, though it regularly closes randomly. Eating in Phở Gà Châm is quite a spectacle, as monied Hanoians turn up in gigantic luxury cars, squeeze into a parking spot & then huddle over fabulously rich bowls of chicken noodle soup (some say the special ingredient is dried squid). Note that *phở* here is twice as much as in similar pavement establishments (but no – you're not being ripped off). $$

Phở Huyền [90 C1] 31 Châu Long; ⌚ 08.00–22.00 daily. Serving *phở gà* throughout the day, Phở Huyền is popular with older Hanoians, some of whom have been coming here for decades. The eatery also serves *phở bò* (beef), though the chicken is what most come for. $$

Machi Ramen [98 B5] No 26, Ngõ 267 Hoàng Hoa Thám; f machi.food; ⌚ 10.30–14.00 & 17.30–21.30 daily. Ramen – the traditional meat version – is served up to the office workers that dominate this part of Ba Đình at lunchtimes. Service is quick & efficient & there are no bad choices on the menu. $$$

Phở Cuốn 31 [98 D2] 31 Ngũ Xã; w phocuonhanoi.com; ⌚ 09.00–22.30 daily. Surrounded by restaurants serving *phở cuốn*, this is the best of the bunch thanks to the extensive menu. Standout dishes include jellyfish salad & stir-fried beef with lemongrass & chilli. If it's full downstairs, head up to the 2nd or 3rd floor. $$$

Quán Cũ [90 C2] 31A Phan Đình Phùng; f quancuhanoi; ⌚ 07.00–14.30 & 16.30–22.00 daily. Simple Northern Vietnamese food done well & catering to a well-heeled clientele of government officials & other middle-class Hanoians. The roasted chicken with honey has a delicious crispy skin & the tofu is especially fresh. $$$

Tầm Vị [91 B5] 4B Yên Thế; f nhahangtamvi; ⌚ 11.00–14.00 & 17.00–21.00 daily. Once an elegant, beautiful & affordable restaurant that somewhat flew under the radar, Tầm Vị was propelled into the spotlight in 2023 when, to the surprise of many, the restaurant was awarded a Michelin Star. The tofu dishes are particularly good. Bookings essential. $$$

Gia [91 A5] 61 Văn Miếu; w gia-hanoi.com; ⌚ 18.00–21.00 Tue–Wed, 11.30–13.30 & 18.00–21.00 Thu–Sat. Overlooking the Temple of Literature, chef Sam is one of the young chefs spearheading the Vietnamese fine-dining movement. The seasonal tasting menus are nothing short of extraordinary. $$$$$

Hai Bà Trưng District

Bún Chả Hương Liên [91 F8] 24 Lê Văn Hưu; f bunchahuonglienobama; ⌚ 08.00–20.00 daily. Better known as Bún Chả Obama thanks to a visit from the erstwhile president in 2016, the *bún chả* here is far from presidential, but the deep-fried crab spring rolls are something special. $

Tanh Tách [91 C7] 3 Yết Kiêu; w tanhtach.com; ⌚ 11.00–14.00 & 17.00–22.00 Mon–Sat, 17.00–22.00 Sun. Fancy & creative seafood served in elegant surroundings in the heart of Hai Bà Trưng District's French Quarter. The canapés are the best things on the menu, & you could consider crafting an entire meal out of these delicious, innovative little dishes. $$$$

Tây Hồ District

Gòn – Bites & Veggies [98 B2] Ngõ 1 Quảng Bá; f gonbitesandveggies; ⌚ 10.00–22.00 daily. Excellent little Vietnamese joint that appeals to a sweeter palette & will remind some of southern cuisine. The rolls are particularly good. $$

Bao Wow [98 B2] 31A Ngõ 12 Đặng Thai Mai; w baowowhanoi.com; ⌚ 11.00–23.00 daily. Hip hipster hangout with well-crafted bao buns & funky tunes in a laid-back outdoor courtyard. $$$

Maii Bistro [98 B2] 46 Tây Hồ; f; ⌚ 11.00–13.30 & 17.30–21.30 daily. Beautifully prepared modern Vietnamese food in an elegant French-style villa within an attractive & leafy corner of West Lake. $$$

Pizza Belga [98 C2] 225 Âu Cơ; w pizzabelga.com; ⌚ 11.00–14.30 & 17.00–22.00 daily. If you didn't know that Belgian pizza was a thing, now you do. This chic pizzeria popular with locals & foreigners serves some of the best pies in town. The creative topping variations, which include walnut, honey & goat's cheese, are admirable. There's also a location in the Old Quarter [90 F4] (47 Hàng Bè). $$$

COFFEE HOUSES

Hoàn Kiếm District

✷ **Bancông Café & Restaurant** [90 E4] 2 Đinh Liệt; w bancongHanoi.com; ⌚ 07.00–23.00 daily. Sprawling café-cum-restaurant encased in a rare Art Deco Old Quarter house with a handful of bucolic balconies that offer views of the anarchic streets below. Try the coconut coffee or creative juices.

Café Đinh [90 F4] 13 Đinh Tiên Hoàng; ⌚ 07.00–22.00 daily. Ancient café with a coveted balcony that overlooks Hoàn Kiếm Lake. Like many of Hanoi's secrets, you'll need to duck down an alleyway & up some rickety stairs to reach it.

✷ **Café Nuôi** [90 E4] 34 Lương Văn Can; ⌚ 07.00–22.00 daily. Atmospheric corner café that's easy to miss, but it has been serving traditional coffee & fresh smoothies to local Hanoians for decades. A rare classic café in the centre of the Old Quarter.

Cộng Cà Phê [91 E5] 27 Nhà Thờ; w congcaphe.com; ⌚ 07.30–23.30 daily. There are several of these tongue-in-cheek communist chic cafés in Hanoi, but this branch allows views of the Gothic

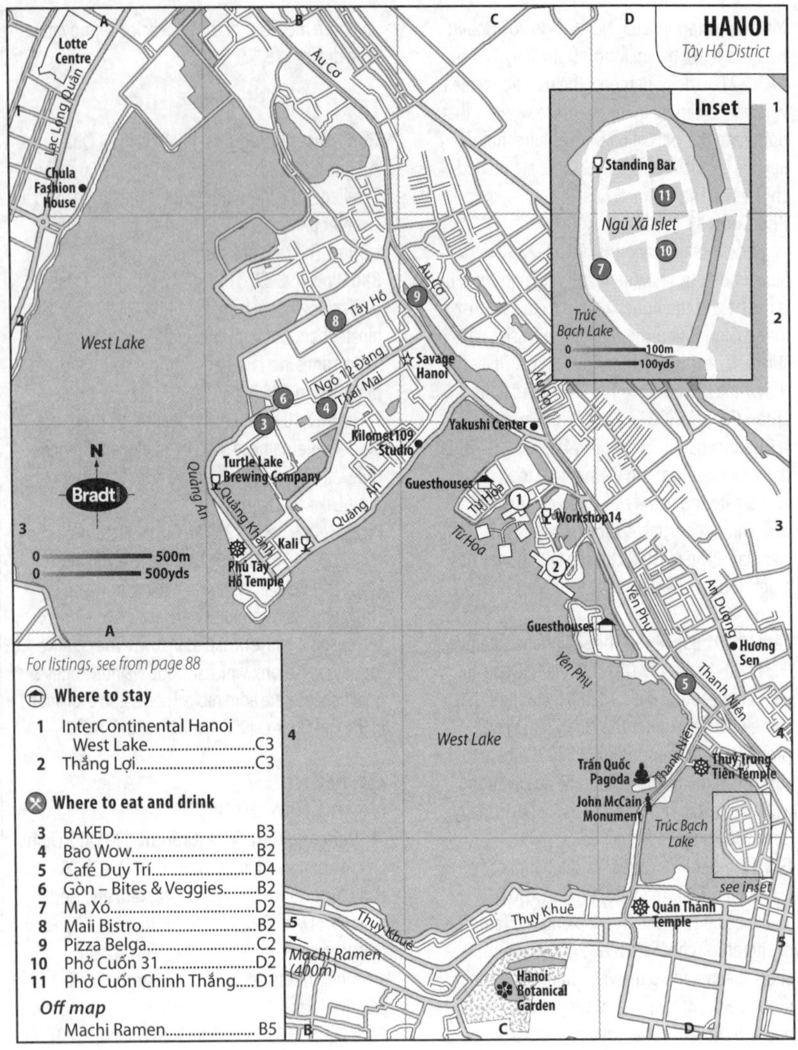

towers of St Joseph Cathedral. The café is often credited with creating coconut coffee.

Habakuk Fine Coffee & Bistro [91 G7] 4 Ngõ Phan Huy Chú; f HabacoffeeBistro; ⌚ 08.00–23.00 daily. Superb single-origin Western coffee in a comfortable room with AC, tucked away down an alleyway. In the evening it morphs into a chic European bistro.

Loading T [91 D5] 8 Chân Cầm; w loadingtcafe.com; ⌚ 08.00–18.00 daily. Alluring café in a grand centenarian house that was appropriated by the socialist government in the 1950s & divided between a dozen or so families. This is a good place to try egg coffee, which the café infuses with cinnamon.

Ba Đình and Đống Đa districts

Ma Xó [98 D2] 120 Trấn Vũ; f Ma.Xo.Cafe; ⌚ 08.00–23.00 daily. Lovely lakeside seating & artsy chic interiors from the same team behind Hanoi Social Club (page 100). There's an on-point playlist, tempting brunches & delicious juices.

✷ **Manzi Art Space & Café** [90 D2] 14 Phan Huy Ích; w manziart.space; ⌚ 08.00–19.00 daily. The modern art & excellent gift shop are the standout reasons to visit this comfortable, light-bathed café, which sits in a whitewashed colonial house on a pretty street just north of the Old Quarter. This is an active hub of contemporary creativity, with occasional evening events.

refined. [91 A5] 43 Văn Miếu; **w** refined.vn; ⌚ 07.30–10.30 daily. Specialises in premium Vietnamese coffee with a few signature creations. Take a stall at the coffee bar or settle into the outside table that overlooks the Temple of Literature.

Hai Bà Trưng District

✷ **Café Thái** [91 E8] 27 Triệu Việt Vương; f cafeThai27TrieuVietVuong; ⌚ 06.30–22.00 daily. A coffee shop institution nestled in an attractive suburb in southern Hanoi, Ca Phê Thái claims to have existed since 1926. Despite the old-school vibes, it's mostly popular with young & trendy Hanoians.

Tây Hồ District

BAKED [98 B3] 46 Xóm Chùa; ⌚ 08.00–18.00 daily. Probably the best cakes in West Lake, if not Hanoi, to munch on with the well-crafted coffee. There's always a reliable spread of classic cookies & cupcakes, with seasonal highlights, too.

✷ **Café Duy Trí** [98 D4] 43A Yên Phụ; ⌚ 06.00–22.30 daily. Recently rebuilt & renovated (though it looks exactly the same inside), Café Duy Trí has existed in some form since 1936. It's the place to go for traditional Vietnamese coffee, yoghurt coffee & tube house architecture.

ENTERTAINMENT AND NIGHTLIFE

Aside from the shows listed here, some tourist sites, including the Temple of Literature (page 118), Hỏa Lò Prison (page 111) and the Imperial Citadel (page 114), have begun **night tours**, which make for an atmospheric evening activity. Check the respective websites for details and booking. There are also **traditional music halls** (page 35) that operate sporadically, including Vietnam Tuồng Theatre [90 D4] and the Chèo Theatre [map, page 81]. **Cinemas** can be found in the big shopping centres (page 100).

Hồ Chí Minh City eclipses Hanoi as a party city, but that doesn't mean that Hanoians don't know how to have a good time. Evening entertainment is mostly relaxed and low-key, revolving around *bia hơi*, cocktail bars and live events, though there are a few notable club options.

EXHIBITIONS AND SHOWS

Goethe-Institut [91 B5] 56–60 Nguyễn Thái Học; **w** goethe.de/ins/vn/de; ⌚ 08.30–18.00 Mon–Fri. Set within a small cluster of whitewashed Art Deco buildings speckled with palm trees, the German cultural centre has an eclectic schedule that includes art exhibitions & film festivals.

L'Espace [91 C8] 8 Thiền Quang; **w** ifv.vn/cac-van-phong-cua-vien-phap/vien-phap-tai-ha-noi; ⌚ 08.30–19.00 Mon–Sat. The Institut Français has a major cultural presence in Vietnam, supporting both local & francophone art exhibitions, music performances, film nights & more. Note that while the website is only in French & Vietnamese, exhibitions also tend to be in English to appeal to Hanoi's wider international community.

THEATRES

Hanoi Opera House [91 G6] Tràng Tiền; **w** hanoioperahouse.org.vn. The eclectic performance schedule includes dance, music and acrobatics; the ticket booth is to the right of the entrance.

Lotus Water Puppet Theatre [91 E5] 16 Lê Thái Tổ; **w** bongsenwaterpuppet.vn; ⌚ showings at 17.15 daily, & sometimes at 18.30. Of the 2 water puppet theatres overlooking Hoàn Kiếm Lake – the other being Thăng Long Water Puppet Theatre [90 F4] on 57B Đinh Tiên Hoàng – this is the recommended one.

Vietnam Puppet Theatre [map, page 81] 361 Trường Chinh; **w** nhahatmuaroivietnam.vn. The Thăng Long Water Puppet Theatre (57B Đinh Tiên Hoàng) overlooking Hoàn Kiếm Lake sees more visitors but the performances at the Vietnam Puppet Theatre were more intimate. Sadly, the Covid-19 pandemic put a halt to regular showings & when we went to print they'd not started up again. Hopefully this will change as tourism rebounds; check the website for details. If out of action, check the Lotus Water Puppet Theatre on page 99.

BARS AND LIVE MUSIC

The 371 Bar [90 D4] 42B Bát Đàn; f; ⌚ 20.00–midnight Fri–Sat. Far & away the best whisky bar in the city, with single malts from across the world served in a cosy space that contrasts with the rowdy *bia hơi* bars nearby.
Beeznees 1920s [90 D4] 163 Phùng Hưng; f; ⌚ 19.00–midnight or later daily. Roaring Twenties-themed speakeasy cocktail bar with an extensive menu & balcony overlooking the train tracks. Think about the theme carefully before pulling back the right book & revealing the secret passageway to the bar.
The Hanoi Social Club [91 D5] 6 Ngõ Hội Vũ; f; ⌚ 08.00–23.00 daily. A café, restaurant & events venue, the Hanoi Social Club does a little of everything. The evening schedule – which you can find on social media – is eclectic & attempts to front music from Vietnam's various ethnolinguistic groups, as well as local & visiting musicians.
Kali [98 B3] 102 Quảng An; f kali.hanoi; ⌚ 17.00–23.00 Tue–Fri, 11.00–23.00 Sat–Sun. Open-air bar & restaurant serving Middle Eastern bites, with regular DJ events on the w/ends.
✷ **Long Waits Jazz** [90 D4] 5 Nguyễn Quang Bích; f; ⌚ 19.00–midnight daily. Intimate & secluded jazz bar supported by a friendly community of music enthusiasts. Music events are mostly on the w/ends; during the week the bar behaves more like a quiet speakeasy.
Nê Boong-ke [90 D3] 12 Cửa Đông; f neboongkehanoi; ⌚ 18.00–01.00 daily. The head mixologist here is credited with creating the *phở* cocktail, which uses the herbs & spices used in Vietnam's national dish to craft a drink.
R7 [map, page 81] No 15 Ngõ 36 Đào Tấn; f; ⌚ 18.00–late daily. Laid-back & friendly rooftop queer bar with an active events calendar, including raucous drag shows on w/end evenings.
Savage Hanoi [98 C2] No 1 Ngõ 9 Đặng Thai Mai; w savage-hanoi.com; ⌚ 22.00–early hours Thu–Sat. Nightclub that has taken over a spooky detached mansion, with different rooms & international DJs. Queer-friendly.
Standing Bar [98 D1] 170 Trấn Vũ; f standingbarhanoi; ⌚ 15.00–midnight Mon–Fri, noon–midnight Sat–Sun. Not under the influence of any brewery in particular, Standing Bar has beers from across the country (& the world). The bar is known for its comedy shows, almost always in English.
Tadioto [91 G6] 24B Tông Đản; f tadiotohanoi; ⌚ 11.00–23.45 daily. Established by journalist & aesthete Nguyễn Quý Đức, who passed away in 2023, Tadioto moved several times before settling in its current location. Frequented by artsy locals, diplomats & journalists.
Turtle Lake Brewing Company [98 B3] 105 Quảng Khánh; f; ⌚ 11.00–midnight daily. One of many craft beer bars in Hanoi, this offers a genuine beer garden experience on the shore of West Lake. Family-friendly during the day, with decent Western food.
✷ **Workshop14** [98 C3] Ngõ 5 Từ Hoa; ⌚ 17.00–midnight daily. Elegant craft cocktail bar that opened at the beginning of 2025 with a refreshingly succinct menu and a front garden filled with pot plants.

SHOPPING

SHOPPING CENTRES Hanoi has long had fewer shopping centres than other large capitals in the region, but that is starting to change. The most numerous are the Vincom centres, two of which are within the central districts [both map, page 81] (191 Bà Triệu; 29 Liễu Giai). A little more upmarket and spacious are the Lotte centres (683 Lạc Long Quân [98 A1]; 54 Liễu Giai [map, page 81]). All the shopping centres have cinemas, arcades, kids entertainment areas and many dozens of shops.

OTHER SHOPS

Art, design and crafts

✷ **54 Traditions** [90 D2] 44B Hàng Bún; w 54traditions.vn; ⌚ 09.00–18.00 Mon–Sat. Antiques shop with various treasures from Vietnam's officially recognised ethnolinguistic groups. Staff members will offer tours of the multi-storey shop & can set you up with the right paperwork if you make a purchase.

✷ **Art Vietnam Gallery** [map, page 81] 2 Ngõ 66 Yên Lạc; w artvietnamgallery.com; ⌚ 10.00–16.00 Mon–Fri. One of Hanoi's most important contemporary art institutions, set up by Susanne Lecht, who moved to Hanoi in 1994. The collection, which can be viewed by appointment only, is considered & eclectic.

Cerender Ceramics [91 E6] 11a Tràng Thi; ⌚ 09.00–22.00 daily. Cerender's flagship store (there are others) is a cavernous trove of ceramics that make good gifts and souvenirs.

Craft Link [91 A5] 51 Văn Miếu; w craftlink.com.vn; ⌚ 09.00–18.00 daily. Cavernous not-for-profit shop with crafts from Vietnam's various ethnolinguistic groups at reasonable prices, conveniently located next to the Temple of Literature.

✷ **Gói Gém Café & Local Art Store** [90 D4] 74 Hàng Nón; ⌚ 08.00–22.00 daily. Prints, mugs, clothes and other knick-knacks crafted by a small team of designers. The products are in a similar vein to TiredCity (see right), though perhaps a little less touristy.

Green Palm Gallery [90 E4] 39 Hàng Gai; w greenpalmgallery.com; ⌚ 08.00–19.00 daily. Established in 1994 by an art critic, this is one of the older galleries in Hanoi, with a neat space close to Hoàn Kiếm Lake.

Hanoia House [90 E4] 38 Hàng Đào; w hanoia.com; ⌚ 09.00–20.00 daily. High-end artisanal lacquerware sporting bold colours presented in an extraordinary antique shophouse that has been lovingly restored. Worth visiting even if you have no intention of buying anything.

✷ **Hiên Vân Ceramics** [91 D5] In the same glorious mansion as Loading T (page 98); w hienvanceramics.com; ⌚ 09.00–18.00 daily. Beautiful artisanal shop selling ceramic bowls, plates, vases & various other objects. It's tucked deep within the mansion so you may need to ask.

✷ **Manzi Art Space & Café** [90 D2] 14 Phan Huy Ích; w manziart.space; ⌚ 08.00–19.00 daily. Not just a modern art gallery & café (page 98), but also a gift shop with 1-of-a-kind pieces. Manzi Exhibition Space, a gallery, is just around the corner.

Thăng Long Art Gallery [90 E4] 41 Hàng Gai; w thanglongartgallery.com; ⌚ 08.00–20.00 Mon–Sat, 09.00–17.00 Sun. Excellent art gallery of mostly contemporary Vietnamese art; they won't mind you snooping around even if you have no intention of buying.

TiredCity Creative Store [90 E4] 97 Hàng Gai; w tiredcity.com; ⌚ 08.30–22.00 daily. Funny & funky designs crafted by a young team of local designers & printed on T-shirts, hoodies, playing cards, postcards, posters & more. There are now more than a dozen locations in the Old Quarter, somewhat lessening the shop's original independent appeal.

Books

✷ **Bookworm Hanoi** [90 C1] 44 Phạm Hồng Thái; w bookwormhanoi.com; ⌚ 09.00–19.00 daily. Hanoi's only English-language bookshop, with tonnes of literature on Vietnam, as well as coffee-table books, travel books & novels.

Nhà Sách Mão [91 F6] 5 Đinh Lễ (head down the alleyway and follow the signs); ⌚ 09.00–17.00 daily. Unless you speak Vietnamese, you won't find much to read here – the only English-language book is one detailing the history of the shop, which has been around since the 1970s. But visiting this hidden bookshop, down an alleyway, feels like stepping into Diagon Alley. Đinh Lễ Street is packed with less atmospheric bookshops, most with English-language sections.

Fashion

Chăn Con Công [90 F3] 37 Đào Duy Từ; f; ⌚ 09.00–21.00 daily. Also at [91 E5] 7A Nhà Thờ; ⌚ 09.00–21.30 daily. Hanoi hipsterism at its finest, Chăn Con Công is named after a famous fabric popular in Vietnam during the communist era. The shop is a jumble sale of stylish secondhand apparel.

Chula Fashion House [98 A1] 43 Nhật Chiêu; w chulafashion.com; ⌚ 09.00–19.00 daily. Vietnamese patterns meet Catalonian creativity for bold, colourful fashion that will turn heads & get people talking. Headed by the effortlessly charismatic Laura Fontan, who arrived in Hanoi with her husband, Diego Cortizas, in 2004. Diego passed away in 2021 & is sorely missed.

Ginkgo [90 F4] 44 Hàng Bè; w ginkgotshirts.com; ⌚ 09.00–22.00 daily. Long-running fashion brand peddling good-quality T-shirts imprinted with iconic images from Vietnam. There are several outlets throughout the country.

Kilomet109 Studio [98 C3] 64 Quảng An; w kilomet109.com; ⌚ 10.00–19.00 Tue–Sun. Slow fashion house led by visionary local designer Thảo Vũ, who skilfully incorporates patterns & techniques from Vietnam's ethnolinguistic groups.

OTHER PRACTICALITIES

BANKS, ATMS AND MONEYCHANGERS Banks and ATMs are everywhere in Hanoi, and there are few reports of scams or machine tampering. Most ATMs charge a fee and most only allow a maximum withdrawal of 3,000,000VND (US$120) at a time, though you can reinsert your card and continue to take out cash until you hit the limit imposed by your bank at home. Banks tend to offer fairly poor exchange rates if exchanging cash. There are usually moneychangers milling around outside Hanoi Post Office [91 F6] on Hoàn Kiếm Lake. There is also a row of moneychangers on Hà Trung Street [91 D5], who offer suspiciously good rates and some consider to be a front for money laundering.

HEALTH ☎ 115 is the state emergency number to request medical assistance. Try to find someone nearby who can speak Vietnamese to help convey the information accurately and quickly.

Family Medical Practice [map, page 81] 298I Kim Mã; ☎ emergencies 24 3843 0748, support line 24 3843 0748; **w** vietnammedicalpractice.com/hanoi/en; ⏲ all day daily
Hồng Ngọc Hospital [90 C1] 55 Yên Ninh; ☎ emergencies 1900 636 555, support line 24 3927 5568; **w** hongngochospital.vn; ⏲ 07.30–17.00 daily
Vinmec International Hospital [map, page 81] 458 Minh Khai; ☎ 24 3974 3556; **w** en.vinmec.com; ⏲ all day daily

POST OFFICE Hanoi Post Office [91 F6] (75 Đinh Tiên Hoàng), the city's main post office, is conveniently located on Hoàn Kiếm Lake, but it's somewhat complicated if you want to do anything more than send a letter. Hanoi has various courier services operated by both private and public companies, including Vietnam Post, Viettel Post, EMS, DHL, Fedex, UPS and Nasco Express. For more on sending post in Vietnam, see page 73.

SPAS Spas come and go in Hanoi, but a reliable, affordable, no-frills massage service is available at **Yakushi Center** [98 C3] (28 Xuân Diệu; **w** yakushicenter.com) in Tây Hồ District. For a traditional Vietnamese spa experience – a process that involves steaming, scrubbing and finishes with a massage – head to **Hương Sen** [98 D4] (68 An Dương; **w** huongsenhealthcare.com), also in Tây Hồ.

WHAT TO SEE AND DO

Carving up a city like Hanoi into manageable chunks is not easy. Guidebooks have long tried to split Hanoi by themed neighbourhood, but as nobody can agree where one ends and the next begins, this can be confusing. While these pages occasionally fall into the same trap of designating neighbourhoods – usually for want of a better word – they are subtitled according to official district delineations (page 86).

HOÀN KIẾM DISTRICT Hanoi's Hoàn Kiếm District has so much to offer that some visitors never explore further afield. To some, the appearance of messy modern buildings, shiny hotel lobbies and anarchic traffic will induce tears of imagined nostalgia for a heritage city that could have been. But for most, the jumble of architectural styles and chaotic street life is part of Hoàn Kiếm's ramshackle appeal. This district, the historical heart of Hanoi, has three parts. Hoàn Kiếm Lake is at the centre of not only the district but also the city, with grandiose colonial edifices,

SO MUCH TO SEE, SO LITTLE TIME

Don't come to Hanoi and expect to cover everything. Ambling around the temples and streets of Hoàn Kiếm Lake and the Old Quarter is essential even for repeat visitors, but design the rest of your itinerary around your interests and broader plan in Vietnam. If exploring the ethnolinguistically diverse parts of the country, such as the northern mountains and Central Highlands, the Museum of Ethnology (page 120) is an important stop. Those with an interest in ancient history will find plenty to dig into at the Temple of Literature (page 118) and Imperial Citadel (page 114). Those whose interests lie in Vietnam's colonial and modern history will want to spend time in the Hỏa Lò Prison (page 111) and Hồ Chí Minh Mausoleum Complex (page 112). If visiting the previous capitals of Cổ Loa, Hoa Lư and Huế, spend time in the southern half of the National Museum of History (page 105). If visiting Điện Biên Phủ in the northern mountains, devote more time to the northern half of that museum. Remember to carve out time to do nothing at all but sit in coffee houses and absorb Hanoi's addictive atmosphere. And if in doubt, look for the 'author's favourite' symbol (✷).

some important spiritual buildings and the setting for Hanoi's best-known myth (page 104). The Old Quarter is the labyrinthine warren of streets and alleyways north and west of the lake. This ancient 13th-century trading quarter (page 107) is where you'll find terraced 'tube' houses, named for their narrow frontage because owners were taxed according to the width of their shop. Hoàn Kiếm's French Quarter (zones built by the French also stretch into Hai Bà Trưng and Ba Đình districts) is east and south of the lake. In the 19th century, much of this area was swampy agricultural land with basic dwellings. When the French took the city at the end of the century, they flattened houses, filled in the swamps and constructed a European-style administrative capital. Today you'll find detached colonial mansions and grand government buildings sitting beside uninteresting blocky skyscrapers on tree-lined boulevards.

✷ **Hoàn Kiếm Lake and around** [91 F5] (Hồ Hoàn Kiếm) This fabled lake is situated at the heart of Hanoi and surrounded by the most compelling parts of the city for visitors. The lake has an adjacent park featuring a 2004 statue of Lý Thái Tổ [91 F5], Hanoi's founder, and two small islands. Ngọc Sơn Temple stands on the larger of the two and is accessible by a wooden bridge on the northeast shore. The iconic Turtle Tower, particularly photogenic on misty days, perches on the inaccessible islet in the southern half of the lake. North of here is the Old Quarter, the ancient part of Hanoi with its legendary 36 guild streets. To the south of the lake is the French Quarter. When they arrived in 1882, the French imposed their own style of neo-Parisian elegance and demolished important city landmarks and pagodas for the glory of France. A sad reminder of what would have existed here sits on the southeast corner of the lake in the form of what is now known as Hòa Phong Tower (Tháp Hòa Phong). Before the French sacking, this was just a small part of the expansive Báo Ân Pagoda.

By 1884, avenues of houses had been completed, the first French hotel appeared one year later, and in 1886 St Joseph Cathedral was inaugurated. Despite their imperialist beginnings and faded ochre exteriors, many of the French villas and terraced houses dotted around the lake are undeniably attractive. First to realise the

LEGEND HAS IT: TURTLES ALL THE WAY DOWN

Hồ Hoàn Kiếm means 'Lake of the Returned Sword', but many Old Quarter residents simply refer to it as Hồ Gươm (Sword Lake). The story goes that, during the 15th century, the divinities sent Lord Lê Lợi a sword, which he used to drive out invaders from the north. After independence was secured and Lord Lê Lợi became King Lê Thái Tổ, the turtle god appeared from the deepest depths of the lake and demanded that the new king return the divine blade. The legend is grounded in truth: giant turtles lived in the lake until quite recently, evidenced by the stuffed specimens in Ngọc Sơn Temple.

commercial potential of accurate renovation was the French company Accor who, in 1990, poured almost US$10 million into completely restoring the **Hotel Metropole** (now the Sofitel Legend Metropole Hanoi) [91 F6] to its former glory. Situated at the intersection of Ngô Quyền and Tràng Tiền, which in its heyday was the most fashionable street in Hanoi, the Metropole first opened in 1901. Over the years, a long list of celebrities have stayed here, including Charlie Chaplin in 1936, Graham Green in 1952, Jane Fonda in 1972 and Brangelina in 2015. Today it is almost as flamboyant as the nearby Opera House and the Government Reception Hall that stands opposite, creating a Petit Paris on the eastern fringe of Hoàn Kiếm Lake.

The roads that circle the lake are traffic-free on the weekends, when tiny children driving toy cars, K-pop troupes filming amateur dance videos, and street performers drawing crowds of onlookers take over the neighbourhood. There are also regular cultural events that dominate the lake's eastern shore. Regardless of whether you visit on a weekend or not, spend one morning walking around the whole of Hoàn Kiếm Lake, preferably at dawn, to take in the almost village-like atmosphere of this great city. You'll spot all kinds of physical activity, including tai chi, Latin dance, aerobics, laughter yoga, calisthenics, badminton and weightlifting. If you're feeling confident, join in.

✷ ***Ngọc Sơn Temple*** [90 F4] (Đinh Tiên Hoàng; 30,000VND/free adult/child) Though this has been a place of worship for at least seven centuries, the temple you see today was built between the 18th and 19th centuries and is accessed by the crimson Thê Húc Bridge. Immediately before the bridge are the Ink Slab and Pen Brush Towers, built in 1864 to commemorate the scholar Nguyễn Văn Siêu. The temple itself honours Văn Xương, the God of Literature, Quan Vũ, celebrated for his remarkable fighting feats, and, perhaps most importantly, the 13th-century national hero Trần Hưng Đạo, who defeated northern invaders. There are also two stuffed turtles that once resided in the lake; one was pulled out in 1968, the other in 2016. Both died of natural causes before their immortalisation.

Turtle Tower [91 E5] (Tháp Rùa; Hồ Hoàn Kiếm) This rather dilapidated but photogenic three-tiered structure was built in the 19th century on an inaccessible islet to honour the legendary turtles that, some believe, still lurk beneath the waters (see above). The French erected a small Statue de la Liberté (Statue of Liberty) atop the structure, but it was pulled down by independence fighters around the time of the Declaration of Independence in 1945.

The Martyrs' Monument [90 F4] (Đinh Tiên Hoàng) This eye-catching communist-era statue celebrates those who fought for Vietnamese independence.

A man wielding a lunge mine is flanked by a woman with an unsheathed sword and a kneeling boy holding a rifle. Lunge mines were used in the war for independence, disabling tanks but also killing the wielder, and the words on the base aptly mean 'Determined to die for the birth of the nation'.

Hanoi Opera House [91 G6] (Tràng Tiền; **w** hanoioperahouse.org.vn) Modelled on Paris's Palais Garnier, Hanoi's garish wedding cake-like Opera House was completed in 1911 with Neoclassical columns and Gothic domes. Arranging a tour to see the building's interiors isn't currently possible, so consider booking to see a performance instead (page 99).

✷ National Museum of History [91 G6] (Tràng Tiền; **w** baotanglichsu.vn; ⌚ Tue–Sun, exc some days over Tết; 20,000VND; 2–4hrs) This mammoth museum, with over 20,000 documents and artefacts, spans two large buildings. You'll need around 2 hours for each section. On the south side of Tràng Tiền Street, a grand 1920s building that blends Eastern and Western styles behind the Opera House details Vietnam's history, from prehistory until the French invasion in the 19th century. On the north side of Tràng Tiền Street, with entrances on both Trần Quang Khải Street and Tông Đản Street, is the second part of the museum in another, less interesting colonial building. Formerly the Revolutionary Museum, this part recounts the history from the beginning of colonialism until the end of the 20th century.

The history of Vietnam spans millennia and those interested could spend a full day here (though be mindful of the long lunch break that was in place at the time of research; check the website). The museum is arranged chronologically and English signage is sufficient. Perhaps the best reason to visit this museum is that it will provide context for where you're going or where you've been in Vietnam.

The south side The first section on prehistoric man on the right as you enter is small but reasonably informative. There are exhibits of primitive tools made from horn, bamboo, coconut shells and bone. Discoveries from Neolithic sites (4000BCE and before) indicate that rice was grown in Vietnam even back then. More attention is given to the Bronze Age civilisations in the larger hall, especially the celebrated Đông Sơn culture, with several large drums (page 8) depicting deer, birds, horses, boats and warriors. Some items come from Cổ Loa Citadel (page 125), about 20km from Hanoi, which has been partly excavated. A highlight is the enormous, 2,000-year-old Hoàng Hạ Drum. By 111BCE, much of Vietnam was under the control of the Chinese, and thus the next section focuses on the various uprisings that took place during this period. It culminates with a small model depicting the 938 battle on the Bạch Đằng River (page 203) that won Vietnam independence.

Until this point, the museum may feel a little incoherent, but a sense of order emerges with the introduction of Vietnam's dynastic era. If you have Ninh Bình on your programme, look out for the small exhibit about the Đinh Dynasty (CE969–80) and Lê Dynasty (980–1009), when Hoa Lư (page 215) was the capital. There is a towering Buddhist statue replica from the Lý Dynasty (1009–1225) when the country's capital was Thăng Long (later Hanoi) and the influence of Buddhism spread widely. A chaotic concave wall mural illustrates the second battle of the Bạch Đằng River, with Mongol ships ablaze, one of the defining moments of the Trần Dynasty (1225–1400). Head upstairs to continue the dynastic chronology.

This next period of Vietnamese history is particularly complicated, with a handful of warring dynasties vying for dominance, though it's possible to piece together a timeline with some standout exhibits. There are some aerial photographs of the short-lived (1400–07) Hồ Dynasty's citadel in Thanh Hóa, some intricate artefacts of dragon heads from the second Lê Dynasty (1428–1527) and two towering twin parrots perched on turtles from the Mạc Dynasty (1527–92). The exhibits from the revived second Lê Dynasty (1533–1788) illustrate the trouble between the Nguyễn clans in the south and the Trịnh in the north. If you're going to Quy Nhơn in Bình Định Province, the Tây Sơn section tells the story of a celebrated rebellion (page 332) that began there in the 1770s and put an end to the Nguyễn–Trịnh rivalry. Alas the Tây Sơn rebels, headed by the new king Quang Trung, proved better at rebelling than ruling, and by 1802 the Nguyễn Dynasty had returned and reunited the country. An artistic flourishing followed, evidenced by wooden screens inlaid with mother of pearl and expertly crafted bronze bells and other artefacts. You may detect some European influence in the later pieces as Western influence intensified and the threat of French colonialism loomed.

Don't leave this part of the museum without taking a look at more than 70 Cham (page 12) artefacts, which are in very good condition, though lacking in contextual information. It's also worth taking a stroll around the leafy garden to enjoy the outdoor displays and the building's grand architecture.

The north side This part of the museum is divided into 25 rooms, which oscillate between being informative and propagandistic. The exhibits start upstairs. The first room has depictions of the French invasion of Vietnam, with epic drawings of various battles, including the sieges of Hanoi and Saigon, and the eventual surrender and subsequent signing ceremony in Huế in 1875. There are also some striking photos, such as one of the Long Biên Bridge when it was finished in 1902.

It then becomes clear why this was once called the Revolutionary Museum. Rooms 2–3 commemorate figures from the resistance movement, chief among them Hồ Chí Minh (then Nguyễn Tất Thành), who began his journey from Saigon to Europe in 1911. There's a nod to the Russian Revolution in 1917. Rooms 4–5 reflect how a resistance movement evolved into a revolutionary movement by the 1930s. Rooms 6–9 introduce the Việt Minh in the context of the Japanese occupation of Vietnam during World War II. An interesting map shows how the organisation began in the northernmost provinces of Vietnam before moving south; this will be of particular interest if visiting Pác Bó in Cao Bằng Province, where Hồ Chí Minh (still Nguyễn Tất Thành) re-entered Vietnam in 1941. A triumphant room then celebrates the declaration of independence with an impressive mural and some black-and-white video footage of this momentous event.

Rooms 10–14 detail the unsuccessful French attempts to retake Vietnam after World War II, culminating in the defeat at the Battle of Điện Biên Phủ in 1954 and the subsequent French exit. There is a notable effort through photographs and art to show that resistance to French rule was nationwide. This section ends with a gruesome room recounting the horrific conditions in French-built prisons in Vietnam, including a ceiling-high guillotine.

Moving downstairs, rooms 15–18 launch into the period when the country was divided into North Vietnam and South Vietnam, with attacks on Ngô Đình Diệm, a 'puppet president' of South Vietnam and his links with Lyndon Johnson, the US president. Photos show the beginnings of American military involvement in 1955 and protests against the South Vietnam government. This is contrasted with images of industrial development in North Vietnam. Rooms 19–24 continue the story of the intense military operation, with some genuine anti-American propaganda posters and horrific photos of bombed buildings and victims. This section climaxes with the famous photo of a tank tearing through the gates of the Independence Palace, then the Presidential Palace, in 1975.

Room 25, the final room, recounts the successes of a reunified Vietnam (without any mention of its failures), showcasing huge infrastructure projects such as Thăng Long Bridge in Hanoi and the gigantic Hòa Bình hydro-electric plant, construction of which began in 1979 but wasn't finished until 1994.

✷ **St Joseph Cathedral** [91 E5] (40 Nhà Chung) Known in Vietnamese as Nhà Thờ Lớn (Big Church), the neo-Gothic St Joseph Cathedral was inaugurated in 1886, and the lofty grey bell towers remain one of Hanoi's iconic images. The plaza in front is a lively place, especially after mass, when churchgoers wearing *áo dài* (Vietnam's national dress) chitchat and take selfies. Mass (look for times on a small sign to the left of the cathedral) is also the only time that you can enter the church via the main gate, though note that this is for worshippers – not sightseers. At other times, head down the quiet road to the left of the cathedral and look for a small raised door on your right to gaze at the golden altar and stained-glass windows. Perhaps the best way to absorb the atmosphere of this corner of Hanoi is to do as the locals do: find a pavement café with a view of the church and sip *trà chanh* (lemon tea) while munching on sunflower seeds.

✷ **The Old Quarter** (Phố Cổ) Beguiling for some and maddening for others, *phố cổ* means 'ancient street(s)' in Vietnamese, and this is the name used by Hanoians to refer to their city's cacophonous, chaotic and pulsating trading quarter. In English the area is more commonly referred to as the Old Quarter. The neighbourhood also goes by the name '36 *phố phường*', referencing the 36 trading guilds that set up shop here from the 13th century. These guilds came from villages across what is now Northern Vietnam and specialised in a particular artisanal craft, from silversmiths and silk weavers to potters and rattan furniture makers. Many streets are named after the produce (*hàng*) originally sold there, and thus the area remains a testament to the city's rich trade heritage. Some streets still peddle the products that have been sold there for centuries. A jewellers' guild was established on Hàng Bạc (Silver) Street [90 F4] in 1428, and jewellery shops flogging trinkets of questionable quality still clog the thoroughfare. This is one of the few streets to maintain a guild communal house – the Đình Kim Ngân (44 Hàng Bạc). Apothecaries and traditional-medicine doctors are still found on Thuốc Bắc (Chinese Medicine) Street [90 D3], evidenced by the aroma of herbs and spices. Metalworkers dominate boisterous Hàng Thiếc (Metal) Street. Other streets are moving on from their original trade. Hàng Mã (Paper) Street [90 D3] sells paper money and replicas of material possessions made for burning ceremonies, but also decorations for the approaching holiday: plastic spiderwebs before Halloween, Fraser fir replicas at Christmas and blood-red wall hangings during the lead-up to Tết (Lunar New Year). Hàng Chiếu (Mat) Street [90 E3] still sells mats, but also rugs, wallpaper and other items for home décor. At the

WHY SO SLIM?

Hanoi, and the Old Quarter in particular, is known for its so-called tube houses, buildings with a narrow frontage that extends both backwards and upwards. These are the physical remnants of a policy that taxed landowners according to the width of their property to ensure that as many families as possible had access to the street.

east end of Hàng Chiếu is the medieval East River Gate (Ô Quan Chưởng) [90 E3], labelled with the Chinese characters 東河門. There were once 16 gates to the city, but this is the only one that remains. Most streets in the Old Quarter, however, no longer sell the products they were named after. Hàng Gai (Hemp) Street [90 E4] sells souvenirs, Hàng Dầu (Oil) Street [90 F4] sells shoes and Mã Mây (Rattan) Street [90 F3] sells cheap knock-offs of well-known brands.

Bia Hơi Corner [90 E3] (Cnr of Tạ Hiện & Lương Ngọc Quyến) At the point where these two roads meet is the notorious Bia Hơi ('fresh beer') Corner, with dozens of noisy bars overlooking a comically chaotic intersection. With almost no return customers, the food here tends to be poor and it's difficult to find true fresh beer; what they serve instead is bottled beer served in cups with a thick head to resemble a glass of fresh beer. For the real deal, see page 95.

✷ ***Bạch Mã Temple*** [90 E3] (76 Hàng Buồm) Nestled deep within Hanoi's Old Quarter is Bạch Mã Temple, or White Horse Temple, regarded by many as the oldest in the city. The temple was commissioned by Emperor Lý Thái Tổ in the 11th century as a tribute to a mythical white horse, whose ethereal guidance led him to the spot where he chose to erect the city walls. However, much of the temple's current architectural splendour can only be traced back to the 18th and 19th centuries, including a sacred shrine dedicated to Confucius added in 1839. Bạch Mã Temple is one of four Hanoian temples that guard against malignant spiritual forces; the other three are Kim Liên Temple (page 120), Voi Phục Temple (page 117) and Quán Thánh Temple (page 116). Once inside the building you won't miss the temple's centrepiece statue: a steadfast interpretation paying homage to the legendary white horse.

Đồng Xuân Market [90 E2] Accessible by riverboat when it was built in 1889 by the French, this market has seen trading with the whole of Southeast Asia. The huge structure was destroyed by fire in 1994, causing millions of dollars in damage, but it reopened in 1996. The standard of the products on offer tends to be pretty poor, but the lively, somewhat local atmosphere makes the market worth a visit.

Heritage House [90 F3] (87 Mã Mây; 20,000VND) This beautifully restored 19th-century merchants' house, once belonging to a Chinese family of jewellers, is one of the best-preserved properties in the area. The interiors boast elegantly decorated rooms adorned with fine wooden furniture arranged around two courtyards. Located on Mã Mây Street, once known for its bamboo and rattan trade, the street now offers cheap souvenirs.

Hanoi Train Street [91 C5] (3 Trần Phú) Hanoi Train Street fever began in early 2018 when a cluster of cafés made it possible to squat next to the tracks and sip a *nâu đá* (iced Vietnamese coffee with milk) or a cold beer while the train rumbled past. As word spread, an influx of travellers and subsequent cafés soon followed, fostering an almost party-like atmosphere along the tracks. Citing safety concerns for its growing fan base, the authorities closed the street in October 2019. With virtually no international tourism during the Covid-19 pandemic, the street reopened in 2020 but closed once more before borders reopened in 2022. At the time of research, Hanoi Train Street was open again, but this will likely change as soon as someone inevitably gets hit by a train. Whatever the current situation, determined tourists always seem to find a way on to the tracks, and the authorities do very little to

LEGEND HAS IT: THE FINAL STRAW

In traditional Vietnamese households, the kitchen is about more than meal prep. The tripod that supports the stove is referred to as Táo, a deity designated by the heavens to oversee the family's well-being. Before any ritual is conducted, traditional families will first inform Táo, who then permits the ritual to proceed unhindered. Known also as Táo Quân, this deity safeguards the household's activities and wards off evil spirits, directly influencing the family's fortune. Folk traditions describe Táo as a triad: two men and a woman. In some regions, they are also honoured as the monarch of the kitchen.

The founding myth of Táo is a curious one. It tells of a woman named Thị Nhi, who was happily married to Trọng Cao. However, after years without children, their relationship soured. In a moment of anger, Trọng Cao struck Thị Nhi, and she left him for another man: Phạm Lang. Wracked with guilt, Trọng Cao abandoned his life and became a beggar. Years later, he arrived at Thị Nhi's new home by chance to beg for food. Thị Nhi recognised him immediately, and after all those years they finally made amends. When Phạm Lang came home, Thị Nhi hid Trọng Cao in a straw pile while she decided what to do. Exhausted, cosy and finally content, Trọng Cao fell asleep in the straw, and, unaware of his presence, Phạm Lang set the pile ablaze. Thị Nhi came outside, witnessed the immolation of her first husband and promptly threw herself on to the fire. Phạm Lang followed suit, and all three of them went up in flames.

Intrigued by the tragedy and touched by their loyalty and love for one another, the heavens transformed Thị Nhi, Trọng Cao and Phạm Lang into Táo Quân. Thị Nhi became Thổ Kỳ, in charge of food shopping. Trọng Cao became Thổ Địa, who managed household affairs. Phạm Lang became Thổ Công, who oversees the chores.

Every year on the 23rd day of the last lunar month (a week before Tết), traditional families perform a ritual to send Táo Quân to heaven, where they report on the family to the gods. They return a week later to resume their duties. The ritual offerings include a hat, shoes, ancestral tablets, a walking stick and a live carp. After the ritual, the carp is released into a river, symbolically transforming into a dragon that Thổ Công uses as a vehicle to travel to heaven.

prevent it. The carnival that has become Hanoi Train Street is the city's most touristed (and touristy) activity. The area north of 3 Trần Phú is always the busiest, so if you find the jamboree here is too much to bear then head south, walking along the railway tracks, until you find a quieter spot to watch the train crawl through the city. Trains pass every 2 or 3 hours throughout daylight hours and into the evening.

Street murals [90 D2] (27 Phùng Hưng) North of Hanoi Train Street, on the northwestern edge of Phùng Hưng Street, are 19 trompe-l'œil street art scenes painted on filled-in railway arches. A 2018 collaboration between local artists, the Hanoi People's Committee, the Korea Foundation and the United Nations Human Settlement Programme, the street murals marked 25 years of diplomatic relations between South Korea and Vietnam. The creative photo opportunities have made these railway arches, which display scenes of local life past and present, a popular selfie spot for both local and international visitors.

Hanoi Ceramic Mosaic Mural [90 D1] Completed in 2010 after a three-year effort by local and international artists to celebrate Hanoi's 1,000th birthday, the Hanoi Ceramic Mosaic Mural runs along the east side of Trần Nhật Duật and Yên Phụ streets. These are busy thoroughfares, making it an unpleasant sight to visit on foot, though worth looking out for in a taxi or on the back of a motorbike. Once completed, it took the Guinness World Record for largest ceramic mosaic. Some of the most colourful and impressive segments, including interpretations of local myths, are near the Chương Dương Bridge, on the east side of the Old Quarter. The mosaic once ran even further north, on to Nghi Tàm Street, but this section was destroyed when the road was widened in 2020.

✷ **Long Biên Bridge and around** [90 G1] Throughout the American War, this remarkable steel structure, completed in 1902 (though *not* engineered by Gustave Eiffel, as sometimes claimed; see below), faced repeated bombings, yet time and again it was swiftly repaired. Trains run through the middle, while motorbikes and pedestrians use the parasitic flanking roads. Use these sideroads to reach Banana Island, a vast tract of farmland in the Red River.

Long Biên Market [90 E2] (Hồng Hà) Hanoi's most vociferous and photogenic market gets going at around 23.00 and runs through to the morning. This is predominantly a fresh food market, also called a wet market, so expect brawny men hacking up animal carcasses, towering mounds of tropical fruit, live fish and seafood in buckets, pallets laden with vegetables and a welcome lack of tourist trinkets. You'll also find street kitchens with market workers huddled over steaming bowls of *phở* and *bún*.

Phúc Tân Public Art Project [90 F2] (Phúc Tân) Overshadowed by Long Biên Bridge is a series of extraordinary and difficult-to-find outdoor art installations. The permanent Phúc Tân Public Art Project was curated by local artist and

LEGEND HAS IT: A BRIDGE TOO FAR

Did you know that the Long Biên Bridge *wasn't* engineered by Gustave Eiffel? For decades tour guides have erroneously claimed that the bridge was built by the same man responsible for the Eiffel Tower in Paris. The myth somehow worked its way into training materials for tour guides, which led to misreporting by parachute journalists and travel writers who looked to link Hanoi with its colonial history through a household name. The error doesn't end at the Long Biên Bridge. Other structures that have been incorrectly attributed to the engineer include the Trường Tiền Bridge (page 261) in Huế, also built with steel girders, and Hồ Chí Minh City's Central Post Office (page 468, which seems especially bizarre as it exhibits nothing of the exposed steel that Gustave Eiffel is known for. Établissements Eiffel, the company Eiffel founded, did design one bridge in Vietnam, which may be the last of its kind in Asia. The Cầu Mống, formerly the Pont des Messageries, is a pedestrian bridge that connects districts 1 and 4 of Hồ Chí Minh City and is in desperate need of repair. As for Long Biên Bridge, it was in fact built by Daydé et Pillé, a rival construction company. For proof, look at the metal manufacturers' plaque on the south side of the bridge, near Long Biên Station. It reads: '1899–1902 Daydé et Pillé Paris'.

university lecturer Nguyễn Thế Sơn, who together with a team of 16 Vietnamese and international artists completed the project in 2020. There is a spread of themes, including the history of the Red River and images of rural life in the delta, all with ecofriendly messaging: recycled materials were used wherever possible. Perhaps most impressive is Vũ Xuân Đông's 'Boats', which was made with 10,000 plastic bottles. The project has met with reasonable success, and is in the process of expanding to neighbouring areas.

✷ **Hoàn Kiếm's French Quarter** Hanoi's French Quarter stretches across several districts, but three of the grandest streets – Trần Hưng Đạo, Lý Thường Kiệt and Hai Bà Trưng – course through Hoàn Kiếm District. Aside from the areas of specific interest (see the next few pages), these broad, tree-lined boulevards make for pleasant walking, despite the traffic, and historical architecture enthusiasts will enjoy gawping at many fine colonial mansions. The prettier houses tend to be embassies or ambassador residences: look out for the Cuban Embassy [91 D6] (65 Lý Thường Kiệt), paradoxically housed in a decadent Art Deco mansion, and the Cambodian Embassy [91 D7] (71A Trần Hưng Đạo), a Beaux-Arts Indochinese structure surrounded by palm trees. Grander buildings include the Supreme Court building [91 D6] (43 Hai Bà Trưng) and the University of Science [91 G7] (east end of Lê Thánh Tông). Of the buildings listed here, only the university, built in a similar Indochinese style to the National Museum of History, is open to the public, albeit rarely; it houses a small biology museum.

Chùa Quán Sứ Pagoda [91 D6] (73 Quán Sứ; f) This impressive Buddhist complex, extensively restored in 1996–98, was originally built to accommodate Buddhists from Cambodia, Laos and Champa, hence its English name, Ambassadors' Pagoda. Its Vietnamese name came from the prestigious title Quán Sứ, which was bestowed on a remarkable monk who cured Emperor Lý Thánh Tông of a terrible disease. The pagoda was the only one left standing after the Lê Dynasty fell into decline. The 15th-century structure decayed and work on a new one, which is a replica of the original, began when the Chùa Quán Sứ was adopted as the national centre of the Northern Vietnam Buddhist Association in 1934. It was completed by 1942 and is now the most important centre of Buddhist teaching in the north. Before you enter cross to the other side of Quán Sứ Street to get a better look at its ornate architecture. Lunar discs, the divine symbol of the emperor, decorate the three-tiered roof, which is topped by three nine-tiered miniature stupas. The centrepiece of the central altar inside the pagoda is a representation of Shakyamuni (Buddha) at birth, protected by nine dragons. He is dwarfed by gleaming figures of the Buddhas of the Past, Present and the Future.

Hỏa Lò Prison [91 D6] (1 Hỏa Lò; w hoalo.vn; 50,000VND; 2hrs) Much of the infamous Hỏa Lò Prison (Maison Centrale) has been destroyed by jackhammers, but enough remains to house a compelling museum with an engaging audio guide (100,000VND). Built in 1896 and originally used by the French to imprison freedom fighters and activists, the exhibits are not for the faint-hearted. Torture techniques are described in vivid detail, and there's a gruesome French guillotine. In the small outside section close to a revered almond tree are sewer tunnels used by escapees. After the French defeat, Hỏa Lò was used to imprison American prisoners of war in the 1960s and 70s, when it was nicknamed the 'Hanoi Hilton'. The late American senator John McCain was held here. The prison has recently started doing weekend night tours; check the website for details.

✷ ***Vietnamese Women's Museum*** [91 E6] (36 Lý Thường Kiệt; w baotangphunu.org.vn; 40,000/10,000VND adult/child; 2hrs) This is one of Hanoi's standout museums, covering the history, fashions, vocations and marriage customs of Vietnamese women across various ethnolinguistic groups. There's a moving section on the female contribution to the war effort, including a fabulous spread of propaganda posters. The museum has a particularly active management board with links to academics and other museums across the world, evidenced by the ambitious temporary exhibition schedule; check the website for details.

Vietnam–Soviet Friendship Palace [91 C7] (91 Trần Hưng Đạo; w cungvanhoalaodonghuunghivietxo.vn) The Soviet Union bestowed this gigantic chunk of architecture upon the Vietnam Trade Union. Construction of the people's palace began in 1978 and it was officially inaugurated and commenced operations in 1985. The compound encompasses an area of 3.2ha; the main building, standing at 96m in length, 60m in width and 33m in height, spans four storeys. Adjacent to the main building is a three-storey structure, connected by a flat-roofed house with a terrace. Today the palace hosts a wide range of events, including performances, conferences, seminars, exhibitions and club activities. Though many events are technically available to the wider public, the website isn't in English and there's no booking system.

Ga Hà Nội [91 B6] (120 Lê Duẩn) Technically in Đống Đa District (page 118), Hanoi's train station (the Vietnamese word *ga* comes from the French *gare*) was built in 1902, though the dominant feature of the current structure looks decidedly modernist. During the American War, bombs ripped through much of this part of the city, causing the central hall of the train station to collapse. It was rebuilt after reunification in 1975 with a perforated façade to allow the building to catch the breeze, but it remains flanked by two stately colonial-era wings.

BA ĐÌNH DISTRICT Ba Đình District looms large in historical significance as well as visitor appeal. The eastern section holds many of Hanoi's big sights, including the Imperial Citadel and the Hồ Chí Minh Mausoleum. This is one of the oldest parts of the city, with archaeological evidence suggesting that there were palaces here as early as the 7th century CE, when modern day Northern Vietnam was under Chinese rule. Ba Đình District is also home to the Trúc Bạch neighbourhood, one of Hanoi's most appealing areas, with cafés, bars and restaurants. As you move west within the district to newer precincts, areas of interest become fewer as the heritage buildings melt away, though there are some worthwhile lakes, including Giảng Võ, Thủ Lệ, Ngọc Khánh and B-52, which holds the remains of a downed American bomber.

✷ **Hồ Chí Minh Mausoleum Complex** (Hùng Vương) Over the years the area surrounding the Hồ Chí Minh Mausoleum has expanded to become one large compound, with a number of sites of interest. There are two entrance points, both on Hùng Vương Street: one near the Presidential Palace and another where the street intersects Lê Hồng Phong Street. It's free to enter the complex (though some sites within it have entrance fees) and note that there is a security and dress code check. Out of respect for Uncle Hồ, you'll be refused entry if showing midriffs, shoulders or knees.

Hồ Chí Minh's Mausoleum [91 A7] Despite his desire for a humble cremation, Hồ Chí Minh's Mausoleum was inaugurated in Ba Đình Square on 2 September

1975, near where he proclaimed the Independence of Vietnam in 1945 after 80 years of colonial domination. The mausoleum operates changeable opening times and is regularly closed for large chunks of the year, so check the current situation with your hotel. Visitors must wait patiently in a line that sometimes stretches for kilometres; they must also be smartly attired and without camera or bag (there are storage lockers). As you enter you are required to be quiet and swiftly follow a route around Hồ Chí Minh's embalmed body and coffin.

Ba Đình Square [90 A2–3] This park is a delightful place for a stroll, but a regrettable lack of shade means it can only be comfortably explored in the evenings or during the cooler winter months. Opposite the mausoleum is the Vietnam National Assembly Building, completed in 2014 to reflect Hồ Chí Minh's final resting place and presumably to connect today's government with modern Vietnam's founding father. South of the assembly building is the Ministry of Foreign Affairs, one of Hanoi's more graceful colonial buildings that blends Western and Eastern styles. The same can't be said for the sunshine-yellow **Presidential Palace** [91 A6], a garish mansion on the northwest corner of the square that was completed in 1906 for the Governor of Indochina. This is where US president Donald Trump met North Korea's Kim Jong-un for a well-publicised summit in 2019.

Hồ Chí Minh's Stilt House [91 A7] (19 Ngọc Hà; 40,000VND) Hồ Chí Minh lived here from 1958 until his death in 1969 after refusing (understandably) to move into the Presidential Palace nearby. It is believed that he died peacefully at home, and everything remains as he left it. He received high-ranking cadres on the ground floor and his bedchambers were above on the raised floor. At the time of research it wasn't possible to enter the house, but the entrance fee allows access to the grounds.

One Pillar Pagoda [91 A7] (Chùa Một Cột) Emperor Lý Thái Tông, son of the founder of Hanoi, had the One Pillar Pagoda built in 1049 because he had a dream in which he saw Quan Âm (or Guanyin in English), the Guardian Spirit of Mother and Child, sitting on a lotus leaf holding a child. The childless emperor saw this as a good omen and, sure enough, after the pagoda was completed, his queen gave birth to a son. You will see a statue of Quan Âm on its altar. Externally, the small building, which is perched on a stone pillar, evokes the form of a lotus, symbol of purity. During the summer lotus blossoms cover the surface of the surrounding pond. The pagoda has been restored several times, in 1105, 1922 and finally in 1955 after being burned by the departing French in 1954. Before you leave, take a look at the dragons on the roof. Between them is a central disc that represents the sun, the symbol of the emperor. Also note the nearby bodhi tree, a gift from the Indian government in 1958.

Hồ Chí Minh Museum [91 A7] (19 Ngọc Hà; **w** baotanghochiminh.vn; 30,000VND; 2hrs) Inaugurated on 19 May 1990 on the 100th anniversary of Hồ Chí Minh's birth, this five-storey building contains displays, photographs and other artefacts relating to his life, as well as his last will and testament. Items on show include his typewriter, a chest of drawers brought from France, a Chinese costume he wore when he fled to Hong Kong, exercise dumbbells, photographs of his exploits and various documents.

Hanoi Botanical Garden [98 C5] (Vườn Bách Thảo; 3 Hoàng Hoa Thám) A short walk from Trúc Bạch Lake behind the Hồ Chí Minh Mausoleum and

Presidential Palace is one of Hanoi's best-kept secrets, the lovely Vườn Bách Thảo, known in English as the city's botanical garden. Here, centuries-old trees provide shade for courting couples among the luscious greenery, which seems somewhat divorced from the lively neighbourhoods nearby. The French landscaped this green patch in 1890, and it became a public park after they left. In the late afternoon and evening, you can watch gymnastic badminton players.

✷ Thăng Long Imperial Citadel [90 B3] (**w** hoangthanhthanglong.com; various entrance fees; 2–3hrs) Constructed by the Lý Dynasty in the 11th century, the extraordinary Thăng Long Imperial Citadel stands on the remnants of a 7th-century Chinese fortress built on reclaimed land from the Red River Delta. Perhaps more than any other structure in Vietnam, the Imperial Citadel is emblematic of Vietnamese independence after it threw off the yoke of 1,000 years of Chinese rule. Archaeological discoveries on the site speak to a unique Southeast Asian culture, known then as Đại Việt, influenced by both China to the north and the Kingdom of Champa to the south. The following is a walking tour of the citadel from north to south that takes a full afternoon or morning. Note that the citadel, which was originally square but is now a distorted rectangle, has two distinct sections with two different entrances, plus the archaeological site at 18 Hoàng Diệu Street. The management authority has recently launched guided night tours that include the northern section of the citadel and the archaeological site at 18 Hoàng Diệu. The tour includes various performances and it's possible to pay extra for an English-speaking guide. At the time of research this tour was in its infancy and only running on Fridays and Saturdays; check the website for up-to-date details.

If on your own, start with the northern section (30,000VND) and enter at 19C Hoàng Diệu Street, on the east side of the road, near the Bắc Sơn Monument. Near the entrance is an air-conditioned hall for temporary exhibitions of varying quality; even if the exhibits aren't particularly compelling, you might use this as an opportunity to cool down before walking around the sun-blasted citadel.

South gate Head north from the entrance to the south gate, also known as the main gate, a grand structure built by the Lê kings, though the elaborate roof was added during the Nguyễn Dynasty. This was one of the entrances to the forbidden city, a space reserved only for royals and their advisers, and the central gate was used only by the king. All the dynasties left their mark on this citadel, brilliantly depicted by the 1999 excavations that sit under a glass roof just inside the south gate. Look down and see pathways built by the Lý, Trần and Lê dynasties. The feudal Vietnamese had the habit of building on top of what came before: the more sunken the stonework, the more ancient it is. After passing through the south gate and veering to the right you'll find a small air-conditioned hall, with the artefacts inside arranged by era. Look out for the dragons and phoenixes, which change according to the dynasty, and an exquisite Lê Dynasty bowl that depicts dragons only when illuminated.

Kính Thiên Palace and Hậu Lâu Pagoda Once the setting for the citadel's grand ceremonies, Kính Thiên Palace, north of the south gate, occupies the central position within the site, its stone dragon steps and foundation remaining as the sole remnants of the palace. Constructed by the Lê kings, this palace held religious festivals until it was destroyed by the French. The remains sit behind blockish French administrative buildings. North of here is the Hậu Lâu, or Princess Pagoda, which may have housed imperial concubines.

General Command Headquarters Bunker Also occupying this central position of the citadel, a little south of the Kính Thiên Palace, is the General Command Headquarters Bunker, the headquarters of North Vietnam's Ministry of Defence during the American War. Also known as the D67 Revolutionary House, here you'll find the office of General Võ Nguyên Giáp, credited for the victory over the French at Điện Biên Phủ, and a basement bunker with antique war equipment and maps within glass cabinets.

North gate The imposing north gate, which overlooks Phan Đình Phùng and Đặng Dung streets, dates back to the dynastic period, though there's been significant restorations and modifications over the centuries. Known as Đoan Môn in Vietnamese, you'll find it at the northern edge of the citadel, with a two-storey watchtower offering commanding views of the complex. Then retrace your steps and exit via the west gate, close to the Kính Thiên Palace remains.

18 Hoàng Diệu Street (18 Hoàng Diệu; 30,000VND/free adult/child) Cross the street to find the archaeological site, which has excavated pillars, wells, tiles and pottery, some of which predate the citadel. These were discovered in the early 2000s when the foundations were being laid for the Vietnam National Assembly Building west of the site. It's difficult to decipher which remains can be attributed to which dynasty, despite efforts from several information plaques. Particular points of interest are a small saline lake which may have been used to keep saltwater fish and a small wooden boat that has been left in situ underground to aid its preservation.

Hanoi Flag Tower (28A Điện Biên Phủ; 20,000VND) The southern segment of the Imperial Citadel used to be dominated by the Vietnam Military History Museum, which has moved to the west of the city (page 120), but it still holds the climbable Cột Cờ Hà Nội, the Hanoi Flag Tower, built in the early 19th century. The octagonal tower is 33m high, has 54 steps and 36 flower-shaped holes for ventilation and lighting. From the vantage point atop the Hanoi Flag Tower you can peer down at Lenin Park, named after a foreign hero who never set foot in Vietnam. The park comes alive at night with teenagers doing tricks on skateboards and toddlers driving miniature Jeeps. The bucolic streets that frame the Imperial Citadel – Hoàng Diệu, Nguyễn Tri Phương, Điện Biên Phủ and Phan Đình Phùng – are some of Hanoi's loveliest.

Vietnam National Fine Arts Museum [91 A5] (66 Nguyễn Thái Học; **w** vnfam.vn; 40,000VND; 1–2hrs) Constructed during the French colonial period, the building that now houses the Vietnam National Fine Arts Museum was once a boarding school for the daughters of French officials, but has been altered considerably over the years. In 1962, the government tasked the Ministry of Culture with transforming the building into a repository for Vietnam's invaluable artistic treasures and the building was adapted to be an art museum. Displays of ancient culture include bronze drums, bronze statues and stone ornaments. Visitors to the museum will also notice the influence of both Chinese and Cham art. There are many works depicting Tết religious scenes, fine landscapes and portraits. While many of the 2,000 or so pieces in the permanent galleries are breathtaking, there's limited information about their contextual significance. An audio guide (50,000VND) helps and is worth the money, but it's far from comprehensive.

The first two galleries exhibit art from the 11th to the 17th centuries. A highlight here is a 16th-century Quan Âm (Guanyin) statue originating from Vinh Phuc, just outside of Hanoi, sprouting a riot of arms. She sits next to a smaller Quan Âm, also from the 16th century, with almost as many arms. Another highlight in the same gallery is the Keo Pagoda doors from the 17th century, with animals hidden among artistic foliage. If you're travelling with kids in tow, see how many creatures they can spot. The collection from the 20th century is more extensive. A highlight from the pre-1945 gallery is a modernist bust from 1931 of an unnamed Vietnamese man in ceremonial mitre by Vũ Cao Đàm. Nearby is a standing screen from 1939 showing exquisite eggshell lacquerwork by Nguyễn Gia Trí. In the post-1945 galleries, subjects shift their focus to heroic scenes of war. There's a noticeable propagandist orientation in the curation, but it doesn't detract from the beauty and skill of the works. From here the galleries are divided by medium: oil, silk, graphic arts and so on. The giftshop is excellent, and there's also a well-curated contemporary art gallery if you have the energy. Sophie's Art Tour (w sophiesarttour.com) used to offer superb Hanoi art tours that included the museum, but they weren't operating when we went to print.

✷ **Trúc Bạch Lake and around** [98 D4] (Hồ Trúc Bạch) Directly opposite the southeastern end of West Lake (page 121) is Trúc Bạch Lake, which is worthy of a leisurely afternoon. Sequestered from West Lake in the 17th century, the Trúc Bạch neighbourhood feels very different from its neighbour, especially on the Ngũ Xã Islet [98 D2], once the epicentre of Hanoi's bronze-making craft. The islet, traffic-free on weekends, is packed with cafés, restaurants, boutiques and art galleries. Encircling the lake are many important sights, including Quán Thánh Temple, Trấn Quốc Pagoda and Thủy Trung Tiên Temple, a rebuilt refuge that perches on a small islet. Trấn Quốc Pagoda and Thủy Trung Tiên Temple sit on either side of Thanh Niên Street, created around 1958 and now one of the city's main arteries along which a teeming mass of humanity surges into the city every morning. The leafy street is attractive and lively, especially on a clear day at sunset. Look out for the John McCain Monument on the southeast side of the road. During the American War, McCain parachuted into Trúc Bạch Lake before being pulled from the water, beaten and imprisoned. He went on to become an American senator, presidential candidate and a fierce Republican critic of Donald Trump.

For a small fee you can rent pedalboats in the shape of swans on the southeast corner of the lake, near Highlands Coffee, and drift around the placid waters.

✷ ***Quán Thánh Temple*** [98 D5] (Thanh Niên; 10,000VND) This attractive sanctuary was first built in the 11th century, although not much remains of its original Lý Dynasty design because of extensive renovations carried out in the 18th and 19th centuries. It houses a towering black bronze statue of Trấn Vũ, a Taoist god, who is bearded, seated and shoeless. Take a look at the red boots in the glass cabinet near the entrance; these were playfully gifted to the god by the Nguyễn Dynasty king Thành Thái. There's also a replica of the bronze bell that baited the mythical golden calf that created West Lake (page 121). Quán Thánh Temple is one of four guardian temples that protected Thăng Long from malicious spiritual forces; the other three are Bạch Mã Temple (page 108) in the Old Quarter, Kim Liên Temple (page 120) in the south of the city and Voi Phục Temple (see opposite) in the west.

✷ ***Trấn Quốc Pagoda*** [98 D4] (46 Thanh Niên) Standing on an islet in West Lake and technically in Tây Hồ District (page 121), this pagoda is the oldest and most dramatically situated in the city. It was constructed 1,400 years ago during a fleeting period of Vietnamese independence in a millennium that was otherwise characterised by Chinese domination. It was moved to this site in the 17th century when floodwater began to eat away at its foundations. The best time to visit is on a clear afternoon to watch the sunset. During festivals like Tết the pagoda erupts in colour as the caretakers decorate the prayer rooms with flowers and trinkets. The pagoda contains a stele with an inscription recording its history, believed to have been written in 1639.

B-52 Lake [map, page 81] (Hồ B-52; Hồ Hữu Tiệp) The rarely visited but completely captivating B-52 Lake derives its name from the remnants of a downed B-52 American bomber that plunged into the lake. The Christmas Bombing, officially known as Operation Linebacker II, was an ineffectual strategic bombing campaign carried out by American forces in December 1972. This intensive operation aimed to pressure North Vietnamese leaders to sign a temporary peace agreement by destroying military targets in Hanoi and Hải Phòng. Despite efforts to evacuate some 500,000 civilians from these cities, over 1,000 civilian lives were lost and the international community condemned the casualties. In defence, North Vietnamese forces launched over 1,200 missiles and downed 15 B-52 bombers. On 27 December 1972, one of them crashed into Hữu Tiệp Lake (the lake's official name) in the Ngọc Hà neighbourhood. While much of the aircraft has burned and eroded away, you can still spot fragments of the rear landing gear and undercarriage eerily rising from the water. A nearby plaque describes the fateful event in Vietnamese and English. Ngọc Hà is now a pleasant, pond-filled neighbourhood with a handful of basic *trà đá* (iced tea) and beer bars that offer views of the wreck. On the neighbourhood's southern edge sits the B-52 Victory Museum, with poor signage but impressive aircraft debris in the front garden.

Voi Phục Temple [map, page 81] (306B Kim Mã) One of four guardian temples (the other three are Bạch Mã Temple, page 108; Kim Liên Temple, page 120; and Quán Thánh Temple, see opposite), Voi Phục sits nestled in Thủ Lệ Park, shaded by trees and topped by a roof that adheres to the traditional style of ancient religious buildings, with corners that gracefully curve upwards. Among the carvings of various mythical creatures is a shrine dedicated to Prince Hoàng Chân, the warrior son of King Lý Thái Tông, who died defending the country in the 11th century. After his death, the king built Voi (Elephant) Phục Temple, naming the spiritual refuge after the stone pachyderms at the entrance.

HAI BÀ TRƯNG DISTRICT An unsung and underexplored but also beautiful section of Hanoi, the northern half of Hai Bà Trưng District (north of Đại Cồ Việt Street) is a somewhat messier extension of Hoàn Kiếm District's French Quarter and shares its destructive origin story (page 103). South of Đại Cồ Việt Street, the grid system gives way to a tangle of small streets interrupted by Bách Khoa University and the National Economics University. This is one of several student enclaves in Hanoi.

Unification Park [map, page 81] (Công Viên Thống Nhất) Directly south of Thiền Quang Lake is one of Hanoi's best parks, with Bảy Mẫu Lake at its heart. Kid-friendly attractions include a house of mirrors, a train that skirts the lake and a few basic fairground rides. For adults, there's an outdoor gym, running track and weekend markets such as book fairs and food festivals. A highlight of the park is on a small island on Bảy Mẫu Lake, where a statue of a sandal-wearing Hồ Chí Minh, modern Vietnam's first president, warmly clasps the hands of Tôn Đức Thắng, the country's second, perhaps representing presidential and revolutionary continuity. The base of the statue reads Bác Hồ – Bác Tôn (Uncle Hồ – Uncle Tôn).

Hai Bà Trưng Temple [map, page 81] (Hương Viên) The Trưng sisters are two national heroines who led an uprising against Chinese oppression some 2,000 years ago and briefly ruled Vietnam. The older sister, Trưng Trắc, may have been the first woman Vietnamese monarch, though her reign only lasted a few fleeting years. Founded in 1142, Hanoi's Hai Bà Trưng Temple, one of many across the country, sits on the west side of an oval lake opposite a nursery and a high school. The lake takes on a lively atmosphere in the afternoons when highschoolers natter over bubble tea in streetside cafés.

ĐỐNG ĐA AND CẦU GIẤY DISTRICTS Were it not for the Temple of Literature, few visitors would make it to Đống Đa, named after the Battle of Đống Đa, which took place here in 1789 during the Tây Sơn Rebellion. The rebellion was led by revered national hero Quang Trung against an immense force of more than 200,000 Chinese Qing invaders. The battle is celebrated for Quang Trung's remarkable speed, mobilising a large contingent of soldiers who journeyed on foot from the south, as well as his ploy to disguise his troops as Qing soldiers and attack while the enemy was intoxicated during the Lunar New Year celebrations. Today, Đống Đa is a hurried, densely populated district. While the main thoroughfares are thronged with traffic, the various lakes are tranquil refuges, with cafés, restaurants and beer bars reflecting ordinary Hanoi life. Particularly pleasant lakes include Xã Đàn, Văn Chương, Ba Mẫu and Đống Đa [all on map, page 81]. Cầu Giấy District, west of Đống Đa District, is best known from a visitor's perspective for what is arguably the country's best museum: the Vietnam Museum of Ethnology.

✷ **Temple of Literature** [91 A5] (Văn Miếu; 58 Quốc Tử Giám; **w** vanmieu.gov.vn; 30,000VND; 1–2hrs) As well as containing special temple sanctuaries for the worship of Confucius and his disciples, this important complex – the image on the 100,000VND note and on Hanoi's street signs – also houses the site of the original School for the Sons of the State (Quốc Tử Giám) which later became known as the National Academy. The French called it Pagoda des Corbeaux (Pagoda of Crows) because of the huge flocks of these birds which gathered in the mango trees near its entrance. It was extensively restored in 1993–94 and has been touched up several times since. The Văn Miếu was built in 1070 and is dedicated to the philosophy of Confucius and his loyal students. It covers just over 3ha, stretches for 350m and is 75m wide at its widest point. It is divided into five main parts by longitudinal walls through which visitors can stroll via elegant gates. As always, the app-based audio guide (bring your own earphones) is highly recommended.

The first, second and third courtyards Enter the site from the Gate of the Temple of Literature (Văn Miếu Môn), which faces south. A terracotta-tiled path runs under the Gate of the Great Middle towards another topped by an impressive wooden pavilion (Khuê Văn Các) that leads to the third courtyard. This decorative structure has an elegant two-floor roof and is one of the symbols of Hanoi. Translated, this gate means Constellation of Literature, and was built in 1805 at the beginning of the Nguyễn Dynasty. Beyond is the Well of Heavenly Brilliance (Giếng Thiên Quang) also called the Heavenly Glory Pond, on either side of which are 82 stone stelae supported by turtle pedestals. The stelae, now protected by roofed pavilions, record the names of successful candidates in the triennial examinations held during the Lê Dynasty (1498–1787).

The fourth courtyard The dragon-adorned Great Success Gate (Đại Thánh) leads into the large fourth courtyard, either side of which are two buildings that were dedicated to the loyal disciples of Confucius. Mandarins and dignitaries of the king would come here to pay respect to these eminent scholars. Both wings were damaged by the French in 1946 but were subsequently restored in 1954 and 1994. These days, the air-conditioned building to the right displays a useful timeline detailing the temple's almost 1,000 years of history. Two dragons flanking a lunar disc adorn the roof of the Great Hall of Ceremonies (Bái Đường), consecrated to Confucius. A lacquered plaque hanging over the central bay bears the words '*vạn thế sư biểu*', which means 'a teacher for all the ages', or more poetically 'master of the universe'. The words are a tribute to the world's greatest teachers. The great bronze bell in this sanctuary to the right as you enter dates from 1768. The High Sanctuary, situated directly north of the Great Hall of Ceremonies, has a similar architectural design. The altar in the centre is dedicated to Confucius and flanked by his four most important disciples. Behind them are ten stelae (five on each side) representing the ten sages. The final enclosure contains the National Academy (Quốc Tử Giám). Reach it by backtracking and moving around to the left or right.

The fifth courtyard The grand finale in the fifth and final courtyard is the Quốc Tử Giám, an impressive structure and an important seat of learning, which was obliterated by French bombs and subsequently reconstructed. It served to educate the sons of the emperor and of court dignitaries in the teachings of Confucius, which had become a kind of state religion. The first commoners to have the privilege of being taught by state professors and lecturers were admitted after the lord Lê Lợi became emperor in 1428. As well as poetry, history and rhythmical prose, the academy attempted to mould its scholars into human beings who showed dignity, integrity and moral principles. It relied on great classical works such as Confucius's *Luận Ngữ* and Mencius's *Mạnh Tử*. The back room holds a shrine to Chu Văn An, a prominent 14th-century principal of the university, and it is often crowded by dozens of praying students hoping for good grades. This is the only building in the compound that you climb. The upper floor holds three shrines to the three kings who contributed most to the Temple of Literature: Lý Thánh Tông (1023–72) oversaw the temple's construction; Lý Nhân Tông (1066–1128) expanded Confucianist worship in Vietnam; and Lê Thánh Tông (1442–97) enlarged the temple. The peasant insurrections that swept the country in the latter part of the 18th century saw the academy decline. Educational standards fell despite the efforts of King Quang Trung. When Gia Long became the new emperor in 1802, he ordered that the capital, along with the academy, be transferred to Huế, where a new academy was formed in 1807 on the banks of the Perfume River.

Đống Đa Mound [map, page 81] (276 Đặng Tiến Đông) This small park commemorates the battle that took place here over two centuries ago and gives Đống Đa District its name. There's a large statue of Quang Trung (otherwise known as Nguyễn Huệ), the victor, and a small temple. Legend has it that the corpses of the defeated were buried here. A huge festival commemorating the victory engulfs the mound on the fifth day of the first lunar month (usually January or February) each year.

✷ **Museum of Ethnology** [map, page 81] (Nguyễn Văn Huyên; **w** vme.org.vn; 40,000VND; 2–4hrs) This museum is located in Cầu Giấy District outside of Ba Đình in the western part of the city. It is one of Vietnam's premier cultural institutions. Focused on the nation's 54 officially recognised ethnic groups across five linguistic families (Austronesian, Tai-Kadai, Hmong-Yao, Sino-Tibetan and Austro-Asiatic), the museum boasts an extensive collection of artefacts. Its interior, thoughtfully arranged across two floors and categorised by ethnolinguistic group, helps visitors grasp this complex ethnic mosaic. The exhibits showcasing women's clothing, funeral customs and weddings are of particular interest.

While one could spend hours inside the museum, the Architectural Garden is perhaps even more extraordinary. Ethnolinguistic groups from across Vietnam constructed houses within it, reflecting architecture from the Bahnar, Cham, Cotu, Ede, Giarai, Hani, Hmong, Tay and Viet (ie: the ethnic majority) peoples. Displays throughout the museum are prominently labelled in Vietnamese, French and English. The museum also offers intimate water puppet shows, but at the time of research this was only at the weekends. Confirm the show times on the website or, failing that, as soon as you arrive. It's also possible to book tours on the website. Visiting the Museum of Ethnology is essential if visiting the country's more ethnically diverse corners, such as the northern mountains and Central Highlands.

✷ **Vietnam Military History Museum** [map, page 81] (Nam Từ Liêm, west of the centre; **w** baotanglichsuquansu.vn; 40,000VND; 3–4hrs) From humble beginnings crammed into a squat building within the Imperial Citadel (page 114), the Military History Museum moved to the western suburbs in late 2024 and has enjoyed a major upgrade. First impressions are of a gargantuan grey monolith with slanting columns fronted by sprightly fountains and saplings. The collection of antique war detritus in the huge front courtyard is intelligently (at least from a propagandistic point of view) arranged into two sections: the oversized weaponry of invaders on one side and the much humbler Vietnamese armoury on the other. The American planes, tanks and helicopters may be the biggest and most impressive, but don't miss the spindly Japanese-made sơn pháo 75mm, which would have been hauled up mountains to flush out the French during the battle at Điện Biên Phủ (page 144).

Once in the grand reception hall, look up at the years carved into the stone, which mark the major battles of Vietnamese resistance. This serves as a roadmap to the museum, which is essentially a museum of Vietnamese history but told through military episodes. The 5-minute video in the next hall is highly worth watching, as a reincarnated geometric bird from a Đông Sơn drum (page 8) flies from its rotund nest to soar over Vietnam's heroes throughout the centuries. From this central hall, various larger halls organised by era fan out in a semi-circle: the founding of Vietnam, 1,000 years of Chinese domination, the dynastic period, the French colonial period, the American War and 1975 until the present. The museum is well organised and easy to navigate, and various military vignettes are creatively told using animations, model exhibits, videos and more traditional signs, most written in good English.

Kim Liên Temple and Communal House [map, page 81] (148 Kim Hoa) Kim Liên serves as the protective bastion in the south; the three others are Bạch Mã Temple (page 108), Voi Phục Temple (page 117) and Quán Thánh Temple (page 116). The temple venerates the god Cao Sơn (High Mountain), one of Lạc Long Quân and Âu Cơ's 100 children (page 10), who later aided Sơn Tinh in overthrowing Thuỷ Tinh, which put an end to the catastrophic floods that were ravaging the nation (page 127). The temple was constructed between the 16th and 17th centuries, and over time, the village of Kim Liên transformed the temple into a communal house, which is why in Vietnamese it's now called Đình (communal house) Kim Liên and not Đền (temple) Kim Liên. Be careful not to confuse this sight with Chùa Kim Liên (Kim Liên Pagoda) in Tây Hồ District.

TÂY HỒ DISTRICT [map, page 98] Informed Hanoians might tell you that their city is embraced by more than 18 lakes, with a surface area totalling over 2,200ha. Indeed, it is impossible to drive anywhere without coming across water. Many are surrounded by tamarind and flame trees and for centuries have provided Hanoians with recreational spots where they enjoy early-morning jogging and badminton and practise tai chi. This spectacle, where even great-grandmothers and great-grandfathers show off their skill with a shuttlecock, gives the city the unique countryside charm that no amount of development will ever destroy. Tây Hồ District, in the northern part of the city, is dominated by West Lake (Hồ Tây), by far the biggest lake in the city, and while development hasn't eradicated the lake's appeal, it has certainly changed it. During the 19th century, Emperor Tự Đức would come to spot arctic herons and Eurasian coots, which have disappeared from the waters. Many ancient precincts were also located in the district, including the flower gardens of Ngọc Hà and Nhật Tân and the incense-making village of Yên Phụ, but the agricultural and artisanal trade has vanished. Today, Tây Hồ District is a leafy, somewhat modern place and, despite ongoing infrastructure projects, remains a desirable place to live.

West Lake (Hồ Tây) West Lake has been the focus of Hanoi's urban development for decades. Here, sumptuous villas and luxury multi-storey apartment buildings compete for space. In a sense this parallels history: a millennium ago the lake was surrounded by ornate pavilions and palaces. Despite the excessive, rapid development, West Lake retains a certain tranquillity, especially on the peninsulas

LEGEND HAS IT: THE CALF AND THE FOX

According to legend, West Lake was created in one of two ways. One myth tells that the chimes of a monk's bronze bell sent a mythical golden calf from the north into a trance. The creature abandoned its mother in search of the source of the sound, but when it reached the area where West Lake now sits, the chimes stopped. Lost and bewildered, the calf walked around in circles and carved out a basin. Water flowed in from the Red River, creating the lake and trapping the doomed calf, which still roams West Lake's murky depths. Another myth claims that a nine-tailed vixen, a common fantastical villain in East Asian folklore, was causing trouble so the Taoist god Trấn Vũ descended from heaven and smote her. The fox's lifeless body had such potency that its grave swelled to the size of a giant crater, which eventually filled with water from the Red River to create West Lake. There's more truth to these stories than one might expect. West Lake was almost certainly created by diverting water from the Red River, and even today it's associated with animal carcasses. Tonnes of dead periodically emerge in West Lake, most recently in 2016, 2018 and 2022. Until the authorities implement a co-ordinated set of long-term solutions to clean the water, this seasonal die-off is likely to persist.

of Từ Hoa, Quảng An and Yên Phụ. The lake remains a firm favourite with the people of Hanoi, who flock here in their thousands on Saturday and Sunday afternoons to slurp coconuts and *nước mía* (sugarcane juice). As with many places in Vietnam, it has interesting (and conflicting) origin stories (page 121).

Phủ Tây Hồ Temple [98 B3] (52 Đặng Thai Mai St) Unfortunately for nearby residents, who bemoan the impassable traffic that swarms around Phủ Tây Hồ during Tết, this is one of Hanoi's favourite places of worship. Outside these chaotic few weeks, Phủ Tây Hồ, which may have been built in the 17th century (accounts differ) and is dedicated to the Mother Goddess, is a calm place that retains an almost rural serenity. Outside the temple is a cluster of *bánh tôm* (page 95) restaurants, a West Lake speciality.

AROUND HANOI

There is easily a fortnight's worth of half- and full-day trips from Hanoi, so those with limited time to explore will need to choose carefully. For years the **Perfume Pagoda** (Chùa Hương) was a popular day trip from Hanoi, and while the river journey to these cave shrines is pretty and the pagoda itself is impressive, the experience has garnered a reputation for overcharging and overcommercialisation, and for now is not recommended. Taking its place are Hạ Long Bay (page 189) and Ninh Bình Province (page 213), now within easy reach from the capital thanks to a vastly improved highway network. But these are both destinations in their own right and will be covered elsewhere in this guide. It isn't possible to list every day trip from Hanoi so what follows is a diverse list of some of the more compelling options, including ancient villages, national parks and religious complexes.

HỒ CHÍ MINH TRAIL MUSEUM (30,000VND; 1–2hrs) A little less than an hour southwest of central Hanoi, the Hồ Chí Minh Trail Museum is easy to tack on to day-trip itineraries that include more far-flung sites, such as Thầy Pagoda, Tây Phương Pagoda or Đậu Pagoda. The museum recounts the story of the so-called Hồ Chí Minh Trail, a convoluted network of trails used to supply the Việt Cộng in the South with weaponry from the North from 1959 to 1975. Despite intense American bombardment, the trail operated continuously throughout the war. The stylish museum building has a sweeping, flowing façade, but the exhibits inside are notably less fluid. The rooms are divided into time periods, or 'campaigns', which offer a lot of detail (including in English) but it can be hard to piece the story of their inception together. The museum does excel at depicting an idealised image of what life was like on the trail. As is often the case in museums like these, the photography steals the show. Behind the museum is a memorial to those lost while serving on the trail, and behind this is an easy-to-miss reconstruction of a tunnel. Also housed in the garden, to the right of the entrance, is some hulking machinery used on the trail.

ĐẬU PAGODA (Chùa Đậu) This unusual pagoda is famous for its lacquer mummies, apparently former Buddhist monks who locked themselves in a room to meditate for 100 days in the 17th century. On the 101st day, disciples entered the room and found that the two monks had passed away, though they were perfectly preserved and still sat in a lotus pose. The transformation was deemed divine, and the two bodies were lacquered and altars built in their honour. Today they sit in decorated glass cabinets. Take care not to confuse this rarely visited pagoda with the larger Chùa Dâu in Bắc Ninh Province.

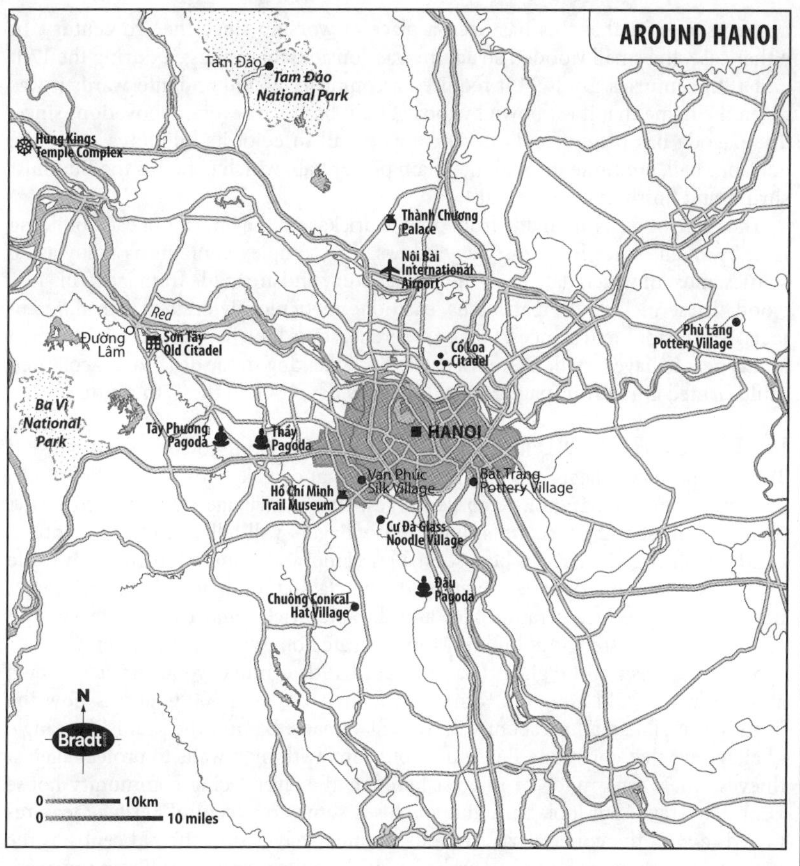

THẦY PAGODA (Chùa Thầy; small entrance fee) Thầy Pagoda is at the foot of Sài Sơn, a karst mountain 10km from Tây Phương Pagoda (see below). The latter half of the journey from Hanoi passes many rice fields surrounded by small karstic peaks and is picturesque if you can look past the factories and warehouses. The original sanctuary dates from the reign of Emperor Lý Nhân Tông (1072–1128) when it was little more than a simple thatched hut belonging to Từ Đạo Hạnh, the pagoda's founder. As you approach you will see the water pavilion, dedicated to the guardian spirit of water puppeteers. In the entrance hall, large guardian figures made out of Red River clay are said to weigh over 1,000kg each. The pagoda is dedicated to Từ Đạo Hạnh in his various reincarnations as monk, king and Buddha. The sprawling complex, which includes a cave, is rather confusing, but there are usually guides milling around at the foot of the pagoda, some of whom speak basic English. If you haven't come on an organised tour, consider employing one of these guides, but agree the price beforehand and factor in a tip at the end. The guides may not have much reliable or understandable information, but they can at least show you parts of the pagoda that you might have otherwise missed.

TÂY PHƯƠNG PAGODA (Chùa Tây Phương; small entrance fee) Also called the 'Pagoda of the West', Tây Phương Pagoda is set on top of a karstic outcrop 10km from Chùa Thầy. An 8th-century temple originally stood on this site, though some accounts suggest that this has been a place of worship since the 3rd century. In either case, the small wooden structure was considerably enlarged during the 17th and 18th centuries. By 1794 it required a complete rebuild and afterwards it was given the name that it is known by today and it has seen several renovations since. The pagoda has magnificent curved roofs on all three of its buildings. After the entrance hall, continue through the main prayer hall, which contains the Buddhist shrine, and finish in the rear hall.

The exterior walls are made from orange bricks and the interior of each building is lit by small lattice lunette-style windows. The complex contains as many as 70 statues, most of which date from the 18th century and are made from jackfruit-tree wood. These include the patriarchs, each one meticulously crafted with different facial expressions and stances. Some are serene, some look happy; a few are worried and appear to have fasted. There is a particularly striking statue of a bronze-coloured multi-armed Quan Âm (page 293), which may date back to the 17th century.

BÁT TRÀNG POTTERY VILLAGE Of the few villages seeking to attract tourists, Bát Tràng, a pottery village, has the most to offer and makes for an excellent half-day excursion from Hanoi. Records suggest that the village was founded in the 14th or 15th century (accounts differ) but villagers will tell you that the potter's guild established themselves here soon after Hanoi was founded in 1010. Over the centuries, Vietnam's dynastic rulers and elite class commissioned the artisans in Bát Tràng to produce ceramic tiles and durable bricks, and these materials still embellish palaces, religious buildings and private homes across the country.

Start your visit at the gigantic and disused 19th-century wood furnace known as Lò Bầu Cổ (Old Dragon's Kiln), which fired clay at 1,300°C and is now the centrepiece of a small museum with decent signage. Behind the kiln is the tangle of alleyways that constitute Bát Tràng's old core, with high walls to protect against thieves. There isn't much of interest here bar the river-facing community house Đình Bát Tràng, but look hard and you'll see some architectural heritage features mixed in with the concrete renovations. Immediately east of the old centre is the Bát Tràng market; the best deals are to be found in the morass of stalls on the north side of the street, but you'll need to bargain. Continue east and find the confusingly named Bát Tràng Museum by National Artist Vũ Thắng (w battrang.museum). Vũ Thắng was perhaps best known for his series of 12 ceramic knee-high boots that showcase a range of traditional craft techniques. The museum only displays one boot at any time and this changes every month. The village's newest offering is the Bát Tràng Pottery Museum (w tinhhoalangnghe.vn; 130,000VND), which opened in 2022 and was built by local firm 1+1>2 Architects. The museum, a collection of tiered cone-like structures, was inspired by the potter's wheel, and it houses a permanent exhibition that recounts the history of the village, a rooftop café and tea room and kid-friendly pottery workshops on the underground floor. The museum is about 500m east of the market on the Bắc Hưng Hải River, an offshoot from the Red River. On your way out from the village, look for award-winning modern architect Võ Trọng Nghĩa's Bát Tràng House, a private home encased in a perforated ceramic façade. Design magazine *Wallpaper** named it 'Best New Private House' in 2021.

HANOI'S OTHER CRAFT VILLAGES Dozens of centuries-old craft villages speckle the countryside around Hanoi, but with the exception of Bát Tràng, few are set up to handle tourists. Visitors will learn little without a guide from a reputable tour agency (page 87). That said, the villages can still make for atmospheric places to visit, and shutterbugs will revel in opportunities to photograph elderly artisans showing off their skills in traditional courtyards. **Vạn Phúc Silk Village**, around 10km southwest of central Hanoi, is geared up for shopping and has some interesting machinery on display. **Cự Đà Glass Noodle Village**, another 8km southeast of Vạn Phúc, makes glass noodles, and you'll spot them draped over huge drying racks and packed on to motorbikes. Some 18km south of Cự Đà Village is **Chuông Conical Hat Village**, where you'll see the hats piled up on street corners and in front porches. An interesting feature of **Phù Lãng Pottery Village** are the dud earthenware coffins that are incorporated into the village walls.

ĐƯỜNG LÂM AND SƠN TÂY Though popular with selfie-stick-wielding students for its atmospheric photo backdrops, the ancient village of Đường Lâm, a little over an hour west of Hanoi, sees few foreign visitors, despite efforts from the Japan International Co-operation Agency (JICA) to promote the village internationally. In 2006, Đường Lâm was designated an official national relic by the Vietnamese government, and it is often referred to as the oldest village in Northern Vietnam (whatever that means). Apart from wandering the narrow centenarian street plan, specific sites of interest include the photogenic village gate and Đình Mông Phụ, a communal house with a richly ornamented ceiling and rooftop. Built in the 17th century, the house was later expanded during the reign of Tự Đức (1847–83). Many of the private homes were also built during the 17th century, and some offer lodgings and lunches if you give them time to prepare. Look out for signs that read 'HOMESTAY'. Also in town is ĐOÀI (w dulichxudoai.com), a nascent artist collective. A little south of Đường Lâm, and within walking distance from the village centre, are two religious clusters of historical interest: the temple and tomb of the hero Ngô Quyền, who secured Vietnamese independence from the Chinese in 938, and, nearby, the temple of Phùng Hưng, another celebrated military leader from the same era. It is believed that both heroes were born in Đường Lâm.

It's worth stopping at the leafy remains of the 19th-century moated citadel in Sơn Tây on your way back to Hanoi. There isn't much in the way of information, but the gates, walls and buildings, some of which are being swallowed by banyan trees, have an almost Angkorian feel about them. Several cafés overlook the citadel, some offering views of the attractive rust-coloured octagonal flag tower. Consider combining a trip to Đường Lâm and Sơn Tây with nearby Ba Vì National Park, where you can stay overnight (page 128).

THÀNH CHƯƠNG PALACE It's easy to while away a good few hours in Thành Chương Palace (150,000VND), which houses a mammoth collection of artefacts in buildings inspired by traditional Vietnamese architecture from across the country. This is the collection of Thành Chương, a commercially successful contemporary artist who has spent decades travelling throughout Vietnam salvaging and safeguarding antiques. The garden is beautiful but jumbled, which is appropriate, believes Thành Chương, who thinks that Vietnam's aesthetic allure doesn't lie in manicured order of the kind you might find in Europe or Japan. A highlight of the 'palace' is a 500-year-old stone bridge that Thành Chương says he saved from neglect from a village in Nam Định Province. You'll also find the artist's own art dotted around the property. It takes around an hour to get to Thành Chương Palace by motorbike or car from Hanoi. If you come by taxi, you'll need to negotiate waiting time.

CỔ LOA CITADEL AND THE TEMPLES WITHIN The scanty remains of this 3rd-century BCE citadel can be unearthed in Đông Anh District, about 15km north of central

LEGEND HAS IT: AN ENAMOURED TRAITOR, BEHEADED

The Chinese dynasties greatly feared An Dương Vương, ruler of Âu Lạc, for they were convinced he had supernatural powers that made him invincible in battle. To discover the secret of his power, Trọng Thủy, the son of a Chinese emperor, was ordered to marry Mỵ Châu, the ruler's daughter, to extract the desired information.

The plan worked. Soon after they married, Mỵ Châu disclosed that when An Dương Vương was building Cổ Loa, a divine turtle gave him a golden claw that he used to forge a crossbow with the power to cut down hundreds of men in a single shot. Trọng Thủy stole the magical crossbow and returned home, sparking a northern invasion of Âu Lạc, and An Dương Vương was forced to flee south.

Upon learning of her husband's treachery, Mỵ Châu confessed what she had done. An Dương Vương decapitated his only daughter in a single blow and threw her head into the sea. Some accounts tell that Trọng Thủy, who still loved Mỵ Châu, found her body, returned it to Cổ Loa and drowned himself in the lake.

Today, Mỵ Châu is understood as a complicated character and, despite her betrayal, is celebrated for the loyalty she showed to her husband. But, as with Theseus, Gilgamesh and other unscrupulous male heroes, An Dương Vương seems to get off scot-free; he is considered a great king, with little attention given to his filicidal act.

Hanoi and across the Red River. This fortification is known for its unusual shape: the ancient city mud walls, very few of which remain, looked like the spiral of a snail's shell when viewed from above. It was built during the reign of Emperor An Dương Vương but was more or less abandoned during the millennium of Chinese domination that began in 111BCE. It briefly became the capital after Ngô Quyền's spectacular defeat of the Chinese in CE938. Archaeological discoveries include axes and arrowheads made from bronze. There is a small museum on site, as well as some placards that give a sense of what the citadel would have looked like and two lavish and storied temples. The 11th-century An Dương Vương Temple (10,000VND) is built on the site of his old palace, which stood in the citadel's southwest corner and overlooks a placid lake. Mỵ Châu Temple (small entrance fee), dedicated to An Dương Vương's daughter, is similarly atmospheric and holds a robed triangular stone that represents the headless body of the princess (see above).

HÙNG KINGS TEMPLE COMPLEX The Hùng kings, Vietnam's somewhat mythical first dynasty (page 10), established the imperial capital of Văn Lang here over 4,000 years ago. Though little evidence of the civilisation remains, several important temples (small entrance fee) have been built here, all of which are connected to the 18 Hùng kings in some way. Most of the structures are newly built and lack the depth and character of older religious complexes like Chùa Tây Phương and Chùa Thầy. The sprawling complex is nevertheless fun to explore, and the area comes alive during a week-long festival on the tenth day of the third lunar month (usually April). Some of the most notable sections of the complex are Hạ (Lower) Temple, Trung (Middle) Temple and Thượng (Upper) Temple, though there are many more.

Hạ Temple is reached from the main gate along a flight of brick steps that ascends through an avenue of tall green turpentine trees. It is dedicated to Âu Cơ, the mother of the Vietnamese people, who awaits you inside the temple on the central altar. Another flight leads up to the Trung Temple, which dates from the 19th century, and the Thượng Temple. According to a local legend, it was on top of this holy mountain that Emperor Hùng Vương VI constructed an altar to ask the gods to provide him with a leader of sufficient strength and character to drive away his northern enemies. This was granted in the form of the courageous Phù Đổng Thiên Vương, popularly known as Thánh Gióng (page 473). The temple is a memorial to this great military hero.

TAM ĐẢO NATIONAL PARK The best time to visit Tam Đảo town was a century ago, when it was a quaint hill station retreat for overheating French colonial administrators. Established in 1907, Tam Đảo once had a large collection of French

LEGEND HAS IT: HOW VIETNAM GOT ITS FLOODS

Eager to secure a suitable husband for his beloved daughter Mỵ Nương, King Hùng Vương (page 10) sought suitors from far and wide. Chief among those vying for the chance to win the hand of a princess were two primordial gods: Sơn Tinh, lord of the lofty mountains, and Thủy Tinh, who presided over the world's watery depths. When summoned, Sơn Tinh conjured a forest from thin air, his mere words commanding verdant mountains to rise from the earth. Thủy Tinh, whom nothing daunted, flaunted his terrible power by invoking tempestuous winds and willing the waters to rise.

The great king found himself impressed, intimidated and reluctant to choose a victor, so he concocted one final test: the first suitor to present a nine-tusked elephant, a cockerel with nine spurs and a horse adorned with nine flowing manes would have Mỵ Nương's hand. As lord of the terrestrial realm, Sơn Tinh pressed his advantage and scoured the land with the speed that only a god could muster. Not a day had passed before he returned with the requested beasts, and he swiftly took Mỵ Nương as his wife.

Despite his criminal disadvantage, Thủy Tinh also found his own set of tellurian mutants, but alas he arrived too late. To his horror, he returned to see that Sơn Tinh had already won the race and claimed the princess as his prize. In a fierce rage – perhaps because the odds were stacked against him – Thủy Tinh summoned torrents of rain, gusts of wind and thunderous bolts of lightning. In his fury, he raised the sea level, unleashing a deluge that ravaged the land. Villages and farmland risked total annihilation in the wake of Thủy Tinh's inconsolable wrath.

To protect his domain, Sơn Tinh, with the support of the lesser god Cao Sơn (High Mountain), raised the foundations of the earth. To shield the people and their crops from devastation, he crisscrossed the land with sturdy dykes that stood defiantly against the advancing waters. This cataclysmic battle went on for an age, but eventually Thủy Tinh wearied, conceded defeat and the oceans receded. However, Thủy Tinh refuses to let go of his desire for revenge. The typhoons and floods that Vietnam endures each year serve as a reminder of Thủy Tinh's eternal vindictiveness – as well as Hùng Vương's grave mistake to devise a contest that favoured one god over another.

Sơn Tinh and Mỵ Nương are said to live in Tản Viên, the highest of the three peaks in Ba Vì National Park (page 128). Sơn Tinh is also one of the Four Immortals (page 210).

mansions, almost all of which were destroyed during the First Indochina War (1946–54). The area became a national park in 1997 and is significantly cooler than Hanoi at any time of year. The resort town, a little less than 2 hours north of Hanoi, has since been rebuilt with an obscene amount of concrete. Tam Đảo makes a good-enough base for countryside walks and remains popular with local tourists on weekends, but it's difficult to find any remnants of charm in the town centre. At the foot of the mountain and within the national park boundaries is the Bear Rescue Centre (w animalsasia.org), arguably a more rewarding experience than visiting Tam Đảo town. Though a rescue centre for indigenous sun and moon bears once farmed for their bile, they arrange educational tours of the facility twice monthly. Spots are limited so check the website for the schedule and book far in advance.

BA VÌ NATIONAL PARK Unlike Tam Đảo, Ba Vì National Park, 2 hours west of Hanoi, doesn't feel like a concrete theme park set up for selfies. This moody, atmospheric and jungled mountaintop has two well-trodden walking trails: one 600-step shlep up to Thượng Temple to worship the mountain god, and an even longer trek to Đền Thờ Bác Hồ (Uncle Hồ Temple). Most Vietnamese visitors, however, stay at the base of the trails and take photos among the spooky ruins of a French church. Like Tam Đảo, Ba Vì National Park was also a French hill station and is colder than Hanoi, so pack at least one extra layer. The more remote parts of the park are home to some fantastic wildlife, including lorises, squirrels, pangolins, primates and dozens of bird species, but don't come expecting to see any. On a rare clear day it's possible to see the three peaks of Ba Vì from Hanoi. The highest peak is Tản Viên, which has mythological connections (page 127). As you near Ba Vì National Park you'll start seeing gigantic signs with the word *SỮA*, which means milk. Stop here for cow's milk, goat's milk and various derivatives, such as *sữa chua nếp cẩm* (yoghurt with black sticky rice). Consider combining a trip to Ba Vì National Park with a visit to nearby Đường Lâm and Sơn Tây (page 125) and overnighting on the mountain at the **Melia** (w melia.com/en/hotels/vietnam/hanoi/melia-ba-vi-mountain-retreat).

4

The Northern Mountains

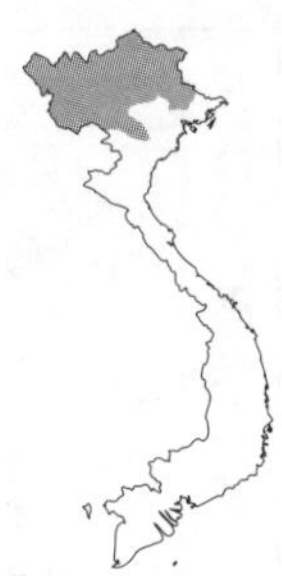

In terms of geographic, historical and cultural complexity, the northern mountains are one of the most enticing areas in Southeast Asia. Coursing upstream along the great rivers of the Northwest or scrambling up the craggy terrain of the Northeast, the smog, noise and chaos of Hanoi melt away. Indeed, though the north's furthest-flung corners are only a few hundred kilometres from the capital, the region's Zomian history (page 5), challenging geography and ethnolinguistic heterogeneity have all contributed to it being seen as the 'other' within the broader Vietnamese context. Some pockets have been discovered, developed and partially despoiled. Most areas still safeguard the thrill of adventure. The walking, driving, boating, kayaking, swimming, caving and (of course) eating opportunities are extensive. But regardless of what you decide to do and where you choose to go (a decision that takes time; page 131), the rewards of travel in the northern mountains can be transformative.

The primary draw tends to be the scenery. This is an unusually mountainous area punctuated by limestone peaks and luscious valleys of terraced paddy fields, maize plantations, tea farms, stilt houses and water hyacinth-quilted rivers. In one valley, large cone-shaped peaks might rise like clusters of weathered pyramids, their steep sides striped with the greens and yellows of the rice crop. In the next, narrow country lanes spiral upwards through Martian slopes before vanishing at nebulous altitudes. While the landscapes are usually the initial attraction, it's often the cultural depth that leaves the greatest impression. Despite the low population density, at least by Vietnamese standards, the northern mountains are one of the world's great ethnolinguistic tapestries; in just a few days it's possible to pass through more than a dozen villages, each nurturing a different language, apparel, cuisine, architecture and belief system.

The northern mountains also feature prominently in the annals of nationalist and revolutionary history. The final battles that secured Vietnam's independence from China in the 10th century were fought on these rugged slopes. Hồ Chí Minh re-entered Vietnam from China and, shrouded by mountains and forests, mustered a revolutionary force that would shake the world. The course of modern history was altered near Laos in 1954 when the Việt Minh forced the French to abandon Indochina, the jewel of their transcontinental colonial empire. And, over a thousand years after shaking off the Chinese imperial yoke, it was from these provinces that Vietnam saw off a potential reinvasion in 1979.

Administratively, Vietnam's northern mountains span two subregions: the Northeast and the Northwest. These have been grouped together for the purposes of this guide. The areas within them can be roughly divided into three groups: west of Hanoi, northwest of Hanoi, and north of Hanoi.

If your time in the northern mountains is limited – anything less than a week – and you don't have your own wheels, it's recommended that you focus on just one of these areas.

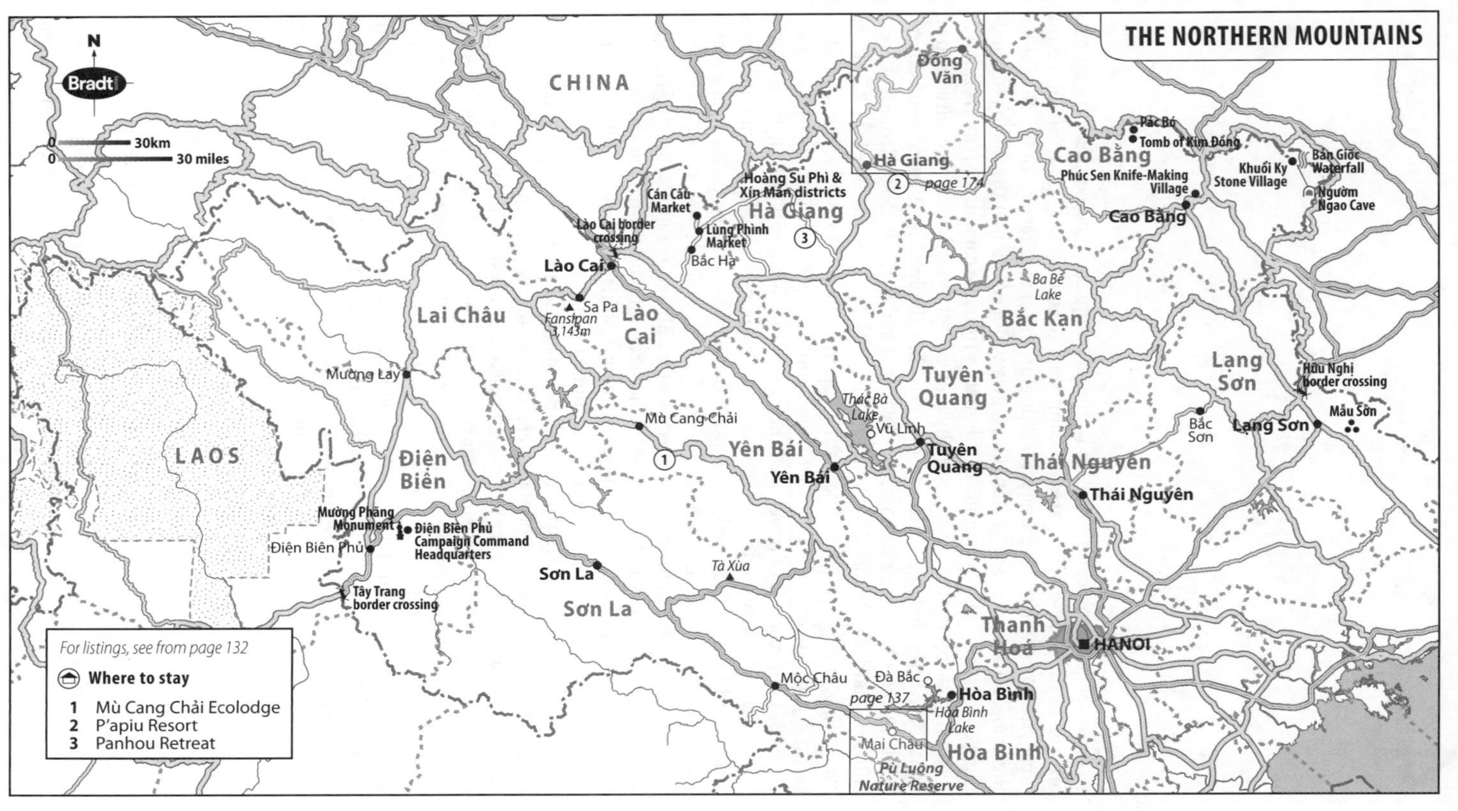
THE NORTHERN MOUNTAINS
N
Bradt
0 30km
0 30 miles
CHINA
LAOS
Đồng Văn
Hà Giang
page 174
Pác Bó
Tomb of Kim Đồng
Cao Bằng
Phúc Sen Knife-Making Village
Cao Bằng
Khuổi Ky Stone Village
Bản Giốc Waterfall
Ngườm Ngao Cave
Hoàng Su Phì & Xín Mần districts
Hà Giang
Cán Cấu Market
Lùng Phình Market
Bắc Hà
Lào Cai border crossing
Lào Cai
Sa Pa
Fansipan 3,143m
Lào Cai
Lai Châu
Ba Bể Lake
Bắc Kạn
Lạng Sơn
Hữu Nghị border crossing
Mẫu Sơn
Bắc Sơn
Lạng Sơn
Tuyên Quang
Thác Bà Lake
Vũ Linh
Tuyên Quang
Thái Nguyên
Thái Nguyên
Mường Lay
Mù Cang Chải
Yên Bái
Yên Bái
Điện Biên
Mường Phăng Monument
Điện Biên Phủ Campaign Command Headquarters
Điện Biên Phủ
Sơn La
Tà Xùa
Tây Trang border crossing
Sơn La
Thanh Hoá
HANOI
Mộc Châu
Đà Bắc
Hòa Bình
page 137
Hòa Bình Lake
Mai Châu
Hòa Bình
Pù Luông Nature Reserve
For listings, see from page 132
Where to stay
1 Mù Cang Chải Ecolodge
2 P'apiu Resort
3 Panhou Retreat

WEST OF HANOI This is the southernmost and least mountainous half of the Northwest subregion. Striking west from Hanoi, closest to the city, the fertile plains are eventually disrupted by the hills of **Hòa Bình Province**, where family homestays and rustic lodges cling to the hills of **Đà Bắc**, nestle in the valleys of **Mai Châu** and perch on the mountainsides of **Pù Luông Nature Reserve**. These highlands are the most accessible from Hanoi, just close enough for a long weekend away from the capital. Further west are the weatherworn and abundant fruit, vegetable, coffee and dairy farms of **Sơn La**. Further still is **Điện Biên**, an underexplored province beyond the sites of Điện Biên Phủ. This section begins on page 135.

NORTHWEST OF HANOI This is the more mountainous half of the Northwest subregion. The transport infrastructure here is better than anywhere else in the northern mountains, with train tracks and a fast, flat highway (CT05) that pierce the Red River Valley. The altitudinous drama begins in **Yên Bái Province**, less than 150km from Hanoi, home to the lowland lake of Thác Bà and fantastical rice terraces of **Mù Cang Chải**. In the same direction, at the end of the highway and train tracks, is Lào Cai Province, with the overtouristed town of **Sa Pa**, from

MAKING THE RIGHT CHOICE

Due to the time it takes to move between provinces, you'd need at least a month to travel across all the northern mountain provinces enjoyably. If you don't have a month to spare, there are two things to consider.

First, extraordinary scenery and cultural depth exist in most corners, so think about the different sights, activities and experiences offered in each place. If you're short on time, consider the homestays and mountain lodges that aren't too far from Hanoi in Đà Bắc, Mai Châu, Pù Luông and Thác Bà. For war history, investigate Điện Biên Phủ. In Lào Cai Province, Sa Pa offers the most comprehensive hiking network and Bắc Hà hosts the most colourful markets. For road trips, northern Hà Giang is unrivalled. The most dramatic and artful rice terraces are in Mù Cang Chải. For relative isolation and a slew of outdoor activities, including some wildlife spotting, there's Ba Bể National Park. Hữu Lũng is the north's burgeoning rock-climbing hub. And, if you have the time, Cao Bằng is an all-round province with ancient villages, historical intrigue, a masterful waterfall and few visitors.

Second, think about how comfortable you are driving – or at least riding on the back of – a motorbike. For many, confidence on a motorbike is the skeleton key that unlocks true adventure in the Vietnamese mountains. If you're happy on two wheels nowhere is off-limits, but if you're not, prioritise Đà Bắc, Mai Châu, Pù Luông, Điện Biên Phủ, Sa Pa, Bắc Hà and Ba Bể National Park. It is still possible to explore other parts of the area without a motorbike, but it may involve a lot of negotiation with hotel receptionists and taxi drivers, who don't usually speak good English. Throughout this chapter are **Hinterlands** boxes, which indicate the parts of the north where there isn't always a huge amount to see or do, but the scenery and lack of visitors invite unplanned, multi-day, do-it-yourself adventures. For these areas, the confidence to ride a motorbike is non-negotiable. These boxes are written for motorcyclists and independent travellers on the hunt for adventure. They are not designed to be comprehensive but should offer enough contextual and practical information to get you started.

which a web of hiking trails fans out in all directions, and **Bắc Hà**, with its endlessly interesting weekend markets. Northwest from here is Lai Châu, a large province ripe for adventurous pursuits. This section begins on page 151.

NORTH AND NORTHEAST OF HANOI In administrative terms, this is part of the Northeast subregion, which also includes the large coastal province of Quảng Ninh, covered in *Chapter 5* (page 187). Directly north of Hanoi begin the hilly provinces of **Thái Nguyên** and **Tuyên Quang**, and just above them **Ba Bể National Park**, where forested hills rise from Vietnam's largest freshwater natural lake. Northwest of here is **Hà Giang**, prime road trip territory both in the province's northernmost extremity and in the lesser-known Hoàng Su Phì. Northeast of Ba Bể is **Cao Bằng**, which looms large in both historical significance and natural beauty (for evidence, look at the cover of this book). East of Ba Bể is **Lạng Sơn**, a relatively prosperous province with a rich food culture, pre-colonial citadels and landscapes for motorbiking and rock climbing. The steep slopes of these northernmost areas, which skirt the Chinese border, have been carved into curving rice terraces with shimmering paddies and patches of corn that cling to the rocky soil. The sparse populations that live here are predominantly ethnolinguistic minority groups and life goes on as it has for years, though tourism is beginning to transform some areas.

MOUNTAIN LODGES IN NORTHERN VIETNAM

Nestled in the northern mountains are a dozen or so remote lodges that are destinations in their own right. Most are far from towns and villages, so you'll rely on the lodge for sustenance, activities and entertainment. Restaurant prices, however, tend not to be extortionate, and most have a tour desk that can arrange trips like visits to nearby villages, swimming in waterfalls and hiking up mountains. These lodges aren't cheap – some are eye-wateringly expensive – but they certainly offer one way to encounter the majesty of the northern mountains.

Mù Cang Chải Ecolodge [map, page 130] Mù Cang Chải, Yên Bái Province; **w** mucangchaiecolodge.com. Rustic little lodge perched on a hill overlooking farms & rice terraces that are especially beautiful in the summer, when they are vibrant green, & Sep, when they are a wheat yellow. The lodges here draw from Hmong architecture, though many are raised on stilts. There's a ramshackle feel about the place that many will find charming; it's also good value for money. **$$**

Mai Châu Ecolodge [map, page 137] Mai Châu, Hòa Bình Province; **w** maichau.ecolodge.asia. Mai Châu Ecolodge, perhaps the closest luxury lodge to Hanoi, has a clutch of bungalows overlooking expansive rice paddies. Popular with families visiting from Hanoi, there's a swimming pool, games room & a decent restaurant. This is one of the few lodges situated close to a tourist-friendly village, so you're not entirely dependent on the property for meals & activities. **$$$**

Pù Luông Treehouse [map, page 137] Pù Luông, Thanh Hóa Province; **w** puluongtreehouse.com. Unusually friendly & homely mountain lodge, with some dreamy, basic treehouses & a handful of bungalows. The views are sublime, as is the food, which is served like a family meal. The Treehouse is in Bản Đôn, one of the most beautiful villages in Pù Luông Nature Reserve, but it gets busy (& noisy) on the w/ends, with visitors from the city with a penchant for karaoke. Still, this is one of the better-value mountain lodges. **$$$**

Panhou Retreat [map, page 130] Hoàng Su Phì, Hà Giang Province; **w** panhouretreat.com. Where others have gone high, Panhou has gone low. This is an unassuming lodge

The provinces of Cao Bằng, Bắc Thái (now Thái Nguyên and Bắc Kạn) and Lạng Sơn formed the famous Cao-Bắc-Lạng resistance zone of the 1947–50 Frontier Campaign. This mountainous region, became the cradle of the revolution during the twilight years of the French colonial period. This section begins on page 164.

WHEN TO VISIT

Summer (May–August) can get very hot, and can be wet, although rainfall doesn't usually last for more than a few hours; autumn (September–November) is cooler and drier; winter (December–February) is cold but manageable (in the cities at least) but can be foggy; and spring (March and April) is unpredictable, and can be wet too. **Waterfalls** tend to be at their fullest at the end of summer or early autumn.

Despite the heat, summer can be a good time to visit **Mai Châu**, as this is when the valley is at its brightest and most beautiful (although it's rarely too cold or too wet, so there's no bad time to visit the area). **Pù Luông** is also at its most beautiful in the summer (May–August) when the rippling rice terraces bulge green. The harvest begins in August and ends in September or October depending on the year.

Mù Cang Chải is at its most mesmerising – and busiest – during the harvest in September. If coming during this month, book your accommodation as far in

encased in a thicket of tropical greenery. There are no views of mountains, but the frog-filled lily ponds & serpentine pathways bespeckled with fluttering butterflies more than make up for it. Though a little rough around the edges in parts, this is the most bucolic & atmospheric of all the mountain lodges. **$$$$**

Avana Retreat [map, page 137] Mai Châu, Hòa Bình Province; w avanaretreat.com. An uber-luxury option built around a waterfall that provides the ever-present sounds of gushing water. The rooms, many with private pools, all have spellbinding views. A remarkable network of elevated platforms & bridges enables exploration of the waterfall, including some corners for reading or yoga. This is surely one of Asia's most fabulous countryside retreats – but it comes at a price. Though technically in Mai Châu, Avana is about an hour by car from the town & villages. **$$$$$**

P'apiu Resort [map, page 130] near Hà Giang city, Hà Giang Province; w papiu.vn. The most luxurious & eccentric lodge of them all, P'apiu is an over-the-top extravagance, with just 4 obscenely large villas, each following a loose theme: unwind in The Mellow with its thick, earthen walls; burrow into Layla Quays, which is almost entirely underground; curl up by the fire in the Alpine-inspired Villa Ravine; or peer over the mountains from The Fluffy, with architecture that curiously blends a Tay stilt house with a Nguyễn Dynasty palace. The property has a gold-standard Travelife sustainability certification, awarded for their environmental & social policies. Note that at the time of research, children under the age of 15 were not permitted to stay at the property, but this may change. **$$$$$**

Topas Ecolodge [map, page 154] near Sa Pa, Lào Cai Province; w topasecolodge.com. One of Vietnam's first luxury lodges, Topas Ecolodge perches on some hills with wrap-around views of the encircling mountains & valleys. The company behind the lodge is Danish, which explains the delicate Scandi touches to the otherwise rustic-chic décor, which draws heavily from the textiles of the Hmong & Dao ethnolinguistic groups that live nearby. The infinity pool here is the stuff of legends, but the never-ending photo shoots from wannabe social media influencers can be tiresome. **$$$$$**

THE NORTHERN MOUNTAINS' SPECIALITY DISHES

BÁNH CUỐN CAO BẰNG Provinces across Northern Vietnam have adapted Hanoi's *bánh cuốn*, wet rice paper rolled with minced pork and mushrooms. To fend off the winter chill, Cao Bằng serves the dish with a hot, herby side soup for dipping. Try it at **Quán Bánh Cuốn Cao Bằng Chị Thi** (page 180), Cao Bằng.

XÔI TRỨNG KIẾN Perhaps originally cooked up by the Tay ethnolinguistic group, sticky rice is fried with black ant eggs and garlic, topped with deep-fried shallots and wrapped in a banana leaf. It's a meal in itself, though some restaurants serve it alongside other dishes. Try it at **Hạt Dẻ Quán** (page 180), Cao Bằng.

VỊT QUAY Due to its proximity to China, Lạng Sơn has become known for its *vịt quay*, or roast duck, which bears similarity to the world-famous Beijing dish. It's not uncommon for visiting Hanoians to buy more than a dozen roast ducks to take to friends and family back home. Try it at **Nhà Hàng Vịt Quay Hải Xồm** and **Phở Vịt Quay Vi Tặng** (both page 184), both in Lạng Sơn.

PHỞ VỊT Duck *phở* is an inevitable combination of Vietnam's national dish and the delicious Chinese-inspired roast duck popular in Lạng Sơn. *Phở vịt* is usually eaten for breakfast. Try it at **Nhà Hàng Vịt Quay Hải Xồm** (page 184) and **Phở Vịt Quay Vi Tặng** (page 184), both in Lạng Sơn, or **Hạt Dẻ Quán** (page 180) in Cao Bằng.

PHỞ BẮC HÀ The market town of Bắc Hà has its own version of *phở*, simply called *phở Bắc Hà* or sometimes *phở hồng* (pink *phở*). The broth is similar to *phở* elsewhere in Northern Vietnam, but the noodles are made with flour from a type of local brown rice that gives them a pink tint. Find it in the markets in and around Bắc Hà and occasionally further afield.

advance as possible and expect crowds. Waiting until October, which is cooler, sunnier and less crowded, is a good idea. The summer months, when temperatures are cooler than in the lowlands and the rice terraces are a brilliant shade of green, are also a good time to visit. In winter, the terraces are muddy and lifeless, though some fill with water to spectacular, reflective effect. Spring is the planting season, and also a good time to visit as the terraces are alive with activity.

Sa Pa town is developed enough that there is no bad time to visit: even when it's bitterly cold or excessively wet there are restaurants, cafés and spas to keep you warm and dry. Some hotels have fireplaces and heaters in the rooms. Fog can descend on the valley at any time during the year, but visibility tends to be best in October and November. With summer temperatures hovering around 20°C, the bracing mountain air is a real tonic after time spent in the lowlands.

There isn't a bad time to visit **Ba Bể National Park** as the flora is evergreen, so the area remains lush throughout the year. Butterfly enthusiasts should try to visit in May or October.

You can motorbike in **Hà Giang** at any time of year, as long as you dress for the weather. The most comfortable months are April, May, October and November, when days are sunny and there shouldn't be too much rain. Winters are cold; bear in mind that Hà Giang city is always a few degrees warmer than the rural districts. Đồng Văn and Du Già can be particularly chilly.

COÓNG PHÙ It's almost impossible to find this Chinese-inspired sweet snack other than at Lạng Sơn's Market Quarter, where it's sold from makeshift street kitchens. Multi-coloured glutinous rice flour balls are boiled and put in a hot sweet soup flavoured with peanuts, coconut and ginger.

LẠP XƯỞNG CAO BẰNG *Lạp xưởng Cao Bằng*, or Cao Bằng smoked sausage, tastes almost central European, but the ethnolinguistic groups of the northern mountains have been preserving meat like this for centuries. Try it at **Hạt Dẻ Quán** (page 180), Cao Bằng.

MẮC KHÉN The northern mountains are known for this wild forest pepper, sometimes called Szechuan pepper, which families forage from trees in the jungle. It's more common in the west of the northern mountains, and is particularly good with grilled meat. Find it in roadside stops in bags to take home.

NGÔ (CORN) *Ngô* is corn, which tends to be greener and a little less sweet than Western varieties. It is usually cooked on makeshift streetside barbecues in towns like Sa Pa and on the roadside.

KHOAI LANG (SWEET POTATO) Often served alongside corn in the same settings, Vietnamese sweet potato, which is usually orange in colour, is sweet and satisfying, especially on a cold winter's day.

BÁNH HẠT DẺ Hazelnut cakes (whether hazelnut is an ingredient is debatable) is a popular sweet snack in towns across the northern mountains, particularly in Lào Cai. You'll see the round, flat, fluffy cakes grilling next to the markets in Sa Pa and Bắc Hà. Take them away and pair them with a coffee from a nearby café.

HÒA BÌNH, MAI CHÂU AND PÙ LUÔNG

Delineated by high karstic peaks, Highway 3 heads past tea and sugarcane plantations on its way to Hòa Bình, the gateway to the mountainous northwest. The province's distinctive geomorphology has been eulogised by many Vietnamese poets, including Nguyễn Du, Thiệu Trị and Hồ Xuân Hương. The non-Viet ethnolinguistic groups who live here – the Muong, Tay, Dao, Thai and Hmong – constitute 75% of its total population of less than 900,000. The Muong (page 136) are the ethnolinguistic majority of Hòa Bình. Towards the west are the ubiquitous stilt houses of the Thai (page 138), which occupy the flat fertile valley of **Mai Châu** and hills of **Pù Luông**. The Kinh mostly reside in Hòa Bình city. The Tay, Dao and Hmong live in more remote corners of the province, including Đà Bắc.

HISTORY Excavations here by the Vietnam Archaeological Institute have uncovered bracelets of shell and bone, strings of polished gemstones and four tombs containing the remains of Bronze Age man. Rice grains from the Neolithic Age have been unearthed in a cave, showing that people in the province grew rice even then; bronze ploughshares have been excavated which are around 4,000 years old. Hòa Bình also holds the Vietnamese record for the oldest wood statuette. The coffin that contained the statuette had artefacts characteristic of

THE MUONG

Of the 1 million Muong people living in Vietnam (making them the fourth largest ethnolinguistic group), around 60% live in Hòa Bình; the rest are scattered around Thanh Hóa and Yên Bái provinces. It is thought that the Muong are descended from the same stock as the Kinh (page 189), but whereas Vietnam's ethnolinguistic majority came under strong Chinese cultural influence, the Muong did not. The Muong belong to the Viet-Muong subgroup of the Austro-Asiatic language family; the roots of their language are closer to Vietnamese than any other in Vietnam.

Traditionally, the Muong practise wet and dry rice cultivation and, where possible, supplement their income with cash crops such as manioc, tobacco and cotton. Weaving is still practised: items produced, usually now for tourists, include pillowcases and blankets. One stark difference between the Kinh and the Muong is in their architecture. The Vietnamese, like the Chinese, build on the ground, whereas the Muong, like the Thai, Tay and many other groups in the north, build on stilts. Organisationally, the Muong are akin to the Thai, living in small villages that constitute bigger units. Muong society was once feudal in nature, with each village cluster coming under the protection of a noble family, and they have a rich literary tradition. Many Muong legends, poems and songs have been translated into Vietnamese. For more about the Muong, visit the Museum of Muong Culture (Bảo Tàng Không Gian Văn Hóa Mường; w muong.vn), which is part ethnography museum, part outdoor art space. This is just south of Hòa Bình city, on the way to Mai Châu and beyond.

Đông Sơn art (page 8), which blossomed 2,000 years ago during the period of the Hùng kings.

The city of Hòa Bình saw some minor battles against the French in 1951. It was also during the 1950s that the Hòa Bình hydro-electric plant was conceived, though the project only began in 1979 – with Soviet assistance – and wasn't completed until 1994. The enormously ambitious dam is 128m high and 970m long, and creates a reservoir of 208km^{2}. The project faced significant challenges, including complex engineering demands and the relocation of thousands of residents, but today plays a crucial role in supplying electricity to huge swathes of Northern Vietnam. The dam has undergone several technological upgrades to improve efficiency and safety over the years and remains a living relic of Vietnam's relationship with the former Soviet Union.

ĐÀ BẮC Đà Bắc is just west of Hòa Bình city, but spent many years overshadowed by Mai Châu and, later, Pù Luông. Today it's a rugged collection of hamlets that rise from Hòa Bình Lake towards the jungled hills. The district is fairly diverse for such a small area, with Tay (page 170), Muong (see above) and Dao (page 172) settlements in close proximity. Tourism here is less than a decade old, and although lodges are beginning to emerge, the best way to explore the district is with **Đà Bắc CBT** (w actiononcbt.com), who offer packages from Hanoi that include all activities, lodgings and meals with local families. If you're looking for a homestay experience, you're short on time and you'd like a hassle-free experience, this is a good option.

MAI CHÂU An isolated farming community until 1993, Mai Châu underwent significant change in just a few short years. Its tranquil valley setting, hospitable Thai (page 138) inhabitants and tasty home-cooked food make Mai Châu a worthwhile stop, but it is now extremely well trodden, with large groups of tourists packed into homestays, guesthouses and lodges – visit during the week if you can. The number of foreign and domestic tourists visiting the area has had a significant impact on the economy of Mai Châu and the lifestyles of its people. The merged villages of Bản Lác and Poom Coọng form the main tourist hub, where many dozens of homestays are crammed into narrow lanes and cavernous shops hawk cheap souvenirs from China. After turning into the villages one's heart may sink at the sight of more than a dozen parked minibuses and stilt houses full of groups gearing up for an evening karaoke session.

Alas, Mai Châu is not a bastion of local life and traditional culture. But the homestays are for the most part run by local families, and stiff competition has increased diversity. It might be best to turn up without a reservation, take a stroll around the village and find a tucked-away house with a view of the paddy fields and then ask if you can stay the night. Mai Châu also offers some of the best homestay cuisine anywhere in Vietnam, as classic Vietnamese dishes combine with the more unusual – and equally delicious – dishes of the Thai. Travellers with a bigger

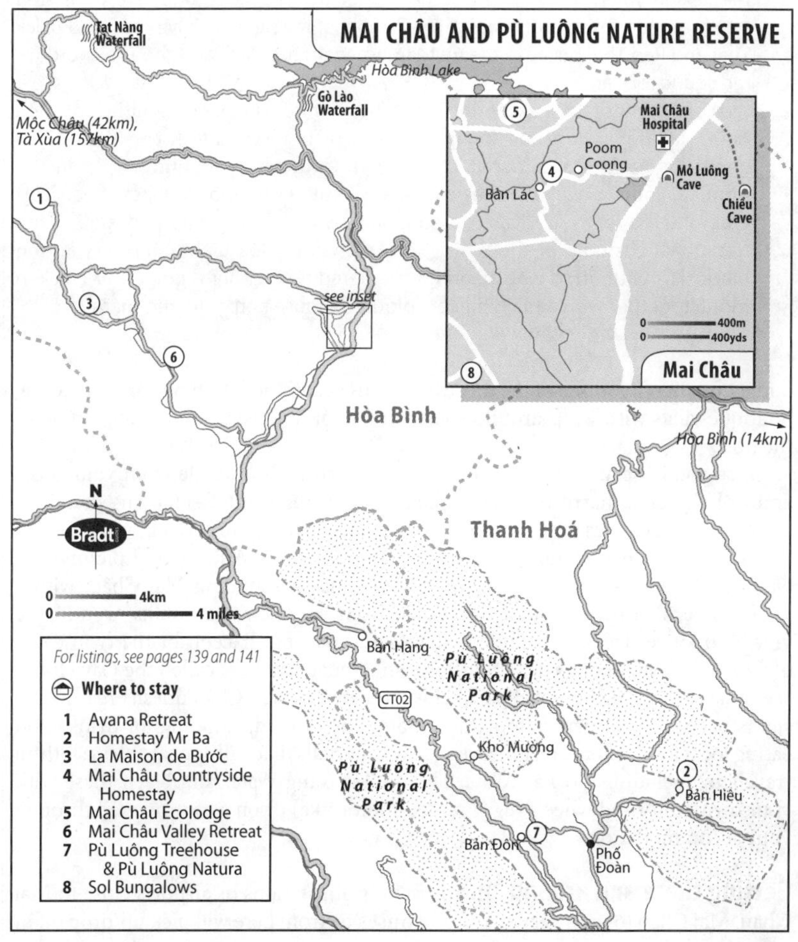

THE THAI

Numbering more than 1 million, this is the third largest ethnolinguistic group after the Kinh (the majority; page 189) and the Tay (page 170). They are distinct from the people of modern-day Thailand, but the language they speak is related to Thai, and, confusingly, it is also called Thai. With a little patience and creativity, it is usually possible for people from Thailand to have basic conversations with the Thai ethnolinguistic group in their own languages. There are two main subgroups: the Black Thai, who settled mainly in present-day Lai Châu, Lào Cai and Yên Bái provinces, and the White Thai, who settled in present-day Hòa Bình, Sơn La and Vĩnh Phúc provinces. Less populous subgroups include the Red Thai, many of whom live in Thanh Hóa Province.

The use of these colour-based classifications has traditionally been linked to the colour of their clothes, particularly the women's shirts. However, there is some confusion over the origins of the terms and it's quite possible that it has nothing to do with the colour of their attire and is, instead, linked to the distribution of the subgroups near the Red and Black rivers. The names become even more perplexing when the Vietnamese names for the Thai subgroups are translated into the Thai spoken in Thailand. For example, some scholars have confused Black Thai and Red Thai because the Vietnamese word for black and the Thai word for red sound similar.

With the notable exception of some White Thai communities of Hòa Bình, traditional costume for the women of both the Black and White Thai generally features a coloured blouse with a row of silver buttons down the front, a long black skirt, a coloured waist sash and a black headscarf embroidered with intricate, predominantly red and yellow designs. The traditional costume of the White Thai women of Hòa Bình comprises a long black skirt with fitted waistband embroidered with either a dragon or chicken motif, together with a plain pastel-coloured blouse and gold and maroon sash.

budget might opt for one of the more luxurious accommodation options, including boutique villas with wrap-around swimming pools and isolated retreats hiding in the hills.

Once you've secured accommodation, you can rent a bicycle from your hosts and wobble across narrow bunds to the neighbouring hamlets, enjoying the views as you go. If the bikes at your accommodation are not up to scratch, you can also rent from Mai Châu Countryside Homestay (page 140). A myriad of picturesque walks and treks can be made in the countryside surrounding Mai Châu, with a wide range of itineraries and durations, from short circular walks around the village to longer treks to secluded villages and beyond. Except for the twin caves of Chiều and Mỏ Luông (the latter hosts an annual rave here called the Cave Rave; see **w** savage-hanoi.com for details) close to Bản Lác, Mai Châu doesn't really have sights per se; a visit here is more about ambling around, stopping for drinks and eating local food. There are, however, a few waterfalls that will appeal to less slothful travellers, including Gò Lào Waterfall and Tạt Nàng Waterfall. Reach these with your own motorised wheels (eg: a rented motorbike) or on a tour booked through your accommodation.

Getting there and around There are no train stations or airports close to Mai Châu. Mai Châu town is very small, and **buses** to/from here will pick up/drop off in

A distinctive feature of Thai women is that they grow their hair long and tie it up in a bun.

The Thai inhabit a large part of Northwest Vietnam, in particular the valleys of the major rivers that spill over into Laos. They arrived in Vietnam between the 4th and 5th centuries from southern China and tend to occupy lowland areas, where they have competed with the Kinh over centuries for good-quality farmland that can be irrigated. They are masters of wet rice cultivation, producing high yields and often two harvests each year. Their irrigation works are ingenious and incorporate numerous labour-saving devices, including watermills made from bamboo that funnel water to plots that are several metres higher than the river. You might spot these outside villages in and around Mai Châu (page 136) and Pù Luông (page 140). When in action, they are a wonder to behold.

Thai villages consist of many dozens of houses on stilts shaded by fruit trees and often surrounded by verdant paddy fields. Commonly located by rivers, a common feature of a Thai village is a suspension footbridge that connects the two sides. Owing to their geographical proximity to and agricultural similarities with the Kinh, it is not surprising to see cultural assimilation – sometimes via marriage – and these days most Thai speak Vietnamese.

Traditionally, when a Thai woman marries, her parents-in-law give her a hair extension and a silver hair pin that she is expected to wear (even in bed) for the duration of the marriage. It is common for Thai women to wear their hair in a bun, and you might spot adapted motorcycle helmets to accommodate the bulge. There are two wedding ceremonies: the first at the bride's house, where the couple might spend their first few years of marriage, followed by a second when they move to the husband's family house. Thai cuisine is also distinct, and many homestay meals in Mai Châu and Pù Luông will include some local dishes on the menu, such as baked fish wrapped in banana leaves.

the centre. From there you can find a taxi, motorbike taxi or perhaps walk to your accommodation, which is most likely in the countryside nearby. Several minibuses each day connect Mai Châu with Hanoi (3hrs). Buses to Mộc Châu (2hrs), Sơn La (3hrs), Điện Biên Phủ (6hrs) and Pù Luông (2hrs) do exist, but they're difficult to book online; ask at your accommodation for details. If heading west, there's a chance you'll need to make your way to the highway that connects Mai Châu with Sơn La, 7km north of town, and wait on the side of the road.

Mai Châu was built for the **bicycle**, and most accommodation options will offer them for free or rent them out for a dollar or two. These bikes are never fantastic, but they are usually good enough for lazy, unscripted romps around the countryside. More adventurous travellers will want to rent a **motorbike** and explore further afield.

Where to stay and eat Most visitors to Mai Châu will eat at their hotel or homestay. If you're staying in one of the hotels and want to try a family-style meal, simply wander into any house with a sign saying 'homestay' and book. Don't expect to eat with the family, though they are generally warm and welcoming. Very little English is spoken here, but the families are used to tourists and will find ways to communicate, often through Google Translate or a young neighbour. Note that homestay meals need to be booked several hours in advance at a minimum, and ideally the day before. More standard Vietnamese restaurants selling *phở* and the like can be found in town.

✷ ***Homestays*** Homestays (**$**) are more numerous in Mai Châu than anywhere else in Vietnam. Most are in and around the congested villages of Bản Lác and Poom Coọng and it's possible simply to turn up and find a room, even during busy weekends. Poom Coọng, the northernmost village, is the more attractive of the two, though the best homestays tend to be in the more isolated hamlets. The more successful and affluent homestays have evolved into boutique hotels with swimming pools and rooftop bars. Generally speaking, the further you are from these villages, the more interaction you'll have with the local family. Homestays are easy to find through Google Maps or online booking agents.

Other places to stay *Map, page 137*

La Maison de Bước 98 Bước village; f lamaisondebuoc. Even more remote than Mai Châu Valley Retreat, La Maison de Bước has simple stilt bungalows set in a pretty garden with a swimming pool. **$$**

Mai Châu Countryside Homestay 30 Pom Coọng; f MaiChauCountryside. At the point where Bản Lác and Pom Coọng meet, the location is far from ideal. But there are panoramic views of the rice fields and mountains, making it a good coffee stop. **$$**

✷ **Mai Châu Valley Retreat** Mai Hịch; w maichauvalleyretreat.com. In a remote corner of Mai Châu that isn't inundated with homestays, the Valley Retreat has simple, rustic rooms & a swimming pool & looks over verdant mountains. Home-cooked meals are prepared with vegetables from the garden. **$$**

Sol Bungalows Chiềng Châu village; w solbungalows.com. Crisply designed, good-value accommodation that isn't quite a luxury mountain lodge – though it comes close. There's a swimming pool that overlooks the rice paddies. **$$**

Mai Châu Ecolodge Nà Chiềng village; w maichau.ecolodge.asia. Mai Châu's established luxury option has attractive rooms & a decent restaurant. See page 132 for more information. **$$$**

✷ **Avana Retreat** Panh village; w avanaretreat.com. At the pinnacle of countryside luxury in Vietnam: expect to pay international prices to stay here. See page 133 for more information. **$$$$$**

Other practicalities Specific activities and hikes are best booked through your accommodation. Souvenir shops are everywhere, but you'll need a discerning eye to find something made by hand. For more sophisticated design items like cushions and wall hangings, try **Mai Châu Designs** (32 Bản Lác; w maichauhome.com). Plucky Mai Châu Hospital (227 QL15; ⌚ 07.30–noon & 13.00–16.30 Mon–Fri & 16.30–18.30 Sat–Sun) is in town on the main road, but for emergencies head to Hòa Bình General Hospital (Tổ 10; w hoabinhhospital.org.vn) or return to Hanoi.

PÙ LUÔNG Pù Luông Nature Reserve, technically in Thanh Hóa Province (page 222) in Central Vietnam, is especially beautiful, even by the high standards set by Vietnam. This is a fantasy landscape of rippling rice terraces and protected limestone forests that harbour the endangered Delacour's langur (*Trachypithecus delacouri*), clouded leopard (*Neofelis nebulosa*), Owston's palm civet (*Chrotogale owstoni*), and possibly some sun bears (*Helarctos malayanus*) and moon bears (*Ursus thibetanus*). There is very little industrial development in this part of the country. Settlements are mostly small villages of stilt houses inhabited by the Thai (page 138), the same ethnolinguistic group that lives in Mai Châu to the west. Pù Luông is undeniably more visually dramatic than its neighbour and yet it sees far fewer tourists, in part because it takes an extra hour or two to get here from Hanoi. Tourism is developing, but less furiously than it did in Mai Châu three decades ago. Like Mai Châu, there

TRAIL RUNNING IN NORTHERN VIETNAM

Trail running has taken off in the northern mountains, with established and popular trails in Sa Pa, Pù Luông and Mộc Châu. Races, which usually happen once a year in each place, range from short fun runs to ambitious ultra-marathons. To see where and when the races are held, visit w vietnamtrailseries.com.

aren't specific sights in Pù Luông; unlike Mai Châu, the reserve is too large to cover on a bicycle. Most of the activities here involve hiking, some of which are self-guided, swimming in streams and waterfalls, visiting villages and waterwheels, and motorbiking. Arrange these through your accommodation.

Getting there and around There are no train stations or airports close to Pù Luông. If travelling by **bus**, there are various villages offering accommodation across Pù Luông Nature Reserve, so when booking make it clear to the driver where you want to go. Prepare to be dropped far from your accommodation and to take a taxi from there. There are regular buses to Hanoi (4½hrs), which usually pass Mai Châu, and irregular buses heading east to Thanh Hóa and Ninh Bình.

Pù Luông is not one town or village, but a series of settlements across a large area, making it particularly difficult to get the most out of it without your own transport. If you're arriving by public transport and don't wish to rent a motorbike, book accommodation at an established lodge in one of the two major settlements: Bản Hiêu or Bản Đôn. Your host should be able to give you enough ideas for villages, waterfalls and rice terraces that you can visit on foot.

Where to stay and eat *Map, page 137*

There are four settlements to research when choosing a base in Pù Luông: Bản Đôn, Bản Hiêu, Kho Mường and Bản Hang. Bản Đôn is the most popular village, with a healthy range of accommodation, from simple homestays to mountain retreats. Bản Hiêu, built around a waterfall, is unimaginably beautiful, but has fewer options to stay and most come just for the day. Kho Mường and Bản Hang are quieter and more remote, each with only a handful of homestays. Only stay in these hamlets if you have your own wheels. There is also an increasing number of homestays and lodges that offer fine views on the main road that runs through Pù Luông, the CT02. Accommodations will also be able to arrange meals and activities, such as hiking and visits to villages.

Homestays tend to come and go so it's impossible to keep a reliable evergreen list, but they are easy to discover through Google Maps or online booking agents and are found across the reserve. The homestay rules apply here: it's usually possible to turn up and find a bed for the night in a shared room, but book meals at least a few hours in advance.

✷ **Homestay Mr Ba** Bản Hiêu; ☎ 379 781 988; f. One of the few reliable homestays that has been in continuous operation for years, this option is highly recommended. It's at the top of the waterfall in the most attractive corner of Bản Hiêu village. If you're visiting for the day, ask your accommodation to call ahead & book lunch. There are both private and shared rooms. **$**

Pù Luông Natura Bản Đôn; w naturabungalow.com. Close to the Treehouse but with less character, Natura nevertheless offers an enviable Pù Luông mountain lodge experience, with a smart infinity pool & comfortable rooms in a garden setting. **$$$**

✷ **Pù Luông Treehouse** (page 132) Bản Đôn; w puluongtreehouse.com. Neverland-like treehouses & excellent food in Bản Đôn. **$$$**

HINTERLANDS: MỘC CHÂU AND TÀ XÙA

For a description of 'Hinterlands' boxes, see page 131.

A rugged and fertile chunk of land west of Mai Châu, most Vietnamese associate Mộc Châu with farming, particularly dairy, though you'll mostly encounter fruit farms that cultivate apricots, plums, apples, pears and many other non-tropical varieties. Mộc Châu is a vast district and sights are dotted all around, making it particularly difficult to get the most out of without your own transport. There are several waterfalls, some of which you can swim in, including Thác Nà Bó, Thác Chiềng Khoa and Thác Dải Yếm. The town of Mộc Châu has restaurants and cafés, but better to stay in one of the accommodation options in the countryside, like the excellent A Chu Homestay (f dulichvanhmong). The road north from Mộc Châu towards the Đà River crossing – possible on a frequent ferry – leads to **Tà Xùa**, one of the highest ridges in Sơn La Province. This is particularly special at dawn during a clear summer's day, when there are views over the morning mist. The photo opportunities here have made Tà Xùa popular with Vietnamese photographers, videographers and motorbikers, and a slew of lodges have popped up to host them, such as the very comfortable **Tà Xùa Ecolodge** (w ecolodgetaxua.com). If you're arriving by public transport and plan to rent motorbikes after arriving, buses to/from Mộc Châu will pick up/drop off on the main road in the centre of town. From there, taxis will take you to your accommodation. Several buses daily connect Mộc Châu with Hanoi (4½hrs), Sơn La (3hrs) and Điện Biên Phủ (7hrs).

Other practicalities There are pharmacies in Phố Đoàn, the main settlement in the reserve. For anything serious, head to Hòa Bình General Hospital (Tổ 10; w hoabinhhospital.org.vn; ⌚ all day daily) or better yet, return to Hanoi.

SƠN LA

Most of the large (14,210km²), wild province of Sơn La west of Hòa Bình consists of a calcareous mamillated plateau. Rarely higher than 1,300m above sea level and averaging 500–700m on the Sơn La Plateau, it experiences less rainfall than the territories of Điện Biên, Yên Bái, Hòa Bình and Laos that surround it. Winter temperatures here can drop to as low as 12°C in Mộc Châu and even lower in Tà Xùa, so come prepared. Sơn La's climate is favourable for growing tea and, more recently, quality Arabica coffee. Deforestation has been a problem, but some valuable trees still flourish towards the border with Laos, including aniseed, yellow pine and small leaf bamboo. Grasslands extend for massive distances and the varieties tend to be tough, although adequate to support small herds of buffalo and oxen. Milk cows are farmed along the Mộc Châu Plateau, where more tender grasses flourish. The Kinh (page 189) tend to live in urban areas, the Thai (page 138) in the valleys at foothills and the Hmong (page 160) at higher altitudes.

HISTORY It was not until the 18th century, under the patronage of the Thai lords, that Sơn La began to develop as a town. During the late 1870s the region was invaded by renegade Chinese Yellow Flag bands taking refuge after the failed Taiping Uprising. Allying himself to Lin Yung-fu, commander of the pursuing

Black Flag forces, Đèo Văn Trị, a Thai chieftain, led a substantial army against the Yellow Flags in 1880, decisively defeating and expelling them from the country. Thus the chieftain established hegemony over all the Thai lords in the Sơn La area, enabling him to rely on their military support in his subsequent struggle against the French between 1880 and 1888.

As the French moved their forces up the Đà River Valley during the campaign of 1888, the chieftains of the area were forced to surrender. A French garrison was quickly established at Sơn La. As elsewhere in the Northwest, the French chose to reward the chieftains of Sơn La for their new-found loyalty by reconfirming their authority as local government mandarins, now on behalf of a colonial rather than royal master.

While large-scale resistance to French rule in the Northwest effectively ceased after 1890, sporadic uprisings continued to create problems for the colonial administration. The French responded by establishing detention centres throughout the area. The culmination of this policy came in 1908 with the construction of a large penitentiary designed to incarcerate resistance leaders from the Northwest and other regions of Vietnam. Just one year after the opening of the Sơn La Penitentiary, prisoners staged a mass breakout, causing substantial damage to the prison itself before fleeing across the border into Laos.

During the final days of colonial rule Sơn La became an important French military outpost, and an airbase was built 20km from the town. The colonial government abandoned Sơn La on the eve of the Battle of Điện Biên Phủ (page 144).

SƠN LA CITY There is little that will keep you in Sơn La, but there's enough to see if you're making an overnight stop. The **Sơn La Provincial Museum** (Khau Cả; w baotangsonla.vn; ⌚ 07.30–11.30 & 13.30–17.30 daily; 30,000VND/free adult/child) is in fact the town's old French penitentiary, constructed in 1908, damaged in 1909, bombed in 1952 and now partially rebuilt for tourists. The original 3m-deep dungeon and tiny cells, complete with food-serving hatches and leg-irons, can be seen together with an exhibition illustrating the history of the place and the key individuals who were incarcerated here.

Buses to/from Sơn La will pick up/drop off in the centre of town, and sometimes at your accommodation. Several buses daily connect Sơn La with Hanoi (4½hrs), and Điện Biên Phủ (5hrs). Sơn La is a small city and most are just passing through. The centre, near Vincom, has most of the **hotels and restaurants**, and from there it's a 30-minute walk to the prison. Sơn La Provincial Hospital (w benhviendakhoa.sonla.gov.vn) is not in the city, but a 20-minute drive southeast towards Hanoi.

ĐIỆN BIÊN PHỦ

Điện Biên Province (9,562.9km^2) is dominated by mountainous terrain, with elevations ranging between 600m and 1,800m. Temperatures here can plummet in December and January, especially in higher altitudes close to Laos, where lows may drop to single digits. Điện Biên's climate and soil conditions are well suited to the cultivation of various crops, with rice paddies filling the valleys and hillsides. The province is particularly noted for its extensive fields of upland rice, which thrive on the terraced slopes, and tea leaves, which grow on trees that billboards claim are more than a thousand years old. Deforestation has taken its toll over the years, but patches of dense forest remain, particularly near the Laos border. The ethnic composition of Điện Biên is diverse, with as many as 19 different ethnolinguistic groups. The most numerous in the countryside are the Hmong (page 160) and

Thai (page 138), who survive primarily on agriculture. The Kinh (page 189), Vietnam's ethnolinguistic majority, constitute only around a third of this province, and are generally concentrated in urban areas like Điện Biên Phủ, the provincial capital, where they engage in trade, government and service industries. For reasons unknown, the people in Điện Biên are especially friendly, making it a particularly compelling province to visit.

For the remote and apparently insignificant little town of Điện Biên Phủ to have earned itself an important place in the history books is a considerable achievement. The Battle of Điện Biên Phủ in 1954 was a turning point in colonial history: it marked the end of French involvement in Indochina and heralded the collapse of its North African empire. Had the Americans, who shunned French appeals for help, taken more careful note of what happened at Điện Biên Phủ, they might have avoided their own calamitous involvement in Vietnam just a decade later. Deep in the highlands of the Northwest subregion, close to the border with Laos and 420km from Hanoi (although it feels further), Điện Biên Phủ lies in the Mường Thanh Valley, a heart-shaped basin 19km long and 13km wide, crossed by the Nậm Rốm River. In contrast to its tumultuous history, foreigners that come in peace will find Điện Biên Phủ to be a friendly city packed with sights related to the 1954 battle.

HISTORY There is evidence that the Thai ethnolinguistic group occupied the Mường Thanh Valley as early as the 4th century BCE, with further infiltration from different Thai groups following in the 11th century CE. During the 15th century much of

THE BATTLE OF ĐIỆN BIÊN PHỦ

On 20 November 1953, after a series of French successes against Vietnamese revolutionaries, Colonel Christian de Castries and six battalions of French and French-colonial troops were parachuted into Điện Biên Phủ. Overseeing the operation was General Henri Eugène Navarre, a celebrated war veteran who served in both world wars. Điện Biên Phủ, situated in a narrow valley surrounded by steep, wooded peaks, was chosen specifically because it was thought by Navarre to be impenetrable. From there, he believed, their forces could begin to harry the Việt Minh close to their bases, as well as protect against incursions from Laos. At the centre of the valley was the all-important airstrip – Colonel de Castries's only link with the outside world. In *Vietnam: A History*, Stanley Karnow describes de Castries as 'irresistible to women and ridden with gambling debts…he had been a champion horseman, dare-devil pilot and courageous commando, his body scarred by three wounds earned during World War II and earlier in Indochina'.

In response, the celebrated General Võ Nguyên Giáp (page 149) moved his forces, some 55,000 men, into the surrounding area, manhandling heavy guns (with the help, it is said, of 200,000 porters) up the impossibly steep mountainsides until they had a view over the French forces. This was unexpected, but the French commander still believed that his forces would have the upper hand in a confrontation and he set about strengthening his position. De Castries created a series of heavily fortified strongholds, giving them women's names (said to be those of his numerous mistresses): Anne-Marie, Françoise, Huguette, Béatrice, Gabrielle, Dominique, Claudine, Isabelle and Eliane. As it turned out, de Castries was not luring the Việt Minh into a trap but creating one for himself and his men.

the far northwest was ruled by these Thai chieftains who gradually extended their territory west, perhaps with support from the Lao king Suliyavongsa (reigned 1637–94), who was the first monarch to welcome European visitors to Laos.

During the 18th century, a great peasant army was formed under the leadership of Hoàng Công Chất from Thái Bình Province to challenge the exploitative overlords of the time, the Trịnh (page 11). Having taken territories along the Mã River he advanced on Mường Thanh District and took the Mường Thanh Valley, where he built the Bản Phủ Citadel in 1752. From these strategic bases he defended the border territories against Burmese, Lao and Chinese bandits. His son, who succeeded him after his death in 1767, fought valiantly against the Trịnh but was eventually forced to flee into neighbouring Laos. The citadel was subsequently razed and for many years the region was in disorder.

Siamese and Laotian troops occupied present-day Điện Biên Phủ in 1795 and again in 1834, but never got a foothold in the lowlands further east, which, by the 19th century, were under the control of the Nguyễn Dynasty. Large numbers of Hmong moved into the area during the Taiping Rebellion (1850–64) in China and many of their descendants remain in remote Tủa Chùa District. Meanwhile, news of a foreign invasion of a different ilk had reached the far northwest. France, a distant European power, attacked Đà Nẵng in 1858, and by 1885 the whole of present-day Vietnam was under the colonial yoke. As France's development and exploitation plans focused on the coast, Điện Biên Phủ was overlooked until 1941, when Hồ Chí Minh re-entered Vietnam from China (page 182) and helped

From the surrounding highlands, Võ had the French at his mercy. The shelling started in the middle of March, and the strongholds fell one by one; Béatrice first and then Gabrielle and Anne-Marie, until de Castries's forces were concentrated around the airstrip. Poor weather, which prevented the French from using their air power, and human wave attacks gradually wore the French troops down. By this time, de Castries had withdrawn to his bunker and command had effectively been taken over by his junior officers. A furious bombardment by the heavy guns of the Việt Minh on 1 May led to the final massed assault five days later. On the final night, the Việt Minh taunted the French defenders by playing the 'Song of the Partisans', the theme of the French Resistance, over the garrison's radio frequencies. The colonel's headquarters fell on 7 May, when 9,500 French and French-colonial troops surrendered. A small force of paratroopers at the isolated southern position, Isabelle, continued to resist for a further 24 hours. De Castries was captured and taken prisoner.

The humiliation at Điện Biên Phủ led the French to sue for peace at a conference in Geneva. On 20 July 1954 it was agreed that Vietnam should be divided in two along the 17th parallel: a communist north and a capitalist south. In total, 20,000 Việt Minh and over 3,000 French troops were killed at Điện Biên Phủ. The Geneva agreement set terms so that the dead from both sides would be honoured in a massive ossuary. But when Ngô Đình Diệm, the president of the Republic of South Vietnam, symbolically urinated over Việt Minh dead in the South rather than bury them with honour, Võ and Hồ Chí Minh decided to leave the French dead to lie where they had fallen. Over the nine years of war between the Việt Minh and the French, the dead numbered somewhere between 250,000 and 1 million civilians, 200,000–300,000 Việt Minh and 95,000 French-colonial troops. Despite all this death, another 20 years of warfare lay ahead.

establish and reinforce various anti-colonial resistance cells in Northern Vietnam. This culminated in the extraordinary Battle of Điện Biên Phủ in 1954 (page 144), resulting in a catastrophic French defeat and the end of colonial Indochina.

GETTING THERE AND AROUND There is no train station in Điện Biên Phủ. Its main bus station is a little over 3km north of the centre, but many bus companies will pick up/drop off in the centre. Booking tickets for next-day travel – including to Laos (see opposite) – is straightforward inside the main terminal. East from here, several buses daily head to Sơn La (4hrs), Mộc Châu (5hrs) and Hanoi (12hrs). For Mai Châu, they'll drop you at a junction nearby, from where you can find a taxi

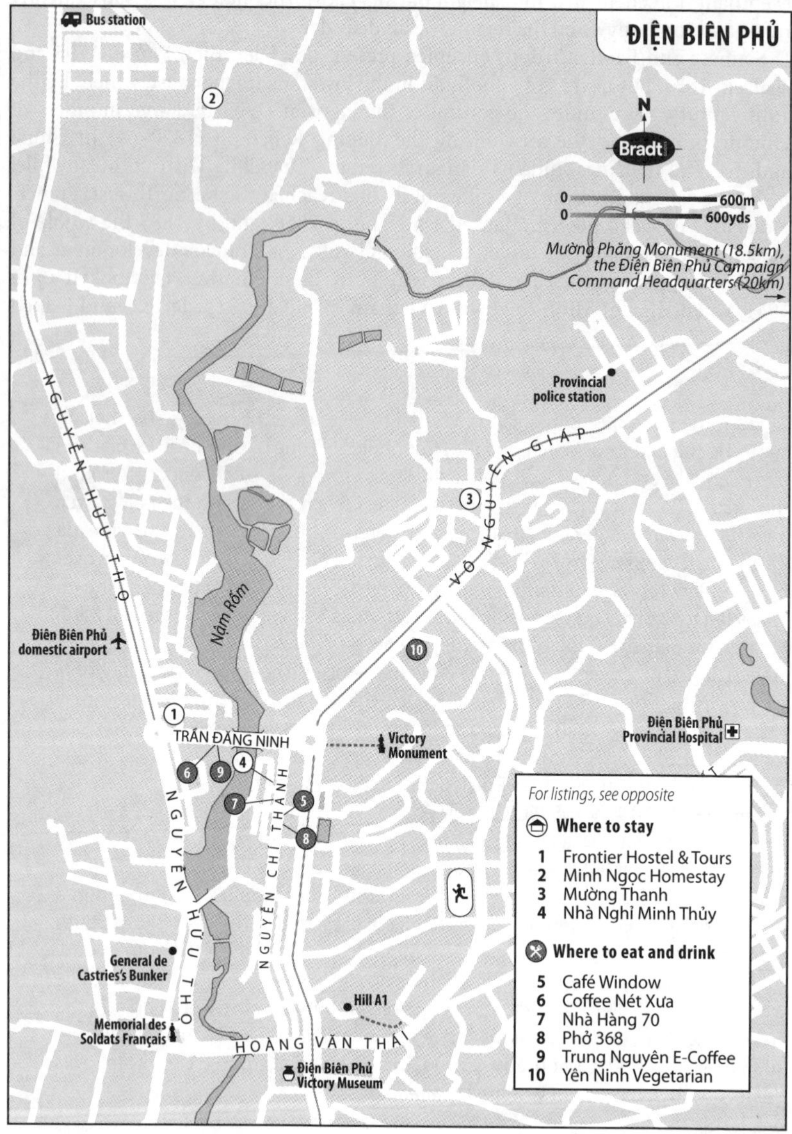

GETTING TO LAOS FROM ĐIỆN BIÊN PHỦ

There is a hassle-free international border crossing (Tây Trang) an hour's drive south of Điện Biên Phủ. Buses to the border and to cities in Laos leave in the morning and pass over a bumpy, winding road used by mining trucks, which may turn a few stomachs. At the time of research, Laos visas on arrival were not available at this crossing, so arrange one at the embassy in Hanoi beforehand. You can book buses a day in advance at the bus station.

into town. North from here, buses head to Mường Lay (2hrs), where you connect to buses heading north and east to Lai Châu and Lào Cai. Travelling by bus in these parts is an adventure but also time-consuming, so come with patience.

Điện Biên Phủ's domestic **airport** (Mường Thanh), 3km from town, is best connected with Nội Bài International Airport in Hanoi. There are two to three flights every day. There are also a few flights a week between Điện Biên Phủ and Tân Sơn Nhất International Airport in Hồ Chí Minh City.

Central Điện Biên Phủ is small and **walkable**, but covering all the sights will require motorised transport. There are taxis in town and ride-hailing apps such as Grab work here, but to explore the sights for a day or two, it's best to rent a motorbike, hire a car with driver or enlist the services of a tour guide.

WHERE TO STAY *Map, opposite*

✷ **CBT Điện Biên Phủ** [not mapped] f dienbiencbt. One of several community-based tourism organisations that work with local families to arrange accommodation in the villages that surround Điện Biên Phủ. Due to the location, it's best to have your own wheels. **$**

Frontier Hostel & Tours 8 Lò Văn Hặc; w frontierhostel.com. New hostel that is spearheading Điện Biên Phủ's burgeoning backpacker scene, with in-depth tours of the city & province & affordable rooms. **$**

Minh Ngọc Homestay No 32 Mó village; f homestayminhngoc. Beautiful & ramshackle property about 4km north of the centre, with delicious home-cooked food & a rustic, wooden charm. **$**

Nhà Nghỉ Minh Thủy 32 Nguyễn Chí Thanh; w booking.com. Standard Vietnamese guesthouse but done well, with clean, simply appointed rooms, some of which overlook the adjacent river. **$**

Mường Thanh 514 Võ Nguyên Giáp; w granddienbienphu.muongthanh.com. Probably the best option in town if peace & quiet is non-negotiable, especially as the rooms are empty most of the time. Some have a faint smell of cigarette smoke, so feel free to keep requesting to see more rooms until you find 1 that fits the bill. **$$**

WHERE TO EAT AND DRINK *Map, opposite*

The city's social life is centred around Nguyễn Chí Thanh Street, a tree-lined thoroughfare with restaurants, cafés and outdoor barbecue restaurants. Điện Biên Phủ is a sleepy place but wander up and down here and you'll likely find what you're looking for.

Restaurants

Nhà Hàng 70 70 Nguyễn Chí Thanh; ⏲ 07.00–23.00 daily. One of a cluster of point-&-pick rice restaurants that serves from late morning & into the night. Truth be told, this place is no better than the others, so come & see which place appears the most appetising. There's no menu so order by pointing at what's available; at busy times you may need to assert yourself to be noticed. **$**

Phở 368 83 Nguyễn Chí Thanh; ⏲ 05.00–14.00 daily. One of Điện Biên Phủ's quintessential *phở* restaurants, which specialises in the beef version, with various cuts. **$**

Yên Ninh Vegetarian Restaurant 257 Tổ 4, Tân Thanh; f yenninhrestaurant; ⌚ 08.00–22.00 daily. Điện Biên Phủ's token vegan restaurant is surprisingly good, with all the usual meatless versions of classic Vietnamese dishes & a few inspired creations. Try the tofu with pineapple & the fried eggplant. Don't be concerned when you see meat & seafood on the menu – they use a soy-based substitute. $

Coffee houses

Café Window 71 Nguyễn Chí Thanh; f window.coffee71; ⌚ 07.00–23.00 daily. Appealing for its total lack of frills, Window offers brusque service, delicious Vietnamese coffee & a bustling morning atmosphere on outdoor chairs & tables.

Coffee Nét Xưa 45 Trần Đăng Ninh; f cafeNetXuaDienBien; ⌚ 06.00–23.00 daily. Điện Biên Phủ's most eclectic café, filled with a fascinating collection of collectibles. Some of it is junk; some is antique; all of it is interesting to examine. They occasionally have live music performances in the evening.

Trung Nguyên E-Coffee 35 Trần Đăng Ninh; ⌚ 07.00–23.00 daily. Reliable coffee shop with a somewhat clinical décor, much like other Trung Nguyên cafés in remote parts of Vietnam. It's better to steer clear of the Western coffee & take a chance on one of their creations, like coffee with green rice, shaved coconut & condensed milk.

OTHER PRACTICALITIES For tours, reach out to Frontier Hostel & Tours (page 147) or CBT Điện Biên Phủ (page 147). Điện Biên Phủ Provincial Hospital (Tôn Thất Tùng; w bvdk.syt.dienbien.gov.vn; ⌚ all day daily) is the biggest medical facility in the province.

WHAT TO SEE AND DO

Điện Biên Phủ Victory Museum (Tổ 1, Mường Thanh Ward; w btctdbp.svhttdl.dienbien.gov.vn; ⌚ 07.00–11.00 & 13.30–18.00 daily; 100,000VND/free adult/child) A futuristic flying-saucer-like building inaugurated in 2014, the exhibits here are dedicated to the 1954 victory, and the museum is a good place to start when visiting the sights in Điện Biên Phủ. Several models depict important scenes from the battle, including Hồ Chí Minh discussing strategy with Võ Nguyên Giáp (see opposite). There are also examples of the Vietnamese artillery, all of which were hauled by pioneer youth volunteers and Việt Minh soldiers along five zig-zag mountain routes. There are displays of wooden wheelbarrows, wooden sledges, bicycles with lengthened handlebars and other methods of transport used to heave the Việt Minh weapons to the battle site. A glance at the mountains visible from the museum gives a sense of how impossible this mission must have seemed. You'll also find weaponry, some damaged beyond recognition, used by Christian de Castries's forces, which included the Foreign Legionnaires. Graphic reminders of the Việt Minh victory are everywhere, including the Việt Minh flag, which was hoisted over the final battlefield. Across the road is the Việt Minh Cemetery, with the graves of some 15,000 soldiers, where Vietnamese tourists come to pay their respects.

✷ **Hill A1** (Road 279, Mường Thanh Ward; ⌚ 07.00–11.00 & 13.30–17.30 daily; 25,000VND/free adult/child) Known to the French as Eliane 2 (named after one of de Castries's mistresses), this was once one of the most important strategic positions overlooking the valley. It housed the headquarters of the French governor and much of the French barracks, protected by tunnels connected with defensive positions and concrete bunkers. Trenches surrounded by barbed wire fences completed the fortifications, which were protected by heavy artillery. During the offensive by Việt Minh commanders, coal miners from Quảng Ninh Province (which holds the country's most important coal reserves) dug a long tunnel under the complex and filled it with explosives. They were detonated on 6 May 1954 and

THE LIFE AND LEGACY OF GENERAL VÕ NGUYÊN GIÁP

Võ Nguyên Giáp was a visionary strategist and Hồ Chí Minh's interior minister in 1945. Together they masterminded the Battle of Điện Biên Phủ, which has gone down as one of the most famous and triumphant anti-colonial victories of all time. Born in Quảng Bình Province in 1912 to an anti-colonial scholar, Võ met Hồ Chí Minh in high school and joined the Revolutionary Party of Young Vietnam in 1926. He was in and out of prison for participating in protests but earned a law degree from Hanoi University in the late 1930s. He married Minh Thái in 1938, and they both worked for the Indochinese Communist Party. When the party was banned in 1939, Võ fled to China, his wife was arrested and died in prison, and his sister-in-law was executed.

During the chaos of World War II and the Japanese invasion of Vietnam, Võ returned to his country in 1941. After Japan's withdrawal, Võ marched with Hồ Chí Minh into Hanoi for Vietnam's Declaration of Independence in 1945. Independence was not won for another nine years, when Võ masterminded the victory in Điện Biên Phủ in 1954, forcing the French to withdraw from Vietnam. Vietnam was divided into North and South that same year, and Võ became deputy prime minister, defence minister and commander-in-chief of North Vietnam's armed forces. Just as he helped expel the French, he also played a part in forcing the withdrawal of the United States and the final defeat of South Vietnam in 1975.

After the end of the American War, Võ became less politically active, until he returned to the fray in 1978 to help remove Pol Pot and the Khmer Rouge from power and defend against the retaliatory invasion from China in the north. Võ served as newly reunified Vietnam's defence minister until 1980 and was a full member of the Politburo until 1982. Ensconced in the leafy grounds of his home on Hoàng Diệu Street in Hanoi, Võ faded from politics in the 1980s but remained an important figurehead. Every war museum in the country worth its salt will have a photo documenting and celebrating Võ's visit. He remained active until he passed away in 2013, aged 102. Unlike other high-ranking Vietnamese officials, Võ was not buried in Hanoi, but was returned to where he was born in Quảng Bình.

Today, Võ remains the most beloved Vietnamese revolutionary hero besides Uncle Hồ himself, though questions hang over his strategies. William Westmoreland, commander of the US forces, famously noted that any American general suffering the same losses as Võ would have been fired immediately. There was a flurry of obituaries in the international media after Võ's death and many of Vietnam's shiny new streets now carry his name.

a tremendous explosion was heard the length and breadth of the valley. Today the crater is still there, but you will see a reconstructed bunker. The site was spruced up in 2014 along with the museum.

Victory Monument (Hill D1; ⏲ 08.00–17.00 daily; 25,000VND/free adult/child) This enormous, 220-tonne bronze sculpture was erected on Hill D1 in 2004 to mark the 50th anniversary of the Vietnamese victory. It was sculpted by acclaimed sculptor Nguyễn Hải and depicts three Vietnamese soldiers, one carrying a child with outstretched arms, standing on top of de Castries's bunker. Reach it by foot along a mighty set of steps from Võ Nguyên Giáp Street, or by car or motorcycle along a lane that runs around the back. The views are as epic as the subject matter, especially on a clear day at sunrise or sunset.

General de Castries's Bunker (Nguyễn Hữu Thọ; 25,000VND/free adult/child) On the battlefield where General de Castries suffered his greatest defeat is this reconstructed bunker protected by a semi-cylindrical roof. There isn't a great deal to see, but scattered around the bunker are examples of artillery used by the French, including an American-made M24 Chaffee tank on the other side of the road. De Castries was captured during the siege and held for four months until after the Geneva peace conference in July 1954. Afterwards he returned to the military, but retired in 1959 and died in Paris aged 88 in 1991. A few blocks south is the Memorial des Soldats Français, which honours the 3,000 fallen French.

Around Điện Biên Phủ Encircling Điện Biên Phủ are battlegrounds, headquarters and memorial sites, usually commemorated with a plaque or sculpture of sorts, but the most engaging sites are in Mường Phăng District, west of the city centre.

HINTERLANDS: THE FAR-FLUNG NORTHWEST

For a description of 'Hinterlands' boxes, see page 131.

Bordering Laos to the west and China to the north, the provinces of Điện Biên and Lai Châu merge to form Vietnam's most westerly enclave and the country's remotest corner. Opportunities for adventure here abound, especially if you're confident on a motorbike, but prepare for all manner of obstacles, including landslides, floods, terrible roads and uncompromising border guards. Do not underestimate how challenging travelling in this part of the country is. Technically, foreigners need permission to enter here, which you may or may not be granted at the gigantic, Orwellian provincial police station (Công An Tỉnh Điện Biên) in Điện Biên Phủ city (312 Võ Nguyên Giáp). But note that even with the right paperwork, you might be refused access to some parts of the area for unknown reasons. There aren't specific sights in the area, but the driving roads are glorious and the sense of adventure is unrivalled. You're highly unlikely to meet any other foreigners; if you do, there's a good chance they will also be armed with this guidebook.

The closest town to this area – a good place to start and finish the adventure, with a few passable hotels and restaurants – is Mường Lay, on the border between Điện Biên and Lai Châu and on the Đà River. Mường Lay formerly occupied a majestic setting in a deep and wide valley cloaked in dense tiers of forest, but it has been moved up the hillside due to the construction of a dam that left this once-idyllic settlement underwater. The road to Mường Lay was built by an energetic French district governor, Auguste Pavie, and was used by soldiers fleeing the French garrison at Lai Châu to the supposed safety of the garrison at Điện Biên Phủ in 1953. Việt Minh ambushes along the Pavie Track meant that the French were forced to hack their way through the jungle, and those few who made it to Điện Biên Phủ found themselves almost immediately under siege again. To extend the adventure, combine the far-flung northwest with eastern Lai Châu Province, close to Sa Pa (page 162).

Some 20km northeast of Điện Biên Phủ and concealed within the forest is the **Điện Biên Phủ Campaign Command Headquarters** ✷ (Mường Phăng; ⌚ 07.00–11.00 & 13.30–17.00 daily; 25,000VND/free adult/child), from where Võ Nguyên Giáp masterminded and guided the victory at the Battle of Điện Biên Phủ. The site is expansive and signage is clear, though contextual information is practically non-existent. The bamboo huts, each with a specific function, are reconstructions and the pathways have been concreted over, offering a safe and sanitised version of what would have been a rather squalid and rudimentary HQ – there are rumours that, in the midst of battle in 1954, Võ Nguyên Giáp was also combatting diarrhoea. Despite the scarcity of information, the historic significance and jungle setting make this one of the highlight sights in Điện Biên Phủ.

More detailed but less dramatic than the monument in town (page 149) is the out-of-the-way **Mường Phăng Monument** (Tượng Đài Di Tích Mường Phăng; Phăng village, on the way to the command headquarters, Mường Phăng; ⌚ 07.00–11.00 & 13.30–17.00 daily; 25,000VND/free adult/child), with 25 figures representing the forces involved in the victory at Điện Biên Phủ. The line-up reflects the youths who dragged cannons up mountainsides and members of the province's various ethnolinguistic groups who transported weaponry using bamboo carrying poles and bicycles with elongated handlebars. Each figure is about 2.7m tall. Front and centre is Võ Nguyên Giáp (page 149), who stands beneath a Soviet-style profile of Hồ Chí Minh. The words above Uncle Hồ read '*Quyết chiến quyết thắng*', or 'Definitive battle definitive victory'.

THÁC BÀ AND MÙ CANG CHẢI

Prior to 1994, Yên Bái Province, together with Lào Cai Province, was called Hoàng Liên Sơn. Covering 6,900km^2, it is home to more than 800,000 people. A route existed for centuries along the valley of the Red River, which allowed direct trading with China and beyond. Steep mountains rise either side of the valley. The notorious outlaws known as the Black Flags used many of the valley's inhabitants to enrich their coffers with gold and relied on slaves to transport much of their merchandise. Yên Bái has always been known as a stronghold for the Vietnamese Nationalist Party (Quốc Dân Đảng; page 14) and the province fought vigorously to oppose the colonial regime in the 1930s.

Rice is grown along the Hồng River valleys, while rattan, bamboo and tea grows in the upland areas. There are also large damson, plum, and pear plantations. As far as tourism is concerned, Yên Bái city, the provincial capital, is one of the least developed in the country, despite being on the train line and having access to Hanoi on a speedy toll road. This is because most bypass the city and head straight to **Thác Bà Lake**, which was created by the damming of the Chảy River, or **Mù Cang Chải**, with its mesmerising array of rice terraces.

THÁC BÀ LAKE This large, scenic stretch of water covers 2,300km^2 and was created when a huge hydro-electric dam was built across the upper Chảy River. Over 10km at its widest area and 80km at its longest, this is fishing utopia: over 80 species have been recorded. With more than 1,000 islets and water that is crystal clear, the lake is also good for swimming. Surrounded by partly forested mountains, the area, best explored by boat, motorbike or on foot, is home to many birds, including wagtails (*Motacilla*), flycatchers (*Muscicapidae*), warblers (*Sylviidae*), finches (*Fringillidae*), shrikes (*Laniidae*), buntings (*Emberizidae*), fulvettas (*Alcippe*), babblers (*Timaliidae*), swallows (*Hirundinidae*), nightjars (*Caprimulgidae*), cuckoos

(*Cuculidae*) and numerous waterbirds. There are several lakeside homestays and lodges, mostly around Vũ Linh, an attractive Dao village. **La Vie Vũ Linh** (Ngòi Tu village; **w** lavievulinh.com; **$$**) is the best established and remains recommended. Many more can be found on Google Maps and on hotel websites. Only 3 hours from Hanoi by car or motorbike, Thác Bà is a good long-weekend option. The easiest way to get here is with your own wheels and some accommodation providers offer a transfer service from Hanoi.

MÙ CANG CHẢI Mù Cang Chải, a sizeable district in Yên Bái Province, holds mesmerising rice terraces: a human-manipulated highland landscape where rock-strewn rivers flow beneath feathery mountains. Huge swathes of these slopes have been carved into spiralling terraces that sometimes ascend to the district's highest peaks – true testament to the ingenuity of human agriculture. These rice terraces, some of which are hundreds of years old, shift with the seasons. Planting in the water-logged strips begins in spring; in summer the terraces slowly swell with the electric green of ripening rice; in autumn they briefly turn wheat-yellow before the harvest; and in winter, when mist descends on the district, the muddy mountains fill with water in preparation for the next cycle. The Hmong (page 160) dominate the area and are responsible for building, maintaining and farming the terraces, but you'll find Kinh (page 189) in the town. There aren't specific sights in Mù Cang Chải, but there are areas where the terracing is especially extraordinary.

Getting there and around There are no train stations or airports close to Mù Cang Chải. Night **buses** (8hrs) connect Hanoi with Mù Cang Chải town. Alternatively, make your way to Yên Bái city and take a bus from there (5hrs). Prepare to be dropped far from your accommodation and then to take a taxi. If you've prebooked accommodation, they should be able to help you with arrival and with onward travel. Irregular buses also connect Mù Cang Chải with the provincial capitals of Sơn La, Lào Cai and Lai Châu for onward travel.

To travel around, one can hike, motorbike or drive. Mù Cang Chải is the name of the biggest town and the district. The better accommodation options are in the more remote areas. Your host should be able to give you enough ideas for villages and rice terraces that you can visit on foot, but you'll need a motorbike or car to find the best views.

Where to stay and eat Budget travellers will find that Mù Cang Chải town is an adequate base, with a litany of cheap homestays and guesthouses. Those with a little more to spend can investigate the lodges that speckle the district. Accommodation providers will also be able to arrange meals, motorbike rental and hiking activities. **Homestays** (**$**) tend to come and go and are concentrated in and around Mù Cang Chải town. Find them on online booking agents.

Lapantan Paradise La Pán Tẩn; f. Scrappy, family-owned lodge with wooden bungalows, many with small balconies. The home-cooked meals resemble those of a homestay & the family will help arrange activities. **$$**

Mù Cang Chải Ecolodge [map, page 130] Nậm Khắt; **w** mucangchaiecolodge.com. Sturdy bungalows perch on stilts & overlook shallow rice terraces & vegetable farms. For more about this lodge, one of the first in the area, see page 132. **$$**

Le Champ Tú Lệ Nước Nóng Community; **w** lechamp.vn. The most comfortable & expensive option in the area is just outside Mù Cang Chải District, but close enough to make half-day trips to the rice terraces. The property is rougher around the edges than it should be for the price & the food is sub-par. **$$$**

Other practicalities There are pharmacies and a hospital in Mù Cang Chải; for anything serious, head to Yên Bái General Hospital (Tiền Phong; w benhvientinhyenbai.vn) or return immediately to Hanoi.

What to see and do The majesty of the area, with its rice terraces, is such that you can travel in any direction and come across outstanding natural and cultivated beauty, but specific visitor-friendly communes have emerged in recent years. Some charge a small entrance fee at certain times of year, particularly during the harvest.

The closest commune to Mù Cang Chải is **Mồ Dề** and it is therefore one of the most visited, particularly by domestic visitors. Móng Ngựa (Mù Cang Chải; 20,000/10,000VND adult/child) – ticketed during the harvest – is the flagship rice terrace viewpoint, but there are more as you head further from the town. Mù Cang Chải Bamboo Forest – also sporadically ticketed – is a small but beautiful patch of slender bamboo blades and provides some diversity to the landscape.

The round top terrace of **Đồi Mâm Xôi La Pán Tẩn**, which sits encircled by expanding and descending rings of further terraces, has become one of the iconic images of Northern Vietnam, and yet few can place it. It's nevertheless one of the most crowded spots in the area and can become unpleasantly busy during the harvest season. Head further northeast for quieter spots.

West of Mù Cang Chải town and south of the main road, **Lao Chải** is as dramatic and beautiful as the rest of the district but sees relatively few tourists. The countryside lane network here is decent, meaning you can climb high for increasingly spellbinding views.

SA PA, BẮC HÀ AND AROUND

Towering over Lào Cai Province are some of the highest mountains in Vietnam. Fansipan (Phan Xi Păng in Vietnamese; 3,143m) is within trekking distance of one of the country's most (in)famous mountain resorts: **Sa Pa**. A large proportion of the province's 781,000 people belong to ethnolinguistic groups other than Kinh, and some live in inaccessible areas close to the Chinese border. In Mường Khương District, at the most northerly tip of Lào Cai Province, are villages of Phu La, Lo Lo, Bo Y, Hmong and Giay. To the northwest, Hmong, Tay and Dao predominate. The province's ethnic diversity has cultivated a colourful market culture, especially in and around **Bắc Hà**, another major draw for visitors. Just north of the Red River Valley is a jagged no-man's land of karstic peaks where wisps of cloud linger like wandering wraiths. In the low mountain areas are mines that produce valuable iron, copper, molybdenum and small amounts of gold and gems. Other resources include the rivers themselves, which have been dammed and exploited to generate hydro-electricity. The province, which covers around 6,384km^2, also has fertile valleys ideal for rice, peaches, plums, pears, apples, bananas and legumes. The provincial capital is Lào Cai, the terminus of the Hanoi rail line.

SA PA AND AROUND Sa Pa is a strange kind of place, a post-modern paradox where everything exists everywhere all at once. Tourism has transformed downtown Sa Pa into a place where villagers in handwoven textiles stroll past glitzy faux French hotels, Ferraris from Hanoi crawl over pothole-ridden streets, and warm neon glows coax in visitors to gorge on karaoke. Keen optimists might relish this bizarre melting pot of backgrounds, nationalities, cultures and socioeconomic groups, but it is hard for the abject poverty not to make an impact. No other Vietnamese town seems to have as many beggars, many of whom are young children. But

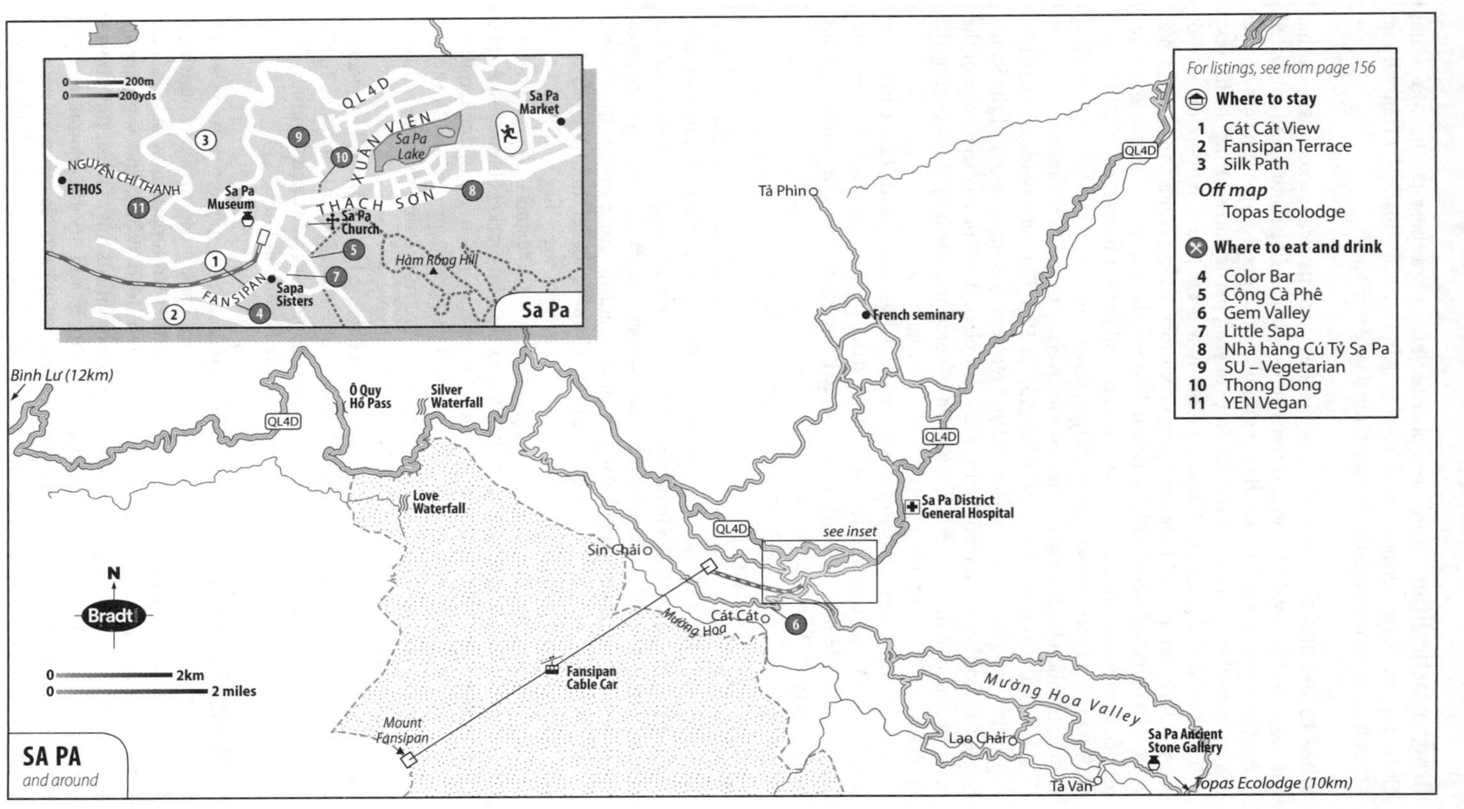

SA PA
and around
For listings, see from page 156
Where to stay
1 Cát Cát View
2 Fansipan Terrace
3 Silk Path
Off map
Topas Ecolodge
Where to eat and drink
4 Color Bar
5 Cộng Cà Phê
6 Gem Valley
7 Little Sapa
8 Nhà hàng Cú Tỷ Sa Pa
9 SU – Vegetarian
10 Thong Dong
11 YEN Vegan
Sa Pa
0 200m
0 200yds
Sa Pa Market
Sa Pa Lake
QL4D
XUÂN VIÊN
THẠCH SƠN
Sa Pa Church
Hàm Rồng Hill
Sapa Sisters
Sa Pa Museum
FANSIPAN
NGUYỄN CHÍ THANH
ETHOS
Tả Phìn
French seminary
Sa Pa District General Hospital
see inset
Cát Cát
Mường Hoa
Mường Hoa Valley
Lao Chải
Tả Van
Sa Pa Ancient Stone Gallery
Topas Ecolodge (10km)
Sín Chải
Fansipan Cable Car
Mount Fansipan
Silver Waterfall
Love Waterfall
Ô Quy Hồ Pass
Bình Lư (12km)
Bradt
N
0 2km
0 2 miles

if you can come to terms with the realities of modern Sa Pa (and do not expect an idyllic alpine refuge), the town makes for a suitable base while exploring the magnificent countryside.

Since the French abandoned the town in the 1950s, property in Sa Pa has been dominated by the Kinh (page 189). Most of the hotel, restaurant, bar and café owners you come across will be from lowland cities and towns south of Sa Pa. Distinct from the Kinh, most superficially by their clothing, are the Hmong (page 160), Dao (page 172) and other groups who come to Sa Pa to trade. The Hmong were the first to seize the commercial opportunities presented by tourism; they can be engaging and occasionally very persistent vendors of hand-loomed indigo shirts, trousers, skull caps and other handicrafts. Some speak better English than Vietnamese. Dao women, their hands stained purple by dye, sell clothing on street corners, stitching while they wait for customers. Weekend evenings are always an occasion for Hmong and Dao youngsters who come from miles around to flirt and socialise. The regular market is at its busiest and best on Sunday morning when some tourists scoot off to Bắc Hà (page 161).

It is important to make the distinction between Sa Pa town and district. While readers of this guide might long for the quieter town of two decades ago, the district, which is nearly 50km long at its widest point, is largely unspoiled. This swathe of land also holds Vietnam's largest network of hiking trails, and it's easy to leave the bustle of the town behind after an hour or so of walking. The key to enjoying (or at least not hating) Sa Pa town – as is the case with most overtouristed places – is to manage your expectations. The visual majesty and cultural diversity of the district, on the other hand, will impress even the most well-travelled visitor.

History The French claimed this former Hmong hamlet in the 1930s after a Jesuit priest chanced upon it in 1918 and boasted of its quasi-European climate and beautiful 'Tonkinese Alps'. Like Đà Lạt in the south, it served as a retreat when the heat of the plains became too much for these delicate Europeans.

By the 1940s, an estimated 300 French buildings, including a sizeable prison and the summer residence of the governor of French Indochina, had sprung up. Until 1947 there were more French than Vietnamese in the town, which became renowned for its parks, lakes and flower gardens. However, as the security situation began to worsen during the latter days of French rule, the expatriate community steadily dwindled. By 1953, virtually all had gone. Those who stayed engaged in skirmishes with the Việt Minh, causing great damage to the architecture. Vietnamese soldiers then sacked the area following their victory at Điện Biên Phủ. By 1955, the French-built electrical station was destroyed, the church was badly damaged, the aerodrome was razed and the hotels were ripped to pieces.

Sa Pa was also one of the places invaded by the Chinese during the 1979 border battles. Chinese soldiers found and destroyed the holiday retreat of the Vietnamese Communist Party secretary-general Lê Duẩn, no doubt infuriated by such an uncomradely display of bourgeois tendencies. Tourism began to recover in the 1990s and has been in overdrive ever since.

Getting there and around There is no airport in Lào Cai Province. The nearest **train** station is in Lào Cai city, to which there are one to two trains daily to/from Yên Bái (4hrs; for Mù Cang Chải and Thác Bà) and Hanoi (8hrs). The station is an hour's bus journey from Sa Pa. Minibuses wait for customers outside the station for when you arrive, and are easy to arrange through your accommodation when you depart. Always agree on the price before getting into the minibus. Alternatively, there is a red-and-yellow public bus (30,000–40,000VND) that leaves every 20–30 minutes from the car park in front of the station. These can be hard to find; if in doubt ask at a café as many others will try to load you into a minibus.

Long-distance **buses** to/from Sa Pa tend to pick up/drop off at their offices close to Sa Pa Lake. Sa Pa is well connected compared with other northern mountain destinations. Several regular buses daily connect the town with Hanoi (6hrs) and Yên Bái (4hrs). Buses aimed at Western tourists also connect Sa Pa with Bắc Hà and Hà Giang, and are best booked through your accommodation.

Central Sa Pa is **walkable**. You'll get much more out of the experience with a guide (see below), but it's possible to walk to the nearby villages of Tả Phìn, Tả Van and Sín Chải without. Note that you will likely pass barriers on the way to all these places and be asked to pay an entrance fee, though these policies change and are loosely enforced. It's never more than a dollar or two, so if stopped by someone looking official it's better not to argue. Hold on to your ticket as you may be asked to present it later.

Tour operators Sa Pa is a mature tourist destination, and it's possible to arrange tailor-made treks at short notice through your hotel. Always request a guide from the countryside, making it clear that you don't want one from Hanoi or Sa Pa town. Guides from the villages know the area best; they will offer a more enriching experience and it's a way of contributing to the village economies. For a more unique experience, contact **ETHOS** (79 Nguyễn Chí Thanh; w ethosspirit.com), the directors of which contributed the section on Vietnam's various ethnolinguistic groups (page 25). They exclusively employ guides from the villages and offer in-depth treks to unknown parts. Try to reach out weeks, or even months in advance to arrange a tailor-made trip. **Sapa Sisters** (Alley 29, 9 Fansipan; w sapasisters.com), an established and reputable tour company, also come recommended.

Where to stay *Map, page 154*

There is no dearth of hotels in Sa Pa and online travel agents will offer some excellent deals. While there is plenty of accommodation east of the lake, there's more happening on the west side near the Sa Pa Church. Alternatively, look at Tả Van and Lao Chải, villages southeast of town, both of which have a growing number of places to stay. Note that many places call themselves homestays, but they are actually small lodges.

Fansipan Terrace 67 Fansipan; f FansipanTerraceCafe. Out-of-the-way hotel on the edge of town that, for now at least, has unencumbered views of the Mường Hoa Valley & beyond. The rooms are simple but attractive & the young staff members are friendly & helpful. There's also a café. **$**

Cát Cát View 50 Fansipan; w catcatview.com. Maze-like hotel with various mid-range rooms across multiple floors. The owners, who have been working in Sa Pa tourism for decades, have a decent network of local guides to lead trekkers across standard routes through the Mường Hoa Valley. **$$**

Silk Path Đồi Quan 6; w silkpathhotel.com/sapa. Sa Pa's luxury option still retains elements of the town's vanishing charms, & it is high enough to offer grand views. This is part of a small, Hanoi-based hotel group, with 2 smart properties in the capital & a slightly garish 1 in Huế. **$$$$**

Topas Ecolodge Lếch Dao village; w topasecolodge.com. This luxury lodge is a 45min drive from town, but for many it's worth the extra effort, with excellent dining, infinity pools & impeccable service. See page 133 for more information. **$$$$$**

Where to eat and drink *Map, page 154*

Sa Pa has the most varied dining scene in Northern Vietnam outside of Hanoi and Hải Phòng. For a taste of the unusual, reach out to ETHOS, who arrange evening food tours of Sa Pa's more exotic offerings. You'll find cheap eats, including grilled corn and sweet potato, close to Sa Pa Church.

Restaurants

Little Sapa 5 Đông Lợi; 10.00–15.00 & 17.00–22.00 daily. Owned by a Hanoian, Little Sa Pa serves simple Northern Vietnamese food done well, even though some dishes have been adapted for Western preferences (eg: expect the chicken dishes – all of which are good – to be made with chicken breast rather than bony chunks). $$

SU – Vegetarian Restaurant 39 Sở Than; 10.00–22.00 daily. New meatless restaurant serving inspired, elevated plates in a gorgeous garden setting. You can't go wrong with the menu, which goes beyond standard Vietnamese fare, but the spicy mushroom soup & braised shitake mushrooms stand out for their rich flavour. $$

Thong Dong 8B Hoàng Diệu; f thongdongveganfood; 08.00–16.00 & 17.30–21.00 daily. This cheap & very cheerful vegan café & restaurant serves Vietnamese dishes, pasta & smoothie bowls. The tasty noodle soups will warm you up on a cold winter evening. $$

YEN Vegan 26 Nguyễn Chí Thanh; f yenvegansapa; 08.00–22.00 daily. Delicate vegan dishes served in a tranquil garden in a biophilic corner of Sa Pa, YEN is a special place. Try the Szechuan tofu with pineapple fried rice. They also serve pastries & coffee in the morning. $$

Nhà Hàng Cú Tỷ Sa Pa 39 Lê Văn Tám; 07.30–22.30 daily. This neighbourhood is very popular with visiting domestic tourists after a warming hotpot, & most of the restaurants are set up for large groups. Cú Tỷ, however, has hotpots designed for 2. Try the sturgeon, which is farmed nearby. $$$

Coffee houses

Color Bar 56 Fansipan; 14.00–late daily. Cosy & eclectic bar with colourful, rustic interiors, comfy corners, cocktails & beers.

Cộng Cà Phê 37 Xuân Viên; w congcaphe.com; 07.00–23.00 daily. Sa Pa's cosy cafés have dwindled in recent years as the visitor profile shifts away from independent travellers & more towards large groups, but popular Hanoi chain Cộng Cà Phê offers a reliable range of Viet coffees.

Gem Valley 10 Cát Cát; 07.00–21.00 daily. One of several cafés on the outskirts of town, but still just about walking distance (25 mins). Come for the decent coffee & stay for the excellent views.

Other practicalities Sa Pa District General Hospital (177 Điện Biên Phủ; w benhviendakhoasapa.com; 09.00–17.00 daily) is northeast of town, on the way to Lào Cai. The provincial hospital (Chiềng On; w bvdklaocai.vn; all day daily) is southeast of Lào Cai city, a little over an hour from Sa Pa.

What to see and do

Sa Pa town There's just enough to keep you busy in Sa Pa before or after a hike. The small **Sa Pa Church** (Hàm Rồng; 06.00–21.00 daily), built in 1930, is the town's emblematic chunk of architecture. Recently rebuilt, the church was wrecked in 1952 by French artillerymen shelling the adjacent building in which Việt Minh troops were billeted. In the churchyard are the tombs of two former priests, including that of Father Jean Thịnh, who was brutally murdered. In the autumn of 1948, Father Thịnh confronted a monk who had been discovered having an affair with a nun at the Tả Phìn seminary. The monk obviously took great exception to the priest's interference, for shortly after this, when Father Thịnh's congregation arrived at Sa Pa Church for mass one foggy November morning, they discovered his decapitated body lying next to the altar. The nearby dusty **Sa Pa Museum** (2 Fansipan; f baotangsapa; 07.30–17.00 daily) exhibits thrown-together displays that are

MOUNT FANSIPAN

At a height of 3,143m, Vietnam's highest mountain Fansipan (Phan Xi Păng) is a two- or three-day trek from Sa Pa. The climb involves some steep scrambles, which are tough in wet conditions. You should be reasonably fit to make it to the summit, and though it's possible to hike the mountain without a guide, this is not advisable. It's also possible to take the Fansipan Cable Car (Nguyễn Chí Thanh; return trip 800,000/550,000VND adult/child Mon–Fri & 850,000/550,000VND Sat–Sun) to the peak, which is now crowded with over-the-top and recently built pagodas and shrines. The crowds and construction can make arriving at the peak a bit of a letdown, but the journey there – either by cable car or on foot – is quite something.

nevertheless informative, and signage is in English. Particular areas of interest are, unsurprisingly, the ethnology sections and the exhibits that recount the founding and development of Sa Pa. **Sa Pa Lake** isn't attractive but is at least ringed by parks and trees. Hàm Rồng Hill (🕘 06.00–18.00 daily; 70,000VND) is a short climb with views of the town, but, like much of Sa Pa, feels overdeveloped. Drop in at **Sa Pa Market** (Lương Định Của; 🕘 06.00–18.00 daily) while circumnavigating the lake, which is just east of the water behind the outdoor sports stadium. While the market is open every day, large sections are unoccupied for much of the week; the best day to visit is Sunday.

Around Sa Pa The main reason to come to Sa Pa is to embark on a hike around the surrounding mountains. Treks can range from a few days to a few weeks. They should only be undertaken with a guide from one of the villages, and ideally through a reputable tour company (page 156) or recommended hotel. They will be able to tailor the tour to your requirements, so be as clear as you can about the number of days, what you'd like to see, the kind of accommodation you're comfortable with, dietary requirements and your fitness levels. The following day trips around Sa Pa can be done independently.

Tả Phìn and the French seminary North of Sa Pa is the Dao and Hmong settlement of Tả Phìn and its derelict French seminary. The names of the bishop who consecrated it and the presiding governor of Indochina can be seen engraved on stones at the west end. Built in 1942, under the ecclesiastical jurisdiction of the parish of Sa Pa, the building was destroyed ten years later by militant Vietnamese hostile to the intentions of the order. Tả Phìn is on the road towards Lào Cai, with clear signs indicating the way to the village on the left. It's 3km to the seminary and a further 4km to Tả Phìn. Beyond the haunting French remnant, the path descends into a valley of beautifully sculpted rice terraces and past Black Hmong settlements to Tả Phìn. One way to approach this village is to take a taxi from Sa Pa to the seminary, walk to Tả Phìn, where there are various places to eat and a few spas, and then walk the 2 hours back to Sa Pa.

Lao Chải and Tả Van Southeast of Sa Pa are the settlement clusters of Lao Chải and Tả Van, two conjoined areas in the Mường Hoa Valley that have become popular with visitors. A leisurely stroll through the villages here is a chance to observe rural life led in reasonable prosperity and view the impacts of tourism on rural Vietnam. Rice cultivation was once the staple income, but weaving, homestays and guiding for the tourist market are quickly taking precedence. Nature was kinder here than elsewhere; there is rich soil and no shortage of water. Like in other villages around Sa Pa, it's possible to see how the landscape has been engineered to suit human needs. The terracing is on a particularly impressive scale (in places there are more than 100 steps), the result of centuries of labour to convert steep slopes into level fields, which can be flooded to grow rice. During summer, in the late-afternoon sun, the rice glows with more shades of green than you would have thought possible, and the lengthening shadows cast the entire landscape into vivid three-dimensional relief. Bamboo is ubiquitous and indispensable: trunks carry water huge distances from spring to village; water flows across barriers and tracks in bamboo aqueducts; mechanical rice huskers made of bamboo are driven by water; houses are held up with bamboo; bottoms are parked on bamboo chairs; and tobacco and other substances are inhaled through bamboo pipes. Any path chosen will lead to some hamlet or other. Lao Chải is 6km away on the far valley side and, armed with Google Maps, is easy to find. Tả Van is 2km further on. All within a 2–3km radius you'll find bamboo forests, waterfalls, streams and the Sa Pa Ancient Stone Gallery (Hầu Thào; ⌚ all day daily), which houses engraved stones that are believed to be inscribed in ancient Hmong. There are also many dozens of homestays and cafés, some of which are artfully positioned with views of the mountains. The whole area might feel rather contrived to well-travelled readers, but there are worse places to visit (eg: Cát Cát). It's possible to swim in some areas, but beware of the water dragon (see below). One way to approach Lao Chải and Tả Van is to walk there – easily done with the aid of Google Maps – wander around enjoying the views and then take a taxi back to Sa Pa. Best to prearrange your return journey with your accommodation before leaving.

LEGEND HAS IT: HIDDEN DRAGON

By Lý Thị Mỷ, Hmong trekking guide for ETHOS (page 156)

There are various groups of legendary entities in the Hmong mythos, and one of the most important is the *zaj*. The *zaj* are dragon spirits that dwell in the rivers, considered by many to be polymorphic gods or goddesses. *Zaj* are generally understood to be benevolent. Some elders say that a *zaj* spirit can grant a person help if they ask for it. In some folkloric tales, *zaj* spirits come to the aid of people in their most desperate times of need.

However, these primordial spirits are ancient, powerful and not to be disturbed or disrespected. Drownings in rivers and lakes are often blamed on these spirits. Some stories recall that encounters with a *zaj* have led to sickness and death – one reason why pregnant women should stay away from rivers.

According to one local legend, the Mường Hoa River, just south of Sa Pa town, shelters one such dark entity, a leviathan of monstrous proportions: the beast of Mường Hoa. Lurking on the riverbed waiting for trespassing swimmers, the beast – said to be a water dragon – will drag these unfortunate souls to their watery graves. The beast strikes when river rapids are at their most ferocious, so after heavy rain it's advised not to swim, or else risk the water dragon's wrath.

Other stories are less morbid. Another legend speaks of the rainbows in the region, which symbolise a dragon spirit in the process of changing from one form to another.

THE HMONG

The Hmong, skilled rice cultivators known for their vibrant traditional attire and embroidery, live across many highland areas in Vietnam, but particularly near the Chinese border. They number well over a million, more than 1% of Vietnam's population, and typically live at higher altitudes. Comparatively recent migrants to Vietnam, the Hmong began to settle in the country during the 19th century after moving south from China. The Hmong language in its various dialects remained oral until the 1930s, when a French priest attempted to Romanise it with a view to translating the Bible. A more successful attempt to create a written Hmong language was made in 1961 but it has since fallen into disuse. Nevertheless – or perhaps because of this failure – the Hmong still preserve an extraordinarily rich oral tradition of legends, stories and histories.

Each branch of the Hmong people preserves its own corpus of songs about love, work and festivals that are sung unaccompanied or with the accompaniment of a small bamboo pipe organ, a two-stringed violin, flutes, drums and gongs. Numerous Hmong dances also exist to celebrate various dates in the social calendar and to propitiate spirits; the Hmong practise Animism, honouring ancestors and spiritual entities through rituals led by shamans.

The Hmong have played an important role in resisting both the French and the Vietnamese. Living at such high altitudes, they tend to be one of the most isolated of all the hill people. Their way of life does not normally bring them into contact with the outside world; the Hmong traders and guides in Sa Pa are the exception, not the rule.

High in the hills, flooding is not a problem so their houses are built on the ground, not raised up on stilts. Hmong villages are now increasingly found along the river valleys and roads as the government resettlement schemes aim to introduce them to a more sedentary form of agriculture. Traditionally, however, the Hmong practised slash-and-burn cultivation, growing maize and dry rice. Though no longer the case, opium was once a valuable cash crop.

There are a number of different groups among the Hmong, including the White, Black, Red and Flower, but many simply identify as Hmong.

Cát Cát and Sin Chải These villages are west of Sa Pa. Cát Cát, once a pretty Hmong settlement just 2km from Sa Pa, has become the most commodified of all the villages in the area. It feels these days like the village exists for shoppers and selfie-takers, but little else. The name Cát Cát may come from the French *cascade*, and there is a fairly impressive waterfall and colonial-era hydro-electric power station at the bottom of the village. Cát Cát might only really be interesting as an example of the bizarre Disneyfication of Vietnamese mountain villages. Sin Chải (also spelt Xin Chải), 4km west of Sa Pa, sees comparatively few visitors and has far fewer homestays than Tả Phìn, Tả Van and Lao Chải, though you'll find simple places serving instant noodles. One approach is to head west, bypass Cát Cát unless the place really appeals, and head straight for Sin Chải. After exploring the pathways around the town and enjoying a simple meal, it won't take much more than an hour to walk back to Sa Pa.

QL4D The road west of Sa Pa, the QL4D that eventually reaches Lai Châu (page 162), makes for a magnificent drive with a few sights to see along the way. Silver

Waterfall (San Sả Hồ; ⌚ 09.00–17.00 daily), just 12km from Sa Pa, is spectacular following rain, but hardly worth a special visit. An extra kilometre along the road leads to Love Waterfall (Sơn Bình; ⌚ 09.00–17.00 daily), a prettier and wilder spot that also sees fewer visitors. A little further along is the Ô Quy Hồ Pass, with sweeping views. The road then descends all the way to Bình Lư. From there you can turn around and head back to town.

BẮC HÀ Bắc Hà is notable for its Sunday market, which thousands of people flock to from across Lào Cai District to shop, sell, socialise and be entertained. Trading is integral to the market, but there's also music, singing, dancing and a load of eating and drinking. This is a village party, weekend market and local talent show all rolled into one weekly multi-sensory spectacle. While tourists have discovered Bắc Hà, it's still very much a local affair. Outside the Sunday market, there are additional markets in villages nearby, plus opportunities to sightsee and hike. Arriving from Lào Cai city, around 18km from Bắc Hà, the scenery features huge expanses of

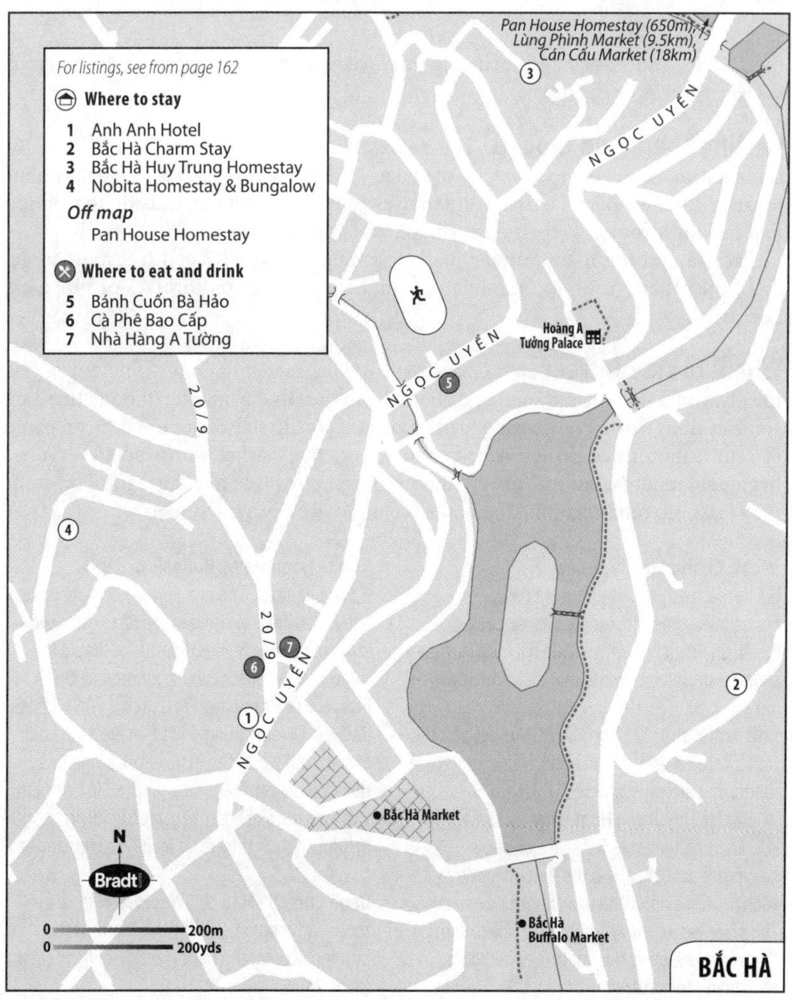

HINTERLANDS: LAI CHÂU PROVINCE

For a description of 'Hinterlands' boxes, see page 131.

Head west from Sa Pa along the QL4D and you'll eventually reach Lai Châu, the modern capital of a sparsely populated province. There are several waterfalls along the way, including Thác Bạc, Thác Tình Yêu and the thundering Thác Tà Tình. Dozens more waterfalls speckle the province away from the main roads. Driving to Sìn Hồ, a town with weekend markets east of Lai Châu city, is hazardous as you need to negotiate hairpin bends and precipitous drops. It is best to drive slowly so you can also witness the extraordinary perpendicular fields. The DT128, the road that connects Sìn Hồ with the main roads, offers one of the most spectacular drives in Vietnam. To extend the adventure, continue to Mường Lay and combine Lai Châu Province with the far-flung northwest, closer to Điện Biên Phủ (page 150).

mountains, pine trees and terracing engraved by the winding road as it climbs skywards towards the town.

Getting there and around The nearest **train** station is in Lào Cai city; for information on trains to Lào Cai, see page 155. From there, it's a 2-hour minibus journey to/from Bắc Hà. These little buses wait for customers outside the station and pick up/drop off at their offices in central Bắc Hà.

Bắc Hà and the main Sunday market is walkable; you'll need transport to get to all the others. Your accommodation can help you rent motorbikes or hire a car and driver.

Where to stay and eat *Map, page 161*

Ideally, you'll stay within walking distance from the Sunday market, though there are some options worth considering further away. If you do stay out of town, be prepared to rent a motorbike. When it comes to eating, the market won't meet everyone's hygiene standards, but it is an extremely atmospheric place to enjoy a meal or, at the very least, sip on a coconut. The best street food is on Ngọc Uyển Street.

Bắc Hà Charm Stay Nâm Cáy; f bachacharmstay. Beautiful but basic bungalows, some with views, & home-cooked meals. Charm Stay feels like it's in the middle of the countryside, but is only a 20min walk from town (up a hill). **$**

Anh Anh Hotel 133 Ngọc Uyển. Nondescript but well-located & good-value hotel, with dozens of rooms that are kept sufficiently clean. **$$**

✷ **Bắc Hà Huy Trung Homestay** Na Quang; f Huytrunghomestay. Trung, the owner, is passionate about Bắc Hà & the surrounding area, & is keen to build tailor-made tours from his experience. This place has a friendly & homestay vibe to it; Trung may move one of his kids out of their bedroom temporarily to make room for you. **$$**

Nobita Homestay & Bungalow Bắc Hà; f NobitaAloxo. One of a slew of new cute garden hotels that are appearing in Bắc Hà to catch the lower mid-range market. Rooms are simple & somewhat ramshackle, but comfortable. **$$**

Pan House Homestay Tả Chải; f PAN-HOUSE-BẮC-HÀ. Dreamy bungalows that are a little out of town but worth the extra effort. Sometimes these places can feel a little unloved in Northern Vietnam, but the hosts here are friendly & helpful, though they cater mainly to Vietnamese travellers. **$$**

Bánh Cuốn Bà Hảo 220 Ngọc Uyển. Ideal for those early-morning starts, this is one of the better places for the Hanoi version of *bánh cuốn* (page 94). **$**

Nhà Hàng A Tường 142 Ngọc Uyển; 345 557 386. Simple, tasty & affordable Vietnamese food & an English menu to boot. Try the roast pork with skin crisped to perfection, with a side of stir-fried vegetables. $$

Cà Phê Bao Cấp 13 20/9 St; CÀ PHÊ BAO CẤP 85-88s BẮC HÀ. Get caffeinated here before, after & during the market, which is just a few steps away. They also have seasonal juices.

Other practicalities Bắc Hà Huy Trung Homestay (see opposite) can arrange trekking and market tours as well as family meals, even if you're staying elsewhere. The provincial hospital (Chiềng On, Lào Cai; w bvdklaocai.vn) is southeast of Lào Cai city, almost 2 hours from Bắc Hà.

What to see and do

Hoàng A Tưởng Palace (257 Ngọc Uyển; 08.00–17.00 daily; 20,000VND/free adult/child) This curious European palace may appear at odds with rural Vietnam, with its Baroque façade, imperial staircase and grand sequence of arches. It was built in the 1910s and appears structurally sound, though very weathered. Like other palaces in the north, most notably the Hmong Palace in Hà Giang (page 175), this folly belonged to a local chief who, in this case, was from the Tay ethnolinguistic group. Though now called the palace of Hoàng A Tưởng, it was conceptualised by his father. Together, they hired French and Chinese architects and designers and flew in – by helicopter – steel and cement from Hanoi. Predicting the imminent French withdrawal from Vietnam, the family abandoned the palace in the 1950s and it passed to the state. Today the palace is a unique and underutilised museum, but it does house a small giftshop and occasionally hosts events.

The markets The main event and a highlight of the week for both visitors and locals, it's possible to explore all the markets over a long weekend in Bắc Hà.

Lùng Phình Market (Friday) [map, page 130] Lùng Phình Market has only recently moved from Sunday to Friday so it doesn't clash with Bắc Hà's, but this may not stick. Ask at your accommodation for updates before making the trip out to this small, local market, which sees few tourists and is about 30 minutes by car from Bắc Hà. You can wander around this market in less than half an hour, but linger a little longer for grilled corn and sweet potato. The market sits on a fork in the road with views of rice terraces.

✷ Bắc Hà Buffalo Market (Saturday) [map, page 161] A reason to spend the whole weekend in Bắc Hà is to experience the town's new Saturday buffalo market. The area used to have two buffalo markets – a Saturday market in Cán Cấu and a Sunday market in Bắc Hà – but organisers decided it would be better to combine them into one market in 2022. This takes place southeast of the site of the main Sunday market, close to the river. The market gets going before sunrise, but it's best to go at around 07.00 so you can see where you're stepping. From a distance, this market appears like a mass of grey and brown as the buffalos, each with an owner, writhe over the mud- and excrement-encrusted streets. Most of the traders are Hmong men, though some women and a few other ethnolinguistic groups participate. You can get as close to the buffalos as you wish, but move slowly and don't make any sudden movements.

Cán Cấu Market (Saturday) [map, page 130] Like the buffalo market, Cán Cấu Market takes place on Saturday morning, and with some planning it's possible to visit both before lunch. Dramatically perched on a mountain road, this is the second largest market in the area, after Bắc Hà. Food is sold on the road, whereas textiles are sold in and around the circular structure. You'll also find medicine, household knick-knacks and a food court of sorts further from the road.

✷ **Bắc Hà Market (Sunday)** [map, page 161] The astonishing Sunday market draws Hmong, Phu La, Dao, La Chi, Tay, Kinh and other ethnolinguistic groups from Lào Cai Province and beyond. It is a riot of chaos and colour: the children wear a kaleidoscope of apparel; the women, as is so often the case in mercantile Vietnam, dominate the commerce; the men consume vast quantities of rice wine while chewing on horse and animal innards that have been cooked in cauldrons. By late morning some of these men can no longer walk, so they are heaved on to motorbikes by their diligent wives and driven home.

On the west side of the market, on Vũ Văn Mật Street, there are makeshift stalls spread out on the floor selling vegetables, fruits, cakes and, most interestingly, natural remedies that resemble the body part they cure: phallic roots for impotency; intestine-like roots for indigestion, and so on. The central square of the market is more orderly: covered stalls laid out in a grid selling fresh produce from the farm, with a raised stage that hosts regular dance and music performances. Nearby cafés serve coffee, coconuts and sugarcane juice. Framing this central square are fabric shops selling local textiles, some clearly directed at tourists, and the food court, where chefs couldn't care less about the fussy hygiene requirements of foreigners. The bold may wish to take this opportunity to try *phở Bắc Hà* (page 134), the town's take on the national dish.

On the east side of the market, near the river, merchants trade in all manner of domesticated animal, including dogs, cats, birds, chickens and the odd cow or buffalo, though most of the bovine trading has happened the day before during the Saturday market. This section is best avoided for those who are squeamish about animal welfare.

The market is best experienced very early in the morning – before 06.00 – so avoid the day trip from Sa Pa, which is a few hours away. It's possible to spend many hours here shuffling between sections, giggling with market sellers, enjoying the stage shows and making a few purchases. Despite the number of visitors, the market is still very much a local affair, and there isn't a huge amount that will appeal to visitors. The textiles, for example, are for the most part poor-quality, factory-made replicas. Try to think creatively about how to contribute to the market in some way by buying items that travel well, like spice mixtures, dried herbs, dried teas and snacks that you can eat on the go, like fruit and nuts. The market starts to wind down before noon.

Hiking and villages There are several walks to outlying villages, including Thải Giàng Phố, Na Hối and Bản Liền. These are difficult to undertake without a guide, so reach out to your accommodation or speak to Trung at Bắc Hà Huy Trung Homestay (page 162).

THÁI NGUYÊN PROVINCE

Immediately north of Hanoi, and the gateway to the Northeast subregion, is Thái Nguyên, a hilly province known for its rolling hills and green tea plantations. It was created in 1997 when the former Bắc Thái Province was rezoned to give the northern provinces greater autonomy. The tea grown here benefits from the province's temperate climate, with cool winters and warm, rainy summers that promote lush, verdant tea trees. Thái Nguyên is ethnically diverse and most groups engage in the tea trade, though the Kinh (page 189) are predominant. The province is also home to significant populations of Tay (page 170) and Nung groups, who typically reside in the rural areas and cultivate rice and other crops. Thái Nguyên city is usually bypassed as visitors make their way to Ba Bể Lake and beyond, but it's worth stopping to dig around the **Cultural Museum of Vietnam Ethnic Minority Groups** (1 Đội Cấn; w vme.org.vn; ⌚ 07.30–11.30 & 13.30–17.00 daily; 40,000VND/free adult/child). Though one of the better museums in Northern Vietnam outside Hanoi, signage is almost too detailed, and it can feel like a slog wading through all the information. Arrive energised, or at least caffeinated after a visit to a nearby café before entering the museum. If looking for somewhere to stay overnight, there's Homestay Suối Cửa Tử (Suối Cửa Tử; f cuatuhomestay) 40km west of Thái Nguyên city and only 2½ hours from Hanoi. The stilt house homestay has a swimming pool, and a 1-hour hike takes you to rock pools you can swim in. You might also investigate Thái Hải Tourism Village (w thaihai.vn), a traditional Tay village that has repurposed itself as a kind of living ethnography museum. There's comfortable accommodation, restaurants, cafés, activities and performances. The project feels artificial - and at times like a cult - but it is undeniably successful and has raised living standards for hundreds of villagers. In 2022 Thái Hải Tourism Village was named one of the world's best tourism villages by the UN World Trade Organization.

BA BỂ NATIONAL PARK AND AROUND

Bắc Thái Province split in 1997 to form Thái Nguyên to the south and Bắc Kạn to the north. While Thái Nguyên is associated with tea plantations, Bắc Kạn is characterised by undulating limestone mountains and deep valleys. Elevations typically range from 500m to 800m. Bắc Kạn's subtropical climate and fertile soils make it ideal for cultivating crops such as corn, rice and various fruit trees. In recent years, efforts have been made to expand the province's tea plantations, which benefit from the cooler temperatures. Deforestation has been an issue, though some areas of dense forest still survive, particularly in protected regions near Ba Bể National Park. The province is as ethnically diverse as others in the north, though the Tay (page 170) tend to dominate the settlements near the lakes and rivers. The Dao (page 172) and Hmong (page 160) typically live at higher altitudes that are out of reach except to the most intrepid travellers. The Kinh (page 189) reside in the province's small urban centres, such as Bắc Kạn city. Bắc Kạn acquired enormous strategic significance during the First Indochina War as the westernmost stronghold of the Cao–Bắc–Lạng battle zone. The town was captured by the Việt Minh in 1944 and its recovery was considered crucial to the success of the 1947 French counter-offensive. Although colonial troops did retake the town, guerilla attacks on its garrison became so frequent that the French abandoned it two years later. Most visitors skip the town and head straight for Ba Bể National Park, regardless of which direction they arrive from.

Ba Bể National Park (Vườn Quốc Gia Ba Bể) was established in 1992 after being declared an area of protection in 1977 and again in 1986. It now comprises an area of more than 100km^2 and is centred on Ba Bể Lake (Hồ Ba Bể, which means 'Three Basin Lake'), a large natural body of water surrounded by limestone hills carpeted in tropical evergreen forest. Hmong and Dao communities live within the national park boundaries, though the settlements nearest the water are all Tay.

LEGEND HAS IT: HOW BA BỂ GOT ITS LAKE

In the early days, Ba Bể was the site of a deep valley surrounded by thick forests and jagged peaks. The people of the region lived in humble wooden homes scattered across the fertile land. One evening, a mysterious beggar, ragged and tired, arrived in the area seeking shelter. Fearful of his appearance, the villagers all turned him away, but a kind widow and her son welcomed him in. They shared with him what little rice they had.

While they ate, the beggar revealed himself as a powerful deity. He warned the widow that a great flood would soon come and swallow the entire valley, destroying the village and all who lived there. However, he told her that if she acted quickly, she could save herself and her son. The deity instructed her to build a raft from bamboo and be ready to flee when the water began to rise.

The widow did as she was told, spending the night preparing the raft. The next morning, dark clouds gathered ominously over the valley. The sky unleashed a torrent of rain that quickly became a flood. Water surged through the valley, submerging the fields, houses and all that stood in its path. The widow and her son climbed aboard the raft just as the floodwaters rose, and they floated safely above the destruction.

By the time the rain stopped, the entire village had disappeared, and in its place was a vast lake, stretching as far as the eye could see: Ba Bể Lake. The land that the widow's small house was on then began to rise above the water to become a small island, a reward from the gods for her kindness and hospitality. This island became known as Widow's Island, standing in the centre of Ba Bể Lake, a reminder of the woman's compassion and the divine intervention that saved her life. The island still exists today, a lone sentinel in the heart of the lake, surrounded by the murky waters of Ba Bể.

FLORA AND FAUNA The thick jungle, which begins at the water's edge, is likely to be the most impressive sight, at least in the first instance. Common species here include beech (*Fagaceae*) and laurel (*Lauraceae*); some rarer species are of Indo-Burman origin, such as tropical almond (*Terminalia*) and commersonia (*Malvaceae*). There are numerous thickets of bamboo, the best represented being *neohouzeaua* and *dendrocalamus*. Medically important species are common, such as *amomum*, *hodgsonia* and *discorea*. In all, almost 400 species of plants have been identified.

The park also contains a high diversity of fauna, including as many as 38 types of mammal. Species include the completely captivating but critically endangered Tonkinese snub-nosed monkey (*Rhinopithecus avunculus*), the black-crested gibbon (*Hylobates concolor*), the stump-tailed macaque (*Macaca arctoides*), the rock monkey (*Trachypithecus francoisi francoisi*), the Asian black bear (*Selenarctos thibetanus*), the clouded leopard (*Pardofelis nebulosa*), the tiger (*Panthera tigris*), the flying squirrel (*Hylopetes alboniger*) and the wild boar (*Sus scrofa*). Many of these discoveries were made decades ago, and today it is unclear which of these species have disappeared. Except for perhaps the boar, it's highly unlikely that you will see any of these animals.

What you will see, however, is dozens of the over 100 species of butterfly and perhaps a few reptiles, amphibians and birds. Among the latter are great egrets (*Ardea alba*), white-eared night herons (*Gorsachius magnificus*) and white-throated kingfishers (*Halcyon smyrnensis*). Birds you'd be lucky to see include the rare silver pheasant (*Lophura nycthemera*), the grey peacock pheasant (*Polyplectron bicalcaratum*) and the great hornbill (*Buceros bicornis*), an extremely shy bird that lives in the highest, most inaccessible regions.

GETTING THERE AND AROUND Ba Bể National Park is a remote destination that sees relatively few visitors; there are no train stations or airports nearby, and no regular bus services. Most travel to the park from Hanoi (4hrs) by **private car**, their own transport or with a **minibus transfer**. To book a minibus, the most economical option, reach out to Mr Linh's Adventures (page 168). Getting to Ba Bể National Park by public transport from elsewhere in the northern mountains is not easy and takes all day. First, book a bus to Bắc Kạn city; from there, buses leave for Chợ Rã, just on the outside of the national park. There are no regular buses from Chợ Rã to the national park, so you'll likely have to get a taxi or motorbike taxi to your accommodation. An alternative route is through Thái Nguyên city (Thái Nguyên Province) or Phủ Thông town (Bắc Kạn Province). This plan of action is only recommended for those with plenty of time and patience. For up-to-date public bus route information to Ba Bể National Park, visit w babenationalpark.com.vn.

It takes around an hour to walk between the accommodation and restaurant clusters (page 168) on Ba Bể Lake, or 10 minutes on a motorbike.

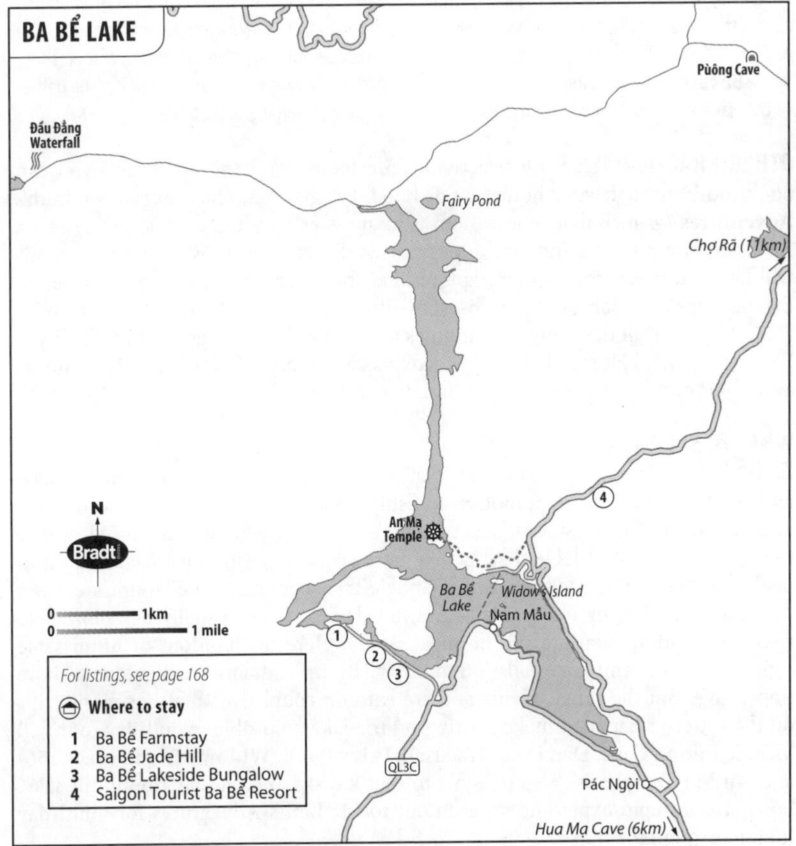

WHERE TO STAY AND EAT *Map, page 167*

Ba Bể National Park offers very few restaurants and cafés. Visitors will have most (if not all) of their meals at their homestay or hotel. Note that decent meals are cooked fresh and need to be booked at least a few hours in advance, otherwise you may have to settle for noodles from a packet.

There are two main clusters of accommodation on Ba Bể Lake, both on the south side of the water. Budget accommodation and most of the homestays are in Pác Ngòi, a small village southeast of the lake that is in a maddening state of constant construction. The lodges and a handful of smaller homestays are in or near Nam Mẫu to the southwest. As elsewhere, look online for an up-to-date list of **homestays** (**$**). For other accommodation, try:

Ba Bể Farmstay Nam Mẫu; w babefarmstay.com. A dreamy, Instagrammable garden retreat with pitched-roof bungalows that are good for families. What your hosts may lack in professionalism they make up for in authentic, uneffusive hospitality. **$$**

Ba Bể Jade Hill Cốc Tốc; f BaBeJadeHill. A kind of budget lodge that can't quite decide whether it's a homestay or a mountain retreat. The family who run the show are friendly, & there's a good chance you'll have the whole place to yourself. **$$**

✷ **Ba Bể Lakeside Bungalow** Cốc Tốc; w babelakeside.com. Built by a local family, some of whom have spent time abroad, so language is not an issue. Rooms are modern & with AC, but are on stilts, so offer sweeping views of the lake & jungles. The food here – which includes a full grilled chicken that you need to order in advance – is particularly good. **$$**

Saigon Tourist Ba Bể Resort 2km northeast of the lake; w saigonbaberesort.com. Ba Bể National Park's only modern-style hotel is a little far from the action, but they have a decent restaurant, café & bicycles for rent. There are dozens of rooms set across lakes & gardens, so this is one of the better options for large groups. **$$$**

OTHER PRACTICALITIES Most activities are focused on the water, and you can book tours through your homestay or hotel. Failing that, reach out to **Mr Linh's Adventures** (w mrlinhadventure.com), the most established tour company in Ba Bể. There are no taxis and Grab does not work here, but most accommodations will let motorbikes for further exploration. There are a few basic pharmacies in the villages on the lake, but the closest medical facility is Ba Bể Hospital in Chợ Rã (Tiểu khu 2; ⌚ all day daily), 45 minutes away. The closest large medical facility is Bắc Kạn General Hospital (Tổ 12; w bvdkbackan.com.vn; ⌚ all day daily), 2 hours away, but for serious issues it's best to return to Hanoi.

WHAT TO SEE AND DO

Ba Bể Lake Most activities in Ba Bể National Park are centred around Ba Bể Lake, and you'll need to charter a motorised fishing boat to explore the extremities. All lodges and most homestays have access to a boat and will be keen to sell private tours, which are affordable. Few people here speak English, but they are used to dealing with foreigners with the aid of Google Translate and printed tour itineraries, so there won't be any issues. Half- and full-day tours can usually be tailored, so select the options that appeal the most, as there are no standout or unmissable sights; the caves and waterfalls found elsewhere in Vietnam are bigger and more impressive. But the range of things there is to do coupled with atmospheric trips on the water in between make boating on the lake enjoyable. A full-day tour will include **Pùông Cave**, Đầu Đẳng Waterfall, **Fairy Pond**, **Widow's Island** (page 166) and **An Mạ Temple**. It's also possible to rent **kayaks** and paddle around the lake. For more intrepid experiences, reach out to Mr Linh's Adventures for multi-day hiking through the hills.

LEGEND HAS IT: THE HEADLESS HORSES

Many centuries ago, a powerful king passed through this area with his entourage. As they approached a nearby cave, the king's horse suddenly froze in fear. No matter how much the king urged it forward, the beast refused to cross the stream near the entrance to the cave. Frustrated, the king turned to the local villagers for answers. They told him that the cave trapped the spirits of those who had been unjustly murdered and that the horse's keen ears could detect their sorrowful cries.

The king vowed to free the trapped souls and bring peace, so concocted a morbid solution. He called upon his soldiers to decapitate their horses and send the heads downstream as offerings to the spirits. While his soldiers carried out this grim task, the king secluded himself in a nearby pagoda and recited Buddhist scriptures. For days he prayed, his voice rising with the wind as it swept through the valley.

Apparently, his efforts were rewarded. The villagers claimed that the cries from the cave had ceased, and the souls must be at peace. Unfortunately, the king, who was unable to hear the cries, could not test to see if his plan had worked, as his horse, of course, had been beheaded. He strolled through the cave and away from the area regardless. Today the cave is called Hua Mạ Cave (Horse Head Cave) as a grim reminder of the perhaps superfluous sacrifice.

Hua Mạ Cave Horse Head Cave (see above) is southeast of Ba Bể Lake on a rough country lane. Steps and pathways make visiting the cave fairly straightforward, thought the multi-coloured lighting system is a little garish. As most visitors stay near the water, it's quite likely that you'll have the entire cave to yourself. The journey up to the cave affords elevated views across the national park.

HÀ GIANG

Covering 7,946km², Hà Giang Province, which is home to around 850,000 people, has a 7,070km-long border with China. During the 1979 conflict, countless shells and rockets fell on the provincial capital Hà Giang, but life here was a hard struggle long before then. Both field and terraced rice is grown; other hardy crops include sweet potatoes, arrowroot, cassava and maize. Most of Hà Giang consists of remote highly mountainous territory where the highlands' ethnolinguistic groups, the Hmong (page 160) and Dao (page 172), live in isolated hamlets. The Tay (page 170), one of the largest groups in the province, live at lower altitudes. The 2019 census showed 22 ethnolinguistic groups living in Hà Giang – each with their own language, architecture, apparel and way of life – making this one of Vietnam's most ethnically diverse provinces. The La Chi, who speak a Tai-Kadai language, are based on the border with China. In Đồng Văn District, the northernmost point in Vietnam, are hamlets of the Pu Peo, who build their houses on stony mountain slopes. In the same district, close to Lũng Cú Flag Tower, are the villages of the Lo Lo (page 175), whose houses are now built on the ground due to a shortage of timber. Other groups include the Bo Y, Co Lao, Phu La and Pa Then.

HISTORY As Vietnam's northernmost province, Hà Giang has long been a bastion of resistance against foreign invaders. In the 11th century, General Lý Thường Kiệt united the disparate groups and won a great victory against the Chinese Song

Dynasty, cementing Northern Vietnam's independence until the 19th century. The original settlement in Hà Giang lay on the east bank of the Lô River and it was here that the French established themselves following the conquest of the area in 1886. The town subsequently became an important military base, a development confirmed in 1905 when Hà Giang was formally established as one of four Northern Vietnamese military territories of French Indochina.

The Hà Giang area saw several important rebellions against the French during the early years of the colonial period, the most important being that of the Dao, who rose up in 1901 under the leadership of Triệu Tiến Kiến and Triệu Tài Lộc. The revolt was quickly put down and Triệu Tiến Kiến was killed during the fighting, but in 1913 Triệu Tài Lộc rose up again, this time marching under the slogans: 'No corvées, no taxes for the French; Drive out the French to recover our country; Liberty for the Dao'. Carrying white flags embroidered with Tổ Quốc Bạch Kỳ (White Flag of the Fatherland) and wearing white conical hats (hence the French name, 'The White Hat Revolt'), the rebels launched attacks in Tuyên Quang, Lào Cai and Yên Bái and managed to keep French troops at bay until 1915, when the revolt was savagely repressed. Hundreds of the insurgents were subsequently deported and 67 people were condemned to death by the colonial courts.

Evidence of the colonial grip on Vietnam is in the form of the crumbling forts that speckle the province. The most well known and impressive are in Hà Giang city and Đồng Văn town, but three additional forts can be found in the small town of Phó Bảng, on the river in Cán Tỷ and in Lũng Hồ District near Du Già.

THE TAY

The Tay are the most populous ethnolinguistic group in Vietnam bar the Kinh (page 189); they number about 1.7 million and are found in the provinces of Northwest Vietnam, stretching from Quảng Ninh to Lào Cai. Tay society was traditionally feudal, with powerful lords able to extract an income from their subjects. Today, traditional Tay society is male-dominated and eldest sons inherit the bulk of the family's wealth.

Economically, the Tay survive by farming and are highly regarded as wet rice cultivators. They are also noted for the production of fruits (pears, peaches, apricots and tangerines), herbs and spices. Diet is supplemented by animal and fish rearing and, where tourism exists, extra income is sometimes earned from producing and selling handicrafts. The Tay live in houses on stilts and tend to live near rivers and lakes in the valleys. Tay architecture is quite similar in design to that of some Thai groups (page 138), but there are important differences, most notably the larger size of the Tay house, the deeper overhang of the thatched or (among more affluent Tay communities) tiled roof and the extent of the railed balcony that often encircles the entire house.

Like the Thai, Tay ancestors migrated south from southern China. Like the Kinh, they follow the three main religions of Buddhism, Confucianism and Taoism, in addition to ancestor worship and Animist beliefs. While Tay people have lived in close proximity to the Viet majority over a period of many centuries, their own language – a Tai-Kadai language related to Thai, not Vietnamese – continues to be their primary means of communication in many communities. Tay literature has a long and distinguished history and much has been translated into many languages.

HINTERLANDS: TUYÊN QUANG PROVINCE

For a description of 'Hinterlands' boxes, see page 131.

Tuyên Quang is a mountainous province covering an area of 5,870km² and home to a population of 780,000, around half of which are Kinh. The rest are members of more than 20 ethnolinguistic groups, including the Hmong, Dao, Tay, Phu La, Pu Peo and Pa Then. The temperature here can fall as low as 10°C in winter, when frequent fogs black out the landscapes. In the summer there is a danger of flash floods, which can make driving along the mountain roads hazardous. Tuyên Quang was once a breeding ground for bandits. The Nguyễn nobles built a fort here; the White Flags made it the centre for their operations in 1867; and between 1868 and the early part of the 1880s it was controlled by the Black Flags. It fell under the colonial yoke between November 1884 and April 1885.

In the early 1930s, revolutionary bases extended throughout the province. On the eve of the August 1945 Revolution (page 14), Hồ Chí Minh set up his main revolutionary base at Tân Trào village, east of Tuyên Quang city, from where he launched a general insurrection. It's now a pilgrimage site. Kim Bình, north of the city, is another important revolutionary base that has been preserved as a heritage site for domestic tourists, though there is some signage in English.

Overzealous logging has denuded much of the landscape, but in parts, and particularly along the border with Hà Giang, the roads are quietly enchanting. The province's fledgling tourism industry is centred in these northern parts of the province, particularly in Na Hang and Lâm Bình districts, which have waterfalls, rivers, lakes and villages with homestays. This is the ideal corner for spontaneous exploration.

GETTING THERE AND AROUND There are no train stations or airports close to Hà Giang city. **Buses** to/from Hà Giang will pick up/drop off either at Hà Giang bus station (19/5 St), 3km south of the centre, or at bus company offices in the centre. Some will pick up/drop off at your accommodation. If booking through your accommodation, ask for clear instructions. Several buses throughout the day connect the city with Hanoi (7hrs). There is a growing number of informal buses aimed at Western tourists that connect Hà Giang with Cao Bằng to the east and Sa Pa to the west. These can take up to 12 hours depending on the route and the condition of the roads.

It's easy to tackle central Hà Giang on foot, but the countryside is built for road trips. Hà Giang is ideal **motorbiking** territory, where roads meander past rippling rice terraces, mountain passes soar above turquoise rivers and countryside lanes thread through forests and limestone pinnacles. The 'Hà Giang Loop' (page 174), an undefined driving circuit that begins and ends in Hà Giang city, usually undertaken on a motorbike, is quickly becoming one of Southeast Asia's quintessential adventure travel experiences. And while some road sections can get busy with both cars and motorbikes, mass tourism has not arrived – yet. There is a huge amount to see along the way, including temples, shrines, viewpoints and villages. There are dozens of motorbike rental shops in Hà Giang, with rental charges ranging from 150,000VND to 500,000VND per day depending on the bike. Ngân Hà Travel (113C Lý Tự Trọng) is recommended, but there are many others. Bear in mind that

THE DAO

The Dao (or Yao, sometimes Dzao) live in Northern Vietnam in the provinces bordering China, particularly in Lào Cai and Hà Giang. They number almost 900,000 and include several sub-groupings, notably the Money Dao and the Red Dao. As these names suggest, Dao people wear highly distinctive clothing, although sometimes only on their wedding day. The Money Dao of Hòa Bình and Sơn La provinces are unique among the Dao in that the women wear black skirts and leggings rather than trousers. A black jacket with red embroidered collar and cuffs, decorated at the back with coins (hence the name), together with a black, red-tasselled, turban-like head garment and silver jewellery are also worn. By contrast, men look rather plain in black jackets and trousers. Head gear tends to be elaborate and includes a range of shapes (from square to conical), fabrics (waxed hair to dried pumpkin fibres) and colours. The women of many branches of Dao shave their eyebrows and the hair above their foreheads before putting on the head garment, as a hairless face and high forehead are traditionally regarded as attributes of feminine beauty.

Dao wedding customs vary with each group. Apart from parental consent, intending marriage partners must have compatible birthdays and the groom has to provide the bride's family with gifts worthy of their daughter. If he is unable to do this, a temporary marriage can take place but the outstanding presents must be produced and a permanent wedding celebrated before their daughter can marry.

The Dao live chiefly by farming: those in higher altitudes are swidden cultivators, growing maize, cassava and rye. In the middle zone, shifting methods are again used to produce rice and maize, and on the valley floors sedentary farmers grow irrigated rice and rear livestock. The Dao draw on a rich history to grow and forage medicinal herbs, and Dao herbal baths and even massage are becoming popular with tourists, especially in Sa Pa.

Spiritually, the Dao have also opted for diversity; they typically worship gods, as well as their more immediate and real ancestors. The Dao also find room for elements of Taoism, and in some cases Buddhism and Confucianism.

most will ask for your passport as a deposit, which is standard. You may also wish to take a tour (see opposite).

WHERE TO STAY

Homestay Field Thôn Châng; **w** booking.com. Basic but friendly mini guesthouse with a dorm & a few rooms run by a confident & charismatic local family. **$**

Kiki's House 134B Lý Tự Trọng; **f** hagiangbackpackhostel. Long-established guesthouse & hostel that can help with motorbike rental, tours & onward travel. There's a friendly backpacker vibe in the downstairs lounge. **$**

Mr Luyen Homestay Hà Thanh village; **f** Mr Luyen homestay. 7km northwest of town, Mr Luyen is one of a number of homestays in the stilt-house villages that surround Hà Giang city. The views & hospitality here are a cut above the rest. **$**

Tom's House Motel & Motorbikes 212 Alley, Tổ 15; **w** booking.com. Tom's is one of Hà Giang's friendliest guesthouses, with clean, modern rooms & helpful advice on motorbike rental & tours. **$**

Yen Bien Luxury Hotel 517 Nguyễn Trãi; **f** khachsanyenbienluxury. One of only 2 large modern hotels in Hà Giang (the other being Phoenix Hotel), this is the better option only because it's in the centre of town. It's a popular wedding venue for Hà Giang's wealthier residents, with capacious, carpeted rooms & a rooftop swimming pool. **$$$**

WHERE TO EAT AND DRINK

Restaurants and street food

Bánh Cuốn Quảng Trường Hà Giang 3 Lê Quý Đôn; 06.00–09.00 daily. B/fast *bánh cuốn* is done extremely well at this park-adjacent spot. **$**

Hương Sen Vegan Restaurant 30A Phùng Hưng; 10.00–21.00 daily. Hà Giang's vegan restaurant, a 10min walk from the centre, is worth the extra effort. Highlights on the menu include hearty steamed dumplings & mushroom sour soup. **$**

Nhà Hàng Phố Bia Nguyễn Thái Học; 06.00–22.00 daily. More of a pub than a restaurant, Nhà Hàng Phố Bia (Beer Street Restaurant) is packed most nights with locals swigging cheap draft beer, who are keen to chat to visitors. The food menu is limited, but there's usually enough to create a meal. **$$**

Bếp Việt Hà Giang 87E Nguyễn Thái Học; bepviethagiang; 09.00–22.30 daily. Hà Giang's poshest restaurant specialises in hotpot, which it serves up to large, rowdy tables of locals & visitors from elsewhere in Vietnam. It's best to come in a group of 4 or more, & ordering anything other than hotpot can be a risk. **$$$**

Coffee houses

Café Núi Cấm Núi Cấm; cafeNuiCam.UongPhaiNham; 07.00–23.30 daily. Come for the views rather than the drinks or service. Café Núi Cấm occupies a gutted bus on the way to the old French fort.

Trung Nguyên E Coffee Hà Giang Sky Bldg, 15 Nguyễn Thái Học; trungnguyenecoffeehg; 08.00–23.00 daily. It's only a matter of time before some comfy café pops up in Hà Giang, but until then, Trung Nguyên E Coffee, on a quiet street close to the river, is one of the better places to grab coffee.

OTHER PRACTICALITIES For bespoke organised **tours** – by motorbike or jeep – that prioritise staying with local families in remote locations, reach out to Flipside Adventures (**w** flipsidevietnam.com), Borderlands (**w** borderlandstours.com) or NoMadders (**w** nomaddershostelhagiang.com). There are plenty of other tour companies offering good-value multi-day tours where you can either drive or be driven, but there are growing concerns about the impact this is having on local communities. Most tours consist of large groups, fail to offer an intimate homestay experience and don't hire drivers from the villages. Important: at the time of research, Hà Giang was one of the few provinces in Vietnam that had set up **roadblocks** to check the paperwork for foreigners. If you don't have an international or local motorbike licence, you will be fined. Negotiating these situations is up to the rider – or consider taking a tour. For more on riding motorbikes in Vietnam, see page 60. The local authorities were also discussing implementing a daily entrance fee for visitors to the Đồng Văn Geopark (the northernmost districts in Hà Giang), but this was yet to be implemented. Hà Giang General Hospital (11 Minh Khai; **w** bvdkhagiang.org.vn; all day daily), which is becoming increasingly used to bashed-up foreigners, is on the east side of the Lô River in the centre of town.

WHAT TO SEE AND DO Almost everyone goes to Hà Giang city to do some kind of road trip, usually to the extreme north of the province by motorbike, but there are a few things to see and do in the city before and after. High above the city, with commanding views, is a 19th-century French fort (Đồng Văn) and a small pagoda. The **provincial museum** (148 Trần Hưng Đạo; BaotangtinhHaGiang; 08.00–16.00 daily; 30,000VND/free adult/child), which received a big upgrade in 2020, is better than most in the northern mountains. English signage is decent and the exhibits serve as a good introduction to the landscapes and ethnolinguistic groups in the province. You might wish to study the timelines that show when the different ethnolinguistic groups arrived in the province and a map indicating the days and locations of the weekly markets.

The following **Hà Giang Loop** route, which starts and finishes in Hà Giang city, is an abridged version of an itinerary from Vietnam Coracle, a website for intrepid travel in Vietnam; for a more detailed itinerary, visit **w** vietnamcoracle.com/ha-giang-extreme-north-motorbike-loop. It assumes you have access to a phone or another device with Google Maps. The itinerary was written for independent motorbikers, but it should also be useful for motorists, cyclists and those trying to design a tour with a driver or company. You will likely cover up to three sections each day, and the entire loop might take anything from three to ten days.

Section 1: Hà Giang–Tam Sơn–Nặm Đăm (52km) Take road QL4C north out of Hà Giang towards Tam Sơn. Drive up the Bắc Sum Pass and then Heaven's Gate Pass, both offering dramatic views, including of the iconic 'Fairy Bosoms', two breast-shaped bumps, before the descent to Tam Sơn, known locally by the

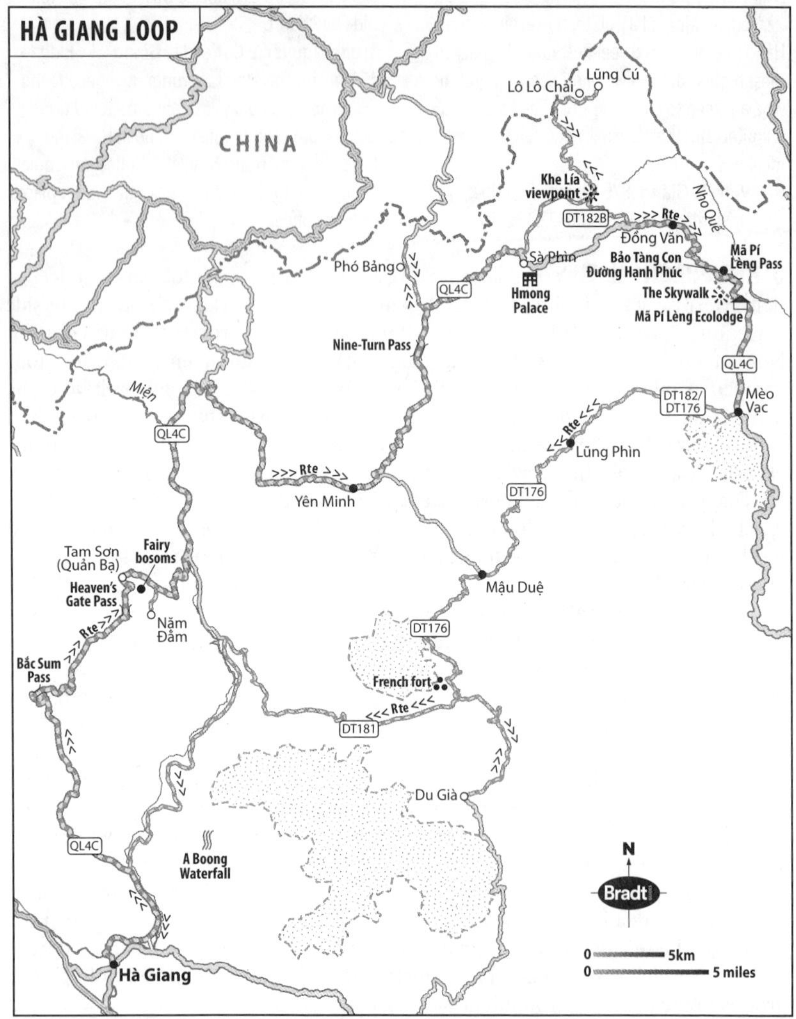

THE LO LO

The Lo Lo number fewer than 5,000 in Vietnam, though in China, where they are known as Yi, there are perhaps as many as 10 million. The Vietnamese Lo Lo are distinctive for the quilted tunics worn by the women, with multi-coloured ribbons and tassels cascading from their waists. Long sleeves are blood red, sky blue and deep purple, and traditional headdresses sport patterned embroidery and more tassels. Women might also wear large, hooped necklaces with low-hanging chains.

district name Quản Bạ. Consider lunch or coffee at the popular Yên Ngọc café (Tam Sơn; 🕘 07.00– 22.00 daily) before visiting the Dao (page 172) village of Nặm Đăm. Here you'll find Dao Lodge (f DaoLodge), a disappointing guesthouse but with attractive architecture from Hanoi-based firm 112 Architects.

Section 2: Nặm Đăm–Yên Minh (36km) Return to Tam Sơn and continue on road QL4C east down to the Miện River Valley. Take a right and climb immediately, passing ancient trees and lofty settlements before reaching Yên Minh, another small, dusty town in a basin surrounded by great limestone pillars. If you're looking for lunch or to stay overnight, try Bống Bang Homestay 2 (Nà Mạ; f Bống Bang Homestay; **$**).

Section 3: Yên Minh–Lũng Cú via Phó Bảng (57km) North of Yên Minh and towards Đồng Văn, the QL4C ploughs through an undulating landscape of dramatic peaks and troughs, formed over millions of years by tectonic activity and erosion. Pinnacles rise and fall at regular intervals, and the shapes are so live and animated it seems as though the landscape had been in fluid motion until it was suddenly petrified, like a frozen sea. After cutting along steep, treeless valleys, the road winds up to the famous Nine-Turn Pass, a helter-skelter stretch of tarmac, before a road to the left leads to Phó Bảng, a picturesque, predominantly ethnic-Chinese town. Return to the QL4C and continue to Sà Phìn, where you can visit the **Hmong Palace**. The Hmong have lived in this border region for many centuries, but the ascendancy of the powerful Vương family in the area is believed to date from the late 18th century, when they established a seat of government near Đồng Văn. In subsequent years the Vương lords were endorsed as local government mandarins of Đồng Văn and Mèo Vạc by the Nguyễn kings in Huế, and later, following the French conquest of Indochina, by their colonial rulers.

Keen to ensure the security of this key border region, the French authorities moved to further bolster the power of the Vương family. Accordingly, in 1900, Vương Chính Đức was recognised as king of the Hmong, and Chinese architects were brought in to design a residence befitting his newly elevated status. A site was chosen at Sà Phìn, 16km west of Đồng Văn; construction commenced in 1902 and was completed the following year.

During the early years of his reign, Vương Chính Đức remained loyal to his French patrons, participating in numerous campaigns to quell uprisings against the colonial government. In 1927 he was made a general in the French army; a photograph of him in full military uniform may be seen within the house. But, as the struggle for Vietnamese independence got underway during the 1930s, Vương adopted an increasingly neutral stance.

Following his death in 1944, Vương was succeeded as king of the Hmong by his son Vương Chính Sính who, the following year, met and pledged his support to President Hồ Chí Minh.

LEGEND HAS IT: UNCHARTED WATER

In the early days, when Đồng Văn was nothing more than a desolate land of jagged rocks and arid cliffs, many groups attempted to settle in the inhospitable terrain, yet the harsh winters and scorching summers drove them away. But when the Tay people arrived, guided by an unknown divine spirit, they were told that this rocky expanse could become a fertile home – but only if they honoured the Water God with a sacred shrine.

The mysterious spirit led the Tay to a hidden spot where a stream gushed forth from the heart of the mountain, a solitary sapling standing guard over the source. Here, the spirit said, the people must build a shrine in reverence to the Water God. As soon as the shrine was completed, the once-barren soil flourished. Fresh water flowed abundantly, nourishing the land and transforming it into a verdant paradise. The lone sapling blossomed into a thriving forest, and the Tay people prospered.

However, prosperity bred complacency. The younger generation, intoxicated by their newfound wealth, grew idle. They turned their backs on the sacred land, abandoning their farms, neglecting the shrine and ravaging the forests for timber and game. The shrine fell into ruin, forgotten and overgrown.

One night, the Water God returned in a furious dream experienced by all the villagers. He warned that if they did not mend their ways, he would reclaim the land and plunge it back into a wilderness unfit for human habitation. When the villagers awoke, they discovered that Đồng Văn's fertile plains were shrinking before their very eyes. The life-giving waters retreated into the earth, leaving behind a parched and barren landscape that was being swallowed by towering mountains and inhospitable canyons.

Terrified, the villagers hastily restored the shrine and offered humble sacrifices, pledging to live in harmony with the land. The Water God accepted their offerings but left a lasting reminder of their folly. Đồng Văn, once a lush expanse, was now reduced to a small, fertile valley surrounded by unforgiving rock – a reminder of the neglected deity's wrath. The water shrine and ancient tree (no longer a sapling) still exist; you'll find them at the western edge of the Old Town on Phố Cổ Street, a little northeast of Quản Hoàng Temple. For evidence of the Water God's retribution, climb the Đồn Cao Fortress and look over Đồng Văn's slender arable strip bordered by unfarmable karst outcrops.

Built between 1902 and 1903, the house of the former Hmong king faces south and was built in accordance with the geomantic principles that traditionally govern the construction of Northeast Asian royal residences, comprising four two-storey sections linked by three open courtyards. The building is surrounded by a moat, and various ornately carved tombs of members of the Vương family lie outside the main gate. Both the outer and cross-sectional walls of the building are made of brick, but within that basic structure everything else is made of wood. The architecture, a development of the late-19th-century southern Chinese townhouse style, features yin-yang roof tiles.

Backtrack a little, leave the QL4C and head north to Lũng Cú – Vietnam's north pole, with a scalable flag tower – via the Khe Lía viewpoint and on to the village of Lô Lô Chải. If you're overnighting here, try Lô Lô Panorama, Homie Homestay or Long Cư Homestay (**$**).

Section 4: Lũng Cú–Đồng Văn (26km) Retrace your steps to the Khe Lía viewpoint and take the DT182B to Đồng Văn. Dồng Văn feels dusty and sprawling until you arrive in the Old Town, which offers some charm, despite a row of fake heritage houses. Đồng Văn is one of the most popular towns on the loop, with a district museum, Quan Hoàng Temple and the Đồn Cao Fortress, which was built by the French at the turn of the 19th century and offers panoramic views. If you're staying here, try Làng Nghiến Homestay (**$**), H'mong Coffee & Homestay (f; **$**), Đồng Văn Eco Stone House (f; **$$**) or the very special Thiên Hương House (f Nk.melanie; **$**), a 20-minute drive north of town. For food, try Ethnic House (15 Dong Van Old Town; f Ethnic House Đồng Văn; **$**).

Section 5: Đồng Văn–Mèo Vạc (22km) This section is a 22km ride along the OL4C on the Mã Pí Lèng Pass (see below), a staggering road clinging to the edge of a wall of limestone mountains, towering hundreds of feet above the craterous Nho Quế River Valley.

After you exit the Mã Pí Lèng Pass, the QL4C straightens out as it heads south to Mèo Vạc, a scruffy, friendly town that sits in a sheltered basin, bathed in blue shadows cast by the ubiquitous looming limestone karsts. The town also hosts a vibrant market on Sundays. Mèo Vạc has plenty of accommodation options, including Hostel Thanh Thành (**$**) and Quang Minh (**$**), both just west of the central market. For some of the most atmospheric boutique lodgings in the entire region, head out of town to the Auberge de Meo Vac (**w** chungpua.com; **$$$**).

Section 6: Mèo Vạc–Mậu Duệ (37km) Leave Mèo Vạc on road DT182 (later marked as DT176) heading west towards Mậu Duệ. This road passes through a stark, rock-strewn limestone valley with some death-defying sections of mountain road. There is at least one town of interest on the way – Lũng Phìn – with a few ancient houses, a bustling morning market and a raised temple built into the rock. Don't stay in Mậu Duệ and push on to Du Già instead.

Section 7: Mậu Duệ–Du Già (38km) After arriving in Mậu Duệ, if may feel as if you've left the dramatic scenery behind. Not so! Head south on DT176, a road leading up a seemingly endless pass over a chain of high, jagged limestone peaks, then down the other side through pine forests and valleys. You'll spot the remains of an unnamed centenarian French fort on the road. Then prepare for a breathtaking

THE SKYWALK

The Mã Pí Lèng Pass was once the most spectacular road in all of Vietnam, but car convoys and construction projects somewhat tarnish the vistas and generate a lot of noise. What was once a blissfully peaceful mountain road has fallen victim to the sounds of jackhammers and boomboxes. To recapture some of Mã Pí Lèng's lost tranquillity, consider hiking the Skywalk. You could do this as a half-day, self-guided trip from Đồng Văn or while driving the Mã Pí Lèng Pass on the way to Mèo Vạc. This 1½-hour trek is one of the loop's most extraordinary experiences and yet few seem to know it's there. After parking at Bảo Tàng Con Đường Hạnh Phúc, a memorial monument to those who died building the road (or Mã Pí Lèng Homestay for a slightly shorter trail), the path climbs to the White Cliff (Vách Đá Trắng) Grotto, which is high above the road. The trail then descends through viewpoints, patches of farmland and a village before re-joining the road close to Mã Pí Lèng Ecolodge (a different property to Mã Pí Lèng Homestay). From there you can walk (1hr) or hitch (10mins) back to where you parked.

HINTERLANDS: HOÀNG SU PHÌ AND XÍN MẦN DISTRICTS

For a description of 'Hinterlands' boxes, see page 131.

These huge districts border Lào Cai to the west and China to the north. The only sensible way to approach them is with your own wheels, and even then travel here is not for the faint-hearted. The road infrastructure is facing an overhaul, and this won't be finished anytime soon. Expect rough roads, controlled and uncontrolled landslides and dubious safety precautions. If this hasn't put you off, there are some extraordinary vistas of terraced farms and roadside waterfalls. Thác Tiên (Fairy Waterfall) in Xín Mần is a pretty spot where you can swim. The peak at Kiou Leou Ti offers fine views. There are also some excellent places to stay. Panhou Retreat (page 132) is a hidden lodge engulfed in jungle and Su Phì CBT has a limited network of homestays and lodges throughout the area. Together these districts offer two or three days of rewarding (but occasionally maddening) driving.

descent into an idyllic valley, where you'll find the tiny hamlet of Du Già, with its glut of accommodation options, including Du Gia Panorama (f; **$$**), Tom's Du Gia Homestay (f; **$$**) and Tớ Dày Du Già (f todayvillage; **$$**). From here you are also close enough to walk to Du Già Waterfall (go at sunrise to avoid crowds; go at sunset for a party).

Section 8: Du Già–Hà Giang city (98km) From Du Già, retrace your steps to the nameless French fort and then head west along the DT181. Once you hit the Miện River, head south along an unnumbered road past the A Boong Waterfall and back to Hà Giang.

CAO BẰNG

Cao Bằng Province consists mainly of wild mountain territory where karst outcrops hug large valleys, terraced fields wind around hills and villages nestle on luxuriantly green slopes. Most of the province's people are Tay (page 170) and Nung, though there are also Hmong (page 160), Dao (page 172) and Kinh (page 189). Indeed, Cao Bằng is one reason why this guidebook avoids the term 'ethnic minority'. While the Kinh are the most numerous ethnolinguistic group in Vietnam, in Cao Bằng they constitute a tiny minority of the population. You're most likely to meet the Tay, who fervently celebrate the Lồng Tồng Festival straight after Lunar New Year. Also well represented are the Nung, who raise carp and pike in fishponds and grow and weave cotton, which they colour with indigo. Many families grow hemp, tea, aniseed and castor-oil plants and raise cattle, goats and horses, which they use to transport produce to local markets. Despite the rich ethnolinguistic diversity, Cao Bằng is best known for two things: Bản Giốc Waterfall (see front cover) and the revolutionary headquarters at Pác Bó, where President Hồ Chí Minh lived from 1941 after returning to Vietnam following decades of revolutionary teaching. Only a fraction of international visitors make it to Cao Bằng, but those who do often find it to be the highlight of their trip.

Virtually none of the late-19th-century French buildings in Cao Bằng city have survived the ravages of war, and redevelopment in the Old Quarter means it holds little of particular interest. Inside the riverbend, between the Bằng and Hiến rivers, is nevertheless pleasant, with a good range of food, drink and accommodation. Kim Đồng Street transforms into a pedestrianised zone on the weekends, with dance performances, market stalls and games. Most of what you've come to see, however, lies in the surrounding districts.

HISTORY Surrounded on three sides by turbulent rivers and tall mountains, this province has always been of interest to strategists. One of the first recorded was Nùng Trí Cao, who set up his little domain here in the 11th century. People knew him as the Emperor of Mind and Virtue, who fought tirelessly against the Chinese. Lord Lê Lợi set up a citadel west of present-day Cao Bằng city in the 15th century, and when the Mạc clan were driven north in the 1590s they established a citadel in the northwest. Virtually nothing of these fortresses remains today.

Before the August 1945 Revolution (page 14), the area had become a French stronghold, and local people were badly treated by the mandarins who governed the area for the colonial authorities. Patriotic movements grew up against them and Hồ Chí Minh began the long road to independence from here (page 182), but it wasn't until 1950 that they were finally ousted and the French retreated to nearby Lạng Sơn. Cao Bằng was badly damaged during the 1979 border war with China and has since been extensively rebuilt.

GETTING THERE AND AWAY There are no train stations or airports close to Cao Bằng. **Buses** to/from Cao Bằng will pick up/drop off in the centre at the bus company offices. Several buses daily connect the city with Hanoi (8hrs), Bắc Kạn (4hrs; for Ba Bể Lake) and Lạng Sơn (4hrs). There are also buses that connect Cao Bằng with Hà Giang for onward travel to Lào Cai Province, but these are less common.

You'll have no trouble covering central Cao Bằng city entirely on foot, but you'll need motorised transport to reach the sights, all of which are in far-flung corners of the province.

WHERE TO STAY

Cao Bang Plant Lady Homestay 224 Bế Văn Đàn; f. A woman from Cao Bằng who loves plants opened this charming little spot to welcome mainly young Vietnamese guests, though her sprightly young team will do everything in their power to make anyone feel at home. **$**

Jodevi Homestay 64 Hiến Giang; f jodevi.homestay.caobang. An increasingly popular spot with young Vietnamese motorbike travellers & Western backpackers, with neat, minimalist rooms in a friendly corner of town. **$**

Lan's Home Lý Tự Trọng; f lanshome.caobang. Simple private & dorm rooms are beautified with local textiles & some genuinely impressive wall murals. The owner speaks English (the staff do not) & can help arrange tours & onward transport. **$**

Mina Homestay Sông Hiến relocation area; f Mina Homestay Cao Bằng. Were it not for the location in a modern, soulless corner of the city, this would be the perfect guesthouse. Rooms are well appointed & the owners are welcoming & keen to converse. **$**

La Maison Boutique 1 Hoàng Đình Giong; **w** maisoncaobanghotel.vn. La Maison has tried with some success to cultivate a luxury Parisian townhouse theme in the middle of Cao Bằng, in a multi-storey, balcony-laden corner building. Rooms are plush, though a little dark. Water pressure can be weak on the higher floors. **$$**

Los Angeles Hotel 93 Xuân Trường; f kslacb2020. Another mid-range hotel in the same vein as La Maison, but with a little more flash & a very slightly better location, close to the central park & statue of Hồ Chí Minh. **$$**

WHERE TO EAT AND DRINK

Restaurants and street food

Phở Chua Gia Truyền Quyên 5 Hiến Giang; ⌚ 07.00–13.00 daily. A Cao Bằng speciality is *phở chua*, which means sour *phở*, though it's probably more sweet than sour. This popular spot serves it with any combination of beef, chicken & duck. **$**

Quán Bánh Cuốn Cao Bằng Chị Thi 4 Hiến Giang; 🕘 06.00–12.30 daily. Serves up fresh *bánh cuốn*, a provincial speciality & hearty variation on the famous Hanoi dish. Finely chopped pork is mixed with mushrooms, rolled in wet rice paper & dipped in a herby side soup. $

Pedro's Pizza Bằng Giang Bridge Cầu Bằng Giang; 🕘 10.00–22.00 daily. Better-than-expected pizza & ice-cold beer is served up on wooden tables attired in red gingham tablecloths. $$

✷ **Yen – Ngon như mẹ nấu** 22 Tổ 12, 1/4 St; f yenngonnhumenau; 🕘 10.00–23.00 daily. The name means 'delicious, just like mum's cooking', which might be an understatement, as the dishes here exceed the expectations of most home kitchens. The fresh, crunchy salads are particularly good. $$

Hạt Dẻ Quán 2 Kim Đồng; f hatdequancaobang; 🕘 11.00–23.00 daily. A big, posh restaurant, popular with Cao Bằng's rising middle class, that serves all the Vietnamese classics along with some mountain speciality dishes, including roast duck from Lạng Sơn. $$$

Coffee houses

✷ **Kim Dong Coffee** 28 Kim Đồng; f; 🕘 08.00–23.00 daily. Part streetside café, part leather shoe repair shop, & with no discernible sign, it doesn't get much hipper than Kim Dong. Look for the trendy & tattooed young things playing with their phones.

Nàng Café 75 Khai Phắt Nà Ngần; f; 🕘 07.00–23.00 daily. A mud house at the front & a garden with pond in the back, Nàng offers various nooks with low tables & chairs. As well as delicious coffee, they make a mean pomegranate juice when they're in season.

Tộc Cà Phê 201 Kim Đồng; f toccaphecb; 🕘 07.00–23.00 daily. Decorated with the textiles made by Cao Bằng's various ethnolinguistic groups & staffed by youngsters in traditional dress, Tộc Cà Phê also has views to the river out the back.

OTHER PRACTICALITIES At the time of research there were no reputable tour companies in Cao Bằng city, but renting a motorbike or hiring a driver and car is easily done through your accommodation. Remember to make it clear exactly where you want to go and how long you want to spend in each place before setting off. Always agree on the price first. Cao Bằng Provincial Hospital (Km2 Đông Khê St; w benhvientinh.caobang.gov.vn; 🕘 all day daily) is south of the city centre, but you may be better off in one of the private clinics, such as Bệnh Viện Đa Khoa Hanoi – Cao Bằng (3/10 St; w benhviendakhoahanoicaobang.com.vn; 🕘 all day daily) or Phòng Khám Đa Khoa Hồng Đức (Tổ 11 Sông Bằng Ward; 🕘 07.00–17.00 daily). Medical care in these parts is lacking; for anything serious, return to Hanoi.

WHAT TO SEE AND DO

Northeast of Cao Bằng city To experience a wild and scenic corner of the country and province, head northeast of Cao Bằng city through riverside roads and across shallow terraced farms to explore unusual villages and scenic spots, including Bản Giốc Waterfall, the grandest cascade in all of Vietnam. Leaving Cao Bằng city early and arriving home late, it's possible to explore this northern corner in a day, though there are some tempting accommodation options near the falls and in Khuổi Kỵ Stone Village. Pack waterproofs even if no rain is forecast: weather can turn quickly in this part of the country and you'll want to stay as dry as possible when approaching the waterfall.

Phúc Sen Knife-Making Village The Nung village of Phúc Sen is 30km east of Cao Bằng city, on the way to Bản Giốc Waterfall. The village's smithery tradition dates back hundreds of years, and you'll see various knifemakers on the side of the road selling their wares.

Khuổi Ky Stone Village The Tay (page 170) community have been building their houses from stone rather than wood, the traditional material, for centuries, but it's not entirely clear why they made the switch. Virtually all of the houses have been changed and adapted in some way, a process that has sped up in recent years as the villagers bank on an imminent influx of visitors. While it's no longer clear which houses are genuinely ancient, they are nevertheless attractive, and many now offer homestay and restaurant services. At the time of research, tourism here hadn't quite taken off yet, and it should be possible simply to turn up and find a local family to stay with.

Ngườm Ngao Cave (near Khuổi Ky Village; 🕘 07.30–17.00 daily; 45,000VND entry, 195,000VND for 90–120min tour) If you've not yet seen a limestone cave in Vietnam, this well-lit underground dominion is worth visiting. The lower fee, which is the option most visitors take, only gives access to a small part of the cave, so if time allows then better to pay the extra dollars for the tour. The guides don't usually speak much English, but that tends not to dampen their confidence or enthusiasm to show visitors around. Without proper surveying, information about the cave is hazy, but it supposedly stretches for more than 2km and was once used as a den by tigers.

✷ ***Bản Giốc Waterfall*** (🕘 07.30–17.30 daily; 45,000VND) A multi-tiered and thundering turquoise cascade of fantastical proportions, ringed by tufts of jungle that creep up limestone pinnacles, Bản Giốc Waterfall is the magnum opus of Vietnam's many waterfalls. The falls, an integral part of the UNESCO-inscribed Cao Bằng Geopark, are shared with China, where they are known as Detian Falls, making them one of the largest cross-border cascades in the world. China hoards the lion's share of the falls, but Vietnam has the better vistas. Indeed, the panoramas here are so dazzling that they feature on the front cover of this guidebook. Few foreign tourists make it to this remote Northern Vietnam nook, but domestic tourists in both China and Vietnam have caught on to this immense natural wonder, resulting in large tour groups, a jovial atmosphere and a theatre of elaborate photo shoots. Water flows throughout the year, including in the dry season (October–April), though an upstream dam may occasionally limit movement. After buying tickets at the visitor centre, stroll down the 500m-long concrete path, bordered by rows of multi-coloured flowering trees and rice terraces that glow green in the summer months, before reaching the falls, which you will hear before they come into view. Spend time here down by the water's edge, taking in views from difficult angles, and pack waterproofs that will enable you to get as close as possible to the spray. Some areas are off-limits, but you can for the most part scramble around wherever you wish. Swimming is banned, but it's possible to pay 100,000VND for a boat journey taking you up close to the falls and a stone's throw from China. Behind the falls is the pagoda **Chùa Phật Tích Trúc Lâm Bản Giốc**, offering elevated views of the waterfall; it is well worth the climb.

Northwest of Cao Bằng city There are two major sites northwest of Cao Bằng, both related to Vietnam's anti-colonial struggle: the Tomb of Kim Đồng, a local revolutionary, and Pác Bó, where Hồ Chí Minh re-entered Vietnam and initiated the independence movement. Visiting the two sites from Cao Bằng will take the better part of a day.

Tomb of Kim Đồng (Trường Hà; 🕘 08.00–23.00 daily) Kim Đồng, a local hero of the Nung ethnolinguistic group, became a symbol of the patriotic youth due to his commitment to the revolutionary cause in the 1940s. Born into a poor family in northern Cao Bằng, he joined the resistance against the French at an early age and carried important messages between different groups of revolutionary forces. He is said to have died at just 14, in 1947. His tomb, nestled beneath towering limestone peaks, is 46km northwest of Cao Bằng city, on the way to Pác Bó.

Pác Bó (Trường Hà; 25,000VND/free adult/child) On 28 January 1941 Hồ Chí Minh crossed the Sino-Vietnamese border, returning home to take charge of the resistance movement after 30 years overseas. In the days that followed, he and his colleagues set up their revolutionary headquarters in a cave in the Pác Bó Valley. A decade ago, Pác Bó was the sort of spot that model carpet-weavers or revolutionary railwaymen might be brought to as a reward. But as disposable incomes have grown, young people have become more adventurous, tourism infrastructure has

FROM CAVES TO CONGRESS

Taking advantage of the surrender of the French administration to the Japanese, the man who would come to be known as Hồ Chí Minh (at that point he was Nguyễn Ái Quốc, the name he adopted in Paris; see page 230) returned to Vietnam. He set up his headquarters at Pác Bó, an area populated mainly by the Nung people. It was from here that Hồ Chí Minh guided the growing revolutionary movement, organising training programmes for cadres, translating *The History of the Communist Party in the USSR* into Vietnamese and editing the revolutionary newspaper *Independent Vietnam*.

The eighth Congress of the Communist Party Central Committee, convened by Hồ Chí Minh at Pác Bó from 10 to 19 March 1941, was an event of great historic importance that saw the establishment of the Vietnam Independence League (Việt Nam Độc Lập Đồng Minh Hội), better known as the Việt Minh. This congress also assisted preparations for the future armed uprising, establishing guerilla bases throughout the Việt Bắc.

The years 1941 to 1945 were a period of severe hardship for the Vietnamese people, as the colonial government colluded with Japanese demands to exploit the country's natural resources to the full, in order to support the Japanese war effort. But, by 1945, the Vichy Government in France had fallen and the French colonial administration belatedly drew up plans to resist the Japanese.

However, on 9 March 1945, their plans were foiled by the Japanese, who had set up a new government, with King Bảo Đại as head of state. At this juncture, Việt Minh guerilla activity was intensified all over the country, with the result that, by June 1945, almost all of the six provinces north of the Red River Delta were under communist control. On 13 August, Japan surrendered to the Allied forces; three days later Hồ Chí Minh headed south from Pác Bó to Tuyên Quang to preside over a People's Congress, which declared a general insurrection and established the Democratic Republic of Vietnam. The **August 1945 Revolution** that followed swept all in its wake; in a matter of weeks the three major cities of Hanoi, Huế and Saigon had fallen to the Việt Minh and King Bảo Đại had abdicated. On 2 September 1945 President Hồ Chí Minh made a historic address to the people in Hanoi's Ba Đình Square, proclaiming the nation's independence.

In Tây Ninh, visit the Great Temple of the Cao Đài religion, a synthesis of Buddhism, Christianity, Taoism, Confucianism and Islam PAGE 392

above (R/D)

The French left many colonial landmarks in Vietnam, including the Notre Dame Cathedral in Hồ Chí Minh City PAGE 468

right (P/S)

The site of the-19th century Thiên Mụ Pagoda in Huế has been a place of worship for centuries PAGE 263

below right (DV/S)

Established in 1070, Hanoi's Temple of Literature may be the oldest university in Southeast Asia PAGE 118

below left (N/S)

above (S/S) Hội An's multicoloured assembly halls, such as Fujian, reflect its rich trading heritage PAGE 310

left (AJS/VT) Circular boats known as coracles are a common sight along Central Vietnam's sweeping coastline

below left (SS) It's still possible to find floating markets in the Mekong Delta, such as at Phong Điền near Cần Thơ PAGE 409

below right (DN/S) Encircling Hanoi are dozens of ancient villages, many of which specialise in just one or two crafts PAGE 124

above (Y/D) Dragon dancing is common during festivals, particularly Tết (pictured) and Mid-Autumn Festival PAGE 68

right (M/S) Hanoi's Museum of Ethnology is an essential stop before heading to the northern mountains PAGE 120

below right (BK) The motorbike is central to Vietnam's aesthetic, both in the cities and the countryside PAGE 60

below left (H/A) The brightly painted Khmer temples in the Mekong Delta, such as this one in Trà Vinh, are rich in iconography PAGE 414

above (A/D) Hồ Chí Minh, modern Vietnam's founding father, is entombed in a vast mausoleum in Hanoi PAGE 112

left (X/S) Điện Biên Phủ, where you can still visit General de Castries's Bunker (pictured), was the site of a humiliating military defeat that brought an end to French colonialism PAGE 150

below (A/S) After obliteration during the American War, Huế's Imperial City began a long restoration process PAGE 256

above (TH/S) Đà Nẵng's Dragon Bridge is a fierce reflection of the city's economic dynamism PAGE 289

right (SF) Hồ Chí Minh City's gilded modernist Independence Palace is an architectural and design marvel and still preserves its 1970s interior PAGE 468

below (DH/S) Đà Lạt is dotted with villas seemingly transported from provincial France, some fit for royalty, such as Summer Palace I PAGE 373

above left (WH/S) A black-shanked duoc in Cát Tiên National Park, one of Southern Vietnam's premier wildlife refuges PAGE 387

top right (DH/D) Vietnam's national parks house a dazzling array of birds, including sunbirds PAGE 7

above right (SO/D) Butterfly populations flourish during the spring and summer months PAGE 7

left (SF) Hike with a local guide through the rice terraces around Sa Pa, in the vast northern mountains PAGE 158

below (LR/D) Though increasingly industrialised, the Mekong Delta is still a labyrinth of fern-fringed waterways PAGE 396

Hạ Long Bay and Lan Hạ Bay (pictured) are where you'll find Vietnam's iconic karst scenery, though choose your cruise carefully PAGE 205

above (GB/S)

River cruising in Ninh Bình, a province of historical and geographical intrigue PAGE 213

right (T/D)

With so few visitors, Bạch Mã is one of Vietnam's most rewarding national parks to visit PAGE 271

below (H/S)

above (H/S) Quy Nhơn is one of the country's most overlooked cities, with sweeping beaches, fishing villages and ancient Cham towers nearby PAGE 326

improved and patriotism remains strong, Pác Bó has become a pilgrimage site for all Vietnamese, especially those from the northern provinces.

The visitor centre and parking is 2km from the sites, and tickets include an electric buggy ride that transports you between the two. The Hồ Chí Minh House of Remembrance contains an altar dedicated to Hồ Chí Minh, while plaques have background information on the Pác Bó area and its historical role in the revolutionary struggle. It also contains information about Hồ Chí Minh's long journey back to Vietnam between 1938 and 1941, culminating in his arrival at Pác Bó in January 1941 and his movements south to Tuyên Quang Province, where a decision was taken in August 1945 to launch a general insurrection to seize power and found the Democratic Republic of Vietnam.

A further 2km by buggy is the Lenin Stream, under the shade of Karl Marx Mountains – both names chosen by Hồ Chí Minh (the place is festooned with commemorative plaques). From here, visitors can walk to Cốc Bó Cave (500m), where Hồ lived and worked after his return from overseas, and visit a few huts in which he sheltered and streams where he fished. The pristine surroundings are beautiful and the area's historical significance only adds to their appeal. Beware that the pathways are very slippery when wet – which is most of the time.

LẠNG SƠN

Lạng Sơn Province covers an area of 8,328km^2 and has a 231km-long border with China. The area is known for its aniseed, peaches, pears, plums, mandarin oranges and roast duck. Mountains in Lạng Sơn Province are fairly low, but much of the province is still immensely attractive. This is particularly true along the border with China and west of Lạng Sơn city, the provincial capital. Lạng Sơn city lies on the Kỳ Lừa River, in a small alluvial plain surrounded by 1,000m-high mountains. The city was badly damaged during the border war of 1979 and has since been substantially rebuilt, but the Old Quarter still contains a few interesting historical buildings and markets.

HISTORY Lạng Sơn looms large in Vietnamese history for several reasons. The first derives from the number of prehistoric artefacts unearthed here. The so-called Bắc Sơn Period (5000–3000BCE) was characterised by the development of pottery and the widespread use of refined stone implements, including distinctive axes with polished edges known as Bắc Sơn axes. In the 15th century CE, it was at Chi Lăng, just south of Lạng Sơn city, that Lord Lê Lợi gained a fantastic victory over the occupying Ming forces with help from a mythical sword (page 104). Later, the area came under the stewardship of the Mạc Dynasty, and the remnants of a 16th-century citadel can still be seen in Lạng Sơn city.

During the colonial struggles it became the main centre for supplying Việt Minh troops. Revolutionary cells were formed as early as 1937, and in August 1945 they were the first to give their support to the Việt Minh. During the Bắc Sơn Uprising in September 1940, revolutionaries detained in Lạng Sơn prison seized the opportunity afforded by the Japanese attack on the town to escape, heading northwest across the mountains to Bắc Sơn, west of Lạng Sơn. With the support of the local Communist Party organisation they fomented a general insurrection in the town, disarming the fleeing French troops and taking over the district centre to set up the first revolutionary power base in Northern Vietnam. The following year, French forces responded by launching a campaign of terror, forcing the leaders of the uprising to retreat into the mountains. The Bắc Sơn Uprising did, however, prove to be an important milestone in the revolutionary struggle and, in the years that followed, the tide turned steadily against the French throughout the region. As a result, it was heavily bombed in a last-ditch effort by the French in July 1953 and considerable damage was inflicted on the railway. The Chinese attack in February 1979 destroyed bridges, hospitals, schools and residences throughout the province.

GETTING THERE AND AROUND There is no airport in Lạng Sơn. There is a train station, but at the time of research there were no passenger trains between Hanoi and Lạng Sơn. These lines were only discontinued in 2020, so it's worth checking for an update. **Buses** pick up/drop off in the centre at bus company offices; several buses daily connect the city with Hanoi (3hrs) and Cao Bằng (4hrs).

Lạng Sơn is just about walkable, but a rented motorbike or taxis will make moving between the sights more comfortable. To give an example, it takes around 45 minutes to walk from Lạng Sơn Citadel in the south of the city to the Mạc Dynasty Citadel and caves in the west. Renting a motorbike is easily done through your accommodation.

WHERE TO STAY AND EAT

Hava Homestay 608B Bà Triệu; f Homestaylangson. Very cheap & friendly hotel that, unfortunately, is inconveniently located in a rather characterless part of town. If you have your own transport, however, this shouldn't be a problem. **$**

Hoàng Thịnh Hotel 319 Bà Triệu. Stay here for the location, which is walking distance to Lạng Sơn's Market Quarter. Otherwise there's little else to keep you, except for perhaps the price; the rooms are fine. **$**

SOJO Hotel Lạng Sơn 297 Phai Vệ; w sojohotels.com. Part of a reliably good modern chain of provincial hotels with small, practical rooms, cooking areas & free washing, but it isn't central. **$$**

4 Points by Sheraton 2 Trần Hưng Đạo; w fourpointslangson.com. The most luxurious place in town, which just about reaches international standards, with a gym, pool, a couple of bars & an obscenely large lobby. The place is empty most of the time, which means they offer good deals. **$$$**

Nhà Hàng Vịt Quay Hải Xồm 42 Bà Triệu; ⌚ 05.30–18.00 daily. One of the best places in town to come for roast duck, which they hack up into chunks & serve with a dipping sauce. **$$**

Phở Vịt Quay Vi Tặng 2 Văn Cao; ⌚ 05.30–11.30 daily. Serves up hearty bowls of duck *phở* for b/fast. Very popular & surely one of the best places in the city to try this local speciality. **$$**

Quán Cơm Anh Thắng Đấu Tơ 34 Lê Lai; ⌚ 10.00–21.00 daily. There's nothing obviously special about this simple rice joint, but it's in the centre of town, always open & the seats spill on to the pavement so you can watch the world go by as you dine. **$$**

OTHER PRACTICALITIES At the time of research there were no reputable tour companies in Lạng Sơn as the city sees so few visitors. Lạng Sơn Provincial Hospital is north of the city centre.

WHAT TO SEE AND DO

The citadels Lạng Sơn Citadel comprises a large section of the ancient city walls, dating back to the 18th century, but there's little to see beyond the brick gate on Nguyễn Thái Học Street. The east- and west-facing walls of the crumbling 16th-century Mạc Dynasty Citadel are located on a limestone outcrop west of Lạng Sơn, and it is the more impressive of the two. The ruin is an atmospheric remnant from a lost world, an era of borderless lands, mountain fortresses and warring feudal lords. The citadel walls are in poor condition despite several renovations over the

HINTERLANDS: MẪU SƠN AND BẮC SƠN

For a description of 'Hinterlands' boxes, see page 131.

The areas around Lạng Sơn city see very few international visitors and will appeal to those with a sense of adventure – and their own transport. Of all the French hill stations in Vietnam, **Mẫu Sơn**, 30km east of Lạng Sơn, is perhaps the most derelict and makes for an interesting day trip from the city. Some 1,541m above sea level, its altitude is like that of Sa Pa and Đà Lạt, but instead of a fully fledged town built around a lake, Mẫu Sơn is a small cluster of crumbling and semi-abandoned buildings. Some of the less weather-ravaged buildings house cafés and a restaurant. The road up and down the mountain is satisfyingly steep and meandering and the ruins are haunting, but there's little that will keep you.

Bắc Sơn, a rural district 85km west of Lạng Sơn, is a constellation of connected valleys sliced by rivers that curl around jungled karst mountains. The plains, which hold all the towns and villages, are a quilt of green and yellow rice paddies in the summer and autumn months – the quintessential image of mountainous Vietnam. There's little to do but drive around while keeping an eye out for signs that point to waterfalls and caves, most of which are pretty, if not remarkable. There are guesthouses in the larger towns and homestays in some of the villages. Two days with an overnight stay in one of the villages is enough time to explore the district.

years, but the views of neighbouring karst mountains rising from rice paddies are impressive any time of the year.

The caves At the Tam Thanh Cave on the road to the Mạc Dynasty Citadel, there are three chambers; the outer one functions as a pagoda with two shrines and another contains a freshwater pool. A poem by Ngô Thì Sĩ (1726–80), military commander of the Lạng Sơn garrison who first discovered this and other caves in the area, is carved on the wall near the entrance. Nhị Thanh Cave, south of Tam Thanh Cave, is perhaps the best known of Lạng Sơn's caves. There are in fact two separate caves here – the one on the right contains the Tam Giáo Pagoda, established in 1777 by Ngô Thì Sĩ, in which are six shrines, while the one on the left follows the Ngọc Tuyền stream deep into the mountain: the latter is particularly dramatic. More of Ngô Thì Sĩ's poetry adorns the walls here.

Climbing in Hữu Lũng Halfway between Hanoi and Lạng Sơn, Hữu Lũng is a burgeoning rock-climbing destination, with dozens of routes up and down the craggy limestone outcrops. Reach out to **Viet Climb** (w vietclimb.vn), the company that pioneered rock climbing in the area, for more information. They've worked with a local family to set up a comfortable homestay and can arrange multi-day, all-inclusive trips from the capital.

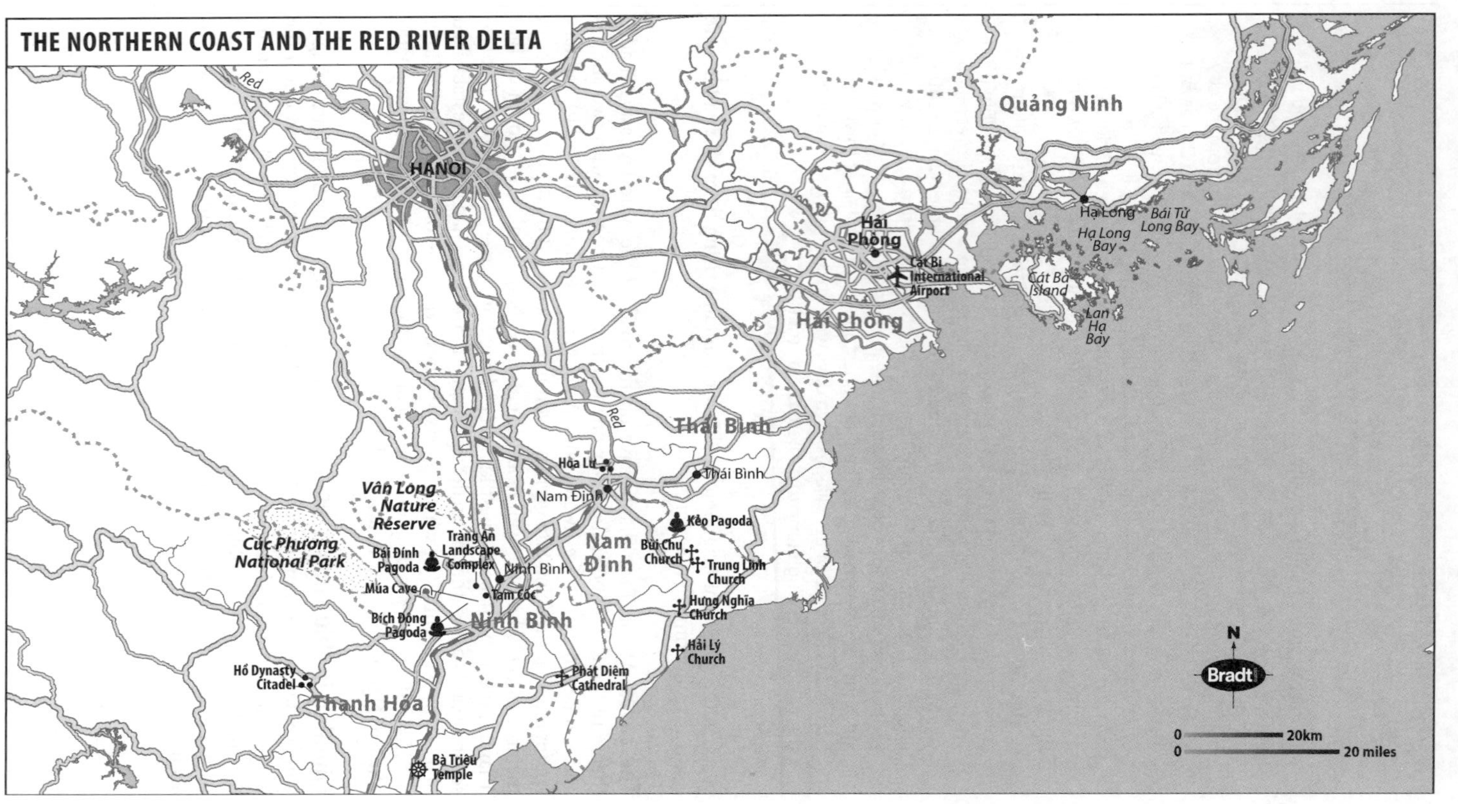
THE NORTHERN COAST AND THE RED RIVER DELTA
Red
HANOI
Quảng Ninh
Hạ Long
Bái Tử Long Bay
Hạ Long Bay
Hải Phòng
Cát Bi International Airport
Cát Bà Island
Lan Hạ Bay
Hải Phòng
Red
Thái Bình
Hoa Lư
Thái Bình
Vân Long Nature Reserve
Nam Định
Kẻo Pagoda
Cúc Phương National Park
Tràng An Landscape Complex
Bái Đính Pagoda
Ninh Bình
Nam Định
Bùi Chu Church
Trung Linh Church
Múa Cave
Tam Cốc
Hưng Nghĩa Church
Bích Động Pagoda
Ninh Bình
Hải Lý Church
Hồ Dynasty Citadel
Phát Diệm Cathedral
Thanh Hóa
Bà Triệu Temple
N
Bradt
0 20km
0 20 miles

5

The Northern Coast and the Red River Delta

Beginning in China's Yunnan Province, the Red River, referred to in Chinese as 紅河 and Vietnamese as Sông Hồng ('Pink River') for its burnt sienna-coloured waters, meanders through the Himalayan foothills and enters Vietnam in Lào Cai Province. Before flowing through Hanoi, it is fed by the Black River from the west and the Lô River from the north and splits to form the Red River Delta. This is Vietnam's great northern delta, and though it's less than half the size of the Mekong Delta in the south, it still covers an area of 15,000km^2 and supports one of the highest agricultural population densities in the world. Nevertheless, from June to October it is prone to extensive flooding which, over the centuries, has necessitated the building of numerous dykes to protect settlements. Northeast of the delta provinces is Quảng Ninh, a largely mountainous province, though it's the coastal areas that draw visitors.

The Red River Delta and northern coastal areas sit squeezed between mountains to the west and the sea to the east. This great strip of land, long considered the cradle of Vietnamese culture and civilisation, holds immense historical significance. Many of the magnificent Bronze Age Đông Sơn drums (page 8) were found here, and all three of Vietnam's ancient capitals – Cổ Loa, Hoa Lư and Thăng Long (Hanoi) – were built close to the banks of one of the Red River's distributaries. Several military victories were won here, most notably the expulsion of Chinese occupiers and Mongol invaders in 938 and 1288 respectively. This northeastern zone is also known for the revolutionary activities from 1945 to 1954 that would contribute to the liberation of Vietnam from colonial rule.

Despite the history, the area is best known for its legends and landscapes. **Hạ Long Bay**, Vietnam's most developed cruise destination, offers layered mythological and geological intrigue. Further south are the equally captivating seascapes of **Cát Bà island and Lan Hạ Bay** and the diverse landscapes and wildlife refuges of **Ninh Bình**. Overlooked areas include historic **Hải Phòng**, dapper **Hạ Long city** and the spiritual enclaves of **Nam Định** and **Thái Bình**, which are home to some outstanding ecclesiastical architecture.

This chapter is organised from north to south, beginning in Quảng Ninh, before moving through the coastal Red River Delta subregion provinces of Hải Phòng, Nam Định, Thái Bình and Ninh Bình.

WHEN TO VISIT

October and November are the best months to visit generally, when days are warm and sunny, evenings are cool and storms unlikely. Winters (December–February)

THE MOTHER GODDESS IN THE RED RIVER DELTA

By Liên Hoàng Lê, PhD candidate at the Institute of Vietnamese Studies and Development Science, Vietnam National University, and founder of Vietlesson, a language school in Hanoi (page 88)

The Red River Delta, the birthplace of Vietnamese civilisation, holds immense historical and cultural significance. For millennia it has been the nucleus of Vietnamese cultural development, with its influences radiating southwards. Given that agriculture is the cornerstone of Vietnamese culture, women have historically played key roles in economic and social life. Unlike nomadic pastoralism, which depends on physical male strength, farming requires sedentary labour and endurance. Additionally, the delta is in a tropical monsoon climatic zone. While the diversity of such zones has meant rich swathes of land capable of nurturing a large population, it also brings natural disasters, like typhoons and disease, that threaten lives. As a result, society has placed great value on female fertility. Large families were important in combating instability and supplying enough labour during the planting and harvesting seasons. Despite the impact of the Confucian patriarchal system, women have long played a crucial role in Vietnam's survival and advancement.

The civilisation that developed in the Red River Delta sought refuge from the unpredictable powers of nature. To make sense of the fickleness of nature, the Vietnamese turned to Mother Goddess worship, or Thờ Nữ Thần, believing that feminine energy brings stability and prosperity. In agricultural civilisations, natural elements such as soil and water were critical to crop development and reproduction. In the Red River Delta, people understood the elements to be feminine primordial deities, giving them titles such as Mẹ, Mẫu, Bà, Mụ and Mạ. All these words mean 'mother'. The most widespread belief system in the Red River Delta was Tam Phủ and Tứ Phủ, also known as Đạo Mẫu. Tam Phủ (Three Places) comprises three realms: Heaven, Earth and Water; Tứ Phủ (Four Places) includes the aforementioned three – plus Mountains. Each realm has a separate Mother Goddess. These Animist principles have been absorbed into Vietnam's broader religions, including Taoism and Buddhism, and you might see this in temples, pagodas and shrines in the Red River Delta subregion and elsewhere in Vietnam. In 2016, UNESCO classified Đạo Mẫu as an intangible cultural heritage.

are cloudy and can be very cold. Spring (March–April) is highly unpredictable and can be drizzly, but optimists will find beauty in the rain. Summers (May–September) tend to be long, hot, sticky and sometimes wet, and in the peak season for domestic tourism (June–August) places can be busy.

As long as you dress intelligently, **Hạ Long Bay** is a year-round destination, but the visuals are different depending on the season. With clear skies and only the occasional storm, the beginning of summer (May–June) offers the brightest colours and most dramatic sunrises and sunsets. Typhoon season usually runs from July to September, but this isn't necessarily a bad time to visit as the storms only hit once every few weeks, if at all. With modern forecasting, cruise companies know if typhoons are hitting the bay days in advance and will refund what you've paid if they need to cancel. Autumn and winter can be foggy, but this is also beautiful in a moody kind of way.

Hải Phòng looks its best in May, when flame trees bloom across the 'Flamboyant City', adding bucolic appeal to the architectural heritage. However, this is also one of the hottest times of year. October, November and December will be less vibrant but more comfortable.

Cát Bà and **Lan Hạ Bay** are at their brightest and most beautiful in the sunny summer months, but this is also the domestic high season and a blisteringly hot time of year, and storms occasionally sweep through the area. Again, autumn is a good alternative weather-wise, and avoids the domestic-tourism rush. This is also the best time of year to hike in Cát Bà National Park, but keep in mind that this is low season, and many hotels only employ a bare-bones operational team. You might need some patience to cope with the poor service.

HẠ LONG CITY AND HẠ LONG BAY

Bordering China to the north and the Red River Delta subregion to the south, affluent Quảng Ninh Province covers an area of 6,200km^2 and is home to nearly 1.5 million people from more than two dozen ethnolinguistic groups. The province's wealth derives from coal mines, fishing fleets, cross-border trade and, increasingly, tourism. While much of the province is mountainous and ethnically diverse, it's the coastal areas dominated by the Kinh (see below) that visitors come to see. Quảng Ninh is home to **Hạ Long Bay** (page 193), one of Vietnam's most successful tourism destinations when measured by income and visitor numbers. The shine of the province's tourism industry is significantly dimmed, however, by serious conservation concerns; whether Quảng Ninh eventually kills the golden goose that has helped make it one of the richest provinces in Vietnam remains to be seen. Most tourists visit Hạ Long Bay (and/or neighbouring Bái Tử Long Bay) on a prebooked cruise from Hanoi that includes transport to and from the capital, but this isn't the only way to explore the area. Independent and intrepid travellers may prefer instead to base themselves in **Hạ Long city** (page 190), the province's capital, an increasingly appealing place.

HISTORY One of the most celebrated waterways in the history of Vietnam forms the border between Quảng Ninh and Hải Phòng Province. The Bạch Đằng River, a distributary of the Red River, is a labyrinth of channels that has witnessed fierce conflict, most famously the battle for independence from China in 938 and the final expulsion of the Mongols in the 13th century. Curiously, the military masterminds of both battles successfully implemented the same strategy (page 203). Bãi Cháy, now part of Hạ Long city, means 'burnt bank', a name originating from the Mongol attack that left the surrounding forest burnt to ashes.

THE KINH

The majority of the people you meet in Vietnam will belong to the Kinh ethnolinguistic group, which constitutes around 85% of the population. The history of the Kinh is marked by a steady southwards progression from the Red River Delta to the southern plains and Mekong Delta. Today the Kinh are concentrated in these two great river deltas, the coastal plains and the main cities and towns. Only in the central and northern highland regions are they outnumbered by other ethnolinguistic groups. Kinh social cohesion and mastery of intensive wet rice cultivation has led to their numerical, and subsequently political and economic, dominance of the country.

Situated towards the province's northern border with Lạng Sơn Province are mountains that, over the centuries, have provided a safe retreat for troops fleeing from Chinese, Mongol and even Cham armies. And it was in Quảng Ninh, arguably, that Vietnam's fate under French colonial rule was sealed. In late 1882 Captain Henri Rivière led two companies of troops to the province to seize coal mines for France. Shortly afterwards he was ambushed and killed and his head paraded on a stake from village to village. His death persuaded the French parliament to fund a full-scale expedition to make the whole of Vietnam a protectorate of France. As the French politician Jules Delafosse remarked at the time: 'Let us, gentlemen, call things by their name. It is not a protectorate you want, but a possession.'

Coal production ramped up under the French, who imposed heinous working conditions on Vietnamese miners. When the French weren't cracking the whip, they luxuriated on junks in Hạ Long Bay, laying the foundations for Quảng Ninh's now-booming international tourism industry. During colonial times, much of the wealth generated in the province was hoovered up by Hanoi and Hải Phòng as Quảng Ninh fell into administrative decline. The province therefore played a lesser role in the fight for independence than Hải Phòng, but also suffered less from American bombing.

HẠ LONG CITY Following the admission of Hạ Long Bay to UNESCO's hallowed roll of World Heritage sites, the towns of Bãi Cháy and Hòn Gai were, in 1994, collectively elevated in status and dubbed Hạ Long city. Conjoined by the outstretched Bãi Cháy Bridge, which opened in 2006 and was financed by Japan, the twin towns still retain distinct personalities. Once the north's premier beach resort, **Bãi Cháy** still bulges with entertainment complexes, open-air seafood restaurants and souvenir shops, but it's dull and listless outside the peak season (May–August). The past decade has seen an explosion in the number of hotels and guesthouses here, but many are badly built, damp and musty. Better to cross the bridge to **Hòn Gai**, with its attractive setting close to the karst islets, a wide boulevard that runs alongside the water, leafy parks, gridded neighbourhoods, some unusual modern architecture and one of the north's more animated market quarters.

Getting there and around There is no operational train station in Hạ Long city. **Buses** leave at least every hour from bus company offices across Hanoi and take 2½–3 hours to reach Hạ Long city. Most drop you off at bus company offices in Hòn Gai or Bãi Cháy. Buses also connect Hạ Long city with Nam Định (2½hrs) and Ninh Bình (4hrs). From either of these cities it's possible to pick up a train heading further south.

The decade-old **Vân Đồn International Airport** (Đoàn Kết Ward, Vân Đồn; w vandonairport.vn) serves Hạ Long city, but it never really got off the ground due to its proximity to Nội Bài International Airport in Hanoi and Cát Bi Airport in Hải Phòng. International flights, only to and from other parts of East Asia, do not run consistently, and at the time of research there was only one flight a week to and from Hồ Chí Minh City. The airport is 50km northeast of Hạ Long city.

Most sights are in or within walking distance of the museum and market quarters, but Hạ Long city is a good place to rent a motorbike and glide around the coastal roads and over Bãi Cháy Bridge. For very informal row-boat cruises to the karst mountains and fish farms near Hạ Long city, you may be able to negotiate with fishermen near the crescent-shaped walking bridge (Cầu Đi Bộ) on the south side of Trần Hưng Đạo Street (page 192).

Where to stay Though across the bridge and further from Hanoi, Hòn Gai is the place to stay in Hạ Long city. You'll have no trouble finding a bed for the night. Particular neighbourhoods of interest include the tight alleyways around Lê Thánh Tông Street near Hạ Long Market and the upmarket neighbourhood behind Quảng Ninh Museum.

✷ **Café Homestay Gốc Bàng** Hồng Hải; f. Cute, cosy & eclectic hotel-homestay tucked down an alleyway, with street food nearby. **$**

Hạ Long Park Hotel Tổ 5, Khu 5, Bạch Đằng; **w** halongparkhotel.com. Adequate budget hotel nestled in a large park & dramatically backing on to a karst mountain. Conveniently positioned halfway between the market & museum quarters. **$$**

MiLaNo Legend Hotel Trần Quốc Nghiễn, Hải Thụy; f milanolegendhotelhalong1. Smart, modern hotel in an affluent gridded neighbourhood close to the ocean & modern museums. **$$$**

Yoko Onsen Tổ 5, Khu 9B, Quang Hạnh; **w** yokoonsenquanghanh.com.vn/en. One of Quảng Ninh's most luxurious accommodation options is 20km outside of the city. This Japan-themed property has a sumptuous onsen, sushi dining & comfortable tatami rooms. An unlikely treat in a remote corner of Vietnam. **$$$$**

Where to eat and drink

Restaurants and street food

✷ **Bánh Cuốn Chả Mực Gốc Bằng** No 189, Ngõ 1 Nhà Hát; f banhcuonchamucgoccaybang; ⏲ 06.00–13.00 daily. Combining the Hanoi speciality of *bánh cuốn* with the Hạ Long speciality of *chả mực* (squid cakes) has proven to be a winning combination at this morning street kitchen, tucked down an alleyway close to the market. **$**

Bún Chả Trang 513 Hạ Long; f; ⏲ 06.00–15.00 Sun–Fri & 06.00–15.30 Sat. If you find yourself in Bãi Cháy at lunchtime, this humble joint cooks up more than decent *bún chả* (page 94) in basic surroundings. **$**

Hạ Long Market Bạch Đằng; ⏲ 02.00–21.15 daily. Around Hạ Long Market there are half a dozen shops & kiosks selling *chả mực* (squid cakes), the local speciality. Most sell *chả mực* frozen & by the kilo to domestic tourists who take them home to cook, but some sell smaller cooked portions that make a tasty snack. **$**

Cơm Niêu Cậu Ấm Cột 5, Lô E, Ô số 5, Hải Thắng; f nhahangcomnieucauam; ⏲ 09.00–23.00 daily. Classic rice restaurant with a huge menu offering all kinds of dishes, from steamed clams & grilled squid to stewed pork & chicken. Rice comes cooked in a clay pot. **$$**

Pizza Pianta Ngõ 2 Hải Phúc; f piantafastfood; ⏲ 08.30–22.00 daily. If you have a hankering for Western food then this is probably your best bet. Many locals will tell you that this is the best pizza & pasta in town. **$$**

✷ **Talata** Số 87, tổ 6, khu 8, Hải Đông; **w** talataseafood.com; ⏲ 10.00–23.00 daily. Large multi-floor seafood restaurant popular with well-heeled locals. The grilled shrimp, which comes on little wooden skewers, & steamed clams that come in a hearty broth are particularly good. **$$$**

Coffee houses

✷ **Coffee Êđê** Lư Hương; f; ⏲ 06.30–22.00 daily. One of the better coffee shops in Bãi Cháy & very popular with locals, especially on Sat & Sun mornings.

Coffee Gió 55 Đặng Bá Hát; f gio.coffee.hl; ⏲ 07.30–23.00 daily. Gió means 'wind', & that's what 1 would hope to catch on a summer's day from this lofty café up in the hills near Bãi Cháy Bridge.

Old Town Coffee 10 Lán Bè; ⏲ 06.00–23.00 daily. Eclectic café overlooking the ocean that attempts an old-world theme with an antique car. There is a limited food menu.

Other practicalities The **central market** is good for basic provisions. **Vinmec Hạ Long** (10 Lê Thánh Tông; **w** vinmec.com; ⏲ all day daily) offers the best medical care in town, but it comes at a price.

What to see and do

Hạ Long Market (Chợ Hạ Long; Bạch Đằng; ⌚ 02.00–21.15 daily) A sprawling area that fans out from the huge yellow market building close to the sea. This is one of the biggest and most bustling markets in Northern Vietnam, especially early in the morning when the fishermen return from a night of fishing. The fish market is at the back, close to the water. Surrounding the market are various shops selling *chả mực* (squid cakes), a Quảng Ninh speciality.

Chùa Long Tiên (Lê Quý Đôn; ⌚ 06.00–21.00 daily) This little pagoda feels old but may only date back to the 1940s. There's not much to see, but it's atmospherically framed by the karst mountain behind it.

✷ ***Cầu Đi Bộ 'bridge' and seaside boulevard*** The semicircular 'bridge' (Cầu đi bộ; Lương Thế Vinh) that juts out into the ocean at the southern end of Trần Hưng Đạo Street is designed to get pedestrians as close to one of the karst islets as possible. From here you'll likely be offered informal (and probably illegal) row-boat cruises to the nearby floating village huts and fish farms, which can be thrilling in an intrepid sort of way. You'll need to negotiate with the captain, which will be a struggle as they are unlikely to speak any English; try not to pay more than 500,000VND for an hour. From the Cầu Đi Bộ you can walk 5km east along a pristine seaside boulevard to Hòn Gai Beach, where you can swim. The walk, which passes Hạ Long city's Museum Quarter, is smart and scenic, with the karst islets of Hạ Long Bay clearly visible.

✷ ***Bảo Tàng Quảng Ninh Museum*** (Trần Quốc Nghiễn; **w** baotangquangninh.vn; ⌚ 08.00–noon & 13.00–17.00 daily; 40,000VND; 1–2hrs) This is a gigantic glass museum that is impressive and unexpected, at least on the outside. The building, which was completed in 2013, was designed by Spanish architect Salvador Pérez Arroyo, with a black glass façade that reflects the sea and sky and symbolises Quảng Ninh's coal-mining industry. Wander around the back of the museum to see how the shiny façade contrasts with the murky waters and rugged karst islands. Exhibits include artefacts from prehistoric times, the feudal period and the revolutionary era; traditional costumes and tools from the province's various ethnic groups; displays on the geological formations, marine life and biodiversity of the area; and displays about coal mining. Truth be told, the dynamic architecture oversells the dull exhibits, but this remains one of Northern Vietnam's more ambitious (and expensive) museum projects.

Trung Tâm Triển Lãm và Hội Chợ Quảng Ninh (Trần Quốc Nghiễn) Next to the Bảo Tàng Quảng Ninh is an even newer building, which is in desperate need of an abridged name. This under-utilised exposition centre coils above the public park like a sea snail (though the Vietnamese call it 'The Dolphin'). The building is often closed to the public, but the space beneath is used by dance troupes and martial arts groups in the mornings and late afternoons.

Bài Thơ Mountain (Hàng Nồi) One of Hạ Long city's more spectacular karst mountains used to be climbable and offered views of the bay, but for some reason the local authorities refused to build a proper footpath and decided that the 200m climb was too dangerous. At the time of research it was not possible to climb the mountain, but it's worth asking around in case something has changed. *Bài thơ* translates to 'poem', originating from 1468 when Lê Thánh Tông, a king but also a

LEGEND HAS IT: DROWNED SORROWS

After King Trần Nhân Tông, the third emperor of the Trần Dynasty, gave up the throne in 1293, he washed the secular dust from his body and entered the Cấm Thục ('Abstinence', or 'Fasting') Pagoda on Yên Tử Mountain. He established monasteries and promoted the practice of Zen Buddhism, emphasising meditation and the integration of Buddhist principles into daily life, and his efforts helped solidify Buddhism as a major spiritual and cultural force in Vietnam.

Trần Nhân Tông's dual legacy as an emperor and a religious figure has earned him a revered place in Vietnamese history. He was also irresistible, according to legend. After arriving in Yên Tử, his 100 concubines traced him here and tried to persuade him of the folly of his ways. Despite their undoubted allure, he resisted all appeals and clung to his ascetic existence. Distraught by their failure and knowing they would never make love to the former king again, the women drowned themselves. Trần Nhân Tông later built a temple to their memory.

poet, visited the area. Inspired by the mountain's beauty, he composed a poem and had it engraved on a rock face on the mountain. Over the centuries, other poets, scholars and vandals also inscribed their questionable works of art on the mountain.

✷ ***Yên Tử Mountain*** Yên Tử (Uông Bí) is 45km northwest of Hạ Long city and climbs to 1,068m. Peppered with pagodas from the 13th to 16th centuries, much has been lost to the ravages of war, climate and neglect, but stupas and temples of more recent foundation survive. The site has attracted pilgrims since the 13th century, when King Trần Nhân Tông abandoned the throne in favour of a spiritual life (see above). During pilgrimage season, immediately after Tết, the mountain can get busy, and these days there is a cable car that takes pilgrims up and down part of the way. But visiting Yên Tử makes a fine day-trip hike from Hanoi, Hạ Long or Hải Phòng in the autumn (October–November) or winter (December–February), when the pagodas are practically empty. The only realistic way to travel here and back is by taxi or with your own transport. There's also accommodation at the foot of the mountain.

HẠ LONG BAY AND BÃI TỬ LONG BAY Loved and loathed, seemingly in equal measure, these days Hạ Long Bay and neighbouring Bãi Tử Long Bay seem to feature on as many no-go directories as they do must-visit checklists. The 1,500km^2 area is undoubtedly one of the natural wonders of Vietnam and is recognised by UNESCO as a World Heritage Site for both its outstanding aesthetic value and as an important example of earth's geological history. The sea here is dotted with myriad rocky islets, all of which have been fashioned into evocative shapes by the elements. Below the deep, limpid waters were once abundant banks of pink, jade and green corals, hundreds of fish species and dozens of shrimp species, but industry has taken its toll on the ecosystem. Most cruise itineraries are for one, two or three days.

In *Việt Nam: Rising Dragon*, former BBC reporter Bill Hayton wrote: 'Hạ Long Bay is not just an icon of the tourist industry, it's a symbol of the country's environmental crisis: the dash for growth, the yearning for a decent living, the lure of cash, the conflicts between business interests and regulations, the confusion between different layers of authority and, above all, the unsustainable rush for reward now, without regard to the future. Hạ Long's beauty endures but beneath the surface it's dying.' Hayton is keen to point out that there is no singular villain, as the lucrative coal

LEGEND HAS IT: HOW HẠ LONG BAY GOT ITS ISLANDS

The legend of Hạ Long Bay is one of Vietnam's most fantastical and well-known tales. The story goes that when the Vietnamese faced an insurmountable threat from northern invaders, they prayed to the divinities. The Jade Emperor, the king of heaven, was moved by their plight and summoned a family of dragons to descend from the heavens. These celestial beings, led by the mother dragon, were tasked with defending the Jade Emperor's favoured nation, which was facing imminent destruction.

Upon their arrival, the dragons unleashed a formidable defence. The mother dragon and her offspring soared over the coast, spitting out thousands of pearls and jade. These precious stones transformed into islands and islets, creating a natural barrier in the sea. The invaders' ships, unable to navigate through this maze of rocky outcrops, crashed and sank, ushering in a period of peace for the Vietnamese people. From that day on, the bay was known as Vịnh Hạ Long, or 'Bay of the Descending Dragons'.

But the story doesn't end there. Having successfully protected the land, the dragons chose to remain on earth and live among the Vietnamese. The mother dragon settled in Hạ Long Bay, while her children ventured a little north to an area now known as Bãi Tử Long Bay, or 'Bay to Honour the Dragon's Children'. The jagged peaks and craggy surfaces of the islands are believed to be the dragons' scales.

industry, destructive overfishing and poorly regulated waste management on cruise ships are all to blame.

More than a decade later, Hạ Long Bay's waste management system has improved, but the number of visitors has increased rapidly. In 2019, a year in which Hạ Long Bay received 4.4 million visitors, an International Union for Conservation of Nature (IUCN) report concluded that, while the geological integrity of the bay is not currently under threat, growth in visitor numbers combined with ineffective waste management will impact the area's aesthetic and scientific value. But the report also acknowledged that the Hạ Long Bay Management Board doesn't have the authority to enforce environmental regulations. If all this is off-putting, consider forgoing a Hạ Long Bay and Bãi Tử Long Bay cruise, as many alternatives abound.

Tour operators Shuttle-bus transfers to and from Hanoi are arranged by the following recommended cruise companies, sometimes for an extra fee. Some cruise ships sail from Tuần Châu island, which is connected to the mainland by a causeway, whereas others depart from the Sun Marina in Bãi Cháy. It makes little difference where you sail from if you're returning to Hanoi after the cruise. However, if you're planning to take the ferry to Cát Bà (page 205) after your cruise then it's better to finish on Tuần Châu island; if you're spending some time in Hạ Long city (page 190) then it's better to end up in Bãi Cháy. For recommended Lan Hạ Bay cruise companies, see page 209.

Ambassador Cruise w ambassadorcruise.com. Ambassador is fairly new on the scene but is challenging the more established cruise companies with their premium service & attention to detail. Cruise ships are massive & luxurious, offering the same activities as others, but with the added benefit of a gigantic water slide. They have banned single-use plastic on board, so if you arrive with a bottle of water then you'll need to check it in & retrieve before you leave.

Au Co w aucocruises.com. Au Co has long specialised in 3-day cruises. The luxury ship sails through Hạ Long Bay & Lan Hạ Bay & offers cabins that blend traditional Vietnamese & contemporary Western décor, some with private balconies. Activities include swimming in quieter beaches, cycling on Cát Bà island & early-morning visits to floating islands. They try to jazz up on-board activities with cooking competitions, a traditional tea ceremony, & an evening barbecue. Au Co is connected to Bhaya Cruises.

Bhaya Cruises w bhayacruises.com. Within tour agency circles, Bhaya is known for its good-value & diverse cruise options. Food tends to be decent, if not exceptional, & cabins, some with balconies, are reliably comfortable. They claim to have exclusive access to Trinh Nữ Beach, but these exclusivity agreements rarely last long in Hạ Long Bay so this information may already be out of date. Bhaya Cruises is connected to Au Co.

Emeraude Cruises w emeraude-cruises.com. Emeraude, under Thiên Minh Group, which has won sustainability awards, has a fleet of 4 reconstructed French paddle steamers. The cabins have comfortable beds & old-style fans, although the bathrooms are on the tiny side. Entertainment includes a Vietnamese cooking demo, squid fishing, evening movies, tai chi on the sun deck at dawn, a massage service & a bar.

Indochina Junk w indochina-junk.com. Indochina Junk tries to offer more off-beat experiences within the confines of the increasingly strict itinerary regulations & claims to be the 1st company allowed access to Bãi Tử Long Bay. Most cruise itineraries avoid Hạ Long Bay completely, choosing instead to ply slightly quieter waters. Activities are standard: kayaking through lagoons, exploring fishing villages & swimming. They also offer a private 4-day cruise that delves deep into Bãi Tử Long Bay.

Paradise Vietnam w paradisevietnam.com. The largest luxury fleet in Hạ Long Bay & Bãi Tử Long Bay, with 7 cruise ship types offering all manner of itinerary. The cabins feature classic European-style décor; some include private balconies & comfortable bathrooms. The food with Paradise Vietnam has always been paramount, with sumptuous buffet b/fasts & lunches & à la carte dinners. Some ships have an on-board spa. Paradise Vietnam is one of the few Hạ Long Bay-based companies that also cruises in Lan Hạ Bay, on the Paradise Grand. They also have a hotel on Tuần Châu island.

What to see and do The better cruise companies will try to offer diversity when it comes to activities in Hạ Long Bay. Note that Bãi Tử Long Bay has long been advertised as the quieter Hạ Long Bay alternative. In reality, there isn't much difference.

Karsts Geologically, the tower-karst scenery of Hạ Long Bay is the product of millions of years of chemical action and river erosion working on the limestone

THE CHEAPEST WAY TO CRUISE THE BAY

A convenient but little-known ferry (w booking.tuanchau-halong.com.vn/#/ferry) connects Tuần Châu, an island close to Bãi Cháy and accessible by a causeway road, with Gia Luận on Cát Bà island. The 1-hour crossing, which runs three to five times a day in each direction, cuts through Hạ Long Bay and at times offers similar views to the cruise ships, including of karst mountains and floating villages. The service is not tourist-friendly, and you may need a friend or hotel receptionist to call the ferry company to confirm times and prices. There's usually no need to book; simply turn up 30 minutes or so before departure. You can bring your motorbike or car on to the ferry. The crossing won't cost more than a few dollars per person and an extra dollar for a motorbike. Cars cost more.

TIPS ON CHOOSING THE RIGHT CRUISE

Choosing the right Hạ Long Bay cruise can feel like charting a course between Scylla and Charybdis, with cheap tourist trap cruises on the left and over-the-top floating palaces on the right. The following tips should go some way towards making the decision at least a little easier.

- **Consider the environmental impact**. This might be a rare example of when it's better to go with a big company, as they tend to operate newer and cleaner boats and have a long-term vested interest in trying to maintain the integrity of the bay. These bigger cruise companies are also more likely to exercise some environmental protection measures.
- **Don't book through your hotel in Hanoi**. And don't book through a travel agent in Hanoi either. You'll have more luck finding what you want and getting what you pay for if you research and book online directly with the cruise company. You might be tempted by the budget cruises touted by hotels and travel agents, but there is no way of knowing that the tour you think you're booking is the one that you'll get.
- **Think carefully about the number of days**. The most popular durations for Hạ Long Bay cruises are one, two and three days. Some cruise companies (notably Bhaya) offer four- and five-day trips as well. Note that this usually includes transport from Hanoi (2½ hours each way), making the one-day and even two-day options feel very short. A two-day Hạ Long Bay cruise means less than 24 hours in the bay, as you board at lunchtime on the first day and alight after breakfast on the second. Dinner cruises have become popular with domestic tourists in recent years, but these tour the bright lights of Hạ Long city, not the karst islands of Hạ Long Bay.
- **Always check the itinerary**. You won't be able to see everything in the bay, but if you have specific interests, make sure these activities are on the itinerary before booking. It's quite common for people to come away from a cruise

to produce a pitted landscape. At the end of the last ice age, when glaciers melted, the sea level rose and inundated the area, turning hills into islands. The jungle-cloaked outcrops are a joy to behold, and it's quite common to see eagles circling above and macaques swinging through the trees below. The most famous karsts, at least for Vietnamese visitors, are the **Fighting Cocks**, two small islets that almost touch at the top. With a little imagination, you'll be able to make out dragons, turtles and other animals as you cruise through the bay. The best way to get close to the karst mountains is on a **kayak**, but bear in mind that not all cruise companies offer this activity. Those that do usually charge extra.

Beaches Since swimming from cruise ships has been banned in the bay, the only way to submerge yourself in the emerald waters is from the safety of a sandy beach. Most cruises will stop on an island with a beach, the most popular of which is **Titov Island**, named by Hồ Chí Minh after he and the Russian cosmonaut Gherman Titov visited in 1962. Most islands with beaches in the bay will also have some form of elevated point offering panoramic views of the seascape. Despite being the busiest, Titov Island offers one of the better views, as the panorama is right in the centre of the island at its highest point.

regretting that they didn't see a floating village or a cave because they didn't check the itinerary.

- **Consider your budget and check what's included**. Prices for Hạ Long Bay cruises vary hugely. Check to see what's included in your tour, but as a general rule, the cruise, basic activities and food are included in the price. Drinks and extra activities like kayaking are not. Always double check to see if pick-up and drop-off in Hanoi is included.
- **Check recent reviews online**, especially for cruise companies not mentioned in this guide. The ones listed on page 194 have earned a good reputation after many years of operation. But if considering cruising with a company not recommended in this guide, always check what the online travel community is saying about them.
- **Book in advance for the popular cruise companies**, and that includes the ones listed in this guide. High season for domestic visitors is June–August and high season for international visitors is October–December. During these times, you may need to book at least a week in advance to guarantee a spot on your desired cruise. Outside these times, a few days should suffice.
- **Question yourself one last time before booking**. Hạ Long Bay cruises are famous the world over and have long been considered something you have to do in Vietnam. However, there are plenty of alternatives that are less impactful on the environment, less touristy and, for many, more enjoyable. Hạ Long city (page 190) is a pleasant place where you can see the karsts of Hạ Long Bay from the broad boulevards on land. A Lan Hạ Bay cruise (page 209) offers similar scenery and you'll have parts of the area entirely to yourself. Cát Bà island (page 205) offers more to see and do, and you can tackle the activities at your own pace. Ninh Bình (page 213), sometimes referred to as Hạ Long Bay on land, also offers cruises through karstic scenery, but on the river in a row-boat.

Caves The islands of the bay are divided by a broad channel: to the east are the smaller outcrops of Bãi Tử Long, while to the west are the larger islands with caves and secluded beaches. Among the more spectacular caves is **Hang Hanh**, which extends for 2km. Tour guides will point out fantastic stalagmites and stalactites that, with imagination, become heroes, demons and animals. **Hang Đầu Gỗ** is the cave wherein Trần Hưng Đạo stored his wooden stakes prior to studding them into the bed of the Bạch Đằng River in 1288 to destroy the boats of invading Mongol hordes (page 203). **Heavenly Palace Cave** (Thiên Cung) is a hanging cave, a short 50m haul above sea level, with dripping stalactites, stumpy stalagmites and solid rock pillars. A truly enormous cave, and the one that features on most itineraries, is **Surprise Cave** (Sửng Sốt Cave).

Floating villages Despite long-term plans to resettle families on land, there are still a couple of floating villages in the bay. **Vung Viêng** in Bãi Tử Long Bay is now one of the largest and most interesting to visit, especially as a few of the floating villagers have pearl farms. Some cruise ships employ local villagers to row visitors around; others have self-paddled kayaks. If the distinction is important to you, make sure you look carefully at the itinerary.

HẢI PHÒNG AND CÁT BÀ

Heading southeast from Hanoi, the northernmost Red River distributaries pass through the provinces of Bắc Ninh, Hưng Yên and Hải Dương, before discharging into the sea through the tiny province of Hải Phòng. Over half of the province's population of around 2.4 million are in Hải Phòng city, the capital. Ugly industrial zones envelop this prosperous powerhouse, but an overlooked historical core of colonial boulevards and merchant quarters hold unexplored appeal for discerning visitors. The rest of the population is scattered through suburban districts, small towns and several islands, the largest being Cát Bà. This 262km^2 island, much of which is a protected area, has decent beaches, thick forests and historic sites. Cát Bà island is also the jumping-off point for trips to Lan Hạ Bay, which challenges Hạ Long Bay's hegemony as Northern Vietnam's ultimate cruising destination.

HẢI PHÒNG CITY Situated only 100km from Hanoi, Hải Phòng is a large city known for its industrial zones, port and factories. As well as the aqua products that are processed in a sea of frozen food factories, manufacturing enterprises include carpets, clothing, lace, handicrafts, footwear and, more recently, cars. The principal manufacturing facility of VinFast, Vietnam's ambitious automobile manufacturer, is here. Perhaps none of this screams tourist appeal, but nestled within all this industry is an attractive, walkable and increasingly well-maintained historical core. Central Hải Phòng, largely a colonial project but with some notable historical Chinese and Vietnamese neighbourhoods, exhibits French mansions, storied religious buildings, a lively Merchant Quarter and some unique local cuisine.

History Hải Phòng was insignificant until the French took control of the area in 1872–73. After 11 years its harbour had been widened and many large international ships docked there. Over the following decades, the European-style city of Hải Phòng began to emerge. During the 1920s, resistance groups started to form and, when the Japanese invaded in October 1940, the French general Georges Catroux could do little to prevent the port falling into their hands. Japanese vessels regularly cruised down the Bạch Đằng Estuary for the next five years, exporting valuable food products, coal, tobacco and iron to Japan.

After the French return at the end of World War II, the Vietnamese resistance movement was in full swing, and cities like Hải Phòng were regarded as a threat by the colonial administration. By November 1946 the situation had reached breaking point, and when French fighter planes appeared over the city, people ran for their lives. The raid killed around 6,000 people, though some put this figure much higher, and the event became known as the Hải Phòng Massacre. One year after the defeat of the French at the Battle of Điện Biên Phủ, Hải Phòng was liberated in 1955. The city that day was plastered with gold-starred red flags as thousands of jubilant people flooded into the centre to celebrate.

American bombs fell on the city in 1966, in an attempt to knock out vital Việt Minh fuel supply lines. During the Christmas Bombings of 18–29 December 1972, Hải Phòng felt the full brunt of Strategic Air Command's B-52 raids, but the city wasn't completely defenceless; it's said that the defence units shot down more than 300 US planes. After the end of the Second Indochina War the port became an exodus point for many refugees fleeing the country, including the city's once-sizeable Chinese population.

Since *đổi mới* (page 21), Hải Phòng has developed into one of Vietnam's more prosperous cities. Like Đà Nẵng and Cần Thơ, Hải Phòng has provincial status, a

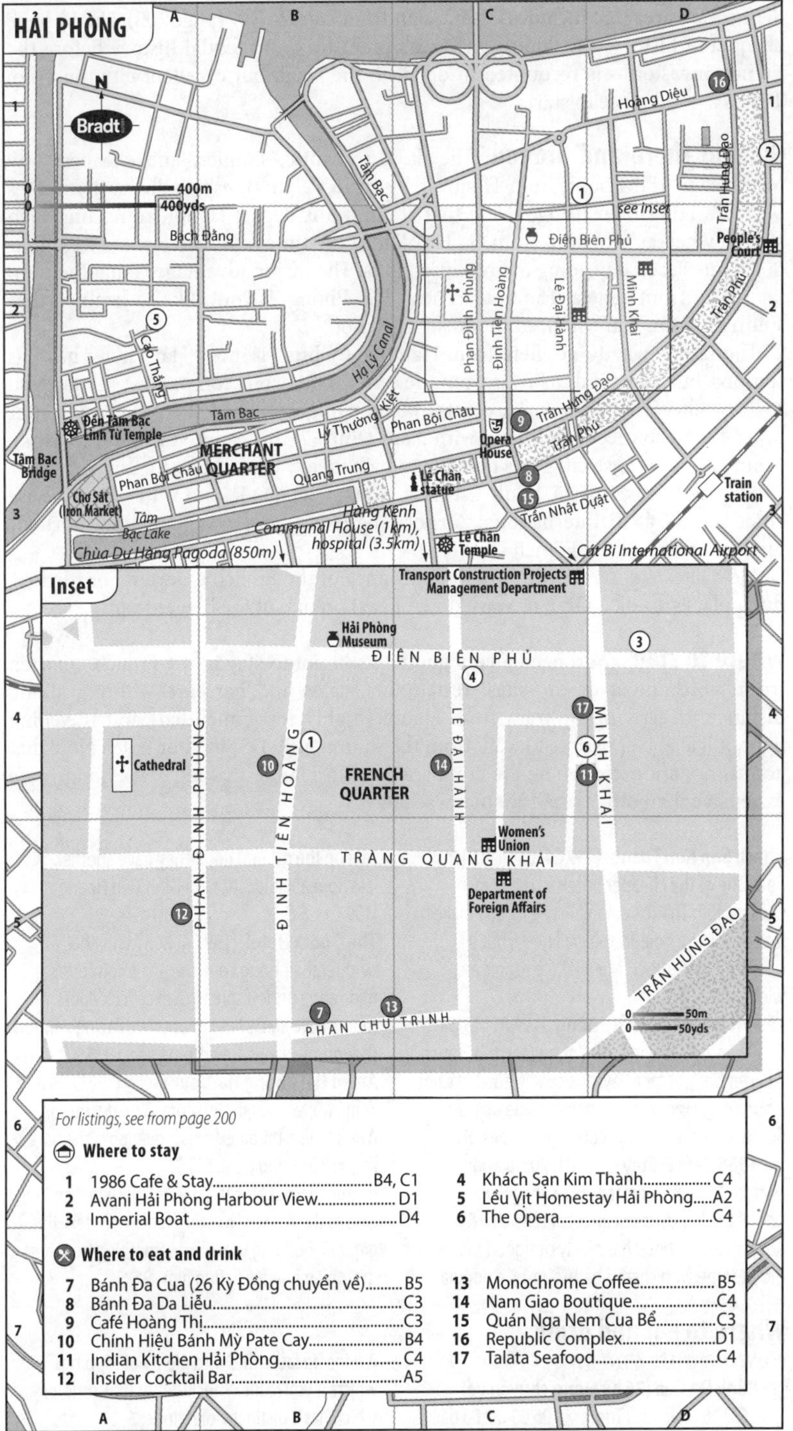
HẢI PHÒNG
A
B
C
D
N
Bradt
0 400m
0 400yds
Hoàng Diệu
Tâm Bạc
Bạch Đằng
see inset
Điện Biên Phủ
People's Court
Trần Hưng Đạo
Trần Phú
Phan Đình Phùng
Đinh Tiên Hoàng
Lê Đại Hành
Minh Khai
Cao Thắng
Hạ Lý Canal
Lý Thường Kiệt
Phan Bội Châu
Đền Tâm Bạc Linh Từ Temple
Tâm Bạc Bridge
MERCHANT QUARTER
Quang Trung
Opera House
Lê Chân statue
Trần Nhật Duật
Train station
Chợ Sắt (Iron Market)
Tâm Bạc Lake
Hàng Kênh Communal House (1km), hospital (3.5km)
Lê Chân Temple
Chùa Dư Hàng Pagoda (850m)
Cát Bi International Airport
Inset
Transport Construction Projects Management Department
Hải Phòng Museum
ĐIỆN BIÊN PHỦ
Cathedral
FRENCH QUARTER
Women's Union
TRÀNG QUANG KHẢI
Department of Foreign Affairs
TRẦN HƯNG ĐẠO
PHAN CHU TRINH
0 50m
0 50yds
For listings, see from page 200
Where to stay
1 1986 Cafe & Stay....B4, C1
2 Avani Hải Phòng Harbour View....D1
3 Imperial Boat....D4
4 Khách Sạn Kim Thành....C4
5 Lều Vịt Homestay Hải Phòng....A2
6 The Opera....C4
Where to eat and drink
7 Bánh Đa Cua (26 Kỳ Đồng chuyển về)....B5
8 Bánh Đa Da Liễu....C3
9 Café Hoàng Thị....C3
10 Chính Hiệu Bánh Mỳ Pate Cay....B4
11 Indian Kitchen Hải Phòng....C4
12 Insider Cocktail Bar....A5
13 Monochrome Coffee....B5
14 Nam Giao Boutique....C4
15 Quán Nga Nem Cua Bể....C3
16 Republic Complex....D1
17 Talata Seafood....C4

delineation area that includes Cát Bà island and Lan Hạ Bay (page 205). Hải Phòng's chequered history – including the area's prehistory and feudal history before the French invasion – is recounted in detail in the small but excellent city museum. This is a good place to start.

Getting there and around The most romantic, simplest and cheapest way to travel to Hải Phòng from Hanoi is by **train** (2½hrs), especially as it rumbles over the Long Biên Bridge. Note that some trains depart Hanoi from Long Biên station whereas others go from Ga Hà Nội. At the time of research there were four departures each day going in both directions. The major advantage is that the train takes you from central Hanoi to central Hải Phòng. If you'd like to head further south by train, you will need to transit in Hanoi.

The fastest way to get here from Hanoi is by **bus** (1½hrs). Hải Phòng has bus stations, but they tend to be far from the centre. Many bus companies will take you to their offices, which are more central, but you might still need to take a taxi to your hotel. Buses connect Hải Phòng with Nam Định (2½hrs) and Ninh Bình (3½hrs). From either of these cities, it's possible to pick up a train heading further south.

Flights from Hồ Chí Minh City, Đà Nẵng, Phú Quốc and other Vietnamese cities serve Cát Bi International Airport (Lê Hồng Phong; **w** vietnamairport.vn) just 7km south of the French Quarter.

Most sites are in or within walking distance of the French Quarter. For further-flung places, book a Grab or wave down a taxi on one of the bigger roads.

Where to stay You'd need a very good reason not to stay in the French Quarter, from which most of the sites, restaurants, cafés and bars are within walking distance. If arriving by train from Hanoi (highly recommended) and travelling light, it'll also be possible to walk from the station [199 D3] to your hotel. Note that accommodation costs here are comparable with Hanoi, making Hải Phòng more expensive than other small Vietnamese cities.

Khách Sạn Kim Thành [199 C4] 67 Điện Biên Phủ. One of the cheaper hotels in the French Quarter, Kim Thành's colonial-style façade makes it appear like a hole-in-the wall hotel, but it opens up at the back. Many of the rooms are windowless. **$**

Lều Vịt Homestay Hải Phòng [199 A2] 15/54 Cao Thắng; **w** leuvit.com. Not quite in the French Quarter but not far away, this cutsey hotel (it's not a homestay) is one of the better-value options. Some rooms have basic cooking facilities. **$**

✷ **1986 Café & Stay** [199 B4] 20 Hồ Xuống Hương; 1986cafenstay. Hồ Xuống Hương is one of the handsomest streets in the city, & this attractive little hotel has nicely designed rooms (note: some with shared bathroom) & a popular café on the ground floor. They have another, less appealing location on Đinh Tiên Hoàng [199 C1]. **$$**

The Opera Hotel [199 C4] 20B Minh Khai; **w** operahaiphong.com. Decent & comfortable mid-range option spread over several floors. All rooms have some kind of outward-facing window, though the views are nothing special. **$$**

Avani Hải Phòng Harbour View [199 D1] 12 Trần Phú; **w** avanihotels.com. A luxury option, Avani feels a bit dated, but it overlooks the park & has a swimming pool. **$$$**

Imperial Boat Hotel [199 D4] 48 Điện Biên Phủ. One of the French Quarter's fanciest hotels, this gigantic building looks like something from a dystopian science fiction film. **$$$**

Where to eat and drink

Restaurants and street food

✷ **Bánh Đa Cua (26 Kỳ Đồng chuyển về)** [199 C5] 16 Phan Chu Trinh; 06.00–22.00 daily. A *bánh đa* favourite, with plenty of toppings which, if you're lucky, includes mantis shrimp, which has a distinct violet tinge. **$**

HẢI PHÒNG'S SPECIALITY DISHES

The places at which to try these dishes are listed opposite/below.

BÁNH ĐA CUA Ask a Vietnamese person what Hải Phòng's culinary claim to fame is and there's a good chance they'll say it's this dish. *Bánh đa* are flat rice noodles browned with sugar, usually served in a soup. *Cua* is crab, which usually takes the form of minced crab and crab cakes. The best *bánh đa cua* places serve up to a dozen other protein toppings, including shrimp, snails, meatballs and *chả lá lốt* (minced pork wrapped in a leaf and then grilled). You can usually point at the toppings, but if you want everything then order *thập cẩm*. In Hải Phòng this is eaten throughout the day and into the night. Try it at **Bánh Đa Da Liêu** and **Bánh Đa Cua (26 Kỳ Đồng chuyển về)**.

BÚN NEM CUA A variation of Hanoi's *bún chả*, but with crunchy deep-fried crab-stuffed square spring rolls instead of (sometimes as well as) grilled pork. As with *bún chả*, the spring rolls are accompanied by sticky rice vermicelli, a green herb salad and a sweet-and-sour *nước mắm* (fish sauce) for dipping. Try it at **Quán Nga Nem Cua Bể**.

BÁNH MỲ QUE More of a snack than a meal and a cute remnant of French cuisine, *bánh mỳ que* are crunchy stick-thin baguettes filled with pâté and dipped in a sweet chilli sauce. Try it at **Chính Hiệu Bánh Mỳ Pate Cay**.

HẢI SẢN *Hải sản* means seafood, and Hải Phòng is predictably good at serving up this Vietnamese favourite. The seafood here is both cheaper and fresher than what you'll find in Hanoi. As is the case elsewhere on the Vietnamese coast, the shellfish tends to outshine the fish. The razor clams and squid are said to be particularly good. Try it at **Talata Seafood Restaurant**.

Bánh Đa Da Liễu [199 C3] 140 Trần Phú; ⌚ 16.00–23.20 daily. Don't let the name put you off (*da liễu* means 'skin disease'; the name comes from the street-food stall's proximity to a skin hospital). This is some of the best *bánh đa* in town, with a huge array of toppings that you can choose by pointing. $

Chính Hiệu Bánh Mỳ Pate Cay [199 B4] 28 Đinh Tiên Hoàng; ⌚ 06.30–22.00 daily. One of many *bánh mỳ que* eateries on this street, serving these pate-stuffed mini-baguettes throughout the day. $

✷ **Quán Nga Nem Cua Bể** [199 C3] 92 Trần Nhật Duật; ⌚ 07.00–20.00 daily. One of the more popular *bún nem cua* on this bustling market street close to the station. The spring rolls are stuffed generously with crab, but if that isn't enough then order a side of grilled pork. $

Indian Kitchen Hải Phòng [199 C4] 22D Minh Khai; f Indiankitchen22D; ⌚ 09.00–22.30 daily. If you stick around long enough to tire of the fabulous local cuisine, this South Asian-run restaurant serves up delicious curries, some of which take advantage of the local seafood. $$

✷ **Nam Giao Boutique** [199 C4] 20 Lê Đại Hành; f NamGiao-boutique; ⌚ 09.00–23.00 daily. Atmospheric old-world restaurant with reproduced Nguyễn Dynasty furniture, serving classic Northern Vietnamese dishes, including deep-fried tofu, stir-fried vegetables & hearty claypot dishes like stewed pork or fish. $$

Talata Seafood Restaurant [199 C4] 20 Minh Khai; w talataseafood.com; ⌚ 10.00–14.30 & 17.00–21.30 daily. Well-run & gigantic seafood restaurant set over several floors & popular with celebrating locals. The grilled shrimp, which comes on little wooden skewers, is particularly good. Don't be scared to eat the shell. $$

Bars and coffee houses

✷ **Café Hoàng Thị** [199 C3] 137 Đinh Tiên Hoàng; ⌚ 07.00–22.30 daily. One of many friendly local cafés that line Đinh Tiên Hoàng & overlook the Opera House. It's best to come 1st thing in the morning, when tables & chairs spill out on to the pavement. As always with these places, expect good Vietnamese coffee & juices.

Insider Cocktail Bar [199 A5] 80 Hoàng Văn Thụ; f; ⌚ 19.00–03.00 daily. Post-modern cocktail bar popular with Hải Phòng's youthful & monied crowd. The menu, as 1 might expect from such a place, is creative & extensive, with both classic & signature cocktails.

Monochrome Coffee [199 B5] 8 Phan Chu Trinh; f monochromecoffeevn; ⌚ 07.30–22.30 daily. Atmospheric café-bar that feels like it should be serving cocktails rather than cappuccinos. There's a balcony upstairs from which you look over the leafy street below.

✷ **Republic Complex** [199 D1] 4 Hoàng Diệu; f republic.complex; ⌚ 08.00–23.00 daily. This hip hangout is like a mini-Shoreditch or Brooklyn, with cocktail bars, a beer garden, cafés, restaurants & occasional live music. Establishments come & go here, so it's best to wander around & find what's right while enjoying the Art Deco balconies of this former residential mansion.

Other practicalities **Vinmec Hải Phòng International Hospital** [199 C3] (Vĩnh Niệm; w vinmec.com; ⌚ all day daily) is 15 minutes south of the French Quarter by car. There is no useful tourist information office, but the kind folks at Hải Phòng Museum may be helpful.

What to see and do

✷ ***The French Quarter*** [199 B4] A tourist destination that never was, and may never be, Hải Phòng's French Quarter is a small neighbourhood that occupies the inner crescent northwest of the park that runs along Trần Hưng Đạo Street. Pedestrians will revel in how walkable this part of the city is, with broad, shaded pavements that function like walkways and not parking spots. Flame trees that bloom bright red in May and June line many of these colonial streets, with the most spectacular display on Điện Biên Phủ. These trees are particularly nostalgic for Northern Vietnamese millennials, as they were planted in school grounds and bloom just before the summer holidays. Despite it being a hotbed of resistance during the First Indochina War, Hải Phòng seems proud of its architectural heritage, and many French buildings have been spruced up to hold different municipal departments. There are far too many to list here, but look out for the **People's Court** [199 D2] (30 Trần Phú), a classic French building with shutters, the **Transport Construction Projects Management Department** [199 C3] (14 Minh Khai), with its decorative porcelain art panels, and the **Department of Foreign Affairs** [199 D4] (15 Tràng Quang Khải), a fabulous Art Deco building inspired by East Asian motifs. Opposite the Department of Foreign Affairs is another handsome but featureless building, the **Women's Union** [199 C5] (14 Tràng Quang Khải), which sits encircled by street barbers trained to offer sexual health advice. Strictly speaking these barbers are not sexual health professionals and their conversations are limited ('Do you use a condom? Do you know where you can get tested?') but it reflects an innovative initiative to invite young men to talk about sexual health in a country where such conversations are often taboo.

✷ ***Hải Phòng Museum*** [199 B4] (66 Điện Biên Phủ; f baotanghaiphong; ⌚ 08.00–11.00 & 14.00–17.00 Tue–Sun; 1–2hrs) Once the Industrial Bank, Hải Phòng Museum (Bảo Tàng Hải Phòng) is an impressive colonial edifice in a wash of sunshine yellow and contains records of the city's storied history. Enter the museum and go right, moving around the first floor in an anti-clockwise circle

STAKE, BAIT, DEFEAT, REPEAT: THE TWIN BATTLES OF BẠCH ĐẰNG

The Bạch Đằng River skirts around Hải Phòng to the north before flowing into the sea east of the city. It feels like every history museum in Vietnam has a piece of this estuary in the form of a haggard wooden stake, so celebrated and consequential are the battles that were fought there. One thousand years of Chinese domination came to a dramatic end here in 938 when Ngô Quyền's army defeated the Chinese navy in true Hollywood fashion. First Ngô's forces embedded iron-headed wooden stakes in the river's muddy bed, with the sharp end pointing upstream. During high tide, he baited the Chinese forces inland until the tide turned, at which point he counter-attacked, driving the ships back towards the sea and into the exposed stakes. With the navy in ruins, the Chinese retreated north, and Ngô Quyền established a new capital in Cổ Loa close to Hanoi.

It is often said that in Vietnam, good ideas replicate quickly. The Vietnamese saw off attempted Mongol invasions throughout the 13th century, but the definitive and final battle came in 1288, when the armies of Kublai Khan, the grandson of Genghis Khan, attempted to penetrate and dominate Northern Vietnam via the Bạch Đằng River. The military commander Trần Hưng Đạo, evidently a keen historian, repeated the same trap set by Ngô Quyền. It worked even better the second time, ending Kublai Khan's ambitious southward expansion. While some of these stakes are still in the river today, many have been dredged up and displayed in museums across the country, including in Hải Phòng Museum. Today, most cities have a Bạch Đằng Street, and it always runs along a canal or river. The names of Ngô Quyền and Trần Hưng Đạo are also forever immortalised not just in street names, but also with statues and in temples.

before heading upstairs. It begins by detailing evidence of the Stone and Iron ages, including excavation information about a nearby Đồng Sơn (page 8) tomb, and then the feudal period, with several excellent photos of ancient religious and communal buildings. Look out for the 13th-century wooden stakes (see above) that were pulled from the Bạch Đằng River, which runs north of Hải Phòng. The colonial period section has some wonderful photos of what Hải Phòng would have looked like a century ago, especially the Merchant Quarter. The museum then charts revolutionary movements, independence and the city's economic and social successes since – with no mention of any hardship. While the museum ends on a somewhat propagandist note, it's still informative.

The Opera House [199 C3] (28 Trần Hưng Đạo) Right in the heart of town is the Opera House, built in 1904 using imported French materials, with a colonnaded front, and facing a wide tree-lined boulevard. In November 1946, 40 Việt Minh fighters died here in a pitched battle with the French, triggered by the government's decision to open a customs house in Hải Phòng. A plaque outside commemorates the battle. The streets around the theatre support the greatest concentration of pavement cafés. Unfortunately, arranging to see anything at the Opera House is a challenge, with no online booking system and shows that seem to book out weeks in advance.

Cathedral [199 A4] (46 Hoàng Văn Thụ) The cathedral's 19th-century square tower is one of Hải Phòng's iconic pieces of architecture, though the grey-blue colour lacks the warmth and whimsy of other colonial buildings in the city. The interiors are rather plain, but it's a good place to escape the heat if visiting in the summer.

✷ ***Merchant Quarter*** [199 B3] West of the French Quarter is the old Merchant Quarter, Hải Phòng's version of the Old Quarter in Hanoi or Chợ Lớn in Hồ Chí Minh City. It sits on a kind of peninsula sandwiched between Tâm Bạc Lake and Hạ Lý Canal and bookended by what used to be Chợ Sắt (Iron Market). A market stood on this site from 1876 until the most recent manifestation – a huge six-storey concrete edifice that never really took off – was demolished in the early 2020s. Apparently a five-star hotel and modern office complex will replace it one day. Despite an empty waste land where the market once was, the neighbourhood east of it is of historical interest. You'll notice some handsome Chinese-style shophouses with shops at the front and homes in the back on Tâm Bạc Street. Some of these houses go all the way back to Lý Thường Kiệt Street, where attractive low-rise 20th-century apartment buildings sit aside modernist two-storey houses.

Đền Tâm Bạc Linh Từ Temple [199 A3] (Hạ Lý) The Merchant Quarter is effectively Hải Phòng's Chinatown, though most ethnic Chinese left in the 1970s. Besides the shophouses and occasional Chinese character written on buildings, another remnant of this once-vibrant community is across Tâm Bạc Bridge at Đền Tâm Bạc Linh Từ, also known as Tam Kỳ Temple. The temple was originally red, like many Chinese-style temples, but was destroyed by the French in 1946. It was rebuilt soon after, only to be obliterated again by American bombs in 1972. Most of what you see today was constructed in 2008.

Lê Chân Temple [199 C3] (53 Lê Chân) Just outside of the French Quarter is this temple, also called the Nghe Temple, which is dedicated to the memory of heroine General Lê Chân who fought with the Trưng sisters (page 118) against the Chinese some 2,000 years ago. The temple is notable for its sculpture and carving, particularly the boggle-eyed dragons, which look more cartoonish and startled than mythical and menacing. A statue of General Lê Chân takes pride of place on the main altar, a notable example of a woman who isn't the Trưng sisters or Quan Âm (page 293) taking precedence in a religious building. Lê Chân is a local hero, evidenced by the big gold statue of her a block north of the temple.

Hàng Kênh Communal House [199 C3] (Đình Hàng Kênh; 55 Nguyễn Công Trứ) The Hàng Kênh Communal House, 2km south of the centre, may be as old as 300 years, though it underwent restorations in the mid 18th century. Originally built as a communal house, its chief function today is as a temple. The main building is supported by 32 columns of ironwood and the wood carvings in the window grilles are especially ornate. From the capacious outside courtyard, the roof is the most dramatic feature, tiled in the fish scale style and ornamented with dragons. The corners of the roof turn up so that it appears that the sheer weight of the tiles is too much for the wooden beams to bear.

Chùa Dư Hàng Pagoda [199 B3] (121 Dư Hàng) Built in the 17th century, this pagoda has been renovated several times since. It is undoubtedly the most ornate sanctuary in Hải Phòng. There are two guardians near the entry to the inner enclosure, one bad and one good. The magnificent central altar has an elaborately carved offering table over which hangs a spiral joss-stick burner. Beyond is the baby Buddha surrounded by nine dragons. Behind are the Buddhas of the Past,

Present and Future. The stone stelae at the rear of the pagoda commemorate the keeper.

CÁT BÀ AND LAN HẠ BAY Occupying a stunning setting in the south of the Gulf of Tonkin and with several pleasant beaches, at least by northern standards, Cát Bà has long been a popular summer holiday spot for Hanoians. Over the past decade or so, adventure activities have proliferated here, including kayaking, swimming, cycling, hiking and rock climbing, making it popular with outdoor enthusiasts, too. The island is rugged and sparsely inhabited, and Cát Bà National Park covers around half of it. Outside Cát Bà town there are only a few small villages. Perhaps the greatest pleasure on the island is to hire a motorbike and explore without a plan, a simple enough project given the island's limited road network.

Cát Bà's remoteness has been steadily eroded, but despite the growth in numbers of karaoke-loving weekenders, it remains an attractive place, though construction that began in 2024 is a considerable blight on the main town's once-scenic bay. The island sits in Lan Hạ Bay, which is one part of a trio of bays (the other two being

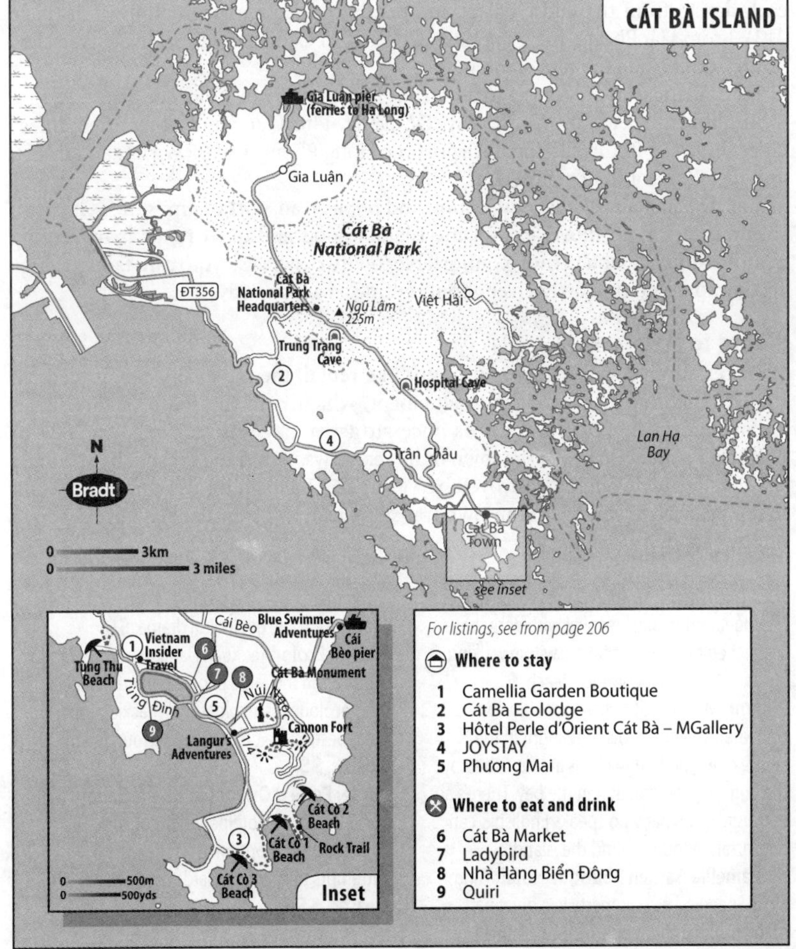

Hạ Long Bay and Bái Tử Long Bay; page 193) directly east of Hanoi. This delineation is important, as Lan Hạ Bay is part of Hải Phòng Province, whereas Hạ Long and Bái Tử Long Bay are part of Quảng Ninh Province and are thus administered differently. Though not as famous or organised as its neighbour to the north, Lan Hạ Bay is a popular alternative. It may be lacking in famous islands and islets, but the scenery is virtually the same and there are far fewer boats.

There are two ways to approach Cát Bà and Lan Hạ Bay. Some opt for a multi-day Lan Hạ Bay cruise, which includes pick-up and drop-off in Hanoi and can include some time on Cát Bà. Another option is to make a base on the island and then arrange day cruises into the bay from there.

Getting there and around The most romantic way to travel to Cát Bà is to take the 2½-hour **train** from Hanoi to Hải Phòng (page 198) and spend some time in the city first. From Hải Phòng, it's possible to catch buses to Cát Bà, which you can usually book through your hotel or online (page 60). The fastest (3½hrs) and simplest way to get to Cát Bà from Hanoi is by **bus**, with a company like Good Morning Cát Bà (w goodmorningcatba.com) which has several departure times each day to/from the Old Quarter and handy connections with Ninh Bình (page 213). From Hải Phòng, there are buses (1½hrs) to Cát Bà town that leave every few hours and include the ferry crossing.

For information on getting to and from Hạ Long city by **boat**, see page 194.

Flights from Hồ Chí Minh City, Đà Nẵng, Phú Quốc and other Vietnamese cities serve Cát Bi International Airport (Lê Hồng Phong, Cát Bi; w vietnamairport.vn), just 7km south of central Hải Phòng.

Cát Bà is not a walkable destination and public transport is almost non-existent, so the best way to move around the island's good and quiet roads is by renting a **motorbike**. If you're not comfortable on two wheels, you can talk to your accommodation or a taxi driver about renting a car for a day.

Where to stay *Map, page 205*

With restaurants, cafés, bars and motorbike rental, the most convenient place to stay is Cát Bà town, the biggest settlement, which is in the south of the island. Unfortunately, however, the town's once-attractive bay was reclaimed in 2024 to construct a hotel that robs the town of its sea views. Avoid the eyesore by staying a few blocks back from the destroyed bay. From Cát Bà town it's also possible to walk to the beaches. If you have your own transport, you can consider staying elsewhere on the island.

JOYSTAY Thôn 1, xã Xuân Đám; w booking.com. A budget option outside town with dorm beds & thatched bungalows that are within walking distance to a reasonably nice beach. **$**

Phương Mai 193 St 1/4; w booking.com. Unbeatable value in this hotel right in the centre of town, though views are tarnished by the ongoing construction in the bay. There's an enthusiastic owner who speaks English & can help arrange tours around the island. **$**

✷ **Camellia Garden Boutique Hotel** Tùng Đình. Sparkling new property in a quiet part of town with a chic modern design & small swimming pool. The property backs on to the karsts for some geological drama. **$$**

Cát Bà Ecolodge Xuân Đám; w catbaecolodge.com. From the same people behind Camellia, this ecolodge is an older, ramshackle property that nestles in a quiet valley surrounded by forests. **$$**

Hôtel Perle d'Orient Cát Bà – MGallery Cát Cò 3 Beach; w hotelperledorient.com. The most luxurious option in Cát Bà, which attempts to keep standards high even in low season. **$$$**

Where to eat and drink *Map, page 205*

The following eateries are all in Cát Bà town.

Cát Bà Market 11 Tùng Dinh; ⌚ all day daily. Tasty budget eats are found in & around Cát Bà Market. Here you'll find simple rice restaurants, *bia hơi* (fresh beer) & *bánh đa cua*, a speciality dish of the area. $

Ladybird 164 1/4 St; f ladybirdrestaurantandbistrot; ⌚ 07.00–23.00 daily. New café & restaurant with colourful décor & a tasty menu of global favourites, from pizza & pasta to rice & ribs. $$

✷ **Nhà Hàng Biển Đông** 8 Núi Ngọc; f biendongcatba; ⌚ 07.00–23.30 daily. Very popular local spot serving fresh fish & seafood. Staff don't always speak English, but there is an English menu & you can point at the fish tanks. Always check the price before ordering as seafood can be more expensive than expected. $$$

Quiri 135B Tùng Dinh; w quirihotelcatba.com; ⌚ 07.00–23.30 daily. Backpacker favourite run by a young team who might challenge you to an arm wrestle. The food is mediocre but the beer menu is larger than normal & the cocktails are perhaps the best on the island.

Other practicalities The closest international **hospital** is Vinmec Hải Phòng International Hospital (page 202) in Hải Phòng.

What to see and do

Cannon Fort High above Cát Bà town sits Cannon Fort, constructed by the Japanese during World War II. Perched at an elevation of 177m, the fort provides panoramic views of Cát Bà island and the surrounding archipelago. The site features several well-preserved gun emplacements and massive cannons, as well as a network of underground tunnels and bunkers. Elevated observation posts offered strategic vantage points for monitoring enemy movements. A small museum and various exhibits showcase historical photographs, documents and military artefacts. These days the fort is renowned for its views, particularly at sunrise and sunset. The hike to Cannon Fort is only 30 minutes, but it's steep and slippery. Comfortable walking shoes are recommended for exploring the site. Unfortunately, the site was closed at the time of research, so ask around for an update. If closed but the sunset is looking promising, you can visit the **Cát Bà Monument** (Biểu Tượng Đạo Cát Bà), perched on a lower hill nearby, instead.

The beaches For an island of its size, Cát Bà has remarkably few sandy beaches – only four within easy access of Cát Bà town: Cát Cò 1, Cát Cò 2, Cát Cò 3 and Tùng Thu. The Cát Cò trinity lie just to the south of town and are popular with locals, especially in the late afternoon. From town, it's a 1km-walk to Cát Cò 1 and a further 1km to Cát Cò 2, which is quieter and more secluded. It's also possible to walk the 1.5km to Cát Cò 3 on a promenade that hugs the coast and heads west from town. One of the highlights of these beaches is the walk connecting Cát Cò 1 and Cát Cò 2, known as the 'Rock Trail'. The views from here are spellbinding, especially at sunrise. Tùng Thu Beach is northwest of town. It's quieter but less dramatic, plus, with no big hotels nearby trying to keep the beach clean, it can fill up with trash. If you drive along the road that hugs the western side of the island (ĐT356) you'll come across other beaches, though few that are especially notable.

✷ ***Hospital Cave*** (Hang Quân Y, Trân Châu; small entrance fee) This wartime facility was built between 1960 and 1965 with the help of Chinese engineers. The multi-level cave served as a secret, bomb-proof hospital and safe house for the Việt Cộng during the American War. The entrance, accessible via a steep staircase, reveals a complex structure with 17 rooms, including operating theatres, recovery rooms and even a small cinema. Today, visitors explore the site through guided tours, which are included in the entrance fee but are only in Vietnamese. Even if you understand nothing from the guide, the signs and mannequins give an idea as to how the cave was used.

Trung Trang Cave (Đường xuyên đảo Cát Bà; ⌚ 07.00–17.00 daily; small entrance fee) This cave nestles in the heart of the island within the lush expanse of Cát Bà National Park, but you can access it from the road a few kilometres south of the park's main gate. Trung Trang Cave stretches for about 300m and has an otherworldly array of stalactites and stalagmites, though it's considerably less impressive than the caves of Phong Nha (page 235). The entrance to Trung Trang Cave is signposted on the road and is easily accessible. The paths are well lit and maintained. It is said that this was a hiding place for Vietnamese soldiers during the various years of conflict.

✷ ***Cát Bà National Park*** (Vườn Quốc Gia Cát Bà; **w** catbanationalpark.vn) The national park, established in 1986, covers roughly half the island, with around a third consisting of coast and inland waters. The park is home to more than 100 **animal species**, including the world's last remaining white-headed langurs (*Trachypithecus poliocephalus poliocephalus*). Their numbers dropped from around 2,500 in the 1960s to 53 in 2000, but since then the number has been rising slowly. These elusive, critically endangered creatures are believed by many zoologists to be a subspecies of a type seen occupying high limestone outcrops in remote parts of southern China. On Cát Bà island they stay well out of view, let alone photographic reach, but still attract world interest. Moose deer and several types of rare macaque (stump-tailed, pig-tailed and red-faced) also roam. Zoologists have identified teeth of the rhesus macaque in a few of the caves, but there have been extremely few sightings. The leopard (*Panthera pardus*) is now thought to be extinct on the island, although their teeth were found in one of the caves, along with those of the Asian elephant (*Elephas maximus*). Some of the larger caves contain Cantor's roundleaf bats (*Hipposideros galeritus*) and horseshoe bats (*Rhinolophidae*). Geckos and other reptiles are particularly common along the paths, though the reticulated python (*Malayopython reticulatus*) has been hunted more or less to extinction. After heavy rain during the breeding season (around July), the whole park is alive with the croaking of frogs.

Many migratory **birds** fly here from further north to avoid harsh winters, making the area a haven for birdlife. There is every chance of hearing several species in the early morning or late afternoon. These include spot-billed ducks (*Anas poecilorhyncha*), white-breasted waterhens (*Amaurornis phoenicurus*), common coots (*Fulica atra*), little grebes (*Podiceps ruficollis*) and pheasant-tailed jacanas (*Hydrophasianus chirurgus*). The primary forest zone is the abode of Indian cuckoos (*Cuculus micropterus*), which have striped underparts and yellow feet. A particularly handsome bird is the orange-breasted pigeon (*Treron bicincta*); the male has a pink neck and a green head. The black-throated laughing thrush (*Garrulax chinensis*) and the scarlet minivet (*Pericrocotus speciosus*) prefer the lower valleys.

The **marine** section of the park is no less bounteous, with fish and shellfish populations that keep the local fishing fleet hard at work and reasonably prosperous. As with Hạ Long Bay, the potential for snorkelling here is zero as visibility is so poor.

After entering through the park headquarters, visitors are free to roam through the forest, but must not wander far from the path. Many hotels arrange treks from the park gate through the forest to the village of Việt Hải for a light lunch, then down to the coast for a boat ride home. This takes a full day and you'll need to take a guide. A short and popular guideless trek leads to Ngũ Lâm Peak behind the park

CRUISE COMPANIES FOR LAN HẠ BAY

Like Hạ Long Bay, there are cruise companies that offer tours of Cát Bà and Lan Hạ Bay with pick-up and drop-off in Hanoi. Cruises tend to be quieter and more flexible than those of the more famous bay, yet offer comparable views and activities. **Heritage Line** (w heritage-line.com/cruise/lan-ha-bay) cruise ships used to operate in Hạ Long Bay, but have found the quieter waters of Lan Hạ Bay more in keeping with their boutique brand. They also offer cruises in Southern Vietnam, Cambodia, Laos and Myanmar. **Orchid Cruises** (w orchidcruisehalongbay.com) were one of the first to focus on Lan Hạ Bay, but now cruise newer routes that combine Lan Hạ and Hạ Long bays. **Paradise Vietnam** (w paradisevietnam.com) is the largest luxury fleet (page 195) in Hạ Long Bay and Bãi Tử Long Bay, but also cruises in Lan Hạ Bay on the *Paradise Grand*.

headquarters. During the wet season (July–October), leeches are a problem and mosquitoes are at their worst. Bring leech socks if you have them and plenty of insect repellent. A collar, long sleeves and long trousers are also advisable.

Cruising One- and two-day cruises around Lan Hạ Bay are easy to arrange in Cát Bà town, and depart from Cái Bèo pier, a 5-minute drive north. It used to be only budget cruises that left from here, but the offerings have started to diversify since the Covid-19 pandemic. For these, reach out to **Việt Nam Insider Travel** (Tùng Dinh St; w vietnaminsidertravel.com; ⌚ 08.30–22.00 daily). More ambitious Lan Hạ Bay cruises are best organised from Hanoi (see above).

✷ ***Kayaking*** Like cruising, self-guided and guided kayaking expeditions are easy to arrange in Cát Bà town and depart from Cái Bèo pier. It's no longer possible to kayak from the pier, so companies take you out on a shuttle boat, from where you pick up your ride. **Blue Swimmer Adventures** (237 Cái Bèo; w blueswimmersailing.com) and **Vietnam Insider Travel** (Tùng Dinh St; w vietnaminsidertravel.com) are two recommended kayak operators.

✷ ***Climbing*** With its karstic geography, Cát Bà island offers superb climbing opportunities. Many routes remain climbable regardless of the weather thanks to natural overhangs that help keep cliff faces dry. Climbing spots are located both inland and in Lan Hạ Bay. Most climbers here are novices, but more challenging climbs can be arranged. Advanced climbers can also try deep-water soloing on the vertical cliffs of Lan Hạ Bay, which involves climbing without ropes and using the ocean as a safety net. Climbers typically finish with a controlled free fall into the sea and swim back to their boat. Do not attempt climbing on Cát Bà on your own, even if you have all the right equipment. Instead, reach out to **Langur's Adventures** (222 1/4 St; w langursadventures.com; ⌚ 08.00–20.30 daily), currently the only operator offering high-quality climbing services with international safety standards.

NAM ĐỊNH AND AROUND

Nam Định is a large and diverse industrial centre, with very few foreign visitors despite its spiritual, historical and culinary intrigue. Most Vietnamese associate

LEGEND HAS IT: THE FOUR IMMORTALS

Nam Định has been shaped by Catholicism, but traditional beliefs about deities in the broader Red River Delta region date back millennia. Key to traditional spirituality in the area is the existence of four immortals: Tản Viên Sơn Thánh (Sơn Tinh), Phù Đổng Thiên Vương (Thánh Gióng), Chử Đồng Tử, and Princess Liễu Hạnh. Sơn Tinh is the mountain god and symbolises the strength and resilience in protecting the land from natural disasters, particularly floods. His legendary battle against Thủy Tinh, the God of Water, represents this struggle (see page 127 for the full story). Thánh Gióng is a legendary folk hero who represents the Vietnamese spirit of resistance against foreign invaders. According to the legend, he grew from a three-year-old child to a giant hero overnight to repel invaders, then flew to heaven after his victory (see page 473 for the full story). Chử Đồng Tử is celebrated for his marriage to Princess Tiên Dung and their dedication to each other despite their different social standings. His legend emphasises themes of love, marriage and the pursuit of wealth and happiness. Princess Liễu Hạnh is a heavenly spirit and one of the principal deities in the Vietnamese Mother Goddess worship (page 188). Liễu Hạnh is venerated for her compassion and protection of the people, embodying the virtues of maternal care and benevolence.

Nam Định with Catholicism, and there are more than a handful of historic churches dotted around the province. The Red River Delta was the first part of the country to be influenced by Western missionaries: Portuguese priests were proselytising here as early as 1627. Christian influence is still strong, despite the mass exodus of Roman Catholics to the south in 1954. Villages (which are built of red brick, often walled and densely populated) in this coastal province may have more than half a dozen churches, all with packed congregations and not only on Sundays. The churches, the shrines, the holy grottoes, the photographs of the parish priest on bedroom walls and the holy relics clearly assume huge significance in people's lives.

However, many residents still subscribe to Eastern religions; Thiên Trường Temple and Phổ Minh Pagoda – both highly regarded – are to be found 3km north of Nam Định. The province may also be the birthplace of *phở*, Vietnam's national dish, though Hanoi disputes the claim. Whatever the truth, *phở Nam Định* remains a version of the dish that is distinct from other *phở* from the north, and it's possible to sample it in humble eateries across the city.

Neighbouring Thái Bình Province also has culinary associations, as it is best known among Vietnamese for its huge rice harvest. Many a Hanoian will say that rice from here is the most fragrant in all of Vietnam (southerners, of course, disagree). Surrounded on three sides by rivers and hemmed in by the ocean on the other, the province often experiences floods that breach dykes and can bring immense hardship. The typhoons can ruin roads, cause salt water to leak into paddy fields, and create swamps.

GETTING THERE AND AROUND There is no airport in Nam Định. Nam Định has a **train** station (Thái Bình does not) and, although it is far from the centre, going by train from Hanoi (2hrs; several daily) is enjoyable. If travelling by train from Hải Phòng, you will need to transit in Hanoi as there is no direct line. Heading south, the train passes Ninh Bình (30mins), Vinh (4hrs), Đồng Hới (8hrs) for Phong Nha and overnight trains to Huế (12hrs), and Đà Nẵng (15hrs) for Hội An.

If there's no traffic, **buses** are the fastest way (1½hrs) to transfer between Nam Định and Hanoi, and they leave regularly throughout the day and night. Buses tend to pick up/drop off in the centre of both cities rather than utilise the bus stations. There are several buses linking Nam Định with Hải Phòng (2½hrs) and Hạ Long (3hrs). Nam Định is close enough to Ninh Bình that you can take a taxi between them. If travelling to/from cities further south by bus, pick-up/drop-off tends to be in the centre.

You will need **motorised transport** to explore Nam Định and Thái Bình. Rent either a motorbike or a private car, which you can do from your accommodation.

WHERE TO STAY AND EAT Nam Định city, particularly the neighbourhoods near the Flag Tower, makes the most pleasant base from which to explore these two provinces. As Nam Định may possibly be the birthplace of *phở*, the noodle soup is reliably good everywhere, but there are no places of particular note. They're easiest to find on the main streets: Điện Biên and Trần Hưng Đạo.

Khách Sạn Dệt 62 Nguyễn Hiền; f dethotel62nd. Simple & clean rooms that look over a courtyard. Plants have been used reasonably successfully to spruce up the otherwise bland space. **$**

✷ **SOJO** 272 Trần Hưng Đạo; w sojohotels.com. Fast-growing & future-forward hotel group that has popped up in Vietnam's smaller cities, offering reliably clean rooms & some tech-driven services. **$$**

Nam Cường Hotel 538 Trần Hưng Đạo; w namcuongnamdinhhotel.com.vn. Nam Định's choice wedding venue & one of the more luxurious hotels in town is a big, nondescript place with views of the surrounding lakes. **$$$**

Không Gian Café Dệt Xưa 5 Hoàng Hoa Thám; f detxuaclaypot; ⌚ 06.30–22.30 daily. Classic Vietnamese 'rice & things' restaurant that doubles as a café with garden. Sits next to one of the few remaining heritage buildings in the city. **$$**

Kohi.Kafei Ven hồ Lộc Vượng; f kohikafei; ⌚ 08.00–22.00 daily. Neat, modern café that offers art classes & overlooks a lake.

WHAT TO SEE AND DO It's just about possible to visit the following sites in one long day – perhaps in the order presented here – if based in Nam Định city. You can combine visiting these churches with Phát Diệm Cathedral (page 220) in Ninh Bình Province.

Nam Định city

Flag Tower (Cột Cờ; Tô Hiệu; ⌚ 07.00–17.00 Mon–Fri) In the heart of Nam Định city is the Flag Tower, built in the early 19th century during the Nguyễn Dynasty as a military observation post and a symbol of authority. Standing at approximately 25m high and made from brick, the tower features a square base that tapers as it ascends, culminating in a flagpole. The octagonal form and flower-shaped air vents echo the flag tower in Hanoi. The surrounding area includes a well-maintained courtyard and gardens, a focal point for national celebrations. Nearby is the **Nam Định Museum** (Cột Cờ; w baotangtinhnamdinh.vn; ⌚ 07.00–17.00 Tue, Thu & Sun), only worth stepping into if you have time to kill.

Phổ Minh Pagoda (Trần Thừa) This pagoda, located 4km from the city centre, was established during the Lý Dynasty and expanded in the Trần Dynasty. The centrepiece of the pagoda is the Phổ Minh Tower, a 13-storey brick tower standing 21m high and constructed in 1305. The tower showcases the zenith of the Trần Dynasty architectural style. The pagoda complex includes several halls, shrines and statues, each depicting various aspects of Buddhist teachings. One of the notable features is the large bronze statue of Buddha, symbolising serenity and spiritual enlightenment.

Thiên Trường Temple (Trần Thừa) The adjacent temple is less high-rise but equally as significant as Phổ Minh Pagoda. It was built in 1238, also to honour the Trần Dynasty, especially Trần Thái Tông, the dynasty's first emperor. Thiên Trường Temple showcases traditional Trần Dynasty architecture with intricately carved wooden structures, red lacquer and gold embellishments. The main hall houses altars and statues of the Trần kings. Surrounded by gardens and courtyards, the temple offers a tranquil atmosphere that contrasts with the busy streets of central Nam Định. It is a significant pilgrimage site, attracting devotees who come to pay respects to the Trần kings during the first lunar month.

✷ **Kẻo Pagoda** (Duy Nhất) North of the main channel of the Red River, 25km southeast of Nam Định but in Thái Bình Province, is the site of the 11th-century Chùa Kẻo, which was destroyed in a flood before being moved to its current location. The present building dates to the 17th century but has been remodelled several times. The pagoda is renowned for its wooden architecture, showcasing intricate carvings and traditional Vietnamese design. The complex includes dozens of compartments, including the main hall, ancestral hall, and the notable three-storey bell tower that stands 11m high. The tower houses a giant bell and drum used during religious ceremonies. Kẻo Pagoda is a major pilgrimage site, especially in the months following Tết.

The churches When touring the churches of Nam Đình, be sure to include Phát Diệm (page 220) in neighbouring Ninh Bình.

✷ ***Bùi Chu Church*** (Xuân Ngọc; **w** gpbuichu.org) This squat neo-Gothic church was built in 1885, making it one of the oldest churches in the area still standing today, though it has been recently renovated and repainted. The church features tall spires, large arched windows and detailed stone carvings. It sits 34km from Nam Định city and just 1km north from Trung Lĩnh Church.

Trung Linh Church (Xuân Ngọc; f GiaoxuTrungLinhBC) Some 33km southeast of Nam Định is Trung Linh Church, one of the province's more elegant churches, particularly on a clear day and viewed from across the pond in front. The church, built in the early 20th century, blends neo-Gothic and Romanesque styles and is notable for its large, symmetrical bell towers and detailed façade. The Ninh Cơ River, just to the west of the church, has some riverside cafés that make a good pit stop.

Hưng Nghĩa Church (Xóm 10, Hải Hưng) Dubbed the Harry Potter church by young Vietnamese fantasy enthusiasts, this massive charcoal-grey, castle-like church is 36km south of Nam Định city. The neo-Gothic structure was originally constructed in the late 19th and early 20th centuries, but has been added to and adapted over the decades. The church's architecture is particularly striking for its tall spires, which are climbable if the church is open, and stained-glass windows. The interior is equally impressive, with vaulted ceilings and ornate altars. The church is not only a place of worship but also a community hub, hosting various religious events, festivals, and gatherings throughout the year. It's garishly lit in December.

✷ ***Hải Lý Church*** (Xóm 3) Located 45km south of Nam Định in Hải Hậu District is Hải Lý Church, a haunting and abandoned structure popular with Vietnamese photographers for its seaside setting. Originally built in the 1940s, erosion and rising sea levels have gradually encroached on the land, causing its Gothic arches to crumble. During high tide, waves that will eventually claim the church lap at the base of the derelict walls. The site is captivating at sunrise, when the play of light accentuates its weathered features. While the church remains in a state of disrepair, the surrounding area is conducive to leisurely walks along the beach.

NINH BÌNH

Ninh Bình Province's classical scenery of karst limestone peaks has inspired countless literary and artistic works, and its distinctive geomorphology extends throughout Hòa Bình and Thanh Hóa. Much of the landscape is due to millennia of erosion by rain, which has leached out calcium carbonate from the densely packed dolomite layers laid down during the Triassic era. Huge caverns have resulted and are particularly striking on the offshoots south of the Hoàng Long River. Here, visitors board sampans in the exquisite watery landscape of **Tam Cốc** (often referred to with the clichéd moniker, developed for marketing, 'Hạ Long Bay on land') to meander through inundated grottoes and past verdant fields of rice. Nearby is **Tràng An**, which UNESCO describes as 'a spectacular landscape of limestone karst peaks permeated with valleys, many of them partly submerged and surrounded by steep, almost vertical cliffs.' In the impressive **Cúc Phương National Park**, the bulk of which is in Ninh Bình though the fringes bleed into Thanh Hóa and Hòa Bình provinces, nature has sculpted massive canyons that shelter all manner of flora and fauna, including some of the oldest trees in the country.

Covering approximately 1,384km^2 and containing 150km of waterways, the province is home to well over a million people and is a treasure trove of religious sanctuaries, pagodas high in the mountains, sacred sanctums of emperors and generals, and more recent reminders that this area was once a stronghold of Catholicism. **Phát Diệm Cathedral**, the most well known, is just one example. Ninh Bình also holds **Hoa Lư**, with temples dedicated to two of Vietnam's earliest kings and the site of the capital of an ancient Vietnam, long before Hanoi, Huế and Saigon were major Vietnamese settlements.

The capital of the densely populated province is Ninh Bình city. Together with Nam Định and Thái Bình, it marks the most southerly point of the northern region. The city itself has little to commend it to the tourist, but it is a useful and accessible hub from which to visit some of the most story-packed areas in all of Vietnam. Travellers can see Ninh Bình on a day trip from Hanoi, but with so much to do, a better choice is to find a base somewhere in the province – perhaps a homestay or retreat in the countryside – to stay several nights and explore by motorbike or private car.

HISTORY Around 12km northwest of Ninh Bình city, King Đinh Tiên Hoàng (968–79) built his royal capital, Hoa Lư. Independence from China had only just been won, so a capital that could be easily defended was crucial. Situated in the narrow, tortuous Hồng River Valley and surrounded by karstic peaks, it was accessible from only two directions. One was blocked by large ditches and the other had high fortifications, with a commanding view. The massive citadel, almost nothing of which remains, had defensive perimeters that surrounded magnificent palaces, perhaps with roof tiles made from solid silver.

The Imperial City was expanded over the following decades and additional palaces with silver roofs and gold pillars were built on mountains. Archaeologists surveying the site have reported that the citadel alone covered 3km^2. The capital was moved to Thăng Long (now Hanoi) in 1010, but Hoa Lư retained its spiritual significance; the Lê Temple you see today was first built during the Lý Dynasty (1010–1225). The area was also important strategically. Countless insurrections have left behind a legacy of ruined citadels that unfortunately offer little to see.

The Tam Điệp Mountains, which extend along Ninh Bình's southern extremity, formed a natural strategic barrier that helped protect the Trần from the Yuân (13th century), the Hồ from the Ming (15th century) and the Lê-Trịnh from the Mạc (16th century). One of Vietnam's greatest military leaders, Quang Trung, built the Tam Điệp–Biên Sơn defence line here in 1788–89 to prevent the northern Qing invaders getting any further south.

GETTING THERE AND AROUND Ninh Bình does not have an airport and is thus served by Nội Bài International Airport (page 85) in Hanoi. It has a **train** station, although it feels far from the city centre. The train station has convenient services, however, with taxis waiting out the front and some little shops renting motorbikes and serving basic food. Hanoi is 2 hours by train, and if travelling by train from Hải Phòng you will need to transit there as there is no direct line. Heading south, the train passes Vinh (5hrs) and there are overnight trains to Đồng Hới (9hrs; for Phong Nha), Huế (13hrs) and Đà Nẵng (16hrs; for Hội An).

If there's light traffic, **buses** are the fastest way (2hrs) to transfer between Ninh Bình and Hanoi; they leave regularly throughout the day and night and tend to pick up/drop off in the centre of both cities rather than utilise the bus stations. There are also several buses between Ninh Bình and Cát Bà (5hrs) and Ninh Bình and Hạ Long (3–4hrs), enabling you to bypass Hanoi. Nam Định is close enough to Ninh Bình that you can take a taxi between them if not taking the train.

Ninh Bình presents an excellent opportunity to rent a **motorbike** and whizz between the sights, which are not walking distance from one another. Some of the closer points of interest are accessible by bicycle and most accommodation providers will lend them for free or rent them out for a small fee. Failing that, talk to your accommodation about renting a car and driver for the day.

WHERE TO STAY AND EAT Ninh Bình city is nothing special, but there are many homestays and garden hotels dotted around near the sites. There are quite literally hundreds of places to stay in the area, and most will let out motorbikes and bicycles. There are also hundreds of places to eat, and fierce competition means that standards are good and prices are low. The speciality here is *dê* (goat) and you'll see signs for it everywhere. *Dê nướng* (grilled goat) or *lẩu dê* (goat hotpot) is a popular way to cook it, but a little-known fresher dish to try is *dê tái lá chanh* (lean goat served with lemon leaf and lemongrass). Artfully placed cafés speckle the landscape.

Amy House Homestay & Hotel 84 Ngõ 190 Trần Phú; **w** booking.com. If you must stay in town & you're travelling on a budget, this is one of the friendliest places around. **$**

Salina Hotel Ninh Bình 205 Phan Chu Trinh; **w** salinahotelninhbinh.com. A step up from Amy is Salina, located in a smart & leafy corner of town & run by a friendly family. **$$**

Tam Cốc Melody Homestay Đam Khê Ngoại; **f**. One of many good-value garden hotels in the Tam Cốc area trying to capture the budget market. The rooms & b/fasts are just fine, but there's a pool & pool table. **$$**

✷ **TOKI Retreat** Gia Viễn District; **f** tokivanlong. An unexpectedly chic hotel attached to a friendly village near Vân Long Nature Reserve, 30mins north of Ninh Bình city by road. A dozen or so carefully designed rooms look over a leafy courtyard, and there's a swimming pool and decent restaurant, too. **$$$**

Jiva Hoa Lư Retreat Thái Vị Temple Valley; **w** jivahoaluretreat.com. Newer garden hotel backing on to karst mountains & with a small swimming pool. Rooms are tastefully designed, with big windows that overlook the gardens & scenery. **$$$$**

✷ **Tam Cốc Garden Resort** Thôn Hải Nhâm; **w** tamcocgarden.com. Beautiful property in a stunning setting surrounded by rice fields & karst mountains. Rooms have stone walls & bathtubs & the common areas have a rustic luxury edge. **$$$$**

Bánh Mì Hanoi Tam Cốc – Bích Động; 🕘 09.00–21.00 daily. Cute establishment selling elevated *bánh mì* (Vietnamese baguettes) & a few other simple dishes. **$**

Hoàng Cuisine Tam Cốc; 🕘 10.00–22.00 daily. Standard Vietnamese restaurant where you can't really go wrong. The menu is too big for anything to be memorable, but the spring rolls & *bò nướng lá lốt* (grilled beef) hit the spot. **$$**

WHAT TO SEE AND DO

✷ **Hoa Lư** (20,000VND) Vietnam's former capital lies about 12km from Ninh Bình. It was the capital of Vietnam from 968 to 1010, during the Đinh and early Lê dynasties. Prior to the establishment of Hoa Lư as the centre of the new kingdom, there was nothing here, but the location in the valley of the Hồng River – on the 'dragon's belly', as the Vietnamese used to say – was strategically desirable. The passes leading to the citadel could be protected with a small force, and defenders could keep watch over the plains to the north and guard against the Chinese, whom the Vietnamese had defeated only a few decades prior.

The first kings of a newly independent Vietnam built massive temples and animals formed the dominant motifs, which were carved in stone. A large part of this former capital, which covered over 200ha, has been destroyed, although archaeological excavations have revealed much of historical and artistic interest. The two principal temples are those of Đinh Bộ Linh, who assumed the title King Đinh Tiên Hoàng on ascending the throne (reigned 968–79), and Lê Hoàn, who assumed the title King Lê Đại Hành (reigned 981–1005).

The Temple of King Đinh Tiên Hoàng This was originally constructed in the 11th century but reconstructed in 1696 and is arranged as a series of courtyards, gates and buildings. The inscription on a pillar in the temple, using the old character

LEGEND HAS IT: THE HEIR AND THE SPARE

The short-lived reign of the Đinh Dynasty came to an end after an apparent spate of gruesome regicidal crimes. The founding emperor of the dynasty, Đinh Tiên Hoàng, bypassed his adult son, Đinh Liên, to make his infant son, Đinh Hạng Lang, heir to the throne. Records attest that the announcement was followed by earthquakes and hailstorms, a sign of disapproval from the heavens, and in 979 an enraged Đinh Liên sent an assassin to kill his younger brother. Years later, during the resulting unease and tumult, a treasonous official named Đỗ Thích sensed an opportunity to seize the throne and killed both Đinh Tiên Hoàng and Đinh Liên as they lay drunk and asleep in the palace courtyard. When Đỗ Thích was apprehended, it is said that he was beheaded and his flesh was fed to the people of the city. Đinh Tiên Hoàng's third son, Đinh Toàn, then became emperor when he was just six years old but ruled (ineffectively, obviously) for only a few months. The powerful general Lê Hoàn then married the queen, thus bringing an end to the Đinh and ushering in the time of the first Lê Dynasty. Another unrelated Lê Dynasty came later, in the 15th century, when the nearby Bích Động Pagoda (page 216) was built.

system, reads 'Đại Cồ Việt' (roughly, 'the great nation of the Việt people'), from which the name 'Việt Nam' is derived. The back room of the temple is dedicated to Đinh Tiên Hoàng, whose statue occupies the central position, surrounded by those of his sons: Đinh Liễn to the left, and Đinh Hạng Lang and Đinh Toàn to the right. In the 960s, Đinh Tiên Hoàng managed to pacify much of the Red River plain, undermining the position of a competing ruling family, the Ngô, who accepted Đinh Tiên Hoàng's supremacy. However, this was not done willingly, and banditry and insubordination continued to afflict King Hoàng's kingdom. He responded by placing a kettle and a tiger in a cage in the courtyard of his palace and decreed: 'Those who violate the law will be boiled and gnawed.' An uneasy calm descended on Đinh Tiên Hoàng's kingdom, and he could concern himself with promoting Buddhism and geomancy, arranging marriages and implementing reforms – although his family's dynasty was not to last long (page 215).

Temple of King Lê Đại Hành The Temple of King Lê Đại Hành is dedicated to the founder of the first Lê Dynasty, who seized power after the regicide of Đinh Tiên Hoàng. To seal the deal, Lê Đại Hành took not only Đinh Tiên Hoàng's throne but also his wife, Dương Vân Nga. Representations of her, Lê Đại Hành and Lê Ngoạ Triều (also known as Lê Long Định), his fifth son, each sit on their own altar in the rear temple.

Tam Cốc (120,000–300,000VND) Tam Cốc means literally 'three caves' and is less than 10km west of Ninh Bình city. The highlight of this excursion is an enchanting boat ride up the little Ngô Đồng River through the eponymous three caves. Those who have seen the film *Indochine*, some of which was shot here, will be familiar with the nature of the beehive-type scenery created by limestone towers, similar to those of Hạ Long Bay. The exact form varies from wet to dry season; when flooded the channel disappears and one or two of the caves may be under water. In the dry season the shallow river meanders between fields of rice, which are sometimes golden. There is a good chance of seeing Chinese pond herons, cinnamon bitterns, black-backed kingfishers and huge phọenix butterflies. You can also spot mountain goats clinging precariously to the rocks and locals collecting snails in the water. Women, and occasionally men, row visitors with both their hands and feet through the caves at a leisurely pace. During the journey you might stop at Thái Vĩ Temple, a simple, serene sanctuary where Emperor Trần Nhân Tông (1279–93) retired after his abdication. On a busy day the boats are nose to tail. To enjoy Tam Cốc at its best, arrive first thing in the morning as soon as it opens. Failing that, visit at midday when other visitors will be having lunch.

Bích Động Pagoda (Ninh Hải) A short drive to the south of Tam Cốc is Bích Động Pagoda, which consists of a series of temples and caves built into, and carved out of, a limestone mountain. The temples date from the reign of Lê Thái Tổ in the early 15th century, but were expanded in the 18th century by Buddhist monks Trì Kiên and Trì Thể. It is typical of many Vietnamese cave temples but with three levels: lower, middle and upper. The lower temple is built into the cliff face, next to which is a pivoted and carved rock that resonates when tapped with a stone. Leading upwards is the middle temple and an 18th-century bell. Here, clear as can be, are the likenesses of a turtle and an elephant. More resonant rock pillars follow and a rock that enables pregnant women to choose the sex of their baby: touch the top for a boy and the middle for a girl. The upper temple consists of two rooms, a forecourt and a pond with healing powers.

Múa Cave (Hàng Múa; Ninh Xuân; 100,000VND) The name Hàng Múa (Múa Cave) is misleading, as instead of going deep underground you ascend 500 steps for a panoramic view of the Tràng An Landscape Complex. The stone and concrete staircase that snakes its way to the top was designed to resemble scales, and at the summit is a small pagoda and a statue of a cartoonish dragon. The climb can be very sweaty, especially in the summer months, but the views are more than worth the effort. Múa Cave means 'Dancing Cave', and it may have been given this name because Trần kings would come here to watch music performances.

Tràng An Landscape Complex (250,000–500,000VND) The Tràng An Landscape Complex, inscribed by UNESCO in 2014, covers an area of 6,226ha and is home to around 14,000 people primarily engaged in subsistence farming and tourism. Like Tam Cốc, Tràng An Landscape Complex is less than 10km west of Ninh Bình city. The area encompasses temples, pagodas, lush paddy fields and quaint villages, but is most famous for an array of limestone karst mountains interspersed with valleys, some partially submerged, surrounded by cliffs. The area is a visual feast, but it also reflects over 30,000 years of human history. Archaeological discoveries within its caves have unearthed evidence of ancient human activities from Neolithic times, when hunter-gatherers seasonally roamed the area, to the Bronze Age. UNESCO recognised Tràng An for its advanced geomorphic evolution of humid tropical tower-karst mountains and because it showcases early human interaction with natural landscapes over extensive periods. The riverboat experience offered from Khu du lịch sinh thái Tràng An is much like the one offered at Tam Cốc (see opposite), though perhaps busier and more dramatic. There are three routes of different lengths to choose from, each priced differently.

✷ **Vân Long Nature Reserve** (100,000VND) This 3,000ha reserve is 17km north of Ninh Bình city and 8km from Highway 1 towards Cúc Phương. It is the home to the endangered Delacour's langur (*Trachypithecus delacouri*), named after a French ornithologist, though the Vietnamese term *voọc mông trắng* (white-bottom langur) is clearly the superior name. One of the 25 most endangered primates in the world and endemic to Vietnam, these whimsical animals are entirely black but for their thighs, which are bright white, giving the appearance that they wear shorts. They also sport mohawk hairstyles, fluffy white beards and pointy ears. The best time to spot the primates is around 16.00 and 2-hour boat tours can be arranged at the visitor centre upon arrival. The likelihood of seeing the hundreds of white-bottomed langurs cavorting on the Vân Long karsts is high, though they may be far away (bring binoculars if you have them). As the boats approach the karsts, most veer right as the scenery is slightly more dramatic. You might wish to ask your captain (with Google Translate) to go left instead, as it's quieter and you have a greater chance to see wildlife. Even if you don't manage to spot any langurs, the boat journey is worth it for the scenery alone, and the experience attracts far fewer visitors than Tràng An and Tam Cốc.

Bái Đính Pagoda A gargantuan pagoda built around the site of a centuries-old place of worship 20km west of Ninh Bình city, Bái Đính Pagoda gets mixed reviews. On the one hand, it is an impressive and photogenic complex, with immense courtyards and halls that stretch up the mountainside. On the other hand, the pagoda, most of which was built two decades ago (though it has expanded since), is a prime example of the commodification of Buddhism in Vietnam. Though technically free to visit, the parking areas (15,000VND for motorbikes; 40,000VND for cars) are so far from the site that the only sensible option to get there is to pay for the electric buggy service (60,000VND) and there are some areas within the compound that you have to pay for. Superlatives are the ultimate goal of the makers of this pagoda. It sometimes claims to be the largest Buddhist complex in Southeast Asia, and although this probably isn't true, it is surely the biggest in Vietnam. It does, however, have the largest bronze Buddha statue in Southeast Asia, as well as the longest corridor, with 500 Arhat statues.

✷ **Cúc Phương National Park** (**w** cucphuongtourism.com.vn) This jungle oasis, which is around 120km south of Hanoi and 45km west of Ninh Bình, is one of the most accessible and well managed of Vietnam's national parks. It is also the country's oldest, consecrated in 1962 by Hồ Chí Minh long before reunification. Located in an area of deeply cut limestone and reaching elevations of up to 800m, the park is covered by 22,000ha of humid tropical montane forest. It is home to an estimated 2,000 species of flora, and although wildlife has been much depleted by hunting, dozens of mammal species and hundreds of bird species remain. The government has resettled a number of the park's 30,000 Mường people (page 136), although some Mường villages do remain. April and May see fat grubs and pupae metamorphosing into swarms of butterflies that mantle the forest in shades of green and yellow. Though it's possible to visit the park on a day trip, you'll get more from the experience if you spend at least one night.

Flora Much of the vegetation here has been preserved in its primeval state. Many species are typical of tropical rainforests but others are rare. Some have been introduced from India, Myanmar and Borneo. Botanists will discover an amazing diversity of species, some of which have never been studied in detail. Many hundreds of varieties of medicinal plants have been discovered in the park.

Parashorea stellata, which can reach 70m, grow in the southern part of the forest. They are extremely old – some more than 1,000 years – and yield a huge amount of timber, which is why they were used in the royal palaces in Huế. Less lofty trees include the *Dracontomelon*, one of which has a diameter of 3.5m, and the *Saraca indica*, which has huge yellow and pink flowers. Large, fruit-bearing trees include mulberry (*Moraceae*), magnolia (*Magnoliaceae*) and custard apples (*Annonaceae*). A fig variety (*Baccaurea oxycarpa*) produces fruit along its trunk, which fall off when ripe. A kind of wild jackfruit (*Sauropus racemosus*) does the same sort of thing and the fruit is usually gobbled up by monkeys. Throughout the park you will see numerous intertwining varieties, some reaching 30cm in diameter. Many are so dense that they block out the sun and nothing can grow below them.

Beautiful clusters of **orchids** grow at the entrance to many of the caves where there is just enough light and a lot of moisture. These include coral orchids, vanilla orchids, snow-white orchids and varieties known as jujube, or 'cosmic sunset'. Rarer but extremely elegant is the sword-like orchid known to the Vietnamese as *quế lan hương* ('cinnamon orchid'; *Aerides odoratum*).

Fauna Cúc Phương National Park has suffered so much from centuries of hunting that jungle and scenery, not the wildlife, is the appeal. Before committing to a trip to Cúc Phương, it's worth remembering that you're highly unlikely to encounter any animals in the wild save some birds, monkeys and insects, though several other species of mammals, birds, reptiles and fish do live here. Some of the conservation centres (page 220), however, are well funded and informative.

Many years ago, it was not uncommon to see **leopard** (*Panthera pardus delacouri*) in some of the more remote areas, though there have been no recent sightings. These swift, ferocious creatures are much smaller than the black variety. At one time **tigers** (*P. tigris corbetti*) were also common in this area, but now a sighting is extremely rare. **Bears** still exist in the park but are rarely seen except in off-the-beaten-track locations. An interesting type of **flying squirrel** (*Hylopetes phayrei*) here has membranes stretching between its fore and hind legs. This enables it to glide for up to 300m between trees. The tiny **mouse deer** (*Tragulus versicolor*), *cheo cheo* in Vietnamese, was rediscovered in 2019 after no sightings by conservationists for almost three decades. These animals have yellow flanks, white bellies and dark yellow backs, and have long been hunted for their meat. Another local delicacy is **wild boar**, which root for underground tubers and feed on banana stems and roots. These can grow to 200kg and can kill a person if threatened. A few species of **fox** may also still live in the park. **Pangolins** (*Manis pentadactyla* and *M. javanica*), made world famous during the Covid-19 pandemic as a potential vector that brought the coronavirus strain from bats to humans, are also being reintroduced to the park after being hunted close to extinction for their meat. Realistically, though, the only (semi) wild mammals you are likely to encounter are gibbons, and perhaps lorises if taking a night tour.

Of the hundreds of **bird** species that occupy Cúc Phương National Park, some are extremely colourful, including the silver pheasant, the red-headed trogon, the pied hornbill and many types of babblers, woodpeckers and thrushes. There are some huge varieties of **beetles** and **butterflies**; one of the most beautiful of the latter is the Kalima, which is about the size of an adult hand. If you come here in April or May, you may see the swarms the national park is famous for. At night there is a huge noise from millions of cicadas. They have dark brown and yellow bodies and orange spots on their wings, and shine at night because of their vermilion lacquer layer.

Practicalities You'll need to arrange private transport to and from Cúc Phương National Park, which is closest to Ninh Bình city but also accessible from Nam Định and Hanoi. Facilities at the park headquarters include comfortable accommodation (**$$**), a restaurant, a café, a visitor centre with bicycles for rent, an information centre and guides headquarters. There is also a range of other accommodation just outside the national park, though nowhere that is particularly noteworthy. If staying in the national park, you'll likely wake up to distant sounds of gibbons singing. It's possible to arrange just about everything through the national park website, though contact them as far in advance as possible as it may take days for them to reply. If you need to make a last-minute booking, you're better off asking a Vietnamese speaker (eg: your hotel receptionist in Hanoi or Ninh Bình) to call one of the phone numbers listed on the website.

Activities There is a 20km-long road from the headquarters to the centre of the park. You can tackle the road without a guide by car, motorbike or bicycle, and the journey goes past a lake, several footpaths to 1,000-year-old trees (mostly *Tetrameles nudiflora*) and the Cave of Prehistoric Man, which is readily accessible via a gentle slope followed by a hundred steps. Locals might tell you that the entrance resembles a giant tiger's mouth. Stalactites in many shapes and sizes hang down from the ceiling like sharp teeth, and scattered in many places on the floor are mollusc shells. Two ancient tombs were discovered here in 1966, as well as remains and tools that date back more than 7,000 years. The tombs are well maintained, and small altars with offerings and incense suggest that they now carry spiritual significance.

The cave has several compartments, one of which is reached by a rickety metal staircase. At the centre of the park is a decent restaurant and several more trails leading to ancient trees and viewpoints. The longest trail leads to Silver Cloud Peak, the highest mountain in the park, but you'll need to prearrange a guide at the park headquarters for the ascent. The journey to the centre of the park, stopping for activities, walks and food, will take the better part of a day.

Conservation centres Endangered Primate Rescue Center (EPRC; **w** eprc.asia; ⌚ 08.30–11.30 & 13.30–16.30 daily) is a big draw in the park. The centre was set up in 1993 and since then they've rescued more than 300 primates from captivity, overseen over 200 births and released over 100 back into the wild. Conservation efforts are focused on gibbons (northern white-cheeked, southern white-cheeked, northern yellow-cheeked and southern yellow-cheeked), langurs (Delacour's, Cat Ba, Hà Tĩnh, Indochinese grey, Francois', red-shanked duoc, grey-shanked duoc and black-shanked duoc) and lorises (pygmy and Bengal slow). The centre is responsible for discovering the grey-shanked douc langur (*Pygathrix cinereus*) in 1997. Its work is extremely interesting and well worth a visit; go in the morning to catch the song of around 30 gibbons (see page 390 for more on gibbon singing). You can book guided tours through the visitor centre and directly with EPRC; you cannot visit independently.

It is possible, however, for you to visit the **Turtle Conservation Centre** (TCC; **w** asianturtleprogram.org; ⌚ 08.00–16.30 daily) independently, though guided tours booked through the visitor centre can provide context and detail. More than 2000 turtles and tortoises across 23 species are cared for here; many have been confiscated from former owners that illegally kept them as pets. Those that are endemic to Vietnam are eventually released in carefully selected areas across the country, though turtles from foreign countries may remain in the centre for the rest of their long lives. One curious resident is a Malaysian giant turtle (*Orlitia borneensis*), which was reportedly found in a nearby river, brought to a temple and worshipped. After the police discovered the illegal alien, they alerted the TCC, who rescued the 27kg tropical specimen and built a heated home so that it might withstand the cold winter. There are plans to repatriate the Malaysian giant turtle this decade. The TCC also operates a successful breeding programme to help boost Vietnam's dwindling numbers.

Other centres include **Save Vietnam's Wildlife** (Cúc Phương; **w** svw.vn; ⌚ 07.30–17.00 Mon–Fri), which offers night tours to see confiscated pangolins and other nocturnal animals.

✷ Phát Diệm Cathedral (Nhà Thờ Đá Phát Diệm; 75 Phát Diệm Đông) Some 28km southeast from Ninh Bình city, Phát Diệm Cathedral is the magnum opus of Christian architecture in Vietnam, partly for its scale but also for its remarkable Eastern style with European stylistic influences. Described as 'more Buddhist than Christian' in Graham Greene's *The Quiet American*, the cathedral was completed at the end of the 19th century. A bell tower takes the form of a Vietnamese pagoda stupa and the nave of the cathedral, stretching for 74m, is supported by 52 ironwood pillars. The cathedral was built under the leadership of parish priest Father Trần Lục between 1875 and 1899. He is buried in a tomb between the bell tower and the cathedral proper. Surrounding the cathedral are several chapels: St Joseph's, St Peter's, the Immaculate Heart's, the Sacred Heart's and St Roch's.

That the church is still standing a century and a quarter later is testament to the integrity of the architecture and Ninh Bình's devotees. In 1953, French action in the area saw artillery shells damage the eastern wing of the cathedral, causing part of the roof to collapse. The cathedral was bombed in 1972 by Americans who despatched eight missiles. St Peter's was flattened, St Joseph's blown to an angle, the cathedral forced to a tilt, the roof tiles hurled to the floor, and 52 of the 54 cathedral doors were damaged. Despite official post-war neglect of Christian buildings in the area, including some recent and dubious fires and demolitions, the foundations of Ninh Bình's stone church have proved unshakeable.

The cathedral is nestled within the friendly town of Phát Diệm. The approach to the cathedral is epic: from the narrow canal that slices through Phát Diệm, you drive down a terraced street to be confronted with a statue of Christ the King in the middle of a rectangular café-fringed pond; behind are the cathedral buildings. Opening hours are sporadic, and if you're allowed to see the interiors, consider it a bonus. Your best bet is early in the morning or late in the afternoon. The cathedral is beautified throughout December and erupts in colour and activity on Christmas Eve.

Phát Diệm is an appealing town, though it's changed markedly since *The Quiet American* was published in 1955. In the novella, Graham Greene's Fowler describes 'the one long narrow street of wooden stalls, cut up every hundred yards by a canal, a church and a bridge. At night it had been lit only by candles or small oil lamps (there was no electricity in Phát Diệm except in the French officers' quarters) and day or night the street was packed and noisy. In its strange medieval way, under the shadow and protection of the Prince Bishop, it had been the most living town in all the country.'

LEGEND HAS IT: A WOMAN'S PLACE

Bà Triệu, or Lady Triệu, is one of Vietnam's most celebrated resistance fighters, as evidenced by the major streets in many cities that bear her name (most streets in Vietnam are named after men).

As with many figures of the time, her story is shrouded in myth. In the 3rd century CE, when Vietnam was under the yoke of the Chinese, Triệu Thị Trinh was born in modern-day Thanh Hóa Province. She lost her parents at a young age and was raised by her brother, but eschewed the conventional life of domestic servitude that was laid before her. Instead, she desired independence for her country. 'My wish is to ride the tempest, tame the waves, kill the sharks,' she reportedly proclaimed. 'I will not resign myself to the usual lot of women who bow their heads and become concubines.'

Seeing opportunity in the chaos that followed the fall of the Chinese Han Dynasty in 220, Lady Triệu mustered a force and took on the weakened occupiers. She is usually depicted as a legendary figure with remarkable strength and large, hanging breasts, riding into battle on an elephant, wearing golden armour and howling her fierce battle cry. Despite some initial successes, the uprisings she sparked were crushed as China reasserted its control over Vietnam, and Lady Triệu was either killed in battle or took her own life to avoid capture.

Lady Triệu's grave is said to be in Thanh Hóa Province, and her life is commemorated with a temple (page 222). Legend claims that the nearby mountain was formed by Lady Triệu's faithful battle elephant. When she died, the elephant refused to move from the site of her grave. It died there and, over the years, the elephant's remains grew to become the mountain.

Thanh Hóa Province Thanh Hóa Province, the northernmost province in Central Vietnam, covers an area of 11,116km^2 and is home to almost 4 million people, yet it gets little attention from travellers. The city of Thanh Hóa offers little of interest, and the nearby beach resort of Sầm Sơn is less scenic than other beaches in Central Vietnam or Cát Bà to the north, but there are two important sites that can be visited as a day trip from Ninh Bình.

The first is the 14th-century **Hồ Dynasty Citadel**, 60km northwest of Thanh Hóa and about the same distance southwest from Ninh Bình. Unlike other citadels such as Hoa Lư and Cổ Loa, which were built from mud, Hồ Citadel was constructed from green granite blocks manoeuvred into place using rounded stones. Looking at the remains today gives an insight into the industriousness of the thousands of workers who built this huge structure with their bare hands. In its heyday, set for strategic purposes between the Mã and Bưởi rivers with a backdrop of mountains, it must have been a magnificent sight. The square structure had walls a metre thick and 5m high, and four gates. Inside was the Royal Palace of the Hồ emperors. Remnants of two stone dragons remain today, seven centuries after it was built, though they both lost their heads under suspicious circumstances.

The second sight is **Bà Triệu Temple**, named after local heroine Lady Triệu (page 221), who fought against Chinese invaders in the 3rd century. It is situated close to Highway 1 in Hậu Lộc District, 19km north of Thanh Hóa, 50km south of Ninh Bình, and 40km east of the Hồ Dynasty Citadel. Originally constructed in the 15th century, the temple was rebuilt during the Nguyễn Dynasty (19th century) and is set in a tranquil area beside a lotus pond.

Part Three

CENTRAL VIETNAM

Central Vietnam: An Overview

Central Vietnam is Vietnam's most diverse region, with a chain of more than a dozen coastal and mountain cities that offer disparate backdrops, histories, cuisines, cultures and climates. As the coastline meanders from north to south, punctuated by these cities but also by broad bays, mountain passes and jungled peninsulas, the weather gets warmer, the skies get brighter, the food gets sweeter and the vegetation becomes increasingly tropical. Away from the East Sea and abutting Laos are the Trường Sơn Mountains, which eventually give way to the foothills and lowlands of Southern Vietnam.

HIGHLIGHTS

PHONG NHA (page 235) Phong Nha-Kẻ Bàng National Park is an arcadia of largely unspoiled natural wonders, chief among them Hang Sơn Đoòng, one of the largest caves on the planet, which remained a secret until little more than a decade ago.

HUẾ (page 244) The erstwhile capital of a feudal, united and pre-colonial Vietnam that still clings to its imperial roots, with one of Southeast Asia's largest walled neighbourhoods, a battle-scarred citadel and a phalanx of imperial tombs that hide in the hills. The cuisine in Huế, some might argue, is the best the country has to offer.

ĐÀ NẴNG (page 277) Central Vietnam's glitziest metropolis, with a ladder of sparkling bridges that speckle the riverfront and a perpetually uncrowded beach. Natural hotspots include the Sơn Trà Peninsula, home to the red-shanked douc langur, the Hải Vân Pass and the Marble Mountains, now a spiritual enclave.

HỘI AN (page 299) A tourism hotspot that needs no introduction, Hội An is Vietnam's best-preserved old town, with the weatherworn walls of heritage buildings built over the centuries illuminated by a pastiche of hanging lanterns. Encircling the Old Town is a patchwork of rice paddies and, a little further afield, lie the millennium-old ruins of Mỹ Sơn.

QUY NHƠN (page 326) A modern city built on a sweeping yellow-sand beach, Quy Nhơn is flanked by fishing villages like Bãi Xép and hidden coves. Away from the coast is Vietnam's largest collection of Cham towers, including the restored site of Bánh Ít and the rarely visited ruins of Dương Long.

KON TUM (page 350) A Vietnamese city unlike any other, Kon Tum is no hassle, low-rise, under-explored and bordered by several Bahnar villages, visible by their lofty and thatched *nhà rông*, or communal houses.

ĐÀ LẠT (page 368) Vietnam's city of eternal spring, romance and a cabinet of architectural curiosities, such as the royal Art Deco Summer Palace, the Neoclassical Đà Lạt Palace Hotel, the fantastical Linh Phước Pagoda and the aptly named Crazy House. Surrounding the city, outdoor activities abound, including hiking, motorbiking, boating and canyoning.

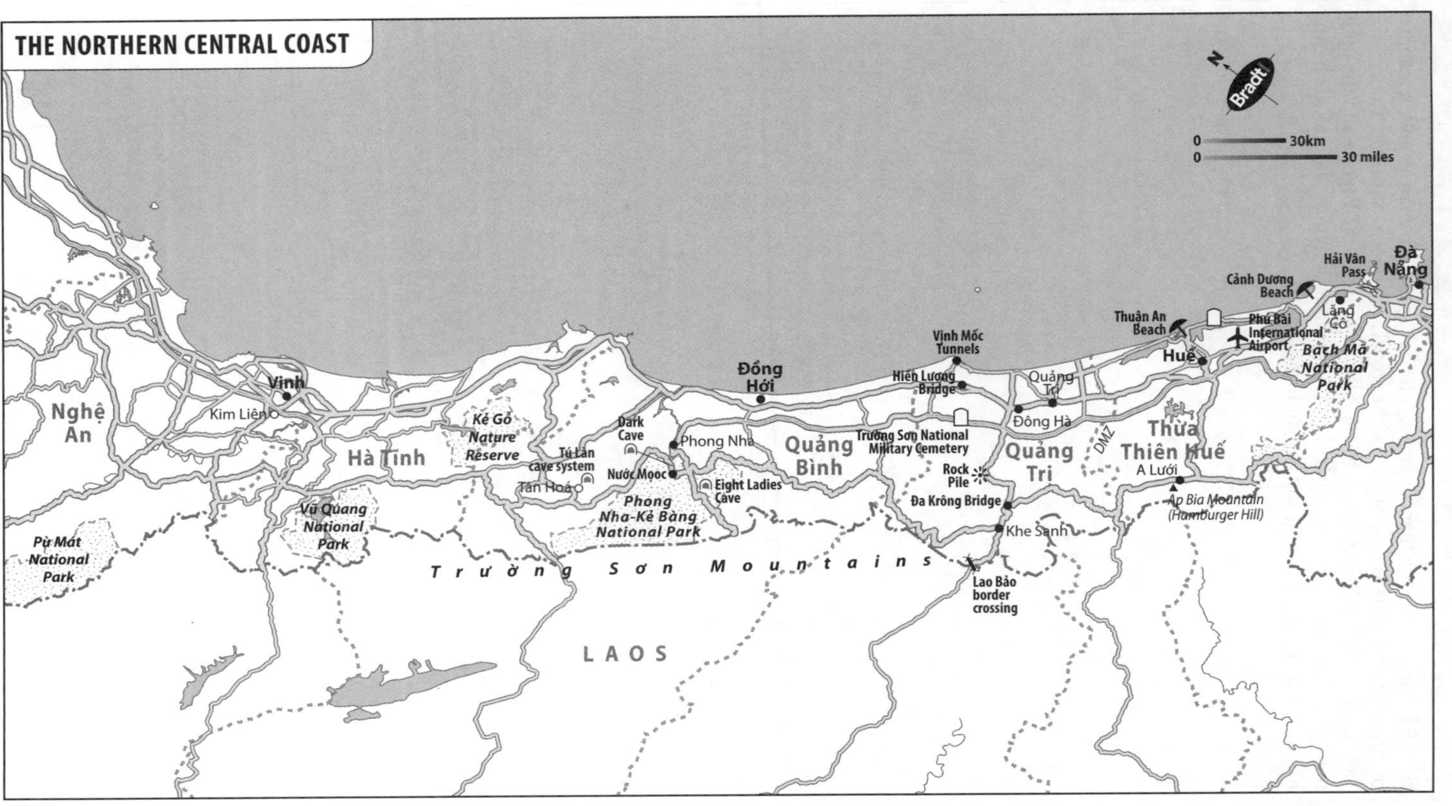
THE NORTHERN CENTRAL COAST
Bradt
N
0 30km
0 30 miles
Đà Nẵng
Hải Vân Pass
Cảnh Dương Beach
Lăng Cô
Thuận An Beach
Phú Bài International Airport
Bạch Mã National Park
Huế
Vịnh Mốc Tunnels
Hiền Lương Bridge
Quảng Trị
Đông Hà
Đồng Hới
Vinh
Kim Liên
Nghệ An
Kẻ Gỗ Nature Reserve
Hà Tĩnh
Dark Cave
Phong Nha
Tú Làn cave system
Nước Mọoc
Tân Hoá
Eight Ladies Cave
Phong Nha-Kẻ Bàng National Park
Quảng Bình
Trường Sơn National Military Cemetery
Rock Pile
Quảng Trị
DMZ
Thừa Thiên Huế
A Lưới
Ap Bia Mountain (Hamburger Hill)
Đa Krông Bridge
Khe Sanh
Vũ Quang National Park
Pù Mát National Park
Trường Sơn Mountains
Lao Bảo border crossing
LAOS

The Northern Central Coast

Moving south from Northern Vietnam, the country's torso bulges briefly in Nghệ An before thinning down to its narrowest point – just 50km wide – in Quảng Bình. This spindly latitude, with Laos to the west and the East Sea to the east, continues through Quảng Trị and Thừa Thiên Huế before the country starts to fatten again near Đà Nẵng. The area from Northern Vietnam to Đà Nẵng is the Northern Central Coast subregion, and although the provinces here are some of the poorest in the country, their inhabitants are among the friendliest.

The Northern Central Coast holds immense natural beauty, with the Trường Sơn Mountains visible from just about anywhere in the subregion. Most of western Nghệ An is taken up by **Pù Mát National Park**, a wild forested expanse. Quảng Bình is home to the UNESCO World Heritage Site of **Phong Nha-Kẻ Bàng National Park**, where the biggest caves on the planet hide beneath a fluffy carpet of thick jungle. The largely untarnished **Bạch Mã Mountain** in Thừa Thiên Huế presides over expansive lagoons that curl around snow-white sandy beaches.

The Northern Central Coast also looms large in historical significance. This coastal strip was the northernmost stronghold of the artistically accomplished Kingdom of Champa before the Vietnamese invasion in the 15th century. The Imperial City of **Huế** was Vietnam's first capital city under Emperor Gia Long, a title it successfully guarded from 1802 until the declaration of independence in 1945. Just north of here was the demilitarised zone, or **DMZ** (the 17th parallel), where Vietnam splintered in two in 1954 and became the abominable theatre for many of the American War's most brutal and consequential battles. Nghệ An, which receives few international visitors, is the *quê* (home town and province) of modern Vietnam's founding father: Hồ Chí Minh. Võ Nguyên Giáp, credited with the victory over the French at Điện Biên Phủ, was born in Quảng Bình. Lê Duẩn, leader of the Vietnam Communist Party after reunification, hailed from Quảng Trị.

The Northern Central Coast is richly rewarding, with immense visitor appeal, and even though the subregion consists of only a handful of provinces, it could easily fill a two-week holiday. This chapter is organised from north to south, beginning with Vinh in Nghệ An Province and concluding with Huế.

WHEN TO VISIT

The best time to visit this area tends to be the spring (March and April), when it is warm and dry(ish). The region heats up from May, a heat that's intensified by what locals call *gió Lào*, hot air from the west, and the summers can be brutal. The heat begins to abate in August and September, but typhoons pummel the region in October and November; note that in Phong Nha, it rains all day every day and there's a good chance the caves will be flooded and the tour companies closed. The autumn rains in Huế are even worse, leading many Vietnamese to refer to the city as *buồn* ('sad' or 'depressing'), though the drizzle lends a certain romantic air to the crumbling imperial sights. Winter (December–February) tends to be cool, cloudy and damp, but otherwise comfortable for those wishing to avoid the heat.

NGHỆ AN PROVINCE

With an area of 16,487km^2, Nghệ An is the largest province in Vietnam, but also one of the poorest. The province has made significant revolutionary contributions: it was the birthplace of the legendary Hồ Chí Minh, the founding father of modern Vietnam, and Phan Bội Châu, who spearheaded the Duy Tân Hội revolutionary movement in 1904. The province also produced the celebrated poetess Hồ Xuân Hương, who wrote during the turbulent years of the Tây Sơn Rebellion (page 332).

Nghệ An's western region is dominated by high mountains that extend along the Laotian border and are rich in natural resources, including tin, antimony, gold and lead. Various ethnolinguistic groups have settled in this mountainous region. The most visible are the Thai (page 138) and the Tay (page 170). The coastline of Nghệ An, which is predominantly Kinh (page 189), features great plains and winding rivers providing water and fertile alluvium for the growing of maize, sweet potatoes, rice and groundnuts.

VINH The province's capital was reduced to rubble by the French in 1952 and by the US and South Vietnam air force between 1964 and 1972, so it has subsequently been rebuilt, East German style. Today it is a reasonably prosperous diversified industrial centre, with a population of around half a million. Vinh lies at the point where the coastal plain narrows, forcing roads and railways to squeeze down a slender strip of coastal land. There is little of historical interest in the city beyond the socialist architecture, but it makes an adequate base from which to arrange a pilgrimage to Hồ Chí Minh's birthplace and adventure to Pù Mát National Park.

Getting there and around The **train** station (1 Lê Ninh) is west of the town centre. North of here is Hanoi (6hrs) and Ninh Bình (4hrs). South of here is Đồng Hới (4hrs), Huế (8hrs) and Đà Nẵng (10hrs). It takes around 28 hours to travel to Hồ Chí Minh City. The track between Vinh and Đồng Hới is one of the most beautiful in the network (page 58). Vinh has a maddening number of **bus** stations, but most companies will drop off/pick up on the street somewhere central, or at

GETTING FROM VINH TO LAOS

Nghệ An has an international border crossing at Nậm Cắn (QL7, Nậm Cắn), right at the northwest tip of the province. At the time of research, the Laos visa on arrival was not available on the border, so if you plan to make this intrepid journey you'll need to arrange a visa at the embassy in Hanoi or consulates in Đà Nẵng and Hồ Chí Minh City beforehand. Since the Covid-19 pandemic, bus routes have been informal and notoriously difficult for foreigners to book, but these situations change fast. Reach out to Vinh Guru Tours (see opposite) for an update. An easier and more popular crossing into Laos is at the Lao Bảo border crossing in Quảng Trị Province (page 250). Buses head there from Đà Nẵng and Huế.

your accommodation if you're lucky. Book long-distance buses to Hanoi (5hrs), Đồng Hới (4hrs), Huế (8hrs) and Đà Nẵng (10hrs) in advance online or through your accommodation.

Vinh International Airport (Nghi Liên Ward; **w** vietnamairport.vn), which doesn't offer international flights, is 8km north of the centre. It is only useful for getting to/from Hồ Chí Minh City.

Vinh is a sprawling city, and although pavements are large and uncluttered, it is too big to cover entirely on foot. Either rent a **motorbike** from your accommodation or rely on **taxis** and Grab to get around.

Where to stay and eat There are no standout hotels in Vinh, but if travelling by train, the **Mường Thanh Vinh** (1 Phan Bội Châu; **w** vinh.muongthanh.com; **$$**) is conveniently located just a few steps from the station. Vinh's biggest hotels are on Quang Trung Street, where there is a more luxurious Mường Thanh (**Mường Thanh Luxury Sông Lam**; 13 Quang Trung; **w** booking.muongthanh.com; **$$$**). The speciality dish in this area is *cháo lươn*, or eel porridge, served in a peppery broth with a baguette on the side. Try it at **Cháo Lươn Bà Ngọ** (Ngõ 4 Đốc Thiết; f; 05.30–13.00 daily; **$**). **Nocenco** (23 Quang Trung; f NocencoCoffee; 06.30–23.00 daily) is a café made from bamboo and designed by modern architect Võ Trọng Nghĩa that perches on a multi-storey shopping mall. Look out the back and you can make out the six-pointed star shape of Vinh Citadel.

Other practicalities **Vinh Guru Tours** (110 Phan Chu Trinh; **w** vinhgurutours.com; 07.30–17.30 Mon–Fri & 07.30–11.30 Sat) is a local company that specialises in tours to Pù Mát National Park. The best **medical** care is offered at Nghệ An General Hospital (Km5 Lê Nin Boulevard; **w** bvnghean.vn; all day daily).

What to see and do Little remains of the 19th-century, star-shaped Vinh Citadel (Thành Cổ Vinh Đào Tấn; 07.00–22.00 daily) save a few (reconstructed) gates. Within the walls are the Soviet Museum (Bảo Tàng Xô Viết Nghệ Tĩnh 10 Đào Tấn; **w** btxvnt.org.vn; 07.00–11.30 & 13.30–18.00 Mon–Sat) and Nghệ An Museum (Bảo Tàng Nghệ An 39 Đào Tấn; **w** baotangnghean.gov.vn; 07.30–17.00 Mon–Sat, 08.00–17.00 Sun), which might appeal only to the most ardent museum enthusiasts. The city's most pleasant green patch is Central Park (Công Viên Trung Tâm, 2 Lê Mao). The lake in the park is surrounded by various miniature models and has a replica of Hanoi's Turtle Tower on an islet in the middle. There's a zone at the northern edge of this park that is pedestrianised on the weekends.

KIM LIÊN (**w** khuditichkimlien.gov.vn; 07.00–11.30 & 13.30–17.00 daily) This commune and open-air museum, 14km west of Vinh, is the place where Hồ Chí Minh (page 230) was born in 1890. There is a reconstruction of the house where a young Uncle Hồ (then Nguyễn Sinh Cung) spent his early years, as well as a memorial altar, in nearby Sen village. Hồ Chí Minh would eventually move to Huế, where he attended Quốc Học, an elite school for gifted students. Although the community and surrounding area were hardly wealthy, he was fortunate to be born into a family of modest means and his father was highly educated. The house where he lived (in fact a replica built in the 1950s) is thatched and simple, offering a glimpse of what rural life was like here over a century ago. This is a pilgrimage site for many millions of Vietnamese and observing your fellow visitors is a highlight of a visit. Most don't spend more than an hour here.

HE WHO ENLIGHTENS

Hồ Chí Minh, one of more than 200 pseudonyms Hồ adopted during his life, was born Nguyễn Sinh Cung, or possibly Nguyễn Văn Thành, in Nghệ An Province near Vinh on 19 May 1890, and came from a poor scholar-gentry family. In the village, the family was aristocratic; beyond it they were little more than peasants. His father, though not a revolutionary, was a dissenter and, rather than go to Huế to serve the French, he chose to work as a village schoolteacher. Hồ must have been influenced by his father's implacable animosity towards the French, although his early years are obscure. He went to Quốc Học College in Huế and then worked for a while as a teacher in Phan Thiết, at the time a fishing village in South Annam.

Hồ did not keep a comprehensive diary, so parts of his life are still a mystery. In 1911, under the name Nguyễn Tất Thành, he travelled to Saigon and left the country as a mess boy on the French ship *Amiral Latouche-Tréville*. He is said to have used a different name so that he would not shame his family by accepting such lowly work. This marked the beginning of three years of travel, during which he visited France, England, the United States (where the skyscrapers of Manhattan both amazed and appalled him) and North Africa. Seeing the colonialists on their own turf and reading such revolutionary literature as the French Communist Party newspaper *L'Humanité*, he was converted to communism. In Paris he changed his name to Nguyễn Ái Quốc (meaning 'patriotic'), and began mixing with leftists and attending meetings of the French Socialist Party. He also took odd jobs: for a while he worked at the Carlton Hotel in London and became an assistant pastry chef under the legendary French chef Georges Auguste Escoffier.

An even more unlikely story emerges from Gavin Young's *A Wavering Grace*. In the book he recounts an interview he conducted with American actress and singer Mae West in 1968, shortly after he had returned from reporting on the Tết Offensive. Upon hearing of Vietnam, Mae West innocently said that she 'used to know someone very, very important there...His name was Hồ...Hồ...Hồ something'. She confided to Young: 'There was this waiter, cook, I don't know what he was... We met in the corridor. We – well...' Young writes that 'her voice trailed off in a husky sigh...'

Gradually Hồ became an even more committed communist, contributing articles to radical newspapers and working his way into the web of communist and leftist groups. At the same time, he remained, curiously, a French cultural conservationist, complaining, for example, about the intrusion of English words

PÙ MÁT NATIONAL PARK (Chi Khê; **w** pumat.vn; ⌚ 07.30–17.30 daily; 10,000/5,000VND adult/child) Pù Mát National Park is a wild, rarely visited chunk of jungled terrain that juts into Laos. It was established in 2001, covers an area of around 911km² and is home to some critically endangered species, including the saola (*Pseudoryx nghetinhensis*; page 232), Annamite striped rabbit (*Nesolagus timminsi*) and white-cheeked gibbon (*Nomascus leucogenys*). Like other national parks in Vietnam, the fauna is very retiring and it's the jungle that people come to experience. There are two ways to explore this national park: independently or with a tour from Vinh. Independent travellers will find clusters of Thai homestays along QL7, the road that cuts through the park, but the more attractive ones are in Môn Sơn village, towards **Khe Kèm Waterfall** (Lục Dạ; ⌚ 07.00–18.00 daily; 30,000/10,000VND adult/child). This is a stunning cascade, where, at the time of research, it was possible to swim, though fish may nibble at your skin. The journey

like 'le manager' and 'le challenger' (referring to boxing contests) into the French language. He even urged the French prime minister to ban foreign words from the French press. In 1923 he left France for Moscow and was trained as a communist activist – effectively a spy. From there, Hồ travelled to Canton, where he was instrumental in forming the Vietnamese communist movement. This culminated in the creation of the Indochina Communist Party in 1930. His movements during these years are scantily documented. He became a Buddhist monk in Siam (now Thailand), was arrested in Hong Kong for subversive activities and received a six-month sentence, travelled to China several times, and in 1940 even returned to Vietnam for a short period – his first visit for nearly 30 years. Despite his absence from the country, the French had already recognised the threat that he posed and sentenced him to death in absentia in 1930. He did not adopt the pseudonym by which he is now best known – Hồ Chí Minh – until the early 1940s, when he clandestinely re-entered Vietnam in Cao Bằng (another important relic and pilgrimage site; page 182) to muster and energise various resistance cells in the north.

Hồ was a consummate politician and, despite his revolutionary fervour, a great realist. He was also a charming man, and during his stay in France between June and October 1946 he made a great number of friends. Robert Shaplen, in his book *The Lost Revolution*, talks of his 'wit, his oriental courtesy, his savoir-faire...above all his seeming sincerity and simplicity'. He talked with farmers and fishermen and debated with priests; he impressed people wherever he travelled. He died in Hanoi at his house in the former governor's residence in 1969.

Since the demise of communism in the former Soviet Union, the Vietnamese leadership have been concerned that secrets about Hồ's life might be gleaned from files in Moscow by nosy journalists. To thwart such an eventuality, they have, reportedly, sent a senior historian to scour the archives.

Today, Hồ's image remains largely untarnished, making him an exception among the tawdry league of former communist leaders. But a Moscow-based reporter has unearthed evidence implying Hồ was married, challenging the official hagiography that paints Hồ as a celibate who committed his entire life to the revolution. It takes a brave Vietnamese to challenge established 'fact'. In 1991, when the popular Vietnamese *Tuổi Trẻ* newspaper dared to suggest that Hồ had married in China in 1926, the editor was summarily dismissed from her post.

there passes Thai waterwheels, ingenious contraptions that irrigate land above the river. Note that beyond visiting this waterfall and driving around the roads and lanes of the national park, other areas are out of bounds to foreigners without visitor permits. The only way to secure these permits is through a tour company like Vinh Guru Tours (page 229), who can arrange multi-day experiences that delve deep into the jungle. One of their signature tours includes a boat trip on the Giăng River – only possible with a permit – and a half-day hike through the jungle.

HÀ TĨNH PROVINCE

The inland journey through Hà Tĩnh Province, either from Nghệ An to the north or Quảng Bình to the south, is tremendously scenic away from the coast. Far towards the west the northern section of the Trường Sơn mountain range rolls into Laos, while the foothills are dotted with church spires and pagodas. Until the 11th century, Hà Tĩnh was the northern border of Indrapura, one of the Champa states (page 12). An ancient citadel once protected this frontier, but it was lost long ago. Many centuries later, when Vietnamese lords wrestled over the area, the Trịnh built a fortress here to protect themselves from attacks by the Nguyễn. The province's biggest claim to celebrity is that it was the birthplace of Nguyễn Du (1765–1820), writer of *Truyện Kiều* (page 35). Mountainous parts of the province suffered the full brunt of the American B-52 raids during the war since these were important chains in the extensive Hồ Chí Minh Trail, which regularly splintered into Laos and Cambodia.

These days, Hà Tĩnh suffers from generally appalling weather. Like the rest of the subregion, summers are brutal, typhoons hit from October and winter (December–February) can be startingly cold. This, coupled with a comparative lack of built heritage, is perhaps why the province's visitor economy has never really taken off, despite tokenistic efforts from development organisations. Indeed, Hà Tĩnh barely gets a mention in other guidebooks. Although Hà Tĩnh should probably not be at the top of your list of priorities, the geography is such that a daytime train journey between Vinh in Nghệ An Province and Đồng Hới in Quảng Bình Province is extremely worthwhile. Hà Tĩnh city does not have a train station.

FLORA AND FAUNA Much of the highland area in Hà Tĩnh Province, which the train tracks skirt around, is dense tropical forest. Some areas in the Vũ Quang National Park, which borders Laos, and the Kẻ Gỗ Nature Reserve are shared with Quảng Bình. Vũ Quang National Park, an isolated, inaccessible area, was identified as one of Vietnam's biodiversity hotspots after the discovery of the Vũ Quang ox, or **saola** (*Pseudoryx nghetinhensis*). Back in 1992, when the biologist John MacKinnon first discovered the skull of the horned mammal, it couldn't be identified. The subsequent discovery of a living specimen in June and July of the same year was confirmation. Superficially, the saola resembles an Arabian oryx, with large eyes, straight sharp horns, a black-and-white patterned head, small feet and a short fluffy tail. Genetic mapping, however, showed that it had greater similarities to an ox, hence the name Vũ Quang ox. With logging now banned in the area, other examples of these endangered species have been seen. More excitement came in 1994 with the discovery of the giant muntjac (*Megamuntiacus vuquangensis*). The national park, which abuts the enormous 3,500km^2 Laotian Nakai Nam Theum Conservation Park, could be the home of other rare and previously undiscovered mammals. In a remote area southwest of Hà Tĩnh, the Kẻ Gỗ Nature Reserve is one of the only locations in the world of the Vietnamese pheasant (*Lophura hatinhensis*), one of the most endangered species on earth. For now, the national parks and nature reserves of Hà Tĩnh are not tourist-friendly.

ĐỒNG HỚI AND PHONG NHA

For centuries, life for most inhabitants of Quảng Bình Province – of which Đồng Hới is the capital – has been a struggle. Although it covers an area of 7,998km^2, very little is suitable for growing crops, partly because the soil is ridden with sand that blows in from the coast. This agricultural scarcity was evident when, after the American War, many risked their lives filling in bomb craters to reclaim patches of land. Compounding the problem are the devastating typhoons and torrential rains that hit the province every year. Dykes, ditches and small dams are continually rebuilt to hold back the seawater that, during the typhoon season, infiltrates the rice fields. During extremely bad years, the area becomes a salty, sandy wilderness where virtually nothing can grow. When aggressive typhoons hit, hundreds of people are left homeless and dozens are killed in landslides. Floodwater extends as far as the eye can see and those with multi-storey houses are forced to abandon the ground floor, sometimes for days. When the floods subside, hundreds of hectares of paddy are spoiled by sand and seawater.

Over millions of years, these typhoons and torrential rains have carved out gargantuan caves, natural wonders that catapulted **Phong Nha-Kẻ Bàng National Park** into the tourism limelight. In 2009, one of these caves, Sơn Đoòng was surveyed and subsequently crowned the biggest cave on earth. Since then, dozens more caves have been surveyed, and more than a dozen are open to the public. On the edge of Phong Nha-Kẻ Bàng National Park is Phong Nha village, where tourism is booming, providing much-needed income and employment opportunities to the people of Quảng Bình. Like Nghệ An, Quảng Bình has also produced revolutionary talent: Võ Nguyên Giáp (page 149), the military strategist who bested the French at Điện Biên Phủ, was born in a small village near the coast. A different revolutionary, of sorts, is the modern architect Võ Trọng Nghĩa (no relation to Võ Nguyên Giáp), who was born just 10km away in 1976 and heads an award-winning firm in Hồ Chí Minh City. Though his architecture is not without its controversies, he has transformed the way modern Vietnamese design is viewed and understood, both in Vietnam and across the world. Today, the province is home to almost a million people.

ĐỒNG HỚI Đồng Hới, the provincial capital, is located at the mouth of the Nhật Lệ River. During the American War, the town was levelled and most of what you see today has been built since 1975. With around 120,000 people, it has successfully evolved into a neat administrative centre for Quảng Bình. More and more tourists come here every year on their way to or from Phong Nha (page 235), 50km northwest of the town. The downtown area is not unpleasant, though there's little to keep you busy – but for those who'd like to bask in the sun, there are beaches nearby.

Getting there and away The **train** station (Thuận Lý St) is 4km west of the town centre and has restaurants and cafés nearby. It is a convenient overnight distance from Hanoi (12hrs), though you should consider a day journey through mountainous Hà Tĩnh (page 231). North is Vinh (4hrs) and Ninh Bình (8hrs); south is Huế (4hrs) and Đà Nẵng (6hrs). It takes around 24 hours to get to Hồ Chí Minh City.

Đồng Hới **bus** station (156 Trần Hưng Đạo) is 1.5km west of the centre – just about walkable if you don't have too much luggage. The bus station is well organised, with different companies occupying glass-fronted booths and prices clearly displayed. There are regular buses to Phong Nha (1hr), which you don't need to book in advance. Book long-distance buses to Hanoi (9hrs), Vinh (4hrs), Huế (4hrs) and Đà Nẵng (6hrs) in advance online or through your accommodation.

Hassle-free **Đồng Hới Airport** (Lộc Ninh Ward; **w** vietnamairport.vn) is 6km north of the city centre and reachable by taxi or Grab. There are a few flights to Hanoi and Hồ Chí Minh City each day.

Central Đồng Hới is small and easy to tackle on **foot**, but you'll need a **motorbike** or **taxi** to travel to and from Nhật Lệ Beach.

Where to stay

Bamboo's House 143 Trương Pháp; f bamboohousevn. Bamboo is a former cave tour guide from Đà Lạt who has given up tunnelling underground for a life on the beach. He can still arrange plenty of adventures, though, but now on kayaks & stand-up paddleboards. A great budget hostel with some private rooms opposite the beach. **$**

✷ **Dolphin Homestay** 42 Nguyễn Du; **w** dolphinhomeqb.com. Highly recommended budget hotel overlooking Đồng Hới's attractive waterfront area, run by a friendly, English-speaking family. They provide maps & can arrange motorbike rental. **$**

Nam Long Hotel 63 Nguyễn Đình Chiểu; **w** namlonghotels.com. On a quiet street in Đồng Hới's most pleasant neighbourhood, surrounded by small, tree-lined streets, restaurants & cafés. Rooms are basic, clean & good value. **$**

Lena Homestay & Villa 110 Dương Văn An; **w** booking.com. Spotlessly clean, upmarket homestay run by a friendly middle-class family. Rooms are larger than in other hotels in the area & the location is ideal. **$$**

Where to eat and drink

There are various seafood restaurants (**$$$**) on Nhật Lệ Beach, some with English menus. If they don't provide them, you can often point at the fish and shellfish you want. As in all seafood restaurants in Vietnam, ask for the price of the dish before placing your order to avoid any surprises when the bill comes. Some other options include:

Restaurants and street food

✷ **Đặc Sản Bánh Lọc Mệ Xuân** 5 Lê Thành Đồng; ⌚ 11.30–22.00 daily. Serving *bánh lọc* (savoury tapioca cakes stuffed with pork & shrimp), a speciality dish that is usually associated with Huế (page 252) but remains popular across this segment of Central Vietnam. **$**

Sophie Homy Café & Food 12 Thuận Lý; f; ⌚ 05.00–22.00 daily. The ideal option if your train is delayed as it sits right outside the station & has comfortable wooden benches. Serves simple, stir-fried dishes, to a foreign crowd for the most part. **$**

Genkan Vegan Café 56 Dương Văn An; ⌚ 07.00–21.00 daily. Probably the best vegan food around, served alongside fresh smoothies & juices. The tofu with corn & 'fish' with tomato sauce come recommended. **$**

Oregano's Pizza 112 Dương Văn An; f OreganoPizzaQB; ⌚ 14.00–21.00 daily. If you must eat something non-Vietnamese while in town, the pizza here is acceptable, the staff are friendly & the streetside location is attractive. **$$**

Coffee houses

CoCo's Coffee 57 Nguyễn Hữu Cảnh; f cocosquangbinh; ⌚ 06.30–18.00 daily. This wouldn't be a café worth hunting out were it not for the eye-catching bamboo canopy, one of the earlier works of modern architect Võ Trọng Nghĩa, who was born in a nearby village.

✷ **Tree Hugger Café & Crafts** 30 Nguyễn Du; f treehuggercafe; ⌚ 08.00–22.00 daily. Perfect little streetside café that appeals to Đồng Hới's creatives, with a bushy front garden & a thoughtful gift shop. Here you'll find young architects drawing up new plans & guitarists wooing their partners.

Other practicalities

Asena Spa (PG18, Cô Tám; **w** asenaspa.vn; ⌚ 08.00–19.00 daily) offers excellent massages, perfect if you've just spent a few days crawling around caves in Phong Nha. The best **hospital** is Quảng Bình Hospital (99 Điện Biên Phủ; **w** benhvientthquangbinh.vn; ⌚ all day daily).

What to see and do

The beach Nhật Lệ Beach, with its plentiful seafood restaurants, is only 2km northeast of town. Around 6km further are the dunes of Nhân Trạch, where you can speed down sand slopes on a rentable sledge or drive around on a quad bike. There are hotels of varying quality, and this is where most domestic tourists tend to stay.

Quảng Bình Museum and around Those who want to get to know Đồng Hới are better off staying in town and tackling the few sites on foot. **Quảng Bình Museum** (30 Quang Trung; **w** baotang.quangbinh.gov.vn; ⌚ 08.00–11.00 & 13.30–16.30 Mon–Fri; 1hr), which has English signage and sprawls across three floors, is a good place to start. The exhibits are not particularly engaging, but they are at least comprehensive, covering natural history, prehistory and ethnic diversity. The most compelling section is the one that focuses on the war effort. The exhibits are very human, focused on the people, who are named, and their deeds during the war. The museum strikes a chord of optimism by skimming over the bombing that flattened the city and instead chooses to focus on the rebuilding efforts. Among the photos of various visiting politicians are some of a very frail Võ Nguyên Giáp (page 149), who visited his home province just before he passed away. The Quảng Bình Museum sits within the moat-encircled Nguyễn Dynasty-era Đồng Hới Citadel, which still forms an attractive pointed star shape from above, though little else remains. South of the citadel is the **Quảng Bình Quan Gate**, also a Nguyễn Dynasty-era remnant and once one of the main gates into the city if coming from the south. It was, of course, flattened during the American War but rebuilt in 1994.

Đồng Hới Park (Đồng Mỹ) Tam Tòa Church (Tháp Chuông nhà thờ Tam Tòa; Nguyễn Du), which sits within Đồng Hới Park, was damaged beyond repair, but the bell tower still stands. The church was built in 1886, destroyed on 11 February 1965 and left in its ruined state as 'evidence of war crimes', says the information plaque. The steeple wallows within the riverside Đồng Hới Park, which comes to life with aerobics, salsa dancing and jianzi in the evenings.

Around Đồng Hới The city is not far from the demilitarised zone (**DMZ**; see page 273 for extensive coverage), one of Vietnam's most important collections of American War sites. While most tourists cover this area from Huế, it's possible to arrange private tours from Đồng Hới with **Heritage Adventure Trails Travel** (Bố Trạch; **w** heritageadventuretrails.com). It's also possible to join their transfer group tour between Phong Nha and Huế, which includes some of the DMZ sights.

PHONG NHA AND TÂN HÓA Phong Nha is a small riverside village that, until recently, saw almost zero international tourism and the population got by on farming, fishing, hunting and logging. Today, tourism is flourishing thanks to the caving opportunities that opened up in the 2010s in nearby **Phong Nha-Kẻ Bàng National Park**. The star attraction is Sơn Đoòng, one of the world's largest caves. Tours of this cave are limited in number, very costly (US$3,000) and last for four days, but visiting other caves is more flexible and affordable; a couple can be explored in an afternoon. The village itself is a sleepy place, with regular kaleidoscopic sunrises and sunsets over the river. Alongside caving, there's hiking, kayaking, cycling and motorbiking.

Tân Hóa, 70km northwest of Phong Nha, is a burgeoning tourism destination that offers easier access to a set of caves outside of Phong Nha-Kẻ Bàng National Park: the Tú Làn cave system and Hang Tiên caves. In 2023, the United Nations World Tourism Organisation (UNWTO) named Tân Hóa one of the world's 'best tourism villages' for its 'pioneering tourism business model that promotes collaboration between enterprises and the local community'. This remains an isolated and remote corner of the province with few places to eat and stay, but if the development of Phong Nha is anything to go by, the number of services for visitors will increase quickly.

Getting there and around Đồng Hới Airport and Đồng Hới train station (page 233) are the nearest to Phong Nha, 45km southeast of the village. Regrettably, there are no shuttle buses; taxis or a regular bus are the only way to travel onwards.

Phong Nha is so small that there is no real **bus** station, and buses tend to drop passengers off or pick them up at their accommodation or on the main

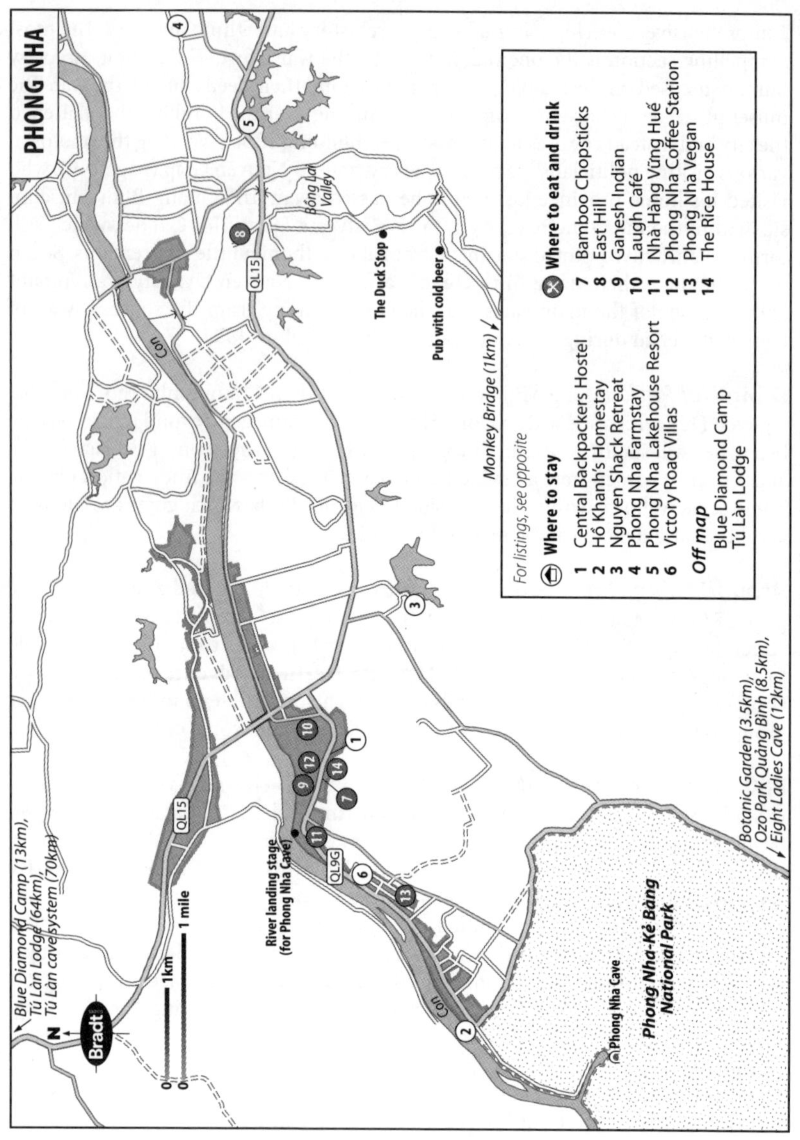

drag. There are regular buses to Đồng Hới (1hr), which you don't need to book in advance, or you can take a taxi. Book long-distance buses to Hanoi (9hrs), Vinh (4hrs), Huế (4½hrs) and Đà Nẵng (6½hrs) in advance online or through your accommodation.

Tân Hóa is 1 hour from Phong Nha and 2 hours from Đồng Hới. Travel here from either place by private car or by reaching out to Oxalis Adventure (page 238) for a transfer.

Phong Nha is small enough to tackle **on foot**, but you'll need a **bicycle, motorbike or taxi** to get to and from some of the better accommodation options outside of town.

Where to stay *Map, opposite*

There are various small guesthouses along the Con River, but other than Hồ Khanh's Homestay, none is particularly noteworthy. This is nevertheless the nicest place to stay in the village.

Central Backpackers Hostel Xuân Tiến; w centralbackpackersphongnha.com. Probably the best backpacker option right now, with dorm & private rooms that are kept clean. There's no backpacker community, but the price & location are right. **$**

✷ **Hồ Khanh's Homestay** Phong Nha village; f hokhanhshomestay. This idyllic spot on the edge of town is owned by the family of Mr Hồ Khanh, the man who led the British caving expedition to discover Sơn Đoòng Cave (page 238). Right on the bank of the river, the views here are especially captivating on a calm, misty morning. Accommodation is simple, but charming & clean. English is limited. **$$**

Nguyen Shack Retreat Cù Lạc 2; w nguyenshack.com. Fairly isolated, ramshackle mid-range option with a lot of wood & thatch. Some bungalows & the restaurant overlook the river & forested hills. It's just about possible to walk into town from here (45 mins) but that includes a stint on a busy road; probably better to rent a motorbike or get a taxi. **$$**

Blue Diamond Camp Xuân Trạch; w bluediamond.camp. Beautiful & apparently net-zero cabin hotel on the outskirts of Phong Nha, with barbecue, kayaking, boating & swimming. Part of the Oxalis Adventure (page 238) family. **$$$**

✷ **Phong Nha Farmstay** Khương Sơn hamlet; w phong-nha-cave.com. The setting of this Aussie/Vietnamese-owned place couldn't be better, right on the edge of beautiful paddy fields in the countryside outside Phong Nha. Alongside a range of rooms, from dorms to family options, there is a great restaurant & bar, plus a pool, a rooftop bar & terrace. The staff are extremely helpful & can provide plenty of information on what to see & do. This is the kind of place people stay for way longer than they had planned. You'll need transport to & from town. **$$$**

Phong Nha Lakehouse Resort Khương Hà; f phongnhalakehouse. In an isolated location overlooking a lake, the waterfront bungalows here are some of the best digs in town. Also has a restaurant with great views, serving a wide range of delicious dishes. You'll need transport to & from town. **$$$**

✷ **Tú Làn Lodge** Tân Hóa; w tulanlodge.com. A new countryside escape put together by the people behind Oxalis Adventure (page 238), Tú Làn Lodge offers fabulous views over the karstic landscape from modern rooms with balconies. Note that this lodge is in Tân Hóa (page 235), a burgeoning tourism destination that is over 1hr from Phong Nha village & 2hrs from Đồng Hới. **$$$**

Victory Road Villas Phong Nha village; w victoryroadvillas.com. The most luxurious option in town, Victory Road Villas is the younger, more refined sibling of Phong Nha Farmstay. If comfort and convenience are your priorities, this is the place. The beds are comfy, there are views to the karsts and there's even a small pool in which to cool off. **$$$$**

Where to eat and drink *Map, opposite*

Laugh Café Cù Lạc 1; 08.00–22.00 daily. Cute little budget restaurant hidden away from the main tourist drag, Laugh (it's not a café) serves simple plates at unbeatable prices. **$**

Bamboo Chopsticks Phong Nha; w bamboochopsticks.com.vn; 07.00–22.00 daily. Long-time popular restaurant serving Vietnamese classics from across the country. The Western dishes are just OK, so stick to rice & noodles. **$$**

East Hill Cầu Bùng; f East Hill Phong Nha; 08.00–22.00 daily. Serves *gà nướng cơm lam*, a speciality of the Central Highlands region (page 348). **$$**

Nhà Hàng Vững Huế Phong Nha; w nhahangvunghue.com; 06.30–22.00 daily. Classic cavernous Vietnamese rice restaurant that is used to serving large groups of domestic tourists, but can also accommodate smaller, non-Vietnamese-speaking parties. Try the tofu with tomato sauce, with or without minced pork. **$$**

PUTTING PHONG NHA ON THE MAP

Back in 1990, two British cavers, Deb and Howard Limbert, landed in Vietnam for the first time. Geologists from Hanoi University had invited the couple with the aim of exploring the country's caves. When they arrived in Hanoi, there were no taxis at the airport, just bicycles and rickshaws, and it took them three days to reach Phong Nha-Kẻ Bàng National Park.

Once in Phong Nha they visited Paradise Cave and Dark Cave and very quickly understood the potential for more underground dominions in the area. They went on to visit other parts of Vietnam and, along with their fellow British Caving Association members, have explored and mapped dozens of caves across the country, but it was to Phong Nha that they wanted to return. Eventually they did and began more comprehensive expeditions to Phong Nha-Kẻ Bàng National Park and beyond.

The area did not disappoint: they surveyed the enormous Hang Én, through which a river flows even in the dry season. Following this river further, the Limberts hoped to find another cave on the same epic scale, but they suffered a setback when they found that the river disappeared underground through an impenetrable pile of boulders. Undeterred, they continued to search the area for a cave entrance, but, despite coming close, they could not uncover an opening. A stroke of luck led to an encounter with local jungle expert Hồ Khanh, who revealed that in 1990 he came across a small cave in the area when sheltering from a storm and felt a fiercely strong wind gusting from within.

In 2008, after a few failed attempts, Hồ Khanh led the Limberts to the small cave, a 7-hour trek from the road, and what they then encountered was much

✷ **Phong Nha Vegan Restaurant** 20 Phong Nha; f phongnhavegan2509; ⌚ 10.00–22.00 daily. Veganised Vietnamese dishes in an outdoor dining room overlooking the lake. Try the grilled mushroom skewers & order a fruit smoothie on the side. $$

The Rice House ĐT20; f thericehousevietnam; ⌚ 10.00–22.30 daily. Neat new joint serving a variety of simple dishes with rice. It's more popular with foreigners than locals, but the food is fresh & well prepared. $$

Ganesh Indian Restaurant ĐT20; w ganesh.vn; ⌚ 10.00–22.00 daily. Surprisingly good South Asian food considering Phong Nha's remote location. Ask the service staff for recommendations & take a break from jasmine rice & noodles, by enjoying basmati & naan instead. $$$

Phong Nha Coffee Station Bố Trạch; f; ⌚ 08.00–18.00 daily. Undoubtedly the best coffee in town & probably inspired by the Australian brunch craze, Coffee Station also serves Western favourites, like muesli bowls with yoghurt & fruit.

Other practicalities The more demanding caves can only be visited as an organised tour with **Oxalis Adventure** (w oxalisadventure.com) or **Jungle Boss** (w junglebosstours.com). For conservation reasons, only one company is licensed to organise tours to any given cave, so the cave(s) you want to visit will dictate which company you'll need to book with. See page 241 for details on the caves and the experiences offered. For trekking tours that focus on flora and fauna away from the caves, contact **Eco Foot** (w ecofoot.com.vn), run by passionate conservationist Nguyễn Thanh Hải. You can also book tailor-made motorcycle trips through the countryside with Phong Nha Riders through **Phong Nha Farmstay** (page 237). The professional tour companies organise extensive first aid training for their staff, but for **medical** emergencies go to Quảng Bình Hospital in Đồng Hới, just under an hour away.

larger than they had dared hope. They surveyed the cave the following year and discovered that this was, in fact, the largest known cave in the world when measured by cross-section. Sơn Đoòng, the exploration of which involves roped climbs and gushing river crossings, is large enough to accommodate jumbo jets and tall enough that a 40-storey skyscraper could stand inside (see page 243 for more on visiting the cave). Giant openings in the cave roof known as dolines allow light to penetrate, birthing jungles that house hornbills, monkeys and flying squirrels.

The Limberts made Phong Nha their home, and by 2013 they were co-leading multi-day public expeditions into Sơn Đoòng with adventure tour guides from the local community, facilitated by Oxalis Adventure. The cave was propelled into the spotlight as the international media descended on the area, but this, inevitably, also led to some undesired attention.

In 2014, Sun Group, a Vietnamese real-estate developer, proposed the construction of a 10km-long cable car to bring mass tourism to the cave. Local officials rejected the plan following opposition from large swathes of society, including politicians, academics, conservationists, business leaders and environmental activist groups like Save Sơn Đoòng, which is still in operation today. In 2016, President Obama visited Vietnam and declared that the cave (which he mispronounced the name of) should be 'preserved for our children and our grandchildren'.

'A Crack in The Mountain', a documentary from 2023, tells the whole story alongside arresting footage of the cave.

What to see and do

Bồng Lai Valley Motorbiking or cycling around Bồng Lai Valley has become Phong Nha's most popular non-caving activity. The hilly and forested landscape is pretty, though highly cultivated, and a handful of local entrepreneurs have set up creative (and occasionally bizarre) things for visitors to do along the way. Exploring the valley and stopping for a couple of activities takes an afternoon.

The Duck Stop (Khương Hà 3 village; 🕘 08.30–18.00 daily) This is a wild and wildly popular activity, where visitors get a theatrical taste of what life in the countryside is like. First slip on a conical hat and grab some animal feed, then prepare to be inundated with fluffy white ducks as they flap around you begging for sustenance. Charismatic young farmer Trần Ngọc Quỳnh began the experience a decade ago as he wanted to give visitors a sense of what his childhood was like, and the experience has since been featured in various international publications. The entrance fee includes a drink and homemade snack, and at busy times you may need to wait for up to an hour.

Pub with cold beer (Hưng Trạch; 🕘 07.00–18.00 daily) Ths popular place received its name when cold beers were hard to come by in the valley. There is no longer anything special about the beer, but the grilled chicken served with a peanut dip and *chéo*, a kind of chilli salt popular in Quảng Bình, is the best in the area. Once a humble roadside check, this 'pub' now has a swimming pool, pool table and some hammocks.

Monkey Bridge – Cường Rừng Farm (Bồng Lai; 🕘 09.00–18.00 daily) Deep in the valley is the Monkey Bridge, a narrow plank stretching over water that the brave can try to cycle across. The idea is the brainchild of Cường Rừng, or Jungle Cường, who will animatedly show you how it's done. There's also a big swing and a shack with views offering drinks, including a delicious honey and herb tea.

Phong Nha-Kẻ Bàng National Park This national park, inscribed on the UNESCO World Heritage List in 2003, originally covered 85,754ha but was extended to 123,326ha in 2015. The expansion means that the park now shares a boundary with the Hin Namno Nature Reserve in Laos, a move that is intended to enhance cross-border conservation efforts. The park's diverse geological landscape is a combination of limestone plateaux and lush tropical forests, but it's the caves that grab headlines (page 238). Among these, the Phong Nha Cave and Sơn Đoòng Cave are of particular interest. Most of those visiting the national park will be doing so on an organised tour to see the caves, but the roads that cut through the park – the ĐT20, ĐT562 and QL15 – are straight out of Jurassic Park, and make for a good day of exploring by motorbike or with a hired car and driver. Along the way there are more than a handful of things to see and do. The caves listed here are those that you don't need to book ahead and you can visit in a couple of hours. See opposite for those 'adventure caves' requiring more of a commitment.

Phong Nha Cave (w phongnhakebang.vn; 150,000VND/free adult/child) Phong Nha's primary tourist attraction, at least for domestic visitors, is a speleological wonder. A team of British divers explored 9km of the main cave system in 1990, but a little less than 1km is accessible to visitors. Coursing through the cave at all times of year is an offshoot from the Con River, which, during the rainy season, can completely submerge the entrance. There are stalagmites and stalactites and those with a powerful torch can pick out the form of every manner of ghoul, god and beast in the rocks. This is a wet cave even in the dry season, and the only way to explore the cave is by riverboat from the river landing stage in Phong Nha village. You'll explore most of the cave from the river, but a small section near the entrance is walkable. Previously, the cave was illuminated in hues of purple and green, lending a Disney-ish feel to the surroundings, but the lighting system was overhauled in recent years to highlight the integrity of the rock formations. The cave formed part of the Hồ Chí Minh Trail (page 275) and a rocket was shot into the cave during the American War. If you look closely, you can make out the damage from the attack. Note that you'll have to pay for the boat as well as the entrance fee. This is charged per boat, not per person, so if there aren't many of you, try to find another group to share with.

✱ **Botanic Garden** (f phongnha.botanic.garden; ⏲ 07.30–16.00 Mon–Sat, 09.00–16.00 Sun; 40,000VND/free adult/child) This is not a botanical garden, but a patch of the national park that has been cordoned off for do-it-yourself hiking trails. There are 30-minute, 90-minute and 3-hour trails to choose from (these times are over-estimations). The trails, which are well marked and easy to follow, include a visit to a waterfall where you can swim.

Ozo Park Quảng Bình (Đông Giang village; w ozoparkquangbinh.com) This is an adventure park with zip lines, kayaking, rope ladders and other obstacle course-type activities. They also serve decent local food.

Eight Ladies Cave (ĐT20) This cave got its name from a tragedy during the American War, when eight young female volunteers and a driver who were clearing the Hồ Chí Minh Trail (page 275) were trapped inside after a bomb caused a landslide that sealed the entrance. Despite rescue efforts, there were no survivors. The site has been transformed into a memorial and shrine to honour their memory; it has become a pilgrimage site for domestic tourists. The Eight Ladies Cave is well signposted on the ĐT562.

✷ **Paradise Cave** (Km16, Hồ Chí Minh Rd; **w** dongthienduong.com; 🕘 07.00–16.00 daily; 250,000VND/free adult/child) This gigantic cave was surveyed in 2005, when it was discovered that it stretched for 31km. Only the first kilometre, however, is accessible to visitors. Coursing through the cave are some of the most spectacular and bizarre-looking stalagmites and stalactites in the area. Visitors explore the formations on a raised wooden walkway, next to which the formations are strategically lit like exhibits in a museum. Some chambers reach up to 100m high and 150m wide. Like Phong Nha Cave, this natural weapons-storage facility also formed part of the Hồ Chí Minh Trail (page 275). Paradise Cave offers a dry, easily accessible experience compared with other caves in the park.

Dark Cave (Hồ Chí Minh Rd; 🕘 08.00–18.00 daily; 80,000VND/free adult/child) Another of the caves first explored by British cavers in the early 1990s, Dark Cave is over 5km in length and reaches heights of around 80m. As the name suggests, this cave lacks natural light so those who venture in will do so with headlamps, which are provided. A new, fun way to reach the cave entrance is to ride a zip line from a high tower into the water before swimming in.

Nước Mọoc (Hồ Chí Minh Rd; 🕘 08.00–16.00 daily; 80,000VND/free adult/child) Here, a pretty trail through woodland leads down to gushing rapids, which are formed by water emerging in a large torrent from an unknown underground source. A series of wooden walkways leads across the rapids to a pleasant spot where it's possible to take a dip – you'll be forced to wear a life jacket and, given the current a few feet away from the swimming area, this is no bad thing.

The adventure caves Some bemoan the fact that the following caves here can only be visited on a tour with a guide, but remember that this provides employment in one of Vietnam's poorest provinces and helps conservation efforts. (These caves are not marked on our map as you cannot visit them independently.) Visiting all the caves that follow would involve several repeat visits and would cost many thousands of dollars. As your time is likely to be limited, select the caves that appeal the most based on your budget and the number of days you have available. Prices are clearly labelled on the corresponding tour company website. Each year undiscovered caves are being found and new tours are being put together; this list is not exhaustive.

✷ Tú Làn cave system

Duration: One to four days. Company: Oxalis Adventure

The Tú Làn cave system offers a diverse array of caves and countryside that featured in the 2017 blockbuster *Kong: Skull Island*. Popular with adventurers, journeying through the system involves walking, crawling, wading and swimming through both wet and dry caves. Dividing the caves are jungle-fringed outdoor rock pools, some of which house campsites. The Tú Làn cave system offers the most diverse range of experiences, with one-, two-, three- and four-day experiences, as well as kid-friendly tours. As it is located outside Phong Nha-Kẻ Bàng National Park, the tours here are good value for money as the national park can't charge the tour companies entrance fees. This system is closer to Tân Hoá village than Phong Nha village.

Hang Tiên

Duration: One to three days. Company: Oxalis Adventure

The twin caves of Hang Tiên ('Fairy Caves'), technically part of the Tú Làn cave system, have enormous chambers that are more befitting a Tolkienian monster than a diminutive, winged creature. The larger Hang Tiên is estimated to be 2.3 million cubic metres. Reaching the caves involves trekking through dense jungle and navigating rugged terrain. Inside, you'll discover clusters of sodden stalactites dripping from the ceiling like freshly watered pot plants. Like the rest of the Tú Làn cave system, the caves offer a varied set of experiences from one to three days. Hang Tiên is also located outside Phong Nha-Kẻ Bàng National Park, closer to Tân Hóa village than Phong Nha village.

Hang Va

Duration: Two days. Company: Oxalis Adventure

Hang Va's highlight is a phalanx of unusual, upside-down ice-cream-cone-shaped stalagmites emerging from emerald waters and creating an ethereal scene that featured in BBC's *Planet Earth III*. Reaching Hang Va is part of the adventure, as you trek through dense jungle, mount razor-sharp rocks, and descend 15m into the cave's entrance. From here you'll wade through subterranean rivers and tiptoe around terraced rock pools. Visit Hang Va between December and March when the pools are at their fullest, though the water can be chilly early on in the year. Tours to Hang Va are combined with Hang Nước Nứt.

Hang Nước Nứt

Duration: Two days. Company: Oxalis Adventure

Hang Nước Nứt's ceiling is adorned with razor-sharp stalactites and bulging columns that formed over 2 million years. The journey to the cave involves trekking through lush jungle before descending into complete darkness, where only the light from a headtorch guides the way. Inside, you'll squeeze through tight river passages and wade through underground pools, linking slender canyons with wide chambers. Sunbeams peek through the roof at times, illuminating the path. It was once possible to visit Hang Nước Nứt on its own, but at the time of research it featured on tours together with Hang Va.

Hang Én

Duration: Two days. Company: Oxalis Adventure

Hang Én (Swift Cave, often wrongly translated as Swallow Cave) is named after the speedy winged flocks that have made nests in the nooks in the cave ceiling. Surveyed in 1994, Hang Én has featured in a live broadcast from ABC News and in the disappointing 2015 Hollywood film *Pan: The Neverland*. In 2023 the cave featured in BBC's *Planet Earth III*, alongside Hang Sơn Đoòng and Hang Va. Located in the core zone of the national park, Hang Én is perhaps the third largest cave in the world, and is accessed by a relatively light jungle trek that traverses rivers and streams and passes through one of the few villages within the national park boundaries. The campsite perches on a sandy beach close to the cave entrance. Hang Én is included in the Hang Sơn Đoòng caving experience.

Tiger Cave

Duration: Three days. Company: Jungle Boss

So-called because the stalactites and stalagmites resemble tiger claws, the 1.6km-long Tiger Cave also boasts dense foliage that has grown in large crevices and a

300m-long underground river that you'll swim through if water levels are deemed safe enough. Like other caves in the park, you'll need to bushwhack through rough jungled terrain to get here. The upper passage of Tiger Cave will have you on your hands and knees as you scramble over boulders. Tours to Tiger Cave usually include tours to Hang Pygmy and Hang Over.

✷ Hang Pygmy

Duration: Two days. Company: Jungle Boss

Hang Pygmy is as long as a football pitch at its widest point, making it perhaps the world's fourth-largest cave by cross-section. Getting to the cave can be intense, with a jungle trek that navigates steep ascents and descents and a long period of darkness in Hang Over. The journey through Hang Pygmy involves a precarious, rope-assisted climb that will test your balance and courage. Within the cave are hundreds of large dead trees that have been ripped up by typhoons and deposited in its vast underground chamber. Once out the other side, you can gaze at the cave's massive entrance, which appears like a gaping mouth of a primordial being frozen in time. Visiting Hang Pygmy is one of the more demanding caving experiences.

Hang Over

Duration: Two to three days. Company: Jungle Boss

Hang Over is a pitch-black 3.5km-long dry passage. The cave was in fact once connected to Hang Pygmy until a collapse millions of years ago cleaved them in two. Navigating Hang Over is part of the adventure, as you plod through its dark corridors without any natural light. Never stray too far from your guide. The journey demands hours spent in the cave before emerging back into daylight, which can be disorientating. At the time of research, it was not possible to visit Hang Over on its own; it's included in tours to Hang Pygmy and Tiger Cave.

Kong Collapse

Duration: Three or five days. Company: Jungle Boss

The Kong Collapse is not a cave but a sinkhole, perhaps one of the largest on the planet. At the time of research the collapse was included in two Jungle Boss tours. The longer one (five days) includes a 100m-high abseil. This is the most thrilling moment of the tours; the rest of the time is spent exploring Tiger Cave, Pygmy Cave and Hang Over.

Hang Ba

Duration: Four days. Company: Oxalis Adventure

Hang Ba is one of six caves in close proximity, the other five being Đại Cáo, Maze, Vĩnh Đại, Light and Circle caves. Far from civilisation, it offers the best chance to view the night sky. The cave sits within the core zone of Phong Nha-Kẻ Bàng National Park, and is relatively remote and untouched, making wildlife here more abundant. The animals are very retiring, but the guides will be able to point the tracks and markings they've left behind. This educational tour was put together with help from UNESCO and the IUCN.

✷ Hang Sơn Đoòng

Duration: Four days. Company: Oxalis Adventure

The magnum opus of Vietnamese caves is hard to conceptualise without making crude size comparisons. Deep within it are stalagmites that would dwarf London's Westminster Abbey. The biggest chamber is higher than the Pyramid of Giza is tall. St Peter's Cathedral in the Vatican could pass through the larger of the two ceiling collapses. These ceiling collapses, called dolines, probably happened around 300,000 years ago, and beneath them flourish jungles with vegetation that differs from that on the surface. The cave is thought to be around 2.5 million years old and animals, including primates and flying foxes, appear to come and go. The cave was likely first discovered in the 1990s, but it wasn't surveyed until 2009. The trek to and through Hang Sơn Đoòng is one of the world's great outdoor adventures, but be prepared to shell out for the experience and book up to a year in advance. The tour includes trekking through Hang Én (page 242), camping under the two ceiling collapses (two nights are spent in the cave) and scaling a 90m-high calcite wall.

HUẾ AND AROUND

Thừa Thiên Huế Province is where the Nguyễn Dynasty authorised the establishment of the new Imperial capital of Vietnam in 1802. Covering an area of 5,009km^2, it consists of one city, two towns and six rural districts, with a total population of more than a million. The province is crisscrossed by numerous waterways, some of which feed the Perfume River (Sông Hương), the most famous of them all, named because of the luxuriant growth of fragrant shrubs near its source. The river skirts rolling hills before running through **Huế**, the cultural, political and religious centre of the province. Most of the province's pagodas are here, along with neatly kept gardens and myriad sites of great historical interest. Approaching from the south over the Hải Vân pass and around various lagoons, it is difficult to imagine that this beauty spot was more than once the site of a tragic seesaw struggle between nations.

With a shoreline over 1,000km long, Thừa Thiên Huế is a tremendous area for breeding and catching shrimps, crabs, squid and fish. Its large saltwater lagoons occur where rivers running off the Trường Sơn Mountains meet the sea, forming the Thuận An, Lăng Cô and Tư Hiền estuaries. These are all areas of outstanding natural beauty. The substrate here is ideal for farming mussels, which are harvested in massive quantities. Linking the province with Đà Nẵng is one of Vietnam's best kept secrets: **Bạch Mã National Park**, a veritable Pandora's box of rare plant and animal species.

Bordering Laos, the district of **A Lưới**, which stretches the entire length of the province, is predominantly virgin forest and areas set aside for commercial timber production and farming. This is traditionally home to more than a handful of the province's ethnolinguistic groups, including the Bru Van Kieu, Co Tu and Ta Oi. Thừa Thiên Huế is also the jumping-off point to visit the **DMZ**, one of Vietnam's most important collections of war sites.

The city of Huế sits ringed by forested hills, bordered by bulging rice fields and sliced in two by the meandering Perfume River, but the city's intrigue goes beyond its evocative natural setting. Despite its status as a cultural and religious hub, many visitors skim over Vietnam's former imperial capital, choosing instead to devote more days to Đà Nẵng's beaches and Hội An's Old Town. This is a mistake. Linger longer than the masses and you'll discover that Huế is a laid-back city of shady streets, eye-catching heritage architecture and proud, curious inhabitants. Đà Lạt may be the country's city of love, but it's hard to name a more romantic Vietnamese city than Huế.

Huế was a riverside fiefdom until 1802, when Emperor Gia Long established the capital here after vanquishing rival claimants to the throne. To impress his imperial authority upon the nation, Gia Long began construction of an immense walled fortress on the banks of the Perfume River, and this citadel still dominates the northern half of the city. Huế's citadel suffered terribly during the war, but a comprehensive rebuilding effort has helped make it one of Southeast Asia's finest walled cities. You could spend days cycling or strolling around within these walls, circling lotus ponds, stumbling upon ruins and escaping the heat (or rain) in beer gardens and cafés.

In addition to the addictive, unhurried café and drinking culture, Huế is one of Asia's culinary behemoths. Some of Vietnam's world-famous dishes – including *bún bò Huế* (beef noodle soup) – hail from here. Vegans and vegetarians will rejoice at the quantity and quality of meatless restaurants, a reflection of the city's Buddhist inclination. Other local specialities include crispy pancakes, various spring roll interpretations and delicate royal savoury cakes, a remnant of the city's past.

Huế's dynastic history is everywhere. Even outside the citadel walls, you'll find opulent palaces, courtly garden houses, extravagant colonial mansions and, perhaps most compelling of all, a set of UNESCO-inscribed monarchic tombs that speckle the hills. The city's conservative and conservationist policies, often bemoaned by the business community, have resulted in a place that lacks the pizazz of Vietnam's more dynamic cities, but instead a landscape where heritage is celebrated and the country's building boom is restrained. During your time here, be sure to spend a morning or afternoon by the sweeping Perfume River – it might be the only urban body of water in Vietnam that is dominated by parks and flower gardens rather than apartment blocks and office buildings.

There are many reasons why tourism hasn't taken off in Huế as it has done elsewhere in the country, but one of them is probably weather. The international high season starts in October, just when the city is pummelled by typhoons. Like the rest of the subregion, winters are cold and damp, and summers brutally hot, when Huế is 'hotter than dragon's breath', a diplomat once remarked. This leaves just three months when the city is pleasant: March, April and September. Huế is definitely worth visiting outside these months, but prepare – both physically and mentally – for extreme heat, rain and damp, depending on the season.

HISTORY Although almost nothing remains, for many centuries the area now known as Huế was a city of reasonable importance during the reign of Champa (page 12). It was practically razed several times in the 5th and 7th centuries by the Chinese rulers that controlled Northern Vietnam. After the Vietnamese finally expelled the Chinese in the 10th century, they immediately attempted to take the area from the Champa, but it didn't become the proud possession of the Nguyễn lords until the 16th century. Following this annexation, the city was known as Phú Xuân.

Another period of long, intense fighting between the Nguyễn and the Trịnh, two arch-rival dynasties, saw the city fall to the latter in 1775. Trịnh control of the area was short-lived, however, as Nguyễn Ánh took back the city in 1802, with considerable financial backing from France. He proclaimed himself Emperor Gia Long and established the new capital of reunited Vietnam here. Gia Long remains a complicated character for whom the government struggles to frame a consistent narrative (page 266). On the one hand, he was a cruel leader and his circumstances left him open to French influence and manipulation. On the other, Gia Long established the first court to control the land from Yunnan (southern China) southwards to the Gulf of Siam. Gia Long coined the name Việt Nam and is surely one of Vietnam's founding fathers. Although the dynasty's power waned over time, Gia Long's descendants exercised considerable control and influence over Vietnam until 1945.

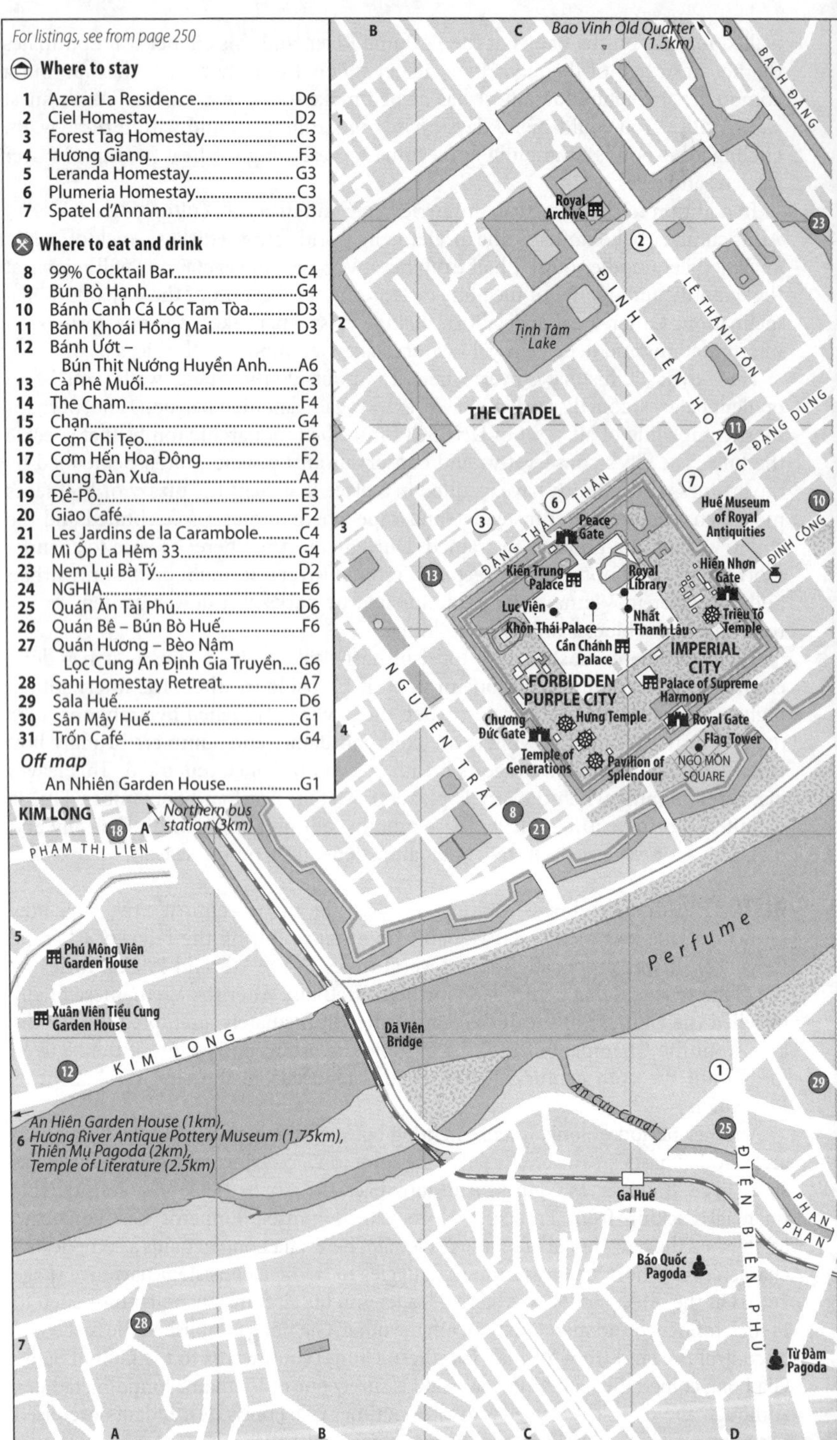
For listings, see from page 250
Where to stay
1 Azerai La Residence D6
2 Ciel Homestay D2
3 Forest Tag Homestay C3
4 Hương Giang F3
5 Leranda Homestay G3
6 Plumeria Homestay C3
7 Spatel d'Annam D3
Where to eat and drink
8 99% Cocktail Bar C4
9 Bún Bò Hạnh G4
10 Bánh Canh Cá Lóc Tam Tòa D3
11 Bánh Khoái Hồng Mai D3
12 Bánh Ướt – Bún Thịt Nướng Huyền Anh A6
13 Cà Phê Muối C3
14 The Cham F4
15 Chạn G4
16 Cơm Chị Tẹo F6
17 Cơm Hến Hoa Đông F2
18 Cung Đàn Xưa A4
19 Để-Pô E3
20 Giao Café F2
21 Les Jardins de la Carambole C4
22 Mì Ốp La Hẻm 33 G4
23 Nem Lụi Bà Tý D2
24 NGHIA E6
25 Quán Ăn Tài Phú D6
26 Quán Bê – Bún Bò Huế F6
27 Quán Hương – Bèo Nậm Lọc Cung An Định Gia Truyền G6
28 Sahi Homestay Retreat A7
29 Sala Huế D6
30 Sân Mây Huế G1
31 Trốn Café G4
Off map
An Nhiên Garden House G1
Bao Vinh Old Quarter (1.5km)
BẠCH ĐẰNG
Royal Archive
Tịnh Tâm Lake
ĐINH TIÊN HOÀNG
LÊ THÁNH TÔN
THE CITADEL
ĐẶNG DUNG
ĐẶNG THÁI THÂN
Peace Gate
Huế Museum of Royal Antiquities
ĐINH CÔNG
Kiến Trung Palace
Royal Library
Hiển Nhơn Gate
Lục Viện
Khôn Thái Palace
Nhất Thanh Lâu
Triệu Tổ Temple
Cần Chánh Palace
IMPERIAL CITY
FORBIDDEN PURPLE CITY
Palace of Supreme Harmony
NGUYỄN TRÃI
Chương Đức Gate
Hưng Temple
Royal Gate
Flag Tower
Temple of Generations
Pavilion of Splendour
NGỌ MÔN SQUARE
KIM LONG
Northern bus station (3km)
PHẠM THỊ LIÊN
Phú Mộng Viên Garden House
Xuân Viên Tiểu Cung Garden House
Perfume
Dã Viên Bridge
KIM LONG
An Cựu Canal
An Hiên Garden House (1km),
Hương River Antique Pottery Museum (1.75km),
Thiên Mụ Pagoda (2km),
Temple of Literature (2.5km)
Ga Huế
ĐIỆN BIÊN PHỦ
PHAN
Báo Quốc Pagoda
Từ Đàm Pagoda

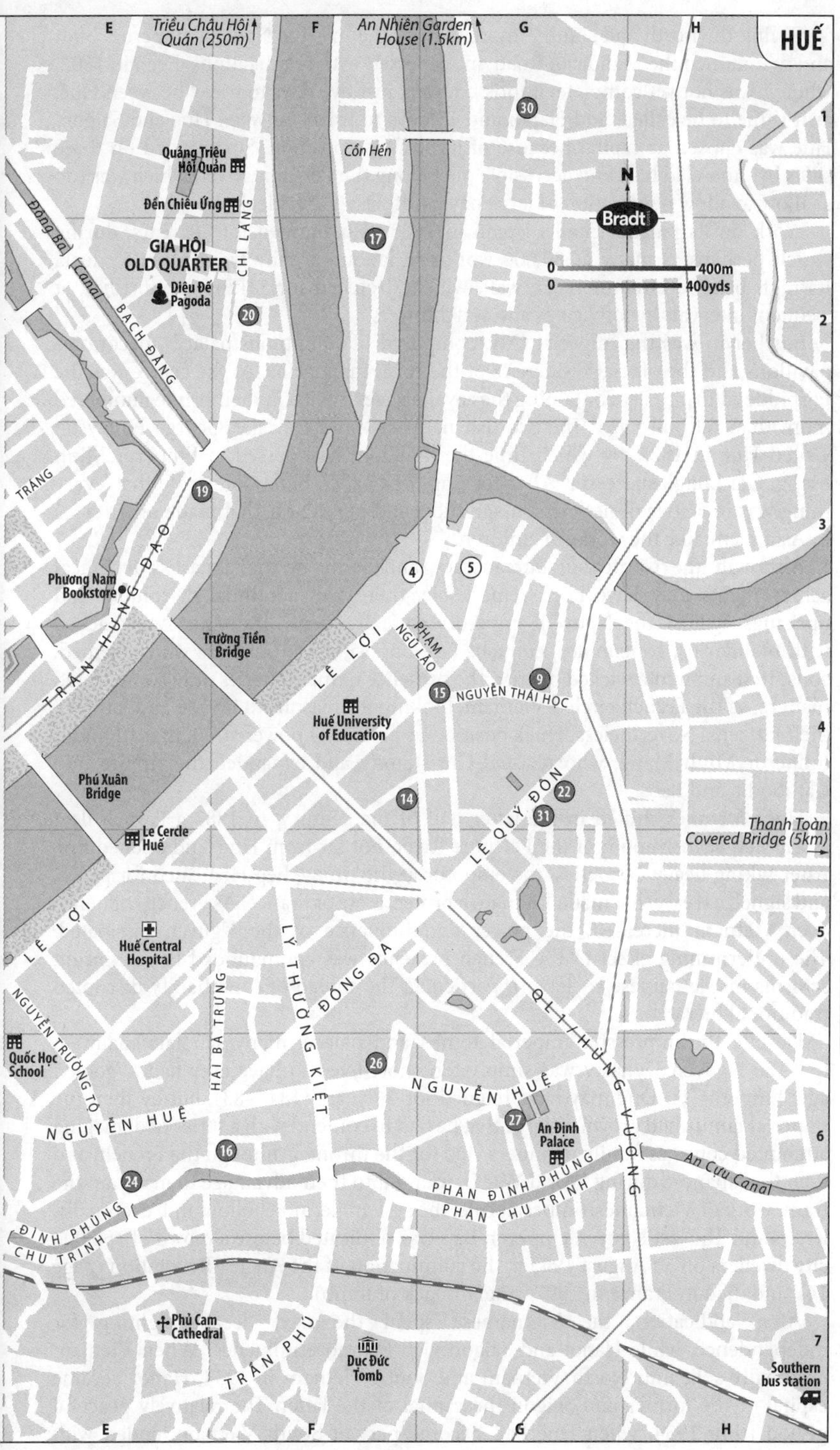
HUẾ
Triều Châu Hội Quán (250m)
An Nhiên Garden House (1.5km)
Cồn Hến
Quảng Triệu Hội Quán
Đền Chiêu Ứng
GIA HỘI OLD QUARTER
Diệu Đế Pagoda
Đông Ba Canal
BẠCH ĐẰNG
CHI LĂNG
0 400m
0 400yds
Bradt
N
TRẦN HƯNG ĐẠO
Phương Nam Bookstore
Trường Tiền Bridge
LÊ LỢI
PHẠM NGŨ LÃO
NGUYỄN THÁI HỌC
Huế University of Education
Phú Xuân Bridge
Le Cercle Huế
LÊ QUÝ ĐÔN
Thanh Toàn Covered Bridge (5km)
Huế Central Hospital
LÝ THƯỜNG KIỆT
ĐỐNG ĐA
HAI BÀ TRƯNG
QL1/HÙNG VƯƠNG
NGUYỄN TRƯỜNG TỘ
Quốc Học School
NGUYỄN HUỆ
An Định Palace
An Cựu Canal
PHAN ĐÌNH PHÙNG
PHAN CHU TRINH
ĐÌNH PHÙNG
CHU TRINH
Phủ Cam Cathedral
TRẦN PHÚ
Dục Đức Tomb
Southern bus station

To link the north and south – more than 1,500km – the Nguyễn emperors built and maintained the Mandarin Road, interspersed with relay stations. Even in 1802, when it was not yet complete, it took couriers just five days to travel between Huế, as it came to be called, and Hanoi and 13 days to travel between Huế and Saigon. Huế was chosen as capital because of its strategic position. Surrounded on three sides by pine-clad hills and accessible only along the Perfume River, which was too shallow to allow penetration of large naval flotillas, it was ideal.

Work on its palatial citadel began in 1805. It continued for 20 years, during which perhaps as many as 80,000 workmen laboured daily from dawn to dusk. Its high bricked circumference wall, which stretched for 11km, was fortified at frequent intervals by lofty gates and watchtowers.

Further in was the Imperial City, composed of sumptuous palaces, decorative pavilions and the official residences of the royal mandarins. At the centre was the Forbidden Purple City containing the royal palaces, which in their prime numbered more than 60 buildings. The Scottish naturalist and traveller George Finlayson visited Huế in 1822, by which time the kingdom had passed to Emperor Minh Mạng, Gia Long's successor. After touring the citadel, Finlayson wrote that 'every thing was in a style of neatness, magnitude, and perfection' that made other cities in Asia seem 'like the works of children'.

Although the Confucian bureaucracy and some of the dynasty's technical achievements may have been remarkable, there was continual discontent and uprisings against the Nguyễn emperors were frequent. The court was packed with mandarins, concubines, eunuchs (see opposite) and scholars who schemed, conspired and wrote wicked poetry. The presence of missionaries only complicated matters, as the French circled Vietnam, looking for reasons to invade and 'protect' their citizens. Nevertheless, Huế's position as an axis of power strengthened under Emperor Minh Mạng, who resisted Christianity and expanded the empire into Cambodia and Laos.

Huế's fortunes shifted in the latter half of the century. In 1883 a French fleet assembled at the mouth of the Perfume River, not far from Huế, and opened fire. After taking heavy casualties, the emperor at the time, Hiệp Hòa, sued for peace, and signed a treaty that made Vietnam a protectorate of France. As French influence over Vietnam increased, the power and influence of the Nguyễn dissipated. The undermining effect of the French presence was compounded by significant schisms in Vietnamese society. In particular, the spread of Christianity disrupted traditional hierarchies.

Despite the impressive imperial tombs and palace, many scholars maintain that the Nguyễn Dynasty was simply too short-lived to have ever had a 'golden age'. Emperor Tự Đức may have reigned for 36 years (1847–83), but by then the imperial family had grown so large that he had to contend with a series of damaging attempted coups as family members vied for the throne. Although the French, and then the Japanese during World War II, found it to their advantage to maintain the framework of Vietnamese imperial rule, the system became hollow and, eventually, irrelevant. The last Nguyễn emperor, Bảo Đại, abdicated before a crowd of 150,000 city dwellers on 30 August 1945 at the culmination of the August Revolution (page 14), and died in France in 1997 (note his lack of tomb).

After abdication, the Vietnamese spent the next decade fighting for independence, while Hanoi and Saigon vied for more influence. When Vietnam eventually split into North Vietnam and South Vietnam in 1954, Hanoi became capital of the former and Saigon the capital of the latter. The relatively peaceful period from 1954, when Huế had become part of South Vietnam, ended with anti-Buddhist propaganda sparking Buddhist demonstrations. Visitors to the Thiên Mụ Pagoda (page 263) can see the car that took Quảng Đức, a senior monk, to Saigon, where he set fire to himself on 11 June 1963 (page 472), to demonstrate dissent against the Ngô Đình Diệm regime. Other Buddhist protest suicides followed in Huế and throughout the country. In 1966 the city was rocked by violent protests against the Saigon military junta.

Early in 1968, the Imperial City suffered substantial damage during the Tết Offensive, when Việt Cộng soldiers holed up in the citadel for 25 days. The bombardment that ensued, as US troops attempted to root them out with napalm, phosphorous bombs and artillery, caused extensive damage to the monuments. It was the South Vietnamese air force that finally flattened what remained of the Forbidden Purple City. As well as destroying much of the city's architectural heritage, the gruesome raids added another 10,000 bodies to the 3,000 already killed in the city by the North Vietnam Army (NVA).

Peace didn't arrive until March 1975, when the Việt Cộng finally took the city. This was an important symbolic piece of Vietnam's reunification, even though the city had lost much of its former glory, and a flag proclaiming '*Quyết chiến, quyết thắng*' ('Determined to fight, determined to win') was raised in what remained of the citadel. Since these dramatic events, Huế has been consistently eclipsed by other towns and cities in Vietnam. Hanoi, already the political capital, reestablished itself as the cultural capital. Đà Nẵng, just 100km southeast of Huế,

THE VARYS OF VIETNAM: LÊ VĂN DUYỆT THE EUNUCH

Lê Văn Duyệt was instrumental in Nguyễn Ánh's successful retaking of Vietnam. A eunuch from infancy, Lê was a talented military strategist and became a trusted adviser to the future emperor. To bolster the army and his influence, Lê simultaneously defended European missionaries and courted French military aid, which ensured an extraordinary naval victory over Nguyễn Ánh's enemies in 1801 that ultimately won him the war.

Eunuchs became key members of the Nguyễn Dynasty court in Huế. They were the only men allowed inside the Purple Forbidden City serving the Son of Heaven, the emperor, alongside his wives and concubines. Eunuchs became quite powerful and would play off the concubines against one another. The castrated men, who wore green and red floral gowns with flat, oval hats, arranged the emperor's nighttime activities and would be bribed by the concubines who wanted to be chosen for that night's sexual adventure.

Lê Văn Duyệt outlived Nguyễn Ánh (who died Emperor Gia Long), but continued to advise his successor, Minh Mạng, though the relationship was strained. Minh Mạng was suspicious of European encroachment on Vietnam and tried to limit French missionary practices, but Lê, perhaps seeing these Christians as a way to access advanced military technology, continued to defend them.

When Lê died in 1832, Minh Mạng began imprisoning and banishing missionaries from Vietnam. He also destroyed Lê's grave, placing a plaque over the ruins that read 'Here lies the eunuch who resisted the law'. In 1836 Emperor Minh Mạng limited the powers of eunuchs so they would not rise to the position of mandarin or become too powerful. The employment of eunuchs was abolished in 1914 by Emperor Duy Tân, who reigned between 1907 and 1916.

soon became Central Vietnam's industrial powerhouse. When tourism took off in the 2000s, Hội An received the bulk of the attention. This overshadowing still exists today. In 2025, the whole of Thừa Thiên Huế Province was elevated to municipality status, granting it the same autonomy as Hải Phòng, Đà Nẵng and Cần Thơ.

GETTING THERE AND AWAY Huế **train** station [246 D6] (2 Bùi Thị Xuân) is central, about 2.5km to both the walking street tourist area and the citadel. It is a convenient overnight distance from Hanoi (16hrs), Ninh Bình (13hrs) and Vinh (8hrs). The extraordinary journey (see opposite) to Đà Nẵng takes 2½ hours. It takes around 20 hours to get to Hồ Chí Minh City.

Huế has a northern **bus** station [246 A4] (Bến Xe Phía Bắc Huế, 132 Lý Thái Tổ; **w** benxehue.vn) and a southern bus station [247 H7] (Bến Xe Phía Nam Huế, 57 An Dương Vương; **w** benxehue.vn) and both are 4km from the centre. Fortunately, though, most bus companies will drop off/pick up somewhere more central, usually near the Perfume River. There are several buses daily heading north to Đồng Hới (4hrs), Phong Nha (4½hrs), Vinh (8hrs), Ninh Bình (11hrs) and Hanoi (13hrs); and south to Đà Nẵng (2hrs), Hội An (2½hrs), Quảng Ngãi (4hrs), Quý Nhơn (8hrs), Kon Tum (10hrs) and Hồ Chí Minh City (18hrs).

Huế is served by **Phú Bài International Airport** [map, page 226] (Zone 8, Phú Bài Ward; **w** vietnamairport.vn), which is not international; there are a couple of flights a day both to Hanoi and Hồ Chí Minh City.

GETTING AROUND Huế is not small enough for visitors to tackle on foot, so you'll need a bicycle, motorbike or taxis to move around. Bicycle is preferred as the streets are relatively orderly, and within the city limits at least there are few inclines. Rent or borrow these at your accommodation. It's possible to cycle to the further-flung sights like the tombs, but bear in mind that these neighbourhoods have hills. If you're proficient on a motorbike, exploring Huế's countryside would be a good reason to rent one.

WHERE TO STAY While most hotels are clustered around Phạm Ngũ Lão Street, the neighbourhoods along the river, within the city walls and out in the countryside make more interesting bases.

Forest Tag Homestay [246 C3] 26 Thanh Hương; **f** foresttaghomestayhue. Tucked down an alleyway in a local neighbourhood. Most guests seem to be Vietnamese & language may cause some issues, but the family is friendly & welcoming. **$**

Plumeria Homestay [246 C3] 3/34 Đặng Thái Thân; **f** plumeriahomestayhue. Cheap,

GETTING TO LAOS FROM HUẾ

The border crossing from Huế to Laos is one of the more popular, especially as the border gate on the Laos side issues visas on arrival. Buses to Savannahkhet on the Thai border leave daily and pass through the Lao Bảo border crossing [map, page 226] (Lao Bảo, Hướng Hóa) in Quảng Trị Province. They are easy to book online or through your accommodation. Some buses originate in Đà Nẵng. Though the distance is short, the journey will take a day, including time spent at immigration, where the officers may ask for bribes to expedite the process.

HUẾ TO ĐÀ NẴNG BY TRAIN

The train journey from Huế to Đà Nẵng, which traverses the Hải Vân Pass (page 294), is regarded as not just one of the most scenic in Vietnam, but in the world. 'The drizzle, so interminable in the former Royal Capital, gave way to bright sunshine and warmth,' writes Paul Theroux, in his 1975 book *The Great Railway Bazaar*. 'Of all the places the railway had taken me since London, this was the loveliest. We were at the fringes of a bay that was green and sparkling in bright sunlight. Beyond the leaping jade plates of the sea was an overhang of cliffs and the sight of a valley so large it contained sun, smoke, rain, and cloud – all at once.'

family-run guesthouse in an ideal location tucked behind the Imperial City & in an attractive, very local corner of town. **$**

✷ **Ciel Homestay** [246 D2] 137 Lê Thánh Tôn; f Ciel Homestay Huế. Upmarket homestay hotel in beautiful grounds & close to the canals & lakes that make the citadel so special. **$$**

Leranda Homestay [247 G3] 75 Võ Thị Sáu; f. Nestled in the touristy corner of town, but it feels a world apart, with a pretty courtyard & rustically designed rooms. **$$**

De Hué Space [map, page 265] 586E Bùi Thị Xuân; f dehue.space. Gorgeous hotel designed by local firm Studio Voi and in an unusual part of the city that sees few visitors. Rooms give a welcome sense of space and are free from clutter. **$$$**

Hương Giang [247 F3] 51 Lê Lợi; w huonggianghotel.com.vn. Art Deco hotel with a history that, like La Residence, played a role in the Tết Offensive (page 249). Now a solid, & stylish, mid-range option overlooking the river &, for better or worse, within walking distance of Huế's tourist hub. **$$$**

Pilgrimage Village [map, page 265] 130 Minh Mạng; w pilgrimagevillage.com. Expansive & atmospheric hotel engulfed in jungle, with a variety of private villas & a broad pool. The hotel isn't new & looks a little tired, but it still oozes charm. In between the tombs & the city, you'll need transport to get to either. **$$$**

Spatel d'Annam Hotel [246 D3] 57 Đặng Dung; w spatel-annam.com. Absurdly named (Spa + hotel = Spatel, apparently) but excellently located garden hotel overlooking a corner of the Imperial City. This is a very local part of the city, close to street food, cafés, parks & lakes. **$$$**

aNhill Boutique [map, page 265] Near Khải Định Tomb; w anhillvietnam.com. Far from the city centre but close to the tombs, this modern hotel is set in a green garden with pool. **$$$$**

✷ **Azerai La Residence** [246 D6] 5 Lê Lợi; w azerai.com/resorts/azerai-la-residence-hue. 1930s Art Deco tour de force, with large, breezy pool. Some rooms, including the opulent top-floor Resident Suite, are nestled in the original residence, though the more comfortable rooms are in the 2 modern wings. **$$$$**

WHERE TO EAT AND DRINK

Restaurants and street food

Bánh Canh Cá Lóc Tam Tòa [246 D3] 45 Đinh Công Tráng; ⌚ 14.00–22.00 daily. This spot serves thick tapioca noodles with fish in a hearty soup flavoured with black pepper. Boiled quail eggs & fermented sausage wrapped in banana leaf are served on the side. These days, most places buy in their noodles, but this place still makes them fresh by rolling out the dough, wrapping it around a cylinder & slicing the noodles straight into the pot. **$**

✷ **Bánh Ướt – Bún Thịt Nướng Huyền Anh** [246 A6] 50 Kim Long; ⌚ 08.00–19.00 (or when they run out) daily. This modest eatery is wildly popular with Huế locals wishing to flaunt their city's cuisine to visiting friends & family. They only serve 2 dishes: *bánh ướt* & *bún thịt nướng*. Go for the former; the latter is better elsewhere. Wash the meal down with *trà đá* (iced green tea) or local Huda beer. **$**

Bún Bò Hạnh [247 G4] Kiệt 56 Nguyễn Công Trứ; ⌚ 05.30–11.00 daily. Popular local street-food spot that is just a few steps from Huế's tourist

HUẾ'S SPECIALITY DISHES

The places at which to try these dishes are listed from page 251.

BÚN BÒ HUẾ Huế's most successful culinary export is *bún bò Huế*, which has been adapted up and down the country. Huế people will tell you that despite the innovations of others, it's still best here, and they're right. This rich noodle soup has a pork- and beef-bone base enhanced with lemongrass and chilli and topped with various beef cuts. Greens are served on the side and dunked. It's usually eaten for breakfast, but some places open in the afternoon. Try it at **Bún Bò Hạnh** and **Quán Bê – Bún Bò Huế**.

BÁNH HUẾ (BÁNH LỌC, BÁNH NẬM, BÁNH RAM ÍT, BÁNH BÈO) Huế's royal savoury cakes, apparently developed to impress the Nguyễn kings, are now available to the masses. These four, similar-tasting dumpling-like cakes are usually served in the same restaurants. They are a combination of rice or tapioca flour, pork and shrimp. Some are wrapped in a banana leaf and steamed. Try it at **Quán Hương – Bèo Nậm Lọc Cung An Định Gia Truyền**.

BÁNH MÌ ỐP LA BÒ Huế's most famous version of the *bánh mì* baguette is not sliced open and packed with cured meat and pickles, but dipped in a plate of fried egg, grilled beef and a sauce. It is only served for breakfast. Try it at **Mì Ốp la Hẻm 33**.

BÁNH BAO *Bánh bao* actually started in China and it is found across Vietnam, but Huế is one of the few places that still has traditional *bánh bao* makers and sellers that flog the fluffy minced pork bun from their bicycles. Listen carefully in the evening and you might hear their portable speaker blaring '*Bánh bao nóng; bánh bao nóng đây!*', which means 'hot *bánh bao*; hot *bánh bao* here!'

BÁNH CANH A noodle soup but made with thick tapioca noodles and usually served with fish (*cá*) or crab (*cua*). The soup tends to be thick and rich, and some have likened the noodles to Japanese udon. Try it at **Bánh Canh Cá Lóc Tam Tòa**.

BÁNH ƯỚT These are often called *bánh cuốn* by Huế locals, which simply means rolled cakes. Lean pork is grilled with sesame and rolled with mint and other herbs

quarter. No English is spoken, but the family running the joint will do their best to take your order. It's at the southern end of the street, close to Nguyễn Thái Học. $

Cơm Hến Hoa Đông [247 F2] 64/7 Ứng Bình; ⌚ 07.00–21.30 daily. One of the busier & more popular spots to try *bún hến* or *cơm hến* on Cồn Hến, the small island where they farm the shellfish. $

Quán Bê – Bún Bò Huế [247 F6] 77 Nguyễn Huệ; f bunbohueobenguyenhue; ⌚ 06.00–09.00 daily. Another *bún bò* option but a little further from where tourists tend to stay. The crab cakes here are especially good; if that's what you want then order '*bò cua*'. $

✷ **Quán Hương – Bèo Nậm Lọc Cung An Định Gia Truyền** [247 G6] Kiệt 148A Nguyễn Huệ; f banhbeocungandinh; ⌚ 08.00–20.30 daily. One of the many places to go for Huế's savoury royal cakes, *bánh Huế*. You order these per plate & each plate is about half a meal, so try & come in a group. $

Bánh Khoái Hồng Mai [246 D3] 110 Đinh Tiên Hoàng; ⌚ 10.30–20.00 daily. Huế's signature savoury pancakes served with shrimp, pork, beansprouts & a peanut dip. An ideal snack while wandering around the neighbourhoods in the citadel. $$

in wet rice paper, then dipped in a garlic and chilli sweet-and-sour fish sauce dipping sauce. Try it at **Bánh Ướt – Bún Thịt Nướng Huyền Anh**.

BÚN HẾN AND CƠM HẾN Two of Huế's most popular dishes – some locals eat this every day – are *cơm hến* and *bún hến*, which is either wet rice (*cơm*) or noodles (*bún*) topped with baby mussels dragged from the Perfume River. It's totally delicious, but has a reputation for causing a funny tummy. Try it at **Cơm Hến Hoa Đông**.

CÀ PHÊ MUỐI Hanoi has egg coffee; Huế has salt coffee. The flavour is hard to pin down: think coffee with salted caramel. The idea comes from a soppy love story (page 255). Try it at **Cà Phê Muối**.

NEM LỤI Versions of this dish are found throughout Central Vietnam. A pork patty is grilled on a stick and wrapped in dry rice paper with greens, pickles and sour fruit such as green mango and pineapple. What makes it special in Huế is the *nước lèo* dipping sauce, made with liver, peanuts and sesame. Try it at **Quán Ăn Tài Phú**.

BÁNH KHOÁI This is like the better-known *bánh xèo* pancake from Hồ Chí Minh City and the Mekong Delta, but is smaller and crispier. Try it at **Bánh Khoái Hồng Mai**.

BÚN THỊT NƯỚNG While northerners eat *bún chả* (page 94), southerners prefer *bún thịt nướng*: grilled sweet pork, salad, pickles, sweet-and-sour fish sauce and peanut and sesame sauce over vermicelli noodles. Try it at **Nem Lụi Bà Tý** and **Quán Ăn Tài Phú**.

VEGAN FOOD Huế is one of Vietnam's centres of Buddhism, and even some non-Buddhists here will eat only vegan food one or two days a month. Interestingly, vegan food in Vietnam traditionally includes no garlic or onions because it is believed that when consumed raw, they may enrage tempers, and if eaten cooked, they might kindle unwanted sexual desire. Huế has a variety of excellent vegan restaurants, from simple street kitchens to fancy restaurants. In particular, try **Sân Mây Huế**, **Sala Huế** and **An Nhiên Garden House**.

Cơm Chị Tẹo [247 F6] 59 Hai Bà Trưng; ⌚ 10.00–20.30 daily. Very popular lunch spot & you'll have to hover while waiting for a table if you come during the lunch rush. The family speaks no English, but this is no trouble as you can point at what you want. $$

✷ **Mì Ốp La Hẻm 33** [247 G4] Hẻm 33, Lê Quý Đôn; ⌚ 06.00–noon daily. This egg b/fast place began as a small restaurant with little more than a handful of plastic tables, but the head chef's secret sauce has provided the capital for several large-scale expansions. $$

Nem Lụi Bà Tý [246 D2] 81 Đào Duy Từ; f quanbaty; ⌚ 14.00–21.00 daily. Serves *nem lụi* & *bún thịt nướng* as an afternoon snack & light dinner. $$

Quán Ăn Tài Phú [246 D6] 2 Điện Biên Phủ; f; ⌚ 08.30–22.30 daily. They serve a few dishes here, but the 1 to order is *nêm lụi*, pork patties grilled on a stick & wrapped in dry rice paper, with shredded pickled carrot & kohlrabi, green mango, various herbs & a kind of green fig. $$

✷ **Sala Huế** [246 D6] 4 Phan Bội Châu; f Nhà hàng SALA Huế; ⌚ 06.00–noon & 15.00–20.00 daily. Good-value vegan restaurant with a huge menu of salads, tofu dishes & stir-fried vegetables. The tofu is good, but the salads served with pour-over dressings steal the show. $$

Sân Mây Huế [247 G1] 8 Thanh Tịnh; f; ⏲ 07.00–14.00 & 16.00–21.00 daily. Superb vegan food served in an old-style house, with a huge menu of veganised Vietnamese favourites & signature innovations. The stewed dishes & fresh green vegetables are particularly good. $$

An Nhiên Garden House [247 G1] Kiệt 11, Tỉnh Lộ 10A; w annhienvegetarian.com; ⏲ 07.00–21.30 daily. Big villa serving vegan dishes in the downstairs dining room, which spills out into the grassy garden. Try the stuffed tofu & the deep-fried silky tofu. $$$

✷ **Chạn** [247 G4] 1 Nguyễn Thái Học; f chancomnieuhue; ⏲ 10.30–21.30 daily. Elevating Huế's dining scene is this large, upmarket, home-cooking-style restaurant, which proved so popular when they opened a few years ago that they launched another restaurant on the same street. They have a rice plate that includes various Huế dishes you might otherwise only find in home kitchens. The chicken & onion salad here is a meal in itself. $$$

Les Jardins de la Carambole [246 C4] 32 Đặng Trần Côn; f; ⏲ 07.00–23.00 daily. There's really no need to eat any Western food in Huế, but if you must, you won't do much better than Les Jardins, which is French-owned & serves European favourites. $$$

Bars and coffee houses

✷ **99% Cocktail Bar** [246 C4] 34 Nguyễn Trãi; w 99cocktail.vn; ⏲ 19.00–midnight daily. Vietnam's cocktail craze has even arrived in the traditional city of Huế. 99% serves up an experiential evening of expertly crafted cocktails & premium service.

Cà Phê Muối [246 C3] 142 Đặng Thái Thân; ⏲ 06.30–noon & 13.30–22.00 daily. Claims to be the birthplace of salt coffee (see opposite) & still one of the best places in Huế to try it. The café is spread across 2 houses & a big garden down an alleyway near the back of the forbidden city.

The Cham [247 F4] 56 Nguyễn Tri Phương; ⏲ 10.00–midnight daily. Craft beer, whisky & snacks served just outside of the tourist ghetto & staffed by a passionate team of late-night tipple lovers.

Cung Đàn Xưa [246 A4] 24/1 Phạm Thị Liên; f cungdanxuahomestay; ⏲ 06.00–21.30 daily. A Kim Long garden house (page 262) that the owner, a chatty retired teacher, converted into a coffee shop. The garden is rich in fruit trees & small ponds.

✷ **Đề-Pô** [247 E3] 2nd Fl, Đông Ba Market, 2 Trần Hưng Đạo; f depocaphe; ⏲ 06.00–22.00 daily. Perched above Đông Ba Market, you have to squeeze through some market stalls to find this huge, new café Đề-Pô, from the French *dépôt* (depo). Sit by the window for views of the leafy street in front.

Giao Café [247 F2] 118 Chi Lăng; f giao.chilang; ⏲ 06.30–22.00 daily. In Huế's former Chinese Quarter & close to the various temples that once served this community, Giao serves quality coffee & juices in a restored modernist building. Popular with Huế's hipsters.

NGHIA [247 E6] Hse No 19, Room 206 Nguyễn Trường Tộ; f nghiabarcafe; ⏲ 06.30–22.00 daily. Housed in the end apartment of a colonial-era terraced block close to the former home of local music legend Trịnh Công Sơn. You can peer at a war-era gun turret from the broad windows.

Sahi Homestay Retreat [246 A7] 245A Bùi Thị Xuân; w sahihomestay.com; ⏲ 07.00–22.00 daily. A boutique hotel & a coffee shop, Sahi serves coffee under a crisply designed modern pavilion made of wood in an unexplored corner of Huế.

✷ **T Roaster** [map, page 265] 7 Sư Vạn Hạnh; f roastercoffeeshop; ⏲ 07.30–17.30 daily. Some of the best coffee in Huế – both Western & Vietnamese – is served in this charming little industrial chic café out by Thiên Mụ Pagoda.

Trốn Café [247 G4] 21 Lê Quý Đôn; f troncoffeehue; ⏲ 06.00–03.00 daily. Coffee by day, cocktails by night, Trốn means 'hidden', so it may take a while to find this secret spot embedded in an alleyway & in a former 1-storey home.

OTHER PRACTICALITIES Two recommended tour companies are **Oriental Sky Travel** (w orientalskytravel.com) and **Slow Travel Huế** (w slowtravelhue.com), who, among many other things, can arrange cruises on the Perfume River. For an audio tour of Huế, download the VoiceMap app (w voicemap.me). For **medical** emergencies, Huế Central Hospital [247 E5] (16 Lê Lợi; w bvtwhue.com.vn; ⏲ 07.00–11.30 & 13.30–17.00 daily) tends to offer the best care.

LEGEND HAS IT: WORTH ITS SALT

Once upon a time, a young Huế boy met a beautiful girl at a party. They felt an instant connection, so the young man asked her out for coffee. During the date, while gazing into the girl's eyes, the boy was overcome with nerves, and he accidentally put salt in his coffee instead of sugar. Embarrassed by his mistake but far too proud to admit it, he gingerly took a sip, hoping the girl wouldn't notice.

But she did. The girl giggled and asked the boy why he put salt in his coffee, so he quickly made up a story to cover up his mistake. He grew up by the sea, the boy explained, and he added salt to his coffee as the taste reminded him of his family and hometown. Touched by the nostalgic story and the love the boy had for his parents, the girl fell head over heels.

The couple eventually married, and throughout their life together, she made salty coffee for her husband every morning. He never told her the truth, and instead chose to stomach what had become a beautiful lie.

Years later, after he passed away, the girl, who was now an old woman, found a letter her husband had written. In the letter he confessed that the salt coffee was just a mistake. He explained that he had kept up the pretence because it had brought them so much happiness. The salty coffee was never a memento of his childhood, but it was a constant reminder that he was lucky enough to marry the love of his life.

As a homage to this soppy love story, cafés across Huế serve salt coffee. Cà Phê Muối (see opposite) claims to be the first.

WHAT TO SEE AND DO

The citadel Like other citadels in Vietnam, Huế Citadel was built to the design of Vauban (a 17th-century fortifications designer from France). Unlike other citadels in Vietnam, it's completely intact, ceaselessly impressive and houses a large chunk of the city's population. Its walls are 6.6m high, 21m thick and 10km in circumference, with ten entrances topped by watchtowers. Construction of the citadel began in 1805. A splendid collection of neighbourhoods sit within its walls, and getting lost among the parks, lakes and heritage streets is one of the highlights of a visit to Vietnam. Within the citadel also lies the Imperial City, now a huge museum and Vietnam's most vivid remnant of the dynastic era. Nestled within that is the Forbidden City. To do the citadel justice, you'll need at least a day to explore.

Ngọ Môn Square and Flag Tower [246 D4] (Thuận Hòa) East Asian custom decreed that the principal gate of the palace should face south (like the emperor) and this is the direction from which visitors approach the site. Over the outer moat, a pair of gates pierce the outer walls either side of the Flag Tower: the Thể Nhân and Quảng Đức gates. It's usually possible to climb the Thể Nhân Gate, affording rare, elevated views of the citadel interior. Just inside the gates are two groups of massive cannons: four through the Thể Ngạn Gate and five through the Quảng Đức Gate. These are the Nine Holy Cannon (Cửu Vị Thần Công), cast in 1803 on the orders of Gia Long from bronzeware seized from the Tây Sơn revolutionaries. The cannons are named after the four seasons and the five elements, and on each is carved its name, rank, firing instructions and how the bronze from which it was made was acquired. They are 5m in length, have never been fired and are meant to symbolise the permanence of the empire. The flag of the National Liberation Front flew at the massive flag tower for more than three weeks during the Tết Offensive in 1968. On hot sunny days this large, exposed square is deserted, but in the late afternoon and early evening it fills with families flying kites. At the same time, the grassy patch to the east becomes a grid of makeshift football pitches used by students.

✷ ***Imperial City*** (Phú Hậu; 🕘 08.00–17.00 daily; 200,000VND/free adult/child; 2–4hrs) UNESCO began the arduous process of renovating the Imperial City in 1983. Vietnam at that time was a pariah state due to its invasion of Cambodia in 1978–79 and the appeal for funds and assistance went unheeded. It was, therefore, fitting testimony to Vietnam's rehabilitation in the eyes of the world when, in 1993, UNESCO declared Huế a World Heritage Site. Although it is the battle of 1968 that is normally blamed for the destruction, the city was in fact gradually destroyed and degraded over a period of 50 years. The French shelled it, fervent revolutionaries burned down its buildings, typhoons and rains battered it, thieves ransacked its contents, termites ate away at its foundations and officials unsympathetic to the Nguyễn Dynasty legacy (page 266) neglected it. Restoration remains ongoing, but the Imperial City and Forbidden City are nevertheless extraordinary places to explore. For an in-depth journey, invest in the audio guide (100,000VND; dry but adequate) or try to find Tim Doling's extremely detailed *Exploring Huế*, which is usually available in bookshops in Huế, including in Phương Nam Bookstore [247 E3] (133 Trần Hưng Đạo St). Within the enclosure, valiant efforts have been made to try and liven up the visitor experience, including a virtual-reality kiosk, opportunities to don emperors' clothing and impromptu traditional music performances. At 08.00 you can watch the changing of the guard, though the historical accuracy of the performance is questionable.

Royal Gate [246 D4] (Ngọ Môn) Over one of three bridges which span a second moat is the Royal Gate, built in 1833–34 during the reign of Emperor Minh Mạng. The ticket office is just to the left. The gate, remodelled on several occasions since its original construction, including in 1921 by Emperor Khải Định, is surmounted by a pavilion from where the emperor would view palace ceremonies. Of the five entrances, the central one was only opened for the emperor to pass through. The other four were for procession participants, elephants and horses. UNESCO threw itself into the restoration of the Royal Gate with vigour and the newly finished pavilion, supported by 100 columns, atop the gate now gleams and glints in the sun during the day. In the evening, the gate is floodlit to spectacular effect.

Palace of Supreme Harmony [246 D4] (Thái Hòa Palace) North from the Ngọ Môn is the Golden Water Bridge – again reserved solely for the emperor's use. This leads to the Great Rites Courtyard (Đại Triều Nghi), on the north side of which is the Palace of Supreme Harmony, constructed by Gia Long in 1805 and used for his coronation in 1806. From here, sitting on his golden throne raised up on a dais, the emperor would receive ministers, foreign emissaries, mandarins and military officers during formal ceremonial occasions. In front of the palace are 18 stone stelae, which stipulate the arrangement of the nine mandarinate ranks on the Great Rites Courtyard: the upper level was for ministers, mandarins and officers of the upper grade; the lower for those of lower grades. Civil servants would stand on the left, and the military on the right. Only royal princes were allowed to stand in the palace itself, which is one of the best-preserved buildings in the Imperial City complex. Its red and gold ironwood columns, decorated with dragon motifs, symbol of the emperors' power, the tiled floor and fine ceiling have all been restored.

The Forbidden Purple City [246 C3–4] Before the horrific damage inflicted upon it in 1947 and 1968, this housed the royal apartments. Only the emperor and his family, eunuchs, concubines and those with special permission were allowed inside its inner enclosure. In its prime there were many buildings and magnificent courtyards. It was entered via the Đại Cung Môn, directly behind the Thái Hòa Palace. Little remains of this gate or the **Cần Chánh Palace** directly beyond, though there are plans to restore both. In this palace the emperor would receive his mandarins and carry out his everyday business. Two small surviving mandarin palaces, **Hữu Vu** and **Tả Vu**, flank the former Cần Chánh Palace and now function as exhibition spaces. Behind the Cần Chánh Palace was the **Càn Thành Palace**, now destroyed. Built by Gia Long in 1802, it served as the emperor's private and primary residence until 1915, when Emperor Duy Tân built the Kiến Trung Palace (see below). The empress lived in the destroyed **Khôn Thái Palace**, a little further north close to the centre of the Forbidden City, while the concubines were literally sidelined in a harem within a complex to the west known as **Lục Viện**. To the east of the royal dwellings is the **Royal Library** (Thái Bình Lâu), a miraculous survivor and one of the compound's most elegant structures. Originally built in 1821, Emperor Khải Định replaced it after a typhoon in 1919–21 and during the reign of Bảo Đại it housed books, manuscripts and Cham artefacts. The library was refurbished in 2014–15. Nearby to the south is the equally attractive **Nhất Thanh Lâu**, another war survivor, which sometimes hosts traditional live music performances. The most eye-catching palace within the Forbidden Purple City is undoubtedly the shiny **Kiến Trung Palace**, a recent and rapidly built replica of the destroyed principal residence of Duy Tân, Khải Định and Bảo Đại. The building is richly decorated both inside and out, reflecting the lavish lifestyles of the last Nguyễn Dynasty kings. Nearby is a **tennis court** with a rather amusing sign that reads: 'King Bảo Đại was under the deep influence of the Western civilisation. He was interested in sports, and especially keen on driving, boat rowing, tennis, golf, shooting, etc...the restoration of king Bảo Đại's tennis court aims at restoring one construction of historic value, serving tourist purposes, positively improving environment, and embellishing the landscape of the Forbidden Purple City.' Despite the disapproval of Bảo Đại's proclaimed proclivity for Western sports, today the tennis court is mostly used by government officials. At the northern edge of the Forbidden City is the **Peace Gate** (Cửa Hòa Bình), a simple structure built in 1833. Outside the Forbidden City but still within the ticketed Imperial City are several more structures of interest. Note that the information below is far from exhaustive.

Pavilion of Splendour [246 C4] (Hiển Lâm Các) West of the Forbidden City, this well-preserved temple, constructed in 1814, was where the emperor came for private prayer. Here he would pay homage to his ancestors, particularly on the anniversaries of their deaths and their birthdays. Notice that its glazed roof tiles are yellow, the imperial colour. The wooden balconies, beams and windows are said to be the originals. In front of the palace stand nine dynastic urns, which were cast between 1835 and 1837 and are Vietnamese national treasures. They are said to be the symbols of nine Nguyễn noblemen. At 2,600kg, Gia Long's urn is the most impressive and stands in front of the others in a central position. All are symbols of stability and have a round mouth (symbolising heaven), bow-shaped handles, straight necks and swollen bellies. Each urn is divided into 17 squares, which are decorated with harmonious scenes such as mountains, rivers, animals and trees, and between them they represent wealth, beauty and unity of the country. In dynastic days, they were used as decorations during coronations.

Temple of Generations [246 C4] (Thế Tổ Miếu) Also west of the Forbidden City and built in 1821, this temple contains altars honouring ten of the emperors of the Nguyễn Dynasty, behind which are meant to be kept a selection of their personal belongings. It was only after the French exit in 1955, however, that the stelae depicting the three revolutionary emperors Hàm Nghi, Thành Thái, and Duy Tân were brought into the temple. The French, perhaps fearing that they would become a focus of discontent, prevented the Vietnamese from erecting altars in their memory. North of this temple is Hưng Temple, built in 1804 for the worship of Gia Long's father, Nguyễn Phúc Luân, the father of the founder of the Nguyễn Dynasty. The temple was renovated in 1951.

Triệu Tổ Temple [246 D3] East of the Forbidden City, this temple was built in 1804 by Emperor Gia Long, to honour the parents of Nguyễn Hoàng, the lord that founded the Nguyễn Dynasty. This twin-roofed structure features a front hall with five compartments and two wings, and a main hall with three compartments and two wings. Study the roof to see yellow enamelled tubular tiles and dragon motifs made from porcelain along the ridges. The central shrine venerates Nguyễn Kim and Nguyễn Thị Mai, Nguyễn Hoàng's father and mother respectively. The left shrine honours the eight other Nguyễn lords and the right shrine their queens. Triệu Tổ Temple was restored in the mid-2010s, with support from the US Ambassadors Fund for Cultural Preservation.

Hiển Nhơn Gate [246 D3] Also east of the Forbidden City and your likely point of exit from the Imperial City, Hiển Nhơn Gate was built a year after Triệu Tổ Temple, renovated by Minh Mạng in 1833 and then completely rebuilt in 1923 by Khải Định. The 1968 Tết Offensive brought terrible damage to the gate, but it was one of the first structures to be restored after the war, in 1977. It is the counterpart to the **Chương Đức Gate** [246 C4] on the west side of the Imperial City.

Huế Museum of Royal Antiquities [246 D3] (3 Lê Trực, close to the Hiển Nhơn Gate; f baotangcovatcungdinh; ⌚ 07.00–17.30 daily; 50,000VND; 30–60 mins) Outside the Imperial City is this museum, founded in 1923 by Khải Định and claiming to be the oldest in the country. The garden has some scattered antiques, mainly centuries-old cannons and imperial statues. Inside, the displays are rather dry, but there is at least adequate signage in English. Items to look out for are Bảo Đại's palanquin, a feudal remnant used to swan around the palace, and Khải Định's bed, a predictably flamboyant piece of furniture designed to reflect French royal extravagance. The king's throne takes pride of place and is refreshingly austere. There is a modest building at the back of the compound that houses Cham (page 12) artefacts, with an interesting map of the various Cham sites in Thừa Thiên Huế Province. Sadly, you'll see virtually all the sites are *phê tích*, which means ruins.

Tịnh Tâm Lake [246 C2] (Hồ Tịnh Tâm) In 1822, Minh Mạng relocated the gunpowder and saltpeter storehouses that his predecessor, Gia Long, had put here and renamed the area Tịnh Tâm Lake, establishing a royal park. The park, inaccessible to the public, was enclosed by a brick wall, remnants of which can be seen on Đinh Tiên Hoàng Street. The largest island in the south pond housed a palace where Minh Mạng and his successor, Thiệu Trị, would relax, read and write poetry. This palace is long gone and today the lake and its islands serve as a public park and popular fishing spot. During the early summer months, the water theatrically blooms with pink and white lotus flowers. The basic streetside cafés and fruit juice stands on Đinh Tiên Hoàng Street are a good place to take in the scenes.

✷ ***The Royal Archive*** [246 C1] (Lầu Tàng Thơ; Đinh Tiên Hoàng St) On the other side of the road to Tịnh Tâm Lake is the Royal Archive, one of Huế's more recently restored buildings. Built in 1825–26 to store official documents, the archive and its collection suffered during the wars of the 20th century and it was eventually abandoned and forgotten. After 1975, homeless families started squatting in the building, creating a close-knit community with neatly compartmentalised dwellings, shared farming areas and a huge garden where kids played jianzi. The government began evicting and relocating the families to tower blocks outside of the city centre in the early 2010s, and by the middle of the decade the archive was vacant and the gate locked. The planned restoration was slow to get off the ground, but the building finally reopened in 2023 as a small museum and reading room used by students. In all fairness, the exhibition of photocopied and enlarged ancient documents is fairly dull and there is no contextual information or narrative flow, but the archive remains a tranquil, somewhat hidden corner in the city.

The Old Quarters Due to the city's importance throughout the 19th and 20th centuries, various merchant and artisanal communities established themselves outside of the citadel walls. Today, the most interesting to visit are Gia Hội, which housed the Chinese community, and the riverside neighbourhood and former trading hub of Bao Vinh, sometimes referred to as 'Little Hội An' on account of its centuries-old shophouses. You might spend up to an hour or two in each.

Gia Hội Old Quarter [247 E2] East of the citadel is Gia Hội, a Chinatown of sorts, with dozens of merchant houses, clan houses and Chinese temples. Most of the ancient residences are found on Bạch Đằng Street, which runs alongside the Đông Ba Canal. On the same street is the rarely visited **Diệu Đế Pagoda** [247 E2] (Bạch Đằng; ⏲ 05.30–21.00 daily), a walled and rectangular compound with parts that feel like the Khmer temples of Sóc Trăng and Trà Vinh. The pagoda was built in 1844 but was completely refurbished earlier this century. Of the various Chinese temples on Chi Lăng Street, Đền Chiêu Ứng [247 F1] (207 Chi Lăng), **Quảng Triệu Hội Quán** [247 F1] (223 Chi Lăng) and **Triều Châu Hội Quán** [247 F1] (319 Chi Lăng) are the most visually impressive. All three were built in the 19th century and are disappointingly difficult to access, with irregular opening hours. If you visit all three, chances are at least one of them will be open.

Bao Vinh Old Quarter [246 D1] North of the citadel is the riverside settlement of Bao Vinh, which dates back to at least the 17th century. Though Bao Vinh has suffered from official neglect for decades, there are just enough historical buildings here to entertain heritage enthusiasts for an hour or two. One of the more visually impressive buildings is the **Bao Vinh Village Communal House** (Hương Vinh Ward), which welcomes you at the southern corner of the village. It's been rebuilt multiple times but retains a wooden frame. Walk (or cycle) north from here along Bao Vinh Street and you'll spot more than a handful of late 19th- and early 20th-century buildings on both sides of the road. Some of the popular 2019 film *Mắt Biếc*

(Dreamy Eyes) was filmed here and more than one coffee shop has sought to benefit from the publicity.

South of the Perfume River The neighbourhoods south of the river hold some of Huế's most storied pagodas, churches and palaces. Exploring them by foot or bicycle, stopping for refreshments along the attractive An Cựu Canal as you go, will take a full morning or afternoon.

✷ ***An Định Palace*** [247 G6] (179 Phan Đình Phùng; ⌚ 07.00–17.00 daily; 50,000VND/free adult/child; 1hr) Facing south and overlooking the An Cựu Canal like some kind of sickly lemon-frosted wedding cake, An Định Palace is set within a 23,000m^2 compound, surrounded by a brick wall and grand entrance gates adorned with gaudy porcelain art. Originally, the compound of ten buildings included a theatre for royal performances, but most ancillary buildings were lost during the war years. The principal three-storey building, known as Lầu Khải Tường (Pavilion of Good Omens), is designed in the style of a French chateau, with richly decorated interiors and six murals painted in 1917 depicting the imperial mausoleums. The ground floor, first floor and unkempt gardens are open to the public, and although information is scarce, the house offers a demonstration of the luxurious lives of Vietnam's erstwhile royal family.

The bronze statue sheltering within the octagonal gazebo depicts Khải Định, Vietnam's penultimate emperor. The original palace was a traditional *nhà rường*, built in 1902 for Prince Nguyễn Phúc Bửu Đảo, but in 1916, when he ascended the throne as Emperor Khải Định, it was demolished. In 1917, construction began for this grandiose neo-Baroque palace to serve as an opulent townhouse for the Europhile emperor. After it was inherited by Bảo Đại, Khải Định's son and successor, it was used as an escape from the formalities of the Forbidden City. When Bảo Đại abdicated in 1945, the palace served as the principal residence of his mother, wife and five children. After 1975, An Định Palace was appropriated by the Provincial Federation of Trade Unions and the building deteriorated significantly. In 2001, the Huế Monuments Conservation Centre took over its care, and restoration began in 2002, with considerable funding and expertise from Germany.

Phủ Cam Cathedral [247 E7] (1 Đoàn Hữu Trưng) While there have been churches on this site since the 17th century, the modernist masterpiece you see today was designed in the 1960s by Huế architect Ngô Viết Thụ, the same man who designed the Independence Palace in Hồ Chí Minh City. Work began in 1962, but due to decades of unrest, war and poverty, the cathedral wasn't finished until 1991. Two bell towers were added at the turn of the millennium. Perched on a hill near the An Cựu Canal, the church's exterior makes a strong impression, but the interior, which accommodates 2,500 worshippers, is even more striking. In *Exploring Huế*, historian Tim Doling writes: 'The inward slant of the buttresses serves to accentuate the wide expanse of vertical space beneath the vaulted ceiling, giving a sense of height designed to inspire worshippers to reach to the heavens.'

Từ Đàm Pagoda [246 D7] (1 Sư Liễu Quán; ⌚ 06.00–21.00 daily) The day after Thích Quảng Đức took his life in Saigon in August 1963, another monk killed himself in the yard of Từ Đàm Pagoda. Savage retaliation by troops loyal to Ngô Đình Diệm followed and many pagodas in Huế were badly damaged. According to the Huế Buddhist Association, the Chinese monk Minh Dung founded this pagoda in the 1690s, but it has been rebuilt multiple times and today feels rather clinical.

During Emperor Thiệu Trị's reign in 1841, it was given the name Từ Đàm, meaning 'Cloud of Buddha'. In the 1950s it became well known as the centre for the Unified Vietnamese Buddhist Association, which was founded here. Today the pagoda is still remembered for the leading example that many of its monks displayed against the Diệm regime.

Báo Quốc Pagoda [246 D7] (17 Bảo Quốc) Báo Quốc Pagoda was probably built in the early 18th century by a Buddhist monk named Giác Phong, though records suggest that some form of religious sanctuary has sat here since 1670. Note the 'stupa' that is behind and to the left of the central pagoda and the fine doors inscribed with Chinese and Sanskrit characters. There is a small monastery to the right. Like Thiên Mụ Pagoda, this pagoda is situated on a small hill, but it is noticeably greener, with fewer visitors.

Along the Perfume River Over two centuries ago, the Scottish traveller George Finlayson wrote about his arrival in the city: 'The most beautiful and luxuriant scenery now burst upon our view, and we were soon agreed that the banks of the river of Huế presented the most beautiful and interesting scenery of any river we had seen in Asia. Its beauties, however, are the gifts of nature more than of art. A vast expanse of water, conveyed by a magnificent river through a fertile valley, not so wide but that the eye can compass its several parts; ridges of lofty and bold mountains in the distance; the cocoa-nut, the areca, the banana; the sugarcane, hedges of bamboos, that wave their elegant tops in the air; rows of that beautiful plant the hibiscus, are the principal materials which, grouped in various forms, delight the eye of the spectator'. Unusually for a Vietnamese city, the river remains undeveloped, though parks, pavilions, sculpture, flower gardens and cycle paths have replaced the sugarcane, hibiscus and areca. Aimlessly strolling along either side of the river between the Dã Viên and Trường Tiền bridges is most enjoyable at sunrise or sunset. The riverside sights are in central Huế and upstream, on both sides of the water. There are a few museums, including the Lê Bá Đảng Art Museum and Hồ Chí Minh Museum, but these are not highlights.

✷ ***Trường Tiền Bridge*** [247 F4] (Phú Hòa) Also called Tràng Tiền Bridge, this attractive, ill-fated structure was named after the royal mint that once stood at its northern end. It was built in 1896 by the French and destroyed soon after by a typhoon. After having been rebuilt it was then razed once more in 1968 during the Tết Offensive. Much like Long Biên Bridge in Hanoi, Trường Tiền Bridge is regularly and erroneously attributed to Gustave Eiffel (page 110). Upstream is the more prosaic (and practical) Phú Xuân Bridge, built by the US army in 1970.

Huế University of Education [247 F4] (34 Lê Lợi; **w** dhsphue.edu.vn; ⌚ 07.00–17.00 Mon–Sat) Just east of Trường Tiền Bridge is this striking modernist university built in 1955 by Ngô Viết Thụ, the prodigious architect who built the Independence Palace in Hồ Chí Minh City. From above the two buildings appear like forked crosses, with perforated façades designed to catch the breeze from the river and funnel cool air through the hallways.

Le Cercle Huế [247 E5] (11 Lê Lợi; **f**; ⌚ 06.00–23.00 daily) This Art Deco riverside pavilion was once a French country club for the city elite. It sat abandoned after the American War, then became government offices, but has recently been renovated to house Le Cercle, a restaurant and café. The architecture is best appreciated from the boardwalk running in front of the building on the water.

Quốc Học School [247 E6] (12 Lê Lợi; **w** thpt-qhoc.thuathienhue.edu.vn; ⌚ 07.45–11.15 & 13.45–17.15 Mon–Sat) This expansive blood-red high school was built in 1916–17, and it may well be the most successful producer of Vietnamese revolutionaries anywhere in the country. Other than Hồ Chí Minh, who studied here when he was still called Nguyễn Tất Thành (a golden statue honouring the young Hồ is in the school courtyard), alumni include Võ Nguyên Giáp, Lê Duẩn, Trần Phú and Phạm Văn Đồng. Continuing the legacy, it became a School for Gifted Students in 1991 and remains one of the country's most elite institutions. Next to Quốc Học is Hai Bà Trưng School (14 Lê Lợi), which was built at the same time as Quốc Học as a school for Vietnamese girls. At the time, it was one of only three schools for non-European girls in all of Indochina. The yellow riverside monument opposite the school commemorates the Vietnamese soldiers who fought in World War I on behalf of France.

✷ ***Azerai La Residence*** [246 D6] (page 251) Huế enjoys a handful of heritage hotels, but this 1930s Art Deco tour de force, with its Streamline Moderne façade and capacious circular lounge bathed in natural light, makes the greatest impact. Like any heritage hotel worth its salt, La Residence overflows with stories. Originally constructed to ensconce the French Resident Supérieure, the mansion was an obligatory target for the Việt Cộng during the Tết Offensive. A cathartic makeover arrived in the early 2000s, which included the construction of two new wings that mirror the Art Deco aesthetic. Even if you don't stay here, it's worth stepping in for a coffee or cocktail in the lounge-lobby.

The garden houses of Kim Long Huế has many garden houses, the most attractive of which are in Kim Long, Huế's greenest neighbourhood on the north side of the river. Exploring this neighbourhood by foot or bicycle will take a full morning or afternoon.

Phú Mộng Viên Garden House [246 A5] (34 Phú Mộng; ⌚ 06.00–22.00 daily) Set amid a large garden that also functions as a café, this French villa was built in the early 20th century and perhaps replaced a traditional style *nhà rường*. The distinctly European style is curious considering the house may have belonged to the family of Tôn Thất Chi, a relative of Tôn Thất Thuyết, who was involved in anti-French movements in the 19th century. It is not possible to enter the house, but buy a coffee or juice and you can wander around the garden at will.

Xuân Viên Tiểu Cung Garden House [246 A5] (22 Phú Mộng) The room holding the family altar of this tucked-away garden house is 400 years old, according to the family that lives here. Wander in and they may invite you for tea and to look around the garden, which sports dragon fruit, pineapple and banana trees. There is no entrance fee, but if you stop to look around then it's polite to leave a little cash for the caretaker family: 100,000VND per small group should suffice.

An Hiên Garden House [map, page 265] (58 Nguyễn Phúc Nguyên; f; ⌚ 08.00–17.00 daily; 50,000VND/free adult/child) Beautifully landscaped but no longer a residential home, An Hiên Garden House was acquired by the Silk Path hotel group in 2018. The entrance fee includes a traditional music performance and a short introduction from a staff member. The house was built in the 1890s by distant relatives of the king but has changed hands several times since. Enter through a large front gate visible from Kim Long Street and along a stone path to reach a square pond and screen, behind which is the house, a classic *nhà rường* made from jackfruit wood and ironwood. The tilework, carved beams and decorative boards are all exceptionally well preserved. The main house served to worship ancestors and welcome guests. These days, there isn't much worshipping, but the house was used to receive foreign delegates, and now welcomes tourists. The flowers are carefully selected so that something is in bloom regardless of the month.

✷ **Hương River Antique Pottery Museum** [map, page 265] (120 Nguyễn Phúc Nguyên; w thaikimlan.com; ⏲ 08.00–17.00 daily; 120,000VND; 1hr) This extraordinarily verdant garden house is over 150 years old, with a family altar, a tea house, some ancient bonsai trees and a collection of more than 5,000 antique pottery pieces. The items, with some that are perhaps 3,000 years old, are placed in glass cabinets with almost no contextual detail, but some of the pieces are exquisitely decorated. The owners of the private museum, Thái Kim Lan and her late brother Thái Nguyên Bá, spent nearly 40 years dredging up pottery pieces from the bottom of riverbeds in and around Huế.

Thiên Mụ Pagoda [map, page 265] (Hương Hòa; ⏲ 08.00–18.00 daily) Thiên Mụ Pagoda, known locally as Linh Mụ Pagoda, is quite simply the finest in Huế. It is beautifully sited on the north bank of the Perfume River, about 4km upstream from the city. The pagoda was established in 1601 by Nguyễn Hoàng, the governor of Huế, after an old woman appeared and said that the site had supernatural significance and should be marked by the construction of a sanctuary devoted to Buddha for the good of the country. Apparently, the Cham had the same idea, as the pagoda replaced an ancient temple. The monastery is the oldest in Huế, and the seven-storey Phước Duyên (Happiness and Grace Tower), built by Emperor Thiệu Trị in 1844, is 21m high, with each storey containing an altar to a different Buddha. The summit of the tower is crowned with a water pitcher to catch the rain, water representing the source of happiness.

Arranged around the tower are four smaller buildings, one of which contains the Great Bell, cast in 1710 under the orders of the Nguyễn lord Nguyễn Phúc Chu, and weighing 2,200kg. Beneath another of these surrounding pavilions is a monstrous marble turtle on which is a 2.6m-high stela, carved in 1715, recounting the development of Buddhism in Huế. Beyond the tower, the entrance to the pagoda is through a triple gateway patrolled by six carved and vividly painted guardians, two on each gate. The roof of the sanctuary itself is decorated with *jataka* stories, which depict the previous births of Buddha. At the front of the sanctuary is a brass, laughing Buddha; behind are an assortment of gilded Buddhas and a crescent-shaped gong cast in 1677 by Jean de la Croix. The first monk to commit suicide through self-immolation, Thích Quảng Đức (page 472), came from this pagoda and the grey Austin in which he made the journey to his death in Saigon is still kept here in a garage in the temple garden. In May 1993, a Vietnamese – this time not a monk – immolated himself at Thiên Mụ. Why is not clear: some maintain it was linked to the persecution of Buddhists; others that it was because of the man's frustrated love life.

Temple of Literature [map, page 265] (Văn Thánh St) Huế's rarely visited and unkempt Temple of Literature, about 750m further from town than Thiên

Mụ Pagoda, was built in 1808, soon after Huế was made capital of Vietnam. The concept was modelled on the more ancient Temple of Literature (page 118) in Hanoi, and thus celebrated the philosopher Confucius and hosted mandarin examinations. The remote location is serene and would have undoubtedly been conducive to study, but the distance proved inconvenient and, 100 years after it was built, in 1908, Emperor Duy Tân moved the educational facility to a site within the citadel. Continue on this road upstream and you'll eventually reach the tombs.

Hổ Quyền Amphitheatre [map, page 265] (373 Bùi Thị Xuân; ◷ all day daily) The Hổ Quyền Amphitheatre lies about 4km upstream of Huế on the south bank of the Perfume River (ie: the opposite side to the garden houses, Thiên Mụ Pagoda and the Temple of Literature). The amphitheatre was built in 1830 by Emperor Minh Mạng as a venue for the popular duels between elephants and tigers. Elephants were symbolic of emperors and strength, whereas tigers were seen as anti-imperial beasts and had their claws removed before the fight. This royal sport was in earlier centuries staged on an island in the Perfume River or on the riverbanks, but by 1830 it was considered desirable for the royal party to be able to observe the duels without placing themselves at risk from escaping tigers. The amphitheatre is said to have been last used in 1904 when, as expected, the elephant emerged victorious: 'The elephant rushed ahead and pressed the tiger to the wall with all the force he could gain. Then he raised his head, threw the enemy to the ground and smashed him to death,' wrote Crosbie Garstin in *The Voyage from London to Indochina*. The walls of the amphitheatre are 5m high and the arena is 44m in diameter. At the south side, beneath the royal box, is one large gateway (for the elephant) and, to the north, five smaller entrances for the tigers. The walls are in good condition and the centre is filled with grass. Houses encircle the amphitheatre, reflecting how people in Huế live among these structures of old.

Temple of the Elephant Trumpet [map, page 265] (Alley 26 Kiệt, 373 Bùi Thị Xuân) Diễn Voi Ré, the Temple of the Elephant Trumpet, dedicated to the call of the fighting elephant, is a few hundred metres away from the Hổ Quyền. It is a modest, crumbling and atmospheric little place with a large pond in front, and contains two small elephant statues. Presumably this is where elephants were blessed before battle, or perhaps where the unsuccessful ones were mourned. Unsurprisingly, the tigers, who represented rebels, received no such temple.

The Royal Tombs and around [map, page 265] As the geographical and spiritual centre of the Nguyễn Dynasty, Huế and the surrounding area is the site of seven imperial tombs, along with the tombs of numerous other royal personages and successful mandarins. Only Bảo Đại who, after abdication, went to live in France does not have a tomb. Designed as peaceful resting places, the exact position of these tombs could only be determined after strict consultation with geomancers. Each of the tombs follows the same stylistic formula, although at the same time they reflect the tastes and predilections of the emperor in question. Many of the tombs were built during the lifetime of each emperor, who took a great interest in the design and construction – after all, they were meant to ensure his comfort in the next life. Each mausoleum, variously arranged, has five design elements: a courtyard with statues of elephants, horses and military and civil mandarins (originally, usually approached through a park of rare trees); a stela pavilion (with an engraved eulogy composed by the emperor's son and heir); a Temple of the Soul's Tablets;

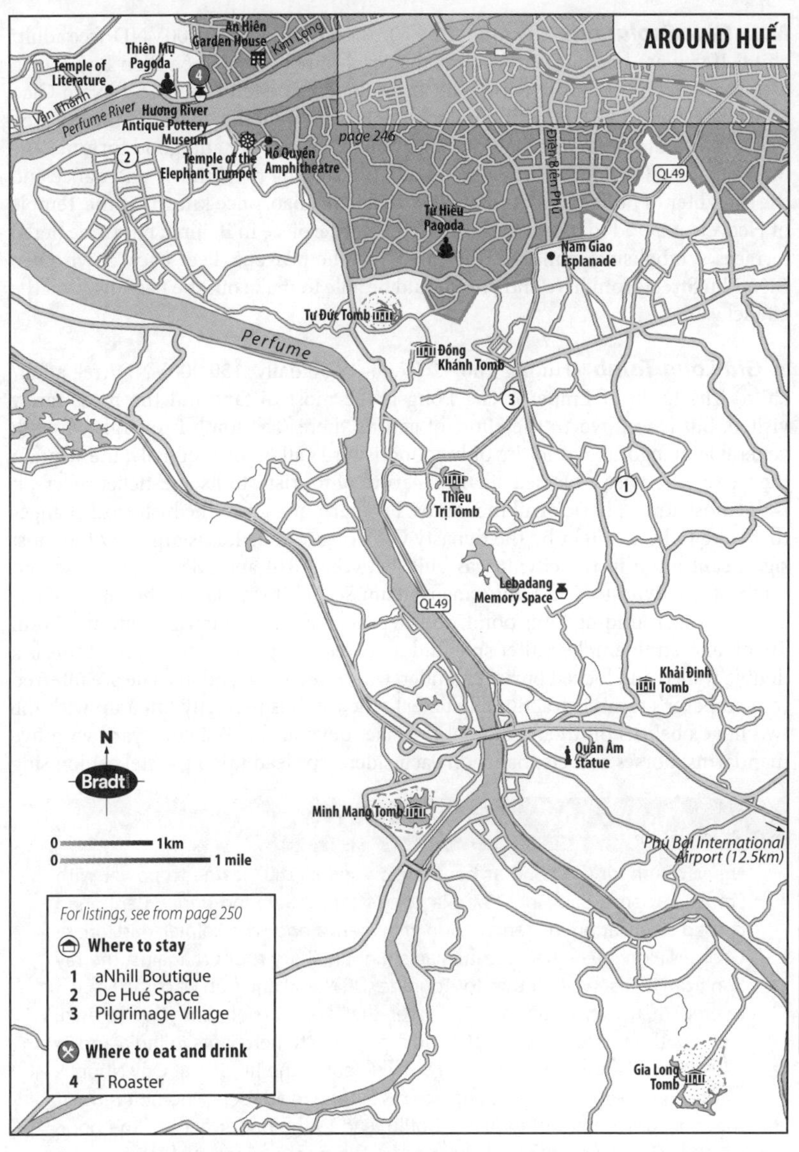

a pleasure pavilion; and a grave. Most of the tombs are outside the city and to visit all seven you would need two full days. If you can spare the time to visit all the tombs, it's highly recommended that you take a chronological approach, starting with the oldest, as it will help frame and structure 150 years of Vietnamese history. This is reflected in the order that follows. As it's the smallest and least impressive – and it is geographically inconvenient for a chronological discovery – you can be forgiven for skipping Dục Đức Tomb. There are restaurants, cafés and even a few notable places to stay on the streets connecting the tombs. You can explore the tombs independently by motorbike, car and driver or on a prebooked river cruise or tour (page 254).

Nam Giao Esplanade (Trường An; ⌚ 07.00–17.00 daily; 50,000VND/free adult/child) If you are heading out towards the royal tombs along Điện Biên Phủ Street, call in at this important religious site at the southern end of the street. Nam Giao Esplanade, built in 1806, is the hillock for heavenly sacrifices where the Nguyễn emperors would pray on behalf of the nation for prosperity and good fortune. The original annual ceremony was a grand affair, including royal music and dance and the slaughter of buffalos, goats and pigs. The Nam Giao, once known as the Temple of Heaven as a nod to its resemblance to the masterpiece in Beijing, has three tiered terraces symbolising mankind, the earth and the heavens. Peer back down Điện Biên Phủ Street from here and you should be able to make out the flag tower on the citadel walls.

✷ ***Gia Long Tomb*** (Hương Thọ; ⌚ 07.00–17.30 daily; 150,000VND/free adult/child) The tomb of Emperor Gia Long is the most distant and the most rarely visited, but is well worth the effort of getting there. The tomb is overgrown with venerable mango trees and the only sound is bird call or, occasionally, the wind in the trees: otherwise a blessed silence. Devoid of tourists, touts and ticket sellers, it is the most atmospheric of all the tombs. Furthermore, given the historical changes that were to be wrought by the dynasty Gia Long founded, it is arguably the most significant tomb in the city. It was built between 1814 and 1820, and as the first tomb of the dynasty, Gia Long's mausoleum set the formula for the later tombs. There is a surrounding lotus pond, and steps lead up to a courtyard with the Minh Thánh ancestral temple, rather splendid in its red and gold. To the right of this is a double walled and locked burial chamber, where Gia Long and his wife are interred (the emperor's tomb is fractionally taller). The tomb is perfectly lined up with the two huge obelisks on the far side of the lake. Beyond this is a courtyard with five mandarins, horses and elephants on each side; steps lead up to the stela eulogising

EMPEROR GIA LONG'S CONTROVERSIAL LEGACY

Nguyễn Ánh, or Gia Long as he was crowned in 1802, came to power with French support. Back in 1787, Gia Long's son, the young Prince Cảnh, had caused a sensation in French salon life when, along with soldier/missionary Georges Pigneau de Béhaine, he had sought military support against the Tây Sơn from Louis XVI. In return for Tourane (Đà Nẵng) and Côn Đảo, the French offered men and weapons – an offer that was subsequently withdrawn. Pigneau then raised military support from French merchants in India and in 1799 Prince Cảnh's French-trained army defeated the Tây Sơn at Quy Nhơn.

Gia Long's reign was despotic – to his European advisers who pointed out that encouragement of industry would lead to the betterment of the poor, he replied that he preferred them poor. The poor were virtual slaves – the price for one healthy young buffalo was one healthy young girl. Flogging was the norm – it has been described as the 'bamboo's golden age'. One study by a Vietnamese scholar estimated that there were 105 peasant uprisings between 1802 and 1820 alone. For this, and the fact that he gave the French a foothold in Vietnam, the Vietnamese have never forgiven Gia Long. And yet he unified the country, began construction of the nation's most impressive citadel and even coined the name Việt Nam. Nevertheless, unlike many important figures in Vietnam's long, legendary history, you are unlikely to encounter a street named after Emperor Gia Long.

the emperor's reign, composed, presumably, by his eldest son, Minh Mạng, as was the custom. This grey monolith, engraved in ancient Chinese characters, remained miraculously undisturbed during two turbulent centuries. Gia Long's geomancers did a remarkable job finding this site; with the mountainous screen in front, it is a textbook example of a final resting place. Visiting this tomb, together with the journey there and back, takes a full morning or afternoon.

✷ ***Minh Mạng Tomb*** (Hương Thọ; 🕘 07.00–17.30 daily; 150,000/30,000VND adult/child) The tomb of Emperor Minh Mạng is the stateliest of all the imperial tombs. Built between 1840 and 1843, it is sited among peaceful ponds, about 12km from the city. In terms of architectural poise, balance and richness of decoration, it has no peer in the area. The tomb's layout, along a single central and sacred axis, is unusual in its symmetry; no other tomb achieves the same unity of constituent parts, nor draws the eye onwards so easily and pleasantly from one visual element to the next. The tomb was traditionally approached through the Đại Hồng Môn, a gate that leads into the ceremonial courtyard containing an array of statuary. Next is the stela pavilion, in which there is a carved eulogy to the dead emperor composed by his son, Thiệu Trị. Continuing downwards through a series of courtyards there is, in turn, the Sùng Ân Temple dedicated to Minh Mạng and his empress, a small garden with flowerbeds that once formed the Chinese character for 'longevity', and two sets of stone bridges. The first consists of three spans, the central one of which was for the sole use of the emperor. The second, single bridge leads to a short flight of stairs with dragon balustrades. At the end is a locked bronze door, which unfortunately always remains locked. This leads to the tomb itself, which is surrounded by ghoulish greenery and a decaying circular wall, only adding atmosphere to this remarkable place.

Thiệu Trị Tomb (Thủy Bằng; 🕘 07.00–17.00 daily; 50,000VND/free adult/child) The tomb of Thiệu Trị was built in 1848 by his son Tự Đức, who took into account his father's wishes that it be 'economical and convenient'. Thiệu Trị's uneventful reign lasted for just seven years and, unlike his forebears, he did not start planning his mausoleum the moment he ascended the throne. Upon his death his body was temporarily interred in Long An Temple, now the Huế Museum of Royal Antiquities (page 258). The tomb is in two adjacent parts, with separate tomb and temple areas; the layout of each follows the symmetrical axis arrangement of Minh Mạng's tomb, which has also inspired the architectural style. The memorial temple area is to the right and reached via a long flight of steps. A gatehouse incorporates Japanese triple-beamed columns (as seen in the Japanese Bridge in Hội An) and at the back of the courtyard beyond is the temple dedicated to Thiệu Trị. The stela pavilion and tomb are a few hundred yards to the left, unmissable with the two obelisks. Just like his father, Thiệu Trị is buried on a circular island reached by three bridges beyond the stela pavilion, though the approach is considerably less grand. This is the only tomb not enclosed by a wall, and a decade ago it was possible to wander into the ruin to find buffalo grazing on the unruly grass and boys fishing in the ponds. Today, it has undergone restoration and is ticketed, like the other tombs.

✷ ***Tự Đức Tomb*** (Đông Ba Bridge; 🕘 07.00–17.30 daily; 150,000/30,000VND adult/child) Tự Đức was the youngest of Thiệu Trị's 24 sons and was known for his extravagances. This is reflected in the ostentatious layout of his tomb, which was built with numerous palaces, temples and pavilions, including imperial-style

LEGEND HAS IT: THE FAKE PHARAOH

To inject some pharaonic intrigue into Huế's dynastic heritage, guides often tell tourists that Tự Đức had the labourers who worked on his crypt killed to keep the location a secret. Delighted tourists expressed a morbid fascination with the story, and somehow the erroneous fact soon made its way into official tour guide training manuals. From there the information went into guidebooks, travel articles and even Vietnam's official tourism website. However, diligent historians have worked hard to debunk what they say is a myth. Their argument? There's not one shred of evidence.

gardens and a lake. You will need quite a long time to explore his mausoleum complex, which is more like a spacious park. It is entered from the east via the Vụ Khiêm Gate. Towards the right you will see the Lưu Khiêm Lake, which has a small islet known as the Tịnh Khiêm. On its northern shore is the Dĩ Khiêm pavilion, also known as the Pavilion of the Emperor's Boats. He often came here to relax, and from the pavilions that reach out over the lake he composed poetry and listened to music. Directly in front of it is the courtyard (Khiêm Cung), which leads via a series of steps to Hoa Khiêm Temple. This commemorates the emperor and his empress, Hoàng Lê Thiện Anh, who used to sit beside him in this room on her tall throne. His smaller throne is still here too, along with their funerary tablets and an assortment of palace paraphernalia, which includes clocks, mirrors, combs and lacquerware. To the left of the building was the emperor's garment store (Ôn Khiêm Đường), where he kept hundreds of garments for everyday and ceremonial use. To the right of Hoa Khiêm Temple was a theatre, where he enjoyed the sensuous performances of his all-female royal dance troupe. Here he would sip chrysanthemum-flavoured tea made only from the dew water collected from the lotus leaves that grew in Lưu Khiêm Lake. Another building behind the Hoa Khiêm Temple, the emperor's mother's apartment (Lương Khiêm Temple), is a fitting memorial to Thiệu Trị's wife, Từ Dụ. To the east of the complex is the Pavilion of Stelae. This is dotted with stone statuary, horses, elephants and mandarins, which are unusually short because they couldn't be built taller than the emperor, who was a mere 5ft. The pavilion contains a massive stone stele, a symbol of his imperial power and majesty, which was transported here from its original site in Thanh Hóa Province. This is inscribed in the emperor's own hand and tells the story of his triumphs and misfortunes. Adjacent to this terraced tomb site is the burial place of one of his adopted sons, Kiến Phước, and his first wife, Empress Lê Thiện Anh. Although he had 104 wives, Tự Đức fathered no sons. He was therefore forced to write his own eulogy, a fact that he took as a bad omen. The eulogy itself recounts the sadness in Tự Đức's life. A flavour of its sentiment can be gleaned from a confession he wrote in 1867 following French seizure of territory. It was shortly after Tự Đức's reign that France gained full control of Vietnam.

Dục Đức Tomb [247 F7] (Phước Vĩnh; ⌚ 07.30–17.30 daily; 50,000VND/free adult/child) Despite ruling for just three days and then dying in prison, Emperor Dục Đức (1852–83) has a tomb, which was built in 1899 by his son, Thành Thái, on the spot where, it is said, the body had been dumped. (Dục Đức was dethroned by the court for his pro-French sympathies.) Emperors Thành Thái and his son Duy Tân are buried in the neighbouring complex. Unlike Dục Đức, though, both were anti-French and were, for a period, exiled in Réunion Island, Africa. Although

Thành Thái later returned to Vietnam and died in Vũng Tàu in 1953, his son Duy Tân was killed in an air crash in central Africa in 1945. It was not until 1987 that Duy Tân's body was repatriated and interred alongside his father Thành Thái. The tombs are in three parts: the Long An Temple; Dục Đức's tomb to the south; and Thành Thái and Duy Tân's tombs adjacent to each other.

Đồng Khánh Tomb (Đoàn Nhữ Hải; ◷ 07.30–17.30 daily; 50,000VND/free adult/child) Đồng Khánh was the nephew and foster son of Emperor Tự Đức. Work on his tomb began in 1889, but was not completed until 1923 under the authority of his son Khải Định. Unusually, it has two separate sections. One is a walled area containing the usual series of pavilions and courtyards. The second, 100m uphill, consists of an open series of platforms. The lower platform has the honour guard of mandarins, horses and elephants, along with a stela pavilion; the third platform is a tiled area that would have had an awning; and the highest platform is the tomb itself. The crypt is enclosed within three open walls, the entrance protected by a dragon screen to prevent malicious spirits from entering. The tomb is notable for its views of pine forested hills and Gothic European touches, a reflection of the colonised country he ruled over.

Khải Định Tomb (Thủy Bằng, Hương Thủy; ◷ 07.00–17.30 daily; 150,000/75,000VND adult/child) Built between 1920 and 1931, this is the last of the mausoleums of the Nguyễn Dynasty and, by the time Khải Định was contemplating the afterlife, brick had given way in popularity to the concrete that is now beginning to deteriorate. Nevertheless, it occupies a fine position on Châu Mountain, facing southwest towards a large white statue of Quán Âm, also built by Khải Định. The valley, used for the cultivation of cassava and sugarcane, and the pine-covered mountains, make this one of the most beautifully sited and peaceful of the tombs. Indeed, before construction could begin, Khải Định had to remove the tombs of Chinese nobles who had already selected the site for its beauty and auspicious orientation. Had the terraced tomb been constructed today, it might be described as post-modern, as the bizarre blend of Vietnamese, Chinese, Cambodian and European styles is difficult to define. A total of 127 steep steps lead up to the Honour Courtyard, with statuary of mandarins, elephants and horses. An octagonal Stela Pavilion in the centre of the mourning yard contains a stone stela engraved with a eulogy to the emperor. At the top of some more stairs are the tomb and shrine of Khải Định, containing a bronze statue of the emperor sitting on his throne and holding a jade sceptre. The body is interred 9m below ground level. The interior is richly decorated with ornate murals and decorations built up with fragments of porcelain. Such was the cost of construction that Khải Định had to levy additional taxes to fund the project. The tomb shows distinct European stylistic influences. Khải Định was emperor only in name: by the early 20th century, the French had complete control over Vietnam. Denied political power, seduced by Western aristocratic decadence and presumably bewildered by his impotence, Khải Định indulged in a lavish lifestyle that is reflected in his flamboyant and muddled tomb.

Lebadang Memory Space (Kim Sơn village; f; ◷ 08.00–noon & 14.00–18.00 daily; 269,000VND/free adult/child; 1–2hrs) Huế's architecture isn't all centred around the Nguyễn Dynasty. Lebadang Memory Space, situated close to Khải Định Tomb in hilly terrain, is dedicated to the life and works of the Vietnamese-French artist Lê Bá Đảng. The modern building showcases a comprehensive collection of

Lê Bá Đảng's art, including paintings, sculptures, prints and mixed-media pieces. An additional part of the space houses up-and-coming artists from Huế and around. Even if you're not taken with the art, the steep entrance fee is worth paying to enter the garden, which is planted with a variety of different flowers so that there's always something in bloom.

✷ ***Từ Hiếu Pagoda*** (Dương Xuân Thượng III village) Từ Hiếu Pagoda is one of the most significant Buddhist temples in Vietnam and yet it receives few visitors. Most who do come are on a pilgrimage to pay their respects to world-famous Zen master Thích Nhất Hạnh, author of various books that have been translated into dozens of languages. Though he spent much of his life abroad, he died here at the pagoda at the age of 95 in 2022. The pagoda was originally established in 1843 by the monk Nhất Định, who built a small hermitage to care for his ailing mother. The site gained prominence with the support of the imperial court during Emperor Tự Đức's reign, which led to its expansion. The pagoda complex features traditional Vietnamese Buddhist and Nguyễn Dynasty architecture, particularly in the various gates. Surrounding the main hall are several ancillary buildings, including living quarters for monks, a bell tower and dozens of tombs. The entrance to the pagoda is through a pathway flanked by pine trees, but unfortunately the main entrance is surrounded by souvenir and incense sellers who are more forceful than they need to be.

Thanh Toàn Covered Bridge (Làng Xá Bầu; 20,000VND/free adult/child) A rare pre-Nguyễn Dynasty heritage site in Huế, this bridge, 6km east of central Huế, was built during the reign of King Lê Hiển Tông (1740–86) by Trần Thị Đạo, a childless woman, as an act of charity, hoping that she might be blessed with a baby. There is a shrine to her in the middle of the bridge, which was installed by Emperor Khải Định in 1925. The bridge, with its shelter for travellers and the homeless, attracted the interest of several kings, who granted the village immunity from a number of taxes. The original yin-yang tiles have been replaced with green enamelled tube tiles and the porcelain art at either end and on the roof is presumably a Nguyễn Dynasty-era addition, but the wooden structure is in good condition (it was most recently rebuilt in 1991). There is a pocket museum exhibiting traditional agricultural tools nearby, but it's often closed.

Around Huế There are various day and weekend trips close to Huế, including beaches, lagoons, mountains and the demilitarised zone (DMZ) in neighbouring Quảng Trị Province.

Thuận An Beach, the cemeteries and the lagoons The closest beach to Huế, just 15km from the city, is not the prettiest or cleanest in Central Vietnam, but nevertheless it makes a good spot to cool down during the brutal summers. The quieter patches are south of Thuận An town, but there's no standout stretch to recommend. The Beach Bar Huế (**w** beachbarhue.com; **$$$**) is the cleanest and most comfortable bar and they offer accommodation, but the food is overpriced and there's a minimum spend. The stick-thin stretch of land between the East Sea and lagoons is also home to one of Huế's more curious sights: entire villages built for the dead. Some Huế families take death very seriously, spending more money on the tombs of their ancestors than they do on their own homes. These are impossible to miss as you head south from Thuận An town with the picturesque lagoons on your right.

✷ ***Bạch Mã National Park*** (Phú Hội; **w** bachmapark.com.vn; ⌚ 08.00–16.30 daily; 65,000/25,000VND adult/child) The hilly woodlands of Bạch Mã National Park stretch from the Laotian border right down to the coast, and although little is virgin forest quite a lot of bird and animal life flourishes within its leafy branches. It is very worthy of a day or two of exploration for anybody interested in seeing Vietnam's nature, but is best avoided during the extremely rainy months of October and November. Indeed, this mountainous enclave experiences some of the highest rainfall in the country. The best time to visit might be March and April for the rhododendron blossom.

The French established a great many hill stations in Vietnam. Đà Lạt was the only one to really develop as a town. Most, like Sa Pa, Bà Nà and Tam Đảo, were rejuvenated, arguably to their detriment. Some others, like Bạch Mã, lay forgotten until recently and as a result have not suffered the curse of concrete. Now, the ruins of French villas have been uncovered, flights of steps unearthed and old gardens and ponds cleared.

Bạch Mã was established as a hill station in 1932, when the construction of a road made it accessible. By the outbreak of World War II there were 139 villas and a hotel. Recognising its natural beauty and biological diversity, the French gave it protected status. In 1991 the Vietnamese government classified it as a national park, with 22,031ha at its core and a further buffer zone of 21,300ha. The area is rugged granite overlain in places by sandstone rising to an altitude of 1,450m at the summit of Bạch Mã. Trails weave past cascades, through rhododendron woods and up the summit trail overlooking the remains of colonial villas.

The park is home to an array of mammals, including the red-shanked douc langur (*Pygathrix nemaeus*) and the buff-cheeked or white-cheeked gibbon (*Nomascus leucogenys*). Birdlife here is particularly interesting. Four restricted-range species are the Annam partridge (*Tropicoperdix chloropus merlini*), crested argus (*Rheinardia*), short-tailed scimitar babbler (*Jabouilleia danjoui*) and the grey-faced tit babbler (*Macronus kelleyi*). The most characteristic feature of Bạch Mã's birdlife is the large number of pheasants. Of the 12 species of pheasant recorded in Vietnam, seven have been seen in the park. A subspecies of the silver pheasant (*Lophura nycthemera*) lives here and Edwards's pheasant (*L. edwardsi*), believed extinct until it was rediscovered in 1996, was seen just outside the park buffer zone in 1998. There are many other species of interest, including the red-collared woodpecker (*Picus rabieri*), Blyth's kingfisher (*Alcedo hercules*) and the coral-billed ground cuckoo (*Carpococcyx renauldi*). For an organised tour from Huế – usually the easiest way to approach the national park – contact Oriental Sky Travel or Slow Travel Huế (both page 254). Phong Nha-based adventure tour company Jungle Boss (page 238) have recently pioneered three-day, two-night trips involving trekking and abseiling.

Lăng Cô and Cảnh Dương Beach The road from Huế to Lăng Cô passes through many pretty, red-tiled villages, compact and surrounded by clumps of bamboo and fruit trees that provide shade, shelter and sustenance. For colour there's bougainvillea, which, through grafting, produces pink and white leaves on the same branch. Just north of the Hải Vân Pass (page 294) lies the once-idyllic fishing village of Lăng Cô (about 65km south of Huế) on a spit of land, which has a number of excellent, beautifully positioned seafood restaurants along the road, especially overlooking Lăng Cô Lagoon on Nguyễn Văn Street. The beach here is attractive, but not extraordinary. Shortly after crossing the Lăng Cô Lagoon, dotted with coracles and fish traps, the road begins the long haul up to Hải Vân Pass, but the majority of traffic now diverts through the tunnel. Apparently, in the first year of his reign, Emperor Khải Định visited Lăng Cô and was so impressed that he ordered the construction of a summer palace. This, it seems, was never carried out, not even by his son Bảo Đại, who was fonder of acquiring palaces than building them. There are several guesthouses and tourist resorts on Lăng Cô. The Banyan Tree Group's Laguna Lăng Cô complex (Cù Dù; **w** lagunalangco.com; **$$$$$**), with its five-star resorts, a spa, shops and a golf course, is on Cảnh Dương Beach, just northwest of Lăng Cô.

A Lưới Huế's most mountainous district stretches the entire length of the province and borders Laos to the east. The drive to A Lưới town from Huế makes for a beautiful ride, especially the final few mountainous kilometres, where the road contorts around mountains and skips over rivers. There's little to do in the one-road town, but just outside is Hamburger Hill (page 276), the site of a brutal battle during the American War that will only really be of interest to war history buffs, and A Nôr Waterfall, a rocky and wild cascade with rock pools where you can swim. It's possible to get to the waterfall and back from Huế in a day, but there are also homestays and hotels close to A Nôr for extending the journey. Huế Crown A Lưới Retreat (Hồng Kim; **f** huecrown.aluoi; **$$**) is modern and appeals to Huế's rising middle class. Anôr House Homestay (A Nôr village; **$**) is one of many simple but comfortable homestays further up the road. The people here refer to themselves as Pa Co, a subgroup of the officially recognised

THE BATTLE OF KHE SANH AND ITS AFTERMATH

Khe Sanh (already the site of a bloody confrontation in April and May 1967) is the place where the North Vietnamese Army (NVA) tried to achieve another Điện Biên Phủ (page 144); in other words, an American humiliation. One of the NVA divisions, the 304th from Hanoi, even had Điện Biên Phủ emblazoned on its battle streamers. US general William Westmoreland would have nothing of it, and prepared for a massive confrontation. He hoped to bury Hồ Chí Minh's troops under tonnes of high explosives and achieve a Điện Biên Phủ in reverse.

The American high command had some warning of the attack: a North Vietnamese regimental commander was killed while he was surveying the base on 2 January 1968 and that was interpreted as meaning the NVA were planning a major assault. Special forces long-range patrols were dropped into the area around the base and photo reconnaissance increased. It became clear that 20,000–40,000 NVA troops were converging on Khe Sanh.

With the US Marines effectively surrounded in a place which the assistant commander of the 3rd Marine Division referred to as 'not really anywhere', there was a heavy exchange of fire later in January. At the height of the battle, 1,000 rounds of artillery rained down on the American defences every day. By 21 January, B-52 sorties were flown out of Guam and Thailand, a rescue mission that was nicknamed 'Operation Niagara'. The Marine artillery fired 159,000 shells; B-52s carpet-bombed the surrounding area. Relying on directions from Air Force Forward Air Controllers (FACs), each would drop 108 high-explosive 500lb bombs from very high altitude on the NVA positions.

Despite the haggard faces of the Marines, the attack on Khe Sanh didn't pan out the way the NVA had hoped. The commanders of the NVA realised there was no chance of repeating their swift and absolute success at Điện Biên Phủ against

Ta Oi ethnolinguistic group, which in Vietnam number around 50,000 and live predominantly in Thừa Thiên Huế and Quảng Trị provinces. Most homestays also sell handwoven crimson textiles, with patterns that differ from those of the ethnolinguistic groups in Northern Vietnam. Note that temperatures here tend to be cooler than in the lowlands, especially at night. For an organised tour from Huế, contact Oriental Sky Travel (page 254).

✷ ***Quảng Trị Province and the DMZ*** The province connecting Quảng Bình with Thừa Thiên Huế is Quảng Trị, infamous as the site of the 17th parallel along the Bến Hải River, where Vietnam was partitioned, and the demilitarised zone (DMZ), the theatre of some of the fiercest fighting during the American War. As the war fades from living memory, so too do the names of the battle sites that once grabbed headlines. The mention of Khe Sanh or Hamburger Hill is enough to give American veterans chills, but these days few visitors to Vietnam have even heard of these places. As nearly all war paraphernalia has been stripped from the DMZ, the visit is more of a pilgrimage than anything else. While it is still possible to explore the DMZ from Đông Hà, the capital of Quảng Trị Province, most visit the area as a day trip from Huế on an organised tour (page 254). Because demand is lower than it was, these tours tend to be private and therefore quite expensive, but this has the benefit of the option to pinpoint where you want to visit. It's not usually possible to see everything there is to see in the DMZ in one day. If transferring between Phong Nha and Huế (in either direction), it's possible to join a half-day group tour

the US military, and instead it was repurposed as a diversion tactic to enable the Tết Offensive (page 249). The siege had diverted over 30,000 US troops away from the cities, which had become the NVA's main target.

The Tết Offensive proved to be a remarkable psychological victory for the NVA – even if their 77-day siege of Khe Sanh cost many thousands (one estimate is 10,000–15,000) of NVA lives, while only 248 Americans were killed (43 of those in a C-123 transporter crash). As was the case throughout the war, a problem for the US military was one of presentation. Even Walter Cronkite, the doyen of TV reporters, informed his audience that, although the siege of Khe Sanh was not an NVA victory, the parallels between Khe Sanh and Điện Biên Phủ were 'there for all to see'.

A year later, 241 soldiers were killed on Ap Bia Mountain (Hamburger Hill) in the A Shau Valley, 65km to the south in Thừa Thiên Huế Province, while the Americans tried to secure the area. The so-called Delaware Operation was unsuccessful and was aborted once the NVA took control of Hamburger Hill. By 1970 it was estimated that over 10,000 tonnes of supplies per day were being transported along the Trường Sơn Highway, part of the Hồ Chí Minh Trail (page 275). The Trường Sơn Cemetery (page 274) contains 20,000 graves of NVA soldiers who had died attempting to liberate their country.

Before the signing of the Paris Accord, early in 1973, the Hồ Chí Minh Trail had suffered more than 800,000 air attacks and 2.5 million tonnes of ordnance. In early spring 1972, Quảng Trị town was pulverised by artillery and rocket fire from four NVA divisions. The B-52 carpet-bombing that followed the NVA occupation four months later finally put paid to what was left. Over 5,000 soldiers from South Vietnam who supported the American raids died in the ruins.

that includes a visit to Vịnh Mốc Tunnels and Hiền Lương Bridge with Heritage Adventure Trails.

History The DMZ was the creation of the 1954 Geneva Peace Accord, which divided the country into two spheres of influence prior to elections that were never held. Like its counterpart in Germany, the boundary evolved into a national border separating communist (the northern Democratic Republic of Vietnam) from capitalist (South Vietnam), but unlike its European equivalent it was the triumph of communism that saw its demise. For more than 20 years until liberation of the South in 1975, no civilian traffic or mail passed this point. On the southern side the Americans built a series of powerful firebases constituting the impenetrable McNamara Defence Line. These included Đông Hà, Cam Lộ, Camp Carroll, Ca Lu, the 230m-high Rockpile lookout site and the famous Khe Sanh Base, which was to suffer one of the longest sieges of the war in 1968 (page 272). The line needed to extend from the coast as far as the Laotian border if it was to destroy the lifeline of the Việt Minh campaign in South Vietnam, the Trường Sơn Highway, better known as the Hồ Chí Minh Trail (see opposite).

✷ Quảng Trị town During the worst fighting, the town of Quảng Trị was wiped out and the **Quảng Trị Citadel** (Lý Thái Tổ; ⌚ 07.00–17.00 daily), built under the orders of Emperor Minh Mạng in 1824, was reduced to a pile of rubble. Sections of it have since been rebuilt. Nearby are the haunting remains of **Long Hưng Church** (Phường 3), which was built in 1955 and taken over by the NVA during the siege of Quảng Trị in 1972. Further south is the bell tower of the **La Vang Church** (Lê Lợi), built in the early 20th century but also largely destroyed during the siege.

Hiền Lương Bridge (Cầu Hiền Lương Vĩ Tuyến 17; Gio Linh town) Hiền Lương Bridge spans the Bến Hải River and marks the 17th parallel, the provisional demarcation line from the 1954 Geneva Accords. After Vietnam's reunification in 1975, the pedestrian bridge became a symbol of unity and domestic tourists come from across Vietnam to have their picture taken here. There is also a memorial and small museum.

✷ Vịnh Mốc Tunnels (Vĩnh Thạch; ⌚ 07.00–17.00 daily; 40,000VND/free adult/child) These visitable tunnels, 13km northeast of Hiền Lương Bridge, eventually served a function like that of the better-known Củ Chi Tunnels (page 481). They began as families in the heavily bombed village dug themselves shelters beneath their houses and then joined up with their neighbours. The tunnels are arranged in three tiers and stretch for 2,034m, with dozens of cubicles. During the war years, 17 children were born here. A few became guides who were able to show visitors exactly where they were born, but they have since retired. Later the tunnels developed a more offensive role when Việt Cộng soldiers fought from them. While exploring the tunnels you will come to a widened area that was used for public meetings, medical treatment or storage of supplies. One of the biggest chambers can hold around 150 people. Amazingly, these tunnels were used long after 1975 as protection from typhoons; during a typhoon in 1985, a baby was born in one of the cubicles.

Trường Sơn National Military Cemetery (Vĩnh Trường; ⌚ 06.00–18.00 daily) This cemetery is 17km west of Hiền Lương Bridge. Here you will see more than 10,000 graves of soldiers and peasants who died while transporting goods or building new arteries of the Hồ Chí Minh Trail. If you look along the tombstones you will see nearly every village in Vietnam mentioned somewhere. Many died not only from US bombs but also from malaria, thirst, hunger, overwork, snakebite and attacks by wild animals.

Rock Pile (Thượng Lâm village) This 230m-high limestone outcrop, just south of the DMZ between Đông Hà and Khe Sanh, served as a US observation post. An apparently unassailable position, troops, ammunition, Budweiser and prostitutes all had to be helicoptered in. The sheer walls of the Rock Pile were eventually scaled by the Việt Cộng. Jon Swain, the war correspondent, describes in his memoirs, *River of Time*, how his helicopter got lost around the Rock Pile and nearly came to disaster in this severely contested zone.

Hồ Chí Minh Trail The Hồ Chí Minh Trail (see below) segments here are an inevitably disappointing 'sight', given that their whole purpose was to be as inconspicuous as possible, but nevertheless this is a worthy pilgrimage considering the sacrifice of millions of Vietnamese porters and the role it played in the American defeat. The trail was more of a shapeshifting network, with many of the concealed pathways running close to Khe Sanh. There is a monument near the Đa Krông Bridge, 16km east of the town.

THE HỒ CHÍ MINH TRAIL

The Hồ Chí Minh Trail was a route used by the North Vietnamese Army (NVA) to ferry equipment from the North to the South, sometimes via Laos and Cambodia. The road, or more accurately roads (there were around a dozen to reduce choke points) were camouflaged in places, allowing the NVA to get supplies to their comrades in the South through the heaviest bombing by US planes. Even the use of defoliants such as Agent Orange only marginally stemmed the flow.

The road was built and kept operational by 300,000 full-time workers and by another 200,000 part-time North Vietnamese peasant workers. Neil Sheehan, in his book *A Bright Shining Lie*, estimates that at no time were more than one third of trucks destroyed, and by marching through the most dangerous sections, the forces themselves suffered a loss rate of only 10–20%.

Initially, supplies were transported along the trail by bicycle, many of which were made in Czechoslovakia; later, as supplies of trucks from China and the Soviet Union became more plentiful, they were carried by motorised transport. By the end of the conflict, the Hồ Chí Minh Trail comprised 15,360km of all-weather and secondary roads. One hero of the People's Army is said, during the course of the war, to have carried and pushed 55 tonnes of supplies a distance of 41,025km – roughly the circumference of the world.

The Hồ Chí Minh Trail represents perhaps the best example of how, through revolutionary fervour, ingenuity and weight of people (not of arms), the Việt Cộng were able to vanquish the might of the USA. But American pilots did exact a terrible toll through the years. Sheehan writes: 'Driving a truck year in year out with 20–25 to perhaps 30% odds of mortality was not a military occupation conducive to retirement on pension.' The cemetery for those who died on the trail at Trường Sơn covers 16ha and contains 10,306 named headstones; many more died unnamed and unrecovered. The most comprehensive museum about the Hồ Chí Minh Trail is in Hanoi (page 122).

✷ **Khe Sanh** This is the site of one of the most famous battles of the war (page 272). The battleground lies along the Hồ Chí Minh Highway that runs 3km from the prosperous town of the same name. There a small museum at the remains of the Tacon military base, surrounded by military hardware. Khe Sanh town makes for a good lunch stop.

Hamburger Hill South of the DMZ and closer to A Lưới in Huế (page 272), this was the site of a brutal battle for high ground in 1969. Hamburger Hill takes its gruesome name from soldiers' perception that they were being ground up like hamburger meat, as the battle involved intense, close-quarters combat. The hill was abandoned shortly after its capture, sparking controversy over its strategic value, and the battle fuelled anti-war sentiment that was a contributing factor to the reduction in American ground involvement. Today there is not much to see.

Đà Nẵng

Clean, green and keen to be seen, Đà Nẵng is often referred to as Vietnam's most liveable city. Sliced in half by the Hàn River, ringed by green mountains that roll into the sea and graced with a sweeping metropolitan beach, Đà Nẵng's setting is undoubtedly preferable to that of Hanoi and Hồ Chí Minh City, but it's how the city has adapted to its surroundings that has won it admirers. In spite of (rather, because of) a decades-long construction boom, the broad river, multi-lane streets and pedestrian pavements give the city a sense of space that is hard to come by elsewhere in urban Vietnam.

Indeed, what modern Đà Nẵng has done better than any other big Vietnamese city is create public space. The metropolitan beach spans more than 10km and is open to all. Behind the beach is not a busy road or an impenetrable wall of glass-fronted hotels, but a chain of grassy parks, pedestrian boulevards and outdoor gyms. In central Đà Nẵng, there are broad public walkways along both sides of the Hàn River with green space like the APEC Park and Điện Hải Citadel speckling the neighbourhoods. For city planners elsewhere in the country, Đà Nẵng is the urban star they look to for guidance.

Another of Đà Nẵng's major appeals is its proximity to nature. The forested Sơn Trà Peninsula is largely undeveloped and home to the striking red-shanked douc langur, a rare creature that is surprisingly easy to spot. The waterfalls and karst caves of the Marble Mountains and the legendary Hải Vân Pass with its hilltop fort are also within easy reach. To top it all off, the city has a rich food scene (as evidenced by the inclusion of some of its restaurants in the Michelin Guide from 2024), a clutch of atmospheric cafés, wonderfully wacky bridges (including one that breathes fire) and some decent museums, including the superb Museum of Cham Sculpture.

Đà Nẵng is not without its problems. The primary offender is, as always, overdevelopment. Poor planning and investment decisions mean that large sections of beach are washed away after abnormally aggressive typhoons, and many construction projects seem to be in a perpetual state of abandonment. In the city centre, many heritage buildings have been pointlessly bulldozed, only to be replaced with dreary substitutes. It's also a place where cultural institutions have not yet had time to mature and develop depth; there's a notable dearth of galleries, exhibitions, live music and other cultural offerings when compared with Hanoi and Hồ Chí Minh City. Some underestimate this when trying to settle in the city long-term and move on after a year or two.

Đà Nẵng, perhaps more than any other city in Vietnam, is a place that eschews the past and embraces the future. While some believe that this philosophy is incompatible with Đà Nẵng's claim to be Vietnam's most liveable city, most accept that this young, fun and geographically dramatic place is worthy of at least a couple of days.

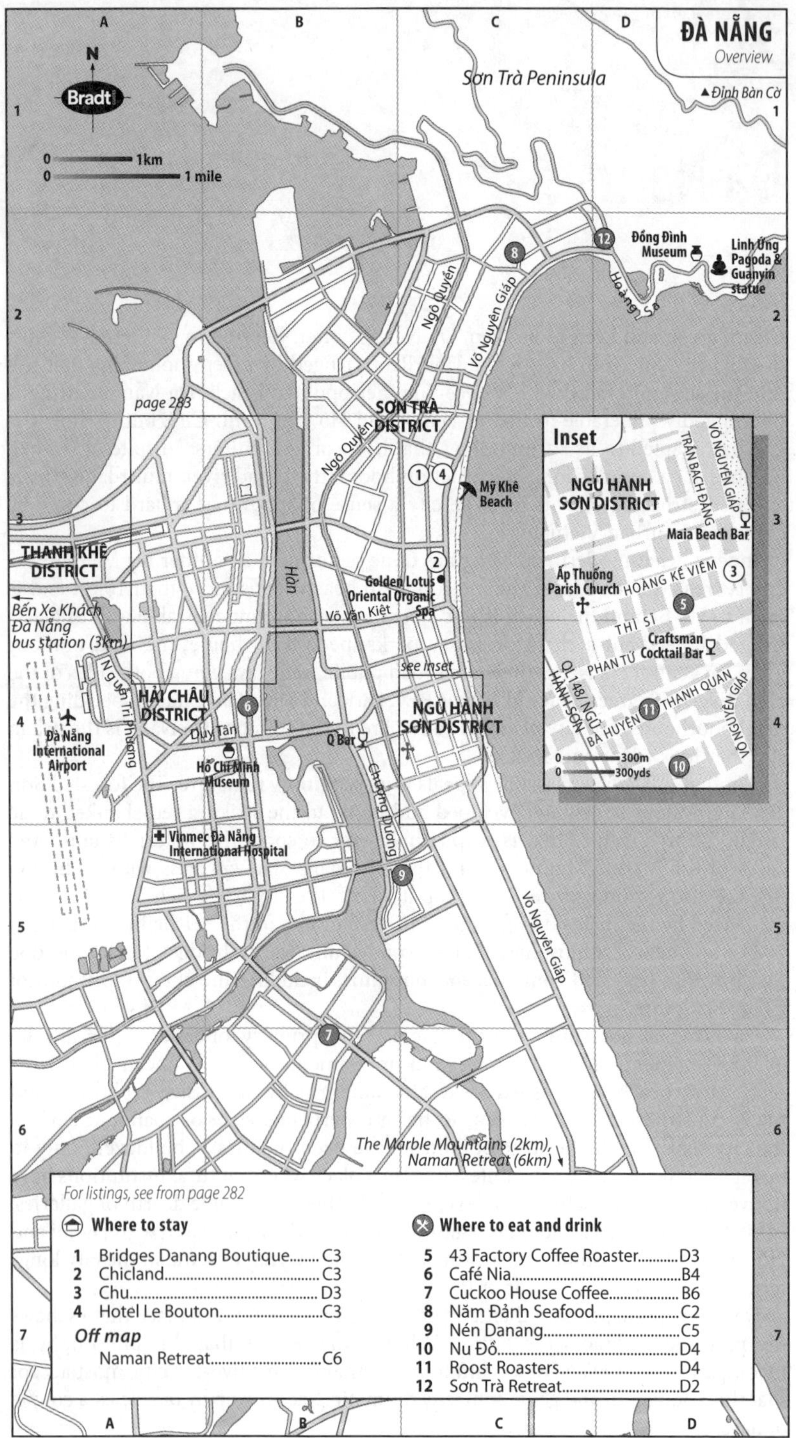

For listings, see from page 282

Where to stay

1	Bridges Danang Boutique	C3
2	Chicland	C3
3	Chu	D3
4	Hotel Le Bouton	C3

Off map

Naman Retreat C6

Where to eat and drink

5	43 Factory Coffee Roaster	D3
6	Café Nia	B4
7	Cuckoo House Coffee	B6
8	Năm Đảnh Seafood	C2
9	Nén Danang	C5
10	Nu Đồ	D4
11	Roost Roasters	D4
12	Sơn Trà Retreat	D2

HISTORY

Đà Nẵng sits in a region of great historical significance. Fairly close to the city in Quảng Nam Province lies Mỹ Sơn (page 314) – the ruins of a sanctuary of the powerful kingdom of Champa, one of the most artistically prolific civilisations in ancient Southeast Asia. The Cham are an Austronesian people with historical connections to the civilisations of Indonesia and Malaysia. According to Chinese texts, in the year 192 a group of tribes formed a union they called Lin Yi, later to become Champa. The area now known as Đà Nẵng became a small coastal settlement in the kingdom.

The polytheistic religion of Champa was a fusion of Buddhism, Shivaism and local elements, producing an abundance of religious sculptures and monuments. Shiva is usually represented as a lingam, an abstract phallic- or disc-shaped representation of the god. The kingdom reached its apogee in the 10th and 11th centuries but, unlike the Khmers, Champa never created a capital city matching the magnificence of Angkor. For long periods the Cham were compelled to pay tribute to the Chinese, and after that they were dominated by the Vietnamese and the Khmers in turn. The Cham state was finally eradicated in 1471, although there are still Cham living in Vietnam, mostly around Phan Thiết (page 342) and Châu Đốc (page 419). Given this turbulent history, it is perhaps surprising that the Cham found any opportunity for the kinds of artistic endeavours found in the Museum of Cham Sculpture (page 289), Vietnam's most comprehensive collection. (For more on the history of the Champa Kingdom, see page 12.)

In Vietnamese, Đà Nẵng was originally known as Cửa Hàn (Mouth of the Hàn River) and it became an important port that acted as a gateway to Huế, the Imperial Citadel. In 1858, its fortified battlements were attacked by the French. Under the command of Admiral Rigault de Genouilly, 2,000 troops overran the An Hải and Điện Hải posts and proceeded up the Hàn River. It was an expedition that had been approved by Napoleon III to push the emperor Tự Đức into allowing trade with France. General Nguyễn Tri Phương successfully resisted the invasion, so the French focused their efforts on Gia Định (present-day Hồ Chí Minh City) instead. By 1889, France had control of the city, renamed it Tourane and expanded its capabilities as a port. The city acquired the name Thái Phiên after the 1945 Declaration of Independence, and then ultimately Đà Nẵng, possibly a Vietnamese version of the Cham term for the opening of a large river. When Vietnam was split in two in 1954, Đà Nẵng fell into what was South Vietnam.

Đà Nẵng became famous when US Marine battalions landed here in December 1965 to secure the airfield. They were the first of a great many more who would land on the beaches and airfields of South Vietnam. The huge American base they built here was protected by 140 military posts and included two new airfields, Nước Mặn and Nón Nước, near the Marble Mountains. This was so heavily pounded by enemy artillery that it was nicknamed 'Rocket City'. It is ironic, then, that when Đà Nẵng was officially taken by the communists on 29 March 1975, it's said that not a single shot was fired in resistance. Originally part of Quảng Nam, the province that surrounds the city, Đà Nẵng gained municipal independence in 1997.

Đà Nẵng Bay is a marvellous natural harbour and today the port is the third busiest in the country, after Hồ Chí Minh City and Hải Phòng. Đà Nẵng represents modern Vietnam better than anywhere else, and many smaller towns and cities, particularly those on the coast, have been forged in its image. The city's transformation in the past 30 years has been remarkable, in part due to party secretary and People's Council president Nguyễn Bá Thanh, an astute and ambitious city leader. It has undergone a whirlwind-like period of growth and continues to expand at a phenomenal rate.

The city was quickly crisscrossed and ringed by huge dual carriageways. Within months of the new roads' arrival, they were fleshed out with factories, shops and houses. A suite of multi-coloured bridges now spans the Hàn River, and even the Sơn Trà Peninsula has seen some development, with the InterContinental group opening a large resort. The beach stretching from Đà Nẵng to Hội An began disappearing under concrete as hotel expansion advanced at a rapid rate. Today the entire stretch is taken up with either five-star resorts or half-finished properties that have seemingly been left for the sea to claim.

One of the many markers of Đà Nẵng's success came in 2017, when the city hosted the APEC (Asia–Pacific Economic Cooperation) Economic Leaders' Meeting. Further investment flooded into the city, widening roads and upgrading the international airport so that Vietnam might put on a good show. The world's most powerful men at the time – including Shinzo Abe, Vladimir Putin, Donald Trump and Xi Jinping – jetted in for the signing ceremony. In the summer of 2020, Vietnam's almost immaculate Covid-19 infection record came to an end in Đà Nẵng when a cluster of infections were detected. Vietnam had implemented a successful zero-Covid strategy from the beginning of the year, but the outbreak led to the country recording its first death from the virus at the end of July. There was an outpouring of support from across Vietnam for Đà Nẵng, a city that many associate with fun family holidays. The city swiftly locked down and managed to stamp out the virus in two months, and Vietnam remained more or less Covid-free until the end of the year. The pandemic battered Vietnam's inbound tourism industry, but Đà Nẵng fared better than nearby Hội An and Huế due to its popularity with domestic tourists. Since the borders opened in 2022, the city's visitor economy has roared back to life, spurring Đà Nẵng's fledgling but promising cultural scenes.

WHEN TO VISIT

Đà Nẵng's long, sunny summers run from April to September. Temperatures heat up in June and July, but a sea breeze is never far away. The city is popular with domestic tourists from June to August, and although hotel prices are higher at

ĐÀ NẴNG INTERNATIONAL FIREWORKS FESTIVAL (DIFF)

DIFF (**w** diff.vn) spans multiple weekends from late April to early June each year, when teams from various countries compete, each presenting a themed display choreographed to music. Past themes have included 'The Legend of Bridges' and 'The Marble Mountains'. During the festival, the city takes on a party-like atmosphere, with cultural performances, traditional music, food stalls – and masses of visitors. Though the city gets crowded, you can enjoy the fireworks from just about anywhere. The best viewing spots, however, are on Trần Hưng Đạo Street, Bạch Đằng Street and various other points on the riverbank. Alternatively, you can watch the fireworks from boats on the river – for a price. If you're coming for the festival and don't plan on taking to the water, find a hotel that is within walking distance to the river so you don't need to contend with the traffic. Note that accommodation prices tend to increase during the festival weekends, and you should book accommodation many months in advance.

this time of year, you shouldn't struggle to find somewhere to stay. The rains begin in October and usually finish in February, so this half of the year is best avoided. Typhoons, which can cause floods, may hit Đà Nẵng in October and November.

GETTING THERE AND AWAY

BY RAIL Đà Nẵng's central train station, Ga Đà Nẵng [283 A4] (202 Hải Phòng; **w** danangstation.com.vn), is only slightly closer to the centre than the airport. Taking a taxi or Grab to and from here will not be an issue, with the journey to and from your hotel unlikely to take more than 15 minutes or cost more than 100,000VND. Note that at the time of research, the train station had no ATM, but plenty of snack stands. If heading straight for Hội An (which has no train station), a taxi down the coast will cost around 600,000VND. For tips and tricks on how to purchase train tickets, see page 59. If you are going north, the train is recommended because the tracks pass over the Hải Vân Pass (page 251).

BY BUS Đà Nẵng's central bus station, Bến Xe Khách Đà Nẵng [278 A3] (Hòa An; **w** benxedanang.vn), is further from the centre than both the airport and the train station, on the border between Liên Chiểu and Cẩm Lệ districts. If you turn up here without a booking and looking like a tourist, everyone will assume that you want to go to Hội An (about an hour) which costs little more than a dollar. Trips to Huế (about 2hrs) will cost double that. You can also travel just about anywhere else from here, including Hanoi and Đồng Hới (for Phong Nha) to the north and Kon Tum, Buôn Ma Thuột, Đà Lạt, Quy Nhơn, Nha Trang and even Hồ Chí Minh City (which can take up to 24hrs). While long-distance bus companies do operate from here and it's possible to turn up and jump on the bus you want within a few hours at most, it's better to book these more ambitious journeys in advance. This usually has the added benefit of a hotel pick-up, so you don't need to contend with out-of-the-way bus stations. For information on how to book buses, including which websites to use, see page 60.

BY AIR Due to its diminutive size, Đà Nẵng's airport is delightfully free of hassle. The terminus for both international and domestic flights, Đà Nẵng International Airport [278 A4] (Nguyễn Văn Linh; **w** vietnamairport.vn), is a mere 2.5km from the Hàn River and central Đà Nẵng; it's usually possible to get there from anywhere in the city in less than 20 minutes. Immediately after baggage reclaim, you'll find kiosks where you can buy a local SIM card, money exchange desks and ATMs. Note that ATMs usually offer better rates than the exchange desks, even when you factor in the charges. As the airport is basically inside the city, few use public transport to travel into the centre; Vietnamese on a budget will usually use Grab or ask a friend or relative to pick them up on a motorbike. A line of taxis is always present outside arrivals, and it shouldn't cost more than 150,000VND to travel to your hotel if you're staying within the city limits. Always ask them to use the meter. You can also attempt to take a Grab taxi or motorbike (page 62) for a slightly cheaper price, though locating your driver can be tricky. The fancier hotels can arrange pick-up at competitive prices. If arriving at the airport and heading straight for Hội An (which has no airport), a taxi down the coast will cost around 600,000VND.

ORIENTATION

Đà Nẵng, with the East Sea to the east, Thừa Thiên Huế Province to the north and Quảng Nam Province to the south and west, is a relatively small city by Asian standards, with a population of a little over a million. There are eight districts: Hải Châu, Thanh Khê, Sơn Trà, Ngũ Hành Sơn, Liên Chiểu, Cẩm Lệ, the rural district of Hòa Vang, and the island district of Hoàng Sa (which is also claimed by China). **Hải Châu** and **Thanh Khê** form central Đà Nẵng, hosting numerous restaurants, cafés, bars, shopping centres, and significant landmarks such as the Museum of Cham Sculpture, the train station, the airport and several of the city's iconic bridges. These districts dominate the west side of the Hàn River. **Ngũ Hành Sơn** and **Sơn Trà** districts dominate the east side of the Hàn River, with Đà Nẵng's clean and accessible beach, the Sơn Trà Peninsula (a rugged and jungled outcrop), and the Marble Mountains, a cluster of five marble and limestone hills named after the five elements. **Liên Chiểu** and **Cẩm Lệ** districts are largely residential and industrial; Hòa Vang District holds the enormous Bà Nà Hills theme park and entertainment complex (page 294) and the highly sensitive Hoàng Sa District is an archipelago (known as the Paracel Islands in English) that is more than 200km east of the city and is nigh on impossible for tourists to visit. Most, if not all, of your time will be spent in Hải Châu, Thanh Khê, Sơn Trà and Ngũ Hành Sơn.

GETTING AROUND

Đà Nẵng is a small but sprawling city. The city's capacious public space is a wonder, but because sights and areas of interest are so spread out, tackling Đà Nẵng entirely by foot can be tedious, especially during the scorching summers and soggy winters. The best strategy is to organise the things you want to do into walkable neighbourhoods, then use a taxi or Grab, which are cheap and ubiquitous, to move between those neighbourhoods. You can flag down **taxis** (there are dozens of companies all offering similar prices) anywhere and journeying between neighbourhoods won't cost more than 80,000VND. It's probably not worth getting your head around the limited public transport system. Another approach is to rent a motorbike. This might be an unthinkable way to move around Hanoi and Hồ Chí Minh City, but motorbiking on Đà Nẵng's broad, congestion-free streets is relatively easy, and perhaps even fun. Some hotels close to the beach will also lend bicycles, but they're usually just for getting to the water and back.

TOUR OPERATORS

Danang Waterfalls (w danangwaterfalls.com) arranges intrepid tours to the various waterfalls in Đà Nẵng and beyond. **Danang Easyriders** (w danangeasyriders.com) is recommended for motorbikes in and around Đà Nẵng. For an audio tour designed and narrated by the author of this guidebook, download the VoiceMap app (w voicemap.me).

WHERE TO STAY

Thanks to Đà Nẵng's building boom, you'll have no trouble finding somewhere to stay. However, as in other fast-changing places in Vietnam, it's impossible to keep an evergreen directory of recommended accommodation. The hotels listed here are special in some way and are likely to see out the decade. Due to the growing popularity of online booking platforms with recent reviews, one option is to decide where in the city you want to be and then to search online. The question to ask yourself is: city or beach?

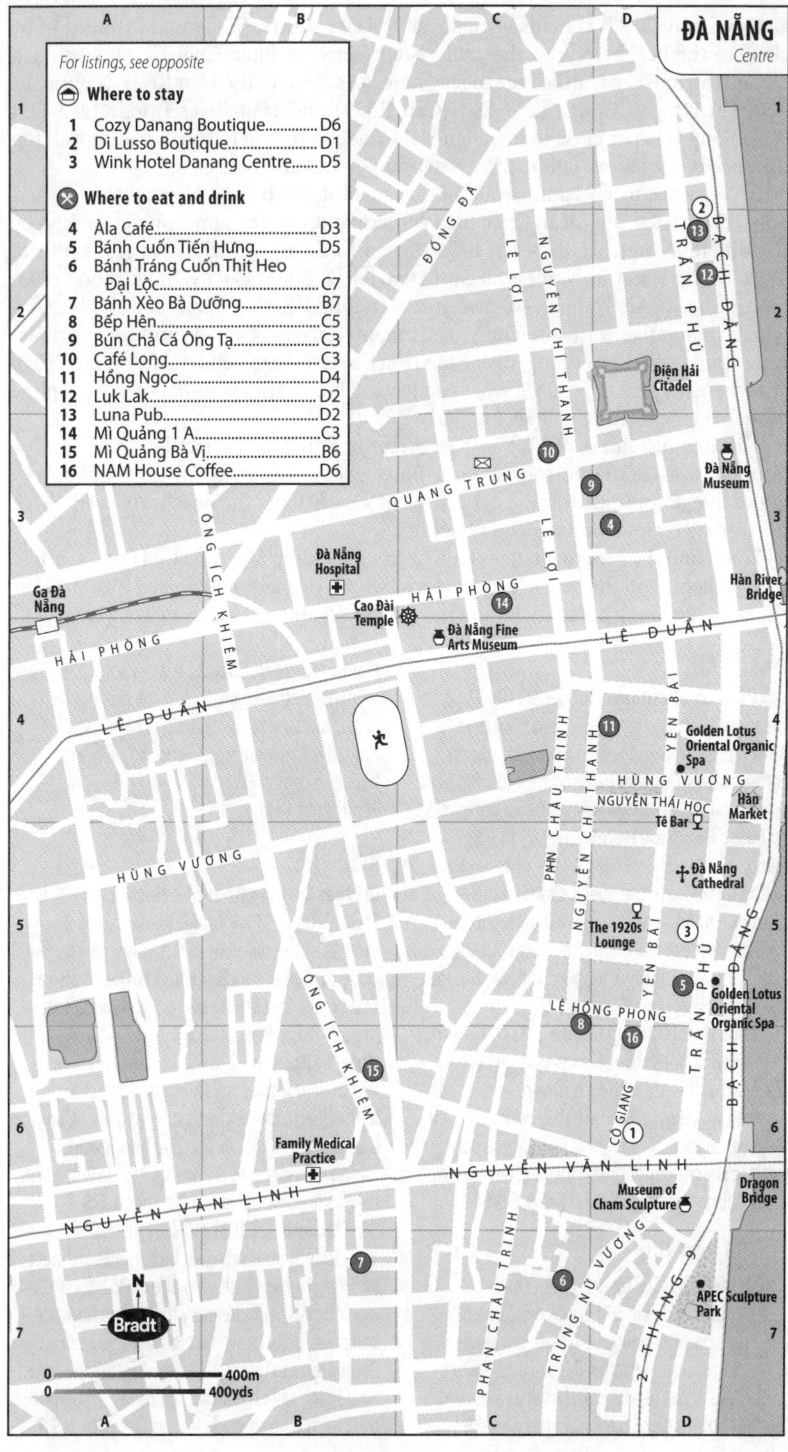
ĐÀ NẴNG
Centre
For listings, see opposite
Where to stay
1 Cozy Danang Boutique.............D6
2 Di Lusso Boutique.......................D1
3 Wink Hotel Danang Centre.......D5
Where to eat and drink
4 Àla Café.......................................D3
5 Bánh Cuốn Tiến Hưng.................D5
6 Bánh Tráng Cuốn Thịt Heo Đại Lộc...C7
7 Bánh Xèo Bà Dưỡng.....................B7
8 Bếp Hên.......................................C5
9 Bún Chả Cá Ông Tạ......................C3
10 Café Long....................................C3
11 Hồng Ngọc...................................D4
12 Luk Lak..D2
13 Luna Pub......................................D2
14 Mì Quảng 1 A...............................C3
15 Mì Quảng Bà Vị............................B6
16 NAM House Coffee......................D6
ĐỐNG ĐA
LÊ LỢI
NGUYỄN CHÍ THANH
TRẦN PHÚ
BẠCH ĐẰNG
Điện Hải Citadel
Đà Nẵng Museum
QUANG TRUNG
ÔNG ÍCH KHIÊM
Đà Nẵng Hospital
Hàn River Bridge
Ga Đà Nẵng
HẢI PHÒNG
Cao Đài Temple
Đà Nẵng Fine Arts Museum
LÊ DUẨN
YÊN BÁI
PHAN CHÂU TRINH
Golden Lotus Oriental Organic Spa
HÙNG VƯƠNG
NGUYỄN THÁI HỌC
Hàn Market
Tê Bar
Đà Nẵng Cathedral
The 1920s Lounge
LÊ HỒNG PHONG
CÔ GIANG
Family Medical Practice
NGUYỄN VĂN LINH
Museum of Cham Sculpture
Dragon Bridge
TRƯNG NỮ VƯƠNG
2 THÁNG 9
APEC Sculpture Park
Bradt
N
0 400m
0 400yds

Hải Châu [278 A4] holds virtually all the **city sights**, so if you don't need to be close to the beach, look in the grid system between Phan Châu Trinh and Bạch Đằng. The most charming area to stay here is as close to the Hàn River as possible, between Dragon Bridge [283 D6] (Cầu Rồng) and Hàn River Bridge [283 D3] (Cầu Sông Hàn) or close to the Điện Hải Citadel. From here you're within walking distance of museums, landmarks, restaurants, cafés and bars.

If you want to be within walking distance of the **beach**, Ngũ Hành Sơn and Sơn Trà districts are ideal. Over the last decade or so, the atmospheres offered by the different stretches of beach have started to diverge. In the area just south of Trần Thị Lý Street in **Ngũ Hành Sơn District** [278 D3] is a neighbourhood often referred to as An Thương – between Ấn Thuống Parish Church and the beach – which is popular with foreigners, with many dozens of hotels and international restaurants within walking distance. Hotel prices here tend to be higher than elsewhere. In general, you get what you pay for, but check up-to-date reviews online as management teams change regularly.

The area just north of Võ Văn Kiệt Street in **Sơn Trà District** [278 C2] is more popular with domestic tourists and hotel prices are lower; you can find very affordable accommodation just a few blocks back from the beach. As ever, check up-to-date reviews online before booking.

You'll find the generic luxury chain hotels, including Marriot and Hyatt, south of the city centre on the beach. Regardless of where you stay, you'll need transport for the more far-flung areas, including the Marble Mountains and Sơn Trà Peninsula.

HẢI CHÂU

Cozy Danang Boutique Hotel [283 D6] 37 Cô Giang; w booking.com. Mere steps from the Cham Museum, Dragon Bridge & a slew of restaurants & coffee houses, Cozy has neat rooms, a rooftop pool, good service & an above average b/fast buffet. **$$**

Di Lusso Boutique Hotel [283 D1] 14 Bạch Đằng; w dilussohotel.com. A little outside the action but close to the river & citadel is this boutique hotel, spread across a handful of floors. There's a film set feel about the lobby, but the rooms are attractively arranged; front-facing ones have small balconies & views. **$$**

✷ **Wink Hotel Danang Centre** [283 D5] 178 Trần Phú; w wink-hotels.com. Funky, modern hotel in the heart of the city, with tech-driven services, co-working space, gym & some handy perks, like 24hr stays (ie: check in for a night at 16.00 & you don't need to check out until 16.00 the next day). Rooms are small, no-nonsense & have views. **$$$**

NGŨ HÀNH SƠN

Chu Hotel [278 D3] 02–04–06 Ấn Thuống 1; f chuhotel.danang. This was once one of the area's premier boutique hotels, but since it was surrounded by taller, flashier and uglier properties, it has repositioned itself as a decent budget hotel a block back from the water. **$**

Naman Retreat [278 C6] Trường Sơn; w namanretreat.com. One of the greener & lusher hotels on a beach strip of high-rises. Naman is conveniently positioned halfway between central Đà Nẵng & Hội An & is only 20mins from either. **$$$**

SƠN TRÀ

Bridges Danang Boutique Hotel [278 C3] 4 Phước Trường 11; w bridgesdanang.com. Each room is a little different in this industrial chic hotel close to a small park & the beach. There's also a small gym, co-working space & café, & staff are friendly & approachable. **$$**

Hotel Le Bouton [278 C3] 12 Trần Đình Đàn; w hotellebouton.com. Quirky design hotel, close to the beach, that eschews straight lines, Le Bouton is a bit of a gimmick, & yet somehow it works. Whitewashed rooms are brought to life with earthy colours from wood, rattan & bamboo. **$$**

✷ **Chicland** [278 C3] 210 Võ Nguyên Giáp; w chiclandhotel.com. Built by biophilic architect Võ Trọng Nghĩa, Chicland is one of Đà Nẵng's iconic hotels, with greenery that bursts from the balconies. Select a sea-facing view if you can. Rooms tend to be small, but intelligently designed with space-saving features. There's a rooftop pool & the beach is just outside (across the road). **$$$**

WHERE TO EAT AND DRINK

RESTAURANTS AND STREET FOOD

Bánh Cuốn Tiến Hưng [283 D5] 190 Trần Phú; 06.00–19.00 daily. Tiến Hưng has been serving Đà Nẵng's version of *bánh cuốn* for decades. Here it's topped with pork floss (dried pork with the texture of cotton wool) & crispy deep-fried shallots, with a green salad & meatballs served on the side. $

✷ **Bánh Xèo Bà Dưỡng** [283 B7] 280/23 Hoàng Diệu; 09.30–21.30 daily. Hugely popular place that specialises in a deep-fried pancake, which is wrapped in leaves & dipped. The grilled pork & beef is also worth ordering. $

✷ **Bún Chả Cá Ông Tạ** [283 C3] 113A Nguyễn Chí Thanh; 06.00–22.00 daily. Surely one of the best places to go for this Đà Nẵng speciality of vermicelli noodles served in a fish broth & topped with fish cake & other delectables. $

Mì Quảng 1A [283 C3] 1 Hải Phòng; 06.00–21.00 daily. A convenient place to try Đà Nẵng's number 1 speciality noodle dish, as it's close to many sights & is open all the time. $

Mì Quảng Bà Vị [283 B6] 166 Lê Đình Dương; 06.00–23.00 daily. Another *mì Quảng* favourite that is out of the way but worth the extra effort. Choose to combine your noodles with fish, beef, pork, shrimp or all of the above. $

Bánh Tráng Cuốn Thịt Heo Đại Lộc [283 C7] 97/148 Trưng Nữ Vương; 08.00–22.00 daily. Probably the best of a cluster of restaurants serving the Đà Nẵng speciality of roll-it-yourself pork belly & greens with dry rice paper. $$

ĐÀ NẴNG'S SPECIALITY DISHES

The places at which to try these dishes are listed from above.

MÌ QUẢNG ĐÀ NẴNG Đà Nẵng used to be a part of Quảng Nam, which is why the province's signature dish is also popular here. The dish is part soup, part salad, part noodle and hugely flexible, often served with pork, chicken, fish and shrimp. Try it at **Mì Quảng 1A**, **Mì Quảng Bà Vì** and **Nu Đỗ**.

BÚN MẮM NÊM Cold rice vermicelli noodles with roasted pork and anchovy fish sauce. Hugely popular with locals, though less so with visitors because of its strong fermented taste and smell. Try it at **Hàn Market** (Chợ Hàn).

BÚN CHẢ CÁ Not to be confused with Hanoian *bún chả*, *bún chả cá* is rice vermicelli noodle soup with fried fish cakes, usually served with a garden salad. Try it at **Bún Chả Cá Ông Tạ**.

BÁNH TRÁNG CUỐN THỊT HEO This is boiled and sliced pork served with vegetables, fruit and a garden salad. Wrap them all together in dry rice paper and dip the parcel into a peanut and sesame sauce. Try it at **Bánh Tráng Cuốn Thịt Heo Đại Lộc**.

HẢI SẢN *Hải sản* means seafood and, thanks in part to Đà Nẵng's roaring domestic tourism industry, this is one of the best places in Vietnam to sample it. Some restaurants have live fish and seafood – prawns, squid, clams, mussels, oysters, and virtually anything else you can imagine – in big tanks. If the menus are confusing, simply point at what you want to eat. Always ask for the price first, as eating seafood in Vietnam can be surprisingly pricey when compared with other dishes (though still a fraction of the price in Europe). Try **Năm Đảnh Seafood** and the restaurants at **Mỹ Khê Beach**.

✷ **Bếp Hên Restaurant** [283 C5] 47 Lê Hồng Phong; w bephenrestaurant.com; ⌚ 09.00–15.00 & 17.00–21.00 daily. Huge menu of Vietnamese dishes served with rice, including tofu, meat & vegetables. Try tofu stir-fried with lemongrass & chilli, grilled eggplant & the *canh chua* (sweet & sour broth). $$

Hồng Ngọc [283 D4] 193 Nguyễn Chí Thanh; ⌚ 06.30–21.30 daily. Chicken & yellow rice are done extremely well in this time-honoured, family-run establishment which, in recent years, has undergone a makeover (prices remain very reasonable). $$

Nu Đồ [278 D4] 11/1 Lưu Quang Thuận; ⌚ 09.00–16.00 Mon–Sat. *Mì Quảng*, Đà Nẵng's speciality noodle dish, is elevated at Nu Đỗ (say it out loud & try & guess why it's called this) by a celebrity chef. $$

Luk Lak [283 D2] 28 Bạch Đằng; w danang.luklak.vn; ⌚ 07.00–22.30 daily. Fresh, tasty, modern Vietnamese cuisine that draws from recipes from Vietnam's mountainous provinces. There are also locations in Hanoi & Hồ Chí Minh City. The salads here are particularly good, as is the grilled chicken with sticky rice. $$$

Luna Pub [283 D2] 9A Trần Phú; f LunaPubDanang; ⌚ 17.00–midnight daily. Casual pizza joint in an open space with young staff, good beers & occasional events. Originally popular with foreigners, Luna now attracts many locals. $$$

Năm Đảnh Seafood [278 C2] 139/59/38 Trần Quang Khải; ⌚ 10.30–20.30 daily. Classic seafood restaurant where you point at tanks of live seafood to order what you want (if you don't speak Vietnamese). Popular with drinking locals, especially during the w/end. Much cheaper than the restaurants on Mỹ Khê Beach. $$$

Sơn Trà Retreat [278 D2] 11 Lê Văn Lương; w sontraretreat.vn; ⌚ 08.00–22.30 daily. Creative menu of fusion dishes served in a quiet garden that overlooks the jungles of the Sơn Trà Peninsula, on the outskirts of the city. $$$

Nén Danang Restaurant [278 C5] 16 Mỹ Đa Tây 2; w restaurantnen.com; ⌚ 05.30–23.30 daily. Đà Nẵng's finest dining experience is at Nén, with daring tasting menus designed by Summer Lê that tell a story. Unlike fine dining restaurants in Hanoi & Hồ Chí Minh City, Nén imports hardly anything, identifying quality ingredients from within the borders. $$$$$

COFFEE HOUSES

43 Factory Coffee Roaster [278 D3] 422 Thì Sĩ; w xliiicoffee.com; ⌚ 06.30–22.30 daily. Expensive but high-quality Western-style coffee in an industrial building that feels as if it should be in Brooklyn or Shoreditch. Many dairy alternatives are served here.

Àla Café [283 D3] K113 Nguyễn Chí Thanh; f alacafe.official; ⌚ 07.30–18.00 daily. One of the best things about Ala, one of a cluster of hip cafés close to the university & therefore full of students, is that you can perch on the roof while sipping your drink. Coffee, both Western & Vietnamese, is reliably good & you can buy beans to take home.

✷ **Café Long** [283 C3] 123 Lê Lợi; w longcoffee.vn; ⌚ 05.00–19.00 daily. Classic café popular with old boys & girls that has been around for at least half a century. Expect tiny chairs, brusque service, cigarette smoke (though you can sit outside), excellent Vietnamese coffee & no cappuccinos.

✷ **Café Nia** [278 B4] 3/14 Phan Thành Tài; ⌚ 07.00–22.00 daily. Dreamlike coffee shop that is particularly captivating in the evenings, with a carp pond in the front garden, fairy lights in the trees & tiny wooden stools & tables.

Cuckoo House Coffee [278 B6] 34 Hồ Phi Tích; w coffeecuckoohouse.wordpress.com; ⌚ 10.00–18.00 daily. Built by up-&-coming Hồ Chí Minh City-based architecture firm Tropical Space, which builds mainly with brick. The café is out of the way & just OK, so it's only really for modern architecture enthusiasts.

NAM House Coffee [283 D6] 15/1 Lê Hồng Phong; f NAMhouseCoffee; ⌚ 06.00–23.00 daily. Cluttered retro café drawing from the 1970s & 80s that whips up (literally) a delicious egg coffee, a speciality of Hanoi.

✷ **Roost Roasters** [278 D4] 57 Bà Huyện Thanh Quan; f; ⌚ 07.00–22.00 daily. Set in a magnificent modernist building with excellent coffee, including some signatures, & a green, tree-shaded garden.

ENTERTAINMENT AND NIGHTLIFE

Đà Nẵng isn't a party city (yet) and the nightlife scene is more about dessert cafés, beach bars and cocktail lounges, with occasional live music. Đà Nẵng's glitzy waterfront makes for a fine night-time stroll, especially between the Dragon and Hàn River bridges. Near the Hàn River Bridge are cheap cafés serving up coconut ice cream, something of a local speciality.

The 1920s Lounge [283 D5] 53 Trần Quốc Toản; f; ⏲ 19.00–01.00 daily. Roaring-Twenties-style cocktail bar with regular live music; you may need to book (send them a message on Facebook or Instagram).

✷ **Craftsman Cocktail Bar** [278 D4] 48 Phan Tứ; f thecraftsmandanang; ⏲ 07.30–01.30 daily. The Craftsman was one of the first craft cocktail bars in the city & continues to outshine many of its rivals with its creative menu.

Maia Beach Bar [278 D3] 290 Võ Nguyên Giáp; f Maiadanang; ⏲ 08.00–00.30 daily. Snazzy, upmarket beach-shack-style bar, with colourful beanbags spread out on the sand in front.

Q Bar [278 B4] 40 An Dương Vương; f qbardanang1; ⏲ 19.00–02.00 daily. New queer bar run by a passionate, community-focused couple. There's occasional entertainment, including drag, & the cocktails are creatively named & well priced.

Tê Bar [283 D4] 3rd Fl, 39–41 Nguyễn Thái Học; f tecocktails; ⏲ 19.00–01.30 daily. Speakeasy nestled above Cộng Café with a narrow balcony offering quiet corners & city views right in the centre of the city.

OTHER PRACTICALITIES

BANKS, ATMS AND MONEYCHANGERS Banks and ATMs are everywhere. Most ATMs charge a fee and most only allow a maximum withdrawal of 3,000,000VND (US$120) at a time. There are usually money-change kiosks in tourist areas and near the beach.

HEALTH

Đà Nẵng Hospital [283 B3] 124 Hải Phòng; w bvdn.danang.gov.vn; ⏲ all day daily

Family Medical Practice [283 B6] 96–98 Nguyễn Văn Linh; w vietnammedicalpractice.com; ⏲ 08.00–17.00 Mon–Fri, 08.00–noon Sat

Vinmec Đà Nẵng International Hospital [278 A5] 30 Tháng 4; w vinmec.com; ⏲ all day daily

POST OFFICE Small post offices dot the city, with the reliable Quang Trung location [283 C3] (96 Quang Trung) in the centre of town.

SPAS For some pampering, head to **Golden Lotus Oriental Organic Spa**, with several locations across the city: [283 D5] 209 Trần Phú; [283 D5] 76 Hùng Vương; and [278 C3] 63 Hà Bổng.

WHAT TO SEE AND DO

✷ **THE BEACH** [278 C3] Mỹ Khê Beach is the city's pride and joy and by most measures the best metropolitan beach in the country. The rules here are strict, which means virtually no litter, and when swimming you must stick to small, cordoned-off sections, under the watchful gaze of the city lifeguards. This means that, even though the beach is more than 10km long, the water can feel crowded at busy times. The beach is technically split into named sections, but locals simply refer to it as *biển* (which means both beach and sea) and use landmarks or street names to specify locations. Once a fabled resort, China Beach was the GI name for this US military R&R retreat during the American War, but locals have never referred to it as such.

At some point in the 2000s, investors recognised the potential to transform the area south of Đà Nẵng and towards Hội An into the Cancún of Asia. This once-empty, wild stretch of beach is now nearly all taken up by resorts. Miles and miles of fine white sand, clean water and a glorious setting (the hills of the Sơn Trà Peninsula to the north and the Marble Mountains clearly visible to the west) have attracted big hotel brands such as Marriott and Sheraton. Sadly, many hotel projects are left half-finished and have replaced views of the sea with ugly construction. Sadder still, only a small section of the 30km-long stretch of beach that connects Đà Nẵng and Hội An is open to the public.

HÀN MARKET [283 D4] (Chợ Hàn; 119 Trần Phú; ⌚ 06.00–19.00 daily) There has been a major market here since at least the 18th century, when Chinese traders established themselves on the riverside area after exiting Hội An in the wake of the town's decline. Under the French, the market expanded in 1895 and again in 1910. In 1991, the city authorities flattened the colonial market and built what you see today. Sections of the market still serve locals, whereas other market traders have found that selling cheap souvenirs to the busloads of tourists that come here is more lucrative.

ĐÀ NẴNG CATHEDRAL [283 D5] (156 Trần Phú; **w** giaoxuchinhtoadanang.org; ⌚ 08.00–11.30 & 13.30–16.30 Mon–Sat) Construction of Đà Nẵng Cathedral, a single-spired Gothic structure with a sugary-pink wash, began in 1923. The stained-glass windows, which miraculously survived the wars, were made in Grenoble in 1927 by Louis Balmet, who was also responsible for the windows of Đà Lạt Cathedral. Đà Nẵng Cathedral was made a diocese in 1963. It's quiet for most of the week, but on Sundays becomes very busy, with worshippers attending mass at several times throughout the day. The church is occasionally overrun with busloads of tourists; if you see coaches out the front, consider coming back later.

ĐIỆN HẢI CITADEL [283 D2] (Thành Điện Hải; ⌚ all day every day) Many pass through Đà Nẵng without knowing that the city has an ancient(ish) citadel. Though modest compared with its contemporaries in Hanoi and Huế, it's worth visiting the citadel for the setting: surrounded by residences and a few glistening skyscrapers. A Vauban-style fortress, Điện Hải Citadel was built as an earthen fortress in 1813 by Gia Long, the first king of the Nguyễn Dynasty. In 1835, Minh Mạng, Gia Long's successor, upgraded the fortress to a citadel. In 1847, Thiệu Trị,, Minh Mạng's successor, rebuilt the citadel after attacks from the French.

The layout is in effect a smaller, less elaborate version of the disappeared Gia Định Citadel in Hồ Chí Minh City. After Đà Nẵng became Tourane and came under the control of the French in 1888, the authorities found the citadel too small to accommodate their needs and converted the grounds into a military hospital. After the French left Vietnam, they were granted permission by the South Vietnam government to open a Francophone school in the old hospital buildings of the Điện Hải Citadel, which eventually spread across the moat to additional buildings. After reunification in 1976, the buildings were taken over by the state pharmaceutical company and in 1988 it became officially recognised as a national monument. In 2004, the pharmaceutical company was relocated to make space for the Đà Nẵng Museum, a decision that the government now seems to regret. The plan is eventually to restore the citadel to its pre-colonial state, though whether this will happen is yet to be seen. Looming over the citadel is the glass-clad Đà Nẵng Administrative Centre, designed to look like a lighthouse and completed in 2014.

ĐÀ NẴNG MUSEUM [283 D3] (31 Trần Phú; [w] baotangdanang.vn; (08.00–11.30 & 13.30–17.00 Tue–Sun; free entrance at the time of research; 1–2hrs) Opened in the 1980s on Lê Duẩn Street and then moved to Điện Hải Citadel, it was decided years ago that the building detracts from the fortress's heritage and that the Đà Nẵng City Museum must relocate again to Bạch Đằng Street. To everyone's surprise, this finally happened in spring of 2025, and the museum now sits within the restored shells of two of Đà Nẵng's last remaining riverfront colonial buildings. Despite the heritage site, the entrance and interiors feel fresh and modern. It begins with natural history and the traditional lives of fishermen, with some rather remarkable photos of Đà Nẵng when it was a humble fishing village. A lot of attention is given to how Đà Nẵng resisted the French, and how the city suffered particularly badly from American aggression during the Second Indochina War. There is also an ethnography section, covering the traditional lifestyles of the Kinh, Co Tu, Gie Trieng, Sedang and others who live in the mountainous areas of the municipality.

✷ **DRAGON BRIDGE** [283 D6] (29 Cầu Rồng) This 666m-long bridge, completed in 2013, is emblematic of Đà Nẵng's flashy economic success and modelled after one of the dragons of the Lý Dynasty, the founders of Hanoi. The yellow bridge is most attractive at night, when it's lit in hues of green, purple and orange. The beast breathes fire from its head on the east side of the river at 21.00 on Saturdays and Sundays, a spectacle that still draws plenty of local families.

✷ **MUSEUM OF CHAM SCULPTURE** [283 D6] (2 Tháng 9; w chammuseum.danang.vn; ◷ 07.30–17.00 daily; 60,000VND/free adult/child; 2–3hrs) Set in a grand French building and surrounded by a sculpture-filled garden, the Museum of Cham Sculpture holds the largest collection of Cham art in the country, and possibly the world. It is also Đà Nẵng's premier museum and unmissable if visiting the Cham sites in Quảng Nam and Bình Định. There is enough signage to make an independent visit worthwhile, but you'll get far more information from a guide, usually (but not always) available at reception. Start left with information about the history of the building, which was completed in 1919 and has always been intended as a museum of Cham artefacts. Don't miss the map, which details just how many Cham sites there are in Vietnam. The exhibits are arranged by site, giving structure to the museum. Especially organised travellers who know which Cham sites they are going to visit (or can remember the names of the places they've been), will want to focus on these sections of the museum. There is a rich selection of sculpture from the popular Mỹ Sơn and destroyed Đồng Dương, including the largest ever Cham Buddha sculpture from the latter. The second floor moves away from sculpture and focuses on the Cham ethnolinguistic group, a distinct minority who live further south, particularly around Phan Rang and Châu Đốc. The display explores festivals, textiles, farming tools and architecture.

APEC SCULPTURE PARK [283 D7] (Bình Hiên) This park came about in 2017, after the city hosted the APEC (Asia–Pacific Economic Cooperation) Economic Leaders' Meeting. Along with an undulating pavilion-type structure that is supposed to resemble a soaring kite, the park holds 18 sculptures from APEC member economies. A fun and nerdy activity is to wander around the park and try to guess which country contributed the sculpture before looking at the sign to reveal the answer.

✷ **ĐÀ NẴNG FINE ARTS MUSEUM** [283 C4] (78 Lê Duẩn; **w** dnfam.vn; 🕘 08.00–17.00 daily; 20,000VND/free adult/child; 1–2hrs) One of only three state fine arts museums in Vietnam, the decidedly modern Đà Nẵng Fine Arts Museum was inaugurated in 2014 and moved to its current location in 2016. The museum houses gently lit and well-organised exhibits over three floors, and despite being one of the city's most important cultural institutions, is overlooked by most visitors. Greeting you at reception is a detailed relief in classic Soviet Realist style depicting the different icons of Đà Nẵng, including Dragon Bridge, the Guanyin statue and a tuft of skyscrapers. Temporary exhibition and children's art spaces flank the reception room, while the upper floors offer a comprehensive introduction to the art and craft works of painters, sculptors and artisans from Đà Nẵng and Central Vietnam. Guides aren't available, but independent visits are rewarding.

CAO ĐÀI TEMPLE [283 C3] (63 Hải Phòng; 🕘 05.30–21.00 daily) Built in 1956–57, this is one of the most important Cao Đài temples in the country, and second in size only to the headquarters in Tây Ninh. If you only visit one Cao Đài temple, this could be the one. Two entrance gates lead to the temple proper. The one marked *nam phái* (on the right) is for men and the one marked *nữ phái* (on the left) for women. Only Cao Đài priests enter through the central part of the main door. The main altar is rather plain, but behind it is an enormous globe with an ever-seeing eye, the symbol of the faith. Note the sign that hangs from the ceiling in front of the main altar: It reads '*Vạn giáo nhất lý*' which, if translated literally, means 'Ten thousand teachings and one principle' (or 'All religions have the same purpose'). The pictures behind the gilded letters are of the founders of the world's great religions. From left to right these are Laozi, wearing blue robes; another figure which is either Moses or Muhammad; Jesus; Buddha, instantly recognisable by his Southeast Asian characteristics; and Confucius. Other portraits in the sanctuary are Ngô Văn Chiêu, the founder of Cao Đài, and other Cao Đài celebrities dressed in white robes.

HỒ CHÍ MINH MUSEUM [278 B4] (Duy Tân; **w** baotanghochiminh.vn; 🕘 07.30–16.30 daily; 20,000VND; 1hr) Hanoi has the best Hồ Chí Minh Museum and Hồ Chí Minh City has the best military museum. Đà Nẵng attempts to combine them both, with a little pre-war history, too. The garden houses some war machinery, which is presumably painted regularly given how it glistens in the sunlight. The history section begins around 1,000 years ago, but it won't make much sense without broader contextual knowledge of famous heroes and battles. The museum then lurches forward to the war of independence and goes to unusually large efforts to showcase resistance from various ethnolinguistic groups in the mountains that surround the city. Move outside to see a replica of Hồ Chí Minh's stilt house in Hanoi, with a renovated section behind it devoted to the man himself.

AROUND ĐÀ NẴNG Day trips from Đà Nẵng go beyond the city's borders. See page 270 and page 314 for trips around Huế and Hội An respectively; both cities are within easy reach.

✷ **The Marble Mountains** [map, page 296] (Huyền Trân Công Chúa; **w** nguhanhson.org; 🕘 07.00–17.00 daily; 2hrs) Layered with myths and legends, this area is one of the highlights of a visit to Đà Nẵng. Under 10km from the city centre, the landscape is dominated by five craggy peaks, the 'Marble Mountains', which are actually limestone crags with marble outcrops. In Vietnamese they are known as the 'Ngũ Hành Sơn', or 'Mountains of the Five Elements', a name possibly given to the cluster in 1825 by Emperor Minh Mạng. The five elements in East Asian philosophy are fire, water, soil, wood and metal, and there is a mountain to reflect each one, though you can't visit them all. A local legend says that the Ngũ Hành Sơn are the eggs of a giant dragon, though more illustrious origin stories also exist (page 292). An important religious spot for the Cham, the peaks became havens for communist guerrillas during the war owing to their commanding view over Đà Nẵng airbase. From here, a force with sufficient firepower could control much of what went on below, and the guerrillas harried the Americans incessantly. Of all the mountains that are possible to visit, Thủy Sơn, the Water Mountain, is the most interesting and extensive. There's not much to see on the other four mountains, but if you have your own transport you might enjoy driving around them in case any of the ten or so pagodas pique your interest. There are two parts to the Water Mountain, and both are ticketed.

Ẩm Phủ Cave (20,000VND) Start with the much smaller Ẩm Phủ Cave, one of the biggest in the mountain and separated into three areas: heaven, earth and hell. In earth, where you enter, you'll find various shrines occupying crannies and dedicated to gods and Buddha. Descend into hell and find various depictions of the gruesome torture techniques devised by demons and used to punish sinners. Ascend to heaven and find many dozens of Buddhas, mythical creatures and eventually a viewpoint. Keep in mind that the staircase is steep and slippery.

Thủy Sơn (40,000VND) To reach the second, more labyrinthine section, exit Ẩm Phủ Cave and turn left. You'll soon see the ticket office, an elevator (15,000VND) and the 150-step staircase that leads to Linh Ứng Pagoda and Xá Lợi Tower. The structures here are not neat or elegant, but the rich clutter of styles and imagery give this section an atmosphere of eccentricity. Don't bypass the easily missed Tàng Chơn Cave, which nestles behind the Linh Ứng Pagoda. When the hill is busy with tour groups, this little cave can provide some solitude.

Leave this cluster and head towards Vạn Thành Cave, a popular and oft-congested cave, before turning right and climbing to Đỉnh Thượng Mài, the highest peak. This offers the best views in the Marble Mountains, yet few bother to make the sweaty climb. At the base of a set of steps leading to the highest peak is another cave, the Huyền Không Cave. Originally a place of Animist worship, it later became a site for Buddhist pilgrimage. The entrance is protected by four door guardians. The high ceiling of the cave is pierced by five holes through which the sun filters and, in the hour before midday, illuminates the central statue of the Buddha Shakyamuni. In the cave are various natural rock formations, which tour guides might point out as being stork-like birds, elephants, a fish and various human body parts. The cave apparently served as a guerrilla base during the American War, and it was here that a team of female fighters hid before destroying 19 American planes on 15 April 1972.

Finally, the Tâm Thái Pagoda, reached from behind, is on the site of a much older Cham place of worship. Constructed in 1825 by Minh Mạng, and subsequently rebuilt in 1946 and then again in 1975 after war damage, the central statue is of the Buddha Shakyamuni (the historic Buddha), flanked by the Bodhisattva Quan Âm (a future Buddha and the Goddess of Compassion; page 293) and a statue of

LEGEND HAS IT: A GOOD EGG

One local legend relates that the Ngũ Hành Sơn are the eggs of a giant dragon that, one day, may hatch. Another entirely different origin myth recounts that a divine turtle once saved a handsome youth from drowning and then gifted him a giant egg. The youth buried it in warm sand and guarded it night and day. One morning he heard a cracking sound, the egg hatched and out popped an ethereal maiden. She was so grateful to him for looking after her that she became his wife. However, the time came when she had to return to the sea. She morphed into her true form – a turtle, of course – but not before leaving behind five pieces of cracked eggshell. These became the five mountains that make up Ngũ Hành Sơn.

Văn Thù (symbolising wisdom). From here you descend to the car park, exiting through a different gate from the entry point.

✷ Sơn Trà Peninsula The Sơn Trà Peninsula is a picturesque area with rich biodiversity, spanning over 60km² and rising to an altitude of 696m. The peninsula, a short ride from central Đà Nẵng, is home to the Sơn Trà Nature Reserve, which protects a diverse range of flora and fauna, including the endangered red-shanked douc langur. Go deep into the peninsula and linger for long enough and you should spot langur families crossing the road or lounging in trees. On the way to the peninsula, consider stopping at **Green Viet** (60 Thành Vinh 2; w greenviet.org; ⌚ 08.00–noon & 13.30–17.00 Tue–Sat), a conservation and education centre whose efforts are focused on protecting the langurs on Sơn Trà. If you contact them in advance, they may be able to help organise tours of the peninsula with a specialist. Beneath the lush forest are near-empty beaches, some of which you can access on muddy pathways that descend from the road (look out for clusters of motorbikes seemingly parked in the middle of nowhere on the side of the road). The peninsula is also home to several sites, including the private Đồng Đình Museum, **Linh Ứng Pagoda** and a towering Guanyin statue, the Đỉnh Bàn Cờ peak and viewpoint, and some ethereal banyan trees (*cây đa*) on the eastern outcrop. Note that the banyan trees are along a dirt road and security guards might block access. It's possible to spend an entire afternoon in this huge, wild corner of glitzy Đà Nẵng. The best way to explore Sơn Trà Peninsula is by motorbike or, if you have legs of steel, bicycle. Alternatively, taxis will take you, but note that cars can't access all corners and you're less likely to see langurs.

Đồng Đình Museum [278 D2] (Hoàng Sa; w dongdinhmuseum.vn; ⌚ 08.00–17.00 daily; 30 mins) Nestled on the scenic slopes of the Sơn Trà Peninsula, this private museum was founded by artist and documentary film maker Đoàn Huy Giáo and opened in 2011. The museum's architecture harmonises with the surroundings and the collection includes pottery, artefacts and artworks from Vietnamese, Sa Huỳnh and Cham cultures. Of particular interest is the Fishing Village Memorial, which showcases traditional tools and early-20th-century photographs. Outdoor gardens and stone paths make this an inviting spot, but the space needs a little love. There is an on-site café offering views of the peninsula and out to sea.

Linh Ứng Pagoda [278 D2] (Hòn Thuỷ Sơn St; ⌚ 07.00–17.30 daily) Linh Ứng Pagoda was built between 2004 and 2010 and it draws worshippers and tourists in equal numbers. The pagoda's most notable feature is the 67m-tall Lady Buddha statue, known in Vietnamese as Quan Âm (see below) and in English as Guanyin (the English comes from the Chinese 觀音). She is the tallest Guanyin in Vietnam, can be seen from almost anywhere on the beach and, together with the Dragon Bridge, is one of Đà Nẵng's iconic structures. The site has been considered sacred since at least the 19th century, when locals built a small shrine here after a Buddha statue reportedly washed ashore. The pagoda will feel more like a tourist sight than a place of worship, but is worth stopping at to gaze up at Guanyin's gentle, gigantic face.

Đỉnh Bàn Cờ [278 D1] Chess Board Peak received its name from the stone Confucian scholar that sits forever at the top of the mountain while contemplating his next move against an invisible opponent. This is a nod to a local legend about two deities that played chess on this peak. When one was distracted by fairies, he lost the game, threw the chessboard into the sea and ascended to heaven in a rage. This is the highest point on the peninsula, and affords views to Đà Nẵng, the Hàn River and the surrounding coastal landscape. Travelling up to the peak along the narrow, winding roads is an adventure. Early risers should come for the sunrise over the water when the peak shouldn't be too busy.

LEGEND HAS IT: DON'T RUN WITH SCISSORS – THE ORIGINS OF QUAN ÂM

Thị Kính was married to a student from a wealthy family. One fateful night when her husband was sleeping, she attempted to trim his chin hair, a fluffy tangle that had always bothered her. In her wisdom she knew that her post-pubertal husband would never be able to grow the thick beard he yearned for, no matter how hard he tried.

While he snored, she ran into the kitchen to grab some scissors. Upon her swift return into the bedroom, Thị Kính's husband awoke in panic at the sight of the blade and assumed she intended to slit his throat. In his fear and anger, he divorced and banished her.

With nowhere to go, Thị Kính disguised herself as a man and took sanctuary in a temple, dedicating her life to religious devotion as a monk. During her time at the temple, a young girl named Thị Màu fell in love with the disguised Thị Kính. When Thị Kính rebuffed her so as not to reveal her secret, Thị Màu found comfort elsewhere, became pregnant and, in an act of revenge, falsely accused the celibate monk of being the father.

The accusation brought disgrace upon Thị Kính. Though she had the opportunity to reveal herself and bring shame on the woman that wronged her, she remained silent, was cast out of the monastery, took the boy from Thị Màu and raised him alone in the mountains. Only after Thị Kính died did the villagers discover the kindness she demonstrated in raising a child that was not her own.

The King of Heaven watched the whole, long episode from above and sanctified her, transforming her into Quan Âm, or Guanyin, the Goddess of Compassion, who brings love and tenderness to all. For reasons unknown, Quan Âm was also adopted by the Buddhist faith, and she's often the central divinity in pagodas across Vietnam, as is the case with Linh Ứng Pagoda. Pilgrims still appeal to Quan Âm for help in bearing sons and fighting unjust accusations.

BÀ NÀ HILLS

Near the top of Chua Mountain (Núi Chua; 1,467m), **Bà Nà Hills** (w banahills.sunworld.vn; from 900,000/750,000VND adult/child) sits at around 1,200m. The views in all directions are unlike anything else in Đà Nẵng, the air is cool and the selfie-stick wielders are relentless. Bà Nà was founded in 1902 by the French, who came here to convalesce, but virtually nothing of the colonial hill station remains. Bà Nà Hills, an investment project from the Vietnamese conglomerate Sun Group, serves as an interesting case study when compared with Bạch Mã National Park (page 271) to the north, which has seen very little development and where French villas abound. The Bà Nà Hills tourism complex includes a fantasy theme park, a 'French Village' (there is nothing French about it), hotels, restaurants, gardens, a funicular railway, a wine cellar-cum-bar and the impossibly popular Golden Bridge.

This 150m-long pedestrian bridge soon became an internet sensation after it opened in 2018 because it appears to be supported by two massive stone hands (they are just for show). The gimmick put Đà Nẵng on the map. While many come away from Bà Nà Hills with fond memories, especially those with kids in tow, others might feel uneasy about the fake heritage buildings that constitute the 'French Village', not to mention the obvious destruction of the forest. If you choose to visit Bà Nà Hills, it's important that you know what you're in for. This is not a quaint mountain retreat, but an ostentatious theme park. The highlight of Bà Nà Hills may well be the journey to it, which is via one of the longest single-wire cable car systems in the world. The cable car affords otherwise unviewable vistas of the densely forested slopes and the steep river that cascades down the hillside.

✷ **Hải Vân Pass** [map, page 226] Those on motorbikes will enjoy tackling the Hải Vân Pass, which rises to an elevation of about 500m and forms the border between Đà Nẵng and Huế. The name Hải Vân means Ocean Cloud, a reflection of the frequently misty conditions that shroud the pass, with views stretching to the East Sea and inaccessible beaches on one side, and forested mountains and panoramas of the Đà Nẵng skyline on the other. The pass also houses some historical sites, including recently rebuilt and restored gates and fortifications at the peak dating back to before the Nguyễn Dynasty. The site is reasonably interesting, with decent signage in English. Driving the pass used to be a treacherous endeavour, but in 2005 the 6km-long Hải Vân Tunnel opened, and the trucks and cars that made driving here so dangerous now use this instead. It's possible to drive up and down the pass from Đà Nẵng in an hour or two. With more time, you might drop down to Lăng Cô Beach (page 271) on the other side of the pass and swim in the sea before making the return journey. If moving between Huế and Đà Nẵng by private car, you can request that the driver take the pass and not the tunnel, but it will cost extra. Another way to tackle the Hải Vân Pass is by train – one of Vietnam's most spectacular train journeys (page 251).

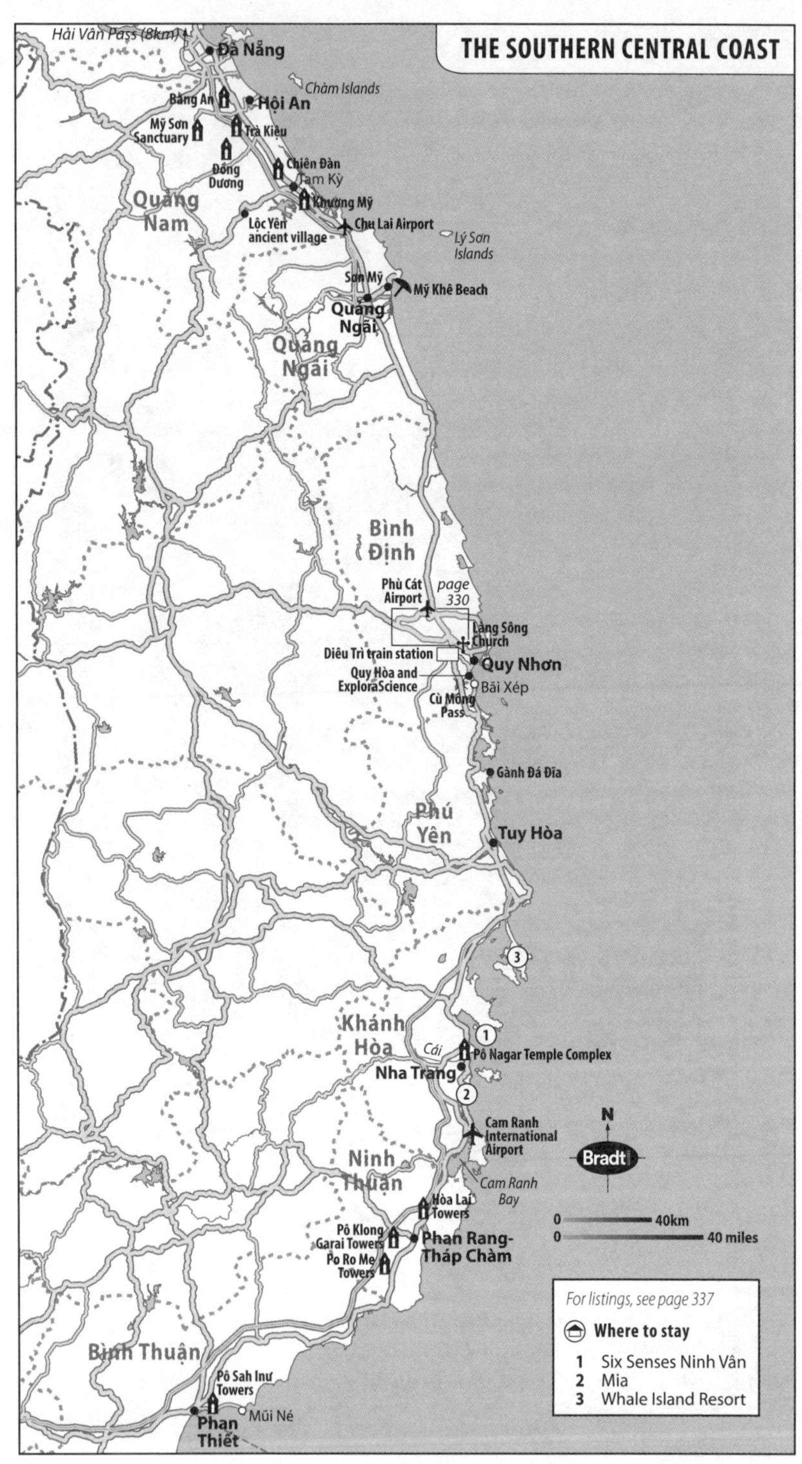
THE SOUTHERN CENTRAL COAST
Hải Vân Pass (8km)
Đà Nẵng
Chàm Islands
Bằng An
Hội An
Mỹ Sơn Sanctuary
Trà Kiệu
Đồng Dương
Chiên Đàn
Tam Kỳ
Khương Mỹ
Quảng Nam
Lộc Yên ancient village
Chu Lai Airport
Lý Sơn Islands
Sơn Mỹ
Mỹ Khê Beach
Quảng Ngãi
Quảng Ngãi
Bình Định
Phù Cát Airport
page 330
Làng Sông Church
Diêu Trì train station
Quy Nhơn
Quy Hòa and ExploraScience
Bãi Xép
Cù Mông Pass
Gành Đá Đĩa
Phú Yên
Tuy Hòa
Khánh Hòa
Cái
Pô Nagar Temple Complex
Nha Trang
Cam Ranh International Airport
Cam Ranh Bay
N
Bradt
Ninh Thuận
Hòa Lai Towers
Pô Klong Garai Towers
Phan Rang-Tháp Chàm
Po Ro Me Towers
0 40km
0 40 miles
Bình Thuận
Pô Sah Inư Towers
Phan Thiết
Mũi Né
For listings, see page 337
Where to stay
1 Six Senses Ninh Vân
2 Mia
3 Whale Island Resort

8

The Southern Central Coast

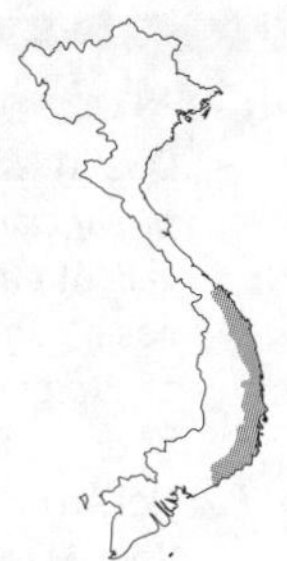

South of Đà Nẵng, Central Vietnam swells to form two adjacent subregions: the landlocked Central Highlands bordering Laos and Cambodia to the west, and the Southern Central Coast hugged by the East Sea to the east. **Quảng Nam**, of which Đà Nẵng was once a part, is the northernmost province in the Southern Central Coast, and as the coast curves south its climate becomes warmer and sunnier, passing **Quảng Ngãi**, **Bình Định**, **Phú Yên**, **Khánh Hòa**, **Ninh Thuận** and **Bình Thuận**. This string of littoral provinces holds the most dramatic of Vietnam's coastal scenery, with outlandishly shaped peninsulas and fjord-like bays, but they also hold many sites of historical significance, most importantly the magnificent vestiges of the lost nation of Champa.

Beginning in the 2nd century CE, the Cham civilisation carved out a niche for itself between the Khmer in the south and the Việt in the north. When they were eventually defeated by the Vietnamese, they left behind some of the richest architectural gems in Southeast Asia. Though Champa was wiped out and few Cham people remain in the subregion, the provinces still reflect the states of the decentralised nation: Amaravati (Quảng Nam), Vijaya (Bình Định), Kauthara (Khánh Hòa) and Panduranga (Ninh Thuận and Bình Thuận). Enthusiasts for ancient civilisations could spend a fortnight exploring the various ruins that pepper the subregion, but the masterpieces are **Mỹ Sơn Sanctuary** near Hội An and the **Cham towers** outside of Quy Nhơn.

The economy of the subregion has depended on the sea for millennia. Champa was a seafaring civilisation that relied on the water for both sustenance and as a conduit for trade between East Asia, Southeast Asia and South Asia. **Hội An**, in Quảng Nam, was for a time Vietnam's most important port and trading hub, and reminders of the city's glorious past speckle its Old Town. For decades, the fishing fleets of Quảng Ngãi, Khánh Hòa and Bình Thuận have been among the largest in the country. Today, **Nha Trang** in Khánh Hòa, **Mũi Né** in Bình Thuận and many smaller seaside settlements elsewhere in the subregion have built resilient visitor economies off the dimpled back of sandy beaches.

This chapter is organised from north to south, beginning with **Quảng Nam**, a crowd-pleasing province with much to offer. **Quảng Nam** has an area of 10,438km^2 and a population of almost 2 million and is one of the few Vietnamese provinces to have two cities: **Hội An**, the tourist hotspot, and **Tam Kỳ**, the provincial capital. Much of the province consists of coastal plains. At the beginning of the dry season, which usually begins after Tết, it is shielded from monsoons by the Trường Sơn mountain range to the east. By October, the Pacific typhoons are beginning and torrential rain whips across the coastal beaches, sweeping sand inland and causing flooding.

It was southeast of Hội An, in Trà Kiệu, that the Cham once built their capital and a huge citadel from the 4th century onwards. Today, sadly, there is nothing to see in

FURTHER INFORMATION

Quảng Nam is one of the few provinces that has a functioning and useful provincial tourism website: w visitquangnam.com. The website makes a valiant effort to draw travellers to the province's lesser-known corners, and has a page dedicated to green travel. For an in-depth guide, pick up a copy of *Exploring Quảng Nam* by Tim Doling in Hanoi or Hồ Chí Minh City. This book, unfortunately, is impossible to find in Hội An. For an audio tour of Hội An designed and narrated by the author of this guidebook, download the VoiceMap app (w voicemap.me).

Trà Kiệu, but elsewhere in the province are remains of the civilisation's architectural and artistic talents. While virtually no Cham remain and more than 90% of the inhabitants of the province are now Kinh, in the mountainous regions there are Co Tu, Sedang, Mnong and K'Ho. Before delving into the art and history of Champa, it's worth looking back at the section on the civilisation's history (page 12).

Đà Nẵng, a part of Quảng Nam until 1997, is where the Americans built the second largest airbase in Southeast Asia, from which they launched air attacks against North Vietnam and southern Laos. They built another at Chu Lai, 30km south of Tam Kỳ, which, during a peak period in 1966, housed 20,000 American GIs. They adopted a 'search and destroy' policy during which enormous damage was inflicted on houses, pagodas, churches and schools. Unprecedented atrocities led to enforced urbanisation as Tam Kỳ (and Đà Nẵng) swelled. Quảng Nam suffered less from the Tết Offensive and bombing raids than the surrounding provinces, however, evidenced by the largely intact Old Town of Hội An and the red tiled rooftops and modernist houses in the villages that surround.

Since 1975, reconstruction has been fast and furious. Forests destroyed by American defoliants have been replaced (some of which has been subsequently logged), cinnamon plantations were replanted and gold mines reopened. Tens of thousands of hectares of farmland have been recultivated after unexploded mines were defused. Tourism is booming, making Quảng Nam one of the most prosperous provinces in Central Vietnam.

WHEN TO VISIT

This subregion is most comfortable in spring (March–April) and immediately before the typhoon season, which is usually October and November. If **Hội An** is hit by a typhoon, it will flood and many businesses are forced to close for a few days. Summer (May–August) is hot, but the paddy fields are at their fullest and an occasional sea breeze will offer some respite. The winter (December–February) is generally cool and damp, but it is warmer and drier the further south you go. Visit **Lý Sơn** in the spring and summer (March–September), when sunny days are all but guaranteed. The islands are best avoided during public holidays and long weekends, when accommodation and transport can be fully booked.

Quy Nhơn is rarely unpleasant, except for perhaps sometimes during the winter. The rest of the year is hot and sunny, with the occasional shower. Typhoons rarely make landfall this far south. **Nha Trang** enjoys the best weather in the country, with a short rainy season, more than 300 days of sunshine a year and, unlike cities further north, a persistent and enviable sea breeze. This far south, the four-season paradigm has effectively disappeared: the 'rainy' season runs from September to December, with cool weather, cloudy skies but regular moments of sunshine. January to August is sunny and clear. **Phan Thiết** enjoys similarly desirable weather.

HỘI AN

If arriving from Đà Nẵng to the north, as most do, Hội An will be your first and perhaps only port of call. The posterchild of Vietnamese tourism, Hội An's Old Town is a bastion of Asian antiquity; a living museum of temples, pagodas, shrines, assembly halls, shophouses and homes. Despite the rising tide of tourism and the unprecedented changes sweeping Vietnam, Hội An still exudes a certain kind of charm, especially in the evening and early morning – but expect to see more tourists here than anywhere else in the country.

Some of the properties along Lê Lợi Street date from four centuries ago. The Japanese Quarter with its covered bridge, now Hội An's most famous landmark, followed half a century later. The Chinese Quarter, encompassing Nguyễn Thái Học, Trần Phú and Phan Châu Trinh, the town's main historical core, came half a century after that. The so-called French Quarter flourished in the late 19th and early 20th centuries. In Hội An's agrarian outskirts, bicycle lanes crisscross paddy fields, leading to laid-back beaches and palm-fringed villages.

Situated 30km from Đà Nẵng, it is an alternative springboard for excursions to the nearby islands, the Marble Mountains (page 290) and Mỹ Sơn. But be warned: Hội An is a contender for Vietnam's most overtouristed place, in part because visitors spend so many nights here (and some never leave). Some travellers spend up to a week in Hội An and only one or two days in nearby Huế (page 244), which easily rivals Hội An in depth of intrigue. Travellers wanting to avoid crowds will want to do the reverse.

HISTORY The Hội An you see today established itself in the 15th and 16th centuries, but the area held significance long before. It was central to the Sa Huỳnh civilisation, which flourished before the 2nd century, and was a trading port of the Champa Kingdom from the 2nd to the 15th centuries. Cultural relics from the ancient Champa Kingdom found on the Chàm Islands and elsewhere show that the foundations of the ancient town of Hội An were built long before the current town came into being.

Though some 30km west of Hội An, the Mỹ Sơn Sanctuary ruins are the greatest evidence of the area's significance. Known then as Amaravati, Quảng Nam was a bastion of Cham culture, art and military power, but pressure from Đại Việt to the north, the Khmers to the south and Mongols from the sea eventually led to the demise of this once-formidable kingdom. By the middle of the 2nd millennium, Amaravati was ceded to Đại Việt (later Vietnam).

Shielded from high winds by the Chàm Islands, Hội Phố (now Hội An and mispronounced by Europeans as Faifo) was selected as a trading post in the 15th century because it is thought that the town was closer to the sea. It became an important port in the 17th and 18th centuries, receiving ships from Siam, Cambodia, Japan, China, Manila and Europe. With them they brought cloth, lead, porcelain, silk, tea, pharmaceutical products and other luxuries, which were traded for sea-swallows' nests from the Chàm Islands, coral from the Hoàng Sa archipelago, pepper from the hill plantations and raw silk from the mulberry farms. Hội An was perhaps the largest trading centre in Vietnam and one of the busiest commercial ports in all of Southeast Asia.

The Chinese, who were allowed to settle here in the 17th century by the Nguyễn lords, left behind many examples of Chinese architecture. The Japanese, who also settled here but in smaller numbers, may have left a remarkable bridge (page 306) with the power to withstand and prevent earthquakes. The Dutch were the first Europeans to trade here, but the Portuguese, French, Spanish, Italians and British soon followed. Virtually all surviving European architecture, however, was built in the early 20th century during the colonial period. Hội An was one of the entry points through which Christianity made its way into the country.

During the mid 19th century the Thu Bồn River began to silt up and trade was transferred north to Đà Nẵng. During French occupation it flourished as a silt and tea processing centre but, after the arrival of the railway early in the 1930s, these important industries were also transferred to Đà Nẵng. Today these economic woes might be seen as a blessing as it helped prevent the town from modernising and losing its architecture.

The war years brought terrible hardship and, during the post-war famine, 3,000 tonnes of rice had to be brought into the town every year to feed the inhabitants. Gradually handicraft industries were revived. The town became known for its excellent-quality bamboo curtains and rattan matting. The post-reunification years saw a revival of the silk industry; many new looms were built and some became electrically operated. Fishermen again took to their boats and Hội An fishpaste became a popular product.

The ancient streets of Hội An are historical relics of world significance, recognised by the government as a National Vestige in 1985. Soon after, and significantly aided by *đổi mới* (page 21) and inbound tourism, the service economy took off and showered Hội An with considerable wealth. In 1999, UNESCO recognised Hội An as a Cultural Heritage Site. In 2008, Hội An became a city, though Tam Kỳ remains the administrative capital of the province.

While a few families still live in Hội An's Old Town, most homes have been converted into restaurants, cafés, museums, galleries, fashion boutiques, souvenir shops and tailors. Indeed, good-value express tailoring was once one of the selling points, but as incomes have risen across the board, it is not as cheap as it once was. During the Covid-19 pandemic, Hội An morphed into an eerie ghost town, one of the many pitfalls of an over-reliance on tourism. This was in stark contrast to Hanoi's Old Quarter, which continued to buzz even without the tourists, and nearby Huế, where life continued more or less as normal, outside periods of lockdown. After Vietnam's borders opened again in 2022, Hội An propelled itself back on to the international and domestic tourism circuit. Once again, the problem the town grapples with is not that there are too few visitors, but that there are too many. The city has swelled to support a population of around 150,000 and receives 4 million visitors a year, the majority of whom are internationals.

GETTING THERE AND AROUND Hội An has no airport or train station, and most travellers get here through Đà Nẵng (see page 281 for getting to Đà Nẵng). If arriving by **train**, disembark at Đà Nẵng, where a row of taxis waits to make the Hội An journey (around 45 minutes at 600,000VND).

There are **buses** that leave for Hội An regularly from Đà Nẵng bus station, which cost little more than a dollar, but take at least an hour. Allow half a day if taking the bus, as you need to allow for waiting times at the station, plus getting to and from the bus station in Đà Nẵng and the pick-up/drop-off point in Hội An (which varies according to the bus you take).

Most of those arriving by **plane** fly to Đà Nẵng and then travel by taxi from the airport to Hội An (also around 45 minutes at 600,000VND). It's also possible to fly to Chu Lai Airport (Tam Nghĩa Ward; **w** vietnamairport.vn) from Hanoi

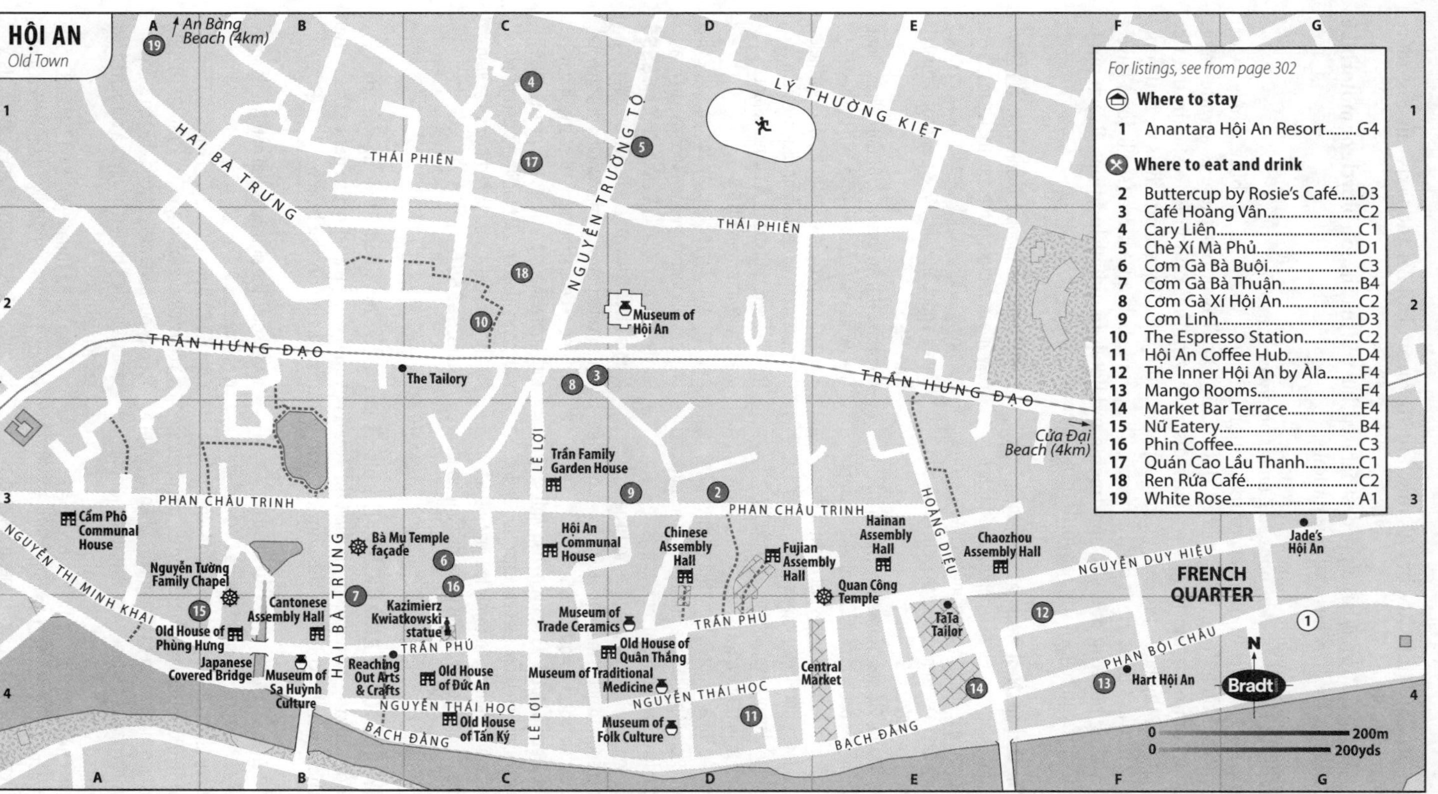
HỘI AN
Old Town
An Bàng Beach (4km)
For listings, see from page 302
Where to stay
1 Anantara Hội An Resort.......G4
Where to eat and drink
2 Buttercup by Rosie's Café.....D3
3 Café Hoàng Vân.......C2
4 Cary Liên.......C1
5 Chè Xí Mà Phủ.......D1
6 Cơm Gà Bà Buội.......C3
7 Cơm Gà Bà Thuận.......B4
8 Cơm Gà Xí Hội An.......C2
9 Cơm Linh.......D3
10 The Espresso Station.......C2
11 Hội An Coffee Hub.......D4
12 The Inner Hội An by Àla.......F4
13 Mango Rooms.......F4
14 Market Bar Terrace.......E4
15 Nữ Eatery.......B4
16 Phin Coffee.......C3
17 Quán Cao Lầu Thanh.......C1
18 Ren Rửa Café.......C2
19 White Rose.......A1
LÝ THƯỜNG KIỆT
HAI BÀ TRƯNG
THÁI PHIÊN
NGUYỄN TRƯỜNG TỘ
TRẦN HƯNG ĐẠO
Museum of Hội An
The Tailory
Cửa Đại Beach (4km)
LÊ LỢI
Trần Family Garden House
PHAN CHÂU TRINH
HOÀNG DIỆU
Cẩm Phô Communal House
NGUYỄN THỊ MINH KHAI
Bà Mụ Temple façade
Hội An Communal House
Chinese Assembly Hall
Fujian Assembly Hall
Hainan Assembly Hall
Chaozhou Assembly Hall
Jade's Hội An
NGUYỄN DUY HIỆU
FRENCH QUARTER
Nguyễn Tường Family Chapel
Cantonese Assembly Hall
Kazimierz Kwiatkowski statue
Museum of Trade Ceramics
TRẦN PHÚ
Quan Công Temple
TaTa Tailor
Old House of Phùng Hưng
Japanese Covered Bridge
Museum of Sa Huỳnh Culture
Reaching Out Arts & Crafts
Old House of Đức An
Old House of Quân Thắng
Museum of Traditional Medicine
Central Market
PHAN BỘI CHÂU
Hart Hội An
Bradt
NGUYỄN THÁI HỌC
Old House of Tấn Ký
Museum of Folk Culture
BẠCH ĐẰNG
0 200m
0 200yds

or Hồ Chí Minh City, but it's much further from Hội An and taxis can cost more than double.

The Old Town is largely pedestrianised, but you may need a **bicycle or motorbike** to access the beaches and rice paddies.

WHERE TO STAY *Map, page 305, unless otherwise stated*

It's no trouble finding accommodation in Hội An, even at busy times. Most central hotels have been priced out of the Old Town, but there is a wide range of accommodation that is walking distance. Another option is to stay in the rice paddies, the large green belt that separates the Old Town from the sea, and some might want to be right on the beach. The people behind Anicca (see below) have a growing network of villas, apartments and hotels in unique locations. Reach out to them if you're looking for something special.

The Cuckoo's Nest Near Trà Quế village; w booking.com. Clean & popular backpacker hostel with dorms & premium communal spaces, including a swimming pool that offers views to the rice paddies. **$**

✱ **Flame Flowers Homestay** 35 Tôn Đức Thắng; w booking.com. One of several simple & affordable guesthouses just north of the Old Town, but Flame Flowers excels for its extraordinary hospitality spearheaded by a welcoming family. **$**

✱ **An Villa** Group 1, Vong Nhi village; w an-villa.com. An Villa has a number of interconnected garden villas nestled in the countryside & surrounded by trees & paddies. You'll need transport to get to the beach & Old Town, but the location makes it worth it. **$$**

✱ **Dechiu Hotel** 23 Nguyễn Phan Vinh; w dechiuhotel.com. Elegant but rustic design accommodation with comfy lounges just a few steps from the beach, this is one of many hotels in that area. **$$$**

La Maison Gao Group 2, Thanh Đông; f. Very cosy villa in a corner of the countryside that is becoming an increasingly popular place to stay. There's a pool, big windows & plenty of natural light. **$$$**

Anantara Hội An Resort [301 G4] 1 Phạm Hồng Thái; w anantara.com. Perhaps not the best Anantara property in Vietnam, this is nevertheless the most luxury hotel walking distance from the Old Town, with rooms & the restaurant overlooking the river. **$$$$**

Anicca Thanh Tây; w aniccavilla.com. Large villa only suitable for big groups, Anicca is part of a family of holiday villas in & around Hội An. **$$$$**

Namia River Retreat 232 Trần Nhân Tông; w namiariverretreat.com. Stunning design hotel and one of Central Vietnam's most stylish stays, with impressive spa facilities and private villas with pools. The tropical bioclimatic design, by Hồ Chí Minh City-based T3 Architects, has won awards. **$$$$$**

WHERE TO EAT AND DRINK

The places in the countryside and along the coast are not walking distance from the Old Town & you'll need transport to get to them. Eat there while exploring the countryside or during a day on the beach.

In and around the Old Town

Restaurants and street food

Cary Liên [301 C1] Hẻm 26, Thái Phiên; 06.00–09.00 daily. Ms Liên serves *ca ri*, or curry, which may have been brought to Hội An by South Asian traders centuries ago. Here it's deliciously spiced & not too sweet. **$**

✱ **Chè Xí Mà Phủ** [301 D1] 115 Nguyễn Trường Tộ; 06.00–21.00 daily. *Chè* is a Vietnamese dessert sometimes translated as sweet soup. The signature dish of this little spot is *chè mè đen*. **$**

Cơm Gà Bà Buội [301 C3] 22 Phan Châu Trinh; f comgababuoigiatruyen; 10.30–21.00 daily. Touristy but nevertheless good chicken & rice served quickly & professionally in a converted old residential home. **$**

✱ **Cơm Gà Bà Thuận** [301 B4] 17/4 Hai Bà Trưng; 10.00–20.00 daily. Lesser-known spot for chicken & rice close to many of the sights &

HỘI AN'S SPECIALITY DISHES

The places at which to try these dishes are listed from opposite.

CAO LẦU A dish found only in Hội An, *cao lầu* used to be reserved for the elite. Now it's an affordable street-food dish of thick chewy noodles topped with sliced pork, greens and crunchy rice squares. The flavour comes from a sweet sauce at the bottom of the bowl, so mix well before tucking in. Try it at **Quán Cao Lầu Thanh**.

MÌ QUẢNG The 'Quảng' in *mì Quảng* refers to Quảng Nam, the province that Hội An lies within. This dish varies considerably from place to place, but essentially it's rice noodles served with egg, chicken, pork, shrimp and sometimes fish. It's usually served with a garden salad and a crunchy rice cracker. As with *cao lầu*, the sauce is at the bottom. Try it at **Mì Quảng Cưng**.

CƠM GÀ Pulled boiled chicken served over yellow rice cooked with the same water used to cook the chicken and topped with coriander. A lot of the dish's flavour comes from the pickles and chilli jam served on the side. Try it at **Cơm Gà Bà Buội**, **Cơm Gà Bà Thuận** and **Cơm Gà Xí Hội An**.

WHITE ROSE Hội An's version of a dumpling, but made with rice flour and stuffed with pork or shrimp, or both. Traditionally it's boiled, but you can also order it fried, transforming it from a soft dumpling into a crispy wonton. Try it, unsurprisingly, at **White Rose Restaurant**.

CHÈ MÈ ĐEN A black, gooey, warm sweet treat made with black sesame that is deliciously comforting, especially on a rainy Hội An afternoon. Try it at **Chè Xí Mà Phủ** or in street stalls in the Old Town.

BÁNH XOÀI Another sweet treat which you can eat on the go, *bánh xoài* means mango cake, and yet there is no mango to be found here. Instead, expect a chewy rice ball stuffed with sweetened peanuts and sprinkled with flour. Find these sold on the street in the Old Town.

run by a traditional family who live in the back. You'll walk through their house to reach the bathroom. $

Cơm Gà Xí Hội An [301 C2] 47/2 Trần Hưng Đạo; ⌚ noon–20.00 daily. Chicken & rice served on the street on little metal tables & chairs, this is Hội An's quintessential street-food experience cooking up a local speciality dish. $

Mì Quảng Cưng [map, page 305] 390 Cửa Đại; ⌚ 06.00–22.00 daily. *Mì Quảng*, arguably the signature dish of the province, is getting harder to find in Hội An, but Ms Cưng still represents. $

✷ **Quán Cao Lầu Thanh** [301 C1] 26 Thái Phiên; f caolauThanh26ThaiPhien; ⌚ 06.00–19.00 Fri–Wed. *Cao lầu*, a thick noodle dish which is believed to have both Japanese & Chinese origins, is difficult to find outside of Hội An, where it was conceived. Nobody does it better than Thanh. $

White Rose Restaurant [301 A1] 533 Hai Bà Trưng; ⌚ 07.30–20.30 daily. Another Hội An speciality restaurant, this time serving White Rose, a boiled & deep-fried dumpling probably introduced to Hội An by the Chinese. $

Cơm Linh [301 D3] 42 Phan Châu Trinh; f comlinhrestaurant; ⌚ 11.00–21.30 daily. Hugely popular with locals & visitors, Linh has a huge menu of Vietnamese favourites, including some local speciality dishes. Best to come outside of usual dining hours to avoid queuing. Vegan & vegetarian friendly. $$

✷ **Nữ Eatery** [301 B4] 10A Nguyễn Thị Minh Khai; f NuEateryHoiAn; ⌚ noon–21.00 Tue–Sun. Delicious & innovative little spot serving contemporary Vietnamese food with clever influences from other parts of the world. The stuffed bao are particularly good. Vegan & vegetarian friendly. $$

Xanh Quán [map, page 305] 138 Trần Quang Khải; ⌚ 09.00–22.00 daily. Classic good-value Vietnamese restaurant serving the whole gamut of local dishes, from steamed fish (recommended) to crunchy salads (also recommended). $$$

Mango Rooms [301 F4] 37 Phan Bội Châu; w mangomangohoian.com; ⌚ 08.00–23.00 daily. Mango Rooms has long been one of Hội An's best restaurants, & its current iteration is right on the river. Chef-patron Đức continues to craft beautiful Vietnamese fare with a creative, contemporary twist. $$$$

Bars and coffee houses

Buttercup by Rosie's Café [301 D3] 71/26 Phan Châu Trinh; w buttercuphoian.com; ⌚ 07.30–16.00 Mon–Sat. Cute café, but also brunch spot popular with Western travellers that serves all the avocado dishes you could ask for, plus a mean cappuccino.

Café Hoàng Vân [301 C2] 49 Trần Hưng Đạo; ⌚ 05.00–18.00 daily. One of the few local haunts left near the Old Town, this café is a no-frills escape for those who are tiring of the pomp of Hội An. Great Vietnamese coffee, obviously.

The Espresso Station [301 C2] 28/2 Trần Hưng Đạo; f; ⌚ 07.30–17.30 daily. Hội An's obligatory hipster coffee spot, which introduced quality espresso-based drinks to Hội An many years ago. It retains the most creative coffee menu in town.

Hội An Coffee Hub [301 D4] Alley 11 Nguyễn Thái Học; ⌚ 07.30–19.00 daily. Cosy coffee spot in the thick of the Old Town & thus an ideal pit stop while exploring the sights, with delicious caffeinated & non-caffeinated drinks.

The Inner Hội An by Àla [301 F4] 54 Phan Bội Châu; f theinnerhoian; ⌚ 07.30–17.00 daily. A little creative hub in & among the European-style buildings of the French Quarter, Àla has a focus on premium Western coffee. They have a sister café in Đà Nẵng.

Market Bar Terrace [301 E4] 2 Hoàng Diệu; ⌚ 16.00–23.00 daily. Not the best bar in the country, but it's hard to beat the location: on top of the market & overlooking the river & old streets of the town.

Phin Coffee Restaurant [301 C3] 132/7 Trần Phú; w phincoffeehoian.com; ⌚ 08.00–21.30 daily. Hidden away down an alleyway in the Old Town, the best thing about Phin is that you can take your coffee up on to the roof & look over the rooftops.

✷ **Ren Rửa Café** [301 C2] 39/3 Alley 144 Nguyễn Trường Tộ; f; ⌚ 08.00–21.00 daily. This beautifully designed café popular with Hội An locals has taken over a mid-19th-century modernist bungalow, with tables & chairs spilling into the garden.

In the countryside and along the coast *Map, opposite*

Restaurants and street food

Cosy Corner Café Tổ 7, An Bàng; f thecosycornercafe; ⌚ 07.30–17.00 daily. Reasonably cheap & cheerful little beach village restaurant not far from the water, specialising in Western brunch food, though there are also Vietnamese dishes on the menu. $$

✷ **Quán A Rồi** Âu Cơ; ⌚ 10.00–22.00 daily. Excellent seafood restaurant serving mainly Vietnamese customers, though the name may come from the Thai word for delicious. No English is spoken, but the animated staff will help create a dinner to remember. Always check the price of the things you order before committing. $$$

Seascape An Bàng; ⌚ 09.00–21.00 daily. Possibly the best place to eat on the beach & far enough away from the more popular sections of An Bàng, with all-day dining, a broad menu & sun loungers. $$$

Mùa Làng rau vườn, Trà Quế; w muatraque.com; ⌚ 11.00–13.30 & 17.00–21.00 Thu–Mon. One of Hội An's most special dining experiences & Vietnam's best restaurants, Mùa serves 2 (vegetarian & non-vegetarian) 'eco-centric' seasonal tasting menus of delicate creations. $$$$$

Coffee houses

✷ **Café Slow Hội An** Thôn Trà Quế; ⌚ 07.30–17.30 daily. Perfect & newly opened garden café that overlooks vegetable patches & has a distinctly relaxed Japanese design theme.

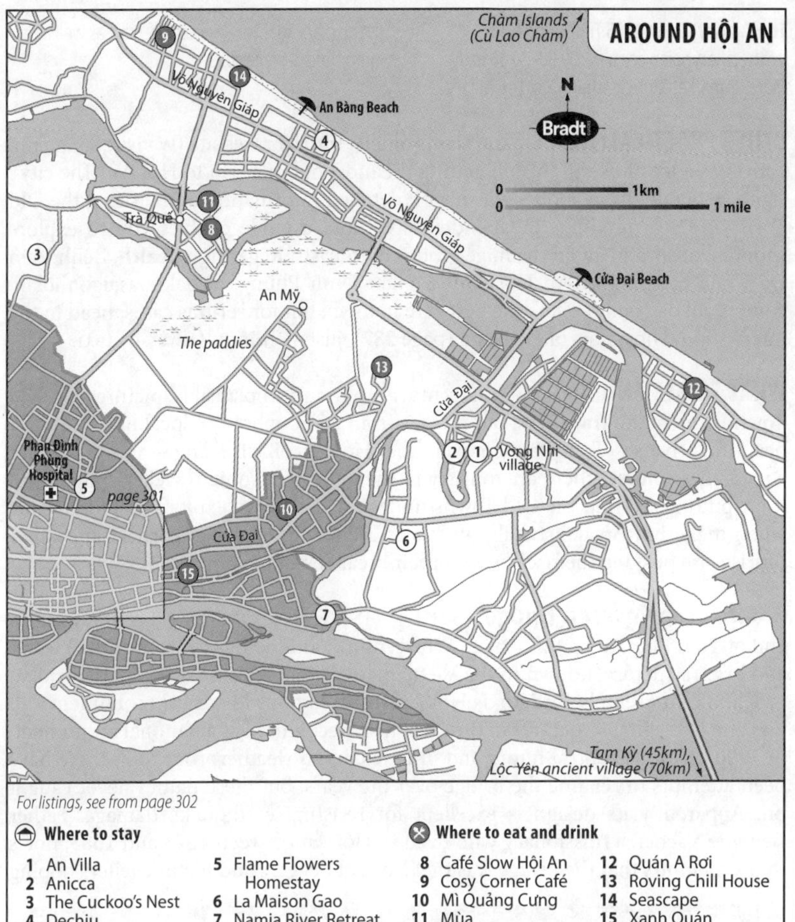

Roving Chill House Nguyễn Trãi, Thanh Tây; RovingChillhouseHoiAn; 08.00–21.00 daily. Popular & Instagrammable spot that began the trend of plonking trendy cafés in the middle of the rice terraces. Many places to sit are mere centimetres from the rice crop.

SHOPPING

Hart Hội An [301 F4] 25 Phan Bội Châu; hartupcycled; 08.30–20.30 daily. Self-described as upcycled home décor, it's as if Hart knows just what you're looking for, including a carefully curated collection from Vietnam's various ethnolinguistic groups.

✷ **Jade's Hội An** [301 G3] 314 Nguyễn Duy Hiệu; 10.00–18.00 daily. Handcrafted clothes, bags and other goodies from a Hanoian with an eye for colourful design. There are particularly good clothes for children.

Reaching Out Arts & Crafts [301 B4] 131 Trần Phú; reachingout.teahouse; 08.00–20.00 daily. Interesting & diverse collection of craft products – from crockery to textiles – made by artisans & people with disabilities. There's also a tea room attached.

TaTa Tailor [301 E4] Old Town; tatatailoring; 09.00–19.00 daily. The place to come for good-value clothing made quickly. TaTa has garnered a well-deserved reputation for quality, price, speed & friendliness.

The Tailory [301 C2] 85 Trần Hưng Đạo; w thetailoryhoian.com; ⌚ 09.00–20.30 daily. More upmarket & pricier than TaTa, The Tailory is the place for more delicate items – as well as ambitious 3-piece suits.

OTHER PRACTICALITIES Quảng Nam's official **tourism** website (w visitquangnam.com) has a lot of useful tips on getting the most out of a trip to Hội An. The city's sights generally have good signage with detailed information and visiting the Old Town and surroundings independently without a guide enables you to explore spontaneously and avoid the huge groups of tourists. Regarding **health**, Bệnh Viện Đa Khoa Saigon Hội An Hospital (6 Phan Đình Phùng; w dakhoasaigonhoian.com; ⌚ all day daily) offers the best care in town, but for serious cases, head to the international hospitals in Đà Nẵng (page 287), just 45 minutes away by taxi.

WHAT TO SEE AND DO Hội An's centuries-old and implausibly picturesque Old Town is the main draw here, but it is far from a stronghold of local life. The most beautiful streets – Trần Phú, Nguyễn Thái Học and Bạch Đằng – and the bigger streets that connect them are touristy to the point that some travellers might find it off-putting. To find the Old Town's understated charms, explore it before 08.00, when makeshift breakfast stalls and cafés are set up on street corners and other tourists are busying themselves with their breakfast buffets.

✷ Japanese Covered Bridge [301 B4] (186 Trần Phú) Situated at the western end of Trần Phú Street, this ornate 17th-century (and perhaps 16th-century) wood and brick structure, known to the Vietnamese as Cầu Nhật Bản (Japanese Bridge) or Chùa Cầu (Temple Bridge), is Hội An's most famous historical monument and was one of the first structures in the town to be recognised as a national monument, in 1990. With its central hump and unique curved weatherproof roof, there have been attempts to rename the bridge over the years, but these names never caught on. Apparently its design is excellent for resisting earthquake damage. Father Bénigne Vachet, a missionary who lived in Hội An between 1673 and 1683, notes in his memoirs that the bridge was the haunt of beggars and fortune tellers hoping

PRICING HỘI AN'S HERITAGE

Hội An has a complicated relationship with entrance tickets. Over the last decade, it has tried several times to implement systems that charge visitors to enter the old core, with the intention that the funds go towards restoration and maintenance efforts. Each time it was met with intense criticism, not usually from tourists but from residents and business owners, resulting in backtracking. At the time of research, it was not necessary to pay to enter the Old Town, but you do pay to enter the sites. Buy a book of tickets for 120,000VND and this gives access to five sites and lasts for three days. If you exhaust the book, simply buy another. There are around 25 ticketed sites, performances and demonstrations. **Sights in this section come under this ticketing scheme unless stated otherwise**. It would take more than a week of intense sightseeing to visit every site. Instead, make sure you always have a valid ticket book on you and only enter the sites you're taken with (or aren't packed with people). Some are more interesting than others but all have something to offer, and at just a dollar per site, it's a good deal. For some of the more compelling or photogenic sights, look for the ✷ symbol.

LEGEND HAS IT: EARTHQUAKE MITIGATION

According to an ancient legend, the foundations of the Japanese Covered Bridge were fastened to the weakest point of an intracontinental dragon. The beast, whose head rested in India and tail writhed around in Japan, had a terrible temper and could make the earth move and the heavens shudder. Some say that he was immobilised by the structure, became helpless and died. Others claim he was merely appeased by the temple that was installed on the bridge. From that day the bridge has been said to have the power to resist earthquakes, but, more importantly, reduce the chance of earthquakes in Japan. Another legend is associated with the bridge's origins: its popular name reflects a long-standing belief that it was built by the Japanese, although no documentary evidence exists to support this. There is also little in the architecture that proves it beyond doubt, says historian Tim Doling, though this is perhaps because the bridge has been rebuilt so many times over the centuries.

to benefit from the stream of people crossing it. These days, you're more likely to see elderly women hawking souvenirs to swarms of tourists. The bridge is also a religious place for the worship of Trấn Vũ, a God of Heaven who protects against demons and prevents disasters, storms and floods (see above). You'll see very little praying and a lot of picture-taking, which might explain why Hội An suffers from typhoons and flooding most years.

While some records suggest the bridge dates back to the 1590s, it probably wasn't built until the 17th century. As for the exact dates, historian Tim Doling writes in *Exploring Quảng Nam*: 'One clue to its construction date is the fact that the bridge is guarded at its west end by a pair of monkey deities (*thần hầu*) and at its east end by a pair of dog deities (*thần cẩu*)…A quick check of the Chinese zodiac reveals that 1632 was the Year of the Monkey, while 1634 was the Year of the Dog, so it's possible that the bridge dates from the period 1632–34. However, this is nothing more than conjecture.' You can find an image of the bridge on the 20,000VND note, reflecting that, despite its name and possible architects, this is one of Vietnam's most iconic structures.

The Central Market [301 E4] (Chợ Hội An; 19 Trần Phú; ⌚ 06.00–20.00 daily; free – not part of the ticketing scheme) Come here early in the morning (before 06.00) and watch hundreds of conical-hatted traders hawk baskets of silvery eels, black tiger prawns, cuttlefish, lobsters, blood ark-shells, periwinkles, numerous types of bivalves, crabs, tunny, snappers and anchovies close to the river. There's also a fruit and vegetable section in the market where you can buy huge durians piled high next to bananas, papaya, custard apples, pineapples, mangosteens and sweet potato. Some stalls are crammed with medicinal herbs, or with untidy lumps of unrefined sugar. Others sell many types of rice and noodles, including the raw ingredients to make *cao lầu*, Hội An's speciality noodle soup. The fabric market is next door, housing many of Hội An's express tailors.

The museums

Museum of Hội An [301 D2] (10B Trần Hưng Đạo; **w** hoianmuseum.com; ⌚ 07.30–11.00 & 14.00–17.00 Mon–Fri) Constructing this big, hulking building on the edge of the Old Town probably seemed like a good idea at the time, but it is now looking rather a clumsy adjunct. Nevertheless, it is an adequate introduction to Hội An's long history, with sections on the area's Sa Huỳnh prehistory, the Champa period (2nd to 15th centuries) and Đại Việt period (15th to 19th centuries). The displays are fairly lacklustre, but photos of 20th-century Hội An are rather special. An additional section is devoted to the resistance movements in the city during the French colonial period and American War. The ground floor is devoted to ceramics, including an interesting display of 600-year-old items dredged up from shipwrecks 25 years ago.

Museum of Trade Ceramics [301 D4] (80 Trần Phú; **w** hoianmuseum.com; ⌚ 08.00–17.00 Mon–Fri) If you were enticed by the ceramics display at the Hội An Museum, don't miss the charming Museum of Trade Ceramics. Vietnamese ceramics have a long history – more than 2,000 years – and evidence of items from the last millennium are found in different corners of the globe. Vietnamese potters and ceramicists were particularly prolific in the 15th and 16th centuries, when pieces made their way to parts of the world that are now Japan, China, Thailand, the Philippines, Indonesia, Malaysia, India, Portugal, Spain, Holland, Italy, England and France. Apparently, from the 17th century Vietnamese ceramics became less important even as Hội An was in its heyday. The museum, which opened in 1995, is housed in a wood-fronted former residence, which was beautifully restored in 1991 with considerable help from Japan.

Museum of Sa Huỳnh Culture [301 B4] (140 Trần Phú; **w** hoianmuseum.com; ⌚ 08.00–17.00 Mon–Fri) Housed in a colonial building from the early 1900s that was owned and occupied by Chinese merchants, Hội An's Museum of Sa Huỳnh Culture opened in 1994 to showcase the area's prehistory. The Sa Huỳnh civilisation, which flourished between 1000BCE and CE200, preceded Champa, and possibly set up the first Thu Bồn River port some 2,000 years ago. There are more than 1,000 artefacts here, which were excavated mostly between 1989 and 1995 in and around Hội An and on the Chàm Islands. The architecture and artefacts are of great historic interest, but signage is generally quite poor and confusing to follow.

Museum of Folk Culture [301 D4] (33 Nguyễn Thái Học; **w** hoianmuseum.com; ⌚ 08.00–17.00 daily) Opened in 2005, this museum exhibits items related to traditional clothing, performance art and occupations. Particular focus is given to the crafts, including lantern making, carpentry and embroidery. Displays include information on traditional weaving, tailoring, pottery, carpentry, farming, music and medicine. The exhibits can feel a little dry, but the building, the largest two-storey house in the Old Town according to the local tourism authority, stretches across an entire block.

Museum of Traditional Medicine [301 D4] (34 Nguyễn Thái Học; ⌚ 08.00–17.30 daily) As a trading hub for communities from across Asia, including Japan and China, it should come as no surprise that Hội An was once home to some of Vietnam's largest apothecaries. Housed in a two-storey residence, this museum is noticeably more intimate than the Museum of Traditional Vietnamese Medicine in Hồ Chí Minh City (page 481), but information is also scarcer. There are more than 200 artefacts and materials related to traditional medicine and a front entrance that replicates a traditional Hội An medicine store, complete with a store counter, herbal medicine cabinets, traditional medicinal plants and sacks of dried herbs.

The Chinese assembly halls Chinese traders in Hội An (like elsewhere in Southeast Asia) established self-governing clan houses, which owned their own schools, cemeteries, hospitals and temples. The *hội quán* (clan houses, or assembly halls) may be dedicated to a god or an illustrious individual and may contain a temple but are not themselves temples. There are five *hội quán* in Hội An, four for use by people of specific ethnicities: Phước Kiến, Cantonese, Hải Nam, Chaozhou and the fifth for use by any other visiting Chinese sailors or merchants. This is the richest collection of *hội quán* in Vietnam outside of Chợ Lớn in Hồ Chí Minh City. Despite heavy taxation, both Vietnamese emperors and later the French colonial administration allowed these communities significant autonomy, recognising their economic contributions.

✷ ***Chinese Assembly Hall*** [301 D3] (Hội Quán Ngũ Bang; 64 Trần Phú; ◷ 07.00–11.00 & 14.00–16.00 daily) This is a good assembly hall to start with, as much of the imagery is repeated across other halls and you can draw parallels. Unusually for an assembly hall, this inclusive refuge was a mutual aid society open to any Chinese trader or seaman, regardless of dialect or region of origin. Chinese vessels tended to visit Hội An during the spring, returning to China in the summer. The assembly hall would help shipwrecked and ill sailors and perform the burial rites of merchants with no relatives in Hội An. Founded in 1741 and refurbished in 1855, it was a meeting place for all five groups (the four listed above plus the Hakka, who did not have their own assembly hall) and also for those with no clan house of their own. The house comprises a front hall, courtyard and main hall, all accessed via a flight of steps and exterior front porch. Interestingly, the front hall lacks shrines. Beyond this is an open courtyard flanked by covered side halls used for meetings.

Access the main hall via a covered incense-burning yard that features a shrine to Quan Âm, the Avalokitesvara Bodhisattva and Goddess of Compassion (page 293), Thiên Hậu Thánh Mẫu, the Goddess of the Sea, and her two demonic assistants Thiên Lý Nhãn and Thuận Phong Nhĩ, here with black skin (see below). To the

LEGEND HAS IT: GIRL POWER

Among the guardians of Thiên Hậu are the protective demons, Thiên Lý Nhãn, or Thousand-Miles-Eye, and Thuận Phong Nhĩ, or With-the-Wind Ear. Thiên Lý Nhãn, typically depicted with red skin and two horns, and Thuận Phong Nhĩ, usually with green skin and one horn, were both deeply enamoured with Thiên Hậu, the Goddess of the Sea. Desiring to win the goddess's favour, the two demons challenged her to a duel. Thiên Hậu, amused but only marginally flattered, agreed that whoever could defeat her in battle would earn her hand in marriage. Despite their formidable powers, neither could best Thiên Hậu, who disposed of them with whimsical ease. Humbled by their defeat and dazzled by her power, they swore lifelong loyalty to the goddess. Ever since, Thiên Lý Nhãn and Thuận Phong Nhĩ have vigilantly watched over the seas, alerting Thiên Hậu to any ships in distress so she might rush to their aid and ensure their safety. The Goddess of the Sea was an important deity for the Chinese diaspora in Southeast Asia, many of whom emigrated by boat. It was common for the community to build temples to thank her for safe passage, and many of these can still be found in Chinese quarters across the region. See page 479 for her origin story.

right of the main hall is a large model ship and flanking the main Thiên Hậu shrine are two additional shrines: the right one honours Thần Tài (God of Wealth), and the left one venerates the hall's founding ancestors. In keeping with its history of inclusivity, this assembly hall is free to visit and is not part of Hội An's ticket scheme.

✷ ***Fujian Assembly Hall*** [301 D3] (Hội Quán Phước Kiến; 46 Trần Phú; ⌚ 07.00–18.00 daily) This is one of the town's most remarkable assembly halls, built around 1690, extensively remodelled in 1795 and 1888, and most recently refurbished in the 1970s. Originally a clan house for a group of ethnic Chinese who came from Fujian (Phước Kiến), it is dedicated to the Goddess of the Sea, Thiên Hậu Thánh Mẫu, whose two-centuries-old effigy built out of papier mâché stands in a glass case centrally on the altar. Also known as the Taoist Queen of Heaven, she is flanked again by Thuận Phong Nhĩ (in red) and Thiên Lý Nhãn (in green this time; page 309). Before reaching the Goddess of the Sea, you'll encounter Quan Âm, the Goddess of Compassion (page 293). On the right-hand side of the courtyard is a beautifully crafted large-scale model of a Chinese war junk dating from the 17th century. A chamber beyond features an altar showing the descendants of six families from Phước Kiến and a glass-enshrined figure of Vietnamese doctor Lê Hữu Trác. A smaller altar, highly venerated by Hội An's childless women, is dominated by the God of Prosperity, Kim Hoa, attended by 12 midwives. The one in red is said to have the power to determine gender. This assembly hall was recognised as a national monument in 1990.

Hainan Assembly Hall [301 E3] (Hội Quán Hải Nam; 10 Trần Phú; ⌚ 08.00–17.00 daily) With a rather colourful history, this assembly hall was founded in the 1870s or 80s and is dedicated to the memory of the 108 sailors and passengers who were killed when three ships were plundered by an admiral in Emperor Tự Đức's navy. In his defence, the admiral claimed the victims were pirates and some sources maintain he had the ships painted black to strengthen his case. The sailors' innocence was revealed to Emperor Tự Đức in a dream, and he swiftly executed the corrupt and criminal naval brigade responsible. The assembly hall is notable for its gilded altar.

Chaozhou Assembly Hall [301 E3] (Hội Quán Triều Châu; 362 Nguyễn Duy Hiệu; ⌚ 08.00–17.00 daily) Near the Hainan Assembly Hall is the assembly hall for the immigrant and merchant community from Chaozhou, in between Fujian and Guangzhou. Exquisite wood carving is the highlight of this hall, constructed in 1845. The altar and its panels depict images from the sea and women from the Beijing court, perhaps intended to console homesick traders. The highly gilded figure of Ông Bổn (the assembly hall is also known as Ông Bổn Pagoda) can be seen sitting on the altar surrounded by delicate filigree, which depicts a veritable jungle of plant and animal life. It would seem that Ông Bổn has been mapped on to more than one historical Chinese figure, but is generally seen as a God of Prosperity.

Cantonese Assembly Hall [301 B4] (Hội Quán Quảng Đông; 176 Trần Phú; ⌚ 08.00–17.00 daily) This assembly hall was built between 1884 and 1885 and refurbished in 1953, 1970 and 1999. The French courted Cantonese immigrants in particular, aiming to harness the entrepreneurial spirit of these settlers. Entering through a three-entrance gateway adorned with protective symbols, you'll find a structure originally built from wood and later reconstructed with brick and concrete. The assembly hall features a main axis with three sections, flanked by two subsidiary axes, reflecting a blend of traditional Chinese and Vietnamese architectural styles. Merchants from Guangdong, now a province in southern China, would meet at this assembly hall, and legend has it that they would gather in front of the central altar before signing a formal contract. This central shrine is dedicated to Quan Công, a legendary Chinese general who helped overthrow the Eastern Han Dynasty. Flanking him are shrines to Thần Tài and Thiên Hậu, fronted by her protectors Thiên Lý Nhãn and Thuận Phong Nhĩ. The hall, with its fine embroidered hangings, is in a cool, tree-filled compound and is a good place to rest.

The communal houses Vietnamese communal houses, or *đình*, are the traditional nerve centres of village or neighbourhood life. They are not *đền* (temples) or *chùa* (Buddhist pagodas), but often have an in-built spiritual element, much like Chinese assembly halls. For more on Vietnamese religious buildings, see page 32.

✷ ***Hội An Communal House*** [301 C3] (27 Lê Lợi; ⌚ 08.00–22.00 daily) This communal house was built in the 18th century but moved to its current location in the early 20th century to make way for Lê Lợi Street. In Vietnamese, it goes by the name Đình Ông Voi, which means 'Mr Elephant Communal House' because of the stone elephant statues that adorn its yard. It underwent significant renovations in 1817 and 1897, an additional vestibule was built in 1942 and after 1975 it became a pre-school. Eventually, the kids were turfed out, and it was only recently restored to become a site for visitors, with a handy floor plan of the structure. The compound includes a front yard, vestibule, west wing, east wing, well and a main hall with a traditional yin-yang tiled roof. Notably, it is the only remaining communal house in Hội An with a two-storey altar and worship space. Most Vietnamese communal houses also had a religious function, and this was dedicated to protective deities.

✷ ***Cẩm Phô Communal House*** [301 A3] (52 Nguyễn Thị Minh Khai; ⌚ all day daily) Though much older, the Cẩm Phô Communal House was moved to the present location in 1817 or 1818, enlarged in 1903 and recognised as a national monument in 1991. The layout is typical of Vietnamese communal houses in Hội An, with a 200-year-old banyan tree, large front yard and east and west wings flanking a central vestibule. Modern Nguyễn Thị Minh Khai Street once ran alongside the river, and this communal house was once served by a nearby ferry wharf. The shrines honour Hoàng Bổn Cảnh, guardian gods of the village and the ancestors of esteemed families.

Old houses and family chapels

Old House of Phùng Hưng [301 B4] (4 Nguyễn Thị Minh Khai; ⌚ 08.00–18.00 daily) A large two-storey shophouse, this was constructed in the late 18th century by Chinese merchant Phùng Hưng and was recognised as a national monument in 1993. Above the main entrance are 'door eyes', which resemble an eight-petalled flower and are believed to serve as protectors against evil. Also look out for the beams, which are adorned with carvings of carp, symbolising the patience and determination needed for business success. The eighth-generation descendants reside in a private family room on the ground floor, while the rest of the house functions as an attraction that is popular with large tour groups. If it's too busy, come back later. Originally, the upper area was used to store goods during floods, as well as the family shrine and a shrine to the Sea Goddess Thiên Hậu Thánh Mẫu (page 479).

KAZIMIERZ KWIATKOWSKI

Nestled in a small park at 138 Trần Phú is a sculpture of a bearded man [301 C4] that you'd be forgiven for thinking was Marx. This is in fact the Polish architect Kazimierz Kwiatkowski, affectionately known as Kazik, who arrived in Vietnam in 1981 with the Polish Conservation Agency. Kazik dedicated much of his life to the restoration of Mỹ Sơn (page 314) and played a crucial role in getting Hội An's Old Quarter recognised as a UNESCO World Heritage Site. He passed away in 1997.

Old House of Quân Thắng [301 D4] (77 Trần Phú; ⌚ 09.30–18.00 daily) Built by a Chinese merchant in the early 19th century, Quân Thắng is a typical example of an ancient shophouse, with the front main entrance used for commerce and the back door leading directly to the family residence. Separating the two zones is the courtyard with bonsai trees and a miniature landscaped garden. The house has many architectural characteristics typical of the period, including *chồng rường giả thủ* (upper beams with upright bars), *cột trốn kẻ chuyền* (hidden pillars and connected rafters) and *vì vỏ cua* (an auxiliary arched roof).

✷ ***Old House of Đức An*** [301 C4] (129 Trần Phú; ⌚ sporadic hours; circle back if closed) The owner of this charming property, built in the mid 19th century, gets overwhelmed by the hordes of tourists that crowd outside his family home, but if you smile and behave courteously then he'll try and explain the house's history in broken English. This former 'bookshophouse' was a hotbed of anti-colonial resistance, with various patriots coming to purchase banned books promoting anti-imperialist ideas. These include Trần Quý Cáp and Huỳnh Thúc Kháng, whom you might recognise in the street names in cities across Central Vietnam. The house is characterised by its traditional tube architecture, consisting of two main sections: a commercial and guest reception area at the front, and a private residential space at the back, connected by a central courtyard. Constructed with a wooden frame, the house features intricately carved pillars and beams, brick and lime mortar walls and traditional tiled roofs. The front building is divided into two sections. The street-facing portion served as a traditional medicine dispensary, and perhaps also as a front to conceal contraband books. Above the shop area is a small attic housing the family shrine. The rear building, accessible through the open courtyard, accommodates the family's living quarters.

✷ ***Old House of Tấn Ký*** [301 C4] (101 Nguyễn Thái Học; ⌚ 08.00–17.30 daily) The Tấn Ký house traded in agricultural products in the 19th century and the design shows influences from China and Japan, particularly in the ornately carved beams. The inside wooden framework is joined with wooden pegs and rests on marble bases and the outside structure is made of thick bricks and tiles, helping to keep the house cool in summer and warm in winter. The house has belonged to the same family for seven generations, and it was recognised as a national monument in 1990.

Trần Family Garden House [301 C3] (21 Lê Lợi; ⌚ 07.00–21.00 daily) Lê Lợi Street was once known as rue Gouverneur-Général-Charles. At 21 Lê Lợi Street is this garden house and chapel, set within a walled compound and built by civil mandarin Trần Tứ Nhạc in 1802, at the beginning of the Nguyễn Dynasty. This might explain its atmospheric similarities with the garden houses of Huế. Remarkably, the house is still owned by the 13th generational descendants of this Chinese mandarin, and was designed as a traditional *nhà rường* with three compartments, two wings and a central courtyard. The two wings have wooden upper beams and upright bars that have been carefully and artistically carved. Access to the reception room, typically through a side door except on special occasions like Tết, reveals a space adorned with intricate wooden carvings, family heirlooms and a portrait of Trần Tứ Nhạc. The rear section of the chapel has been converted into an antiques and gift shop that some visitors might feel uneasy about considering this family house is not free to visit.

Nguyễn Tường Family Chapel [301 B3] (8 Nguyễn Thị Minh Khai; 🕘 08.00–21.00 daily) This family chapel was built in 1806 (restored in 1909 and 2005) by Nguyễn Tường Vân, the head of the Royal Army. When he died in 1822, a family temple with three shrines was constructed. The central shrine is dedicated to Nguyễn Tường Vân, the shrine to the right as you face it is dedicated to male family members and the shrine on the left is dedicated to female family members. A portrait of Nguyễn Tường Vân still sits on the central shrine. The temple's façade features windows with carvings of *phật thủ*, or 'Buddha's hand' fruit, which resemble a Buddhist mudra and symbolise blessings and friendship. The family temple also showcases the *mái vỏ cua*, an arched roof commonly used in Nguyễn Dynasty palaces in Huế. This distinctive design links various roof sections and serves as a gutter.

✷ ***Quan Công Temple*** [301 E4] (24 Trần Phú; 🕘 07.30–17.30 daily) Built in 1653 by Ming refugees, this kaleidoscopic and ornate temple is dedicated to Quan Công, a highly esteemed Chinese general who epitomised loyalty, sincerity and integrity. The main hall is dedicated to the general and his adopted son, Quan Bình, and weapon-bearer Châu Xương. Notable features include two horse statues: a white horse on the left symbolising Quan Công's steed before he received a red one from the gods, depicted on the right. The temple also contains shrines to the mother goddess Bà Chúa Tiên Nương Nương, one of the Four Immortals. The temple has been refurbished multiple times, including in 1906, when the Minh Hương Ancestor Worshipping Temple moved to a neighbouring plot, and in 1940, when a passageway was added to connect the two buildings (this was later blocked after 1975). The temple reportedly still holds 18th-century poems composed by Nguyễn Nghiễm and other generals who visited Hội An from Northern Vietnam.

Bà Mụ Temple façade [301 B3] (675 Hai Bà Trưng; 🕘 all day daily) The grand façade is all that remains of this 17th-century pagoda, also built by the Minh Hương community. During colonial times it was known as the Pagode de Maternité, or Maternity Pagoda. Viewed from the street, it's clear the façade fronted two sanctuaries: the gate on the left led to a temple built in dedication of the midwifery deities and Thiên Hậu Thánh Mẫu (page 479); the gate on the right led to a temple dedicated to a suite of gods and generals, including the God of Medicine. The temple was extensively restored in the 1920s and 30s with help from the École Française d'Extrême-Orient, but it was badly damaged by war in the 1940s and subsequently abandoned. The façade you see today was most recently restored in 2018 and is fast becoming an iconic photography spot. The courtyard in front is packed with cafés and restaurants, and is a good spot to rest away from the central streets of Hội An's Old Town.

The French Quarter [301 F3] Just like Hanoi, Huế and Hồ Chí Minh City, Hội An has a French quarter, though it's noticeably smaller and is named after the architecture, not the previous neighbourhood tenants, who were mainly Chinese. The French Quarter stretches west from Hội An Market along Phan Bội Châu Street. You'll find notable French shophouses on both sides of the street, most of which have been repurposed as cafés and restaurants.

Outside the Old Town *Map, page 305*

The beaches A white-sand beach with a host of simple restaurants, beach bars and sun loungers, **Cửa Đại Beach** is 4km from Hội An, east down Trần Hưng Đạo Street, which eventually becomes Cửa Đại Street, and is a pleasant 25-minute bicycle ride or 1-hour walk from Hội An. At **An Bàng Beach**, 4km north of Hội An, off the dual carriageway, a collection of popular beach bars (page 304) and hotels (page 302) have opened. It's an easy cycle north on Hai Bà Trưng Street past paddies, though the road has become busy in recent years. If you drive, park your vehicle in one of the parking spots at the end of Hai Bà Trưng Street and walk to find a beach bar that appeals, but always agree on the parking price. The quieter and arguably nicer spots are those that are furthest from Hai Bà Trưng Street. Seascape Restaurant comes recommended.

The paddies Separating Hội An's Old Town from the coast is a crescent of rice paddies crisscrossed by countryside lanes. In the summer months these paddies bulge with ripening rice and make for idyllic walks, especially at sunrise and sunset. There's also a growing number of hotels (page 302) in this neighbourhood, as well as restaurants and cafés (page 304) that can serve as pit stops. Particularly pretty areas are the adjacent An Mỹ neighbourhood and Trà Quế farming islet. You could spend a day exploring these enclaves, especially with the aid of a bicycle, or visit them on your way to one of the beaches.

Around Hội An *Map, page 296*

Captivated by the lantern-strewn streets, glistening beaches and gleaming paddies like hypnotised moths to a tantalising flame, not many tourists take the time to make excursions outside Hội An. This is a great shame, as surrounding the Old Town are fairytale villages, a paradisical archipelago and Mỹ Sơn Sanctuary, an extraordinary set of ruins and Vietnam's premier archaeological site.

✷ ***Mỹ Sơn Sanctuary*** (Duy Phú; **w** mysonticketonline.vn; 🕘 06.00–18.00 daily; international visitor 150,000VND) *As Mỹ Sơn is one of Vietnam's most important archaeological sites, this section was written with considerable input from Dr Nguyễn H H Duyên (page 12).* Declared a World Heritage Site by UNESCO in 1999 and dating from the 4th to the 13th centuries, Mỹ Sơn is one of Vietnam's most ancient monuments. Weather, jungle and years of strife have wrought their worst on Mỹ Sơn. But the jungle under which the sanctuary remained hidden to the outside world provided it with its best protection: more has been destroyed in the past 60 years than in the 600 before that. Today, far from anywhere, Mỹ Sơn is a tranquil archaeological treasure with some exceptional details to look at. The site is located about 60km south of Đà Nẵng, 30km west of Hội An, and consists of dozens of monuments spread over a large area.

A startling number of visitors don't make it to Mỹ Sơn, making it all the more appealing for those who do. The thin red bricks used in the construction of the towers and temples were exquisitely carved, and this craftsmanship of many centuries remains obvious today. The trees and creepers have been pushed back but Mỹ Sơn remains cloaked in green and backed by forested mountains. Many of those who take the time to soak in the site and go at the right time of day (ie: first thing in the morning) find Mỹ Sơn to be one of the highlights of their experience in Vietnam.

Cham architecture The characteristic Cham architectural structure is the tower, built to reflect the divinity of the king: tall and rectangular (usually but not always), with four porticoes, each of which is blind except for that on the west face. Because Cham kings were far less wealthy and powerful than the Khmer kings of Angkor, the monuments are correspondingly smaller, but also more personal.

Originally built of wood (none of these remain), they were later made of brick, of which the earliest are located at Mỹ Sơn. Although little of these early examples remains, the temples seem to show similarities with forms from India, while also embodying Khmer and Javanese stylistic influences. Bricks are exactly laid and held together with a form of vegetable cement, probably the resin from trees. It is assumed that on completion, each tower was surrounded by wood and fired over several days in what amounted to a vast outdoor kiln.

Mỹ Sơn architecture is notable for its use of red brick, which has worn surprisingly well. Indeed, it remains a mystery to this day why the original structures seem more resistant to moss than the rebuilt and restored ones. Sandstone plinths are sometimes used, as are sandstone lintels, the Cham seemingly – like the Khmer of Angkor – never having learned the art of arch building, one of the few architectural techniques in which Europe was centuries ahead of Asia. Linga, phallic sculptures, and yoni, the female receptacle into which the carved phallus was normally inserted, are also usually made of sandstone. Overwhelmingly, however, brick is the medium of construction and the raw material from which Hindu, Shivaist and Buddhist images and ornaments are so intricately carved.

They would all have been supplied with water channels, ramifying like tentacles from the main stream that ran through the centre, and visitors will still get a sense of this today.

An Indianised land It is important to see Mỹ Sơn in the broader context of the Indianisation of Southeast Asia. Not just architecture but spiritual and political influences are echoed around the region. Falling as it did so strongly under Chinese influence, it is all the more remarkable to find such compelling evidence of Indian culture and iconography in Vietnam. Indeed, this was one of the criteria cited by UNESCO as justification for its listing. Nevertheless, one of the great joys of Cham sculpture and building is its unique feel, its graceful lines and unmistakable form. Angkor in Cambodia, Bagan in Myanmar, Borobudur in Java and Ayutthaya in Thailand, all of which are broadly contemporaneous with Mỹ Sơn, are temple complexes founded by Hindu, Shivaist or Buddhist god kings.

The process whereby new ideas and beliefs are absorbed into a pre-existing culture is known as syncretism. The Hindu cult of devarāja was developed by the kings of Angkor and later employed by Cham kings to bolster their authority. The king was the earthly representative of the god Shiva. Shivaist influence at Mỹ Sơn is unmissable. Shiva is one of the Hindu holy trinity, impermanent destroyer of the universe. Shiva's dance of destruction is the very rhythm of existence and hence also of rebirth. Shiva is often represented, as at Mỹ Sơn and other Cham relics throughout Vietnam, by the lingam, the phallus. Surrounding Mỹ Sơn was obviously a settled city with an unknown population, but it seems to have had a holy or spiritual function rather than being the seat of power, and it was possibly a burial place for its god kings.

Discovery and destruction Much that is known of Mỹ Sơn was discovered by French archaeologists from the École Française d'Extrême-Orient. Their rediscovery and excavation of Mỹ Sơn revealed a site that had been settled from the early 4th to the 13th centuries, one of the longest uninterrupted periods of development of any monument in Southeast Asia. The site was first cleared at the end of the 19th century, after being neglected for more than 500 years. When the French started excavating they discovered that several dozen buildings were in a remarkable state of repair, considering their age. They bestowed an unromantic identifying sequence of letters and numbers to the site in 1898, and this naming system remains today. Unfortunately, Mỹ Sơn was a Việt Cộng field headquarters and therefore located within one of the US 'free fire' zones, and it was extensively damaged in the American War. In particular, the finest sanctuary in the complex, A1, was demolished. After especially intense B-52 bombing raids and artillery bombardments in 1969, around 20 structures remained. Many statues, altars and linga have been removed to the Museum of Cham Sculpture in Đà Nẵng. There has been an admirable international effort to help restore Mỹ Sơn, with aid programmes organised by India, Italy, Poland and Japan (but the United States is absent from the list).

Exploring the ruins This is the finest Cham site in Vietnam, but don't expect anything as grand as Angkor. It may well be the setting, ringed by jungle-carpeted mountains, that leaves the greatest impression. Archaeologists who have studied the site in considerable detail think that originally there were 12 large sanctuary complexes here. Intricately designed, they were fairly haphazardly arranged, all within an area covering around 1km. The site is divided into ten groups (A, A', B, C, D, E, F, G, H and L) and two towers (N and K). The best preserved and most impressive are groups B, C and D. Groups A, H, G, E and F and tower K are in varying states of repair. Virtually nothing remains of groups A' and L and tower N.

You'll need 2 hours at least to explore the whole site. If it's sunny, it's highly recommended that you go as early as possible (gates open at 06.00) and failing that, leave it until the end of the afternoon (gates close at 17.00). This way you beat both the crowds and the heat, but the real prize is that the jungle is at its most alive in the early morning and late afternoon. If it's raining, you can be a little more relaxed about timings. If you didn't come with a guide, it's sometimes possible to hire one at the entrance gate. Alternatively, pay 79,000VND for the informative app-based audio guide, from which much of the information on these pages was taken. You'll need to bring your own headphones.

After entering there is a small museum on your right, built with aid money from Japan, and worthy of 10–15 minutes to help contextualise the site. You can then opt to walk the 2km road through the jungle to the site or take a 5-minute electric buggy. The route around the site is 3–4km. There are several dance performances that take place throughout the day; if this is of interest, check the day's timings at the ticket office and plan accordingly. The stage is near Group H.

The site proposes an anti-clockwise route, starting at Group H and finishing with Tower K. You might, however, choose to do the opposite, leaving the most impressive complexes, groups B, C and D, towards the end. There has been some attempt to make the site accessible for those who use wheelchairs, but this remains far from an accessible site for those with physical disabilities.

Group H If taking the route proposed by the site authorities, this is the first group you come across: look for some ruined towers poking over treetops on a small hill on the right. There isn't much to see, but some towers have been somewhat restored with help from India in 2018–19. This is one of the highest temple groupings in the sanctuary, together with Group G. Today, H1 is the most impressive. This was the main temple in the group, which is called a kalan. The structures show building techniques that may have been borrowed from the Khmer.

Group C Groups B, C and D are clustered together in the biggest complex anywhere in the site. After leaving Group H, you'll pass the outdoor theatre and see this group cluster in front. Built between the 8th and 13th centuries, the prosperous period of the Champa kingdom, restoration work started here in the 1930s, largely by French archaeologists. A lot of this work was undone by bombing campaigns in the 1960s, and then restoration began again in the 1980s. Group B is the most impressive, so work up to it by starting with groups C and D.

Group C consists of seven towers. C2 is the gate tower, built in the 10th to 11th centuries, which is when wood stopped being used as a building material. Group C contains the 8th-century primary sanctuary (C1), probably built with wood and then later rebuilt in the 10th and 11th centuries with brick. Visitors to Đà Nẵng's Museum of Cham Sculpture will see the statue of Shiva in human form, which was removed from this kalan. It has a boat-shaped curved roof, the only one. Unlike B1 this kalan is not completely surrounded by secondary sanctuaries. There are, however, four ruined temples (C4–C7) directly to the north of it, with very narrow entrances and interiors, possibly because they were only used by priests. C7, built in the 8th and 9th centuries, is likely to be the oldest. Note the wall pillars have stylised carvings of leaves and other foliage, a decorative theme of Mỹ Sơn that may have been influenced by Javanese art.

Group D There were originally six buildings that stood between groups B and C and the river. D1 and D2 were the most important buildings. Known as reception houses or retreat houses, these were likely a place where the royal family, dignitaries and perhaps other worshippers would prepare to pray. A representation of the threshold separating the real world from the spiritual world, worshippers would come here to cleanse themselves before worshipping in groups B, C and possibly A. These days they now hold various pieces of poorly labelled sculpture, the most captivating of which is the dancing Shiva, known as Nataraja, in D2. This piece dates from the 13th century, is made of sandstone and originally lived in H1 (see above). Shiva is shown in a soft and fluid movement, in contrast to the often sterner and more rigid

LEGEND HAS IT: TAKE NOTHING BUT MEMORIES

Some believe that Mỹ Sơn holds supernatural powers. A long-serving security guard tells of a young girl who visited Mỹ Sơn and spirited away a small piece of brick as a souvenir. The girl's mental health soon started to deteriorate, causing great concern in the village. Eventually, the girl's mother found the piece of brick in her room and suspected that it might be the culprit. She took it to fortune tellers, who confirmed that this sacred object was the reason for her daughter's illness and that it must be hastily returned. The woman returned to Mỹ Sơn, gave the piece of brick to the security guard and told him the story. He quickly placed it back where it belonged. Unfortunately, the security guard never learned whether the return of the relic restored the girl's sanity.

depiction in Indian art. The knees form an equilateral triangle and eight arms move in a circle to reflect the eternal and unstoppable movement of the universe. The dance in its entirety represents the restless cycle of birth, life and death.

Group B If you look carefully around the square perimeter of this complex, you will be able to see 13 buildings, one of which is the main gate to the complex (B2). This is directly opposite the meditation house (D1) which you'll recognise because it is the only slated structure. In the centre of this enclosure, past the gate, you will see the huge remains of the main sanctuary, B1. Though a structure may have existed prior, the main sanctuary was rebuilt in the 7th and 11th centuries. The fine brickwork of the 11th-century base can still be appreciated, but the rest was built with large stone blocks, a unique feature in the Mỹ Sơn complex. Archaeologists excavating here in 1985 discovered the sacred linga and yoni, which were ceremonially cleansed with holy water. Surrounding B1 are 11 other temples that contribute to the worship of Shiva. One of the best preserved is auxiliary temple B3, in the southwestern

ANCIENT AMARAVATI

This section was written with considerable input from Dr Nguyễn H H Duyên (page 12).

Champa was a decentralised country consisting of five states that took names from areas of India: Indrapura, Amaravati (Quảng Nam), Vijaya (page 329; Bình Định Province), Kauthara (page 339; Khánh Hòa Province) and Panduranga (page 341; Ninh Thuận and Bình Thuận provinces). Amaravati was perhaps the most important, but outside of Mỹ Sơn, little of it remains beyond the Bằng An, Khương Mỹ and Chiên Đàn towers. Though smaller than the towers of Vijaya, they are a satisfactory substitute if you don't have time to visit Bình Định.

TRÀ KIỆU This nondescript little place en route to Mỹ Sơn was, in fact, the first Cham capital in the 4th century. That it supported a flourishing artistic and religious life can be gleaned from the exhibits in the Museum of Cham Sculpture in Đà Nẵng. Trà Kiệu was sacked by the Chinese in the 5th century but appears to have flourished again in the late 10th century. Excavations in this valley in 1927–28 by the École Française d'Extrême-Orient showed that there was once a huge citadel here with a circumference of 4km. This protected a royal citadel inside. Today, alas, there is nothing to see.

ĐỒNG DƯƠNG This site, 20km southeast from Mỹ Sơn and known as Indrapura, supplanted the sanctuary as the centre of Cham art and culture when King Indravarman II built a large Buddhist monastery there at the end of the 9th century. Artistically, little changed – the decoration of the towers simply became more ornate and involved, and the reliefs more deeply cut. There is a room in the Museum of Cham Sculpture in Đà Nẵng devoted to sculptures from Đồng Dương, including carved Buddha images. Cham Buddhism saw its finest artistic flowering in the 10th century. In the early 10th century, the focus of Cham art returned to Mỹ Sơn once again under the patronage of Indravarman III (once evident in obliterated towers of Group A). Nothing much of Đồng Dương remains either, except the remnants of an old gate that will probably be forever under scaffolding. Out of the way and with little to see, only the most ardent admirers of Cham ancient history will get much from visiting Đồng Dương.

corner, which has a distinctive pyramidal roof. This is dedicated to Ganesh, God of Good Fortune and Wisdom, and son of Shiva. It was built in the middle of the 10th century. B4 was constructed at the end of the 9th century in honour of Ganesh, but also Skanda, the God of War and another son of Shiva. It is believed that B5, situated at the southeasterly corner and probably the most photographed structure in the site, was a temple sanctuary used to house the sacred scriptures and objects used in ritual worship. Note the twin elephant carvings on the east and west sides and carved birds hiding in tree foliage. B6 has a water tank, probably used to store holy water to perform the cleansing ceremony for idols, such as the sacred linga in B1. The remaining B buildings are various small temples. Look very carefully at the exterior walls in Group B and you will see the remains of some exquisite wall carvings.

Groups A and A′ There were originally 13 towers here, but only three – A1, A10 and A13 – have been somewhat restored after American bombing raids in 1969. The restoration project took place from 2018 and 2022 with significant help and

✱ BẰNG AN Dating from the 11th century, Bằng An Cham Tower belongs to the Bình Định style, and thus is similar to the much larger towers close to Quy Nhơn (page 329). This unique octagonal tower, possibly designed to resemble a linga, is the only type of its kind still surviving since the Chánh Lộ kalan in Quảng Ngãi Province was destroyed by bombs during the American War. You won't find any elaborate ornamentation or pilasters and you may notice that the vestibule has been restored with a different brick pattern from the original. Two mythical animal statues with lion bodies and elephant heads (known as *gajasimha*) stand before the entrance gate. They have different mane patterns suggesting that they belong to different periods. Just 13km west of Hội An, you can visit this tower on the way back from Mỹ Sơn.

CHIÊN ĐÀN The Chiên Đàn Cham Towers (Tam An; ◷ 08.00–18.00 daily; 20,000VND/free adult/child) were built in the 10th and 11th centuries, and are just off Highway 1, 40km south of Hội An. The oldest, the south tower, is badly damaged. The north tower, which is slightly larger, is in a similar condition but still has part of its vestibule intact. The middle tower, the largest, has a crumbled vestibule, but the body, decorated with plain pilasters, is in quite good condition. It features some attractive examples of bas-reliefs, possibly depicting scenes from the Hindu Ramayana epic.

KHƯƠNG MỸ These ruined, sapling-studded towers are on the outskirts of Tam Kỳ, a small city 50km south of Hội An and the capital of Quảng Nam Province. The site includes three kalans: a largish, well-preserved south tower, a smallish, badly damaged north tower and a small middle tower. It would seem that these towers, probably built at the turn of the 10th century, have suffered from some particularly clumsy restoration work, as the bricks at the base clearly pave over the decorative features higher up. The south tower is the most impressive, with a relatively intact vestibule, and the colossal pilasters on the body of the tower are lavishly adorned with grape-leaf patterns. Although the lines are softer, the decorative style of the middle tower is similar. The north tower has deteriorated badly but still shows some interesting patterning.

funding from the Indian embassy. A1 was one of the finest towers in all of Mỹ Sơn, a soaring masterpiece at 28m tall. It dates to the 10th century and held a linga and yoni, which are now lost. The intricate carvings would have reflected the glory of the royal family. A10, to the left of A1, dates from the 9th century. Inside is the largely intact square and terraced pedestal that forms part of the yoni and linga. Assembled from 17 sandstone blocks, this is the largest of its kind in Champa art and in 2021 it was recognised as a national treasure by the Vietnamese government. A13, to the other side of A1, was also built in the 9th century, and would have once sported a soaring Garuda. Thanks to the renovation project aided by the Indian embassy, it is now possible to understand the layout of the rest of this group. The brickwork at the base of many of the larger temples is now in good shape. The interiors of the Group A temples, surrounded by a brick wall, may have been adorned with precious gifts for the god king, such as magnificent sculptures of female heavenly dancers (known as *apsaras*). Next to Group A1 are the destroyed remains of Group A', giving a sense of what most of the site looked like after the war.

Group G It may not match the grandeur of Group B, but the 12th-century Group G, perched on a small hill, is serene in the morning light. Look for the stele with ancient Champa script and carved faces on the base of G1, the largest structure. From here you can peer down over groups A, B, C and D. G1 is the kalan, G2 is the gate tower, G3 is the retreat house and G4 is the storehouse. Constructed on a low hill similar in height to the Group H hill, the towers here have three entrances, with perhaps the central entrance reserved for the king and important dignitaries. The kalan is large, with four lion statues, built in the 12th century, at the four corners and there would have been a sequence of 52 masks representing Kala, God of Time and a reincarnation of Shiva. Many of these masks, each one different, are visible thanks to restoration efforts with support from Italy, which took place from 2003 to 2013. Within Group G you'll also find one of Mỹ Sơn's only surviving steles, which details the purpose of the group and methods of construction.

Groups E and F These two groups form a conjoined complex. Group E's nine structures, built in the second half of the 7th century, were some of the oldest towers in Mỹ Sơn. The group has a restored temple and some attractive sculptures that are left open to the elements, including Nandi, Shiva's sacred bull, made from sandstone. Nandi is the mediator between Shiva and the followers. Note the four legs tucked underneath and the exposed hooves and tail. E7 is the best preserved, and functioned as a warehouse tower to hold scripture and other items used in worship. The only notable structure in Group F is a towering pile of brick rubble protected by a roof. To understand the offender, look for the huge dips in the ground – these are bomb craters that have now filled with water to make lotus and lily ponds. This was built in the 8th and 9th centuries.

Tower K Built in the 11th and 12th centuries, this was perhaps built after the main temples as a gateway to the site. This is the last structure if taking the anti-clockwise route, and at the time of research was undergoing excavation and restoration, with help from India.

✷ ***Lộc Yên ancient village*** (Tiên Cảnh) A fairytale village that is actually closer to Tam Kỳ (see opposite), Lộc Yên has an extraordinary collection of ancient houses – some more than 100 years old – that perch on elevated plots overlooking landscaped gardens and framed by palm trees. Though some parts of the village show signs of age and wear, the overall ambience remains enchanting. For now the village remains quiet, with few services save a couple of roadside cafés, but given the setting and proximity to Hội An, tourism will develop quickly. Nhà Hàng Lộc Yên (Old Lộc Yên village; ⌚ 09.00–22.30 daily; **$**) serves delicious food (try the grilled chicken) and has a few basic but clean rooms. There are several ancient houses and all of them are inhabited by families who are not yet used to receiving visitors, but remain very welcoming and proud: this is the kind of village where serendipitous encounters can still happen. One of the more attractive and visitable houses is Nhà Cổ Tiên Cảnh (Tiên Phước), with a broad courtyard and family altar demonstrating a traditional Kinh vernacular. The gate claims that the house was only built in 1940, but parts of the house, according to the owner, date back to the 19th century. Lộc Yên is 70km south of Hội An and 26km west of Tam Kỳ.

THE CHÀM ISLANDS (CÙ LAO CHÀM)

The Chàm Islands, part of a UNESCO World Biosphere Reserve, are 15km from Cửa Đại Beach and clearly visible offshore. Hòn Lao, the largest island, boasts beaches, coral reefs and a rainforest; in the warm water that surrounds it there are more than 945 marine species. The island appeals principally to divers and snorkellers, but is also popular with those seeking a slice of small island and community life. The Chàm Islands are pioneering a no-plastic policy, which is still taking time to take hold, but remember to take away any single-use plastic that you take. There are also small marine conservation and environmental cleaning fees, which are paid upon arrival or are included in the boat ticket fee. Important: The Chàm Islands are one of the few places in Vietnam without a bank or ATM, so be sure to bring **cash** from the mainland. Some visit the islands on a day trip, but spending at least one night on the island is preferable. Once on Hòn Lao, walking is possible for short distances but a motorbike (with an optional driver) is needed for the further-flung corners of the island. Arrange boat trips to explore secluded beaches and snorkel in hidden coves at your accommodation. For more information, visit **w** visitquangnam.com/experiences/beaches/traveler-guide-to-cham-islands. The weather here matches that of Hội An (page 298).

GETTING THERE AND AWAY **Speedboats** are the fastest option (30 minutes) to travel to the Chàm Islands; they depart daily from Cửa Đại Wharf at around 08.00 and 13.00, and return at 13.00 and 19.00. For a slower, cheaper and more scenic option, travellers can take the ferry (90 minutes), which takes motorbikes. This information is subject to change, so check at your accommodation in Hội An, who should also be able to book your tickets.

WHERE TO STAY AND EAT There is no dearth of homestays and simple restaurants in Bãi Lăng, the main town, most of which you can walk to after disembarking. You can arrange motorbike rental and basic tours through your host. **Monkey Homestay** (Tân Hiệp; **$**) and **The Coral** (Tổ 10 khối Thịnh Mỹ; **$**) come recommended. **Ray Ong Bàng** (⌚ 06.00–20.30 daily; **$$**), 2km south of the main town and signposted from the road, offers decent food and drinks with elevated views across the island.

TAM KỲ

Tam Kỳ, home to around 125,000 people, is the administrative capital of Quảng Nam and the province's second largest city after Hội An. In many ways, Tam Kỳ plays second fiddle to its celebrity neighbour to the north, but it has nevertheless developed into a prosperous and welcoming city. Severely damaged during the American War, the city was largely rebuilt in the decades that followed, bulldozing the historical architecture that had survived. Few visitors stop in Tam Kỳ as it lacks the historical allure of Hội An, but the city does offer a few attractions for those who are willing to spend a night or two. The weather patterns here are similar to those of Hội An (page 298).

GETTING THERE AND AROUND **Tam Kỳ train station** (Nguyễn Hoàng) is central. North of here is Đà Nẵng (90 mins), Huế (4hrs) and Hanoi (20hrs). South of here is Quảng Ngãi (90 mins), Diêu Trì (for Quy Nhơn; 5hrs), Nha Trang (10hrs) and Hồ Chí Minh City (around 24hrs). **Buses** tend to pick up/drop off in the centre of town on the side of the road, at bus company offices and some at the Bến Xe Quảng Nam (1 Phan Bội Châu), a local bus station just north of the city centre. From here, frequent and regular local buses head to Hội An (1hr). Heading further north, there are regular buses to Đà Nẵng (90 mins), Huế (3hrs) and beyond. Heading south, there are buses to Quảng Ngãi (90 mins), Kon Tum (6hrs) and beyond. **Chu Lai Airport** (Tam Nghĩa Ward; w vietnamairport.vn), 30km south of the city, serves both Tam Kỳ and Quảng Ngãi, and is only connected with Hanoi and Hồ Chí Minh City. Central Tam Kỳ is walkable, but you'll need a taxi or motorbike to reach the Cham towers (page 318), tunnels, beach and Lộc Yên (page 320).

WHERE TO STAY AND EAT There are dozens of hotels in the city centre, which are easy to find on and around Phan Bội Châu Street, though nowhere of particular note. You may prefer to base yourself in one of the beachside properties in Tam Thanh, like the ramshackle but charming **You-Retreat** (Tam Thanh; f youretreatvietnam; **$$**).Tam Kỳ is a good place to try one of the provincial specialities: *cơm gà*, or chicken rice. There are various places in town serving the dish, but perhaps none more beloved than **Cơm Gà Bà Luận** (707 Phan Châu Trinh; ⌚ 09.00–22.00 daily; $). **Bếp Đỏ** (45 Trần Hưng Đạo; f bepdovn; ⌚ 06.00–22.00 daily; $$$) offers a more elevated dining experience, with kombucha and craft beer, though prices remain very reasonable.

OTHER PRACTICALITIES **Quảng Nam Provincial Hospital** (1 Nguyễn Du Lê Hữu Trác; w bvdkquangnam.vn; ⌚ all day daily) is central.

WHAT TO SEE AND DO The **Quảng Nam Museum** (281 Phan Bội Châu; w baotang.quangnam.gov.vn; ⌚ 07.30–17.00 Mon–Fri, 09.00–17.00 Sat–Sun) is well organised, with an extensive section on the province's various ethnolinguistic groups, many of whom live close to the border with Laos. Gold-sand **beaches** are just 11km east, as is the coastal village of **Tam Thanh** and its gallery of street art and painted houses, a project that began with Korean support in 2016. About 30km south, close to Chu Lai Airport, is Bãi Rạng, a broad, clean beach that is yet to see much development. Closer to Tam Kỳ are two important – but decrepit – clusters of Cham towers, **Chiên Đàn** and **Khương Mỹ** (page 319), which lie northwest and southeast of the city centre respectively. Near the Chiên Đàn towers are the **Kỳ Tân tunnels** (Thạch Tân village), a wartime underground network with limited accessible areas and information when compared with the tunnels of Vịnh Mốc (page 274) and Củ Chi (page 481), but connected to an attractive 300-year-old communal house. Though many make the trip to the bucolic village of **Lộc Yên** (page 320) from Hội An, the journey from Tam Kỳ is significantly shorter.

QUẢNG NGÃI AND SƠN MỸ

Quảng Ngãi Province is famous internationally for one of the worst reasons imaginable: the Mỹ Lai Massacre. On that dreadful day, 16 March 1968, more than 500 civilians were brutally killed in **Sơn Mỹ village** by a unit of the United States Army. More than five decades later, tens of thousands of domestic tourists come to pay their respects every year. Few international visitors penetrate the province, however, as it sits surrounded by the more obviously appealing provinces of Quảng Nam (and Hội An), Bình Định (and Quy Nhơn) and Kon Tum.

Many of the province's 1.5 million inhabitants are farmers, fishermen and forestry workers. Cinnamon and sandalwood is grown and pigs and cattle raised in the hilly districts in the west of the province. At lower levels, rice, fruit and sugarcane are the favoured crops. Many coastal communities live on the edge of vast salt marshes, where they tend salt lagoons. The dramatic and volcanic **Lý Sơn**, somewhat undiscovered island oases 25 nautical miles from the coast, are famous for their garlic plantations.

Quảng Ngãi city is a modest provincial capital situated on the south bank of the Trà Khúc River. Few people spend the night here, but it makes an adequate base from which to explore Sơn Mỹ village and Lý Sơn. The city has one or two things to see, including the popular Mỹ Khê Beach, backed by fresh seafood restaurants, and the inevitable provincial museum, centred on a largely reconstructed citadel that was originally built during the early years of the Nguyễn Dynasty. The weather here is similar to that of Hội An (page 298).

GETTING THERE AND AROUND **Quảng Ngãi train station** (1 Nguyễn Chánh) is on the west side of the city. North of here is Tam Kỳ (1½hrs), Đà Nẵng (3hrs), Huế (6hrs) and beyond. South of here is Diêu Trì (for Quy Nhơn; 3hrs), Nha Trang (8hrs) and Hồ Chí Minh City (around 16hrs). **Quảng Ngãi bus station** (2 Trần Khánh Dư) is south of the centre, where taxis and buses wait to ferry people into town. Kon Tum (7hrs) is the closest city in the Central Highlands. **Chu Lai Airport** (Tam Nghĩa Ward; w vietnamairport.vn), with flights to Hanoi and Hồ Chí Minh City, is 45km north of Quảng Ngãi. You'll need motorised transport to reach Sơn Mỹ village, the main reason people come here.

WHERE TO STAY AND EAT The best place to stay is close to Phạm Văn Đồng Square; try the simple and very reasonable **Hotel Đông Phát** (20 Trương Quang Giao; **$**). Various cafés and restaurants are walking distance from here, including the delicious do-it-yourself rolls at **Quán Ram Nướng Dưới Cống** (19 Nguyễn Năng Lự; 07.00–21.30 daily; **$**). Vegans can head a little further to **Sala Vegetarian Restaurant** (1 Lê Lợi; f nhahangvietchaysala; 06.00–14.00 & 16.30–20.30 daily; **$**).

OTHER PRACTICALITIES The large **Quảng Ngãi Provincial Hospital** (Lê Hữu Trác; w bvdk.quangngai.gov.vn; all day daily) is 3km west of the centre.

WHAT TO SEE AND DO

Central Quảng Ngãi The **Citadel** (99 Lê Trung Đình; w thanhcoquangngai.vn; 08.00–20.00 daily) is a Vauban citadel built in the early years of the Nguyễn Dynasty, though very little of this relic remains and it feels semi-abandoned. In the centre of the citadel is **Quảng Ngãi Museum** (99 Lê Trung Đình; w baotangquangngai.com; 08.00–11.30 & 13.00–17.00 daily), a jumbled attic of a museum with little to no English signage. Interesting exhibits include an unusual dual burial site found on Lý Sơn (see opposite), some prehistoric jewellery and some Cham relics, including an example of their ancient script. There is also a small section on some of Vietnam's lesser-known ethnolinguistic groups that inhabit the mountainous areas, including the Hre and Co.

Around Quảng Ngãi The memorial site of **Sơn Mỹ village** (Tịnh Khê), one of the most harrowing spots in the country, is 13km east of Quảng Ngãi city, over the Trà Khúc River and before you reach Mỹ Khê Beach. Sơn Mỹ is where one of

THE MỸ LAI MASSACRE

The massacre at Sơn Mỹ was a turning point in the world's view of the American War and the role that the USA was playing. Were American forces defending Vietnam and the world from the evils of communism? Or were they merely shoring up a despotic government that had lost all legitimacy among the population it ostensibly served?

The massacre occurred on the morning of 16 March 1968. Units from the 23rd Infantry Division were dropped into the village of Sơn Mỹ, which was made up of hamlets including Mỹ Lai (after which the massacre was named). The area was regarded as an area of intense communist presence – so much so that soldiers referred to the villages as Pinkville. Only two weeks beforehand, six soldiers had been killed after stumbling into a minefield. The leader of the platoon that was charged with the job of investigating the hamlet of Mỹ Lai was 2nd Lieutenant William Calley. Under his orders, 347 people, all unarmed and many women and children, were massacred. Some of Calley's men refused to participate, but most did.

Neil Sheehan, in his book *A Bright Shining Lie*, wrote: 'One soldier missed a baby lying on the ground twice with a .45 pistol as his comrades laughed at his marksmanship. He stood over the child and fired a third time. The soldiers beat women with rifle butts and raped some and sodomized others before shooting them. They shot the water buffalos, the pigs, and the chickens. They threw the dead animals into the wells to poison the water. They tossed satchel charges into the bomb shelters under the houses. A lot of the inhabitants had fled into the shelters. Those who leaped out to escape the explosives were gunned down. All of the houses were put to the torch.'

In total, more than 500 people were killed at Sơn Mỹ, most in the hamlet of Mỹ Lai, but another 90 at another hamlet (by another platoon) in the same village.

The story of the massacre was filed by Seymour Hersh, but not until November 1969 – 20 months later. The subsequent court martial only convicted Calley, who was by all accounts a sadist. He was sentenced to life imprisonment, but had served only three years before President Nixon intervened on his behalf (he was personally convicted of the murder of 22 of the victims). As Sheehan argues, the massacre was, in some regards, not surprising. The horrific nature of the war had led to the killing and maiming of countless unarmed and innocent peasants; it was often done from a distance. In the minds of most generals, every Vietnamese was a potential communist; from this position it was only a small step to believing that all Vietnamese were legitimate targets.

the worst, and certainly the most publicised, atrocities committed by US troops occurred during the American War. The massacre of innocent Vietnamese villagers is better known as the Mỹ Lai Massacre after one of the four hamlets of Sơn Mỹ. The memorial is essentially in two parts: the museum and the garden. The museum holds some truly grotesque photographs from the massacre, but also testimony from both demonic and repentant American GIs. The garden reflects the layout of the hamlet at the time of the massacre: a pretty cluster of thatched houses connected by a network of pathways. These foot and bicycle paths have been concreted over and poignantly imprinted with the large footprints of American boots. The creek where many villagers were dumped after being shot has been preserved. The immense horror and historical significance of the site aside, the garden gives a sense of what mid-20th-century Vietnamese coastal villages might have been like.

There are several places to eat here, but the best might be **Quán Cao Hải Biển Mỹ Khê** (Thôn Cổ Lũy; ◷ all day daily, but hours depend on the number of customers; **$$$**). Nearby is Minh Đức Pagoda, which is in the process of constructing what will be the biggest statue of Quan Âm (page 293) in Vietnam.

LÝ SƠN ARCHIPELAGO

The Lý Sơn Islands – there are three: Big Island (Đảo Lớn), Small Island (Đảo Bé) and Mù Cu islet – are known for their volcanic landscapes, clear waters and garlic farms. For many years the islands were beyond the reach of tourists, as foreign visitors needed to apply for permission to visit due to the presence of a military base. These days, the military base is still in operation but the islands are open to all, presenting a tempting option to put the sea between you and the subregion's overdeveloped coast.

Small Island is prettier and quieter and has nicer beaches, with only a handful of rustic accommodation options. The beaches on Big Island are not especially inviting, but all the sights are there (providing a day or two of things to do), as well as seafood restaurants and two inactive volcanoes, both of which are scalable. The larger of the two is on the east side of the island, with a steep road leading up to the crater lake (swimming is forbidden) and some grassy viewpoints from which to catch the sunset and look over the patchwork of garlic farms. Nearby is **Cave Pagoda**, or Chùa Hang (Lý Sơn), an atmospheric and active place of worship built in the 17th century, with many old frangipani trees. The smaller volcano is on the west side of the island, near the lofty statue of Quan Âm, the Goddess of Compassion (page 293) and a popular deity in the subregion. Park under her watchful gaze to make the 10-minute climb up to the crater, past small shrines and grottoes. Nearby is Lý Sơn's sky-blue fishing fleet, which is illuminated to spectacular effect at sunset. The island's chaotic fish market begins every day at sunrise and lasts until about 07.00 on the east side of the island on the small pier near Bình Yên Hotel (page 326). There is little to do in the evenings, but makeshift streetside cafés and snack stands are set up on the main square near the Mường Thanh Hotel, creating a jovial, family-friendly atmosphere.

GETTING THERE AND AWAY **Boats** to Big Island leave from Sa Kỳ Port, a 30-minute taxi journey from Quảng Ngãi, and the journey time is around 45 minutes, depending on weather conditions. Booking tickets to Lý Sơn in advance is by phone and therefore not yet easy for non-Vietnamese speakers, but you might ask your hotel receptionist in Quảng Ngãi (or Hội An, Quy Nhơn or Đà Nẵng) for help. However, with a handful of companies making the route daily, it's usually possible to turn up and be on a boat within an hour or two. If taking your chances, try to arrive at the port by 07.00. Once on the island, you can book your return, and onward travel to Small Island (20 mins), through your accommodation.

WHERE TO STAY AND EAT On Big Island there are are various cheap homestays and guesthouses, which include **Bình Yên Hotel** (opposite Lý Sơn Port; f nhanghilyson.khachsanlysonqn; $), **Hoàng Sa Resort** (on the east of the island; f hoangsahealinghome; $) and, if a certain level of comfort is required, **Mường Thanh Holiday** (on the island's south coast; f MuongThanhHolidayLySon; $$$). Small Island has far fewer places to stay, which is part of its appeal, but this includes **Bé Ecolodge** (Small Island; f; $$), one of the most compelling places to stay in the small archipelago, with simple thatched cottages and excellent food, including seafood barbecues. Seafood is, of course, the speciality on both islands, and there are various restaurants serving visitors, including the excellent **Quán Hải Sản Phát Hải** (Thôn Đông; ⌚ 07.00–23.00 daily; $$$) and **Cơm Hải Sản Út Ngọc** (Thôn Tây; ⌚ 06.00–22.30 daily; $$). English menus had not yet materialised at the time of research, but it's possible to point at the live seafood you want to devour. A speciality food of the islands – aside from the garlic – is the delicious and crunchy *gỏi rong biển* (seaweed salad).

QUY NHƠN AND THE CHAM TOWERS OF VIJAYA

Quy Nhơn is the capital of Bình Định Province, which looms large in Vietnamese history for two reasons: the ancient Cham city of Vijaya and the Tây Sơn Rebellion. It has also made significant cultural contributions: both *tuồng*, Vietnamese classical opera, and *võ Bình Định*, a martial arts form that developed during the aforementioned rebellion, originated here. The area's heritage, combined with the capital city of Quy Nhơn, a prosperous city with a fine beach, make Bình Định one of Vietnam's standout provinces for visitors. See opposite for the more remote beaches in the province.

The opening paragraph that introduces Quy Nhơn in a Bradt guide from 1998 demonstrates how Vietnamese cities have transformed in such a short period of time. 'Qui Nhơn,' the introduction reads, 'is not a pleasant city to stroll around in: crowds of rag-tag houses bunched together in a higgledy-piggledy fashion, electric wires strewn everywhere and too much traffic. The locals are not as friendly as many and some can be downright rude. Only a decade ago the beach was ideal for bathing. Now even a short stroll will see you side-stepping human turds as you hold on tightly to your security belt.'

Today, this city of almost half a million is one of Vietnam's urban success stories. The beach is not merely free of excrement, but one of the cleanest in the country, with gentle tides, few crowds and an attractive promenade. The streets behind are orderly and neatly kept, and the sense you get from the friendly residents is that they are fully aware that they live in one of Vietnam's most desirable cities. A number of high-end resorts and low-key guesthouses have found their home here, but the city has so far avoided the rampant building booms seen in Đà Nẵng and Nha Trang.

GETTING THERE AND AROUND **Quy Nhơn train station** (Lê Hồng Phong) is no longer operational, but passengers can use Diêu Trì train station, 10km west of Quy Nhơn. North of here is Quảng Ngãi (7hrs), Đà Nẵng (10hrs) and beyond. South of here is Nha Trang (4hrs), Tháp Chàm (6hrs), Bình Thuận (for Phan Thiết and Mũi Né; 8hrs) and Hồ Chí Minh City (13hrs).

Quy Nhơn has an organised **bus** station – Bến Xe Quy Nhơn (71 Tây Sơn) – on the southern edge of town, but some bus companies will pick up/drop off at your accommodation. Quy Nhơn is well connected, and you can get just about anywhere on

THE TRANQUIL, TRASH-FILLED COVES OF BÌNH ĐỊNH, PHÚ YÊN AND KHÁNH HÒA

More than a dozen scenic beaches bespeckle the serrated coastlines of Bình Định, Phú Yên and Khánh Hòa provinces. The sad truth, however, is that the wildest, most dramatic and least developed beaches tend also to be the dirtiest. With no hotels and few visitors, there's little incentive (or budget) for the provincial governments to rid the beaches of the trash that washes in from the sea day after day. That said, the situation is highly dependent on weather patterns, ocean currents and shifting local policies. A beach could be clean and pleasant one month but resemble a dump the next. Đà Nẵng has demonstrated that good policies that are strictly enforced can turn a dirty beach into a clean one quickly. One can only be hopeful that smaller, poorer local governments can find their own ways to tackle the issue.

Not wanting to put off visitors, many guidebooks and promotional materials only extol the natural blessings of a particular beach without even touching on the issue of manmade harm. Below is a selection of some of the more beautiful beaches across these three provinces. At any given time, some might be spotless whereas others may be filthy. Checking very recent reviews online can be a good idea. If making the trip to any of them, it is wise to come with low expectations that can be exceeded rather than high ones that can be crushed. Naturally beautiful beaches with basic services, arranged from north to south in the three provinces, include:

BÌNH ĐỊNH
Đề Gi (45km north of Quy Nhơn)
Kỳ Co (20km north of Quy Nhơn)

PHÚ YÊN
Xuân Hải (20km south of Quy Nhơn; 75km north of Tuy Hòa)
Vịnh Hòa (30km south of Quy Nhơn; 65km north of Tuy Hòa)
Vũng Rô (40km south of Tuy Hòa)

KHÁNH HÒA
Đại Lãnh Vũng Rô (45km south of Tuy Hòa; 85km north of Nha Trang)
Điệp Sơn Islets (65km north of Nha Trang and a boat trip)
Dốc Lết (45km north of Nha Trang and a boat trip)

If you don't want to take the risk, you're less likely to be disappointed if you seek out clean metropolitan beaches like those in Quy Nhơn or Nha Trang, both of which have diligent and well-funded local authorities that keep their stretches of sand clean and free of trash – or save your beach time for the Côn Đảo archipelago (page 438).

Like all environmental problems, beach trash is a complex issue that requires a set of solutions. To learn more or see how you can help, visit Hanoi-based NGO Keep Vietnam Clean (w keepvietnamclean.org).

the bus, including Quảng Ngãi (3hrs), Hội An (5hrs), Đà Nẵng (6hrs) and beyond to the north, and Nha Trang (4hrs), Phan Thiết (8hrs), Vũng Tàu (10hrs) and Hồ Chí Minh City (10hrs) to the south. The closest city in the Central Highlands is Pleiku (4hrs).

Tiny **Phù Cát Airport** (Cát Tân Ward; w vietnamairport.vn) is 30km (45 mins by car) northwest of the city, a mild annoyance considering how convenient other city airports are in the subregion. Fly from here to Hanoi or Hồ Chí Minh City.

Central Quy Nhơn is **walkable**, but you'll need motorised transport to explore most of the sights, which lie outside the city. Rent either a **motorbike or car with driver** from your accommodation or talk to a **taxi** driver about commandeering their vehicle for the day.

WHERE TO STAY When looking for hotels, it's sensible to try and be as close to Xuân Diệu, the street that runs alongside the beach promenade, as possible. This is where you'll find most of the cafés and restaurants, and it's close to the water.

Sông Suối Homestay 2 10/2 Lê Thánh Tôn; f songsuoi.homestay. A solid budget option run by a friendly & enthusiastic owner. They cater mainly to Vietnamese guests & there's very little English spoken, but it hardly matters. If they're full, try the Sông Suối 1, a kilometre away but also close to the beach. **$**

Odin Hotel 6 Trần Cao Vân; w odinhotel.com.vn. Modern, clean & inexplicably named after the Norse king of the gods, Odin probably isn't suited to royalty, but it's excellent value – & there's a rooftop pool. **$$**

✷ **An House Quy Nhơn** 186 Xuân Diệu; f. A neon dolphin dives over this lovely little beachfront property, which offers unincumbered views of the sunrise & promenade. **$$$**

Anantara Bãi Dài Bridge; w anantara.com/en/quy-nhon. One of the most luxurious hotel chains in Vietnam, the Anantara here is relatively understated & blissfully peaceful, with low-rise beachside villas (with private pools) that give direct access to the beach. It's just south of Bãi Xép fishing village, 14km from Quy Nhơn. **$$$$$**

WHERE TO EAT AND DRINK

Food street Ngô Văn Sở; 🕘 10.00–23.00 daily. Quy Nhơn's 'food street' won't win any awards for quality, but it's one of the cheapest places in town. Restaurant owners can be pushy, but feel free to shop around. It's open all day but busiest in the evenings. **$**

Nhà Hàng Quê Hương 2 185 Lê Hồng Phong; f nhahangquehuongquynhon; 🕘 10.00–21.00 daily. Classic 'rice & things' restaurant. Most dishes are served as individual plates like Western food, but the food is 100% Vietnamese. **$**

Quán Cơm Bảy Quán 199 Nguễn Huệ; 🕘 09.00–20.00 daily. Popular all-day rice restaurant that is famous for its *cơm sườn* (rice with grilled pork chop), which they grill outside to tempt in customers. **$**

Xi An Lau 51 Nguyễn Huệ; f Xian.dimsum; 🕘 06.00–11.00 & 15.00–21.00 daily. Unexpected & delicious Chinese street restaurant tucked away behind red lanterns. Dim sum seems to be the speciality, but they also have noodle soups. **$$**

Hoa Hoa Seafood Restaurant 8 Nguyễn Dữ; 🕘 10.00–22.00 daily. Classic seafood restaurant serving all the superb fruits of the sea dishes that you can imagine, including grilled shrimp, steamed squid & deep-fried fish. **$$$**

Sisters Tavern & Pizzeria 94 Trần Phú; f SistersQuyNhon; 🕘 11.00–20.30 daily. Pizza, salads, steaks & craft beer to satisfy those cravings for Western food. The atmosphere is relaxed in this restaurant, which appears to cater mainly for local families. **$$$**

Adiuvat Coffee Roaster 57A Nguyễn Huệ; f adiuvatcoffeeroasters; 🕘 07.30–21.30 daily. Serves the best coffee in town in cool, quiet surroundings. Bar-side seating means you can watch the baristas at work.

OTHER PRACTICALITIES The large **Bình Định Hospital** (39A Phạm Ngọc Thạch; w benhvienbinhdinh.com.vn; 🕘 all day daily) is in the centre of town.

WHAT TO SEE AND DO

Quy Nhơn city Most of Quy Nhơn's premier sights lie outside the city, but there are some areas of interest in the centre. The **beach** is barely ever crowded, and

LEGEND HAS IT: NOT BY THE HAND OF ANY MAN

Mahishasura was a powerful monster born from the union of a demon king and a cursed buffalo, and later gained formidable power from the fire god Agni, making him invincible to attacks from any man. Emboldened by this power, Mahishasura unleashed terror across the heavens, driving the gods from their celestial realm.

Desperate to reclaim their home, the gods united their energies to create a divine warrior – the goddess Durga. Radiant and fierce, Durga was armed with celestial weapons: Shiva's trident, Vishnu's discus and Indra's thunderbolt. Mounted on a mighty lion, she set off to challenge Mahishasura.

A battle of epic proportions ensued, with Mahishasura constantly shifting forms, from fierce buffalo to armed warrior, but Durga countered his every move. When Mahishasura was in the midst of transforming, Durga seized the moment, driving her trident into his shifting form and trampling him, striking him down during the brief moment when he was most vulnerable. Agni's divine blessing made Mahishasura invincible against attacks from male entities, but Durga was female, and thus was able to overpower him.

the promenade that wraps around it comes to life in the afternoon and early evening. The **Bình Định Museum** (26 Nguyễn Huệ; **w** baotangtinhbinhdinh.vn; ⌚ 07.00–11.00 & 14.00–17.00 daily; 10,000VND/free adult/child) is small and fairly dull, but with an intriguing collection of sculptures taken from the nearby Cham towers. One piece depicts the goddess Durga trampling a buffalo demon (see above), though it's not clear which tower she was taken from. **Quy Nhơn Square** is a large, sun-blasted plaza during the day, but in the early evening it fills with families and dance troupes.

Around Quy Nhơn Between the ancient sites of Vijaya, the Quang Trung Museum and other sights, there are two or three full days' worth of exploring outside of Quy Nhơn.

Làng Sông Church (Quảng Vân village; ⌚ 07.30–11.30 & 14.00–17.00 daily) is one of the oldest Catholic churches in Vietnam, dating back to 1868. It is part of the Làng Sông Seminary, which played a significant role in Catholic education and the printing of Vietnamese-language books during the colonial period. The typical Indochinese architecture and layout is attractive, with tall trees and grassy patches. It sits 9km northwest of central Quy Nhơn.

The Cham towers of ancient Vijaya *These site details were written with considerable input from Dr Nguyễn H H Duyên (page 12).* Vijaya was one of the five states of the Indianised country of Champa, south of Amaravati (page 318; Quảng Nam). Known to the Vietnamese as Chà Bàn, the Cham people moved their capital to Vijaya from Amaravati in the 11th century after being hounded by a newly independent Vietnam to the north. A thousand years ago, the defensive capital would have been quite the sight. It was surrounded by a 5km enclosure in an area shielded by hills to the north and a deep river to the south. The walled enclosure had four access gates and many lookout towers. These proved invaluable when the city was attacked by the Vietnamese in 1044 and by the Khmer in the following centuries. The walls of the enclosure suffered some damage, but the vast Cham

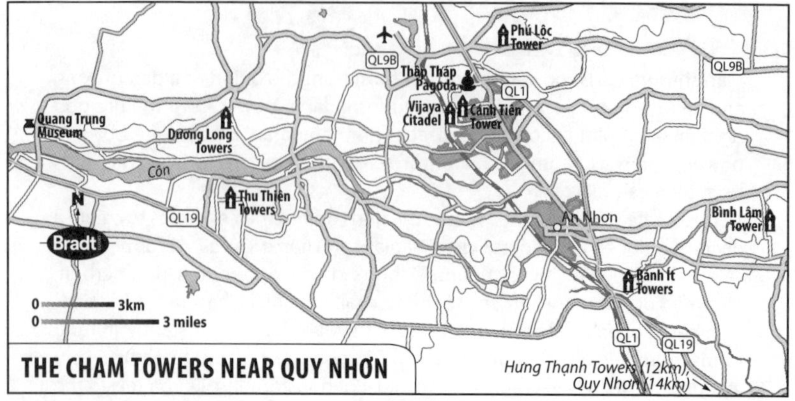

THE CHAM TOWERS NEAR QUY NHƠN

army inside repelled the invaders. Another attack came in 1377, when a strong Vietnamese army once again failed to take the city.

By 1471, however, the Vietnamese had mustered one of the strongest forces ever seen in Vietnam and they breached the citadel's walls. This catastrophic loss led to the eventual destruction of the Champa state. One could spend a full day exploring the myriad archaeological sites of ancient Vijaya. Unlike Amaravati (Quảng Nam), there is no sanctuary on the scale of Mỹ Sơn (page 314), but the Cham towers here are the finest in all of Vietnam. Visiting them takes some independent planning and background reading as there are no audio guides or information plaques. Those confident on a motorbike or scooter will be able to rent one in their hotel in Quy Nhơn and spend the day hopping between temples. Those who are less confident should rent a car for a day. Start as early as you can (before sunrise if possible) to take advantage of the early-morning light.

Hưng Thạnh Towers (Trần Phú; 🕘 07.00–11.30 & 13.30–17.00 daily; 20,000VND/free adult/child) More commonly known as Tháp Đôi (meaning twin towers), the Hưng Thạnh Cham towers, standing 18m and 20m high and just 2km from central Quy Nhơn, were built at the end of the 11th century. Their curved pyramidal roofs are distinctly Khmer style, the North Tower having six storeys. Its twisted decorations are reminiscent of the Bánh Ít Towers. The smaller tower has suffered badly and climbing plants are now damaging its superstructure.

✷ **Bánh Ít Towers** (Phước Hiệp; 🕘 07.00–18.00 daily; 20,000VND/free adult/child) These are the most manicured of all the towers in Bình Định, and the most popular. They sit 16km northwest of Quy Nhơn city, and approaching them is an epic experience as they loom over the QL19 road on top of a hill between two branches of the Côn River. Four structures, all restored, remain on the site. Once you have climbed a little up the hill, you will see the main kalan, once surrounded by a brick enclosure. The three-storey roof is in remarkably good condition. A close look at the recessed niches, also known as false doors (bricked-up cavities in the shape of doors), will reveal human figures praying. Examination of the repository for offerings shows an impressive image of Garuda, Vishnu's mount, at the western end of the boat-shaped roof. The gate tower has plain pilasters and two doors opening towards the east. The stele tower with its four large doors has undecorated pilasters. The complex represents a style of Cham architecture that is intermediate between those seen in Quảng Nam Province and in Bình Định

Province. The structures were built after the imperial Cham capital was transferred from Amaravati to Vijaya around the beginning of the 11th century.

Bình Lâm Tower (Phước Hòa; ⌚ 07.00–11.30 & 14.00–17.00 daily) The 20m-high Bình Lâm Tower, one of the first to be built in the Vijaya area and 20km north of Quy Nhơn, is typical of the transitional period in Cham art (11th century). It does not sit atop a hill but would have been within the boundary walls of a defensive citadel. If there were any other structures within the walled fortress, they were likely built of perishable materials as no evidence of them remains. Northwest of the tower is a ruined, 200m-long wall, once part of the citadel walls. This area was an important port city of the Kingdom of Champa from the 11th to the 15th centuries. It is noted for its highly decorative friezes and floral designs. Close examination will reveal images of gods seated on lotus-shaped thrones, prancing lions, human figures and the heads of mythical sea monsters with mammalian paws and fish tails (known as *makara*). The arcature of the false doors is richly decorated. Low down and near the ocean, the tower probably flooded every time a typhoon hit the area, which may account for the more heavily weathered lower sections. The tower was restored around the same time as Cánh Tiên Tower with new bricks to replace missing sections, but the result is more pleasing as the same-coloured bricks were used.

✷ Phú Lộc Tower (Nhơn Thành; ⌚ all day daily) Majestic Phú Lộc Tower (sometimes Phước Lộc Tower) sits atop a hill 30km northwest of Quy Nhơn. One of the furthest from the city, it's also one of the most dramatically situated, with wrap-around views of the surrounding hills and rice paddies. The site is not yet ticketed and thus there are no opening hours – arrive at sunrise for spellbinding views. Though you'll see the tower as you approach the hill, finding the path up is a challenge. Your best bet is to first visit the nearby Phước Lộc Pagoda on the south side of the hill, then ask around for the pathway up. If you're sent through a cemetery (where you can park a motorbike), you're going the right way. From here, a dirt path leads up to the tower. The east-facing kalan echoes the architectural style of the nearby Cánh Tiên Tower, which you can make out from the top of the hill if you look southwest. It stands on two rectangular terraces carved into the mountainside, though time and the elements have rendered them almost indiscernible. Originally enclosed by a vanished brick wall, the tower rises with straight pilasters framing false doors on three sides. The interior once held a linga, but now houses a small cauldron of bats.

Cánh Tiên Tower (Nhơn Hậu; ⌚ 07.00–11.30 & 14.00–16.30 daily; 10,000VND/free adult/child) Cánh Tiên Tower, 26km northwest of Quy Nhơn, probably dates from the end of the 12th century or beginning of the 13th century. The tower has a pyramidal roof made up of ten small storeys and is notable for its delicate decorative sandstone components. The site was renovated quite recently, and it presents as one of the most 'complete' towers other than the Bánh Ít complex. The renovation was controversial, however, as crude replicas replaced the missing stonework, enabling visitors to distinguish between the 12th-century original sections and the 21st-century replacements. The effect is rather jarring. It's believed that Cánh Tiên Tower was once surrounded by ten other Cham towers, but they were destroyed and their parts repurposed to build the Thập Tháp Pagoda (page 333). From the hillock on which it stands, you can look out over an agricultural landscape, which was once the site of the Vijaya Citadel.

Vijaya Citadel (An Thành–Cù Lâm) Vijaya Citadel, known to the Vietnamese as Chà Bàn and which later became Hoàng Đế Citadel, is about 27km north of Quy Nhơn. Originally a Cham capital, it was repeatedly attacked by the Vietnamese and eventually, in 1471, overrun and left to ruin by Emperor Lê Thánh Tông after he defeated the Cham. The ruins were then taken over by the Tây Sơn brothers in the 18th century (see below) and made the capital of their short-lived kingdom. Not much remains except for some Cham ruins, as well as a few structures that appear to be from the Nguyễn Dynasty. According to archaeologists, the enclosure of the Royal Champa Citadel was extended long after the last Cham army was defeated here. Historians confirm that in 1776 Nguyễn Nhạc ordered this extension and renamed Chà Bàn as Hoàng Đế, the Tây Sơn Citadel. Records from the 19th century report a new citadel with a perimeter of 7,400m, much larger than that of the Chà Bàn city within. Excavations have shown that Hoàng Đế was composed of three concentric parts. Walls of the Forbidden City in the centre of the complex were 1.5m thick and had only one access gate. The Inner City walls surrounding it were 7m thick, with three access gates. Outside this was the Outer City wall, 11m thick at the bottom and 4m thick at the top. This also had three access gates. The whole complex offered considerable protection against advancing armies. The few earth and laterite walls that remain belong to the citadel that was built in 1776. Only a few bricks now remain, since most were removed and used to construct the nearby Thập Tháp Pagoda (see opposite). Sculptural works removed from the site during the 1934–35 excavations are now on display in the Museum of Cham Sculpture in Đà Nẵng (page 289).

THE TÂY SƠN REBELLION (1771–88)

At the time of the Tây Sơn rebellion in 1771, Vietnam was in turmoil as the Trịnh and Nguyễn lords battled and conditions in the countryside were deteriorating to the point of famine. The three Tây Sơn brothers – Nguyễn Nhạc (the oldest), Nguyễn Huệ (the youngest), and Nguyễn Lữ – found a rich lode of dissatisfaction among the peasantry, which they successfully mined. Exploiting the latent discontent, they redistributed property from hostile mandarins to the peasants and raised a motley army of clerks, cattle-dealers, farmers, hill people and even scholars, to fight the Trịnh and Nguyễn lords. Brilliant strategists and demonstrating considerable leadership skills, the brothers and their supporters swept through the country. In the south, Saigon was captured by Nguyễn Nhạc while his brothers headed north to challenge the Trịnh. Around 1784, it was clear that a Siamese army, in support of the Nguyễn lord Nguyễn Ánh, was assembling in the Mekong Delta. Hearing of this risk to the succeeding rebellion, Nguyễn Huệ sailed south and the Siamese and Nguyễn Ánh were overwhelmingly defeated.

The Chinese, sensing that the disorder and dissent caused by the conflict gave them an opportunity to bring the entire nation under their control again, sent a 200,000-strong army southwards in 1788 and occupied Thăng Long (Hanoi). In the same year, the most strategically minded of the brothers, Nguyễn Huệ, proclaimed himself emperor under the name of Quang Trung and began to prepare for battle against the cursed Chinese. On the fifth day of Tết in 1789, the brothers attacked the Chinese near Thăng Long, catching them unawares as they celebrated the New Year. (The Việt Cộng were to do the same during the Tết Offensive nearly 200 years later.) With great military skill, they routed the enemy, who fled in panic back towards China.

✷ **Dương Long Towers** (Tây Sơn District; ⌚ 07.30–11.00 & 14.00–16.30 daily; 15,000VND/free adult/child) This haunting and magnificent triad of temple towers sits 41km northwest of Quy Nhơn, halfway between the Quang Trung Museum and the Vijaya Citadel. Whichever direction you come from, the approach is extraordinarily dramatic. Known to the French as the Ivory Towers, this is one of the most fantastic Cham sites in Vietnam and not to be missed. Much influenced in style by Khmer art, these three kalans were built in the 12th and 13th centuries. The magnificent Middle Tower, the highest at 24m, has windows opening towards the east. Close examination of the lower part reveals carvings of female breasts. The upper part has a string of dancing monkeys. The distinctive four-storey roof is shaped like a lotus throne. The South Tower, standing at 22m, is similar but has badly damaged false doors. The North Tower, also 22m high, has its own decorative style, with seven pilasters and intricate decorations on the false doors. The stonework here is particularly detailed, and on the temples' upper cornices are figures of animals. It's unclear who these temples were dedicated to, but it's been speculated that Dương Long was a Tantric Buddhist site, another Khmer influence.

Thập Tháp Pagoda (Vạn Thuận 1 Bridge) Located in the area of the Chà Bàn rampart, this Frankensteinian pagoda stands on a hill surrounded by lotus ponds and was built from the red bricks taken from ten Cham towers that once stood near Cánh Tiên Tower. Construction began in 1665. Three wells in the grounds were also built from Cham bricks. The outer façade is very plain but the interior is lavishly decorated with colourful roof hangings.

Rather than face capture, one of the Chinese generals committed suicide. This victory at the Battle of Đống Đa is regarded as one of the greatest in the annals of Vietnamese history. Quang Trung, having saved the nation from the Chinese, had visions of recreating the great Nam Việt Empire of the 2nd century BCE, and of invading China. Among the reforms that he introduced were a degree of land reform, a wider programme of education, and a fairer system of taxation. He reportedly even tried to make all peasants carry identity cards with the slogan 'the great trust of the empire' emblazoned on them.

These greater visions were not to be, however. Quang Trung died suddenly in 1792, when his son, Nguyễn Quang Toản, was just ten years old. Nguyễn Ánh, who had survived the humiliating defeat in the Mekong Delta, saw his opportunity to retake the throne, and swept through the country, murdering Nguyễn Nhạc, Nguyễn Lữ and Nguyễn Quang Toản. Once victory was assured, Nguyễn Ánh proclaimed himself Emperor Gia Long, ushering in the Nguyễn Dynasty, and moved the capital to his ancestral family home in Huế in 1802. (See page 266 for information on Gia Long's controversial legacy.) Interestingly, today the end of the so-called Tây Sơn Dynasty is regarded in Vietnam as a great national tragedy. While today's government-sanctioned history books regard that Nguyễn Dynasty as weak and unable to resist colonisation, it is assumed (with little proof) that the Tây Sơn Dynasty would have had the strength and resolve to overcome the French.

Quang Trung and the other Tây Sơn brothers – like many former nationalist and peasant leaders – are revered by the Vietnamese and honoured by the communists. Most cities will have a Nguyễn Huệ or Quang Trung Street, but rarely both.

✷ ***Quang Trung Museum*** (Tây Sơn District; **w** baotangquangtrung.com.vn; ⌚ 07.00–11.30 & 13.30–17.00 daily; 50,000VND/free adult/child) Vietnam has a penchant for celebrating the exploits of the poor, and those of the Tây Sơn brothers (page 332) are displayed in the Quang Trung Museum, approximately 45km from Quy Nhơn, not far from the Dương Long Cham Towers. This museum, a worthwhile interlude while exploring the sites of ancient Vijaya (page 329), is dedicated to Nguyễn Huệ, a national hero of the 18th century and one of the three brothers who led the Tây Sơn insurrection. Exhibits are clear and easy to follow, and the epic episodes of the rebellion are brought to life with some extraordinarily detailed wall murals.

Quy Hòa and ExploraScience (10 Science Avenue; **w** explorascience.vn; ⌚ 08.00–11.00 & 14.00–17.00 Tue–Sun; 60,000VND–120,000VND depending on activities) The former site of a leper colony, 8km south of Quy Nhơn, has an attractive, empty beach, as well as the unlikely ExploraScience, an interactive museum that promotes scientific knowledge and curiosity for young visitors. Visitors can participate in innovative experiments, explore astronomy through observatories and learn about the natural world in an engaging and educational environment. It was clearly designed for Vietnamese school groups, but will also appeal to parents travelling with kids in tow.

Bãi Xép Some 14km south of Quy Nhơn is the fishing village of Bãi Xép. Once a hidden spot with two quiet beaches – one used by fishermen and the other for swimming – Bãi Xép is busier and dirtier than it was. These days, the village has more hotels than it probably needs and trash is a problem, but the tight alleyways are nevertheless atmospheric, interesting and free of cars. In the evenings, the south side of the village, where you can swim, hosts a row of basic seafood restaurants.

TUY HÒA

The coastal province of Phú Yên has a population of around a million. Most are fishermen, rice farmers, forestry workers and mineral miners. A growing number work in service industries as the province's beaches cultivate a budding domestic tourism industry. Phú Yên's scenery rivals that of its neighbour, Khánh Hòa (see opposite), especially along the Cù Mông Pass, which connects the province with Bình Định to the north. A tunnel now cuts through the pass, leaving the mountain road more or less free of traffic. See page 327 for the more remote beaches in the province.

At the mouth of the Đà Rằng River, which meanders down from the Central Highlands, is the provincial capital **Tuy Hòa**. A low-rise and sprawling city with less than a handful of things to see and do and an inferior metropolitan beach, Tuy Hòa is less appealing than other coastal hubs. Unlike Quy Nhơn and Nha Trang, which sit comfortably nestled in bays, Tuy Hòa is not built around the beach, and the coast feels separated from the happenings of the city. The sea can be rough in this exposed and mercurial yellow-sand stretch and there are few waterside services.

If you do find yourself here for a night or two, spend the day exploring the city's two towers. The first is the largely rebuilt but attractive **Tháp Nhạn** (72 Lê Trung Kiên; ⌚ 06.30–22.30 daily), the city's Cham tower, which is near the train station. The second is a nod to the Cham towers of the subregion, the **Nghinh Phong Tower** (Bình Kiến; ⌚ all day daily), a modern structure on the coast close to the hospital. Some 35km north of Tuy Hòa is **Gành Đá Đĩa** (An Ninh Đông Ward; ⌚ 08.00–

18.30 daily; 20,000/10,000VND adult/child), a natural formation consisting of thousands of hexagonal basalt columns created millions of years ago from volcanic eruptions. The lava, after cooling rapidly upon contact with the sea, crystallised into these geometric shapes, which appear manmade and resemble a giant beehive. The sight is popular with domestic tourists.

Like Quy Nhơn, Tuy Hòa is rarely unpleasant, though it can be drizzly from October to February. The rest of the year is hot and sunny with the occasional shower. Typhoons rarely make landfall this far south.

Tuy Hòa train station (149 Lê Trung Kiên) is on the west side of the city. North of here is Diêu Trì (for Quy Nhơn; 2hrs) Quảng Ngãi (5hrs), Đà Nẵng (8hrs), Huế (11hrs) and beyond. South of here is Nha Trang (3hrs) and Hồ Chí Minh City (around 12hrs). **Phú Yên bus station** (277 Nguyễn Tất Thành) is just north of the train station and buses to most corners in the country pass through here. Buôn Ma Thuột (5hrs) is the closest city in the Central Highlands. Tuy Hòa Airport is just south of the city centre, with flights to Hanoi and Hồ Chí Minh City. The most pleasant place to stay is within the gridded Phường 7 neighbourhood, just east of Hùng Vương Street, which also has many restaurants and cafés. Phú Yên General Hospital (15 Nguyễn Hữu Thọ; **w** benhvienphuyen.vn; ⌚ all day daily) is 2.5km north of here.

NHA TRANG

Once an important part of the Kauthara Champa Kingdom, prosperous Khánh Hòa Province – of which Nha Trang is the capital – covers an area of more than 5,000km^2 and is home to approximately 1.5 million people. The biggest earners are tourism, focused around Nha Trang, and fishing, with one of the largest fleets in the country. Numerous shrimp farms are also dotted along its coastline, the favoured varieties for cultivation being tiger and banana shrimps, and salt from various salt fields is exported worldwide. The hilly province has huge reserves of minerals, including black titan, diorite, rock crystal and iron. Agricultural communities grow rice, avocado, dragon fruit, cassava, tobacco, beans, sugarcane and peanuts.

Economic development has taken an undeniable toll on the province. With tourism booming as early as the 1990s, households collected Torocea, Hippopus and Tridacna, spectacular-looking shells which fetched good prices. Coral began appearing in the tourist shops, along with endangered seahorses, which are also used in traditional medicine. Forests were felled at an alarming rate, the most exploited species being sandalwood, which provides oil for the province's perfume industry. While the province continues to grapple with the impact of tourism, the superb beaches of Nha Trang and Cam Ranh, close to the airport, remain an undeniable draw. See page 327 for the more remote beaches in the province.

Nha Trang's days as an undiscovered treasure seem like a distant memory. It is a firmly established favourite of Vietnamese as well as foreign visitors, particularly from Russia, and Nha Trang is now well set up to indiscriminately relieve them of their tourist dollar. Bookended by tall mountains and a calm bay with a sweeping crescent of powdery golden sand, it was only a matter of time before this city – Vietnam's sunniest – became loved by holidaymakers. Over the last two decades or so, Nha Trang has changed beyond recognition. Huge international hotels now line the riverfront, while construction in the hotel quarter is ongoing.

Nevertheless, beyond the main tourist zones the city has some charming spots and the areas to the north and south offer rugged coastal drives, Cham ruins and long beaches. The name Nha Trang is thought to be derived from the Cham word

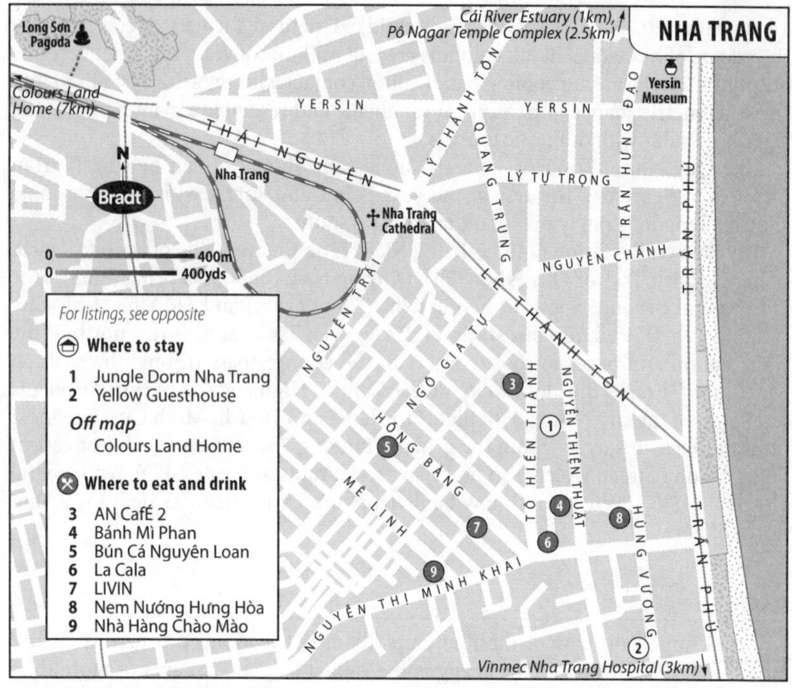

'*yakram*', meaning 'bamboo river', and the surrounding area was a focal point of the Cham Kingdom – some of the country's best-preserved (ie: reconstructed) Cham towers lie close by. South of Nha Trang lies Cam Ranh, a Vietnamese version of Cancun, with gigantic resorts that ensconce visitors within their confines. North of the city sits a geographically dramatic series of peninsulas and outcrops that hide the province's less-developed treasures – for now.

GETTING THERE AND AROUND **Nha Trang train station** (17 Thái Nguyên) is central. North of here is Diêu Trì (for Quy Nhơn; 4hrs), Quảng Ngãi (7hrs), Đà Nẵng (10hrs) and beyond. South of here is Tháp Chàm (90mins), Bình Thuận (for Phan Thiết and Mũi Né; 4hrs) and Hồ Chí Minh City (9hrs).

Nha Trang is big enough to warrant more than one **bus station**, and some bus companies will have a shuttle bus service for pick-up/drop-off at your accommodation. Nha Trang is well connected, and you can get just about anywhere on the bus, including Quy Nhơn (4hrs), Quảng Ngãi (7hrs), Hội An (9hrs), Đà Nẵng (10hrs) and beyond to the north, and Mũi Né (4hrs), Phan Thiết (4hrs), Vũng Tàu (6hrs) and Hồ Chí Minh City (6hrs) to the south. The closest city in the Central Highlands is Đà Lạt (3hrs).

Cam Ranh International Airport (Cam Nghĩa Ward; **w** vietnamairport.vn) is 40km south of the city, with multiple flights a day to Hanoi, Hồ Chí Minh City and some other domestic cities. There is a limited number of international flights to other parts of Asia and to Russia.

Nha Trang is **walkable**, and you can travel to most of the city sights and back by **taxi or Grab**. For day trips from the city, rent either a **motorbike or a car with driver** from your accommodation or talk to a taxi driver about commandeering their vehicle for the day.

WHERE TO STAY *Map opposite, unless otherwise stated*

Jungle Dorm Nha Trang 8/19 Nguyễn Thiện Thuật. Friendly & well-run backpacker hostel, with all the thoughtful extras that make shared accommodation comfortable, including private curtains & pillow-side power sockets. **$**

Colours Land Home Xuân Phú village, Vĩnh Phương Ward; **w** booking.com. Out of the centre but close to the river, Colours is a little garden retreat with a swimming pool, run by a charismatic team. **$$**

Yellow Guesthouse 186 Hùng Vương; **f** YellowHouseNhaTrang. Clean & crisp no-nonsense accommodation with interior balconies that let in the light but keep out the city noise. **$$**

✷ **Whale Island Resort** [map, page 296] Đầm Môn village; **w** whaleislandresort.com. This basic but beautiful resort close to Nha Trang has the whole island to itself. If you're fed up with the overdevelopment of the coastline, this is the place to come. The beaches are empty & kept clean, & the beach hut rooms are simple but comfortable. **$$$**

Mia [map, page 296] Cam Hải Đông Ward; **w** mianhatrang.com. A modern design hotel that clings to cliffs between Nha Trang & Cam Ranh. Many of the villas, which sit in tree-studded gardens, have private pools. **$$$$**

Six Senses Ninh Vân [map, page 296] Ninh Vân Bay; **w** sixsenses.com. Uber-luxurious seaside retreat with everything you'd expect to get when spending hundreds of dollars a night, including an organic garden, private beach, decent gym & so on. Some of the timber villas are built over the water. **$$$$$**

WHERE TO EAT AND DRINK *Map, opposite*

Bánh Mì Phan 164 Bạch Đằng; **f** banhmiphannhatrang; ⏲ 07.00–20.30 daily. Nothing but Vietnamese baguettes done well in this take-away joint close to the beach. **$**

Bún Cá Nguyên Loan 123 Ngô Gia Tự; **f**; ⏲ 06.00–22.30 daily. Serving the popular Nha Trang take on *bún cá*, fish noodle soup, with generous portions of fish & seafood & a sweet, rich broth. **$**

Nem Nướng Hưng Hòa 46/21 Hùng Vương; **w** nemnuonghunghoanhatrang.com; ⏲ 08.00–22.00 daily. *Nem nướng* is a Nha Trang speciality similar to *nem lụi* in Huế & Đà Nẵng – grilled pork sausage wrapped in rice paper with salad & pickles & served with a dipping sauce. **$$**

La Cala 172/16A Bạch Đằng; **w** la-cala.com; ⏲ 11.00–23.00 daily. Family-owned restaurant with some of the best pizza, pasta & other Italian dishes you'll find anywhere in Vietnam. **$$$**

LIVIN 5A Ngô Thời Nhiệm; **w** livinbbq.com; ⏲ 11.00–23.00 Mon–Fri, 09.00–23.00 Sat–Sun. The owners of LIVIN grew up in the US, where they became barbecue experts, a skill they put to good use when crafting the menu. **$$$**

✷ **Nhà Hàng Chào Mào** 166 Mê Linh; **f**; ⏲ 10.30–14.30 & 17.00–21.00 daily. Excellent little Vietnamese restaurant serving specialities from across the country, which has somehow become popular with Korean tourists. It's not a dish from the area, but try the *bánh xèo*. **$$$**

AN Café 2 24 Nguyễn Trung Trực; **f** ANCAFE24NGUYENTRUNGTRUC; ⏲ 06.00–22.30 daily. One of a number of AN cafés serving good coffee, tropical fruit juice & dessert milkshakes in stylish surroundings.

OTHER PRACTICALITIES The **diving** in Vietnam is not as good as elsewhere in Southeast Asia, but Vietnam Active (**w** vietnamactive.com) is a professional outfit in the centre of town that knows the best sites. **Boat trips** around the area can be arranged at your hotel, or pay a visit to Emperor Cruises (**w** emperorcruises.com/emperor-cruises-nha-trang), an established and reputable cruise company. The large **Vinmec Nha Trang Hospital** (Trần Phú, Vĩnh Nguyên Ward; **w** vinmec.com) offers the best care and is used to foreigners, but medical costs are high. Nha Trang has received international visitors for years, and a comprehensive, competitive health-care ecosystem has developed in the city, with several decent private clinics and multilingual pharmacists.

WHAT TO SEE AND DO

The beach Nha Trang's banana-shaped sandy strip is its pride and joy. The bay is more protected than other metropolitan beaches, in part due to Hòn Tre, the large island in front that has been transformed into a theme park. The central area is rarely unpleasantly busy, but if it is, simply head a few hundred metres north.

Long Sơn Pagoda (22 23 Tháng 10; 🕘 all day daily) The best-known pagoda in Nha Trang, perhaps because it can be seen from many corners of the city, is the Long Sơn Pagoda, built in 1963. Inside the sanctuary is an unusual image of the Buddha, backlit with natural light. Murals depicting the *jataka* stories of Buddha's birth and life decorate the upper walls. To the right of the sanctuary, stairs lead up to a big white Buddha, perched on a hillock, from where there are fine views. Before reaching the white pagoda, take a left on the stairs. Through an arch behind the pagoda you'll see a 14m-long reclining Buddha. Commissioned in 2003, it is an impressive sight. The pagoda commemorates the monks and nuns who died demonstrating against the Diệm government – in particular those who, through self-immolation (page 472), brought the despotic nature of the Diệm regime and its human rights abuses to the attention of the world.

Nha Trang Cathedral (1 Thái Nguyên; 🕘 08.00–11.15 & 14.00–16.15 daily) Granite-coloured (though built of concrete) and imposing, the cathedral was built between 1928 and 1933 on a small rock outcrop. It was not until 1961, however, that the building was consecrated as a cathedral for the diocese of Nha Trang and Ninh Thuận. The cathedral has a single crenellated tower and a fine vaulted ceiling, with stained glass in the upper sections of its windows and pierced metal in the lower. The windows over the altar depict Jesus with Mary and Joseph, Joan of Arc

ALEXANDRE YERSIN

Alexandre John Emille Yersin was born in 1863 in Canton Vaud, Switzerland. He enrolled at the University of Lausanne and completed his medical education in Paris, where he became an assistant to chemist and microbiologist Louis Pasteur. In 1888, Yersin adopted French citizenship. To the astonishment of all, he became a ship's doctor; he visited Asia and in 1891 landed in Nha Trang. Two years later, as part of his exploration of Vietnam, he came upon the Đà Lạt Plateau, which he recommended for development as a hill resort owing to its beauty and temperate climate. The following year, in 1894, he was urged to visit Hong Kong to assist in an outbreak of the plague. He identified the bacillus, which was named *Yersinia pestis*. In 1895 he set up a laboratory in Nha Trang which, in 1902, became a Pasteur Institute, the first to be established outside France. Here he developed an anti-serum for the treatment of plague. He established a cattle farm for the production of serum and vaccines and for the improvement of breeding stock at Suối Dầu, 25km south of Nha Trang. Yersin was responsible for the introduction to Vietnam of commercial crops such as coffee, rubber and the cinchona (quinine) tree. In his retirement he indulged his passions – astrology, photography and observation of the hydrographic conditions of Nha Trang Bay, and he died in 1943. He is one of very few Europeans to have streets named after them, including in Nha Trang, and there is a **museum** (10 Trần Phú; 🕘 08.00–noon & 14.00–16.30 Mon–Fri; 26,000VND) devoted to his life and contributions to Vietnam.

ANCIENT KAUTHARA

This box was written with considerable input from Dr Nguyễn H H Duyên (page 12).

Kauthara was a state in the Champa Kingdom that sat between Vijaya (page 329; Bình Định Province) and Panduranga (page 341; Ninh Thuận and Bình Thuận provinces). The **Pô Nagar Temple Complex** (61 Hai Tháng Tư; 🕘 06.00–17.30 daily; 30,000VND) in Nha Trang are the most visible remnants of the state, situated on a hill just outside the city. Originally the complex consisted of eight towers, four of which remain. Their stylistic differences indicate they were built at different times between the 7th and 12th centuries, though an inscription on one stele suggests that the site was first constructed in 591. The largest (at 23m high) was built in 817 and contains a statue of Thiên Y A Na, originally a Cham goddess known as Pô Nagar, a great goddess born from the sea with 97 husbands and 39 daughters and, according to the scholar Nguyễn Thế Anh, the personification of the nurturing earth for the Cham. Pô Nagar was absorbed into the traditional Vietnamese worship of the mother goddess (page 188) and became Thiên Y A Na, a process that Nguyễn Thế Anh has referred to as 'Vietnamisation' and 'Confucianisation'. 'Neither her polyandry nor the large number of her children was mentioned,' he writes. 'She was, moreover, depicted as an immortal (*tiên nữ*)...She devoted herself to the task of instructing the inhabitants, while not hesitating to resort to supernatural powers in order to impose respect. Such an image was assuredly more familiar to the mentality of the Vietnamese governing class than the naturism with which the deity was originally permeated.' The other towers are dedicated to gods: the central tower to Cri Cambhu (which has become a fertility temple for childless couples); the northwest tower to Sandhaka (woodcutter and foster-father to Lady Thiên Y A Na); and the south tower to Lady Thiên Y A Na's daughter. This is an important site during the three-day Kate Festival (page 342), Cham New Year (seventh month of Cham calendar, tenth month of lunar calendar).

and Sainte Thérèse. Like the windows in Đà Lạt and Đà Nẵng cathedrals, they were made in Grenoble by Louis Balmet. There are 14 rather fine pictures depicting the stations of the cross.

Cái River Estuary En route to the Pô Nagar Temple Complex (see above) and visible from the small hill where they sit is the Cái River Estuary, home to Nha Trang's aquamarine fleet of fishing boats, lined with red and complete with painted eyes for spotting the fish, and circular coracles for getting to the boats and mechanical fish traps. The traps take the form of nets that are supported by long arms; the arms are hinged to a platform on stilts and are raised and lowered by wires connected to a capstan which is turned, sometimes by hand but more commonly by foot.

Around Nha Trang In addition to the places mentioned here, see page 327 for some of the more secluded beaches close to Nha Trang.

Cam Ranh Bay One of the world's largest natural harbours lies 34km south of Nha Trang. Highway 1 skirts around the bay – a centre for Vietnam's salt industry; for miles around the scenery is white with salt pans (looking like wintry paddy fields) producing pure, crystalline sea salt. During the American War, this was an important US naval base and subsequently taken over by the Soviets. In fact the Soviets, or at least the Russians, were here before the Americans: they used it for re-provisioning during the Russo-Japanese war of 1904, which they emphatically lost. After reunification in 1975, the Vietnamese allowed the Soviets to use this fine natural harbour once again as part-payment for the support (political and financial) they were receiving. However, from the late 1980s, the former Soviet fleet began to wind down its presence here as Cold War tensions in the area eased and economic pressures forced the former USSR to reduce military expenditure. Now the port is almost deserted as the area has pivoted towards beach tourism. Nha Trang's airport is now here and there is a new coastal road linking the city to the airport. Lining the road are gigantic resorts of all sorts, from high-rise concrete monoliths to capacious garden retreats. If you want nothing more than to luxuriate in comfort on a beach, Cam Ranh is one of Vietnam's finest choices. You'll have your pick of good-value, international standard hotels that offer a myriad of services, but The Anam (Nguyễn Tất Thành; **w** theanam.com; **$$$$**) comes recommended.

Ninh Thuận Province Famous for its vast vineyards, Cham towers and white, sandy beaches, this province nevertheless attracts far fewer visitors than neighbouring Khánh Hòa. Reminders that this is Cham territory will never be far away. Tens of thousands of Cham still make up a significant percentage of the province's half a million people; many of the 100,000 or so people who live in the provincial capital, Phan Rang-Tháp Chàm, are children of mixed marriages between Kinh and Cham. The lofty towers dotted throughout the province are reminders of different periods in their colourful history. Virtually nothing remains of Panduranga (see opposite), their 4th-century kingdom, part of an empire that once stretched from Phan Thiết to the 17th parallel. Those that remain (9th–16th centuries), although decayed from the passage of time, still demonstrate the artistry and building skills of these Indianised people.

Ninh Thuận claims to be the driest (and sunniest) province in Vietnam, and at times feels more like a rocky Mediterranean island than the tropical coast. Grapes are grown in vast quantities and are said to be the best in the country. Some farmers also grow onions and hot peppers. Phan Rang-Tháp Chàm divides into three loosely connected areas: Phan Rang, Ninh Chữ (the beach) and Tháp Chàm. Ninh Chữ and Phan Rang beaches are 6km east of the city centre. Together they form a sweeping golden crescent that is mainly for local beachgoers. There are several cafés that let

KITE SURFING

Ninh Thuận is Vietnam's windiest, sunniest province with a long, rocky coastline, so it should come as no surprise that it is also developing as a kite-surfing destination, particularly at Mỹ Hòa, just north of Phan Rang-Tháp Chàm. Mỹ Hòa offers reliable winds between November and April, with speeds often reaching 30–40 knots. The bay features a desirable setup, with a combination of flatwater lagoons and small waves that cater to different styles and skill levels, including complete beginners. **Phi Kite School** (Vĩnh Hải; **w** phikiteschool.com) comes recommended, but there are many others, so shop around. **Panduranga** (Mỹ Hòa village; **w** panduranga.vn; **$$**), named after the ancient Cham kingdom, is an excellent little boutique hotel in the area.

chairs and umbrellas, in addition to selling drinks and food. For accommodation there's a variety of odds and ends including some local guesthouses and there are inexpensive restaurants on the beach. North of the capital is a large, rocky, windy outcrop with kite-surfing camps (see opposite) and the picturesque fishing settlement of Vĩnh Hy.

Ninh Thuận is just within day-trip distance of Nha Trang (and Cam Ranh) and you can talk to your hotel about arranging a car to see the Cham sites, beaches and vineyards, with a stop for a seafood meal in Vĩnh Hy. If you'd like to overnight here, look at accommodation in Phan Rang-Tháp Chàm, which has a range of options, homestays in Vĩnh Hy, or Panduranga (see opposite) in Mỹ Hòa village. For an exceptional resort experience (at obscenely high prices), there's the **Amanoi** (Vĩnh Hy village; **w** aman.com; **$$$$$**), part of Aman (not to be confused with Anam in Cam Ranh), one of the world's most luxurious hotel groups. Ninh Thuận is just as accessible from Mũi Né (page 345), another beach resort further south.

Ancient Panduranga *Details on the sites in this section were written with considerable input from Dr Nguyễn H H Duyên (page 12).* Panduranga (Ninh Thuận and Bình Thuận provinces) was the southernmost state in the decentralised state of Champa, the other three being Amaravati (page 318), Vijaya (page 329), and Kauthara (page 339). The most impressive remnants of the state are three complexes of Cham towers within easy reach of Phan Rang-Tháp Chàm, each representing different periods of Cham history: Hòa Lai, Pô Klong Garai and Po Ro Me. Visit from north to south in the order presented here to discover the three historical periods of Panduranga chronologically.

Hòa Lai Towers (🕘 all day daily) The earliest, the Hòa Lai group, date from the 9th century, a time when relations with the feuding Chinese were restored. These towers have a similar 'classic' style to the Pô Sanu towers near Phan Thiết, which belong to the same period. Situated close to Highway 1, about 14km north of Phan Rang-Tháp Chàm, the towers are both easy to reach but suffer from noise pollution from the road. Of the three original towers, the north has best withstood the ravages of time. The weathered masterpiece still shows delicate decorative patterns, intricately carved friezes and unique false doors. The south tower is well preserved but plain by comparison. The middle tower was completely destroyed by bombs and shells during the American War.

Pô Klong Garai Towers (Đô Vinh Ward; 🕘 07.30–17.30 daily; 20,000/10,000VND adult/child) The poster-child, the popular Pô Klong Garai group was constructed during the 13th and 14th centuries, when the wars with the Khmer had just ended and new religious edifices were erected. These towers represent a high point in Cham architectural achievement, and are some of the last towers built before the takeover of Champa. They are about 7km from Phan Rang-Tháp Chàm and dominate a hill that looks out over a barren, cactus-filled wilderness. The kalan tower consists of three sections. To the Cham, the foundations symbolise the human world, the body the spiritual world and the pyramidal tower the sacred world. The focal point would have been a sacred image of linga yoni, a representation of Shiva the Destroyer. Attached to it is the repository, which contained a statue of the god Nandin, Shiva's sacred bull. The site is fairly active and you might spot Hindu-following Cham pilgrims making offerings before proceeding to the inner sacred sanctuary at the heart of the kalan. The Cham kings were deities, and here the god-king to be worshipped is Pô Klong Garai, who is seated in the centre of the main temple. In the

KATE FESTIVAL

One of the most interesting times to come to Phan Rang-Tháp Chàm is for Cham New Year (seventh month of Cham calendar; usually October). On the eve of the festival, a huge procession consisting of Cham religious leaders, local dignitaries, and dance and music troupes heads to Pô Klong Garai and Po Ro Me. Local people transport gifts and clothes for the highly venerated god-kings of the past, which are presented to them during the clothes offering ceremony that follows. A Cham priest will bathe the linga yoni with holy water and people entering the kalan will attempt to sprinkle themselves with what remains, since it is believed by some that it has the power to promote health and happiness. The festivities continue for three days.

past worshippers would have washed themselves in the purifying water held inside the mandapa, the smaller tower to the right of the repository. Devout pilgrims to the site might bring their own water to clean themselves and use the mandapa as a meditation hall, a function for which it was also originally intended. If you stand at the western side of the mandapa and look upwards at the kalan, you will see a famous bas-relief just above the eastern entrance to the repository room. This is the dancing six-armed Shiva, guardian deity of this temple-tower. A careful look at the sandstone pillars of the entrance gate will reveal ancient inscriptions written in the Cham language, dating from the 13th–14th centuries. Above, on the tower wall, are beautifully carved pilasters, some with delicate lotus petals. Seated gods look down on you from stone perches (known as *amalaka*) and tower top. The temple plays an important role in the Cham Kate Festival (see above).

Po Ro Me Towers (Phước Hữu; 🕘 all day daily) Standing on a solitary hill are the 17th-century Po Ro Me Towers, dedicated to Po Ro Me, one of the last kings of Champa (1629–51). This ritual sanctuary, 19km southwest from Phan Rang, also comes alive during the Kate Festival. The towers were built after the fall of the Cham capital Vijaya (page 329) in present-day Bình Định Province. This victory by the huge Viet army of Lê Thánh Tông in 1471 had led to a drastic reduction in the size of the Kingdom of Champa, whose people were forced further south. Near here they established their last imperial capital. Representing the final period of tower construction, the complex bears some resemblance to the Pô Kloong Garai complex. The mandapa and the repository for offerings have long vanished, but the three-storey kalan is relatively intact. The architectural design is simpler with no pilasters and three false doors. Its most outstanding feature is a bas-relief showing the king as an incarnate of the god Shiva with two regular arms and six rear arms. Also in the complex, represented as deities, are his wives. Sadly, the statues here are replacements of the stolen originals. Virtually nothing remains of the rest of the imperial capital.

PHAN THIẾT

Phan Thiết is a fishing town at the mouth of the Cà Ty River and, despite its modest appearance, it is the administrative capital of Bình Thuận Province. The province spans 7,992km^2, is home to around 1.7 million people and its economy was traditionally driven by fishing and fish sauce production. More recently the service sector, particularly tourism in Mũi Né, has begun to make significant contributions.

The coastal area also supports salt production and the cultivation of dragon fruit, cashews and rice. Offshore, oil exploration is underway. The province also retains a strong Cham cultural presence (see below). Around a quarter of the 180,000 or so Cham people living in Vietnam live here.

For many visitors the fish and seafood are the main attraction of Phan Thiết. At times, pavements are piled high with dozens of species of shellfish, including cuttlefish, razor clams, mussels and shrimp, and fish, including mackerel, cod and mullet. Many of the fish end up in *nước mắm* factories, which have a reputation for producing both delicately flavoured and pungent fish sauce. Though there isn't much that will keep you in town, Phan Thiết has some of the best – and best-value – seafood restaurants in the country.

GETTING THERE AND AROUND **Phan Thiết train station** (1 Lê Duẩn) is 4km northwest of the centre, on a spur that only connects with Hồ Chí Minh City (4hrs). At the time of research, this only ran once a day in either direction on Friday, Saturday and Sunday. To travel by train during the rest of the week and to head north, take a 20-minute taxi journey west of the centre to **Bình Thuận train station** (Mương Mán Ward), which is on the main north–south line. North of here is Tháp Chàm (3hrs), Nha Trang (4hrs), Diêu Trì (for Quy Nhơn; 8hrs), Quảng Ngãi (11hrs), Đà Nẵng (14hrs) and beyond.

Phan Thiết has a few **bus** stations, including Bến Xe Phan Thiết and Bến Xe Bình Thuận. Some bus companies will pick up/drop off at your accommodation. Popular cities south of here include Vũng Tàu (5hrs) and Hồ Chí Minh City (4hrs). Cities

THE CHAM TODAY

With the over-running of Champa in 1471, Cham identity was diluted by the more numerous ethnic Vietnamese. The Cham were dispossessed of the more productive lands and found themselves in increasingly marginal territory. Economically eclipsed and strangers in their own land, Cham artistic creativity atrophied, their sculptural and architectural skills, once the glory of Vietnam, faded and decayed, like so many Cham temples and towers. It is estimated that there are, today, 180,000 Cham people in Vietnam, chiefly in Central and Southern Vietnam in the coastal provinces extending south from Quy Nhơn. Important communities are also to be found in Hồ Chí Minh City and in the Mekong Delta around Châu Đốc.

Their forebearers demonstrated astute artistic creativity, and skills in weaving and music live on. The Cham of the south are typically engaged in fishing, weaving and other small-scale commercial activities; urban Cham are marginalised and live in slum neighbourhoods. Further north the Cham are wet or dry rice farmers, according to local topography; they are noted for their skill in wet rice farming and small-scale hydraulic engineering. In Southern Vietnam the majority of Cham are Muslim, a comparatively newly acquired religion, although familiar from earlier centuries when many became acquainted with Islamic tenets through traders from India and the Indonesian isles. In Central Vietnam many Cham are Hindu and the linga remains a feature of spiritual life. The Museum of Cham Sculpture in Đà Nẵng (page 289) has a floor dedicated to the ethnolinguistic group, and there is also a comprehensive Cham Cultural Centre (Trung Tâm Trưng Bày Văn Hóa Chăm) 70km north of Phan Thiết on the way to Phan Rang and Nha Trang.

north of here include Phan Rang-Tháp Chàm (2hrs), Nha Trang (5hrs), Quy Nhơn (8hrs), Quảng Ngãi (12hrs), Đà Nẵng (15hrs) and beyond. The closest city in the Central Highlands is Đà Lạt (5hrs).

Phan Thiết Airport opened in 2024, but at the time of research civilian flights had not yet started

Central Phan Thiết is **walkable** and you can travel to Mũi Né and back by **taxi**.

WHERE TO STAY AND EAT Near the market is the nicest place to stay, but most hotels are the other side of the river, a short walk away. Try **T's House** (43 Nguyễn Đình Chiểu; f THouseHomestayMuiNe; **$**) for something simple, or **Đồi Dương Hotel** (209 Lê Lợi; w doiduonghotel.com; **$$**) for a classic mid-range Vietnamese hotel. Trawl for seafood restaurants along Phạm Văn Đồng Street. **Hải Sản Thuận Phát** (109–111 Phạm Văn Đồng; ⌚ 08.00–midnight daily; **$$$**) is recommended.

OTHER PRACTICALITIES The large **Bình Thuận Provincial Hospital** (Trường Chinh; w benhvienbinhthuan.vn; ⌚ 24hrs) is near Phan Thiết train station, 4km northwest of the centre.

WHAT TO SEE AND DO

Phan Thiết The neighbourhood around **Phan Thiết Market** is pleasant to walk around. The most distinctive landmark is the municipal **Water Tower** (Long Khê village), completed in 1934 and situated across the river. It is an elegant structure with a pagoda-like roof and features in the logos of many local businesses and agencies. Nearby is the **Bình Thuận Museum** (4 Bà Triệu; w baotangbinhthuan.com; ⌚ 07.00–11.00 & 13.30–17.00 Mon–Fri, 07.00–11.00 Sat–Sun), a clean and orderly building with clear exhibits that few people see. There are a few Hồ Chí Minh relics, including a **museum** (39 Trưng Nhị) on Trung Nhi Street and the Đức Thanh School (Trưng Nhị St; ⌚ 07.30–11.30 & 13.30–16.30 daily) next door,

LEGEND HAS IT: WHALE OF A WARTIME

According to legend, while fleeing the carnage of the Tây Sơn Rebellion (page 332), Nguyễn Ánh, the future founder of the Nguyễn Dynasty, encountered a fierce storm at sea. When his boat was close to being ripped apart, a giant whale appeared and lifted the vessel on its back, carrying it to safety. In gratitude for the divine intervention, Emperor Gia Long (page 266), as he came to be known after taking the throne, decreed the whale to be a sacred animal, leading to the practice of whale worship.

The practice is most prevalent in the Southern Central Coast subregion, where whales are now revered as guardians of fishermen and are believed to rescue sailors during storms. When whales occasionally wash up on the beach, elaborate funerals can take place where the bones are buried, dug up three years later and moved to a temple. These whale temples pepper the subregion, especially in Bình Thuận, Ninh Thuận and Khánh Hòa provinces, where the annual festival **Lễ Hội Nghinh Ông**, usually held in August, honours the creatures. Colourful rituals involve offering prayers and sacrifices to Cá Ông (grandfather fish) to ensure safe voyages and abundant catches.

While Gia Long's support for whale worship is well documented, it may have originally been a Cham belief that was adopted by the Việt as they moved south in the 15th century.

where Hồ Chí Minh taught in 1910 and 1911. **Vạn Thủy Tú Temple** (54 Ngư Ông; 07.30–11.30 & 13.30–16.30 daily; 15,000/5,000VND adult/child), first built in 1762, is probably the oldest whale temple (see opposite) in Vietnam and houses more than 100 whale skeletons, including one specimen more than 22m long. Like all whale temples, it was originally built by the sea but, as sea levels have receded in Phan Thiết, this temple is now stranded in the middle of a neighbourhood. The **Fish Sauce Museum** (360 Nguyễn Thông; f baotangnuocmam; 08.00–18.00 daily; 100,000VND/free adult/child), 7km east of town on the way to Mũi Né, provides a comprehensive introduction to Phan Thiết's most famous commodity, with guided tours.

Around Phan Thiết

Mũi Né Mũi Né is the name of the touristy sandy cape and the small fishing village that lies at its eastern end. Mũi Né's claims to fame are its *nước mắm* (fish sauce) and its beach, where it is possible to do a host of watersports including kite surfing, for which it is justly famous. Bodyboarding and surfing are better in December to January when there are more waves. The wind dies down at the end of April, and May has virtually no wind. The cape is also dominated by some impressive and visitable sand dunes; some are golden but in other parts quite red, a reflection of the underlying geology. Like other mature beach destinations in Central and Southern Vietnam, there is a range of hotels offering competitive room rates. The **Pit Stop** (122 Nguyễn Đình Chiểu; f pitstopvietnam; 08.00–23.00 daily) is a rare example of a food court done well in Vietnam, serving affordable cuisine from across the world. Mũi Né is within taxi-ride distance of Phan Thiết.

Pô Sah Inư Towers (Phú Hài Ward; 07.00–17.00 daily; 15,000/7,000VND adult/child) There are many relics of the Champa Kingdom's Panduranga state (page 341) here in Bình Thuận Province, the best and easiest to find being Pô Sah Inư, two Cham towers dating from the late 8th century or early 9th century close to Phan Thiết. They have undergone restoration and the road leading up to them makes a nice evening ride; you can watch the sun set and from this vantage point you'll see the physical make-up of the coastal plain and estuaries to the south and the Central Highlands to the north. Driving up the long climb towards Mũi Né from Phan Thiết, the towers are on the right-hand side of the road and quite unmissable. There are two towers (kalans) at this site. The South Tower is well preserved, with two of its three tiers remaining. The smaller North Tower shows features typical of Khmer art characteristic of the 8th-century transitional period. Like Cham towers elsewhere in this part of the country, they were constructed of brick bound together with tree resin. Once the tower was completed timber was piled around it and ignited; the heat from the flames melted the resin, which solidified on cooling.

9

The Central Highlands

The various plateaux of the Central Highlands, or Tây Nguyên in Vietnamese, reach an altitude of 1,500m. These craggy and fertile elevations are part of the Trường Sơn Mountains, which undulate throughout Central Vietnam and beyond. To the west of this landlocked swathe of land is southern Laos and eastern Cambodia; to the east is the Southern Central Coast. The subregion's knobbly terrain contrasts with the fleshy rice paddies and soft sand of the Southern Central Coast, earning it the nickname 'the backbone of Vietnam'.

This backbone has long been associated with more than a dozen ethnolinguistic groups. French missionaries were active among these groups (the colonial administration deterred the Kinh from settling here) although with uneven success. Towards the end of the 19th century, missionaries from Quy Nhơn were dispatched to Đắk Lắk, where they received a hostile reception from the Mnong. They then travelled north to Kon Tum where, among the Bahnar, one of the largest groups in the subregion, they found more receptive souls for their evangelising. The Bible was swiftly translated into Bahnar and, as a result, they are one of the few ethnolinguistic groups in the country with a written language that is in everyday use: you might spot it on museum signboards in Kon Tum and Gia Lai. Other sizeable ethnolinguistic groups include the Jarai, Ede and K'Ho.

While missionaries engaged in the enterprise of religious conversion, French businesses were hard at work establishing plantations to supply the home market. Rubber and coffee were the staple crops. The greatest difficulty they faced was recruiting sufficient labour; people here understandably preferred to cultivate their own small plots rather than accept the hard labour and slave wages of the plantation owners. The cities of the subregion suffered disproportionately during the American War; Pleiku was flattened whereas Đà Lạt emerged relatively unscathed. After reunification in 1975, and particularly during the 1980s, there was a scramble for land. Groups from other parts of Vietnam, most notably the Kinh but also the Hmong from Northern Vietnam, have encroached on land throughout the subregion, sometimes leading to violence.

The Central Highlands is one of Vietnam's most important areas for nature. It contains part of the Cát Tiên National Park, which creeps into the subregion from Đồng Nai Province, and the Yok Đôn National Park, one of the largest in Southeast Asia. As new species are still being discovered here, it appears that the Central Highlands' natural history could be even richer than previously thought. In many areas along the border with Cambodia and Laos, there are primeval forests and they remain a source of precious timbers, including tough ironwood and rosewood, despite logging clampdowns. Protected areas nurture rare pine species and important medicinal plants.

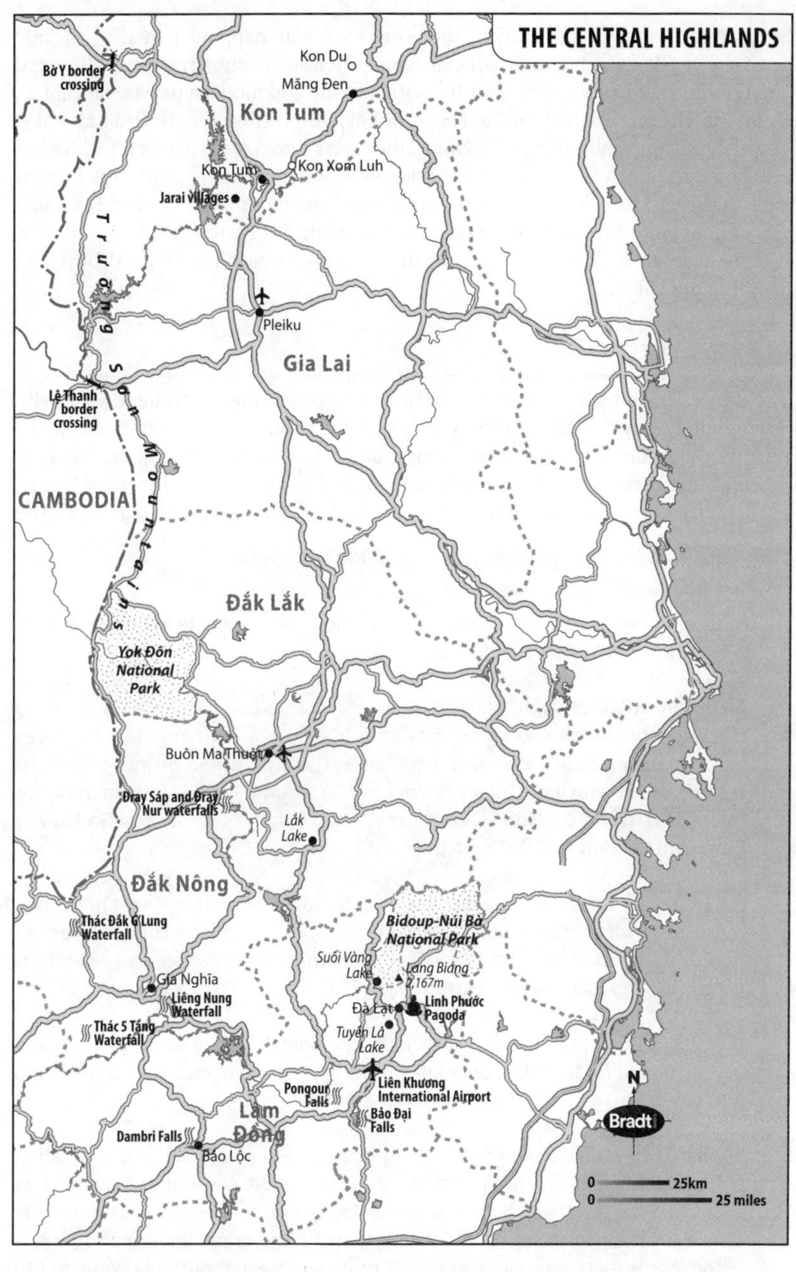

Administratively, the Central Highlands is divided into five large provinces: Kon Tum, Gia Lai, Đắk Lắk, Đắk Nông and Lâm Đồng. From a traveller's point of view, the Central Highlands is visually less dramatic and more cultivated than the northern mountains, but certainly no less interesting. **Kon Tum** is an unassuming, friendly place that can feel more Laotian than Vietnamese, with a low-rise capital surrounded by small hamlets and the unsung mountain retreat of Măng Đen.

Several important battles during the American War happened in the volcanic province of Gia Lai, and its provincial capital **Pleiku** was subsequently obliterated and rebuilt. Đắk Lắk is coffee country, with a flashy and modern provincial capital, **Buôn Ma Thuột**, and the protected areas of **Yok Đôn National Park** and **Lắk Lake**. Together with neighbouring Đắk Nông (they were once one province), Đắk Lắk is also home to some of Vietnam's most impressive waterfalls. Lâm Đồng, the highest and southernmost province, is where you'll find the mountain resort of **Đà Lạt**, a city of honeymooners, adventure sports and a cabinet of curiosities.

This chapter is arranged from north to south, beginning in Kon Tum and finishing in Đà Lạt.

WHEN TO VISIT

The dry season, which runs from November to April, is the best time to visit, with warm, sunny days – the beginning of the dry season in particular is when the region's waterfalls will be at their loudest and lakes are at their fullest. But bear in mind that there are frequent cold and windy days in January. The wind can be particularly deceptive, as the province can look perfect on paper (eg: 20°C and

THE CENTRAL HIGHLANDS' SPECIALITY DISHES

Most of the speciality dishes in the Central Highlands originate in Đà Lạt, though a few are found further afield.

GÀ NƯỚNG CƠM LAM The Central Highlands' most ubiquitous speciality is grilled chicken served with sticky rice cooked in a hollowed-out bamboo tube. Sides include cucumber and herbs, and the dip is usually crushed peanut with roast sesame or salt with lime. Try it at **Cơm Lam Gà Nướng – Thảo Nguyên** in Đà Lạt (page 371), **Quán Gà Nướng Cơm Lam** in Kon Tum (page 352) and **Gà Nướng Cơm Lam Cô Sinh** in Măng Đen (page 356).

GỎI LÁ A little-known Bahnar dish that is only found in Kon Tum. To eat *gỏi lá*, one must select some leaves, shape them into a cone, then fill the cone with boiled pork and shredded pig ear and top it with a fermented soy sauce and a short, fat green chilli. Try it at **Gỏi Lá Út Cưng** (page 352).

BÚN CUA ĐỒNG A pungent, brown-coloured noodle dish popular in Kon Tum and usually served for breakfast or at lunchtime. The rich, divisive flavour comes from fermented field crab. Try it at **Kon Tum Market**.

BÁNH ƯỚT THỊT NƯỚNG A little-known speciality of Buôn Ma Thuột is a variation of fresh spring rolls. The rice paper arrives on your table wet and stretched across circular plastic trays, which are stacked on top of one another on a custom-made rack. Pack the rice paper carefully with grilled pork, green papaya and pickles before harnessing your chopstick skills to make a neat, mouthful-sized wrap to dip in a sweetened fish sauce. Try it in Buôn Ma Thuột at **Bánh Ướt Thịt Nướng** (page 361).

BÚN ĐỎ A speciality of Buôn Ma Thuột, *bún đỏ* means red noodles, in reference to the crimson-coloured broth. The recipe for this dish seems to be flexible, as

sunny) but the gusts cut like sharpened ice. In the warmer, rainy season (May–October), it rarely rains for days on end but there is no escape from the mud. **Măng Đen** is almost always refreshingly cool, though it sits engulfed by cloud and drizzle for much of the rainy season, while Gia Lai is the wettest Central Highland province, making **Pleiku** the region's grimiest city in those months. Đắk Lắk also gets very muddy in the warm rainy season, though **Buôn Ma Thuột** remains a neat and orderly regional capital despite the mess. Other good months to visit Đắk Lắk Province are July – durian season – and October, when the coffee beans are picked.

One of **Đà Lạt**'s (many) eyerolling monikers is 'the City of Eternal Spring', which gives the impression of cool, sunny and bright days throughout the year, with only a few brief showers to keep things fresh. This is not the case. Like the rest of the region, the start of the dry season tends to offer the best weather, while January and February can be very cold. It has the same rainy season as elsewhere. But there is so much to do in Đà Lạt that it is enjoyable to visit at any time of year, as long as you have the right clothes. This is the highest city in the Central Highlands, so it's also the coldest. Whatever the temperature in the rest of Southern Vietnam, here you will need at least one additional layer. Due to its visitor appeal, the only time to avoid Đà Lạt would be during long local-holiday weekends.

long as it produces a hearty soup. Blood cake, crispy pork fat, deep-fried tofu and a meagre heap of greens usually tops the noodles. Try it at **Bún Đỏ, Riêu Hồng** (page 361).

BÁNH CĂN Cup-shaped fried rice batter topped with a quail's egg and served with a herby broth. A popular breakfast treat served on the streets of Đà Lạt. Try it at **Bánh Căn Cây Bơ** (page 370).

BÁNH MÌ XÍU MẠI Đà Lạt's preferred way to eat baguettes is dipped in a clear soup with a few meatballs. Make sure you spice the soup with chilli oil before you dip. Try it at **Bánh Mì Xíu Mại Bé Linh** (page 371).

BÁNH TRÁNG NƯỚNG Also known as Đà Lạt pizza and more of a snack than a meal: a crispy rice flour cracker is topped with an undefined array of toppings, from sausage to tinned tuna, and covered in mayonnaise, ketchup and chilli sauce. Popular with teenagers and eaten in the evening. Find it along **Nguyễn Văn Trỗi Street**.

MÌ QUẢNG *Mì Quảng* began in Quảng Nam, but many immigrants arrived here from the province over the decades and recreated their homeland speciality noodle dish. Some might tell you that Đà Lạt serves the best *mì Quảng* in all of Vietnam. Thick yellow noodles are topped with shrimp, pork, fish, beef and greens. Try it at **Ms Xi Noodle Shop** (page 371).

PHỞ KHÔ GIA LAI A delicious, deconstructed *phở* variation is found in Gia Lai Province. The *phở* noodles, which are thinner and spongier than those from the north, are served separately from the broth, the beansprouts and the greens so you can construct your own bowl. Try it at **Phở Khô Hồng** in Pleiku (page 357) and **Phở Khô Hai Tô** in Buôn Ma Thuột (page 361).

KON TUM

Bordered on the west by Laos and Cambodia, Kon Tum Province is in the extreme north of the Central Highlands. More than 50% of the province's half a million people are not Kinh (page 189), and belong chiefly to the Bahnar (page 354), Jarai (page 355) and Sedang (page 358) groups. The province is also home to the smallest ethnolinguistic group in Vietnam, the Brau, with only a few hundred members. The Bahnar live in villages surrounding the provincial capital, **Kon Tum**. The Jarai are further from the city, and the Sedang further still. The small city of Kon Tum is predominantly Kinh, who moved here decades ago to set up rubber, tea, sugarcane, coffee, mulberry, peanut and cinnamon farms. The Kinh still dominate business today, owning and running most of Kon Tum's hotels and restaurants. Northwest of Kon Tum city, close to the border with Quảng Ngãi Province and at 1,200m above sea level, is **Măng Đen**, a burgeoning mountain retreat that receives few international visitors. The province covers an area of 9,614km^2.

Situated on the Đăk Bla River, the interesting frontier town of Kon Tum has a population of around 170,000. Many are Bahnar, and in the Bahnar language, Kon means settlement and Tum means lake or pond. Dotted throughout the city are legacies left by the French, who invaded Kon Tum in the 19th century. Here they built a prison to house revolutionaries and anyone who resisted their cause. Many were used as slave labour to construct one of the main roads linking Kon Tum with other parts of the Central Highlands. Still standing are various ecclesiastical heritage structures, like the iconic wooden church with its stained-glass windows, golden arches and the statue of Christ that looks down from above the entrance porch. In the garden is a statue in memory of missionaries who came here, first in 1651 and then in 1835. Slow-paced, low-rise and not entirely flattened during the American War years like Pleiku to the south, Kon Tum is undoubtedly appealing, and the atmosphere of the place is reminiscent of a small provincial city in Laos or northern Cambodia. Added to the mix are artful cafés and some local speciality foods.

GETTING THERE AND AROUND There are no long-distance **trains** in the Central Highlands. The bus station, Bến Xe Kon Tum (281 Phan Đình Phùng), is 3km northwest of the central market, but some bus companies will pick up/drop off closer to the centre. Several buses daily connect Kon Tum with Đà Nẵng (7hrs; most are overnight), the closest big city, and Quảng Ngãi (5hrs), the closest coastal city and train station. Several buses daily also connect Kon Tum with the other Central Highland cities further south, including Pleiku (1hr), Buôn Ma Thuột (5hrs), and Đà Lạt (12hrs). Pleiku is also close enough that you might consider going by private car, which you can book through your accommodation.

There is no airport in Kon Tum, so the province is served by **Pleiku Airport** (3 17/3 St; **w** pleikuairport.vn) in Gia Lai Province, 44km south of the city. This domestic airport is connected with Hanoi and Hồ Chí Minh City.

Central Kon Tum is small, and it's possible to explore the churches, seminary and museum **by foot**. Bear in mind that at the time of research there were very few **Grab** drivers in town, though the number is likely to increase over time. For the Bahnar and Jarai villages, you'll need to rent a motorbike, private car or join a tour. To travel to Măng Đen, rent a motorbike and head up the mountain pass along QL24 or take a **local bus** at 482 Nguyễn Huệ Street (depart every 1–2hrs). Buses heading for Quảng Ngãi also pass through this mountain retreat.

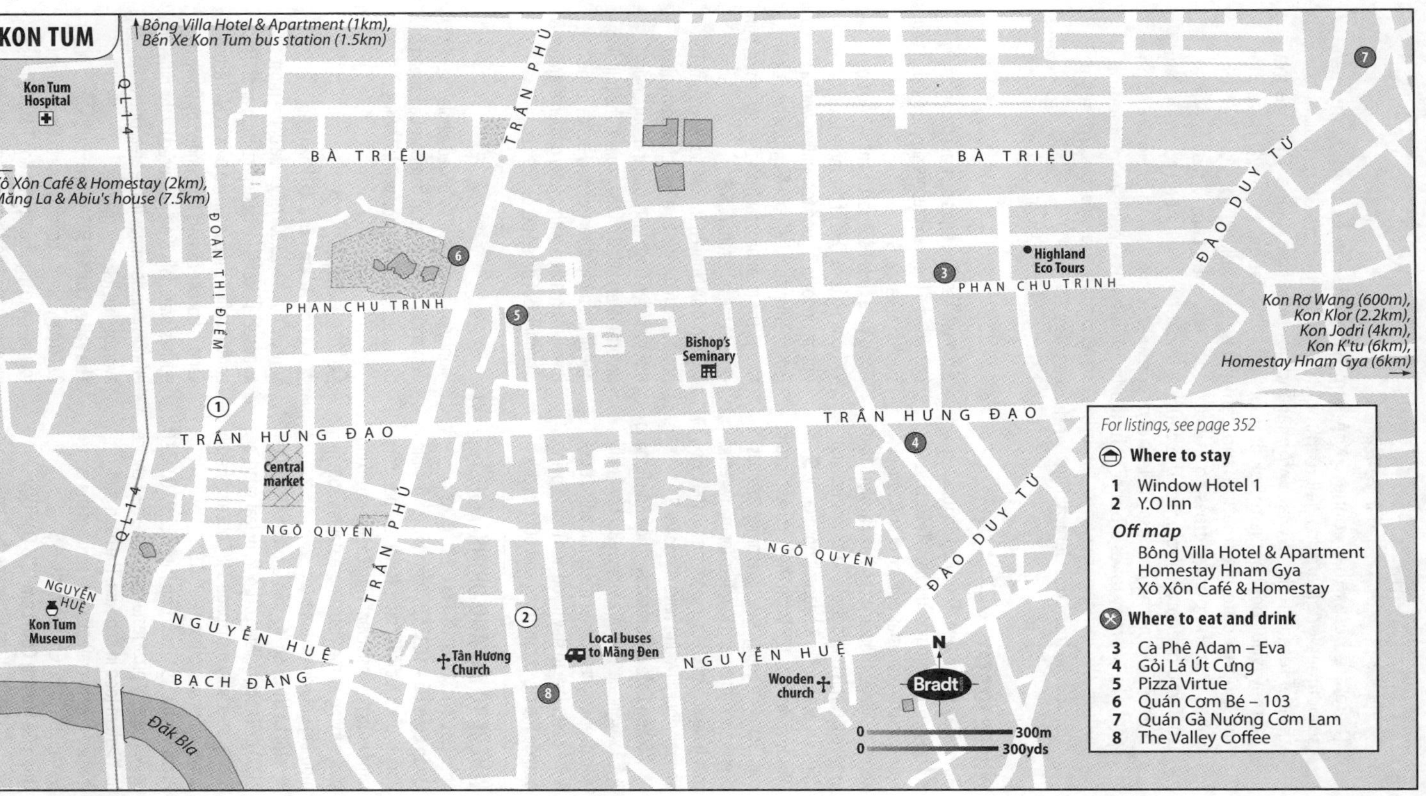
KON TUM
Bông Villa Hotel & Apartment (1km), Bến Xe Kon Tum bus station (1.5km)
Xô Xôn Café & Homestay (2km), Măng La & Abiu's house (7.5km)
Kon Rơ Wang (600m), Kon Klor (2.2km), Kon Jodri (4km), Kon K'tu (6km), Homestay Hnam Gya (6km)
Kon Tum Hospital
Kon Tum Museum
QL14
BÀ TRIỆU
TRẦN PHÚ
ĐOÀN THỊ ĐIỂM
PHAN CHU TRINH
TRẦN HƯNG ĐẠO
NGÔ QUYỀN
NGUYỄN HUỆ
BẠCH ĐẰNG
ĐÀO DUY TỪ
Đăk Bla
Central market
Bishop's Seminary
Highland Eco Tours
Tân Hương Church
Wooden church
Local buses to Măng Đen
N
Bradt
0 300m
0 300yds
For listings, see page 352
Where to stay
1 Window Hotel 1
2 Y.O Inn
Off map
Bông Villa Hotel & Apartment
Homestay Hnam Gya
Xô Xôn Café & Homestay
Where to eat and drink
3 Cà Phê Adam – Eva
4 Gỏi Lá Út Cưng
5 Pizza Virtue
6 Quán Cơm Bé – 103
7 Quán Gà Nướng Cơm Lam
8 The Valley Coffee

GETTING TO LAOS FROM KON TUM

There are buses that connect Kon Tum with Pakse in Laos (though they sometimes originate in Pleiku) through Bờ Y border crossing, but at the time of research these were informal and not bookable online. To make the journey, your best bet is to ask at your accommodation, as they'll have the most up-to-date information and can make the booking for you. Keep in mind that the border crossing at Bờ Y does not issue Laos visas on arrival, so if you need a visa to enter the country (most do) you'll need to arrange it beforehand at the embassy in Hanoi or consulates in Đà Nẵng or Hồ Chí Minh City. The journey takes around 12 hours, including time spent at immigration, where the officers may ask for bribes to expedite the process. To get to Cambodia from the Central Highlands, see page 357.

WHERE TO STAY *Map, page 351*

Homestay Hnam Gya Thôn Kon KơTu; f homestayhnamgya.dulichKonKoTu. Lovely little genuine homestay outside of Kon Tum in Kon K'tu village, though it can be difficult to book in advance. This is village life, so expect barking dogs, crowing cocks & heartfelt hospitality. **$**

Window Hotel 1 189 Đoàn Thị Điểm; w booking.com. Standard good-value hotel group that has been knocking around Kon Tum for many years; they have at least 2 other properties in the city. Ironically, not all rooms have windows. **$**

✷ **Xô Xôn Café & Homestay** Thôn Kon Rơbang 1; f xoxoncafe. Run by a French-Bahnar family with deep connections in the community, this is the best place to stay if you don't mind being outside the city centre (they rent out bicycles & motorbikes). The tours here are thoughtfully organised & they can prepare simple meals if you book in advance. **$**

Bông Villa Hotel & Apartment 41 Âu Cơ; w booking.com. One of the more luxurious options in town & good for families, with a (cramped) swimming pool & crisp, white, clean rooms. The location is far from the city centre, but close to the bus station. **$$**

Y.O Inn 16A Nguyễn Trãi; w booking.com. This hotel used to be run by a French organisation that provided hospitality training, but Covid unfortunately killed off the project. The building, one of the more attractive new builds in the city, is well maintained, with a leafy garden entrance & charming but dated décor. **$$**

WHERE TO EAT AND DRINK *Map, page 351*

Restaurants and street food

Quán Cơm Bé - 103 526 Trần Phú; ⌚ flexible during lunch & dinner time. Reliable & popular family-run rice restaurant with English-speaking staff, serving all the Vietnamese staples from mid-morning until dinnertime. **$**

✷ **Gỏi Lá Út Cưng** 45 Trần Cao Vân; ⌚ 09.00–21.00 daily. Specialising in *gỏi lá*, or leaf salad, a Bahnar speciality dish (page 348), but also freshly grilled chicken & other meat. **$$**

Pizza Virtue 191 Phan Chu Trinh; ⌚ 07.00–22.00 daily. This new pizza restaurant is the best choice for Western food in Kon Tum. The head chef learned how to craft pizzas in some of the best restaurants in Hồ Chí Minh City. **$$**

Quán Gà Nướng Cơm Lam 206 Đào Duy Từ; ⌚ 08.00–21.30 daily. Serves the Central Highland's favourite dish: grilled whole chicken with sticky rice cooked in bamboo. Call ahead & pre-order to cut down on waiting times. **$$**

Coffee houses

✷ **Cà Phê Adam - Eva** 80 Phan Chu Trinh; ⌚ 09.00–23.00 daily. One of the most atmospheric cafés in the Central Highlands. This garden coffee shop is owned by a local artist, with various bucolic corners surrounded by flowering bushes, waterfalls & art produced by the different ethnolinguistic groups in the area. Drinks are average, but it hardly matters.

The Valley Coffee 505 Nguyễn Huệ; f; ⌚ 06.30–22.00 daily. Serene coffee house in the centre of town serving high-quality (for Kon Tum) coffees & juices in, & underneath, a new house on stilts.

OTHER PRACTICALITIES Xô Xôn Café & Homestay (see opposite) runs highly recommended in-depth **tours** with local guides to explore Bahnar and Jarai villages in the province. Highlands Eco Tours (41 Hồ Tùng Mậu; w vietnamhighlands.net) can also arrange tours of the area, including multi-day hikes. There is no useful tourist information office in Kon Tum, but the provincial museum is a good place to start, and if you happen upon an English-speaking member of staff then you can put questions to them. **Kon Tum Hospital** (224 Bà Triệu) is central.

WHAT TO SEE AND DO

Kon Tum Museum (Nguyễn Huệ; ⌚ 07.30–11.00 & 13.00–16.30 Tue–Sun; 20,000VND/free adult/child) The focus here is on Kon Tum Province's ethnic diversity. English signage on the first floor is generally poor, but there are photos of festivals and other cultural practices from ethnolinguistic groups that you're unlikely to come across, like the Ro Mam and Brau. The quote from Hồ Chí Minh upstairs, which reads: 'Kinh or Tho, Muong or Man, Gia Rai or E De, Xe Dang or Ba Na, all are descendants of Vietnam, all are brothers and sisters. We are happy together, we suffer together, we aid one another...' is telling, as some ethnolinguistic minority communities sided with the French and Americans during the war years, seeing the Kinh majority as their true colonisers. The exhibit upstairs, which covers apparel, architecture and a display of gongs, is labelled in English. About 500m west of Kon Tum Museum, along the river, are the remains of a colonial prison, now serving as a memorial.

✷ **Wooden Church** (Nhà Thờ Gỗ; Nguyễn Huệ; ⌚ 07.00–17.00 daily) Built by the French with Bahnar labour in 1913, the fine Wooden Church remains largely unaltered, with the original wooden frame and wooden doors carefully cared for over the decades. In the grounds stands a statue of Stephen Theodore Cuenot, the first Roman Catholic bishop of East Cochinchina diocese. The French missionary endeavoured to convert the highland groups to Christianity, a mission that succeeded, as many Bahnar still identify as Christian today. He was arrested on the orders of Emperor Tự Đức, who harboured mistrust of foreign missionaries, and died in Bình Định prison on 14 November 1861, a day before the beheading instructions arrived. He was beatified Saint Étienne-Théodore Cuenot in 1909.

Tân Hương Church (92 Nguyễn Huệ; ⌚ all day daily) At first glance, this cream cake of a church appears similar to other centenarian Vietnamese churches, but the stilt foundation (crouch down and look under one of the little arches) and the depiction of St George and the dragon are highly unusual. The glass in the windows is all old, as the rippling indicates, although one of the two stained-glass windows over the altar has required a little patching up. The roof is a modern replacement, but the original style of fish-scale tiling can still be seen in the tower. The interior of the church is exquisite, with dark wooden columns and a fine vaulted ceiling made of wattle and daub. The altar is a new but rather fine addition, made of a jackfruit tree, as is the lectern. The original building was erected in 1853 and then rebuilt in 1860 following a fire. The current church dates from 1906.

Bishop's Seminary (146 Trần Hưng Đạo; ⌚ 07.30–11.00 & 14.00–17.00 Wed–Mon; w giaophankontum.com) The architecturally remarkable and prominent building is set in lovely gardens, with pink and white frangipani trees. The seminary was founded by French missionary Martial Jannin Phương and completed in 1935, and it skilfully blends architectural styles, with a grand imperial staircase leading to the reception room. There was once an upstairs exhibition room, but in recent years it has been closed to the public.

Around Kon Tum

✷ ***Bahnar villages*** There are scores of Bahnar villages around Kon Tum that are best reached by motorbike. The villages largely feature wattle and daub houses, mostly on stilts with outdoor porches, but central to the village is the *nhà rông* communal house, a towering structure usually with a thatched roof and accessed by ladders made from a single tree trunk. In the evening the elderly folk of the village might go for communal prayers while the young people gather at the foot of their longhouses for a sunset chat or play volleyball, the unofficial sport of the Central Highlands. Most families have a few pigs, dogs and chickens that roam loose in the villages when they're not tucked away beneath the houses. Considering the tiny spaces in which many Vietnamese city dwellers live, some houses are positively palatial. There is a large living room in the centre, a kitchen (with no chimney) at one end and bedroom at the other.

East of Kon Tum and on the outskirts of town, **Kon Rơ Wang** has a relatively small and pretty *nhà rông* that is dwarfed by the adjacent banyan tree. Strike east on Bắc Kạn Street, passing the much larger *nhà rông* in **Kon Klor** that overlooks the river. Cross the suspension bridge nearby and continue east to **Kon Jodri** (or **Kon K'ri**), another Bahnar community with a particularly photogenic *nhà rông* dominating the hamlet on a small hill. Nearby **Kon K'tu**, near the river, is especially attractive, but the village's traditional way of life is under threat from tourism development, evidenced by the large hotel complex on the left before you arrive at the village. Another slender *nhà rông* sits in a village square bustling with activity in the late afternoon. From the square, a small lane leads to the village's squat wooden church, while another leads to **Homestay Hnam Gya** (page 352), an excellent option if you'd like to stay overnight in a village.

West of Kon Tum, other Bahnar villages are worth exploring. **Măng La** has an extraordinary peach and cream-coloured concrete church that, from the front,

THE BAHNAR

The Bahnar are a Mon–Khmer-speaking group concentrated in the Central Highland provinces of Gia Lai–Kon Tum, numbering about 300,000. Locally powerful from the 15th to 18th centuries, their influence was eroded by neighbouring groups during the 19th century (see the Sedang, page 358). Like the Ede (page 362), Roman Catholic missionaries influenced the Bahnar greatly and they came to identify closely with the French. Many converted to Roman Catholicism, but Christianity is usually an adjunct to Bahnar Animism. Bahnar houses are built on stilts and, in each village, there is a communal house, or *nhà rông*, which is the focus of social life. Bahnar settlements are instantly recognisable by the tall, thatched roofs of these *nhà rông*. The height of the roof is meant to indicate the significance of the building and the financial standing of the village. It is a focal point of the village for meetings of the elders, weddings and other communal events. There is an imposing and well-maintained Bahnar *nhà rông* in the garden of the Vietnam Museum of Ethnology in Hanoi. The 'Kon' in Kon Tum is the Bahnar word for settlement, so if you see a village that starts with the word then there's a good chance that it had Bahnar beginnings.

THE JARAI

Primarily living in Gia Lai and Kon Tum provinces (especially near Pleiku) and numbering half a million, the Jarai are the largest group in the Central Highlands, with smaller numbers in Cambodia. They are settled cultivators and live in simple, thatched houses made from wood and bamboo. Over the centuries, Jarai architecture has begun to look increasingly Bahnar (see opposite), with symmetrical houses with a front porch and high-roofed *nhà rông* communal houses. The Jarai are Animist and recognise the spiritual dimension of nature, but many communities have also accepted Christianity to a degree. This ethnolinguistic group is notable for their complex funeral process. Like with the Kinh in Huế, Jarai cemeteries resemble villages for the dead, with elaborate tombs. But unlike the Kinh, Jarai tombs are guarded by wooden statues, often carved from new wood, that form a protective fence around the burial site. The dead and their personal possessions are placed within the tomb as a final send-off to the afterlife. Traditionally there are gong performances and ceremonial dances that might last for days, and jars of rice wine and plates of food are shared among participants. These days, tombs are less embellished and the ceremonies more informal, but the cemetery remains an important component in Jarai villages. There is a model of a traditional Jarai tomb in the garden of the Vietnam Museum of Ethnology in Hanoi. The 'Plei' in Pleiku is Jarai for settlement, so if you see a village that starts with 'Plei' or 'Pley' then it's probably Jarai.

presents as a traditional *nhà rông* but stretches back to form the shape of a cross. The façade features an image of the last supper beneath a huge white cross and images of daily Bahnar life. Further west is the house of **Abiu** (xã Ngọk Bay; ☎0333 929240, although it may not work), a talented Bahnar musician and local celebrity who can sing in Bahnar, Jarai, Vietnamese, English and French. The setup isn't designed for drop-in guests, but try your luck when exploring the area. He has very basic accommodation and the family can prepare meals in the shaded garden, but you need to book in advance.

Northeast of Kon Tum, on the QL24 on the way to Măng Đen, are several more Bahnar villages with some fabulous architecture. There is a bold blue church in *nhà rông* style with Bahnar geometric patterns in **Kon Xom Luh**, 17km from the centre of town. Further on by 20km, closer to Măng Đen than Kon Tum, is the attractive village of Kon Du, with one of the widest communal houses in the province.

Jarai villages The Jarai villages are further afield and are worth visiting for their cemeteries (see above). **Ia Chim** is about 10km southwest of Kon Tum, and the cemetery can be found close to the central market (Chợ Ia Chim) across from the sports pitch. **Plei Weh**, even further west, also has a cemetery but finding it is tricky. People here are unaccustomed to visitors, but they can be extremely friendly. If you show them a photo of a Jarai cemetery then they'll likely take you to visit and try to explain to you (in Jarai or Vietnamese) what you're looking at.

Măng Đen Affectionately referred to as 'Little Đà Lạt', Măng Đen is a small, foggy mountain retreat that enjoys cool temperatures throughout the year. It's on the bucket list of many domestic tourists, but few foreigners know of its existence. If you have your own transport, you can spend a few hours here if driving the road between Kon Tum and Quảng Ngãi, a dramatic and winding mountain pass that is a joy to ride on a motorbike (less so in a bus). There is also just enough to do here to warrant an overnight stop. The most popular activity is visiting **Pa Sỹ Waterfall** (Măng Cành Ward), a jungle-fringed stream cascading into a deep pool that, unfortunately, is no longer possible to swim in. The manicured gardens adorned with animal statues are probably unnecessary, but the waterfall is full for most of the year, and the atmosphere is often jovial, with large groups of domestic tourists taking creative photos on the bridge in front. **Thác Lô 3 Waterfall**, which is still very wild but easy to access down an overgrown concrete staircase, has a quiet rock pool where you can swim. **Hồ Đắk Bla Lake** is a pretty, popular spot that is, for better or worse, becoming increasingly Instagrammable, with flower-filled backdrops and lakeside cafés. The old mountain pass road (Đèo Măng Đen), reached via a pine forest (**Rừng Thông Măng Đen**), enjoys light traffic, panoramic views and a few makeshift cafés and camping spots. There are many places to stay in Măng Đen, most targeting the domestic market. Try **HeniSi Homestay** (62 Phạm Văn Đồng; f henisihomestaymangden; **$$**) – not a homestay, but small alpine villas – and enjoy grilled chicken with sticky rice, a Central Highlands speciality, at **Gà Nướng Cơm Lam Cô Sinh** (QL24, Đắk Long Ward; **$$**).

PLEIKU

Covering 15,495km², the volcanic province of Gia Lai – of which Pleiku is the capital – is the largest in the Central Highlands. It is as ethnically diverse as other provinces in the region, though the Jarai (page 355) and Bahnar (page 354), who live in villages in the countryside, and the Kinh (page 189), who live in towns and cities, are the most numerous ethnolinguistic communities. Although travelling through the province has been eased by extensive road improvements, it can be miserable in September and October, when there is frequent torrential rain. Locals might tell you, perhaps with a tiny trace of pride, that Gia Lai is the wettest province in the Central Highlands. In the highland forests there are vast reserves of bamboo and rattan, while in the valleys cereal crops compete for space with sesame, cassava, peanuts and mulberries. Tea, coffee and tobacco are also grown here.

During the American War, Pleiku was strategically important as an American military base and the headquarters of the South Vietnamese Army in the Central Highlands. As a sad consequence, the city was virtually wiped out and the town you see now consists of concrete-block buildings erected in the 1980s with cash donated by the Soviet Union, in and among more modern architectural creations. From a visitor's point of view, Pleiku, which is dusty in the dry season and soggy in the rainy season, is the runt of the litter of Central Highlands provincial capitals. But if you're here for a night then there are a few things to keep you occupied, while volcanoes and waterfalls pepper the encircling countryside.

GETTING THERE AND AROUND The **bus** station, Bến Xe Đức Long Gia Lai 43 Lý Nam Đế, is 4km southeast of the central market, but most bus companies will pick up/drop off closer to the centre. Several buses daily connect Kon Tum with Pleiku (1hr), and the city is close enough that you might consider going by private car. Several buses daily also connect Pleiku with Đà Nẵng (8hrs; most are overnight), Quy Nhơn (4hrs), Buôn Ma Thuột (4hrs) and Đà Lạt (11hrs).

The province is served by **Pleiku Airport** (17/3 St; w pleikuairport.vn), 6km north of town, which handles flights to/from Hanoi and Hồ Chí Minh City.

GETTING TO CAMBODIA FROM PLEIKU

There is technically an international border crossing with Cambodia near Pleiku at Lệ Thanh, but at the time of research there was no consistent bus service making the journey. Come prepared and ask at your accommodation in Kon Tum or Buôn Ma Thuột for up-to-date information before arriving in Pleiku, as hotels here see so few foreign visitors. As is usually the case with remote borders, you'll need to prearrange your Cambodian visa as they are not issued on arrival. Getting to Laos from the Central Highlands is a little more organised; see page 352.

Central Pleiku is **walkable** but you'll need to rent a **motorbike** to explore further afield. As there are so few tourists in Pleiku, you might struggle to rent a private car.

WHERE TO STAY AND EAT There are various standard hotels close to the Market Quarter, or head a little further out of town to **Pleiku Highlands Boutique Hotel** (157 Thống Nhất; **w** booking.com; **$$**). The local speciality is *phở khô*, which you can try at **Phở Khô Hồng** (22–24 Nguyễn Văn Trỗi; 05.00–14.00 daily; **$**). **Passata Bistro** (43 Võ Thị Sáu; f; 09.30–14.00 & 16.00–21.30 daily; **$$**) does decent Western food. Outside the centre, **Tiệm Café Ngày Bình Yên** (109 Tô Vĩnh Diện; 06.30–22.00 daily) is a rustic viewpoint café that overlooks the quiet airport runway and a patchwork of surrounding rice terraces.

OTHER PRACTICALITIES There is no useful tourist information office in Pleiku. **Gia Lai Hospital** (132 Tôn Thất Tùng) is east of the centre.

WHAT TO SEE AND DO

Market Quarter Though redeveloped in the early 2000s, Pleiku's Market Quarter feels decades older. The spire of the central building curves up like a Theravada Buddhist pagoda stupa, sheltering a tangle of market stalls that spill into the surrounding streets.

Museum Quarter There are two museums of note in Pleiku if you have time to kill: the **Gia Lai Museum** (21 Trần Hưng Đạo; **w** baotangtinh.gialai.gov.vn; 08.00–11.00 & 13.30–16.30 Tue–Sun; 10,000VND/free adult/child) and the **Hồ Chí Minh Museum of Gia Lai and Kon Tum** (6 Phan Đình Phùng; 07.00–17.00 Mon–Fri; 40,000VND for foreign visitors). Both are housed within the same park, which borders a noisy road, and neither had English signage at the time of research. Nevertheless, it's possible to glean some information about the natural history, ethnolinguistic make-up and revolutionary efforts of the province through models and photography in the Gia Lai Museum. The most compelling exhibit is the set of miniature houses in the garden, one for each major ethnolinguistic group in the province. The Hồ Chí Minh Museum is also lacklustre, though there are some interesting photos of Uncle Hồ, including one of him playing volleyball, a popular pastime in Gia Lai villages.

Minh Thành Pagoda (348 Nguyễn Viết Xuân; 07.00–17.00 daily) This ever-expanding, somewhat clumsily arranged modern Northeast Asian-style pagoda has concrete gardens, fishponds, bonsai trees and a host of Buddha statues. The pagoda was established in the 1960s and has swelled over the decades.

THE SEDANG

Concentrated in Gia Lai and Kon Tum provinces and numbering about 127,000, the Sedang traditionally lived in extended family longhouses like the Ede (page 362), though society is patriarchal. Once a war-like people, the Sedang and the Bahnar were fierce rivals throughout much of the 19th century. Kidnapping people from neighbouring villages for sacrifice was commonplace, and there is documentation indicating that this practice was subsequently put to commercial use and formed the basis of a slave trade with Siam (Thailand). Sedang villages were once well defended, presumably for fear of reprisal, with thorn hedges supplemented with spears and stakes.

One curious episode in the history of the Sedang tells of their self-anointed king. French adventurer Marie-Charles David de Mayréna arrived in Indochina in 1863, serving in the French navy in Saigon. In 1888, amid Siam's territorial expansions in the Central Highlands region, de Mayréna convinced the Governor of Cochinchina to let him lead an expedition to negotiate with the Sedang and Jarai. Remarkably, instead of securing their submission to France, he persuaded the Sedang chiefs to establish the Kingdom of Sedang, with him as King Marie I. The kingdom had its own constitution, flag and capital. Human sacrifices were banned and freedom of religion was assured. Despite his grand ambitions, his attempts to gain French recognition failed, leading him to approach British authorities in Hong Kong in 1889. He created various royal regalia but ultimately returned to France and then Belgium to escape legal troubles. By 1890, de Mayréna's attempts to return to Indochina were thwarted by the French and Siamese authorities. He convinced a friend and colleague, de Villenoy d'Augis, to lie low in an uninhabited island in the Strait of Malacca. Later that year, both men were found dead; one poisoned and the other shot. De Mayréna has been referred to as the Kurtz of Vietnam, based on the literary and cinematic characters from Joseph Conrad's *Heart of Darkness* and Francis Ford Coppola's *Apocalypse Now*. In both stories – Coppola based his film on the book but set it in the context of the American War – Kurtz is a Westerner who proclaims himself leader in a remote jungle.

Around Pleiku Pleiku enables plenty of adventures for intrepid travellers with their own transport. Of the various inactive volcanoes that surround Pleiku, **Chư Đăng Ya**, 23km north of the city, offers the most picturesque views from its craterous peak. Walking up and down the volcano takes little more than an hour, but it's also possible to make the trip on a motorbike if the path isn't too muddy. Impressive waterfalls with few visitors (except for at weekends) include **Thác Lă G'rang** (Lă G'rang Ward), 30km west of Pleiku, **Thác Xung Khoeng** (Lă Me Ward), 39km southwest, and **Phú Cường Waterfall** (Dun Commune), 44km south. It's best to visit the waterfalls at the beginning of the dry season (November) and it's possible to see all three in one sweeping quarter circle on a day trip from the city.

BUÔN MA THUỘT

With an average altitude of around 500m, the highland province of Đắk Lắk covers an area of 13,062km^2, with Buôn Ma Thuột at its heart. The province has a population of more than 2 million and is ethnically diverse, with Jarai, Mnong, Ede, Bru-Van Kieu, Sedang, Khmer, Thai, Lao, Chu Ru, Muong, Hmong, Dao and

Bahnar communities. When you travel away from the main roads in Đắk Lắk you will see buffalo herds, pig farms and oxen grazing at the roadside. It was also once common to see large herds of elephants with their infants crossing the road, but today they live almost exclusively in protected or inaccessible areas. Elephants here used to be trapped in the wild by skilful Mnong hunters using huge ropes attached to their domesticated cousins, but the practice is now illegal (page 366).

The province contains one of the country's biggest tropical forests, which includes parts of **Yok Đôn National Park**, the most diverse habitat in the Central Highlands. Much of Đắk Lắk is relatively unexplored, especially its high mountains. Tributaries

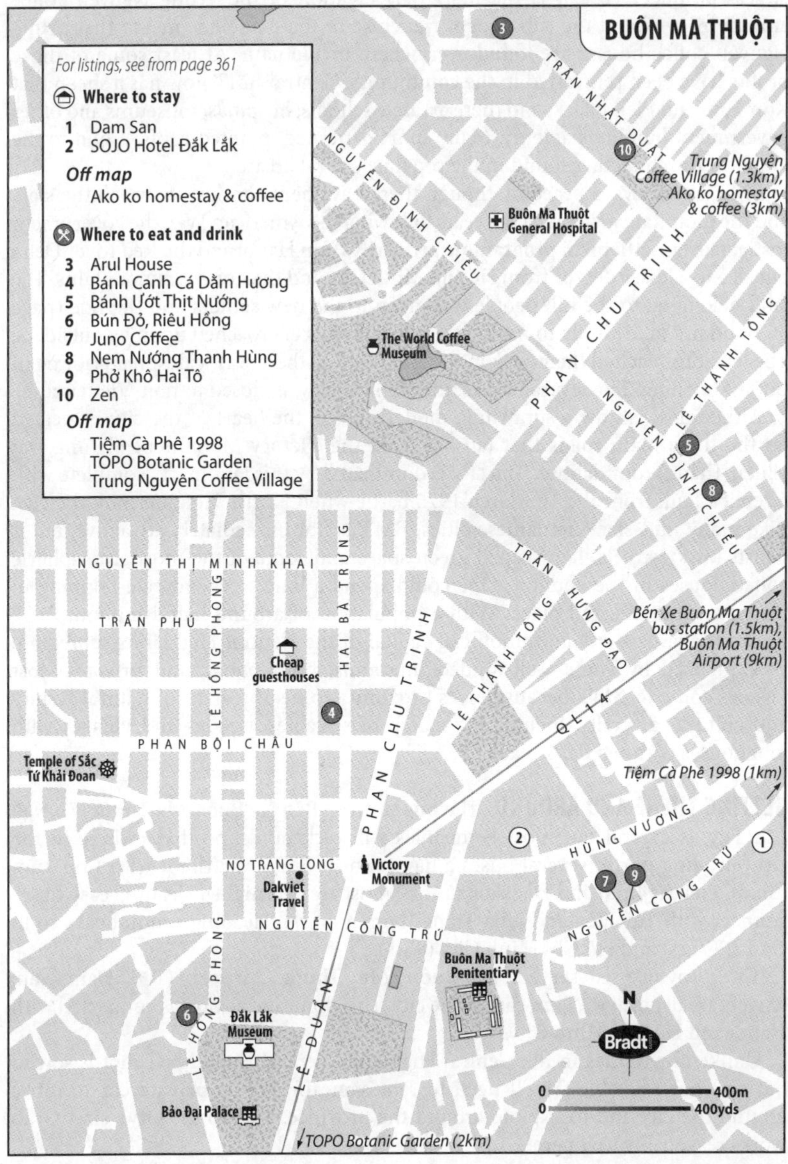

from Mount Chư Yang Sin (1,244m) form the 330km-long Srepok River, which flows northwest through Yok Đôn National Park and into the mighty Mekong in Stung Treng Province, Cambodia. This is just part of an intricate water-web. During the rainy season, between April and October, **Lắk Lake** and the province's various **waterfalls** are at their magnificent best.

Buôn Ma Thuột (or Buôn Mê Thuột or Ban Mê Thuột or simply BMT) is the administrative capital of the province and the coffee capital of Vietnam. It has surpassed its illustrious and renowned neighbour Đà Lạt to be the main centre for coffee production, propelling Vietnam into the position of the world's second largest producer (Brazil is the first). The creation of the Trung Nguyên coffee empire in 1997 and the subsequent franchise of the name has meant that Trung Nguyên coffee houses are found everywhere in Vietnam. At least some of those profits have been reinvested in the community. Central BMT now has a sheen that Kon Tum and Pleiku lack, and there are new schools, hospitals, museums and other government buildings aplenty. Many sport patterned, pointed roofs, a nod to the longhouse architecture found in the province's rural areas.

BMT nowadays is peaceful, though there have been tensions between the state and the mountain groups. In the years following the American War, the government instigated a resettlement programme primarily from Hanoi and the Red River Delta but also to a lesser degree from Hồ Chí Minh City and the northern mountains. The land belonging to the hill people was given to the new settlers and the Ede (page 362) did not take kindly to having their livelihoods encroached upon by outsiders. The tensions reached their peak in the 2000s, when there was widespread rioting in Buôn Ma Thuột. For several weeks, the whole area was closed to non-Vietnamese.

Although it is now a sprawling, modern place, the heart of the city is located on the three main roads that fan out from the Victory Monument (Tượng Đài Chiến Thắng) roundabout. The city is dominated by this landmark, complete with a replica tank from the 10 March 1975 battle when North Vietnam took the city. Like many mid-size Vietnamese cities, BMT is not immediately attractive, but it boasts bosky streets, landscaped green space and some of the most atmospheric coffee houses in the country. One could spend a long weekend café-hopping in this sprawling, relaxed place. With a population of around half a million, BMT is also the largest city and unofficial capital of the Central Highlands subregion, as evidenced by some well-funded museums, both public and private. Most visitors come to BMT because of its proximity to nearby areas of natural beauty and cultural diversity, including a clutch of sizeable cascades and villages with longhouses within a day's reach.

GETTING THERE AND AROUND The **bus station**, Bến Xe Buôn Ma Thuột (72 Ngô Gia Tự), is central but most companies will pick up/drop off elsewhere in the city. Heading north, several buses a day connect Buôn Ma Thuột with Kon Tum (5hrs), Pleiku (4hrs) and Đà Nẵng (13hrs; most are overnight). Heading east, buses connect with Tuy Hòa and Nha Trang (both 4–5hrs). Heading south, buses go to Đà Lạt (7hrs) and Hồ Chí Minh City (8hrs).

The province is served by **Buôn Ma Thuột Airport** (100 Đam San; w vietnamairport.vn), 9km east of the city. This domestic airport is connected with Hanoi and Hồ Chí Minh City.

Unlike other cities in the Central Highlands, central Buôn Ma Thuột is spread out and not walkable. You'll need to rent a **motorbike or private car** to move around the city and to explore around the province. Due to the city's size, **Grab** works reasonably well here.

WHERE TO STAY *Map, page 359*

There are dozens of cheap guesthouses (**$**) in the gridded neighbourhood west of Phan Chu Trinh Street, on and around Phan Bội Châu Street, though none comes especially recommended. The area is speckled with simple cafés and eateries, so it makes a good base from which to explore the city.

Ako ko homestay & coffee Hẻm 451/19 Y Moan Ênuôl; f dulianeban2008. Far from the centre but worth the extra effort, this experiential homestay is set in a well-maintained longhouse in the countryside. Accommodation is simple: a mattress on the floor underneath a mosquito net. But the Ede family running the homestay are passionate about their culture, & keen to share their music, food & customs with visitors. **$**

✷ **Dam San Hotel** 212 Nguyễn Công Trứ; **w** booking.com. Huge hotel with clean, quiet, good-value but worn-out rooms overlooking a swimming pool & tennis court. The hotel leans into the Ede design motif rather successfully. **$$**

SOJO Hotel Đắk Lắk 15 Hùng Vương; **w** sojohotels.com. Sterile, modern hotel for those who value cleanliness, convenience & comfort over charm, but bear in mind that rooms are small. **$$**

WHERE TO EAT AND DRINK *Map, page 359*

Drinking coffee in the eclectic collection of cafés in BMT is a highlight of a visit to the city, as it should be in Vietnam's capital of coffee. The Western coffee tends to be just OK but the Vietnamese coffee is almost always excellent.

Restaurants and street food

Bánh Canh Cá Dằm Hương 63 Hai Bà Trưng; 🕘 noon–21.00 daily. A noodle soup served with fish in a slightly sour broth. Very popular with locals & you might need to share a table. **$**

Bánh Ướt Thịt Nướng 90A Lê Thánh Tông; 🕘 14.30–22.00 daily. A little-known BMT speciality is *bánh ướt*, or wet rice cakes. Rice paper arrives wet, spread on plastic disks & stacked high on a special rack. Fill it with grilled pork, pickles & greens. **$**

Bún Đỏ, Riêu Hồng 31–33 Lê Hồng Phong. Serving 'red noodles', a BMT speciality dish & popular as a late-afternoon snack. This is a noodle soup with a rouge-tinted broth topped with various add-ons. Hồng is one of several street kitchens in the area. **$**

Nem Nướng Thanh Hùng 12B Nguyễn Đình Chiểu; 🕘 08.00–22.00 daily. *Nem nướng*, or grilled pork patties wrapped in rice paper & stuffed with greens & pickles, is associated with the adjacent Southern Central Coast subregion, but the dish has made its way across the country, including here. **$**

Phở Khô Hai Tô 99 Nguyễn Công Trứ; 🕘 05.30–10.00 daily. A popular b/fast eatery that serves Gia Lai Province's most well-known dish, *phở khô*. The broth is rich, the beef is tender & you can choose between noodle types. **$**

✷ **Arul House** 17–19 Trần Nhật Duật; 🕘 08.00–22.00 daily. Arul House is masterfully built around a large longhouse in an Ede village that has been absorbed by BMT. The food is very well prepared, & there are a few Central Highlands speciality dishes on the menu, too. The dining room looks over a garden where you can relax before or after the meal. **$$**

Coffee houses

Juno Coffee 97 Nguyễn Công Trứ; 🕘 06.00–22.00 daily. Spruced-up old-school café that has somehow modernised in a ramshackle kind of way but still appeals to middle-aged, suit-wearing men. The traditional Vietnamese coffee is particularly good here.

Tiệm Cà Phê 1998 98 Ama Sa; 🕘 07.00–22.00 daily. A neat garden with views that will make you think you're in the middle of the countryside, despite being on the edge of the city. Clientele is young & phone obsessed.

✷ **TOPO Botanic Garden** Hẻm 347 Lê Duẩn; 🕘 06.30–22.00 daily. Labyrinthine garden coffee shop with tables & chairs scattered around ponds & under trees. An unexpected oasis south of the city centre.

Trung Nguyên Coffee Village 163 Lý Thái Tổ; **w** trungnguyenlegend.com; 🕘 07.00–22.00 daily. Vast coffee hamlet with various places to sit & absorb the luxury surroundings, including an ancient-style wooden house & miniature waterfall. This is the flagship coffee shop of Trung Nguyên, Vietnam's main coffee producer. They advertise coffee plantation tours, but this wasn't possible at the time of research.

Zen 103 Trần Nhật Duật; f ZenCoffee103; ⌚ 06.00–23.00 daily. Trendy & rustic street coffee shop that is effortlessly hip, with comfortable wooden chairs & an unkempt garden.

OTHER PRACTICALITIES There is no useful tourist information office in Buôn Ma Thuột, but you can find some free information from the travel desk at Dam San Hotel (page 361). They also offer a wide range of **tours**, but the quality is not consistent and the prices tend to be high. You'll have better luck at **Dakviet Travel** (32 Nơ Trang Long; w dakviettravel.vn), which specialises in elephant-riding tours (never recommended) but they can also arrange tours to villages, Lắk Lake and Yok Đôn National Park. You can ask about coffee plantation tours at the Trung Nguyên Coffee Village (page 361). **Buôn Ma Thuột General Hospital** (62 Nguyễn Đình Chiểu) is 2km north of the city centre.

WHAT TO SEE AND DO

✷ **Bảo Đại Palace** (2 Y Ngông; ⌚ 08.00–17.00 daily; 10,000VND/free adult/child) Bảo Đại, Vietnam's last king, was enamoured with the Central Highlands, as evidenced by more than a handful of palaces across the subregion. This is perhaps the most architecturally interesting, as it draws so heavily from the longhouse architecture of the province. Nestled within a site of 6.5km^2 of land with several trees over 100 years old, the palace stands nearly 2m above ground level. Like Bảo Đại's other palaces, the king acquired it rather than commissioned it. It was built in 1905 to house the Maison Lefévre Restaurant, but from 1914 to 1949 it served various administrative functions. From 1949 to 1954, Bảo Đại, then Head of State of South Vietnam, used this place as his retreat and hunting lodge during the rainy season. Following reunification in 1975, the palace became the first headquarters of the Đắk Lắk Provincial Party Committee. It became a museum in 1999. Signage is in Vietnamese, English, French and, interestingly, Ede.

THE EDE

Primarily concentrated in the Central Highlands province of Đắk Lắk and numbering more than 300,000, the Ede, like the Bahnar (page 354), came into early contact with the French and were keen adopters of Christianity. Today they might be considered polytheist: they recognise the Animist spirits of rice, soil, fire, water and so on, but identify as Christian and regularly attend mass. The Ede are notable for their matriarchal way of life, though this may be eroding as they gradually assimilate with the Kinh. The commune falls under the authority of an elderly, respected woman who is responsible for communal property, especially the gongs and jars that feature in important festivals. Traditionally, after the girl's family selects a husband, he then comes to live with her in a longhouse on stilts that accommodates the matrilineal extended family all under one roof. The rectangular architecture lends itself to extension; if there's no space in the existing structure, the family constructs another compartment in the house, lengthening the longhouse. There is a model of a traditional Ede house in the garden of the Vietnam Museum of Ethnology in Hanoi. In traditional families, wealth and property are inherited solely by daughters.

LEGEND HAS IT: THE SONG OF ĐĂM SĂN

By Biên Nguyễn, a Hanoi-based travel writer, photographer and enthusiast for the Central Highlands.

Of the various heroes from epic stories told by the peoples of the Central Highlands, no one is more well known than Đăm Săn. His story is recounted in 'The Song of Đăm Săn' (or '*Klei khan y Đăm Săn*' in Ede and '*Trường ca Đăm Săn*' in Vietnamese), an epic Ede (see opposite) poem that reveals some of the beliefs and customs of the group, in particular their matrilineal traditions. Familiar mythological themes of preordained destiny, heroic hubris and divine rebirth are explored throughout the epic, often with what today's audience might consider to be progressive gender role reversals.

The poem tells the story of a promising but rebellious Đăm Săn, whose destiny was to marry two nymph-like sisters: Hơ Nhị and Hơ Bhị. When Đăm Săn tried to resist, the gods intervened, forcing him to submit to their will, but he could never accept the mild misery of spousal servitude. When Đăm Săn arrived at his wives' house, he refused to tend to the household duties and, in a tantrum, cut down the sacred tree that had birthed Hơ Nhị and Hơ Bhị, an act that killed them instantly. Fearful of a rootless existence – and realising that he had loved his wives all along – Đăm Săn begged the gods to return the sisters to him. Still seeing heroic promise in this prodigious but headstrong young man, they obliged.

The gods, in all their wisdom, were right. Đăm Săn became a heroic chieftain and decent husband, at least for a time. He tamed untameable elephants, farmed unfarmable land and caught uncatchable fish. In one of the most heroic acts of his early years, Đăm Săn rescued his kidnapped wives from two powerful and villainous chieftains, enhancing his fame in the heavens.

Celebrity only fed Đăm Săn's ego and arrogance – and rekindled his wandering eye. The hero decided to embark on an unthinkable quest: to journey to the divine realm and make the Sun Goddess (often a masculine deity in other cultures) his third wife. Armed with magic weapons and undeterred by advice from the elders, Đăm Săn eventually found the goddess, who lived in an infinitely long golden longhouse. She rejected him immediately, refusing to return to earth. As the deity of a matrilineal culture, the Sun Goddess, of course, must remain in her familial home. Besides, if she descended to earth, the forests would burn, the land would split and the seas would evaporate. Life on earth would cease to exist.

Rebuffed, Đăm Săn attempted the perilous journey back to earth, but he ignored the advice of the Sun Goddess and drowned in a swamp along the way. Here his story becomes even more curious. After his death, Đăm Săn's soul transformed into a fly, soared into his sister's mouth and impregnated her. Eventually, Đăm Săn's sister gave birth to a boy, who continued his uncle's legacy.

✷ **Đắk Lắk Museum** (2 Y Ngông; **w** daklakmuseum.vn; ⌚ 08.00–16.00 Tue–Sun; 30,000VND/free adult/child) North of the Bảo Đại Palace and within the same park, the Đắk Lắk Museum appears like a gigantic spaceship from a 1980s science fiction film. This is the biggest and best museum in the entire subregion, and you could spend hours exploring the various sections. At the time of research there was a ground-floor semi-permanent photography exhibition by French photographer Jean-Marie Duchange, who took engrossing photos of the Central Highlands and its people in the 1950s. There is a history wing, which is refreshingly concise, starting from Đắk Lắk's Neolithic period and culminating in the province's modern-day industrialisation. The most interesting wing is devoted to the ethnic diversity of the province; apparently there are over 49 ethnolinguistic groups in Đắk Lắk (ie: over 90% of all the officially recognised groups in all of Vietnam). This is likely because so many northerners – including from the ethnically diverse northern mountains – migrated here after 1975. A lot of detailed information on the traditional daily lives of the different groups, covering fishing, farming, music, textiles and pottery, is available. There is a particularly interesting section on the Mnong and how they used to capture wild elephants with sophisticated but brutal strategies and equipment (this practice is now banned). A final wing focused on biodiversity is less impressive.

The World Coffee Museum (Nguyễn Đình Chiểu; **w** baotangthegioicaphe.com; ⌚ 07.00–17.45 daily; 150,000VND/free adult/child) The privately owned and rather expensive World Coffee Museum is, unfortunately, very flashy but with little substance. The exhibits cover coffee culture from around the world and feel disjointed and incoherent, though you'll find nuggets of information. The building is a contemporary take on Ede longhouse architecture, was completed in 2018 and funded by the Trung Nguyên coffee empire.

Temple of Sắc Tứ Khải Đoan (117 Phan Bội Châu; ⌚ 06.00–19.00 daily) Established during the Nguyễn Dynasty under the patronage of Queen Mother Đoan Huy (Bảo Đại's mother), this pagoda combines traditional Vietnamese architecture with serene natural surroundings. The main hall houses statues of Buddha and other important Buddhist figures and is richly decorated with murals and woodwork. Adjacent to it stands a multi-tiered pagoda, symbolising spiritual ascent, and it is surrounded by gardens featuring bonsai trees and stone lanterns.

Buôn Ma Thuột Penitentiary (18 Tán Thuật; ⌚ 07.00–17.00 Mon–Fri; 20,000VND/free adult/child) Visiting this prison, which was built by the colonial administration in 1930–31, is probably an 'if time' activity as there is barely any information, even in Vietnamese, despite recent renovations. The signage that is there makes the point that Đắk Lắk was a remote and isolated place at the time, and imprisoning independence fighters here was a form of psychological torture that ripped them from their coastal communities. The same barbaric ideas motivated the construction of the better-known prison on Côn Đảo (page 438). The rooms are hauntingly bare, aside from a few models reflecting the torture endured by the inmates.

Around Buôn Ma Thuột The waterfalls can be seen in one long day trip, but for the other areas around BMT it's better to stay overnight.

Đray Sáp and Đray Nur waterfalls These waterfalls, 25km southwest from BMT and the primordial manifestations of eternal love (see opposite), are the most popular day trip. The waterfalls consist of several different cascades all next to each other, forming a 100m-wide cascade. They are particularly stunning late in the wet season and justify the moniker 'waterfall of smoke', although the falls are also impressive in the dry season. The falls may occasionally be closed as the paths are too treacherous to use, and swimming is no longer permitted at any time of year.

LEGEND HAS IT: THE STAR-CROSSED LOVERS

Long ago, in a village by the Srepok River, there lived a beautiful girl named H'Hương and a handsome young man named Y'Bi. They were deeply in love, but their families were sworn enemies and forbade their union, leading to a tragic separation. Determined to be together, H'Hương and Y'Bi decided to escape and find an isolated place where they could live in peace away from their warring families. One night, under the cover of darkness, they fled their village and ran towards the dense forests and rugged terrain surrounding the Srepok River.

As they reached the river's edge, a powerful storm hit the land, causing the Srepok to swell and rage. The heavens wept for the plight of these ill-fated lovers, who clung to each other as they clung to their lives. The gods, moved by their devotion, decided to intervene. They transformed H'Hương and Y'Bi into two waterfalls – Đray Sáp and Đray Nur – that would forever cascade side by side, never to be separated again.

You can enter the falls from either side of the river (**Đray Nur** in Đắk Lắk Province; **Đray Sáp** in Đắk Nông Province), but the Đắk Lắk side tends to be better managed. Nevertheless, trash remains an issue.

Lắk Lake The serene but heavily deforested Lắk Lake is about 50km southeast of Buôn Ma Thuột. In the winter months, early-morning mists hang above the calm waters and mingle with the columns of woodsmoke rising from the longhouses. The lake is an attraction in its own right, but makes for a more compelling visit because of the surrounding Mnong settlements (page 366). Lakeside villages like Buôn Lê, Buôn Jun and Buôn Liêng have been developed as attractions and feel rather commodified, but these are the villages that tour guides are familiar with and it's still possible to learn a little of the Mnong way of life. There are also a handful of homestays spread across these villages, though none is notable or consistent; it's best just to turn up and look for signs. For the independent traveller on a motorbike there are plenty of more remote villages to visit, as you move west from the lake on the DT687 road, but do not expect much in the way of restaurants and places to stay. Despite the tourist setup, the lakeside setting of Liên Sơn, the largest settlement on the south side of the water, is tranquil, especially in the late afternoon when you might catch men bringing back the fish of the day to the lakeshore, alongside giggling children, bathing buffaloes and snorting pigs. If it's clear, you can gaze at multi-coloured sunrises and sunsets. One of the most atmospheric accommodations in the Central Highlands – **Lak Tented Camp** (193 Nguyễn Tất Thành; **w** laktentedcamp.com; **$$$**) – is here, but it's on the other side of the lake and only accessible by boat. Book in advance and they'll come to pick you up. The camp can arrange hikes and village visits, and they have music performances on Saturday and Sunday. The restaurant offers a surprisingly large menu with plenty to choose from.

Yok Đôn National Park (Krông Na; **w** tour.yokdonnationalpark.vn; ⌚ 07.00–17.00 daily; 60,000VND/free adult/child) Situated close to the Cambodian border in a remote corner of the province, this national park is only just beginning to realise its tourism potential. Inaugurated in October 1991, Yok Đôn was Vietnam's largest national park, with an area of 1,155km^2, until 2015, when the boundaries

THE MNONG

The Mnong of Lắk Lake have been influenced by the Ede, with many living in longhouses, though traditionally they would have constructed straw and mud- or wood-thatched homes. The Mnong have long constructed dugout canoes, which are painstakingly hollowed out from tree trunks by axe and used to fish on Lắk Lake. But they are perhaps better known for their skills in hunting and taming elephants, which they would use to drag logs from the forest. The practice of catching wild elephants in Vietnam is now illegal, but there is an exhibit of the equipment once used in the Đắk Lắk Museum (page 363) in Buôn Ma Thuột. The Mnong number fewer than 100,000 and, like the Ede, are matriarchal. The 'Buôn' in Buôn Ma Thuột means 'settlement' in the Mnong language, so if you see a village that starts with the word then it's probably Mnong. The Mnong are also associated with buffalo sacrifice ceremonies, though these are fast disappearing.

of Phong Nha-Kẻ Bàng National Park (page 240) were extended. Covering predominantly flat terrain with an average elevation of just 100–150m, it has an annual rainfall of 1,500–1,600mm. The area includes three mountains: Yok Đôn (482m), Yok Da (472m) and Rơ Hêng (425m), which are covered in dense, green, semi-deciduous forest. Of the dozens of tree species, the Dipterocarpaceae family covers more than a third of the forest's total area. Among the plant species seen are *Shorea obtusa*, *Xylia xylocarpa*, *Dalbergia bariensis*, *Hopea odorata* and subtropical families of Indian origin such as camphor (*camphora*) and almond (*combretaceae*) species. Around 60 species of tall grasses grow in thin forest.

The grassy areas on the forest edges extend around the boundary zones where many ethnolinguistic groups live, including the Mnong, Ede, Jarai and Bahnar. Because they rely partly on their natural surroundings for their way of life, a certain amount of exploitation has been tolerated by the national park authorities, though regulations are getting stricter. Bamboo from the forests is still sometimes used to make floors and walls for the stilt houses that fringe the area. Orchids flourish on higher ground; particularly striking are sword orchids (*Cymbidium* species), buffalo ear orchids (*Dendrobium* species) and leopard skin orchids (*Renanthera* species).

There are 63 species of mammal, 17 of which are on the worldwide endangered list. Several highly protected zones have been set up to guard against poaching of endangered species such as banteng (*Bos javanicus*) and gaur (*Bos gaurus*), two types of wild cattle, and Asian elephant (*Elephas maximus*). Yok Đôn is also home to the rarely seen Asian tiger (*Panthera tigris*) and Indochinese leopard (*Panthera pardus delacouri*), and the more recently discovered golden jackal (*Canis aureus*). More common animal species include sambar deer (*Cervus unicolor*), wild boar (*Sus scrofa*), and wild buffalo (*Bubalus bubalis*). Deep in the primary forest you may see red flying squirrel (*Petaurista petaurista*), a red-shanked douc langur (*Pygathrix nemaeus*) and even hear, though are unlikely to see, one of the rarest gibbons in Asia: the black crested gibbon (*Hylobates concolor*).

At least 250 species of bird are found here. Since much of the forest is primary, it provides an ideal habitat for hornbills (Bucerotidae family), recognisable by their banana-shaped bills. These impressive birds are represented by no fewer than seven species. The mountainous region is preferred by brown hornbills (*Ptilolaemus tickelli*) while the striking white-tailed wreathed hornbill (*Rhyticeros undulatus*) prefers the lower deciduous forest zone. Small flocks of green peafowl (*Pavo muticus*) were discovered more recently. Hiking through the long grass, there is a good chance of disturbing pheasants, shrikes, tailorbirds and coucals, or even rare endangered species of peacock pheasant, such as the magnificent Germain's peacock-pheasant (*Polyplectron germaini*) and grey peacock-pheasant (*Polyplectron bicalcaratum*). Note that the (very) rainy season is from April to October.

The national park is not as organised or responsive as those closer to Hanoi or Hồ Chí Minh City, but the headquarters do offer accommodation in their simple guesthouse or outside in tents and hammocks. **Tours** include half- and full-day treks, cycling, fishing, birdwatching and 1-hour boat rides along the river. The standout activity is the so-called ethical elephant experience, where you track rehabilitated elephants for a half- or full-day experience. Contact the national park through their website to book. If they don't reply to your first email, send another. And if that still doesn't work, reach out to the tour companies in BMT (page 362).

Đắk Nông Province This province gained independence from Đắk Lắk in 2004 and Gia Nghĩa became the provincial capital. While there isn't much of note in the city, it sits surrounded by rugged terrain and some astonishing waterfalls that see few visitors, including the cacophonous **Thác Đắk G'Lung** (Thác 72, thôn 5; w dakglung.vn; ⌚ 07.00–17.00 daily; 60,000/40,000VND adult/child). More wild,

THE CONTROVERSIAL BUFFALO SLAUGHTER FESTIVALS

Some communities in the Central Highlands have carried out buffalo slaughter festivals for centuries. The significance, sequence and specifics change slightly depending on the area, but they usually take place after the spring harvest in February or March. Mnong buffalo slaughter festivals tend to be the most well documented. A few days before the festival, selected youths are sent to fetch a tall tree from the forest, which is brought back to the community and highly decorated. The finished pole, about 9m high, is erected in the middle of the sacrificial area. The following day, the strongest buffalo bull available is harnessed to the pole. Women and young men dance around the pole to the rhythm of gongs while older men sit and drink rice wine through long straws out of a vase. An official ceremony is held early the next day in which the bull's owner gives up his prize possession in an act of gratitude to the gods. A strong young man then strikes the bull in the heart with a sharp spear. A gong is placed over its head while agile young men cover the ceremonial pole with the bull's blood. A string is then attached to the bull and the loose end tied to the rice storehouse. Buffalo blood is mixed with wine and water and sprayed on the rice storehouse. Traditionally, the belief is that this age-old ritual will guard against evil and bestow health and happiness on the community. The bull is then cut into equal slices and distributed among the villagers. The ceremony usually ends with a dance around the blood-covered ceremonial pole to the sound of gongs. As one might imagine, the ceremony is at odds with progressive Vietnam. Many pressure groups – both Vietnamese and international – have achieved some success in lobbying the government to ban the festival. In 2016, international charity Animals Asia, one of the pressure groups, reported that Lâm Đồng Province and Buôn Hô District in Đắk Lắk Province had prohibited the ceremony. But without an enforced nationwide ban, the festivals continue to take place in more remote parts of the subregion.

unticketed waterfalls include **Thác 5 Tầng** (Đắk Sin Ward), which translates to Five Floor Waterfall, and the elegant, singular cascade of **Liêng Nung Waterfall** (Buôn N'Jriêng). This list is just a snippet; detailing every waterfall in the province is far beyond the scope of this book. If you're looking for a remote corner of Vietnam full of adventure that few have heard of, let alone been to, you'll find it in Đắk Nông.

ĐÀ LẠT

Đà Lạt is the capital of the mountainous province of Lâm Đồng, which covers an area of 9,765km^2 and is part of the Trường Sơn mountain range that extends north into Đắk Lắk, Kon Tum and beyond. Often shrouded in mist, it's an area of forests, waterfalls and tea, coffee and fruit plantations. More than 1.5 million people across more than 40 ethnolinguistic groups live in the province – remarkable when you consider that there are 54 government-recognised groups in total across the whole of the country. Lâm Đồng's vast forest land is cultivated for its precious woods. Much sought-after are mahogany, ebony and teakwood, as well as large quantities of bamboo.

The province contains a small section of the Cát Tiên National Park (page 387), inaugurated in 1992, which extends over the border from Đồng Nai Province. Its semi-deciduous wet tropical forest is home to many rare animals such as gaur (*Bos gaurus*), Siamese crocodile (*Crocodylus siamensis*) and, until 2010, the Javan rhino (*Rhinoceros sundaicus*). Lang Biang Mountain to the north is home to emerald cuckoos (*Chrysococcyx maculatus*), ochraceous bulbul (*Criniger ochraceus gutturalis*), many species of pheasants (Phanianidae family), babblers (Timaliidae), pigeons (Columbidae) and thrushes (Turdidae). Agricultural land supports rice fields, corn, sugarcane, potato, strawberries and mulberry, which is used to feed silkworms. While Đắk Lắk Province to the north has come to be associated with cheap Robusta coffee beans ground up for instant coffee, Lâm Đồng is quietly carving out a reputation for higher-grade Arabica. The province's two major urban areas are Đà Lạt and Bảo Lộc, close to Dambri Falls.

Đà Lạt, Vietnam's 'City of Love', has always been a mecca for honeymooners. Two decades ago, newlyweds might have spent their holiday strolling through pine forests, perching on pony-drawn carriages and splashing around in a pedal boat shaped like a swan. These days courting couples whizz between design restaurants and artisanal coffee houses on motorbikes and frolic in flower gardens while being bossed around by photographers.

With its cool mountain air, Đà Lạt was once a tranquil city where one could escape Hồ Chí Minh City's chaotic madness. Today, it is less chaotic than Vietnam's big cities, but in some ways it's madder. Đà Lạt has long been a theatre of eccentricities, from flamboyant French palaces and Gaudí-esque pagodas to psychedelic hotels and maze-like cafés.

Backed to the north by mountains and to the southeast by valleys, it was the favourite holiday resort of many Vietnamese elites, including Madame Nhu, the de facto First Lady of South Vietnam from 1955 to 1963. Evidence of the city's popularity with aristocrats is the legacy of Emperor Bảo Đại, who used to hunt tigers near here with his son Bảo Long. From their base at one of the summer palaces (page 373) they would march out of Đà Lạt in grand ceremonial style on the backs of elephants. These days their homes are museum showpieces. Nearby is the Pasteur Institute, a respectful reminder of Louis Pasteur's student, Dr Alexandre Yersin (page 338), who founded a health spa here in 1893. Looming over Xuân Hương Lake is the single-spired cathedral and some grand old hotels that have been around since colonial times, including the Đà Lạt Hotel and Hotel du Parc. The rolling hills around the lake

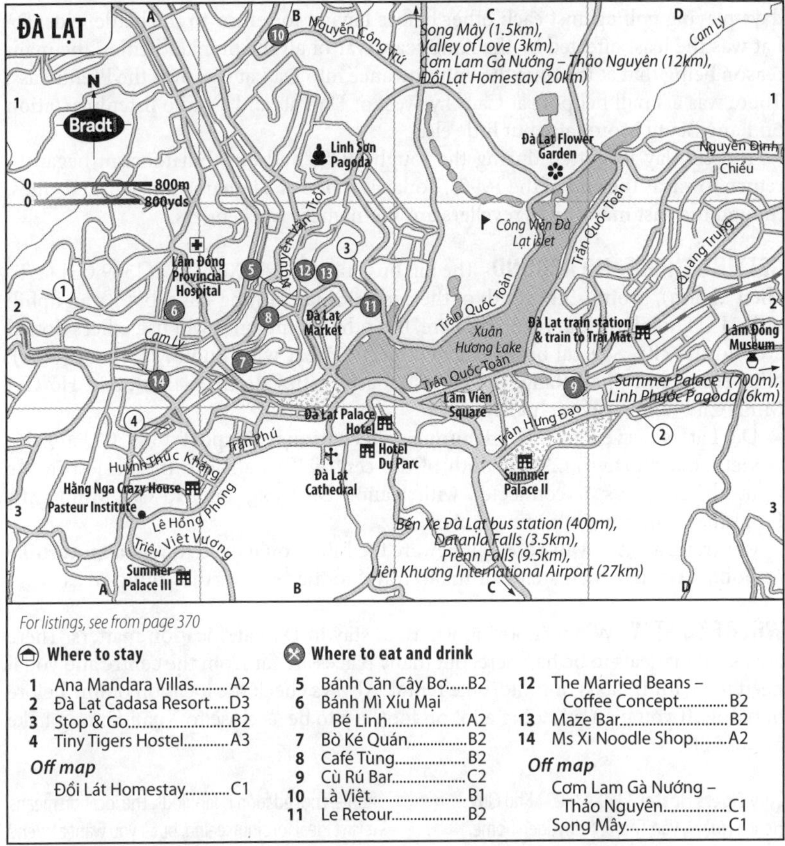

are dotted with more than 2,000 timber-framed French villas and an abundance of flower gardens blossoming with orchids, roses and other temperate flora.

While late-Nguyễn Dynasty and French colonial heritage abounds, so do opportunities to lose yourself in the great outdoors. In the area are forests, lakes and waterfalls for hiking, kayaking, camping, motorbiking and canyoning.

HISTORY Probably on the orders of Gouverneur Général Paul Doumer, Dr Alexandre Yersin, a protégé of Louis Pasteur, is credited with 'founding' Đà Lạt in 1893. This is of course nonsense, as Lâm Đồng Province was already populated by various ethnolinguistic groups who have lived here for centuries.

Yersin stumbled across the area when he was trying to find somewhere cool to escape from the sweltering summer heat of the coast and lowlands. The lush alpine scenery of Đà Lạt agreed with the French overlords and it soon became the secondary city in the south after Saigon. In the summer months, the colonial administration moved lock, stock and barrel to Đà Lạt, where it was cooler. Đà Lạt was also the favourite city of Bảo Đại, Vietnam's last emperor, and it is possible to see his former imperial residences.

The French felled trees and cleared land to make way for a golf course and luxury hotels that you can still see today. In both World War II and the American War elite officials of the opposing armies would apparently while away a pleasant couple of days playing golf against each other before having to return to the battlefields. Đà Lạt was the least affected by the American War of all the highland cities, the main reason being that at the time the only entrance into Đà Lạt was over the Prenn Pass. There was a small heliport at Cam Ly, west of Đà Lạt, and a radio listening station on Lang Biang Mountain, but little else.

The city lay forgotten during the tough 1970s and 80s, but tourism began to return towards the end of the 1990s. Today it is one of Vietnam's most visited cities, though the vast majority of revellers are Vietnamese weekenders.

GETTING THERE AND AROUND The big **bus** station, Bến Xe Đà Lạt [369 C3] (1 Tô Hiến Thành), is only 2km south of the central Xuân Hương Lake, but it's an uphill walk. FUTA will pick up/drop off here, but other companies will use offices dotted around the city. Several buses daily connect Đà Lạt with Buôn Ma Thuột (6hrs); Nha Trang and Phan Rang, the closest coastal cities (both 3–4hrs); and Hồ Chí Minh City (7hrs; leaving hourly).

Đà Lạt is served by **Liên Khương International Airport** [369 C3] (QL20; w vietnamairport.vn), 29km south of the centre. This airport, the busiest in the Central Highlands, is connected with Hanoi, Đà Nẵng and Hồ Chí Minh City. From there you can get a taxi to town.

Central Đà Lạt is **walkable**, but beware the hills. You'll need to rent a **motorbike or book a Grab**, which are plentiful, to travel to the city's further-flung areas.

WHERE TO STAY When choosing where to stay in Đà Lạt, location matters. There are excellent deals to be had here, but many places are far from the centre and you'll need to factor in taxis or motorbike rental. Always check the location online before booking. If you plan on doing a lot on foot, try to be as close to Xuân Hương Lake as possible.

Tiny Tigers Hostel [369 A3] C32 Khu Quy Hoạch Hoàng Văn Thụ; f tinytigershome. Friendly backpacker vibes in this converted neighbourhood family house, with both private rooms & dorms. Almost daily communal dinners are a good place to meet people. This is the home of Rew Rew (see opposite) & as a result the tours on offer are very comprehensive. **$**

Đà Lạt Cadasa Resort [369 D3] 16 Trần Hưng Đạo; f resort.cadasa. The budget version of Ana Mandara (see right), with a collection of hillside heritage villas. The buildings need a lot of work, but the run-down architecture lends the place a sort of charm. **$$**

Đồi Lát Homestay [369 C1] Thôn Đạ Nghịt; f doilat.homestay. Situated 20km (40mins) northwest of town is this collection of cabins nestled in pine forests. The hosts are friendly & the home-cooked food is fabulous. The location means it isn't ideal for sightseeing, but if you want a w/end of doing nothing then this is the place. **$$**

✷ **Stop & Go** [369 B2] 88 Lý Tự Trọng; w stopandgohotel.com. Close to the action but surrounded by pine trees, Stop & Go is a genuine boutique hotel with only a few rooms, each 1 a little different & artfully decorated. **$$**

✷ **Ana Mandara Villas** [369 A2] 2 Lê Lai; w anamandara-resort.com. Restored French hillside villas built in the 1920s & 1930s, each with a couple of bedrooms & some with a living room &/or dining room. The furnishings are reminiscent of Shaker-style furniture; the beds are heavenly; the baths are on feet. The heated pool, buried amid the secluded hillside villas, is a treat; a night swim in the cool air is invigorating. There's a luxurious spa on site & the restaurant is reasonably priced. **$$$$**

WHERE TO EAT AND DRINK

Restaurants and street food

✷ **Bánh Căn Cây Bơ** [369 B2] 56 Tăng Bạt Hổ; ⌚ 05.00–noon daily. The place to come for Đà Lạt's fried pancake dish topped with a quail egg. This little establishment serves the dish on the pavement on a hilly lane. **$**

Bánh Mì Xíu Mại Bé Linh [369 A2] 37 Hoàng Diệu; 🕘 06.00–noon daily. Arguably the best place in town for Đà Lạt's take on *bánh mì* (baguettes), with simple streetside seating. Here the bread is served with a hot meatball broth to fend off the early-morning winter chills. $

✷ **Ms Xi Noodle Shop** [369 A2] Lô A26, Mạc Đĩnh Chi; 🕘 13.30–16.30 daily. Perhaps it's criminal to say that Vietnam's best *mì Quảng* is in Đà Lạt, not Quảng Nam or Đà Nẵng, but you read it here first. The thick yellow noodles are served with a richer-than-usual broth & topped with peanuts. $

Bò Ké Quán [369 B2] 73/3A Ba Tháng Hai. Simple family restaurant with a big menu of meat, vegetable & tofu dishes served with white rice. This is one of those places that seems to get everything right: great food, agreeable ambience & very reasonable prices. $$

Cơm Lam Gà Nướng – Thảo Nguyên [369 C1] Ankroet. Delicious grilled chicken & sticky rice, a Central Highlands speciality, served in a family roadside restaurant on the way to Suối Vàng Lake, a few kilometres from the city. $$

Song Mây [369 C1] 98 Trần Quang Khải; 🕘 08.00–22.00 daily. Upmarket & often quiet Vietnamese restaurant with views over the farms on the outskirts of Đà Lạt. The salads here are particularly good. $$$

Bars and coffee houses

✷ **Café Tùng** [369 B2] 6 Khu Hòa Bình; 🕘 07.00–21.30 daily. Classic Vietnamese coffee shop that has been around since the 1950s, with smartly designed seats ideal for people watching. The coffee is good, as is the homemade yoghurt.

Cù Rú Bar [369 C2] 2 Phạm Hồng Thái; f curulocalwine; 🕘 09.00–midnight daily. Both a café & a bar, ramshackle & makeshift Cu Rú is also a hub for artists. There are exhibitions happening throughout the year.

Là Việt [369 B1] 200 Nguyễn Công Trứ; w laviet.coffee; 🕘 07.00–22.00 daily. A newish chain of stylish coffee shops with outlets in cities across the country began in Đà Lạt, & this comfortable, warehouse-style café & roastery is their flagship store.

Le Retour [369 B2] 38 Phan Bội Châu; f LeRetour.WineBar; 🕘 16.00–midnight daily. Fancy wine bar that feels like it belongs in central Hồ Chí Minh City instead of provincial Đà Lạt. One of the best wine & cheese selections in the city.

The Married Beans – Coffee Concept [369 B2] 6 Nguyễn Văn Trỗi; w themarriedbeans.com; 🕘 07.00–21.00 daily. High-quality coffee served in a cosy space in an attractive corner of town. There's also a small gift corner selling souvenirs.

Maze Bar [369 B2] 57 Phan Bội Châu; f 100roof.mazebar; 🕘 08.00–midnight daily. Part maze, part cave, this popular but gimmicky bar-pub-café doesn't adhere to any design theme, & that's all part of the fun. There are several ways up & down the building & exploration is encouraged.

OTHER PRACTICALITIES There is no useful tourist information office in Đà Lạt, but there is more English spoken here than anywhere else in the subregion. Ask your accommodation provider for tips as they'll likely be a trove of local knowledge. There are two particularly good adventure **tour** companies to note. For canyoning (abseiling down waterfalls), hiking, camping and other physical activities, reach out to Highland Sport Travel (w highlandsporttravel.com). For motorbike trips around Đà Lạt and beyond, contact Rew Rew Adventures (w rewrew.vn). **Lâm Đồng Provincial Hospital** [369 A2] (1 Phạm Ngọc Thạch) is northwest of the lake.

WHAT TO SEE AND DO

✷ **Xuân Hương Lake** [369 C2] Originally the Grand Lake, Xuân Hương Lake was renamed in 1954 after an illustrious female poet who lived through the Tây Sơn Rebellion and first two decades of the Nguyễn Dynasty. The lake was created in 1919 after a small dam was constructed on the Cam Ly River. It is the mostly attractive centrepiece of the town and a popular exercise area for the local inhabitants; many will, first thing in the morning, walk around the lake or perform tai chi exercises. Power walking and jogging at dusk is also popular. At the northeast end of the lake is the free **Đà Lạt Flower Garden** [369 C1], which has orchids, roses, lilies

LEGEND HAS IT: SWOON AND SUICIDE

About 4km east of Xuân Hương Lake is Than Thở Lake, which was once popular with flirting couples. This Lake of Sighs, as the name translates to English, may be named after the swooning girls that were courted here by handsome young men from the military academy in Đà Lạt. Another more colourful theory is that the name was coined after a young maiden, Mai Nương, who drowned herself in the lake in the 18th century. The story is that her lover, Hoàng Tùng, had joined the army of Emperor Quang Trung to fight the Chinese, who were mounting an invasion of the country after the chaos of the Tây Sơn Rebellion (page 332). Before leaving for battle, Hoàng Tùng had thoughtlessly failed to tell his lover. Devastated, and thinking that Hoàng Tùng no longer loved her, she committed suicide by drowning herself in the lake. Unfortunately, the lake was drained in recent years and is no longer worth visiting. If you do happen upon it, you'll likely sigh with disappointment.

and hydrangeas. Opposite is the Công Viên Đà Lạt islet, behind which is a more manicured flower garden that has a small entrance fee. On the south side of the lake is Lâm Viên Square, with two bizarre modern structures: one resembling a swirled ice cream scoop and another looking like a wilting yellow lotus flower.

Đà Lạt Palace Hotel [369 B3] (2 Trần Phú; w dalatpalacehotel.com) Located near Xuân Hương Lake is this symbol of colonial luxury, built between 1916 and 1922. Clearly designed by French architects who drew no inspiration from the local vernacular, its architecture is Neoclassical with Art Deco elements, featuring grand façades and gardens. The hotel quickly became a favourite among French colonial officials and international travellers. It was once the epitome of Indochinese luxury, on a par with the Metropole in Hanoi and the Continental in Hồ Chí Minh City, hosting lavish parties and high-profile guests. Despite the challenges of the 1950s, 60s and 70s, the hotel remained a prominent fixture in Đà Lạt. Following a period of decline after 1975, the hotel underwent extensive renovations in the 1990s and reopened in 1995. In the evening you can sip mediocre cocktails in the hotel bar while sitting on a spongy sofa and listening to a pianist play pop song renditions. Behind the Đà Lạt Palace Hotel is the overlooked **Hotel Du Parc** (15A Trần Phú; w dalathotelduparc.com), with an elegant Art Deco façade and old-fashioned elevator. After enjoying a refreshment in either hotel you can usually wander around the property without attracting too much attention. Just look like you belong.

Đà Lạt Cathedral [369 B3] (15 Trần Phú; ⌚ sporadic hours) The single-tiered cathedral is visible from the lake. At the top of the turret is a weathercock, which is why it is sometimes referred to affectionately by locals as the 'Chicken Cathedral'. Construction began in 1931, although the building was not completed until the Japanese occupation in 1942. The stained-glass windows, with their vivid colours and use of pure, clean lines, were crafted in France by Louis Balmet, the same man who made the windows in Nha Trang and Đà Nẵng cathedrals, between 1934 and 1940. Sadly, most have not survived the ravages of time, but those that remain glisten in the midday sun. Lining the nave are blocks of woodcarvings of Christ and the crucifixion.

✷ Trần Hưng Đạo Street [369 C3] Many of the large colonial villas – almost universally washed in pastel yellow – are 1930s and 1940s vintage. Some have curved walls and railings and are almost nautical in inspiration, an Art Deco offshoot known as Streamline Moderne. Others have taken inspiration from countryside homes in Provence in southern France. Many of the larger villas can be found along Trần Hưng Đạo Street, with many of these converted into hotels, restaurants and cafés. Some remain in private ownership, while others are government offices and a few appear to be abandoned. Sadly, some of the villas have fallen into a very sorry state and are looking decidedly unloved, perhaps a reflection of the understandable animosity directed towards the French colonial legacy, but given their architectural significance, this is a great pity. Perhaps the largest and most impressive house on Trần Hưng Đạo is the former residence of the governor general at 12 Trần Hưng Đạo, now known as Summer Palace II (Dinh II), an unfriendly and not recommended government hotel. The villa is 1930s in style, with large airy rooms and furniture, and occupies a magnificent position set among mountain pines and overlooking the town and lake. A ramshackle collection of smaller villas separated by gardens is up the road at the Cadasa Resort (page 370). They offer a friendlier welcome, and although the restaurant is nothing special, you can enjoy a drink in the garden café.

Lâm Đồng Museum [369 D2] (4 Hùng Vương; w baotanglamdong.com.vn; ⌚ 07.30–11.30 & 13.30–17.00 daily; 10,000VND/free adult/child) A statue of Hồ Chí Minh standing on a bed of fake lotus flowers welcomes you to Lâm Đồng Museum, which is disappointing given the size, diversity and visitor appeal of the province. It begins with a natural history section, with some pretty photos of waterfalls and the pitiful and gruesome stuffed remains of animals who once roamed Lang Biang Mountain. The history section exhibits some black-and-white photos of Đà Lạt in the 1930s and 40s and details the province's role in the revolutionary struggle, but the most interesting section might be the ancient Đông Sơn relics and artefacts from Funnan-era temples. Amazingly, these were only discovered this century in Cát Tiên National Park. There's also a detailed section covering the various ethnolinguistic groups in the area, which is worth investigating if exploring the more remote corners of the Central Highlands. You should find a K'ho xylophone made from thin stone slabs and then another musical instrument, a *khen bầu,* made out of a large gourd shell. One exhibit made from bamboo tubes is a K'ho scarecrow. Baskets made from split bamboo are exhibited alongside others made from rattan. Look out for the small section on apparel as it's unlikely that you'll see people in the Central Highlands wearing their traditional attire, and these are displayed together with jewellery, rings, necklaces of bronze, silver and ivory and bracelets.

Summer Palace I [369 D2] (Dinh I; Trần Quang Diệu; ⌚ closed at the time of research – check online; 50,000/25,000VND adult/child) The first owner of this alpine chateau was Robert Clément Bourgery, who had it built in 1929. It wasn't until 1949 that the palace was acquired by the crown and used as a residence and office for Bảo Đại, Vietnam's last emperor, who was exiled in 1954 and died in France in 1997. He renamed the palace 'Gia Long Palace' after arguably his most important ancestor, the founder of the Nguyễn Dynasty (page 266). The gaudy golden entrance gates, certainly not original, lean perhaps a little too keenly into the palatial colonial theme, but the manicured gardens are a lovely place to stop for a breather. Sitting within them is the 12-room house, which was divided into two parts: the ground floor for the reception and official offices and the first floor for the royal family living quarters. After the signing of the Geneva Agreement that led to Bảo Đại's exile and the partition through the country, Ngô Đình Diệm became prime minister of South Vietnam and chose this palace as his residence. He renamed the building Bạch Hóa Palace and built a secret escape tunnel. It's possible to see the entrance, but unfortunately the passageway is off limits to visitors. This 'tunnel', which is perhaps more like a bunker, is apparently very elaborate, with an office, a lounge, a radio room and offshoot tunnels that lead to the various guard stations. The main purpose of the tunnel, however, was to connect the master bedroom with the heliport behind the palace, enabling Ngô to be whisked away like a Bond villain. Dotted around the villa are pictures of Đà Lạt from a century ago, long before the population exploded, with lonely detached colonial buildings surrounded by pine forests. They give a sense of how this mountain resort would have been for its former proprietors. Note that at the time of research this sight was closed due to an ownership dispute so check online or ask at your accommodation for updates.

✷ **Summer Palace III** [369 A3] (Dinh III; 1 Triệu Việt Vương; ⌚ 07.00–17.30 daily; 30,000/15,000VND adult/child) Bảo Đại built this palace between 1933 and 1938, about 2km from the town centre. Perched on a hill with views on every side, it is Art Deco in style both inside and out, and rather modest for a palace. The stark interior contains little to indicate that this was the home of an emperor – almost all of Bảo Đại's personal belongings have been removed. The impressive dining room contains an etched-glass map of Vietnam, while the study has Bảo Đại's desk, a few personal ornaments and photographs, notably of the family who, in 1954, were exiled to France, where their descendants still live. One of the family photos shows Bảo Đại's son, the prince Bảo Long, in full military dress. He died in July 2007 in France aged 71. Emperor Bảo Đại's daughter, Phương Mai, in a spirit of reconciliation, was invited back to visit Vietnam in the mid-1990s. The princess, who married an Italian duke and died in 2021, politely declined on account of her age. The emperor's bedroom and bathroom are open to public scrutiny, as is the little terrace from where, apparently, on a clear night he would gaze at the stars. The family drawing room is open, with a little commentary on which chair was used by whom. The gardens are colourful and well maintained, with a few benches to sit and enjoy the cool mountain air. From the moon balcony you can see the garden was arranged into the shape of the Bảo Đại stamp.

Pasteur Institute [369 A3] (16 Lê Hồng Phong; ⌚ 07.00–11.30 & 13.00–16.30 Mon–Fri, 07.00–11.30 Sat) The yellow-wash institute, built to produce vaccines for keeping the colonial population healthy, was opened in 1935. Although small and modest, it is an attractive Art Deco building fashioned in a series of cubes. Remarkably, the building still operates as a vaccine centre today, and some foreigners associate it with getting their Covid-19 jabs in 2021. It's not always open to visitors (unless you have an appointment), but you can admire the architecture from the outside.

Hằng Nga Crazy House [369 A3] (3 Huỳnh Thúc Kháng; **w** crazyhouse.vn; ⌚ 08.30–19.00 daily; 80,000/30,000VND adult/child) Wealthy and well-connected architect Đặng Việt Nga has, over a period of many years, built up her hotel in organic fashion. Guests sleep inside mushrooms, trees and giraffes and sip tea under giant cobwebs. There is also a honeymoon room (obviously), an ant room and plenty more. Fortunately for the guests, the private rooms are not available to the public, but the gardens, resembling scenes taken from the pages of a psychedelic fairytale book, are accessible. From these gardens you can step through a shell into an underwater wonderland before scaling a vine-like exterior staircase that

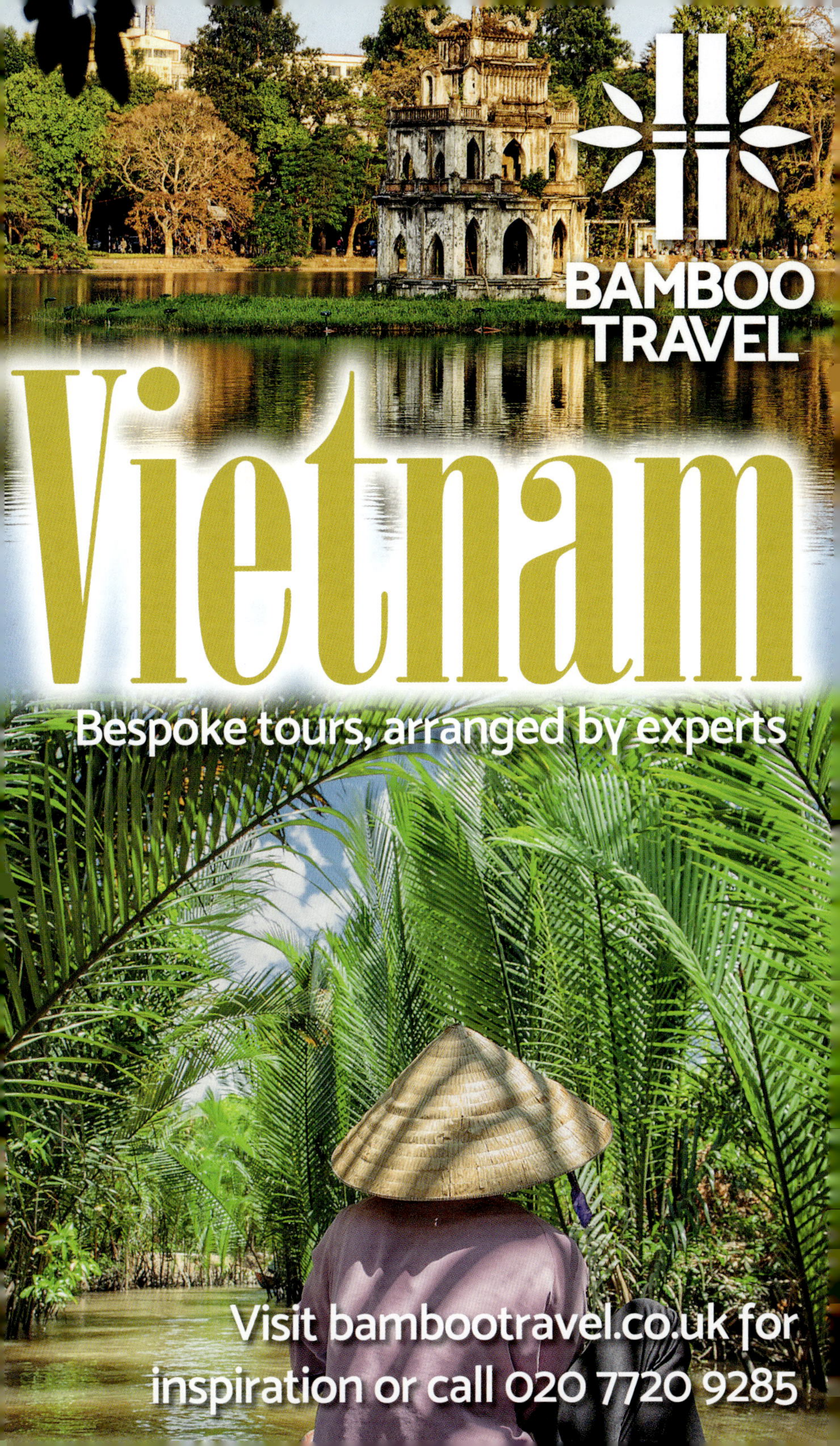
BAMBOO
TRAVEL
Vietnam
Bespoke tours, arranged by experts
Visit bambootravel.co.uk for
inspiration or call 020 7720 9285

connects a witch's cabin with what looks like a gigantic dollop of melting ice cream. This is one of Đà Lạt's most popular sights; if there's a queue or you spot tour buses outside, consider coming back later.

Đà Lạt Market [369 B2] (Chợ Đà Lạt; 1 Nguyễn Thị Minh Khai; ⌚ early morning–midnight daily) Đà Lạt Market sells a dazzling array of exotic (for Vietnam) fruits and vegetables grown in the temperate climate of the area – plums, strawberries, carrots, potatoes, loganberries, artichokes, apples, onions and avocados. The forbidding appearance of the market is masked by the riot of colour of the flowers on sale, including gladioli, irises, roses, gerbera, chrysanthemums and marigolds. Sampling the immense variety of candied fruit here is the highlight of any visit to Đà Lạt.

✷ **Ana Mandara Villas** [369 A2] (page 370) Unlike the Hotel Du Parc and Palace Hotel, you will need to pre-arrange a visit to this heritage hotel if you're not staying there. There is an atmospheric restaurant and café with views, and if you spring for afternoon tea or a meal then the reception team will usually throw in a free tour of the grounds. After the French founded Đà Lạt they began crafting houses based on their respective regions back home, contributing to the city's eclectic architecture. Ana Mandara Villas was originally called Cité Bellevue, and it belonged to Jean Neill, a retired French colonel who moved to the area in 1920 and became rich off plantations and infrastructure projects. He built his first villa in 1929 on this pine-filled hill and soon after his French friends and colleagues, attracted by his elite colonial lifestyle, decided to join him. Two years later Neill built another villa for hosting guests, now Le Petit Restaurant, the site of the restaurant and tea room. Perched on the edge of the hill, the house enjoyed views over Đà Lạt and its mushrooming ecclesiastical architecture, with a large reception room and an attic for storing wine. Many more villas followed throughout the 1930s and 40s. The hill began to fall into decay after 1954, but almost half a century later Ana Mandara began the process of salvaging and renovating 15 villas, which they eventually converted into hotel rooms. The hotel opened in 2006 and now has 26 villas, including the original 15. Each one is a little different. While touring the property, look out for the Architect's Villa, with a ground-floor archway and imperial staircase built entirely of split stone, two symmetrical attics and tall chimneys.

Đà Lạt train station [369 D2] (Quang Trung) Đà Lạt train station, built in the 1930s, is located about 2km from the town centre. Designed by French architects, the station showcases an Art Deco style blended with traditional elements; the most distinctive feature is its three-peaked roof, reportedly inspired by Lang Biang Mountain and the communal houses of the Central Highlands. Inside, the station features high ceilings and large arched windows, reflecting the architectural trends of the interwar period. Originally serving as a link between Đà Lạt and other regions, the railway played a crucial role in the city's development as a hill station. During the American War, the railway line suffered significant damage, and services were halted in the 1970s, but restoration efforts in the early 1990s revived a portion of the line for tourism. Today, you can sometimes enjoy short train rides to Trại Mát village and Linh Phước Pagoda (page 377). Irritatingly, train times shift, and they only happen if there are enough customers, two features that are seemingly incompatible with one another. If this train trip is of interest, be prepared to take a back-up (eg: a taxi or a rented motorbike). The station also

LEGEND HAS IT: RULE THE ROOST

If exploring south of Đà Lạt, you may come across the huge wooden chicken statue of Làng Gà (Chicken Village). This rather touristy K'ho village is only worth visiting if it's on your way to one of the waterfalls. There are, however, a few basic places to have coffee and several weaving shops that provide good-quality products at a fraction of what they would cost in Đà Lạt or Hồ Chí Minh City.

The village's claim to fame is the 5m-high concrete chicken statue that gives Làng Gà its name. There are numerous stories concerning its inspiration. The most popular one is that it was constructed in honour of a local village wench who was tragically killed while searching in the surrounding mountains for an engagement present to give to her fiancé. She had apparently been searching for a nine-clawed chicken, presumably inspired by the wedding gifts presented to Mỵ Nương by Sơn Tinh in one of Vietnam's most famous myths (page 127). Another version of the story of its origin is that it was built to commemorate the heroic peasant chicken farmers who fought for independence.

houses exhibits on the history of the railway, with old photographs and artefacts. Cafés and souvenir shops within the station offer refreshments and locally produced products, including chocolate.

Linh Sơn Pagoda [369 B1] (120 Nguyễn Văn Trỗi) This pagoda, built in 1942, is kept in immaculate condition. Perched on a small hillock, two dragon balustrades front the sanctuary, themselves flanked by two ponds with miniature mountain scenes. To the right is a small, Dutch-looking pagoda tower. Behind is a school of Buddhist studies attended by dozens of young, grey-clad men and women.

Around Đà Lạt

Waterfalls Đà Lạt is surrounded by waterfalls, some more worthwhile than others depending on the season. Cam Ly Waterfall (8B Hoàng Văn Thụ; 🕘 07.00–17.00 daily; 40,000/20,000VND adult/child), 2km from the centre of town, is the closest to Đà Lạt town centre, but is poorly maintained and at times filled with rubbish. Instead, head to **Datanla Falls** (QL20 Đèo Prenn; 🕘 07.00–17.00 daily; 50,000/25,000VND adult/child), 5km out of town on Highway 20 towards Hồ Chí Minh City. From the entrance the path leads steeply downwards into a forested ravine; it is a fairly easy hike there but can be tiring on the return journey. The falls are hardly spectacular, but the Alpine Coaster, a toboggan on rails, adds some thrills to the experience. Further along Highway 20 are Prenn Falls (20 Liên Khương–Prenn Highway; 🕘 09.00–17.00 daily; 50,000/25,000VND adult/child), 12km from the town centre, which were dedicated to Queen Sirikit of Thailand when she visited in 1959. Though they underwent some renovations, the falls began to be degraded and suffer from pollution because dredged silt from Xuân Hương Lake in Đà Lạt was being dumped at the source of the falls. Unfortunately, the falls remain unimpressive. For genuinely impressive waterfalls, you'll need to head further south to Bảo Đại Falls (Tạ Hine Ward), which at the time of research was free and unmanaged, and Pongour Falls (Tân Hội Ward; 🕘 07.00–17.30 daily; 20,000/10,000VND adult/child). Both are about an hour from Đà Lạt and about half an hour from each other. Canyoning (abseiling down waterfalls) has become Đà

Lạt's flagship adventure activity and is a thrilling way to explore more inaccessible spots. Reach out to Highland Sport Travel (page 371).

Lakes The environs of Đà Lạt are also dotted with lakes, and unlike the lakes in the city, they haven't been heavily manipulated or built upon. **Suối Vàng Lake** (Dankia village) is a long, thin stretch of water surrounded by hilly pine forests. There isn't a whole lot to do, but the journey there and back, passing several spots serving *gà nướng cơm lam* (grilled chicken and sticky rice cooked in bamboo; page 348), is pleasant. Consider buying the grilled chicken to take away and finding a spot in the pine forest with a view of the water. **Tuyền Lâm Lake** (Phường 4) is a little more developed, with artful coffee houses perched on the lake's northeast corner. From here it's possible to take a boat tour around the lake and swim in its more remote corners. Camping on Tuyền Lâm Lake has become popular and there are some short trekking routes. Book a tour with Highland Sport Travel (page 371).

✷ ***Linh Phước Pagoda*** (120 Tự Phước; ⌚ 07.00–17.00 daily) Topping Đà Lạt's list of oddities is Linh Phước Pagoda, 9km west of the city centre. Established in 1952, the pagoda is known for its mosaics made from literally millions of pieces of broken glass, pottery and porcelain. The 49m-long dragon statue, for example, was made from 12,000 beer bottles. There is a standing Buddha statue made with 600,000 dried (possibly fake) flowers. The climbable seven-storey bell tower, standing at 37m, houses the largest bell in Đà Lạt, weighing 8,500kg. The most curious section of the pagoda is its horrifically detailed depiction of hell and the nightmarish carnival of scenes of torture conducted by grinning and grotesque demons. This horror house is behind the main hall and not immediately obvious; if you see a red, horned man-donkey brandishing a trident then you're in the right place.

Lang Biang Mountain (305 Lang Biang; ⌚ 07.00–17.00 daily; 50,000/25,000VND adult/child) This mountain (2,167m) is around 15km north of Đà Lạt. You can drive or take a taxi to the visitor centre (Khu Du Lịch Lang Biang). From

LEGEND HAS IT: THE STAR-CROSSED LOVERS (THE SEQUEL)

Long ago, two neighbouring ethnolinguistic groups (accounts differ as to which ones) living in the region maintained a fierce rivalry. H'Biang, a young woman from one group, and K'Lang, a young man from the other, met by chance while collecting water in the forest. Their encounter quickly evolved into fierce passion, but their respective groups forbade their union. Determined to be together, H'Biang and K'Lang decided to defy their families and flee to a mountain and live in isolation.

Their happiness was short-lived, however. H'Biang fell ill, and K'Lang, unable to elicit help from either community, watched helplessly as she passed away. Overwhelmed with grief, K'Lang also succumbed to sorrow and died beside H'Biang. When their families found the bodies, the chiefs of both groups decided to end their feud to honour the couple. In a symbol of reconciliation, the mountain where H'Biang and K'Lang died was named Lang Biang, a combination of both names.

For the Central Highlands' other tale of ill-fated love and eternal devotion, see page 365.

here you can hike to the peak, which housed an American radar listening post during the war, in about 2 hours.

Bidoup-Núi Bà National Park (Đạ Nhim; f VuonQuocGiaBidoupNuiBa; ⌚ 08.00–16.00 daily; 40,000/20,000VND adult/child) Some 35km northeast of Đà Lạt, Bidoup is a well-organised national park covering an area of over 700km^2. Named after Mount Bidoup, the park is part of the Lang Biang Biosphere Reserve. Though heavily logged at lower altitudes, Bidoup hosts a variety of ecosystems, including evergreen forests, pine forests, and montane subtropical forests. It is home to numerous plant species, some of which are rare and endangered. The park's diverse flora includes pine trees, orchids and medicinal plants. The park is also a sanctuary for several endangered species such as the yellow-cheeked gibbon (*Nomascus gabriellae*), the Asian black bear (or moon bear; *Ursus thibetanus*) and the gaur (*Bos gaurus*). Do not expect to see any of these. Perhaps as many as 300 bird species also live in the national park, including the rare Vietnamese pheasant (*Lophura hatinhensis*) and the black-hooded laughingthrush (*Garrulax milleti*). Do not expect to see these either.

Hiking trails vary from leisurely walks to challenging treks through forests and up viewpoints. One self-guided option, which takes 2–3 hours, is the hike to Thiên Thai Waterfall and back. The visitor centre can provide a map and there are signs to guide you along the way. The most popular guided trek is the two-day ascent and descent of Mount Bidoup (2,287m). Longer tailor-made trips are also possible; reach out to the helpful park team over Facebook to enquire. The park facilities include visitor centres, camping grounds, picnic areas and attractive lodge accommodation around a small pond. If you plan to do anything other than the self-guided hike to Thiên Thai Waterfall, you will need to book in advance on Facebook. It's often possible to turn up and find somewhere to stay, but there's no guarantee that the restaurant will be serving. Bidoup limits karaoke noise from guests, a first for national parks in Vietnam.

Bảo Lộc and Dambri Falls As the road descends towards Hồ Chí Minh City to the Bảo Lộc Plateau, the forest is replaced by tea and coffee plantations, fruit orchards and mulberry farms used in silk production. Many of the farmers on the plateau settled here after fleeing from the north following partition in 1954. At the centre of the plateau is the town of Bảo Lộc, 200km from Hồ Chí Minh City and 120km from Đà Lạt. With a population of 170,000, this is Lâm Đồng's second settlement. Most buses moving between Hồ Chí Minh City and Đà Lạt pass through here, making it a good place to break up the 7-hour journey. The town is pleasant, especially around the Đồng Nai ponds, though there isn't much to do. The area's prime attraction is **Dambri Falls** (14 Village Lý Thái Tổ; w dambri.com.vn; ⌚ 07.30–16.30 daily; 250,000/150,000VND adult/child), highly Disney-fied but often considered the most impressive in the subregion. Hotels in Bảo Lộc will let motorbikes that you can use to reach the falls, 20km northwest of town. Otherwise, negotiate with your hotel receptionist for a private car that includes waiting time (2 hours is plenty). The falls are the centre point of an amusement complex designed for families with young children, with slides, an alpine coaster and Ferris wheel. The waterfall is impressive even in the dry season, though an elevator that sits next to the cascade detracts considerably from its beauty.

Part Four

SOUTHERN VIETNAM

Southern Vietnam: An Overview

From the dichotomous climate (rainy or dry) to the delectable cuisine (sweet and spicy), Southern Vietnam smells, looks and feels more like the rest of Southeast Asia. Most roads lead to Hồ Chí Minh City, a rollicking megalopolis that is every bit as dynamic as Bangkok. To the north is the Southeast, with thick jungles reminiscent of Borneo. To the south is the Mekong Delta, with cultural and geographical landscapes akin to those in Cambodia. Out in the East Sea and Gulf of Thailand are tropical islands that rival those of Indonesia, Malaysia and the Philippines.

HIGHLIGHTS

CÁT TIÊN NATIONAL PARK (page 387) A true jungle and one of Vietnam's better-organised national parks, Cát Tiên has night safaris, cycle lanes, hiking trails and, perhaps best of all, wildlife rehabilitation centres like the Đảo Tiên Endangered Primate Species Centre.

CẦN THƠ (page 403) Cần Thơ is one of Vietnam's five major cities, but that doesn't supersede the mellow vibes that characterise the Mekong Delta subregion. This laid-back, amiable city acts like a subregional hub, offering easy access to Sóc Trăng, Đồng Tháp and Bạc Liêu, and, at a push, Trà Vinh and Châu Đốc.

TRÀ VINH (page 411) Surrounding the unhurried provincial capital, the countryside of Trà Vinh is where centuries-old Khmer pagodas, like Hang Pagoda and Chùa Angkorajaborey, rise above lofty trees topped with messy stalk nests.

CHÂU ĐỐC (page 419) Châu Đốc is like a microcosm of Mekong Delta life, with the spiritual enclave of Núi Sam, the ethnolinguistic diversity of the Cham and Khmer villages, the waterscape of Trà Sư Cajuput Forest and several vestiges of the subregion's complicated history, like the Ba Chúc Pagoda.

CÔN ĐẢO ARCHIPELAGO (page 438) Côn Đảo holds sublime natural beauty and remains one of the few coastal tourism spots that hasn't suffered from overdevelopment. It also fosters a dark history as a major incarceration destination during the revolutionary years.

HỒ CHÍ MINH CITY (page 449) Hồ Chí Minh City on paper but Saigon to those who know and love the place, this emerging megacity is twice the size of Hanoi and yet there's less than half the history. Nevertheless, the sights of the city's central districts, like the Independence Palace, War Remnants Museum and colonial-era hotels, reflect an important chapter of Vietnam's broader story. West of here is Chợ Lớn, or Chinatown, surely one of the most rambunctious neighbourhoods on earth, but also with a clutch of atmospheric temples and pagodas.

10

The Southeast

The small diagonal strip of land framed by Hồ Chí Minh City, Central Vietnam, Cambodia and the East Sea is the Southeast. With just five provinces – Đồng Nai, Bình Dương, Bà Rịa-Vũng Tàu, Bình Phước and Tây Ninh – and with a total area of 21,800km^2, only the Red River Delta subregion is smaller. Phan Thiết and Mũi Né in Bình Thuận Province are sometimes considered part of the Southeast, including in Vietnam's official tourism literature, but due to the province's Cham heritage, this guide covers this province in *Chapter 8*.

The Southeast is within easy travelling distance of Hồ Chí Minh City and offers many diverse areas of interest, making it a favourite spot for weekenders. One of the most popular places, at least for locals, is the small city of **Vũng Tàu**, a seaside resort with some unexpected colonial and post-colonial heritage sites. To its east is **Hồ Tràm**, an unassuming coastal strip that has been somewhat spared the frenzy of Vietnam's resort-building craze. Offshore and still within Bà Rịa-Vũng Tàu Province is the 14-island Côn Đảo archipelago, covered in *Chapter 12*.

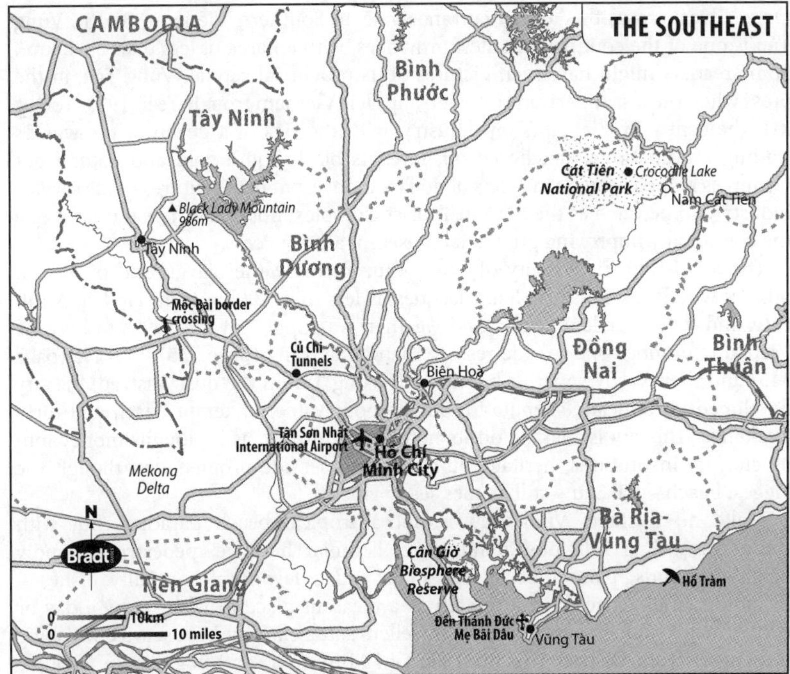

Only a few hours from Hồ Chí Minh City, at the other end of the subregion, is **Tây Ninh**, headquarters of the Cao Đài religion where an ever-seeing eye, the symbol of the faith, looks out from a huge sphere dotted with 3,072 stars. Near the Cambodian border is the Black Lady Mountain, visited every summer by tens of thousands of pilgrims who come to honour the mysterious Lý Thị Thiên Hương. From its almost 1,000m summit, one can look out over the fruit gardens of Bình Phước, the largest province in the region but with the fewest visitors.

Between Tây Ninh and Bà Rịa-Vũng Tàu is Bình Dương, a province with industrial zones of great interest to investors, and Đồng Nai, the gateway to **Cát Tiên National Park**, one of Vietnam's richest wildlife refuges. This chapter is organised from east to west, beginning with Vũng Tàu in the coastal province of Bà Rịa-Vũng Tàu and concluding with Tây Ninh.

WHEN TO VISIT

Vũng Tàu, Hồ Tràm and Tây Ninh are year-round destinations in terms of weather as it's rarely too hot or too rainy. However, try to avoid the coastal areas during the weekend, especially if a public holiday day or two are attached. Due to its many churches and active Christian community, Vũng Tàu is a good place to spend Christmas. The best time to visit Cát Tiên National Park is December or January, the beginning of the dry season. March, April and May are also dry, but hot. The rainy season, June to November, can be an atmospheric time to go, but expect mud and some waterlogged areas. Leeches are there all year, but are worse during the rainy season.

VŨNG TÀU

Once advertised as the 'tourist entrance gate' to Southern Vietnam, Bà Rịa-Vũng Tàu is one of the country's smallest provinces, with an area of less than 2,000km^2. Some readers might have seen pictures of its provincial capital, Vũng Tàu, in the press when the last American combat troops left Vietnam from here in 1973. Today, it is the centre of Vietnam's oil industry, with the rigs of a dozen of the world's leading multinationals anchored offshore. Its black liquid gold and natural gas resources helped provide millions of dollars to invest in new ventures in the service industry. Some, such as the Bãi Sau Tourist Complex, flopped, whereas others, like the continually improving provincial museum, are a success.

The good-time riviera city of Vũng Tàu, formerly the playground of French officers who knew it as Cap Saint Jacques, is less than 100km from Hồ Chí Minh City, and with excellent year-round weather, was tipped in the 1990s to become Vietnam's number one seaside resort. Then Nha Trang (page 335), Mũi Né (page 345) and their vastly superior beaches left Vũng Tàu in the dust. Instead, the city developed an undesired reputation for its poor-value, unkempt beach and dirty weekends. The city is shaking off its notoriety, however, as it ploughs money into its cultural institutions, heritage buildings and seaside promenades, though the biggest beach – Bãi Sau – still exudes seedy vibes.

Make no mistake: Vũng Tàu is not a tropical beach paradise. But with some compelling religious architecture, colonial heritage, pedestrian-friendly neighbourhoods, panoramic sunset spots and a few local speciality dishes – including fabulous seafood – the city is a pleasant place to while away a day or two. A major boon for no-nonsense travellers is the efficient boat service whisking passengers from District 1 (central Hồ Chí Minh City) to Vũng Tàu in a couple

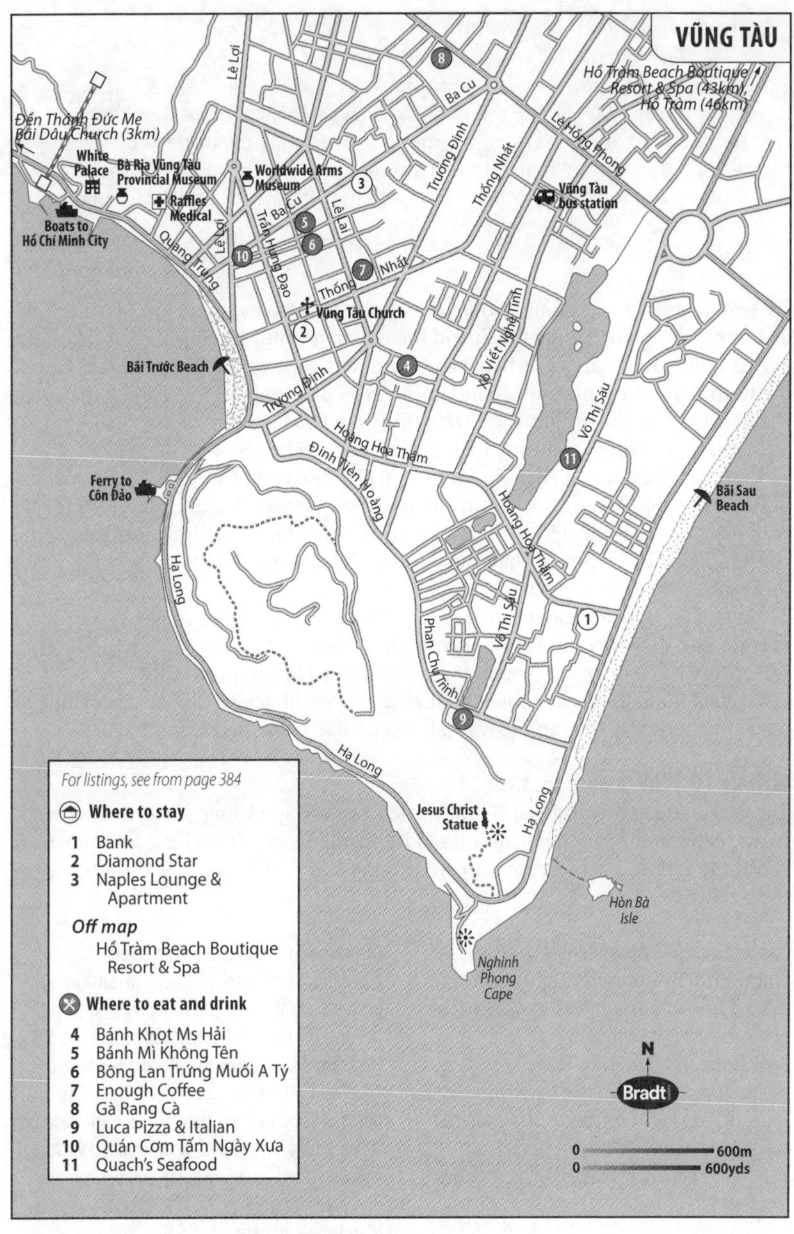

of hours. This is far preferable to contending with bus stations and traffic jams. If you're really craving a beach, head to Hồ Tràm, just an hour northeast by road.

GETTING THERE AND AROUND Vũng Tàu has no train station or airport. The most enjoyable way to travel here from Hồ Chí Minh City is by **boat**. Greenlines (**w** greenlines-dp.com) offers passenger-only boat services from Bến Bạch Đằng (10B Tôn Đức Thắng, District 1) in central Hồ Chí Minh City to Vũng Tàu. There

GETTING TO CÔN ĐẢO FROM VŨNG TÀU

If the seas are calm, there is a comfortable ferry service between Bãi Trước in Vũng Tàu and Côn Sơn in the Côn Đảo archipelago, with **Côn Đảo Express** (w phuquocexpress.com) on a large ship that made its maiden voyage in 2024. If the seas are rough, the ferry might not run. The journey takes 4 to 5 hours and runs every other day. Check the website for up-to-date prices and times.

are two boats each day going in both directions, with boats from Hồ Chí Minh City to Vũng Tàu leaving before lunch and the return journey leaving after. It takes just over 2 hours. Boats arrive at Bến Tàu Greenlines close to Bãi Trước Beach. Check the website for the most up-to-date times, prices and for booking. Failing that, visit the ticket office, also at Bến Bạch Đằng. You can usually jump on the boat without a reservation, except for during national holiday weekends.

Vũng Tàu **bus** station (Bến Xe Vũng Tàu, Nam Kỳ Khởi Nghĩa) is 2km northeast of Bãi Trước Beach and 1km northwest of Bãi Sau. Regular buses connect Vũng Tàu with Hồ Chí Minh City (3hrs). There are also regular buses heading north along the coast to Phan Thiết (3hrs), Phan Rang (6hrs), Nha Trang (8hrs) and beyond. From those cities you can switch to the train.

Vũng Tàu is close enough to Hồ Chí Minh City that you might spring for a **private car**. If you're moving between the other destinations in this chapter, a private car is the only way to avoid transferring in Hồ Chí Minh City.

Central Vũng Tàu is just about **walkable**, but you'll need a **taxi or motorbike** to reach further-away sites and to travel between Bãi Trước Beach and Bãi Sau.

WHERE TO STAY *Map, page 383*

The leafy streets behind Bãi Trước Beach are an appealing place to stay, with parks, cafés and restaurants, and it's close to the sights. If looking for your own accommodation, try the streets close to Vũng Tàu Church. Prices can double on the weekends.

Naples Lounge & Apartment 152/4 Ba Cu. Self-contained studio apartments & rooms with basic cooking facilities & a clean, fresh look. If you have trouble booking, try Airbnb. **$**

Bank Hotel 174 Hoàng Hoa Thám; w nganhanghotel.vn. Gigantic government hotel in one of Vũng Tàu's most spectacular modernist buildings. Service & facilities are lacking, but architecture enthusiasts will enjoy the attractive façade. **$$**

Diamond Star Hotel 4 Thống Nhất; f diamondstarhotel. The location outshines the property at this gleaming white hotel, with views of Vũng Tàu Church & a neat square in front. **$$**

Hồ Tràm Beach Boutique Resort & Spa Hồ Tràm; w hotramresort.com. In Hồ Tràm, 1hr north of Vũng Tàu, this superb beachside oasis is beautifully landscaped, with secluded villas, lily-filled ponds, reading library, games room & play areas for the kids. An ideal couple- & family-friendly w/end getaway. **$$$**

WHERE TO EAT AND DRINK *Map, page 383*

Restaurants and street food

✷ **Bánh Khọt Ms Hải** 42 Trần Đồng; 06.00–13.00 daily. One of dozens of humble family-owned establishments selling local speciality *bánh khọt*. **$**

Bánh Mì Không Tên 58 Lý Thường Kiệt; 18.00–23.00 daily. Nameless corner building kiosk selling what many Vũng Tàu residents will tell you is the city's best *bánh mì*. You'll need to queue, but it's worth the wait. Take-away only. **$**

Bông Lan Trứng Muối A Tý 2 Đồ Chiểu; ⌚ 08.00–20.30 daily. This part of town is known for *bông lan*, a kind of cupcake with savoury toppings like cheese, salted egg & pork floss (salted dried shredded pork with a cotton wool-like texture). This establishment is one of many. Take-away only. $

Quán Cơm Tấm Ngày Xưa 3 Trung Nhi; ⌚ 06.00–20.30 daily. All-day eatery that gets busy at lunchtimes & sells *cơm tấm* (page 460), a dish associated with Hồ Chí Minh City but popular across the south. $

Luca Pizza & Italian 230 Phan Chu Trinh; f LucaPizzaItalianRestaurant; ⌚ 11.00–22.30 daily. Pizza, pasta, grilled vegetables & other Italian favourites, including ice cream & other delicious desserts. $$

✷ **Quách's Seafood Restaurant** 187 Võ Thị Sáu; ⌚ 09.00–22.00 daily. Excellent quality but quite pricey seafood in a relaxed, almost diner-like setting. The staff speak English & the picture menu is easy to navigate, or you can go outside & point at the fish tanks. $$

Coffee houses

Enough Coffee 42/12 Lê Lai; ⌚ 07.00–19.00 daily. Cute 1-room hideaway coffee house. They specialise in Western coffee favourites, so flat whites, lattes & the like. The coffee beans are imported.

✷ **Gà Rang Cà** 242A Lê Hồng Phong; ⌚ 07.00–17.00 daily. Casual streetside café with excellent coffee brewed from quality local beans. They also sell the beans they use at very reasonable prices.

OTHER PRACTICALITIES There are no tourist information offices and travel agencies of note in town, but you'll hardly need one as you can access **tourist** services (eg: motorbike rental) through your hotel. VTVFCF (w vtvfcf.org), a volunteer fund that helps disadvantaged families, also runs tours. **Raffles Medical** (1 Lê Ngọc Hân) have a location in Bãi Trước, but return to Hồ Chí Minh City for serious health problems.

WHAT TO SEE AND DO

Bà Rịa Vũng Tàu Provincial Museum (4 Trần Phú; w baotangbrvt.org.vn; ⌚ 07.30–11.30 & 13.30–17.00 daily; 40,000VND/free adult/child) Huge institution that adds to Vietnam's lengthening list of comprehensive provincial museums. The museum only opened in 2021 but received a facelift at the end of 2023. English signage is good and full of detail, only occasionally rambling into the esoteric. The museum is set up chronologically and pinpoints pivotal moments in history,

VŨNG TÀU'S SPECIALITY DISHES

BÁNH KHỌT Vũng Tàu's number-one speciality dish is *bánh khọt*, a shallow cup-shaped pancake topped with shrimp and spring onion. Eat it with pickles, herbs and lettuce and dipped in a sweet-and-spicy fish sauce dipping sauce. Try it at **Bánh Khọt Ms Hải** (see opposite).

BÔNG LAN Vũng Tàu's secondary claim to culinary fame are these little cupcakes, an innovative blend of traditional European baking and Asian sweet treats. Salty eggs and/or pork balance the sponge. Try it at **Bông Lan Trứng Muối A TÝ** (see above).

HẢI SẢN Some people from Hồ Chí Minh City come to Vũng Tàu just for the seafood (*hải sản*), though in reality it's a similar standard to anywhere else on the coast – and not particularly cheap. The crab and clams are said to be particularly good in Vũng Tàu. Try some at **Quách's Seafood Restaurant** (see above).

including civilisations, the feudal period, the French invasion and resistance, American invasion and resistance and Vũng Tàu after 1975. A highlight of the museum is the atmospheric aquatic chamber with salvaged antiques on the uppermost floor. As is often the case when arriving somewhere new in Vietnam, the provincial museum is a good place to start.

Bãi Trước Beach Front Beach is far smaller than Bãi Sau (Back Beach), but with fewer hotels in this part of the city it has a congenial local vibe, especially at sunset. Behind the beach is a park, playground and various modern art sculptures. Either side of the small patch of sand, fishermen set up makeshift market stalls and try to flog their catch directly to haggling housewives.

Vũng Tàu Church (6 Thống Nhất; w giothanhle.net/gio-le/nha-tho-vung-tau) Though the structure of this church, established in 1889 and adapted several times since, is quite simple, it has some notable Asian touches, such as the dark green roofs with gently curving corners. The church community is very active, particularly during Easter and Christmas, and is welcoming to newcomers of all faiths. There are two services (in Vietnamese) a day Monday to Thursday, one on Friday, three on Saturday and five on Sunday. The times are published on a board to the right of the entrance. Outside the services, the church opening hours are sporadic.

Jesus Christ Statue (Núi Nhỏ; ⌚ 07.15–11.30 & 13.30–16.30 daily) This Rio de Janeiro-style figure of Jesus, built in 1971 with outstretched arms, looks out over the East Sea from its perch on top of Small Mountain (Núi Nhỏ). The statue rests on a raised platform, is 28m high and was built with an internal spiral staircase that reaches a viewing platform at the level of the outstretched arms. The sweaty climb from the coast begins close to the Nghinh Phong Cape, Vũng Tàu's southernmost point and an excellent sunset spot, but it's also possible to drive some of the way on a motorbike. The view directly east looks out over Hòn Bà Isle, where there is a small shrine.

Hòn Bà Isle This Maldivian experience is only reachable at low tide, when you can stroll across the rocky isthmus to the small tidal islet. This has been a place of worship since at least the 19th century and was originally visited by fishermen to pray to Thủy Long Thánh Mẫu, a water goddess, for a bountiful catch. These days it's more popular with domestic tourists than worshippers. The pathway is at its most accessible during the full moon.

✷ White Palace (Bạch Dinh; next to the provincial museum; ⌚ 07.30–11.30 & 13.30–17.00 Tue–Sun; 15,000VND/free adult/child) Emphatically French in its design, 'Villa Blanche' was built between 1898 and 1902. It was originally intended to be the summer residence of Paul Doumer, the French governor-general, yet he returned to France before having the opportunity to luxuriate within its white walls. The Nguyễn kings have a closer connection to this site than any colonist. In 1788, Nguyễn Ánh (later Emperor Gia Long) ordered the installation of a beacon to warn Gia Định Citadel of invasion. In 1824, King Minh Mạng upgraded this and built Phước Thắng Fortress to exert control over the Cần Giờ estuary. Barely anything of this fortress remains, though there is a plaque commiserating its destruction. In the early 20th century, the White Palace was used as a prison to house Emperor Thành Thái, who fiercely resisted the French, for a decade before his exile to Réunion Island. In 1934, Bạch Dinh became one of Emperor Bảo Đại's lavish resorts. During the Indochina Wars, the palace fell into disrepair, but in 1992 it was recognised by the Ministry of Culture as a cultural relic. Set among white frangipani, fragrant magnolia and *Bougainvillaea spectabilis* blossoms, its archaic European façade adorned with stylistic Greco-Roman figures looks out over the bay. The grounds make for a pleasant stroll, but beware the unfriendly macaques.

Worldwide Arms Museum (98 Trần Hưng Đạo; w baotangroberttaylor.com; ⌚ 08.00–17.00 daily; 70,000VND/free adult/child) Vũng Tàu is the unlikely home of one of Vietnam's most expansive collections of military uniforms and arms. The private collection belongs to Robert Taylor, something of a local celebrity. If he's around, he'll be enthusiastic about chatting to visitors and answering questions. The highlight might be the detailed and fearsome Japanese armour from the Samurai period, but the museum also houses Chinese, Greek, Mongol, Napoleonic, Persian and Roman exhibits. There are some magnificent rifles, many of which are ornate and beautiful despite being weapons of war. The museum is extremely well signposted and war history aficionados will spend many happy hours here. For others, the seemingly endless wardrobes might prove to be overkill. Local guides are available, though they don't always speak English.

Around Vũng Tàu

✷ ***Đền Thánh Đức Mẹ Bãi Dâu Church*** (140A Trần Phú; ⌚ 04.00–21.30 daily) You could spend a whole afternoon motorbiking around Vũng Tàu's westernmost jungle-clad peninsula, stopping at the various seaside cafés, colourful pagodas and stylish churches. A highlight of the trip is the exceptionally stylish Đền Thánh Đức Mẹ Bãi Dâu, a seemingly well-funded church with an intelligent, self-cooling interior.

Hồ Tràm Beach An hour north of Vũng Tàu, Hồ Tràm is a rugged beach destination; if you're making the trip here it's worth staying at least one night. The sand strips here are large and quiet, punctuated by rocky outcrops that extend into the sea. Though not as paradisical as those further north, they are calm, quiet and relatively close to Hồ Chí Minh City.

CÁT TIÊN NATIONAL PARK

Located east of Hồ Chí Minh City, Đồng Nai Province, which has more than 3 million inhabitants, covers almost 5,890km^2. Its main administrative centre, Biên Hòa, is a highly industrialised town. The province's brown-red soils are rich in minerals, especially basalt, and agricultural communities produce rice, corn, cassava, soya beans, sugarcane, cotton, tobacco, coffee, sweet potatoes and raffia. These days, if the province makes an appearance in local media, it's usually with updates on the progress of Long Thành Airport. A landmark project set to transform Vietnam's aviation landscape and just 40km from Hồ Chí Minh City, the airport will finally relieve pressure on Tân Sơn Nhất International Airport, which has long operated beyond capacity. In early 2024 Prime Minister Phạm Minh Chính demanded that Long Thành be ready for 2026, but like many large public infrastructure projects in Vietnam, the airport is marred in controversy related to land acquisition, environmental impact, financial concerns, project delays and issues of transparency. Despite this enormous development project in the south of the province, much of northern Đồng Nai is covered in dense forest, some of which is protected by **Cát Tiên National Park**.

Cát Tiên, 150km northeast of Hồ Chí Minh City, is one of Vietnam's largest national parks, covering an area of close to 800km^2. It was established in 1992 and is currently managed by a team of rangers who have the daunting task of policing its strict protection zone. The park first hit conservation headlines in 1991 when a World Wildlife Fund (WWF) survey discovered the presence of the Javan rhino (*Rhinoceros sundaicus*), at the time one of the world's rarest endangered large mammals. Further surveys in 1992 and 1994 showed that the population was successfully breeding. The park hit headlines again in 2010, but this time for the wrong reasons: the body of a Javan rhino had been found with its horn removed. The following year it was confirmed that *Rhinoceros sundaicus* was extinct in the country – a tragic day indeed. Now only those in Ujung Kulon National Park in West Java remain.

The park's diverse ecosystems support hundreds of plant species, including medicinal herbs and rare orchids. It is home to more than a hundred bird species and dozens of mammals, including one of the country's largest elephant populations. The forests are also home to macaques, gibbons and gaur, otherwise known as Indian bison, all of which are quite easy to see. Pied storks and night herons inhabit the park's numerous lagoons and lakes. Many are preyed upon by Siamese crocodiles, which are also easy to spot. Rich forest covers most of the park's total area. The predominant species is the bamboo (*Bambusa procera*), which occupies around a third of the terrain. Many of the larger species such as the red sindora tree, *hopea*, *shorea* and *dipterocarpus* species reach a height of 40–50m and were of great economic importance before logging was curtailed. A small resident population of the Ma and Stieng ethnolinguistic groups lived here and would burn down trees to grow corn, sesame, pumpkins and gourds, but these groups have since been resettled outside the national park boundaries.

There is enough to do to justify a few days here, including cycling to the Crocodile Lake, tracking elephant footsteps on a hike, kayaking through narrow rivers to spot birds, jumping on a jeep at night to find gaur and visiting reserves that shelter gibbons, lorises, langurs, macaques and bears.

HISTORY AND CONSERVATION Cát Tiên National Park was established by combining three smaller reserves in 1992, when Western governments and organisations started taking an interest. An integrated conservation programme was instigated in 1995 with funding of US$6.3 million from the Dutch government, going some way to improving socioeconomic development and reducing deforestation, over-utilisation, illegal hunting and rare-plant collecting. Anti-poaching activities funded and facilitated by the WWF began the following year. In the late 1990s, Fauna & Flora International (FFI) started working on habitat restoration and species conservation projects in the park, including reforestation and community engagement activities; soon after the Global Environment Facility, International Union for Conservation of Nature, Conservation International and the International Rhino Foundation began various conservation projects, including biodiversity conservation, monitoring and protecting endangered species, sustainable land management, and building on anti-poaching measures. The Endangered Asian Species Trust, a UK charity, opened its flagship project, the Đảo Tiên Endangered Primate Species Centre (page 390), within Cát Tiên National Park in 2008. In the same year, Australian charity Free The Bears opened Cát Tiên Bear Rescue Centre. Despite these positive movements in animal conservation, the Javan rhinoceros was declared extinct in Vietnam in 2010, marking a significant loss for biodiversity in the park. Nevertheless, international conservation efforts, particularly from the WWF and FFI, continued and strengthened. In more recent years, community-based conservation and reforestation projects gained momentum, involving local communities directly in conservation to ensure that they benefit from protecting the park. This remains a challenge, particularly for the Mạ and Stieng communities, who have been resettled in squalid villages just outside the national park.

GETTING THERE AND AROUND The small village of Nam Cát Tiên is the launchpad for Cát Tiên National Park. To travel into the national park from here, there is a small pier that ferries people across the river. The national park is 150km northeast of Hồ Chí Minh City, a little more than halfway to Đà Lạt. To get to and from here independently, book a Futa Hồ Chí Minh City–Đà Lạt **bus** and ask them to drop you at Tân Phú town. From Tân Phú, you can find a taxi to the national park. If you're booking accommodation before you arrive, ask about transport as they can often offer good deals for **private cars or minibuses** and might link you with other guests to save money. If you're moving between the other destinations in this chapter, a private car is the only way to avoid lengthy transfers. Cars and motorbikes are not permitted within the national park, but many hotels lend bicycles, and it's also possible to rent them for a small fee at the visitor centre. Make sure you spend a few minutes inspecting and riding the bikes before deciding on which one to take.

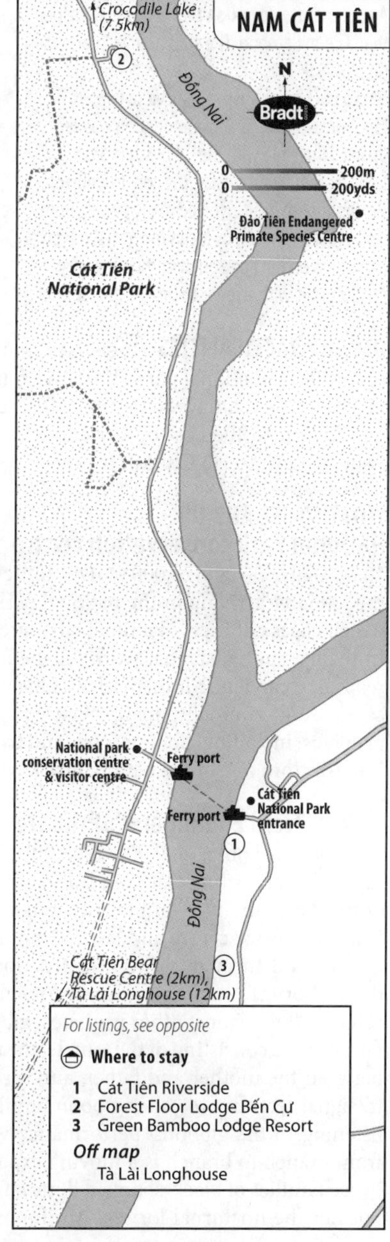

WHERE TO STAY AND EAT *Map, right*

You will likely eat most of your meals at your accommodation. Activities available to you are different depending on where you stay. Kayaking, treks to the bat cave, elephant path tracking, and activities with local communities are best done from Tà Lài Longhouse. Cycling and hiking to Crocodile Lake, the night safari and visiting the conservation centres is easiest from Forest Floor, the park headquarters and the various accommodation options in the village.

Green Bamboo Lodge Resort Ấp 1, Nam Cát Tiên; f Green Bamboo Lodge Enjoy Nature. Rustic & good-value accommodation, with bungalows on stilts overlooking the river, decent food & friendly, English-speaking staff. There are cheaper options for budget travellers here. **$**

Cát Tiên Riverside Hotel Ấp 1, Tân Phú; f. Another riverside option that is newer & crisper than Green Bamboo. The staff here are particularly helpful. **$$**

✱ **Tà Lài Longhouse** Tà Lài; w ta-lai-longhouse.com. This accommodation was set up in partnership with the WWF & has proved to be extremely successful. The construction of the longhouse itself involved many people from the area & is now run by locals too. You sleep on a mattress on the floor, but it's otherwise very comfortable, with screens to provide privacy between groups. It's become popular with international school groups from Hồ Chí Minh City, so avoid the w/ends & holidays. Homestay-style meals are generous & delicious, & the English-speaking team can organise various tours. **$$**

✱ **Forest Floor Lodge Bến Cự** f vn.forestfloorlodge. Tented lodge accommodation in the jungle, overlooking a stream & close to the visitor centre within the national park boundaries. The tents are as sealed as they can be, but this won't stop geckos & insects coming in & making some noise (don't worry, though – you're safe inside your mosquito net). There is a wooden deck where you can spot birds, including toucans if you're lucky. Meals are tasty home cooking, but a little on the small side. Since Forest Floor is inside the national park, there's no need to keep crossing the river. **$$$**

OTHER PRACTICALITIES There is no tourism information office beyond the visitor centre in the national park. There's also no ATM in town, so come with **cash**. Bear in mind that you have to pay 60,000VND each day you spend in the national park in addition to the cost of any entrance fees or activities. If you have any **health** issues, return to Hồ Chí Minh City.

WHAT TO SEE AND DO

National Park conservation centre

(w cattiennationalpark.com.vn; ⏲ 07.00–19.00 daily; 50,000/25,000VND adult/child) The visitor centre, which is just to the left after arriving in the national park, has a small conservation centre of sorts which cages confiscated animals that are about to be released back into the world. In theory, specialists that work for the national park decide when the animals are ready and can fend for themselves. One would hope that is as soon as possible as the cages seem criminally small. What you see is pot luck, but there are usually some primates, including gibbons, boas and tropical birds. There is a short tour in broken English from one of the national park employees.

✱ Đảo Tiên Endangered Primate Species Centre

(w go-east.org; ⏲ by appointment only; 400,000/200,000VND for foreign adult/child) One of the highlights of visiting Cát Tiên National Park are the expert- or volunteer-led tours of this large and well-run facility. English-language tours run daily at 08.00, leave from the visitor centre and last 2–3 hours; always book a few days in advance and they'll send through visiting instructions. The tour is early enough to hear the dawn chorus from the white- and golden-cheeked gibbons, both in and outside the reserve. Unlike most other primates, gibbons are monogamous and live in nuclear family units consisting of the female, the male and their offspring. The song is a duet between the mother and father, and serves as both a bonding exercise and a way to signal territory to other gibbon families. The song is extraordinarily loud, and listening to the gibbons' performance while watching them gymnastically swing from branch to branch is a moving experience not to be missed. You're also likely to see families of black-shanked douc langurs, who are generally not monogamous, but not the nocturnal lorises. An important part of the tour is learning how the primates are rehabilitated into the jungle after being rescued, through the use of semi-wild transitionary areas.

Cát Tiên Bear Rescue Centre (w freethebears.org; ⌚ 07.30–16.30 daily; minimum donation 1,100,000/550,000VND adult/child) This rescue centre, run by Australian charity Free the Bears, offers half-day tours of the sanctuary that provide 'special behind-the-scenes access'. You'll learn the harrowing stories that led to the bears finding themselves in the rescue centre and meet the team looking after them. The tours are pricey, but one can assume that is to limit numbers and that the money goes towards looking after the bears. Book directly on the website a few days in advance.

✷ **Cycling and hiking to Crocodile Lake** (250,000VND) Come here to see a freshwater crocodile, in this case the Siamese crocodile (*Crocodylus siamensis*), an endangered species endemic to the wetlands and slow water streams of Southeast Asia. The freshwater crocodile life cycle is around 40 years and an adult can reach over 3m long. These crocodiles lay eggs throughout their lives, with the reproductive season lasting from April to October. According to signs, each year a female can lay 30 to 40 eggs, with a hatching success rate of 75–95%, which seems unlikely considering they are endangered. The crocodiles hunt at night and sun themselves during the day. To reach Crocodile Lake (Bàu Sấu), rent a bicycle from the visitor centre and cycle 4km north, where you'll see a sign pointing to the lake on the left. Leave your bike behind and walk a well-marked trail for around 45 minutes to the lake. You'll pass an ancient tree on the way. It's also possible to stay overnight at Bàu Sấu; inquire at the visitor centre. There is a small hut serving coffee, cold drinks and instant noodles overlooking the lake.

Night safari (500,000/300,000/200,000/150,000VND pp for 1/2/3/4+ people) The night safari is designed for seeing the endangered gaur, otherwise known as Indian bison (*Bos gaurus*), though you may also see deer and, if you're very lucky, lorises. The safari isn't particularly intrepid: an open-air truck simply drives up and down the road that tracks south from the visitor centre while the 'guide' (don't expect any information) looks for animals with a big torch. But the chances of seeing gaur herds are fairly high. These large herbivores congregate in groups in the grasslands. Gaurs can be aggressive so if you happen upon one while walking anywhere in the park then keep your distance.

✷ **Trekking and kayaking** Trekking and kayaking experiences are best organised through and from Tà Lài Longhouse (see opposite). At the time of research they were running two tours: one to follow elephant paths to see footprints and scratching posts (don't expect to see elephants) and another to a bat cave. Tours are rewarding, though not in English. Tà Lài Longhouse also rents kayaks to explore the narrow rivers that branch off from the Đồng Nai River. Go in the evening and spot kingfishers and egrets.

TÂY NINH

Sharing a 240km border with Cambodia to the northwest and covering an area of 4,030km^2, Tây Ninh Province was part of the Khmer Kingdom until the 17th century. This border territory is where Vietnamese-American photo-journalist Nick Út shot his Pulitzer Prize-winning photo documenting the horrific scene of a young girl, Phan Thị Kim Phúc, running up the road naked to escape a napalm attack. The province made front-page news again between 1975 and December 1978, when soldiers of Pol Pot's Khmer Rouge periodically attacked villages in this province, killing the men and raping the women. Ostensibly, it was to stop these incursions that the Vietnamese army invaded Cambodia in December 1978, taking Phnom Penh by January 1979. Today, Tây Ninh is famous because of its Cao Đài Cathedral.

You can visit the province at any time of year. Most people visit Tây Ninh as a day trip from Hồ Chí Minh City, and it's just about possible to see both the Cao Đài Great Temple and Black Lady Mountain in one day. If you decide to stay overnight, there are plenty of accommodation options in Tây Ninh city, but nowhere of particular note.

WHAT TO SEE AND DO

✷ Cao Đài Great Temple (Phạm Hồ Pháp; f toathanhtayninh.official; ⌚ all day daily) The idiosyncratic Cao Đài Great Temple, the cathedral of the Cao Đài religion (page 33), is the main reason to visit Tây Ninh. The Cao Đài Great Temple, built in the 1930s and 40s, is set within a very large complex of schools and administrative buildings, all washed in pastel yellow. The twin-towered cathedral seems European in inspiration but with distinct Asian features. On the façade are figures of Cao Đài saints in high relief and at the entrance is a painting depicting Victor Hugo flanked by the Vietnamese poet Nguyễn Bỉnh Khiêm and the Chinese nationalist Sun Yat Sen. The latter holds an inkstone, symbolising, strangely, the perceived link between Confucianism and Christianity. British travel writer Norman Lewis was amusingly unimpressed with the structure, writing in *A Dragon Apparent*, published in 1951, that the 'cathedral must be the most outrageously vulgar building ever to have been erected with serious intent'.

Just before midday, a procession forms outside the cathedral. After removing shoes and hats, women enter the cathedral through a door to the left, men to the right, and they then proceed down their respective aisles towards the altar, usually accompanied by a Cao Đài priest dressed in white with a black turban. During services they don red, blue and yellow robes, signifying Confucianism, Taoism and Buddhism respectively. The men in coloured robes sporting an embroidered divine eye on their clothes are more senior. During services, on the balcony at the back of the cathedral, a group of men play a stringed instrument between their feet using a bow; women sing as they play. The ceremony unfolds like a séance from a fictional cosmic cult in a Lovecraftian short story. Novelist Graham Greene, who was reportedly inspired to visit Vietnam after reading Lewis's *A Dragon Apparent*, referred to the procession as 'The Walt Disney Fantasia of the East' in *The Quiet American*.

Inside, two rows of pink pillars entwined with green dragons line the nave, leading up to the main altar, which supports a large globe on which is painted a single staring eye – the divine, all-seeing-eye and master of the universe. It is to this Supreme Being that the congregation bows to the sound of a loud bell. The roof is blue and dotted with clouds, representing the heavens, and the walls are pierced by open, latticework windows with the divine eye as the centrepiece to the window design. At the back of the cathedral is a sculpture of Phạm Công Tắc (see opposite), the last pope and one of the religion's founders, who died in 1957. He stands on flowers surrounded by huge brown snakes and is flanked by his two assistants; one is the leader of spirits, the other the leader of the material world.

There are nine columns and nine steps to the cathedral, representing the nine steps to heaven. Above the altar is the Cao Đài pantheon. At the top in the centre is Sakyamuni Buddha. Next to him on the left is Lao Tzu, master of Taoism. Left

THE FOUNDERS AND FOLLOWERS OF CAO ĐÀI

The Cao Đài religion was founded in 1926 by Ngô Văn Chiêu after he was visited by the Supreme Being in 1919 during a séance in Phú Quốc that reportedly shook the tables in the room. When he died in 1943, his successor, Phạm Công Tắc, suffered greatly under the French and was eventually deported to the Comoros Islands. He returned in 1946, but during the pro-Catholic Ngô Đình Diệm period was forced to flee into neighbouring Cambodia. Ngô was so opposed to the sect that it is rumoured he, along with his brother, Ngô Đình Nhu, had the Cao Đài chief-of-staff killed. Some think this barbaric act was the reason they were assassinated in Chợ Lớn in November 1963 (page 17). Today, there are perhaps as many as 6 million members of the sect across the world, as against only 26,000 initially. Many famous people such as Victor Hugo, Brahma, Confucius, Buddha, Sir Winston Churchill, Moses, Sun Yat Sen, Li Bai, Quan Công, Charlie Chaplin, Allan Kardec and Admiral Duclos are now worshipped as saints. In theory, followers of this religion are strict vegetarians, obey the rules of chastity and live very simple, altruistic lives. Some followers hold séances in which they communicate with the spirit world. Through a medium, generally a learned monk, they talk to dead relatives and well-known Cao Đài advocates who illuminate the way forward. For more on the Cao Đài religion, see page 33.

of Lao Tzu is Quan Âm, the Goddess of Compassion (page 293), sitting on a lotus blossom. On the other side of the Buddha statue is Confucius. Right of the sage is the red-faced Chinese military general Quan Công. Below Sakyamuni Buddha is the leader of Chinese saints. Below him is Jesus.

The biggest ceremony is held at midday, but smaller ones take place at 06.00, 18.00 and midnight. The best viewing position is a balcony that overlooks the chequered floor of the nave. Visitors should not enter the central portion of the nave – keep to the side aisles – and should not wander in and out during services. If you go in at the beginning of the 1-hour service, stay until the end. The temple is 96km northwest of Hồ Chí Minh City and 64km from Củ Chi town. Visiting the great temple used to be easily combined with a trip to the Củ Chi tunnels (page 481), but worsening traffic in and around Hồ Chí Minh City has made this a long and unpleasant day. These days it is preferable to see Tây Ninh as a separate trip.

Black Lady Mountain (Núi Bà Đen; 🕘 06.00–18.00 daily; 10,000/5,000VND adult/child; cable car prices vary) Black Lady Mountain, sometimes translated as Black Virgin Mountain (page 394), is 10km to the northeast of Tây Ninh and 106km from Hồ Chí Minh City. The peak rises dramatically from the plain to a height of 986m and can be seen in the distance on entering Tây Ninh. The Black Lady was perhaps a certain Lý Thị Thiên Hương, a semi-mythical figure. Throughout history, the mountain has been fought over because of its strategic importance as the highest spot in Cochinchina. The Trịnh and the Nguyễn fought fierce battles here, followed by the French and the Vietnamese. During the American War, it frequently switched between the Việt Cộng and the South Vietnamese Army. Today, a war monument sits at its base. The Black Lady's commemorative temple, Linh Sơn Tiên Trạch, is about 600m up the mountain. Restored several times over the decades, it contains some beautiful Avalokitesvara Bodhisattva (Quan Âm; page 293) figures made out of fine porcelain. Those with energy can climb to the

LEGEND HAS IT: VIRGIN TERRITORY

The legend behind Núi Bà Đen, or Black Lady Mountain, has several conflicting threads. The accepted version tells of Lý Thị Thiên Hương, the daughter of either a 17th-century mandarin or a high-ranking Cambodian guard. Eager to find a husband for his beloved daughter, the wealthy father sought suitors from near and far.

Among those who pursued the chance to win her hand was a young scholar named Lê Sỹ Triệt, whose charm and intellect captured the young girl's heart. Another version claims that she fancied a fierce warrior who was off fighting occupying forces. The love between Hương and this mysterious young man blossomed, but was unfortunately met with ardent opposition. Hương's father, disapproving of their union due to social disparities, arranged for her to marry someone else and forbade her from seeing the man she loved.

Here the story becomes even more unclear. One legend tells that Hương agreed to end things with her lover but rejected her father's chosen suitor and fled to the remote mountain. Seeking solace in the mountain's secluded caves, she devoted herself to a life of solitude and meditation. She transformed into a black-robed deity, becoming the guardian spirit of the mountain, known as Bà Đen.

Another story suggests that rather than complying with her father's wishes, she threw herself from the mountain. A further version of this story is that Hương was kidnapped and raped by local scoundrels and her body was dumped on the mountainside. One final version claims that, after fleeing to the mountain, she devoted her life to helping the sick and poor, and was given the name Linh Sơn Thánh Mẫu (Mother Goddess of the Mountain) by the villagers.

Whatever the truth, many believe that Bà Đen now grants protection to visiting pilgrims.

top, which takes a very sweaty 60 minutes. The rest can take the 5-minute cable car journey. At the peak is a vast pagoda complex with views of Cambodia, as well as Bình Dương and Bình Phước provinces. The government recognised the Linh Sơn Thánh Mẫu Festival, which takes place during the fifth lunar month (June or July), as an intangible national heritage in 2019.

11

The Mekong Delta

The Mekong Delta lacks the topographical verticality of other subregions in the country, with the horizon in most provinces beginning at the closest copse. It is also highly populated, cultivated and industrialised, so pockets of unsullied natural beauty are thin on the exceptionally flat ground. Away from the urban sprawl, however, at the subregion's verdant best, the delta is a riot of greens: chameleon-coloured rice seedlings deepen in shade as they sprout ever taller, while palm trees and orchards make up an unbroken belt of viridescent hues. For many visitors, the appeals of the subregion lie in the tranquillity of its hinterlands, but also in the richness of its cultures. The delta's cultural intrigue is in its depth, not its breadth: only a handful of Vietnam's ethnolinguistic groups are represented here, but some pockets feel more like other parts of Southeast Asia. The Muslim Cham villages in the west, for example, are akin to rural neighbourhoods in Malaysia and Indonesia; the lofty pagoda stupas of the Buddhist Khmer provinces in the east wouldn't look out of place in Cambodia or Thailand.

Close to Hồ Chí Minh City and popular places for day trips (not recommended for an in-depth experience) are the provinces of **Tiền Giang**, **Vĩnh Long** and **Bến Tre**. **Cần Thơ**, the beating heart of the delta, offers all the benefits of a big city, from a range of hotels to varied dining options, and is within easy reach of **Sóc Trăng**

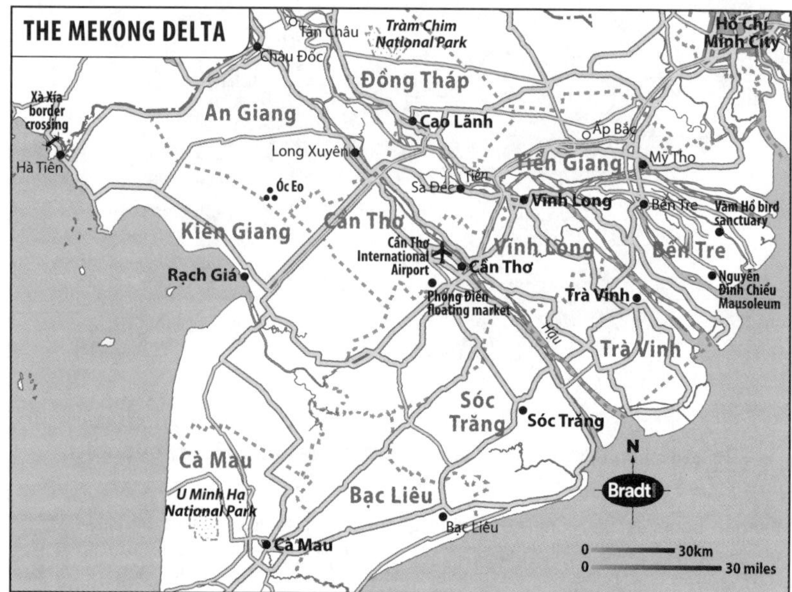

MAKING THE RIGHT CHOICE

Much like the northern mountains, it usually isn't possible, or even desirable, to go everywhere. All the provinces give a sense of what life is like in the Mekong Delta, though each offers different things to see and do. There are two things to consider: how much time you have and what you want to do. If you have three days or less, including transport time, restrict your area to the provinces closest to Hồ Chí Minh City: Tiền Giang, Vĩnh Long, Bến Tre, Cần Thơ and Đồng Tháp. With more time, you can explore the further-flung provinces: Trà Vinh, Cà Mau, Kiên Giang and An Giang.

In terms of things to do, the touristy provinces of Tiền Giang, Vĩnh Long and Bến Tre all offer typical Mekong Delta experiences, with boat journeys, visits to islands, waterside temples and some hidden-away lodges. Cần Thơ, a city with many sights of its own including a floating market, makes the best base, as the restaurant and hotel offerings are the best in the subregion. From here you can make trips to Sóc Trăng, Trà Vinh and Đồng Tháp. This guide does not suggest ✷ for places, but if it did, they would be: Cần Thơ because it makes for a comfortable base; Trà Vinh and its dozens of Khmer pagodas; Hà Tiên with its tombs and temples; and Châu Đốc, which offers spiritual intrigue, ethnolinguistic diversity, nature reserves and historical sites.

and beyond. East of here is **Trà Vinh**, with some of the finest Khmer temples in the country and a laid-back provincial capital. South is **Cà Mau**, a wild corner of the country that receives few visitors but has some important nature reserves. West of Cần Thơ is **Sa Đéc** in Đồng Tháp, one of the delta's most attractive towns; **Hà Tiên** in Kiên Giang, with its vestiges of an unusual history; and perhaps the most culturally and spiritually rich corner in all of Southern Vietnam: **Châu Đốc** in An Giang.

The Mekong Delta, which the Vietnamese refer to as Miền Tây (Western Region), or more poetically đồng bằng sông Cửu Long (Delta of the Nine Dragons, because the Mekong is said to split into nine distributaries upon reaching Vietnam), has long been Vietnam's rice bowl. Before the partition of the country in 1954, rice was traded from the south, where there was a surplus, to the north, where there was a deficit, as well as internationally. Even prior to the creation of French Cochinchina in the 19th century, rice was being transported from here to Huế, the imperial capital. The delta covers 67,000km^2, more than half of which is cultivated. In the Mekong Delta there is nearly three times as much rice land per person as there is in the north.

The Mekong Delta was not introduced to agriculture on an extensive scale until the late 19th and early 20th centuries. Initially it seems that this was a spontaneous process: peasants, responding to the market incentives introduced by the French, slowly began to push the frontier of cultivation southwards into this wilderness area. The process gathered pace when the French colonial government, seeing the subregion's potential, began to construct canals and drainage projects to open more land to wet rice agriculture. By the 1930s the population of the delta had reached 4.5 million, with 2,200,000ha of land under rice cultivation. The Mekong Delta, along with the Irrawaddy (Burma) and Chao Phraya (Thailand), became one of the great rice-exporting areas of Southeast Asia.

Given their proximity to prosperous Hồ Chí Minh City, the inhabitants of the Mekong Delta might have expected some of the benefits of development to trickle their way and help diversify away from agriculture. In this they have largely been disappointed. However, most of the Mekong Delta provinces are trying, and to a degree managing, to secure investment. Be it hotels, cafés and karaoke in Bến Tre or canning and storage plants in Cần Thơ, they are trying to improve their collective lot. The traditional problem they faced was that each year during the monsoon season wide areas of the delta would flood. The government builds and maintains river defences against the annual floods, but it is a laborious process. A novel and potentially more serious concern is the climate crisis: some of the more terrifying predictions put the Mekong Delta under water by the end of the century.

This chapter is organised as if approaching the subregion from Hồ Chí Minh City. It moves south through Mỹ Tho, Vĩnh Long, Bến Tre, Cần Thơ and Trà Vinh, before moving west to Sa Đéc, Hà Tiên and Châu Đốc. Though administratively a part of the Mekong Delta, Phú Quốc island is divorced both in geography and in character from the rest of the subregion, and is covered on page 427.

WHEN TO VISIT

The Mekong Delta has two seasons: a warm wet season (May–November), and a cooler dry season (December–April). January tends to be the most comfortable month.

The bird sanctuaries – **Vàm Hồ** in Bến Tre, **Tràm Chim** in Đồng Tháp and **Trà Sư** in An Giang – are best immediately after the rainy season, in December. **Ok Om Bok Festival**, usually in November, and Khmer New Year, usually in April, are most fervently celebrated in Sóc Trăng and Trà Vinh, close to Cần Thơ. One of the most colourful festivals in all of Vietnam is **Bà Chúa Xứ Temple Festival** (page 424), which takes place in April. Châu Đốc's Muslim Cham community also celebrates **Eid al-Fitr** at the end of Ramadan.

RIVERSIDE LODGES IN THE MEKONG DELTA

In some corners of the Mekong Delta there are lodges that can shape an experience in the subregion. In many cases you'll rely on the lodge for meals and activities, and most have some kind of tour desk to arrange excursions.

The Island Lodge 390 Thới Bình Hamlet, Tiền Giang; w theislandlodge.com.vn. A French-owned boutique lodge with colonial-style rooms with views of the Mekong River, gourmet fusion cuisine & an infinity pool. This is one of the delta's oldest luxury properties & its age is beginning to show, but in some ways this adds to the rustic charm. **$$$**

Mango Home Riverside Mỹ Thạnh Commune, Bến Tre; w mangohomeriverside.com. Mango Home Riverside is a good-value garden lodge with a pool, games room & decent dining. Like much of the Mekong Delta, the property is a little rough around the edges, but at these prices you can hardly complain. **$$$**

Victoria Núi Sam Núi Sam, An Giang; w victoriahotels.asia/en/destination/victoria-nui-sam. Part of the Victoria network, Núi Sam is not situated on the river but perched on one of the only hills in the subregion, on the border with Cambodia. It's fairly basic as lodges go, but comfortable, with 36 bungalows dotted across the mountain offering knock-out views. The service is excellent & the restaurant here is one of the best in the province. Also has a swimming pool with unobstructed views of the paddy fields. **$$$$**

Azerai Cồn Ấu, Cần Thơ; w azerai.com. Set on a private islet, this is the most luxurious place to stay in the subregion (outside of Phú Quốc). Getting here involves a *Mission Impossible*-style speedboat journey. The rooms are simple but with a touch of Scandinavian design elegance, & the grounds offer a gym, games room, pool, spa, restaurants & plenty of greenery. **$$$$$**

MỸ THO

Tiền Giang Province, of which Mỹ Tho is the capital, has an area of 2,500km^2 and a population of almost 2 million. A large part of the province is used for rice growing: the paddy is cropped two to three times per year and yields are extremely high. One of the main reasons for this is the abundance of fresh water delivered by the rivers: this is one of the only provinces in Vietnam to touch both the Mekong Delta and the mouth of the Saigon River. Saltwater fish farms are common in the coastal districts, a favoured variety being *tai tượng* (elephant's ears), found on most restaurant menus (usually shallow fried). Households also farm carp and prawns. Markets bulge with mango, watermelon, papaya, pomelo, grapefruit, longans, oranges, plums, apples, coconuts, jujube, bananas, rambutans and durians.

If arriving in the Mekong Delta from Hồ Chí Minh City, Mỹ Tho is the first city you'll encounter. This important riverside market settlement has been largely rebuilt after a horrific pounding during the American War. Old wooden buildings that once overhung the waterfront have been demolished and more humdrum architecture has taken their place. Modern cafés and restaurants have sprung up in the town centre, offering sweet coffee and fresh seafood. Along the waterfront, hotels accommodate tourists, though as Mỹ Tho has become busier and more cluttered, many bypass the city and head for lodges elsewhere in the province or in Bến Tre (page 401) and Vĩnh Long (page 400).

GETTING THERE AND AROUND There are no trains in the Mekong Delta. It takes 90 minutes to get to Mỹ Tho from Hồ Chí Minh City or Cần Thơ by **bus**, which leave at least every hour. To travel to other destinations in the Mekong Delta, Futa (w futabus.vn) is the best bet, but for the Hồ Chí Minh City–Mỹ Tho leg, you might be better off using Thảo Châu (w xethaochau.com), which you can book through Bao Lau (w baolau.com). Grab doesn't work well in Mỹ Tho, but you can ask your accommodation to book **taxis** for you.

WHERE TO STAY AND EAT Standard hotels can be found on the riverfront, but **The Little House** (357/10/13 Nguyễn Thị Thập; w thelittlehouse.my.canva.site; **$**) is recommended. Staying out of town in **Cồn Phụng Resort** (Cồn Phụng; w booking.com; **$$**) or **The Island Lodge** (see opposite; **$$$**) is preferable. **Hủ Tiếu Sate Mỹ Tho** (206A Nam Kỳ Khởi Nghĩa; 06.30–23.00 daily; **$**) does good noodles and **Nhà Hàng Hải Sản Sông Tiền** (Lãnh Binh Cẩn; w nhahangsongtien.tiengiangtourist.com; 10.00–22.00 daily; **$$$**) has excellent seafood.

OTHER PRACTICALITIES For informal **river cruises and activities**, you'll be able to negotiate with hawkers at the pier at the southern end of Nam Kỳ Khởi Nghĩa Street. There is no tourist information office. For **medical care**, Hồ Chí Minh City (page 465) and Cần Thơ (page 406) are not far away.

WHAT TO SEE AND DO

Vĩnh Tràng Pagoda (Ấp Mỹ An; 06.30–19.00 daily) Mỹ Tho's number-one attraction and worth a detour if merely passing through the city is this peach-and-cream pagoda. First built in 1849, it was rebuilt after fire damage in 1907 and 1930 and extensively renovated in 1992. It has an architectural style that blends Vietnamese, Chinese and French motifs, with highly sculptured columns and a fairytale façade. The pagoda was once known for its wooden statues, but new gargantuan Buddha statues now dominate the area.

THE COCONUT MONK

Phoenix Island (Cồn Phụng) was the sanctuary of Ông Đạo Dừa, the Coconut Monk. He got his name because, when he meditated for a period of three years, he apparently ate nothing but coconuts. He headed a religious sect known as Tịnh Độ Cư Sĩ, which practised a mixture of Christian and Buddhist doctrines. You will see both a cross and a reverse swastika in the grounds of his overgrown sanctuary on the east side of the island. They compete for attention with decorative columns that feature colourful, eccentric-looking dragons. Some say he was educated in France, others that he became a monk when he was only ten years old. One story is that he once put himself forward as a presidential candidate. Ridiculed and much talked-about because of his eccentricities, he is still remembered throughout the country. The sect was persecuted by both the South Vietnamese government and after reunification, and the monastery has fallen into disuse.

Ấp Bắc 20km west of Mỹ Tho is the hamlet of Ấp Bắc, the site of the communists' first major military victory against South Vietnam's forces. The battle demonstrated that without direct US involvement the communists could never be defeated. US lieutenant colonel John Paul Vann was harsh in his criticism of the tactics and motivation of the South Vietnamese Army who, in his eyes, failed to dislodge a weak Việt Cộng position. As he observed from the air, almost speechless with rage, he realised how feeble his Vietnamese ally was, an opinion that few senior US officers heeded – to their immense cost. Khu Di tích Chiến Thắng Ấp Bắc is a small museum that commemorates the victory, with weaponry and artefacts relating to the battle and a dark grey monument in a fitting socialist Realist style.

The islands There are four islands in the Tiền River between Mỹ Tho and Bến Tre that are named after Vietnam's four most important mythical animals: Dragon, Turtle, Phoenix and Unicorn. The best way of getting to them is to take a tour, but bear in mind that these islands are extremely touristy. Those seeking a quieter and less touristy river experience would do well to look elsewhere and go deeper into the delta. A vast pier and boat service centre has been built at the southern end of Nam Kỳ Khởi Nghĩa, where all the tours are now concentrated. To avoid the tens of thousands of visitors now descending on these islands, go in the afternoon after the tour buses have left and overnight in Mỹ Tho after the trip. If the above hasn't put you off, you'll find that all four islands are little gardens of Eden, stuffed with longan, durian, roses, pomelo, honey and rice wine (and tourists).

VĨNH LONG

Vĩnh Long Province, of over 1 million inhabitants, relies heavily on rice cultivation. Coconuts are also farmed extensively and jujube, plum, durian and longan trees grow well in the highly fertile alluvial soil deposited by the Tiền and Hậu rivers. Many communities also grow pepper, cashew and cacao trees. Industries in the province produce bricks and tiles, pottery, garments, agricultural machines, medicinal products, mats and rugs. Mỹ Tho and Vĩnh Long provinces are the gateway to the Mekong Delta from Hồ Chí Minh City; virtually all visitors to the area will pass through here.

Busy Vĩnh Long city has witnessed a modest high-rise trend when compared with Mỹ Tho and Bến Tre. Restaurants have been modernised and the ramshackle wooden stilt houses clustered on the waterfront have been replaced with concrete varieties. Streets are crammed with motorbikes, but down at the waterfront the pace of life is less hurried. Vĩnh Long was once a launchpad for boat trips through islands and to homestays and lodges, but this activity is now largely concentrated in Mỹ Tho. Some guidebooks and websites continue to peddle the small floating market at Cái Bè in Tiền Giang Province, but this closed during the Covid-19 pandemic and it is unlikely to reopen.

GETTING THERE AND AROUND It takes 2 hours to get to Vĩnh Long from Hồ Chí Minh City and 1 hour from Cần Thơ by **bus**. Vĩnh Long is too small for Grab, but you can ask your accommodation to book **taxis** for you.

WHERE TO STAY AND EAT Vĩnh Long's hotel and restaurant offerings are lacking, but you'll find most of what you need on the riverfront, close to Vĩnh Long Museum. **Khách Sạn Saigon – Vĩnh Long** (2 Trưng Nữ Vương; **w** saigonvinhlonghotel.com; **$$**) is a characterless but practical hotel, but for something special head out to **Mekong Pottery Homestay** (209A/15 Thành Mỹ 1; **w** mekongpotteryhomestay.com; **$$**), run by an artisanal family of potters.

OTHER PRACTICALITIES For informal **river cruises and activities**, sometimes you can negotiate with boat operators near the river. There is no tourist information office. For **medical care**, Hồ Chí Minh City (page 465) and Cần Thơ (page 406) are not far.

WHAT TO SEE AND DO

Văn Thánh Miếu (Trần Phú) Overlooking a river 2km southeast of the town centre, this complex was built with mustard-yellow walls in a Sino-Vietnamese style. If you only have time to visit one religious building in Vĩnh Long, this should be it. The complex is associated with the story of local hero Phan Thanh Giản, a mandarin-diplomat born in the province in 1796. It was he who signed the Treaty of Saigon, which formally handed over the rule of a large part of Cochinchina to the French in 1862. Later, in 1867, after leading an unsuccessful revolt against the French, he committed suicide rather than surrender. This is a Confucian temple, which are rarer in the south than in the north.

Vĩnh Long Provincial Museum (1 Phan Bội Châu; **w** baotangvinhlong.vn; 🕘 07.30–11.00 & 13.30–16.30 Tue–Sat) One of the better provincial museums in the subregion and located in the heart of Vĩnh Long, this building is simple and functional and the exhibits focus on the area's revolutionary history. Wartime relics on display include weapons, including some antique tanks, and photographs of local resistance fighters, many of whom played a role in the region's battle for independence. Another section of the museum focuses on the lives, past and present, of the three major ethnolinguistic groups in the eastern Mekong Delta: the Kinh (page 189), the Hoa (page 477) and the Khmer (page 411).

BẾN TRE

Of the three northeasternmost Mekong Delta provinces (the other two being Tiền Giang and Vĩnh Long), Bến Tre is probably the most attractive as it sits furthest from the busy Hồ Chí Minh City–Cần Thơ highway. Once separated from the mainland by the Mekong River, Bến Tre is no longer an island province; a bridge links it from just outside Mỹ Tho. It depends heavily on farming, fishing and coconuts, although there are some light industries engaged in processing the local farm output and refining sugar. During the wars of resistance against the French and Americans, Bến Tre earned itself a reputation as a staunch Việt Minh and Việt Cộng stronghold. The province's main claim to fame is that it is the birthplace of Nguyễn Đình Chiểu, a blind poet.

Bến Tre city has a relaxing riverfront feel, where bountiful fruit stalls are laid out on the waterfront and locals sell potted plants on barges by the river, though there's little to keep you occupied. Most come here to escape Hồ Chí Minh City and settle into a Mekong Delta lodge or homestay outside the city. Bến Tre is more amiable than Mỹ Tho and Vĩnh Long, however, and like all Mekong Delta settlements over a certain size, there are plenty of places to eat, drink coffee and slurp coconuts by the water.

GETTING THERE AND AROUND It takes a little over 2 hours to travel to Bến Tre from Hồ Chí Minh City by **bus**, which leave every hour. Bến Tre bus station (QL60, Hữu Định) is 4km north of the centre. The best bet for buses to and from Bến Tre is Thảo Châu (w xethaochau.com), which you can book through Bao Lau (w baolau.com). Grab doesn't work in Bến Tre, but you can ask your accommodation to book **taxis** for you.

WHERE TO STAY AND EAT There's no shortage of cheap, adequate hotels on the riverfront, as in other Mekong Delta cities. For something a little more special, head out to the countryside to design hotel **Haven Nest Retreat** (Nhơn Thạnh Ward; f; **$$$**) or **Mango Home Riverside** (page 398; **$$$**). Bến Tre has a number of good vegan restaurants, one of which is **Ẩm Thực Chay Tạ Ơn** (Mỹ Tân; ⌚ 08.00–21.00 daily; **$$**).

OTHER PRACTICALITIES There is no tourist information office. For medical care, Hồ Chí Minh City (page 465) and Cần Thơ (page 406) are not far.

WHAT TO SEE AND DO

Viên Minh Pagoda (Nam Kỳ Khởi Nghĩa; ⌚ 07.00–11.00 & 13.00–21.00 daily) This was rebuilt out of bricks and mortar in 1951–59. In the courtyard you will be greeted by a pure white statue of Quan Âm, the much-venerated Goddess of Compassion (page 293). The squat building is attractive and the interiors are orderly and colourful.

Bến Tre Museum (146 Hùng Vương; ⌚ 07.00–17.00 daily) Housed in what appears to be a colonial building but with significant modifications, Bến Tre Museum showcases the province's revolutionary contributions, including the Bến Tre Uprising of 1960, one of the first large-scale, co-ordinated revolts against the South Vietnamese government in the Mekong Delta. The uprising involved local guerrilla fighters, many of them women, using hit-and-run tactics to attack government targets. Though eventually suppressed, it inspired similar uprisings across Southern Vietnam and boosted support for the Việt Cộng. Unfortunately there is very little signage in English.

Around Bến Tre

Nguyễn Đình Chiểu Mausoleum (An Đức) Some 36km east of town, this tomb and shrine is dedicated to Nguyễn Đình Chiểu, a blind, prodigious poet from the 19th century. An epic and vivid poem of his tells of Lục Vân Tiên, who became blind while weeping over the loss of his beloved mother, and most cities have a street named after him. The mausoleum and temple are not remarkable, but the journey there and back from Bến Tre city traverses the province's lush countryside. You can combine the site with a visit to the bird sanctuary below.

Vàm Hồ bird sanctuary (Tân Quy, Tân Mỹ Commune; w sanchimvamho.vn; ⏲ 08.00–18.00 daily) Also situated east of Bến Tre city, this sanctuary of the winged class hosts pied storks, night herons, plovers, copper herons, white storks and wild ducks. Spotting them is not guaranteed, and birders that come from far and wide just for this may be sorely disappointed. Both Tràm Chim (page 416) and Trà Sư (page 424) offer much more rewarding experiences. You can, however, combine the sanctuary with a visit to the mausoleum (see opposite) as part of a larger exploration of the province, and the sanctuary has valiantly tried to diversify their offerings with river tours and farm visits. As always with bird sanctuaries in Vietnam, visit early in the morning or late in the afternoon.

CẦN THƠ

With a population of almost 2 million and with a fully fledged second-tier city, Cần Thơ Province is the economic, technical, geographical and cultural centre of the Mekong Delta. The main farming area between Cần Thơ city and the Hậu River is ideally suited to rice cultivation, where it's possible to grow three crops a year. Many other crops are cultivated, including jute, bananas, sugarcane, coconuts, pepper, tangerines, oranges, cashews, cacao, lemons and beans. Animal husbandry in the province is advanced, thanks originally to the efforts of Cần Thơ University, the most active educational institution south of Hồ Chí Minh City. Pigs are a big business and cattle are bred in large numbers. Improved biological and chemical control has eliminated many pests and given villagers a better standard of living, though the effects of climate change (page 5) pose real threats to this newfound prosperity.

Around three quarters of the province's inhabitants live in Cần Thơ city. Some of the foreign business dollars that have flooded into Hồ Chí Minh City have trickled into Cần Thơ, but it is far from living up to the city's nickname of 'Western Metropolis', and it lacks the urban dynamism of Đà Nẵng and Hải Phòng, Vietnam's other second-tier cities. Nevertheless, when compared with the rest of the Mekong Delta, hotels are smarter and more numerous and restaurants are plusher and more widespread. For those travellers who require comfort, variety and urban buzz in the delta, the city is a good choice, especially as old Cần Thơ is still there – though in many cases hidden by a more modern façade. Although it's a far cry from the fluid and bustling commercial romance peddled by tour companies and travel media, Cần Thơ's floating market is at least still operating, and remains interesting.

GETTING THERE AND AROUND The global ambitions of **Cần Thơ International Airport** (179B Lê Hồng Phong; w vietnamairport.vn) are yet to be fully realised, but it has several direct daily flights to various domestic destinations, including Hanoi, Phú Quốc, Côn Đảo, Đà Nẵng and Hải Phòng. Cần Thơ, which is 3 hours from Hồ Chí Minh City by **bus**, is a transport hub within the Mekong Delta, with connections to most cities, including Cà Mau (4hrs), Sóc Trăng (2hrs) and Châu Đốc (3hrs) with Futa. The city has a number of bus stations, but most companies will arrange pick-up/drop-off by shuttle bus. See page 405 for information on

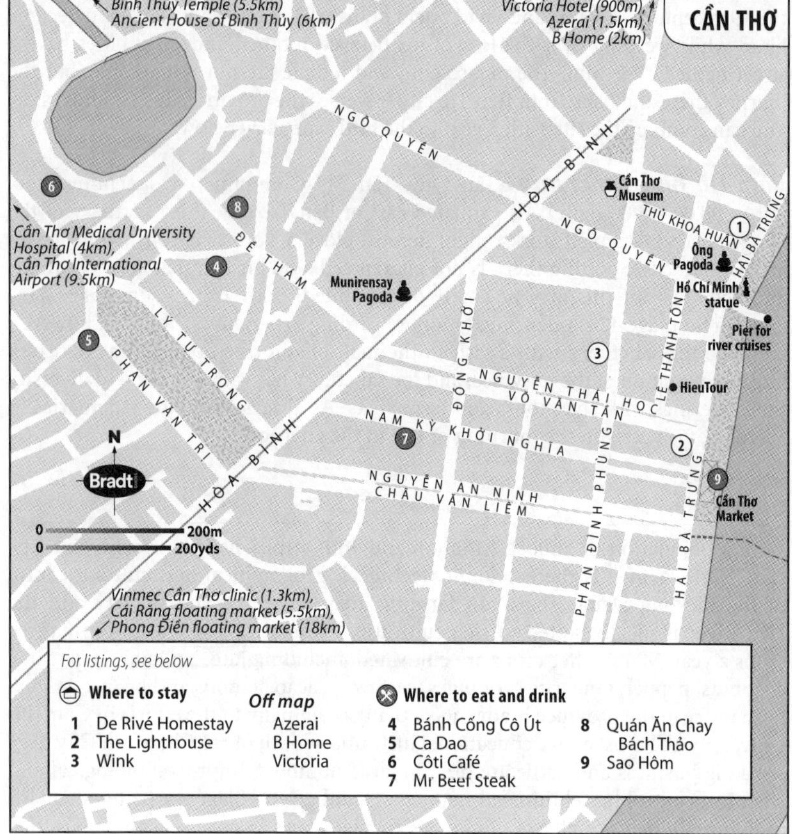

getting around the Mekong Delta by **boat**. It's also possible to take the ferry from Cần Thơ and Sóc Trăng to the Côn Đảo archipelago (page 438). **Grab** works well in Cần Thơ and **taxis** are plentiful.

WHERE TO STAY *Map, above*

When looking for basic accommodation in Cần Thơ, it's wise to be as close to the market as possible. This pedestrian-friendly neighbourhood is known as Ninh Kiều.

B Home 16 Tôn Thất Tùng; f bhomecantho. Modern, clean dorms & private rooms run by an enthusiastic team. The location isn't especially close to the market, but the facilities & service make up for it. **$**

De Rivé Homestay 10 Thủ Khoa Huân; f HauGiangBamboo. Friendly, simple & temptingly cheap, De Rivé has a handful of rooms overlooking the river & waterside promenade. **$**

The Lighthouse 120 Hai Bà Trưng; f thelighthousecantho. New apartment hotel that is ideally located in the centre of town & just a few steps from the market. There's a popular restaurant & café on the ground floor. **$$**

Victoria Cái Khế; **w** victoriahotels.asia. A classic colonial-style hotel, with capacious gardens & a swimming pool, that is suited to families. Rooms are showing their age but carry a certain charm. **$$$**

Wink Hotel 14 Phan Đình Phùng; **w** wink-hotels.com. The Saigonese tech-hotel group has recently branched out to Cần Thơ, bringing its combo of crisp design, hip staff & techy services. $$$

✷ **Azerai** See page 398. Simply superb riverside lodge with all the frills you could want, set in bucolic gardens. $$$$$

WHERE TO EAT AND DRINK *Map, opposite*

Bánh Cống Cô Út 28 Lý Tự Trọng; 13.00–21.00 daily. Serves *bánh cống* (page 407), a savoury rice cake probably with Khmer origins. $

Quán Ăn Chay Bách Thảo 86A Đề Thám; f ComChayBachThao.CoHieu; 06.30–21.30 daily. Simple vegan food done very well & friendly on the pocket. Try one of the noodle soup dishes. $

Ca Dao 2 Phan Văn Trị; f CADAORestaurantCoffee; 06.00–23.00 daily. Ca Dao somehow manages to pull off being both a restaurant & a café – a rare feat in Việt Nam. The service is good & they serve many subregional specialities, including a solid *cá kho tộ* (braised fish). $$

Mr Beef Steak 59 Nam Kỳ Khởi Nghĩa; f mrbeefsteakcantho; 07.00–22.00 daily. One of the better restaurants serving Western food, which includes not only steak but also pasta & salads. $$

Sao Hôm Restaurant Hai Bà Trưng; f saohomrestaurant; 06.00–22.30 daily. Touristy but acceptable due to the location in the market & overlooking the water, Sao Hôm has been serving satisfied visitors for years. They do a light & crispy *bánh xèo* (savoury pancake), a local speciality. $$$

Côti Café 180 Huỳnh Cương; f cotioicafe; 08.00–02.00 daily. Little café serving sweet drinks & savoury snacks with a rooftop terrace that overlooks a small, circular lake packed with waterside restaurants.

OTHER PRACTICALITIES For informal **river cruises and activities**, you'll be able to negotiate with tour hawkers on Hai Bà Trưng Street, who will no doubt approach you with plastic signs and broken English to illustrate their offerings. Feel free to

CRUISING THROUGH THE MEKONG DELTA

Though not as popular or affordable as it was, cruising through the Mekong Delta is still a tempting way to explore a part of the world where, up until quite recently, waterways were the principal transport routes. Cruises run from one to seven days, and some can deposit you (or pick you up) in neighbouring Cambodia. There are several cruise companies that ply these subregional waters; below is just a selection. Some, but not all, are based in Cần Thơ or nearby.

Bassac Cruises w transmekong.com. Bassac Cruises specialises in small-group river cruises on traditional wooden boats with simple but comfortable cabins. Their itineraries take guests through the quieter canals of the Mekong Delta, with visits to local villages & markets.

Jahan Cruises w heritage-line.com/ship/the-jahan. Part of the Heritage Line family with boutique cruises across Southeast Asia, Jahan Cruises offers a luxurious (& expensive) experience along the Mekong between Hồ Chí Minh City & Phnom Penh.

Song Xanh Sampan w victoriamekong.com. Offering intimate, private sampan boats, Song Xanh Sampan, a member of the Victoria family, delivers a somewhat personalised cruise experience in the Mekong Delta. Ideal for couples or families, these vessels are small enough to wind through narrow canals.

Victoria Mekong Cruises w victoriamekong.com. A luxury & comfortable cruise option, Victoria Mekong offers spacious cabins with river views, an onboard pool, spa & nightly cultural performances. The cruise ships are very polished & feel like large, floating hotels.

THE MEKONG DELTA'S SPECIALITY DISHES

DỪA *Dừa* means coconut, and this is the unofficial symbol of the Mekong Delta: it's a rare moment when you scan your surroundings and not see one (or at least a tree that produces one). Sip on these at basic roadside hammock cafés before returning the waterless fruit to the vendor, who will hack it open and hand it back with a spoon so you can scoop out the flesh.

TRÁI CÂY Vietnamese has two words for fruit: *hoa quả* (literally 'flower fruit') is more common in the north, whereas *trái cây* (literally 'fruit [of the] tree') is more common in the south. The fruit in the south – including pineapple, mango, rambutan, durian, mangosteen and more – tastes sweeter here than anywhere else in the country. Find fruit everywhere, but the markets have the most variety.

HỦ TIẾU Southern Vietnam's quintessential noodle dish is *hủ tiếu*, a rice noodle dish with origins in southern China. In the Mekong Delta, the broth (served on the side if requested) is sweeter, the proteins are varied and the side of greens is especially bountiful. Try it at **Hủ Tiếu Sate** in Mỹ Tho (page 399), **Quán Hủ Tiếu Bà Sẩm** in Sa Đéc (page 415) and **Hủ Tiếu Nam Vang (Quến Hà Tiên)** in Hà Tiên (page 418).

BÁNH XÈO It may not have originated in the Mekong Delta, but the savoury pancakes here are larger, thinner and crunchier than in the provinces further north. Shrimp, pork and beansprouts come as standard, but some establishments add their own special touches. Try it at **Sao Hôm Restaurant** in Cần Thơ (page 405).

shop around, but take name cards and phone numbers as they may not be there the next day. There is no tourist information office, but **HieuTour** (27A Lê Thánh Tôn; w hieutour.com) has a handle on Cần Thơ and around; they may struggle with longer itineraries across the delta. **Victoria** (w victoriamekong.com) is an altogether more professional outfit, with links across the subregion. As for **health care**, Vinmec Cần Thơ (150A 3/2 St; w vinmec.com; ⌚ all day daily), a major private hospital, was being built at the time of research but should be completed by the time you're reading this. Cần Thơ Medical University Hospital (179 Nguyễn An Cư; f bvdhydct; ⌚ all day daily) is nearby.

WHAT TO SEE AND DO

Cần Thơ Market and Hai Bà Trưng Street Inside the covered market on the waterfront there is hardly room to move in the mornings as traders in conical hats vie for custom. The early-morning arrival of boats at Ninh Kiều Wharf, laden with pink potatoes, purple sesame, giant fleshy prawns, yellow catfish and silver mackerel plus a kaleidoscope of countless fruits, is a spectacle not to be missed. The market stays open all day and into the early evening. Nearby, on shophouse-lined Hai Bà Trưng Street, everyone is greeted by a huge silver gleaming statue of Uncle Hồ.

Cần Thơ Museum (1 Hòa Bình; w baotangtpcantho.cantho.gov.vn; ⌚ 08.00–11.00 & 14.00–17.00 Tue–Thu, 08.00–11.00 & 18.30–21.00 Sat–Sun) The largest city in the Mekong Delta is also home to the subregion's biggest museum. Truth be told, this isn't saying much in a part of the country not known for its educational

BÁNH CỐNG More of a snack than a meal, *bánh cống* is a savoury, deep-fried rice cake made with mung beans, pork and shrimp. *Bánh cống* is usually served with a plate of fresh herbs, lettuce, pickled vegetables and a tangy fish sauce dipping sauce. Popular in Cần Thơ – where you can try it at **Bánh Cống Cô Út** (page 405) – and Sóc Trăng.

CÁ TAI TƯỢNG Known as *cá tai tượng* in Vietnamese, 'elephant ear' fish is so-called for its broad, flat shape. The fish, usually deep-fried whole and presented standing upright on a rack, is served in local restaurants everywhere. Ideally, the skin is golden, the meat is tender and it's served with rice paper, herbs and vegetables so diners can make their own fresh spring rolls. Try it at **Nhà Hàng Hải Sản Sông Tiền** in Mỹ Tho (page 399), **Sao Hôm Restaurant** in Cần Thơ (page 405) and **Bassac Restaurant** in Châu Đốc (page 421).

BÚN NƯỚC LÈO Popular in Trà Vinh, but also Sóc Trăng and Bạc Liêu, this is a noodle soup fusion dish, with Khmer, Vietnamese and Chinese influences. The broth is made with fermented fish, giving it an earthy flavour, and is topped with pork, fish and sometimes shrimp. Try it in Trà Vinh at **Bún Nước Lèo Cô Ba** (page 412).

CÀ RI A curious speciality brought to the Mekong Delta by South Asian immigrants during colonial times, curry here is richly spiced without a hint of sweetness, which is a welcome break from a regional cuisine dominated by sugar. Goat is the protein of choice, but chicken is also available. Try this in Trà Vinh at **Quán Cơm Cari Ja** (page 412).

institutions, but the museum is at least comprehensive, with exhibits highlighting the history of the Mekong Delta's ethnolinguistic groups, including the Kinh, Khmer and Hoa communities. A significant section of the museum, of course, is dedicated to the region's role in the American War, while another section focuses on the economic development of the region, particularly its agricultural backbone.

Ông Pagoda (32 Hai Bà Trưng; ⌚ 07.00–20.00 daily) Dating from 1894 and built by Chinese from Guangzhou, Chùa Ông is not freestanding but part of a terrace of buildings, setting it apart from other Chinese temples in Southern Vietnam. The layout is a combination of pagoda – with a small open courtyard for the incense smoke to escape – and meeting house for overseas Chinese.

Munirensay Pagoda (36 Hòa Bình; ⌚ all day daily) Those not venturing to the Khmer cultural strongholds of Trà Vinh, Sóc Trăng and An Giang will want to visit Munirensay Pagoda. Built in 1948, the pagoda stands out from Cần Thơ's otherwise Vietnamese aesthetic with its striking Theravada Buddhist architecture, characterised by golden spires and colourful murals that depict scenes from the life of Buddha. Inside, you'll find a serene prayer hall adorned with statues of Buddha and detailed frescoes. See page 414 for a guide on Khmer iconography.

✸ **Bình Thủy Temple** (46/11A Lê Hồng Phong; ⌚ all day daily) Situated at the corner where a river and canal meet, 7km northwest of the centre, Bình Thủy Temple was built in 1844 to honour the village's founding ancestors and local deities. The architecture of Bình Thủy Temple is a blend of traditional Vietnamese styles with some Chinese influences, featuring intricate wooden carvings, roof tiles and dragon motifs. The temple is a hub of cultural activities, especially during major festivals like the Lunar New Year.

Ancient House of Bình Thủy (Nhà Cổ Bình Thủy; 144 Bùi Hữu Nghĩa; ⌚ 07.30–noon & 13.30–17.00 daily) Near the Bình Thủy Temple is the Ancient House of Bình Thủy, which was used as a setting in the 1992 film *The Lover*. Built in 1870 but adapted since, it blends French and Vietnamese design and is renowned for its façade featuring large arched windows. Various antique pieces of furniture are scattered around inside, and surrounding the house is a large, well-kept garden with bonsai trees.

Cái Răng floating market (An Ninh) Cái Răng floating market is 7km from the town centre and one of the most popular (ie: touristy) markets in the delta. An animated affair, the vendors here attach a sample of their wares to a bamboo pole to attract customers. Up to seven vegetables can be seen dangling from staffs – winter melon, pumpkin, spring onions, giant parsnips, grapefruit, garlic, mango, onions and Vietnamese plums. Housewives paddle their sampans from boat to boat and barter, haggle and gossip. At the back of some boats, washing is hung out, tiny children play and motors are stranded high above the water. Most hotels in Cần Thơ will offer a trip to this floating market, but to explore it independently, wander down to Hai Bà Trưng Street (page 406) and negotiate with one of the hawkers; 100,000VND is a good price. The market starts before sunrise and it's best to arrive there by 06.00.

LEGEND HAS IT: THE FLOATING MARKET MYTH

In the quiet embrace of dawn, when the first light of day kisses the river's surface, the floating markets of the Mekong Delta awaken. Boats laden with tropical fruits drift gently across the shimmering water, their bows piled high with mangoes the colour of sunset and watermelons as round as the moon. From above, it appears as if a thousand colours dance upon the water. Traders call out to one another, their voices rising and falling with the splash of oars and the rustle of wind in the palm trees. Vendors prepare bowls of noodle soup, passing them from boat to boat; the river is not just a market, but a communal space where food and community flow together…

Waxing lyrical about Vietnam's fabled floating markets is easier than keeping them afloat. Floating markets were once the linchpin of commerce in the Mekong Delta, but as road infrastructure has improved and more families live on land, the tradition is, for better or worse, quickly dying. By the end of the decade, Vietnam's floating markets may have vanished, except for perhaps those that provincial authorities try to prop up for tourists. And yet travel writers and content creators who tell it like it isn't continue to sustain this floating market myth. At the time of research, there were still three worthwhile floating markets: Cái Răng and Phong Điền near Cần Thơ, and Long Xuyên in An Giang. Long Xuyên floating market (page 425) is the least touristy, most interesting and hardest to visit. When it comes to Cái Răng, the most popular floating market with tour companies, don't be misled by decades-old photos that show an ocean of tightly packed boats. These days, you're only likely to see two or three dozen boats at most.

OK OM BOK FESTIVAL

At the end of the rainy season, usually in November, the Ok Om Bok Festival season begins. Flower Dedication ceremonies are followed by the Welcome the Moon Festival, which takes place on the 15th day of the tenth lunar month. This features boat races at dawn, when 24m-long pirogues with 40–50 oarsmen from all over the delta race each other in Sóc Trăng (see below). The event is part of a religious festival so the monks from each community competing are in charge of choosing the oarsmen and the assistants. Before the racing starts, the oars are blessed and a flower vase is placed on the stern of the boat.

Around Cần Thơ

✷ ***Phong Điền floating market*** (Nhơn Ái Ward, Phong Điền District; ◷ 04.30–07.00 daily) This daily floating market is probably on its last legs but will hopefully see out the decade. Around 20 or so small boats gather from around 04.30 to sell fruits and vegetables before their customers – also on boats – glide away. It's possible to gaze at the exchange unnoticed from a nearby bridge. The market is usually over by 07.30, at which point you can head back to Cần Thơ, possibly stopping at one of the many roadside noodle eateries for breakfast on the way. The best way to travel there is on a rented motorbike. If you want to take a taxi, organise it with your accommodation the day before.

Sóc Trăng The province of Sóc Trăng, the capital city of which goes by the same name, is 60km southwest from Cần Thơ and makes for an engaging day trip to visit the Khmer pagodas. Although integrated into Vietnamese society, the Khmer have retained their cultural identity, and many Buddhist sanctuaries contain schools where resident monks educate the young in their language, customs and myths. Their festivals, often very lavish affairs, are distinctly different from those of the Vietnamese. Many of the province's inhabitants (just over 1 million), depend on agriculture and fish production, though rice is farmed extensively, and in 2023 a variety of rice known as ST25, which developed and is farmed across the province, was named 'World's Best Rice' by The Rice Trader. The Khmer new year's festival, known as Chol Chnam Thmay and taking place in April, is one of the most colourful on the delta. Led by Buddhist monks in saffron-yellow cloaks, it proceeds through the streets and past Khmer pagodas. The entourage – men in red silk sarongs dotted with yellow and violet and women in coloured or plain blouses – transport offerings of flowers, rice, fruit and wine, accompanied by drummers in vivid red costumes. The small and unreliable **Khmer Museum** is worth visiting if open, displaying everything from garments and cummerbunds to agricultural tools and pottery. **Chùa Khleang Pagoda** (53 Tôn Đức Thắng) is a typical Khmer sanctuary. Its three-tiered roof has generously extended eaves and porches crowned with elongated curved spires. Rows of plain pillars support the bottom tier, which appears to be held in place by decorative apsaras (heavenly maidens). A fine wood carving on the pagoda's doors depicts fairies fighting against ogres. The pagoda may date from the 16th century, but if so has been updated several times since. The central exhibit in the main hall, a magnificent golden seated statue of Sakyamuni, looks down from its perch on the high altar. **Mahatúp Pagoda** (418 Văn Ngọc Chính), sometimes called Bat Pagoda in English, is built in a similar style. The crowning glory of this sanctuary is the colourful painting of the Sakyamuni Buddha, his head highlighted

CÀ MAU: THE END OF THE ROAD

Vietnam's most southerly province and the eastern flank guarding the Gulf of Thailand, is literally the end of the road. Very few make it this far south and independent travel is hard for non-Vietnamese speakers. The best way to explore Cà Mau is probably through a local tour provider (page 405), though don't be surprised if they try to put you off and offer trips to a more manageable province instead. Of primary interest to visitors is not the city, but U Minh Hạ National Park, west of Cà Mau city and a favoured hiding place for the Việt Cộng during the American War. Fascinating in its complexity and vast in its extent is an apt summary of U Minh Hạ National Park. The water in the area is almost black due to its high peat content; the name Cà Mau may derive from an old Khmer word meaning 'black water'. Many mangroves can grow to over 30m in this salty mire and in places where there is hardened soil, species such as *Lumnitzera* and a saltwater fern *Acrostichum* take hold. In June and November the cajeput flowers and the place turns into creamy-white wonderland. Bees are numerous, resulting in a fairly lucrative honey industry, and you will find bottles sold in and around Cà Mau city. It's also possible to catch shrimp and crab at certain times of year. In the 1990s, the Hanoi Institute of Ecology carried out research in U Minh Hạ to survey the bird species after the extensive war damage. In some of the worst affected areas, where repeated defoliation had severely stunted growth, they discovered cranes were living happily. Since then, some of the larger bird species that were common here before the war, including the spot-billed pelican or grey pelican (*Pellecanus philippensis*) and the greater adjutant (*Leptoptilos dubius*), which breeds in Cambodia, have been seen.

by a psychedelic halo and protected by an umbrella. Inside there is also an ancient stone statue of Lord Buddha. As evening approaches, it becomes evident how this place earned its nickname, as hundreds of bats fly from their resting places in the adjacent trees. A reason to spend time in Sóc Trăng is to see the annual Ghe Ngo boat race, which coincides with the Ok Ọm Bok Festival (page 409), usually held in November. If overnighting, hotels are easy to come by in the centre, but you'll need to book weeks in advance during the festival. If visiting for the day from Cần Thơ, it's best to book a car for the day through your accommodation. It's also possible to go by motorbike, but the road is far from scenic.

Bạc Liêu About 2½ hours from Cần Thơ and 1 hour from Sóc Trăng, Bạc Liêu is a pleasant, rarely visited town with a population size of 150,000 and just about close enough to Cần Thơ to explore as a day trip. It is not as rich in rice production as other Mekong provinces due to its proximity to the sea, so many enterprising locals make a living from salt farming and fishing. Agriculture has always been hard in Bạc Liêu Province due to saltwater intrusion, and this will surely worsen due to rising sea levels. In the centre of town along the Bạc Liêu River is **Nhà Công tử Bạc Liêu** (13 Điện Biên Phủ; **w** congtubaclieu.com.vn; 🕘 07.00–18.30 daily; 45,000/20,000VND adult/child), an early 20th-century French mansion and now a well-looked-after museum. **Bạc Liêu Bird Sanctuary** (Nhà Mát Ward), 3km southwest of town, is home to a large white heron population; the best times to visit are December and January. As with other bird sanctuaries in the region, visit early in the morning or late in the afternoon and apply plenty of mosquito repellent as the place is inundated with biting insects. **Xiêm Cán Pagoda** (Vĩnh Trạch Đông), 12km west of Bạc Liêu, was built in 1887 and a small group of monks still resides here. There are hotels and restaurants in the city, but few tourists overnight here and there is nowhere of note. As with Sóc Trăng, the best way to visit Bạc Liêu is by chartering a car for the day in Cần Thơ.

TRÀ VINH

Trà Vinh is the capital of the province of the same name and around a third of the population of 1.4 million people are Khmer (see below). This large population is a bit of an enigma, for while Khmer people can be found across the Mekong Delta, the concentration is highest in Trà Vinh, despite it being the most distant Mekong province from Cambodia. For whatever reason, Trà Vinh established itself as a centre of population some 500 years ago; then, as Vietnamese settlers began fanning across the delta, displacing the Khmer, the population of this area somehow remained. Families that fled the Khmer Rouge in 1978–79 further boosted the community. Many who have settled in Trà Vinh have adopted Vietnamese versions of Khmer family names, but the population nevertheless remained firmly rooted in their traditions, creating a little pocket of Cambodian ethnicity and culture far from home.

Travelling through the province, visitors will notice the distinctive Khmer temples, with their extravagantly extended roof eaves and golden-orange tiles flashing in the sun. Indeed, there are so many of these that sources have a hard time settling on a precise number, but 150 is an adequate estimate. Goods in the province were once transported along a massive web of fine channels which open out into the Trà Vinh sea territory, though improving road infrastructure has diminished the waterways' usefulness. The main land areas grow coconuts, rice, sugarcane and fruits such as bananas, pomelos, mango, longans, sapodillas, oranges and tangerines in the fertile alluvial belt between the Tiền and Hậu rivers. Industries in Trà Vinh include shipbuilding, food processing, weaving, engraving, poultry raising and fertiliser production. Remains of the Funan civilisation (page 9), including jewels, golden sculptures and early sandstone figures, have been found across the province.

THE KHMER

The Khmer are the ethnic majority of Cambodia. With the fall of the Khmer empire in the 15th century, following the sack of Angkor by the Ayutthaya Kingdom, Khmer cultural and ethnic identity in the Mekong Delta gradually became overshadowed by the expanding Việt from the north. Much like the Cham (page 343) of Central Vietnam, Khmer economic power diminished over time and many of their once-majestic temples and monuments fell into disrepair. Today, around 1.3 million Khmer people live in Vietnam, primarily in the Mekong Delta provinces of Trà Vinh, Sóc Trăng and An Giang, with smaller communities in Hồ Chí Minh City and Cần Thơ. A proportion of these are the children of victims of the Khmer Rouge regime, who fled here in the 1970s. The Khmer are typically involved in agriculture, particularly rice farming, and they are known for their festivals (page 409) and religious architecture. The Khmer, like those from Thailand and Cambodia but unlike many from Northern Vietnam, practise Theravada Buddhism.

For those interested in religious edifices, Trà Vinh is the place to visit. Attractive buildings coupled with tree-lined boulevards – some trees are well over 30m tall – make this one of the more attractive cities in the delta. Điện Biên Phủ Street is the city's main thoroughfare, along with the Trà Vinh River, a relatively small branch of the Mekong compared with most delta towns. Streets in Trà Vinh city are wider but quieter than in other subregional towns and business is centred around Trà Vinh Market. Close to the Trà Vinh River, some stilt houses look out over the muddy waters, which teem with small boats in the early morning. The modern market building, adorned with a huge picture of Hồ Chí Minh, is the heart of the city. A walk through the market and along the riverbank makes a pleasant late-afternoon or early-evening stroll. One could spend days in Trà Vinh exploring all the pagodas, but for most visitors two to three nights is sufficient.

GETTING THERE AND AROUND From Saigon, it takes 4 hours to travel to Trà Vinh by **bus**. Connections between Cần Thơ and Trà Vinh are less organised and you may need to transit in Vĩnh Long or Mỹ Tho, meaning the journey could take most of the day. If you're making this journey, ask at your hotel in either city for the best route, or consider springing for a private car. There are a few bus pick-up/drop-off points in town, but if booking with Futa (recommended; w futabus.vn), they will send a shuttle bus.

Trà Vinh is small enough to walk around, but you'll need to rent a **motorbike** or hire a **car and driver** to see the Khmer pagodas, the vast majority of which are out in the countryside.

WHERE TO STAY

Khách Sạn Thanh Trà 1 Phạm Thái Bường. Humdrum hotel but close to the market, the beating heart of this small city. It's fairly large, so if the 1st room you're shown isn't to your liking, request another. **$**

Khách Sạn Thủy Nguyên 354 Đồng Khởi Nối Dài. This clean & comfortable hotel is not in the centre, but the canal-side location close to some sparkling Khmer pagodas is appealing. Better suited to those with transport. **$**

✷ **Bích Ngoan Hotel** 22 19/5 St; f. Probably the best place to stay in town, with a range of rooms that overlook a park & a ground-floor café. This park is a mixed blessing, though, as it's noisy with dance groups in the early morning & late afternoon. **$$**

Villa Basi Phương Thạnh; f vilabasi. Rustic & charming shack-like rooms set in a verdant garden a few kilometres from the city centre. You'll need your own wheels to stay this far out. **$$**

Trà Vinh Lodge 12/6 Ấp Đôn; w travinhlodge.com. Currently the province's most luxurious accommodation, with comfortable villas overlooking a palm tree-fringed pond. 15km north of the city centre so the location isn't ideal. **$$$**

WHERE TO EAT AND DRINK

Bếp Chay Nhà Ruma 559 Kiên Thị Nhẫn; ⌚ 08.00–14.00 & 16.00–20.00 daily. Almost 100 hearty vegan dishes served up in a decorated front garden. The tofu dishes are reliably good, as are the salads. **$**

Bún Nước Lèo Cô Ba 19/5 St; ⌚ 06.30–20.00 daily. One of the best places in the city to try the city's famous noodle soup dish, with lots of sides designed for dunking. **$**

Quán Ăn Chi 163 Võ Nguyên Giáp. Do-it-yourself fresh spring rolls in a no-nonsense streetside restaurant close to Chùa Angkorajaborey & the Museum of Khmer Ethnic Culture. **$**

Quán Cơm Cari Ja 159 Điện Biên Phủ; ⌚ 06.00–noon & 15.30–19.30 daily. Cari, or curry, is a curious speciality dish of the area with South Asian roots. There are a number of restaurants that serve the dish in town, but this particular one is housed in a modernist house. **$**

Núp Concept Alley 71 Phan Đình Phùng; ⌚ 08.00–18.00 daily. Tiny café with just a few tables, but also AC for those roasting Mekong Delta summers.

OTHER PRACTICALITIES The tourist office appears to have disappeared, but the friendly folks at Bích Ngoan Hotel (see opposite) and the ground-floor café keep materials printed by the province. They can also arrange **tours** with English-speaking tour guides. **Trà Vinh Provincial Hospital** is west of the city centre.

WHAT TO SEE AND DO

✷ Ông Mẹt Pagoda (1 Lê Lợi) The Ông Mẹt Pagoda north of the town centre dates back to the mid 16th century. It is a gilded, highly photogenic and well-maintained pagoda where the monks may ply you with tea to give them an opportunity to practise their English. In the mornings there are sometimes street kitchens where schoolchildren stop by for their noodle breakfasts.

✷ Hang Pagoda (Châu Thành) The two most striking aspects of Trà Vinh are the storks and the Khmer temples. Fortunately, these can be combined at the nearby Hang Pagoda, also known as Ao Bàn Om, about 5km south of town and 300m off the main road. It is not particularly special architecturally, but the sight of the hundreds of storks that rest in the grounds and wheel around the pointed roofs at dawn and dusk is quite something.

Museum of Khmer Ethnic Culture (Nguyễn Du; ⌚ 07.00–18.00 daily) The architecture of this museum, built in 1992, seems to channel the style of celebrated modernist Cambodian architect Vann Molyvann, with cantilever staircases and ponds. Some of the antique items are exquisite, but with little English signage and only rough dating (eg: '20th century'), it's easy to get bored after 30 minutes or so. Opposite is the **Angkorajaborey Pagoda** (Ang; Lương Hòa, Châu Thành District; ⌚ 09.00–17.00 daily), dating from 990. There is no structural evidence of its millennium-old beginnings, but it's a huge, impressive compound and makeshift cafés and juice stands with hammocks skirt the adjacent square pond. This area is 5km southwest from town, and one could spend the whole afternoon here.

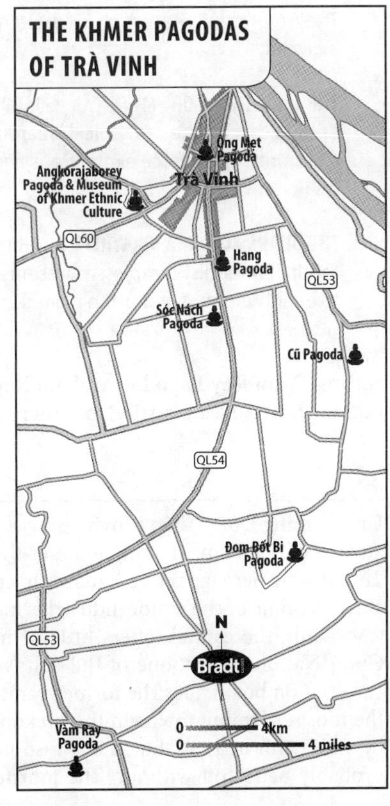

Further afield To get the most out of Trà Vinh, rent a motorbike or hire a taxi and explore south of the city. There are more than a hundred pagodas to visit, and they appear everywhere. Information is virtually non-existent, and the plaques that do exist are usually written in Khmer, and sometimes Vietnamese. Some of the more attractive pagodas include **Cũ Pagoda** (Old Pagoda; Kim Hòa, Cầu Ngang), **Đom Bốt Bi Pagoda** (Nhị Trường, Cầu

DECODING KHMER ICONOGRAPHY

Khmer pagodas (*chùa* in Vietnamese) are rich in iconography, but very few have signage, and if an English-speaking monk isn't around to help, it's hard to know what you're looking at. The images found on Khmer temples are rooted in Theravada Buddhism, and many of the symbolic elements are tied to Buddhist teachings.

THE NAGA, OR SERPENT In Khmer temples, the naga, a multi-headed serpent, is often seen on staircases, railings or temple entrances. It represents protection and is a symbol of fertility, water and the connection between the earthly and divine worlds.

GARUDA The garuda, a mythical bird-like creature, represents strength, power and wisdom, symbolising victory over negative forces.

APSARAS Apsaras are celestial dancers and are often carved on walls and pillars. They represent the beauty of divine beings and are believed to embody the grace of spiritual enlightenment. While more common in ancient Angkorian temples, apsaras still appear as decorative motifs in some modern Khmer Buddhist temples.

THE SINGHA, OR LION Stone lions often guard the entrances to Khmer temples. They represent protection and strength, guarding the sacred space from evil spirits.

THE CHINTHEY, OR MYTHICAL GUARDIANS Often found flanking temple entrances, chinthey (mythical guardian creatures) protect the temple from evil spirits. Their fierce expressions and powerful postures are meant to ward off negativity.

THE DHARMACHAKRA, OR WHEEL OF DHARMA The Wheel of Dharma, a common motif in Buddhist temples, represents the teachings of Buddha and the path to enlightenment. It is often placed at key points in temple architecture.

Ngang), **Vàm Ray Pagoda** (Ấp Vàm Ray, Trà Cú District) and **Sóc Nách Pagoda** (2/9 St; ⌚ 04.30–22.00 daily), but there are many more.

SA ĐÉC

Unassuming Đồng Tháp Province has a population of over 1.5 million and covers an area of 3,390km^{2}, making it larger than Mỹ Tho, Vĩnh Long, Bến Tre and Cần Thơ. People here farm rice, catch fish, cultivate mulberries, weave mats and raise shrimp. Some of the major industries include rice milling and feather processing. Cao Lãnh, the capital, offers little of interest, but north of the capital is Tràm Chim National Park, one of the delta's largest sanctuaries for birds, which you can spot on boat trips. The former capital of Sa Đéc, on the other hand, is one of the most charming towns in the Mekong Delta. The title of capital was snatched by Cao Lãnh in 1984, but it is a responsibility that the small town of Sa Đéc is probably better off without. The journey between the two towns passes flower gardens, brick kilns and bikers transporting their wares. For international visitors, Sa Đéc's biggest claim to fame is that it was the birthplace of French novelist Marguerite Duras, and the town's three main frangipani-garlanded avenues – Nguyễn Huệ, Trần Hưng Đạo and Hùng Vương – together with some attractive colonial villas betray the French influence on the town. For domestic tourists, Sa Đéc is most famous for its flower cultivation. Many nurseries regularly send white lilies, roses, gladioli, Japanese daisies and carnations to the markets in Hồ Chí Minh City.

GETTING THERE AND AROUND By **bus**, it takes 3 hours to get to Sa Đéc and 4 hours to get to Cao Lãnh from Hồ Chí Minh City, with Futa (**w** futabus.vn). It's also possible to travel there from Cần Thơ (90mins), Long Xuyên (90mins) and Châu Đốc (3hrs), but you may need to transit in Cao Lãnh (45mins). Talk to your hotel about which buses are making the routes. Sa Đéc bus station (Nguyễn Sinh Sắc) is 1km southwest of the centre, so just about walkable. Sa Đéc is very small and pedestrian-friendly.

WHERE TO STAY AND EAT It used to be possible to pay a few dollars to stay in Sa Đéc's most storied building, **Nhà Cổ Huỳnh Thủy Lê** (see below), but this wasn't an option at the time of research. **Khách Sạn Sa Đéc** (499 Hùng Vương; **$$**) and **Khách Sạn Thảo Ngân** (4 An Dương Vương; **$$**) are both standard and acceptable hotels, with the latter slightly preferred due to its proximity to the market. Sa Đéc is famous for its *hủ tiếu* (noodle soup), and you'll find it at **Quán Hủ Tiếu Bà Sẩm** (188 Trần Hưng Đạo; ⏲ 06.00–21.00 daily; **$**). **Mai Café** (behind Vincom; **w** maicafe.vn; ⏲ 07.00–22.00 daily) is a pot plant-filled café serving drinks and snacks.

OTHER PRACTICALITIES There is no tourist information office. For medical emergencies, return to Hồ Chí Minh City.

WHAT TO SEE AND DO

Sa Đéc Market Quarter (Nguyễn Huệ; ⏲ 02.00–18.00 daily) Sa Đéc's bustling riverside market on Nguyễn Huệ Street is worth a visit. Many of the scenes from the film adaptation of Duras's novel *The Lover* were filmed in front of the shop terraces and merchants' houses here, though two new practical buildings – Sa Đéc Fish Market (Chợ Cá Sa Đéc) and Sa Đéc Vegetable Market (Chợ Nông Sản Sa Đéc) – now dominate the area. Away from these orderly commercial buildings you can sit in one of the many riverside cafés to watch the world float by – which presumably, as a young woman, is what Duras did.

Huỳnh Thủy Lê Ancient House (255A Nguyễn Huệ; ⏲ 08.00–17.00 daily; 40,000VND) Duras's lover Huỳnh Thủy Lê's house is an unmissable Sino-influenced building on the main street. There are intricate gold-leaf carved animal figures framing arches and the centrepiece is a golden shrine to Chinese warrior Quan Công. The house was built in 1895 and restored in 1917. There are photographs of the Huỳnh family (after his exploits with Duras he married and had five daughters and three sons; he died in 1972), Duras and the Sa Đéc school. Duras's childhood colonial home no longer exists, but she lived in a house near the École de Sa Đéc (now Trường Vương Primary school on the corner of Hùng Vương and Hồ Xuân Hương streets), which is pictured inside the ancient house.

Phước Hưng Pagoda (Ấp Phú Sơn) This is a sunshine-yellow Chinese-style pagoda constructed in 1838 when Sa Đéc was a humble one-road village. Surrounded by ornamental gardens, lotus ponds and cypress trees, the main temple to the right is decorated with animals assembled from pieces of porcelain rice bowls. Inside are wooden statues of Buddhist figures made in the same year that the pagoda was constructed. There are also some superbly preserved gilded wooden beams and two antique prayer bells. The smaller one was made in 1888.

Tư Tồn Rose Garden (Khu Du Lịch Vườn Hồng Tư Tồn; Vòng xoay làng hoa; 🕘 07.00–18.00 daily) Sa Đéc's entrepreneurial flower farm owners have realised that they can earn extra income from visiting tourists, mostly domestic photography and selfie enthusiasts. One such farm is the Tư Tồn Rose Garden, a 6,000ha nursery on the river that is home to dozens of varieties of rose and hundreds of other types of plant, including medicinal herbs. Wander amid the potted hibiscus, beds of roses and bougainvillea, and enjoy the visiting butterflies.

Tràm Chim National Park (Khóm 4, Tam Nông; 70km northwest of Sa Đéc; w tramchim.net.vn; 720,000VND–1,200,000VND including activities) Once known as the Sarus Crane Reserve, this famous sanctuary was set up by Professor Võ Quý (Hanoi University) in 1988. Thanks to work carried out by George Archibald of the International Crane Foundation, it later received international funding. This went a long way towards protecting the extremely rare and elegant sarus crane (*Antigone antigone*), which can be recognised by its red head, grey plumage and reddish legs, though it remains unlikely that you'll spot them. Other birds seen here are the common crane (*grus grus*), which is similar but smaller than the sarus and has a black head and white hindneck. It is also quite likely that you'll see white-throated kingfishers (*Halcyon smyrnensis*) skimming across the water, Chinese pond herons (*Ardeola bacchus ralloides*), brown dippers (*Cinclus pallasii*), buff-throated warblers (*Phylloscopus subaffinis*) and tailorbirds (*Orthotomus* species), as well as egrets, flycatchers, wagtails, shrikes, babblers and waterhens. For the best birdwatching, visit early in the morning or late in the afternoon.

HÀ TIÊN

Hà Tiên falls within Kiên Giang Province, which, with an area of 6,300km^2, is the Mekong Delta's largest. With sunshine all year round, temperature averaging 28°C, a 200km-long coastline, idyllic islands and excellent seafood, it's no wonder that this province has propelled itself into tourism stardom. This boom is almost entirely restricted to Phú Quốc island (covered in the next chapter; page 427), however, leaving the rest of the province almost free of visitors. The population exceeds 2 million, and many of those who don't work in the service industry on Phú Quốc are pepper growers, rice farmers, coconut plantation workers, salt harvesters and fish and seafood cultivators. The provincial hero is Nguyễn Trung Trực, who led a rebellion against the French and died in Rạch Giá in 1868.

Rạch Giá is the provincial capital, not an unpleasant place but with little of interest to tourists. Visitors will have more to explore in Hà Tiên, a quaint town with a slow pace of life, by urban Mekong Delta standards. Though hotels clutter the riverbank and there is a lot of construction, a boom that has no doubt been helped by the opening of the border with Cambodia at Xà Xía, step back off the main thoroughfare and you will find vestiges of its appeal. Hà Tiên's history and heritage is strongly coloured by its proximity to Cambodia, to which the area belonged until the 18th century. The numerical and agricultural superiority of the Vietnamese allowed them to gradually displace the Khmer occupants, and eventually military might, under Mạc Cửu, prevailed. But it is not an argument the Khmer are prepared to walk away from, as their incursions into the area in the late 1970s showed.

GETTING THERE AND AROUND There is no airport or train station on mainland Kiên Giang (there is an airport in the province, but it's on Phú Quốc island). From Hồ Chí Minh City by **bus**, it takes 7 hours to get to Hà Tiên (5hrs to Rạch Giá). Consider an overnight bus if you're short on time. Cần Thơ to Hà Tiên is 5 hours (3hrs to Rạch Giá). The bus station (QL61, Vĩnh Hòa Hiệp) is a few kilometres southeast of the town centre. There are several **boats** moving between Hà Tiên/Rạch Giá and Phú Quốc (1–2hrs); book them through Bao Lau (w baolau.com). The Hà Tiên ferry terminals (Kim Dư) are southeast of the town centre, on the other side of the river.

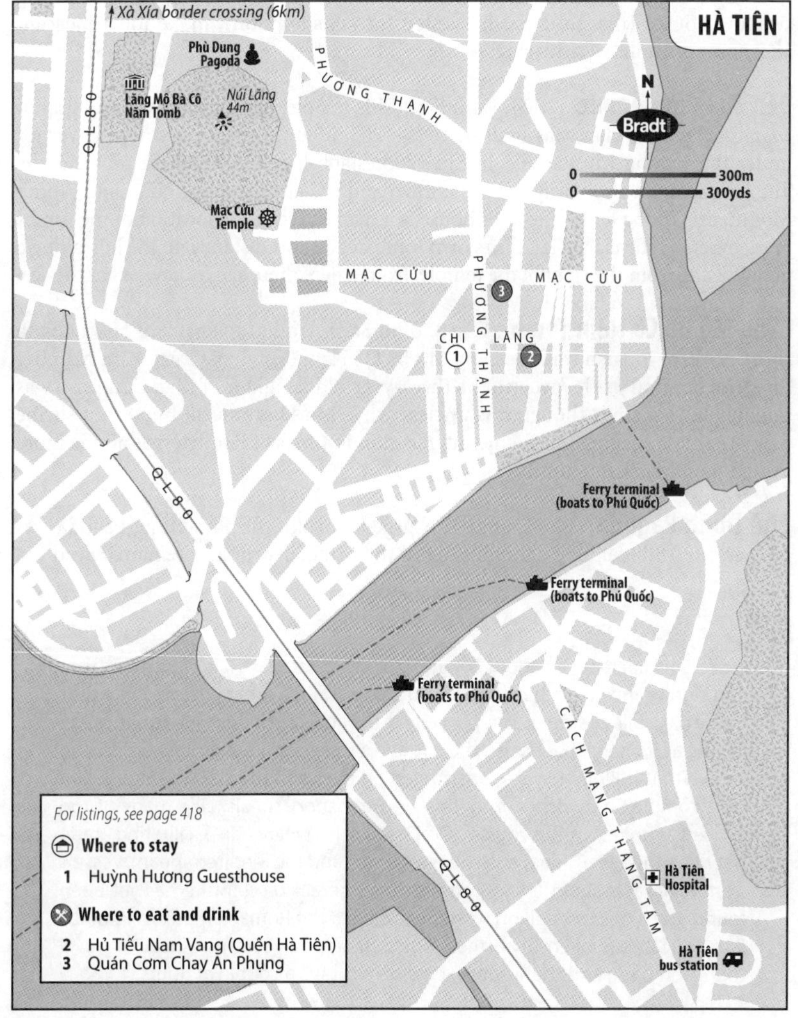

Grab doesn't work well in Hà Tiên, but you can ask your accommodation to book **taxis** for you.

WHERE TO STAY AND EAT *Map, page 417*
The better area to stay is in the older part of town, just northeast of the market. **Huỳnh Hương Guesthouse** (47 Chi Lăng; **w** booking.com; **$$**) is a good option. Cheap eats are also dotted around this neighbourhood; try **Hủ Tiếu Nam Vang (Quến Hà Tiên)** (32 Mạc Công Du; 🕘 05.30–noon daily; **$**) for noodles or **Quán Cơm Chay An Phụng** (14 Mạc Cửu; **$**) for vegan.

OTHER PRACTICALITIES There is no tourist information office. The underfunded **Hà Tiên Hospital** is near the bus station.

WHAT TO SEE AND DO Hà Tiên's waterfront is dominate by massive market buildings, but the streets behind, with a few heritage buildings and towering swallow houses (the nests are harvested for consumption), make for a pleasant afternoon of aimless wandering.

Đền Mạc Cửu Temple (28 St, Bình San) This temple, dedicated to the worship of Mạc Cửu and his clan, was built in 1898–1902. Mạc Cửu was provincial governor under the waning Khmer rule and in 1708 established a Vietnamese protectorate. The temple lies a short way from the town and sits at the foot of Núi Lăng (Tomb Mountain). To the left of the altar house is a map showing the location of the tombs of members of the clan. Mạc Cửu's own tomb lies a short distance up the hill, along a path leading from the right of the temple, from where there are good views of the sea.

Lăng Mộ Bà Cô Năm Tomb (QL80, Bình San) Around the back of Núi Lăng (a short drive, or longish walk) is Lăng Mộ Bà Cô Năm (Tomb of Great Aunt Number Five), an honorary title given to the three-year-old daughter of Mạc Cửu, who was possibly buried alive, though it is unclear why. It has become an important shrine to Vietnamese seeking her divine intercession in times of family crisis and is more visited than Mạc Cửu's tomb.

Phù Dung Pagoda (Phù Dung) The large and colourful Phù Dung Pagoda was built in the 18th century, though little of the original structure remains. Find it a

ÓC EO

Óc Eo is an ancient city about 20km inland from Rạch Giá. It is of great interest and significance to archaeologists, but there is not a great deal for the visitor to see bar a pile of stones. This port city of the ancient kingdom of Funan (page 9) was at its height between the 1st and 6th centuries CE. Excavations have shown that buildings were constructed on piles and the city was interlinked by a complex network of irrigation and transport canals. Like many of the ancient empires of the region, Óc Eo built its wealth on facilitating trade between the East (China) and the West (India and the Mediterranean). Vessels from Malaya, Indonesia and Persia docked here. No sculpture has yet been found, but a gold medallion with the profile of the Roman emperor Antonius Pius (CE152) has been unearthed. You'll need your own transport to travel there and back, and the whole excursion will take a couple of hours.

GETTING TO CAMBODIA FROM HÀ TIÊN

Hà Tiên is a mere 6km from the no-nonsense Xà Xía border crossing (QL80, Mỹ Đức) with Cambodia. Make sure you have a prearranged visa for entering Cambodia, and note that this puts you in a remote part of Cambodia, more than 150km from Phnom Penh. You may need to take a taxi to Kep Beach, 20km away, to find a bus to the Cambodian capital.

short distance along a path to the northwest, just off Phương Thạnh Street. A lengthy Shakespeare-esque story is attached to this temple, the name of which translates to 'Cotton Rose Hibiscus Pagoda'. In 1730, newly widowed Nguyễn Nghi fled invaders from Laos and landed in Hà Tiên with his son and ten–year-old daughter, Phù Cừ (the ancient form of Phù Dung, with the same floral meaning). Nguyễn Nghi was soon appointed professor of literature and poetry to Mạc Cửu's son, Mạc Tử, and privately tutored his own little daughter, who had taken to dressing as a boy in order to be able to attend school. After Mạc Cửu's untimely death in 1735, his son was granted the name Mạc Thiên Tích and the title Great Admiral Commander-in-Chief, Plenipotentiary Minister of Hà Tiên Province. Later he inaugurated a poetry club at which young Phù Cừ, still in the guise of a boy, declaimed exquisitely, setting passions ablaze. Surreptitious investigations put the Great Admiral's mind at rest: 'he' was in fact a girl. A long poetic romance and royal wedding followed. After years of happy marriage the angelic Phù Cừ one day begged her husband to let her break with their poetic love of the past and become a nun. The Great Admiral realised he could not but comply. He built the Phù Cừ Pagoda, wherein his beloved wife spent the rest of her life in prayer and contemplation. The towering pagoda was built so high that it served as a constant reminder and could, in due course, be seen from his own tomb.

CHÂU ĐỐC

Bordering Cambodia and split by the Hậu River, An Giang is one of the most diverse provinces in the delta. Save Kiên Giang (page 416) to the south, An Giang is the only province southwest of Hồ Chí Minh City where you'll see hills and mountains, a chain known as Bảy Núi (Seven Mountains). There's also extraordinary religious and cultural diversity: the province is home to communities of Cham (page 343), Hoa (page 477), Khmer (page 411) and Kinh (page 189) that follow Animism, Buddhism, Hòa Hảo (page 34), Taoism and Islam. This is one of the only places in the country where you'll hear the Adhan (the Islamic call to prayer). Long Xuyên is the province's capital, but most will head straight for Châu Đốc, a scruffy but appealing riverside border town and the focal point of the province's visitor economy. From this friendly, laid-back town you can explore diverse villages, shrine-studded hills, bird sanctuaries, glistening temples and poignant reminders of the brutal Khmer Rouge regime in Cambodia in the 1970s. While Châu Đốc, with markets that swell with activity in the mornings and a sunset-facing riverside promenade ideal for evening strolls, makes a comfortable base, it's also worth visiting Long Xuyên to see the untouristed floating market. Most visitors only stop in Châu Đốc for a night on their way to or from Cambodia, but the town should not be reserved only for border crossers. Though half a day from Hồ Chí Minh City by bus and even longer by boat, Châu Đốc has enough to keep curious travellers busy for at least a few days and is one of the Mekong Delta's standout places to visit.

GETTING THERE AND AROUND Châu Đốc is 6 hours from Hồ Chí Minh City by **bus**; consider an overnight bus if you're short on time. If travelling during the day, the scenery along the way is fairly lacklustre, but the road does pass by other areas of interest, including Mỹ Tho and Sa Đéc, if you want to break up the journey. Cần Thơ, where there is an airport, is 4 hours from Châu Đốc. Châu Đốc bus station (91 Boulevard, Khóm Hòa Bình) is 3km east of town, but shuttle buses will run you to the centre.

If you wish to travel by **boat**, Victoria Mekong Cruises (**w** victoriamekong.com) have pricey itineraries on luxury cruise ships that depart Cần Thơ and pass through An Giang on their way to or from Phnom Penh in Cambodia.

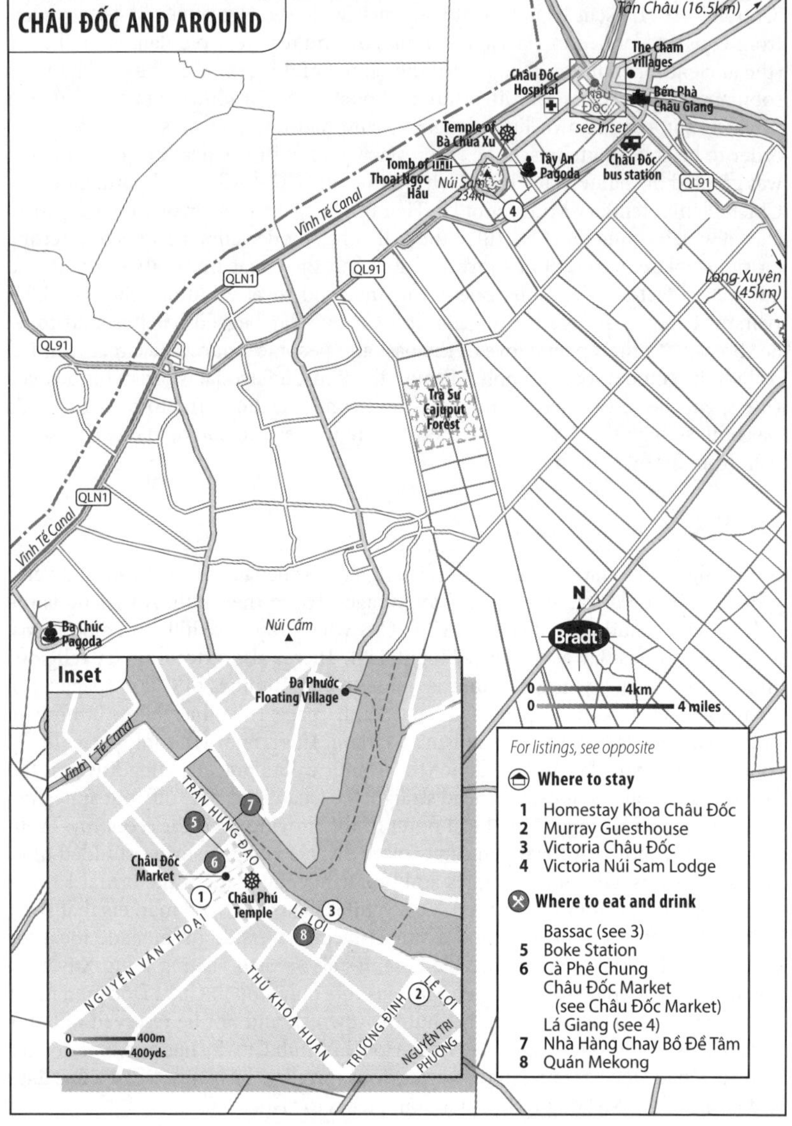

ONWARD TRAVEL TO CAMBODIA BY BOAT

Hãng Châu (w hangchautourist.vn) operates daily boat departures from Châu Đốc to Phnom Penh in Cambodia. The journey takes around 6 hours and leaves in the mornings (the return journey takes place in the afternoons). Visit the website for the most up-to-date information and book tickets or inquire at Victoria Châu Đốc (see below).

Grab doesn't work in Châu Đốc, but you can ask your accommodation to book **taxis** for you.

WHERE TO STAY *Map, opposite*

Homestay Khoa Châu Đốc 116–118 Nguyễn Văn Thoại; f homestaykhoachaudoc. Charming, quirky & friendly guesthouse in the centre of town. The family-run joint will do what they can to make your stay as comfortable & hassle-free as possible, including help with transport. **$**

Murray Guesthouse 11 Trương Định. Tired but clean hotel with decent beds & good AC. Refillable water bottle stations & the rooftop garden are a plus, as is the riverside walk into town. **$$**

✷ **Victoria Núi Sam Lodge** See page 398. A fantastic hideaway in the Mekong. **$$$**

Victoria Châu Đốc Hotel 1 Lê Lợi; w victoriahotels.asia/en/destination/victoria-chau-doc. Scenic riverfront deck, pool complete with loungers & sunset views of the river. All rooms are attractively decorated, though a little dated. The hotel group runs a daily speedboat to & from Phnom Penh. A refined place with superb service. **$$$$**

WHERE TO EAT AND DRINK *Map, opposite*

Châu Đốc Market 44 Phan Văn Vàng; ⌚ all day daily. In & around Châu Đốc Market there are dozens of street-food joints, including those selling *bún cá*, fish noodle soup & a local speciality dish. **$**

Nhà Hàng Chay Bồ Đề Tâm 275 Trần Hưng Đạo; ⌚ 07.30–20.30 daily. Local dishes made vegan, with tofu & seitan instead of meat. Try the tofu with lemongrass, deep-fried mushrooms or hotpot. **$**

✷ **Bassac Restaurant** Within the Victoria Châu Đốc (see above); ⌚ 06.00–22.00 daily. Overlooking the river, this might be the best restaurant in Châu Đốc. They do a fabulous sweet & sour *lẩu cá* (fish hotpot), a local speciality, but also tender stewed pork & Khmer-influenced chicken coconut milk curry. Western options also available. **$$**

Lá Giang Within Victoria Núi Sam (see above); ⌚ 06.00–22.00 daily. Lá Giang is every bit as good as Bassac. The stewed fish is a standout, or for a Vietnamese dish inspired by Western cuisine, try *bò lúc lắc* (stir-fried beef & vegetables) served with rice or chips. **$$**

Quán Mekong 41 Lê Lợi; ⌚ 06.00–22.00 daily. Housed within the courtyard of a colonial house & serving Mekong Delta favourites like boiled crab & shellfish in tamarind sauce. **$$**

Boke Station 1 Phan Đình Phùng; w bokestation.com; ⌚ 06.30–22.00 daily. Châu Đốc's hipster hangout, with beers, juices & coffee. The colonial building is elegantly lit in the evenings.

✷ **Cà Phê Chung** 8 Phan Đình Phùng; ⌚ 06.00–18.00 daily. Local café on the ground floor of a handsome colonial corner building. There's an old-world charm about Cà Phê Chung that is fast disappearing in Vietnam.

OTHER PRACTICALITIES Unsurprisingly, given their presence in the province, Victoria Châu Đốc (w victoriamekong.com) has the best **tour** desk in town. For a more personal experience, reach out to Ms San at Mekong Châu Đốc Travel (w mekongchaudoctravel.com), but note that she can get booked up weeks, sometimes months, in advance. For more informal river cruises and activities, you'll be able to negotiate with tour hawkers on the riverside promenade south of the market. There is no tourist information office. **Châu Đốc Hospital** (Tân Lộ Kiêu Lương) is 2km southeast of the city centre.

WHAT TO SEE AND DO

Châu Phú Temple (228 Trần Hưng Đạo) Built in 1926 under the Nguyễn Dynasty, this splendid temple and communal house has bright yellow walls, attractive orange and green roof tiles and Chinese decorative features that may remind visitors of the imperial buildings in Huế. The temple is a good place to start a tour of Châu Đốc as it was constructed to worship the official **Thoại Ngọc Hầu**, who is something of a local hero and will continue to pop up throughout your stay. The mandarin oversaw the construction of the Vĩnh Tế Canal (see below) and is buried at Núi Sam (see opposite). Look out for the fine carved pillars and shrine to Hồ Chí Minh, which was added more recently.

Vĩnh Tế Canal (Kênh Vĩnh Tế) This remarkable feat of engineering took 800,000 workers five years to build and was completed in 1824. It is 90km long and stretches all the way to Hà Tiên on the southwest coast. Its purpose was two-fold: navigation and defence. So impressed was emperor Minh Mạng in the achievement of the canal's builder, Thoại Ngọc Hầu (see opposite), that he named the canal after his wife, Châu Thị Vĩnh Tế. The workers, many of whom were ethnic Khmer, were subject to terrible working conditions, resulting in the deaths of thousands. This mistreatment was later used by the Khmer Rouge to motivate the atrocities committed at Ba Chúc Pagoda (page 424) more than 150 years later. Some river tours include a quick visit to the canal.

Châu Đốc Market (Trần Hưng Đạo) Separated into two parts (wet goods by the river; dry goods in the town), Châu Đốc Market is at its busiest early in the morning but continues operations throughout the day. Some of the more attractive colonial buildings in town, such as those hosting Cà Phê Chung and Boke Station (page 421), are on the streets that fan out from the dry market.

Around Châu Đốc It's best to group the sites around Châu Đốc by location. Perhaps spend one day exploring closer areas of interest like Đa Phước Floating Village, a Cham village and Núi Sam. Spend the next exploring further afield, with a hike up Núi Cấm. Spend a third day boating through Trà Sư Cajuput Forest and visiting the harrowing Ba Chúc Pagoda. The easiest way to explore An Giang is by organised tour (page 421), but those with their own transport and a sense for adventure will have no problems designing their own itineraries.

Đa Phước Floating Village (Sông Hậu) You'll see the colourful floating houses and fish farms of Đa Phước from the riverside promenade in Châu Đốc. A farm can house as many as 70,000 fish (mostly carp, tilapia and catfish), which writhe around in cages that are up to 6m deep beneath the wooden structures. The colours are a fairly new addition to the village: the local government implemented the idea and paid for the paint in 2023 to spruce up the place for tourists. Take a tour here with Victoria or negotiate with one of the hawkers on the promenade.

The Cham villages (Phú Hiệp & Phủm Soài) Across the river from Châu Đốc is a cluster of Cham (page 343) villages, an extraordinary Islamic enclave in a part of mainland Southeast Asia that is dominated by Buddhism and Taoism. The most popular village for visitors is Phú Hiệp, thanks to its accessibility and the impressive

THE QUEEN OF SILK

Lãnh mỹ a is a black, shimmering silk that adorned Vietnamese royalty in the early 20th century and is produced in Tân Châu, north of Châu Đốc. Often referred to as the 'Queen of Silk', its aesthetic is achieved from an intensive dyeing process using the fruit of *Diospyros mollis* trees. Today it's almost exclusively used by Vietnamese fashion boutiques, such as Metiseko (page 464). It's sometimes possible to visit the ateliers of Tân Châu, but what you see depends on where the artisans are in the process. Ask at Victoria Châu Đốc or Ms San (page 421) for more information.

green and white Mubarak Mosque. To reach here, hop on a ferry at Bến Phà Châu Giang. Another lesser-visited village, also with a number of handsome mosques and musallas, is Phủm Soài, but it's difficult to access unless on an organised tour. Look out for women making *nâmpārang* (*bánh bò nướng* in Vietnamese), a kind of pancake made with coconut milk, duck egg and rice flower. The discerning reader may wonder if the Muslim Cham are the same group that constructed the magnificent Hindu structures in Central Vietnam, like Mỹ Sơn close to Hội An and the towers in Bình Định Province. The Cham were in fact originally an Indianised Hindu civilisation that ruled much of Central Vietnam, but they began converting to Islam in the 11th century. Take a tour here with Victoria (page 421) or negotiate with one of the hawkers on the promenade.

✷ ***Núi Sam*** (Núi Sam) Aptly named because, from the air, it resembles a horseshoe crab (*sam* in Vietnamese), this mountain, really a barren, rock-strewn hill, has great religious significance. A newly asphalted road leads to the top, bypassing various religious complexes, statues and even a couple of dinosaur statues. A hike up and down this road, stopping at areas that interest you along the way, makes for a fine early-morning or late-afternoon activity, especially when combined with a drink at Victoria Núi Sam Lodge (page 421). From the summit (234m) you can look out over Cambodia (3km northwest) and the patchwork fields to the southwest. The more storied sites, however, are actually at the foot of the mountain. **Tây An Pagoda** was built in 1847, but has clearly been extended multiple times, now exhibiting Chinese, Islamic, Khmer and perhaps even Italian Renaissance styles. The highlight here is perhaps not the gaudy exterior, but the plethora of detailed statues within. The nearby **Temple of Bà Chúa Xu** (925 Phạm Văn Bạch) was built between 1820 and 1825 and restructured several times over the years. What you see today is a featureless modern structure from the 1970s, but the interiors are extremely vivid. Taking pride of place on the central altar is the bedecked and bejewelled statue of Bà Chúa Xứ (page 424), who gazes over an endless line of worshippers asking for good fortune. Opposite this temple is the **Tomb of Thoại Ngọc Hầu** (see opposite), flanked by those of his two wives. Núi Sam is about 6km southwest of Châu Đốc, which would make for a very long and boring walk along a main road. Take a taxi or motorbike instead. When you're ready to return, you should have no trouble finding another at the foot of the mountain to bring you back again.

Núi Cấm (Núi Cấm) Núi Cấm, more than 700m high, is part of the Bảy Núi (Seven Mountains) chain that dwarfs Núi Sam to the north. There are several sites dotted around, including some gaudy pagodas, humble shrines and a cable car (120,000/80,000VND per route adult/child), which you can explore independently.

LEGEND HAS IT: BÀ CHÚA XỨ AND THE STRENGTH OF NINE VIRGINS

The origins of Bà Chúa Xứ – meaning 'the Lady' – are genuinely unclear, but the myths may date back to the Funan period (page 9). One story goes that, millennia ago, a South Asian royal was looking to establish a new kingdom when he chanced upon Núi Sam, which back then was an island surrounded by water. He marked his discovery with a statue – the Lady – which he'd brought from home. There she lived for thousands of years, bringing prosperity to the local villagers, until a few centuries ago, when a group of jealous foreigners tried to spirit her away.

The Lady, imbued with divine heft, proved impossible to carry and in a fit of anger the thieves broke her arm. The locals saw that she was vulnerable at the top of an unguarded mountain and tried to carry her to the village, but they too couldn't muster the strength. After asking the Lady what to do, a spirit medium explained that it would take nine virgins to bring her down.

Nine unmarried women were summoned for the task, and for them the statue was so light that they carried the Lady down the mountain with ease. Once at the bottom, the Lady suddenly became too heavy to carry again, and the villagers concluded that this was where she belonged. At the top of Núi Sam you can still see the empty plinth where the Lady once stood. To celebrate the story, each year towards the end of the fourth lunar month (usually in May) there is a ceremony where a replica Lady is carried down the mountain by a festooned litter of young women.

However, the best way to conquer Núi Cấm is on a hike (10–20km), especially as this is one of the few parts of the Mekong Delta where climbing a mountain is possible. For this you'll need a guide, which you can arrange through Victoria (page 421). Núi Cấm is about an hour south of Châu Đốc by road.

Ba Chúc Pagoda (Chùa Ba Chúc, An Định) As soon as the Khmer Rouge took power in Cambodia in 1975, skirmishes began on the border with Vietnam. In 1978, the Liberation Army of Kampuchea crossed the border and brutally massacred upwards of 3,000 people. Some villagers took sanctuary in Ba Chúc Pagoda, where they were discovered and murdered in truly horrifying ways, and the site now stands as a memorial. This makes for a harrowing visit, with photos of the massacre's aftermath, blood-stained walls and the bones of the victims arranged in a tomb that resembles a closed white lotus flower. These remains are arranged by age, from grandchildren to grandparents, reflecting the sheer horror and thoroughness of the massacre. This was one of the events that propelled the Vietnamese military to invade Cambodia at the end of 1978, leading to the ousting of Pol Pot at the beginning of 1979. By road, the pagoda and memorial site are an hour southwest of Châu Đốc, or 45 minutes from Núi Cấm.

✱ ***Trà Sư Cajuput Forest*** (Rừng Tràm Trà Sư, Ấp Văn Trà; **w** trasu.vn; ◷ 06.30–17.30 daily; 120,000VND) Fabulous Trà Sư Cajuput Forest is a birders' paradise, with over 70 species across 850ha. Like other protected areas, the site is well organised, with ticket offices and clear pricing. It is divided into two parts. One part is accessed by motorboat, which takes you deep into the forest to eat local specialities, mainly different types of hotpot. Unless you are particularly hungry, skip this section, as the noisy boat and human activity drive away any chance of seeing birds. The second part is reserved only for row-boats and is the highlight of a visit, as a local person (usually a woman) gently propels you through the water. The sheer number of birds – perhaps tens of thousands – is surreal and at times cacophonous. Storks, egrets and other large waterbirds are the most numerous, but spotted doves, pied bush chats and anhinga (snake birds) also inhabit the forest. Look for white-throated kingfishers, which appear as flashes of turquoise. The most eye-catching river scenes from the 2023 film *Đất rừng phương Nam* (*Song of the South*) were filmed here. Only visit in the morning (07.00–09.00) or in the afternoon (15.00–17.00); if you arrive at midday many of the birds will be hiding from the heat. It's an enjoyable journey at any time of year, but the waterscape is particularly pretty when water levels are at their highest, usually in September to November. December and January are cool and dry, making them the most comfortable months to visit. It's about 45 minutes by road from Châu Đốc.

✷ ***Long Xuyên floating market*** (Sông Hậu, access from Bến Phà Ô Môi; 🕘 05.30–09.00 daily) Long Xuyên's floating market will appeal to those in search of a more local experience than the trips offered at Cái Răng floating market in Cần Thơ. Like Cái Răng, Long Xuyên's market is wholesale, so you'll see mostly large boats loaded with coconuts, pineapples, bananas, sweet potatoes and other goods. Smaller vessels in the market for tropical fruits and vegetables motor up to the wholesale boats, who advertise their offerings by strapping a representative item to a pole, usually at the bow of the ship. Unlike Cái Răng, the number of market boats outstrips the number of tourist ones many times over. Look out for the breakfast sellers, who move from boat to boat peddling noodle soup and iced coffee. It's fairly easy to visit Long Xuyên floating market independently, as buses leave Châu Đốc regularly from 04.00 for the 60-minute journey. After arriving in Long Xuyên, head for the Ô Môi jetty, where boat owners will approach you offering a ride. Try not to pay more than 200,000VND per person for 1–2 hours. After visiting the market and

HÒA HẢO WHO?

In 1939, Huỳnh Phú Sổ founded the Buddhist sect known as Hòa Hảo in Phú Mỹ, about halfway between Châu Đốc and Long Xuyên, on the border with Đồng Tháp Province. It's difficult to reach even with your own transport, but then there isn't much to see because Huỳnh Phú Sổ demanded that followers practise this religion in the privacy of their homes, with little to no pomp. You may, however, see male followers of the sect in An Giang and the surrounding provinces, with their goatee beards and hair tied back in a bun. If you are lucky enough to visit a house of a Hòa Hảo worshipper, you will see relatively simple altars to honour heaven, Buddha and the family ancestors.

Nicknamed the 'Mad Monk' for his nationalism and unusually austere worship practices, Huỳnh Phú Sổ is still thought of by followers as a saint with messianic qualities. He became a considerable threat to the French, who used his assumed insanity as an excuse to imprison him in a mental institution in Saigon, where he's said to have converted one of his doctors. The French then tried to exile him to Laos before they lost control of Indochina during World War II. After his release he became head of a powerful revolutionary organisation that attempted to ally with the Việt Minh. This alliance ultimately failed, and the Việt Minh assassinated Huỳnh Phú Sổ in 1947. The Hòa Hảo faithful still anticipate his rebirth at a time of need.

before returning to Châu Đốc (or moving east towards Hồ Chí Minh City or Cần Thơ), stop for a coconut near the jetty and observe the morning bustle of the town. Then wander up to **Long Xuyên Cathedral** (9 Nguyễn Huệ A), which was built in the 1960s and depicts two elongated arms clasping a cross between outstretched fingertips. If you're in need of a bed in Long Xuyên, Đông Xuyên (9A Lương Văn Cù St; **w** dongxuyenhotel.vn; **$$**) is a huge, adequate option in a pleasant part of town, walking distance to the market, riverside and cathedral.

12

The Southern Islands

By Tom Divers

Either side of Vietnam's tapered southernmost tip lie two tropical archipelagos with contrasting characters. To the west, in the balmy waters of the Gulf of Thailand, **Phú Quốc** is the focus of major investment and construction, a globally connected island and an engine of Vietnam's beach tourism industry. To the east, far out in the turbulent waters of the East Sea, **Côn Đảo** is a rugged, isolated and sparsely populated cluster of islands that so far have dodged the intensive development of Phú Quốc, perhaps in part out of respect for the thousands of Vietnamese political prisoners incarcerated here during the colonial era. While Phú Quốc embraces its future as a place of leisure and entertainment, Côn Đảo preserves its past as a memorial to the ghosts that haunt its rocky shores. But there are also similarities. Both islands are densely forested and protected by national parks, providing inland activities such as hiking and visiting waterfalls, as well as traditional seaside revelry, and both are associated with Nguyễn Ánh, who became the first emperor of Vietnam's last imperial dynasty.

Of the two, Phú Quốc has the longer, softer, sandier beaches, with more entertainment options (including safari parks, themed resorts and cable cars), making it more conducive to family getaways and relaxing breaks. Here you'll find honeymooners and young families whiling away their days playing on the coast, swimming in jungle-engorged waterfalls and marching around theme parks before retiring to the comfort of a resort for seafood and cocktails. Côn Đảo has fewer archetypal tropical beaches but a more dramatic coastline and a better-preserved natural environment. Here, forest-piercing hiking trails and offshore dive sites will appeal to independent, active travellers, not to mention the ever-present reminders of its dark past in the form of heritage buildings and museums. Flecking the sea off the Mekong Delta's west coast, **Hòn Sơn** and **Nam Du** are sparkling mini-archipelagos that maintain a local vibe, and **Hải Tặc** (Pirate Island) is a fledgling domestic tourist destination with a rustic edge.

PHÚ QUỐC

Vietnam's largest island, Phú Quốc has a 150km coastline that is a halo of sand and cerulean seas, forging dozens of beaches that dissolve into the motionless waters of the Gulf of Thailand. Phú Quốc translates as 'rich land', an apt description of its lush interior, which remains mostly forested, with around half the island under national park protection and much of it designated a UNESCO Biosphere Reserve. The island's north and east coasts are backed by jungle-covered mountains, while its western flank features gentle slopes sliding down to long, sandy shores. Phú Quốc is part of the Mekong Delta province of Kiên Giang, 40km from the nearest mainland

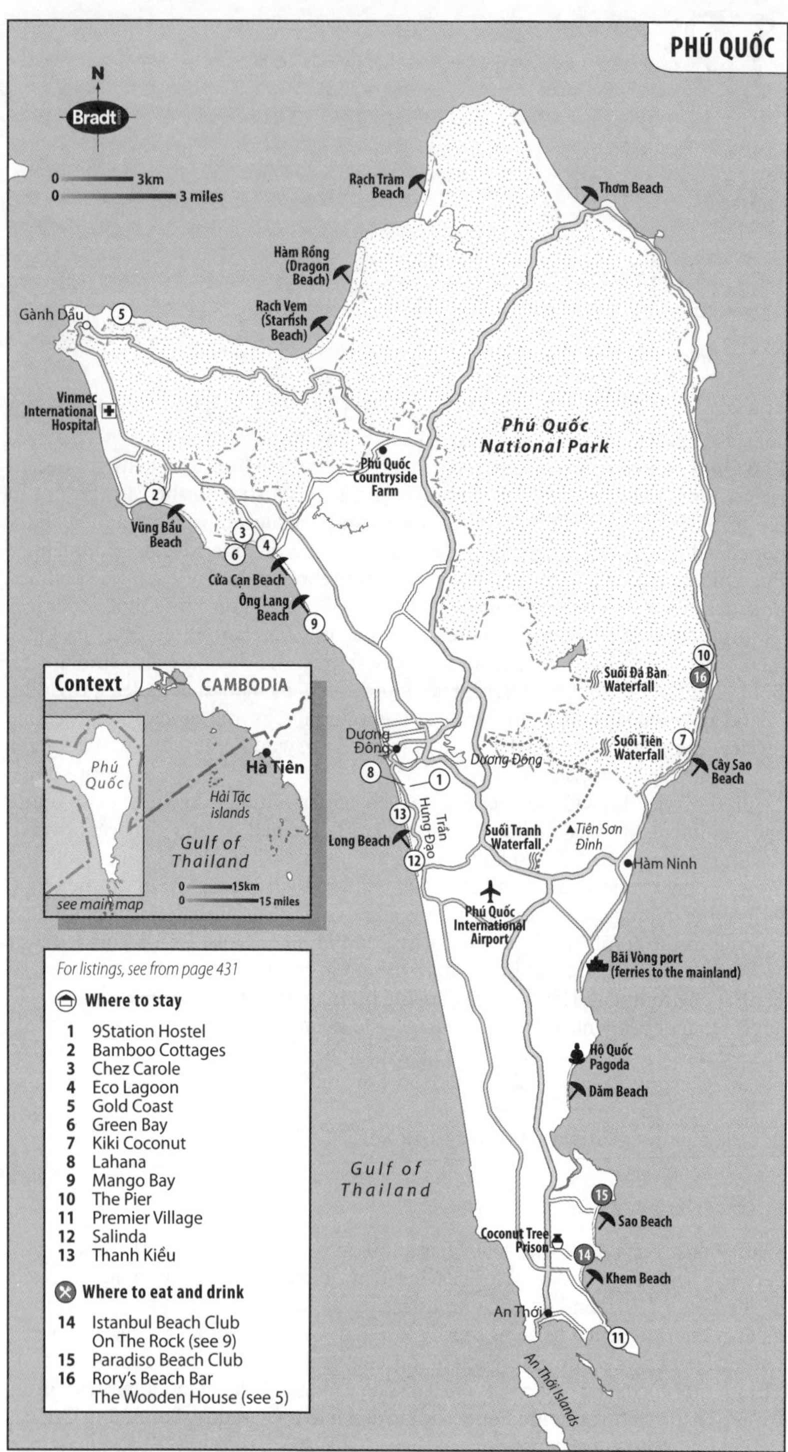
PHÚ QUỐC
N
Bradt
0 3km
0 3 miles
Rạch Tràm Beach
Thơm Beach
Hàm Rồng (Dragon Beach)
Rạch Vẹm (Starfish Beach)
Gành Dầu
Vinmec International Hospital
Phú Quốc National Park
Phú Quốc Countryside Farm
Vũng Bầu Beach
Cửa Cạn Beach
Ông Lang Beach
Suối Đá Bàn Waterfall
Suối Tiên Waterfall
Cây Sao Beach
Dương Đông
Dương Đông
Trần Hưng Đạo
Long Beach
Suối Tranh Waterfall
Tiên Sơn Đỉnh
Hàm Ninh
Phú Quốc International Airport
Bãi Vòng port (ferries to the mainland)
Hộ Quốc Pagoda
Dăm Beach
Gulf of Thailand
Sao Beach
Coconut Tree Prison
Khem Beach
An Thới
An Thới Islands
Context
CAMBODIA
Phú Quốc
Hà Tiên
Hải Tặc islands
Gulf of Thailand
0 15km
0 15 miles
see main map
For listings, see from page 431
Where to stay
1 9Station Hostel
2 Bamboo Cottages
3 Chez Carole
4 Eco Lagoon
5 Gold Coast
6 Green Bay
7 Kiki Coconut
8 Lahana
9 Mango Bay
10 The Pier
11 Premier Village
12 Salinda
13 Thanh Kiều
Where to eat and drink
14 Istanbul Beach Club
On The Rock (see 9)
15 Paradiso Beach Club
16 Rory's Beach Bar
The Wooden House (see 5)

port of Hà Tiên, but only 4.5km from Cambodia. In the context of regional tourism rivals like Phuket, development on Phú Quốc is still in its early stages, but the island is by no means pristine. Tourism gained momentum at the turn of the millennium, with backpackers celebrating the rustic quality of Phú Quốc compared with the crowded Thai islands. In the 2010s, mass development began in earnest, with an international airport, new roads and dozens of large-scale integrated resorts.

Today, the population is 180,000 and the capital, **Dương Đông**, is a busy urban centre. Apart from tourism, the island's economy is buoyed by high quality black pepper, fish sauce and seafood, all of which can be sampled by visitors. At the end of 2020, Phú Quốc became Vietnam's first 'Island City' (Thành Phố Đảo), a special administrative title that's testament to the pace of development over the last decade. Vast swathes of the coastline and interior remain undeveloped, but litter in the sea and on the beaches combined with relentless construction and environmental destruction in concentrated areas is a growing concern that has led to an increasingly negative perception of Phú Quốc. However, it's a big island and visitors can choose what side of it they want to experience: low-key resorts, empty beaches, forest trails and fresh seafood at local eateries, or sprawling, multi-storey entertainment complexes, casinos and overpriced tourist restaurants.

HISTORY For much of the first millennium CE, Phú Quốc was in the sphere of influence of the Mekong-based Indianised kingdom of Funan (page 9). It wasn't until the early 17th century that the island is mentioned in surviving documents from the Khmer empire, who called it Koh Tral. From the 1680s, Phú Quốc came under the control of the Mạc Dynasty, a small kingdom founded by a Chinese immigrant in Hà Tiên, who formed an alliance with the Nguyễn lords, rulers of Southern Vietnam. In 1775, French bishop and missionary Pierre Pigneau de Béhaine set up a Catholic seminary on the island, where he lived and taught for several years. While on Phú Quốc, Béhaine befriended Lord Nguyễn Ánh

THE PRINCE AND THE PRIEST

Formed on the island in the late 1770s, the friendship between French missionary Pierre Pigneau de Béhaine (1741–99) and Vietnamese lord Nguyễn Ánh (1762–1820) changed the course of Vietnamese history, leading to the establishment of Vietnam's last imperial line and providing the pretext for French colonialism. Béhaine was running a seminary on Phú Quốc when 15-year-old Nguyễn Ánh arrived in 1777, seeking refuge after being deposed by the Tây Sơn Rebellion. The two formed an alliance and in 1787 Béhaine travelled to the court of Louis XVI in France to sign the Treaty of Versailles, agreeing French military support for Nguyễn Ánh in exchange for economic and territorial concessions in Vietnam. The political turmoil of the French Revolution in 1789 meant that the treaty was never implemented, leaving Béhaine to support his friend through his own means by providing a mercenary force and modern weaponry, which helped defeat the Tây Sơn and establish Nguyễn Ánh as emperor in Huế, taking the royal title Gia Long. Upon his death in 1799, Béhaine was honoured by the emperor with a royal-style tomb in Saigon, which stood for more than 180 years: the site is still known today as Lăng Cha Cả (The Father's Tomb). Later, in the 1850s, the French used the unimplemented Treaty of Versailles as the basis on which to claim legitimacy for their colonial ambitions in Vietnam.

(page 429), who fled to the island in 1777 after being overthrown by the Tây Sơn Rebellion. Their alliance would ultimately lead to the defeat of the Tây Sơn and the establishment of Nguyễn Ánh as emperor Gia Long, the first ruler of the Nguyễn Dynasty, while also paving the way for French colonial expansion in Vietnam. Phú Quốc was part of French Indochina from the 1860s; a prison was established for political dissidents near the end of their rule in 1953 and was thereafter used by US-backed South Vietnam for the same purpose, incarcerating tens of thousands of people and becoming known as 'Nhà Tù Cây Dừa' – 'Coconut Tree Prison' – until the end of the war in 1975. Cambodia has long contested Vietnamese ownership of Phú Quốc, a dispute that flared intermittently over the decades, most recently in May 1975 when Khmer Rouge troops crossed the sea to conduct raids on the island.

WHEN TO VISIT During the **dry season** (November–May), the sea can be as calm as an infinity pool, offering ideal conditions for swimming, snorkelling, boat trips and beach-hopping. The island is busiest in December and January. Throughout the **monsoon** (June–October), strong winds whip up waves and heavy rains feed inland waterfalls and rivers that nourish the tropical canopy hanging over steamy hiking trails. Note that in the high season (November–March) hotel rates can double.

GETTING THERE AND AWAY

By sea Phú Quốc is connected to two mainland ports, both in the Mekong Delta. **Hà Tiên** (page 416) is the shorter crossing (1½hrs) and conveniently located on the Cambodian border for onward international travel; **Rạch Gía** is longer (2½hrs) but the city is a better-connected hub for onward domestic travel. Phú Quốc Express (w phuquocexpress.com) and Superdong (w superdong.com.vn) operate modern, fast boats three to five times daily with coach-style seating in air-conditioned cabins, with outside deck space. Online booking is efficient, as is buying tickets in person at offices across the island. All boats arrive/depart at **Bãi Vòng** port on the southeast coast. Most hotels can arrange pick-up for guests, or taxis and VinBus meet passengers at the port entrance.

By air **Phú Quốc International Airport** (w vietnamairport.vn) is served by all airlines that operate out of Vietnam, creating a network of daily domestic connections to most mainland hubs. However, routes come and go depending on the season. Regular international routes include major Asian cities. The airport is 15–30 minutes by road from Dương Đông town and most of the island's major resorts on the west coast, but it's a 45- to 60-minute drive to the northern beaches. Most hotels will arrange complimentary airport pick-up/drop-off for their guests. Alternatively, metered taxis wait outside the arrivals hall, and ride-hailing apps, such as Grab and Xanh SM, are easy to use. The VinBus network (see below) also regularly stops at the airport.

GETTING AROUND **VinBus** (run by Vingroup; w vinbus.vn) operates a free, island-wide electric bus network serving passengers 24 hours a day, with buses running every 15–30 minutes. Useful stops include the airport, ferry port, Dương Đông town and most of the popular hotels and beaches. Download the VinBus app for up-to-date routes, schedules and live tracking. **Xanh SM** (w xanhsm.com) is an all-electric vehicle ride-hailing app, with a large volume of electric vehicles. **Grab** cars and motorbikes can be booked via the app, but it's often more convenient just to ask your accommodation to book a local taxi for you. Good roads traverse the

OTHER ISLANDS IN THE GULF

Scattered off the western coast of the Mekong Delta, in what is technically the Gulf of Thailand, several mini-archipelagos offer travellers the chance to experience a more rustic, less-developed island life than what you find on Phú Quốc. **Nam Du** and **Hòn Sơn** can be reached by daily fast boats from the Mekong city of Rạch Gía, while Đảo Hải Tặc (Pirate Island) has daily connections to Hà Tiên. Of the three, Hòn Sơn is the prettiest, with hiking opportunities in the forested hills, fishing hamlets that maintain age-old household craft businesses such as fish sauce and pottery, and a few boulder-strewn sandy beaches. Unfortunately, household rubbish in the ocean can take the shine off all three archipelagos.

length and breadth of the island, making self-ride exploration on **rented scooters** or **bicycles** a joy. Scooters are available to rent from most accommodation options.

WHERE TO STAY *Map, page 428*

Phú Quốc has a wide range of accommodation and choosing where to stay will be a significant factor in determining your overall impression of the island. For this reason, the list of options here is longer than in other regional chapters. As a rule, the west coast has the highest concentration of hotels and is home to some of the most ostentatious resort complexes on the island. The east and north coasts are sparsely populated and developed. The best all-round option is Ông Lang Beach, while Gành Dầu, Cửa Cạn and Vũng Bầu are all very tranquil. In the high season (November–March) rates can double.

9Station Hostel 91/3 Trần Hưng Đạo; f 9station.hostelbar. Clean, modern, tasteful & smart, 9Station is a cut above the average hostel. It is 5–10mins' walk from the beach, but guests can use the infinity pool at its sister property (Lahana; see right). The bar is a good hangout for meeting other travellers. **$**

Bamboo Cottages Vũng Bầu Beach; e bamboophuquoc@gmail.com; w booking.com. Cool, airy concrete & tile bungalows on the beach or thatched-roof wooden cabins set back by a stream beneath casuarina trees, Bamboo Cottages is calm, understated & great value. **$$**

Chez Carole Tổ 1, Ấp 4, Cửa Cạn; w chezcarole.com.vn. Cosy wood, tile & stone bungalows on a bank overlooking the long arc of Cửa Cạn Beach. Rooms feature sea or river views from their verandas. The beach is good & there's a pool. **$$**

Eco Lagoon Lê Bát, Cửa Cạn; w ecolagoonphuquoc.vn. Referring to itself as a 'boutique homestay', Eco Lagoon is set on a serene brackish inlet 5mins from Cửa Cạn Beach. Rooms are contemporary rustic, with wooden flooring, bamboo blinds & scatter cushions. **$$**

✷ **Gold Coast** Chuồng Vích, Gành Dầu; w goldcoastphuquoc.com. At the northwestern tip of the island, Gold Coast occupies a scenic position on a crescent of white sand beneath coconut palms, with vistas across the gulf to the jungles of Phú Quốc's empty northern bays. **$$**

✷ **Kiki Coconut** Cây Sao, Hàm Ninh; f KikiCoconutBeach. With only 4 tile-roofed bungalows on the white sand beneath a shady canopy of coconut palms, Kiki is a serene spot on the largely undeveloped east coast. Beach activities & watersports are all free for guests. **$$**

Lahana 91/3 Trần Hưng Đạo; w lahanaresort.com. Lahana is located down a quiet alleyway, a 10min stroll from the seafront, & rates are very reasonable. Spacious, tastefully appointed thatched wood & concrete bungalows grace a hillside overflowing with tropical foliage. **$$**

The Pier 168 Ấp Cây Sao, Hàm Ninh; f thepier.phuquoc.resort. Cosy, modern villas & seafront bungalows on stilts above the water with sweeping coastal views. Sunrises are picturesque & the jungle-clad escarpment rising up behind the resort offers a dramatic backdrop. **$$**

✷ **Thanh Kiều** 100C/14 Trần Hưng Đạo; **w** thanhkieuresort.com. Long-running & family-owned, this modest, understated & well-organised resort sits on a prime stretch of beach shaded by coconut palms right at the heart of Phú Quốc's most popular seafront. **$$**

✷ **Green Bay** Tổ 1, Ấp 4, Cửa Cạn; **w** greenbayphuquocresort.com. A low-rise resort in large grounds, Green Bay's 81 rustic-chic villas are spread along the beach & hillside. The villas have sunken outdoor bathtubs & large terraces, some with private pools. There are 2 restaurants & 2 infinity pools. The bay is a mix of sandy beach, rocky inlets & some decent coral. **$$$**

✷ **Mango Bay** Ông Lang Beach; **w** mangobayphuquoc.com. The epitome of a tropical island getaway, Mango Bay is set in lush grounds with a long beachfront, sparingly peppered with thatched wood & rammed-earth bungalows. Preservation of the natural environment is a priority: there's no swimming pool & no AC, but there's an air-cooling system above the beds. **$$$**

Salinda Cửa Lấp, Dương Tơ; **w** salindaresort.com. Situated on a palm-lined stretch of Long Beach, this stylish, contemporary resort features tasteful décor, a good pool, a spa & outstanding dining, including a high-quality Indian & Italian restaurant & complimentary sparkling wine with b/fast. **$$$**

Premier Village Mũi Ông Đội, An Thới; **w** premiervillage-phuquoc.com. This luxurious resort consists of 215 large modern villas with private pools dotted on the hillside & beachfront. 2 sandy beaches – 1 each side of the promontory – enable both sunrise & sunset views. **$$$$**

WHERE TO EAT AND DRINK Thanks to its expanding population and global links, Phú Quốc has a varied and increasingly sophisticated dining scene. Many of the resorts have good restaurants, Dương Đông town is abuzz with tempting street-food options, and Trần Hưng Đạo Street is lined with eateries serving an impressive range of Vietnamese and international cuisines. When it comes to drinking, there are many opportunities for sunset cocktails across the island. **Rạch Vẹm**, a remote northern bay also known as Starfish Beach and accessed via a dirt road, hosts dozens of local seafood restaurants (⌚ 10.30–22.00 daily; **$$**) on wooden piers or floating offshore; Nguồn Sống and Ngàn Sao are recommended. The majority of listed places fall within Dương Đông, Gành Dầu and Hàm Ninh towns and along Trần Hưng Đạo, and are therefore not mapped individually.

PHÚ QUỐC'S SPECIALITY DISHES

BÚN KÈN A light and refreshing dish featuring a rich broth of pulverised fish mixed with coconut milk and poured over a base of shredded green papaya and rice noodles, with a variety of aromatic fresh herbs on top. Try it at **Bún Kèn Út Lượm** (see opposite).

BÚN QUẬY Seafood soup whose name means 'stirring noodles' on account of the need to mix and stir in your own dipping sauce of salt, chilli, calamansi and MSG. Try it at **Bún Quậy Kiến Xây** (see opposite).

GỎI CÁ TRÍCH A standout dish, this herring salad is served with sheets of rice paper to roll before dipping in a special fish sauce. The dish is available at most seafood restaurants, with a standout version at **The Wooden House** (see opposite).

HẢI SẢN Fresh seafood (*hải sản*) is available at most restaurants but is best sampled at local *quán hải sản* (seafood eateries), particularly those near Hàm Ninh and Rạch Vẹm fishing villages.

Restaurants

✷ **Bún Kèn Út Lượm** 42 30 Tháng 4, Dương Đông; ⌚ 06.00–noon daily. Part salad, part soup, *bún kèn* has been served at Út Lượm for 45 years. If you only try 1 local dish, this should be it. $

Bún Quậy Kiến Xây 28 Bạch Đằng, Dương Đông; w bunquay.vn; ⌚ 07.00–23.00 daily. Serving *bún quậy* with squid, shrimp paste, fish cake or beef, Bún Quậy Kiến Xây claims this Phú Quốc speciality as its own & has a chain of trendy, visitor-friendly restaurants across the island. $

Phở Sài Gòn 31 30 Tháng 4, Dương Đông; ⌚ 06.30–11.30 & 17.00–22.30 daily. Get your obligatory bowl of beef noodle soup at this noodle house in Dương Đông town. For a treat, order *phở xương* – slow-cooked beef on the bone. $

Dr Sweetsmoke 129 Trần Hưng Đạo; f DrSweetsmoke; ⌚ noon–22.00 daily. If you've had enough of seafood, try this American-style barbecue restaurant with a long list of good-quality steaks & ribs all cooked in a large smoker on site. $$

The Home Pizza 128 Trần Hưng Đạo; f thehomepizzapq; ⌚ 11.00–22.30 daily. Very good, freshly made pizza in a contemporary, minimalist setting, with lots of imaginative toppings. Try the special *gỏi cá trích* (herring salad) pizza or, if you dare, the durian pizza. $$

✷ **Quán Tình Biển** TL48 Hàm Ninh; ⌚ 08.00–23.00 daily. Standing out from the other local restaurants in the area, Tình Biển has dozens of tanks of live fish & shellfish to choose from before dining in the open air on a wooden pier. $$

Saigonese Eatery 129 Trần Hưng Đạo; f saigoneseeatery; ⌚ 08.00–22.00 daily. A pleasant, relaxed spot popular with visiting expats from the mainland, this restaurant serves interesting riffs on Vietnamese classics & some good Western dishes too. $$

The Wooden House At the Gold Coast resort (page 431); ⌚ 07.30–21.00 daily. Set on the sand beneath coconut palms, the resort restaurant boasts large portions & one of the best versions of *gỏi cá trích* (herring salad) on the island. $$

✷ **On The Rock Restaurant** At Mango Bay (see opposite); ⌚ 07.00–22.30 daily. Ever popular for sunset dinners, the restaurant at Mango Bay is set on a wooden deck above a rocky beach. The international menu is created using as many ingredients as possible sourced from the island, featuring seafood, Vietnamese fusion & Mediterranean dishes. Very romantic, but it's often busy, so book ahead. $$$

Bars and coffee houses

Bittersweet 185 Trần Hưng Đạo; w bar.bittersweet.vn; ⌚ 18.00–01.00 daily. Enter the shop front of a chocolatier & open the hidden door to access this 1920s-style speakeasy bar with cushioned booths & low lighting.

✷ **Chill Bistro & 40Six Beach Haus** Tổ 01, ĐT45, Gành Dầu; f 40sixbeachaus; ⌚ 08.00–22.00 daily. On the beach at the northwestern tip of the island, these 2 relaxed bars offer cocktails, Vietnamese rums, teas, smoothies, a young crowd & great views towards the Cambodian islands.

Chuồn Chuồn Sao Mai, Dương Đông; f chuonchuonbistro; ⌚ 07.30–23.00 daily. Chuồn Chuồn is positioned on the hillside behind Dương Đông town, with good views over the green hills & ocean, plus a menu of cocktails, craft beer and juices.

Istanbul Beach Club [map, page 428] Bãi Khem; f istanbulbeachclub; ⌚ 08.00–23.45 daily. Set on the rice-white sand of Khem Beach, this thatched-roof bar has a deck & beanbags on the sand.

Paradiso Beach Club [map, page 428] Bãi Sao; ⌚ 09.00–18.00 daily. An attractive, pastel-toned villa opening on to a patio beneath tall palms, this open-sided bar is the best place to enjoy the white sands of Sao Beach with a cocktail in hand. Quality is average, but the setting is unbeatable.

✷ **Rory's Beach Bar** [map, page 428] Group 3, Cây Sao; f RorysBarPhuQuoc; ⌚ 09.00–22.00 daily. A sprawling beach club, this long-standing Phú Quốc institution recently relocated to the low-key east coast. Spacious & laid-back with a social vibe, Rory's has a large open deck, big indoor drinking & dining area, a rock pool, mini-golf & a wooden pier. The drinks list is extensive.

Xốm Coffee & Bar 149 Trần Hưng Đạo; f; ⌚ 07.00–23.00 daily. A wooden house with pastel-toned shutters raised on a platform above the road, this café has a calm ambience & good coffee.

OTHER PRACTICALITIES Most accommodation options can assist guests in arranging a variety of island **tours**. Many hotels outsource to established Phú Quốc operators, such as John's Tours (143 Trần Hưng Đạo; w phuquoctrip.com; ⏲ 07.30–21.00 daily) and Red River Tours (379 Trần Hưng Đạo; w redrivertours.com.vn; ⏲ 08.00–22.00 daily). A much smaller and more personal option is Tommie Local Tours (e hoangthienanhtuan@gmail.com; f Tommie Phu Quoc Local Tours), an island resident doing his best to show visitors his home.

Cards are widely accepted in most accommodation, but **cash** is generally best for dining and shopping. **Vinmec International Hospital** (DT45 Bãi Dài, Gành Dầu; ☎ 0297 3985 588; w vinmec.com; ⏲ 24hrs), in the northwest, is the best place to go if you have a medical emergency.

WHAT TO SEE AND DO Try to find the latest version of the free, annually updated **Phú Quốc Island Visitor Map**, available from many cafés, hotels and tour desks. The map is an excellent way to familiarise yourself with the island's topography and where all the sights are in relation to each other. For beachcombers, there's enough coastline to stretch out a week of exploration, as well as the smaller **An Thới Islands** (Quần Đảo An Thới) off the southern tip, where some of the best snorkelling and diving is found. Inland, the hills, forests, streams and plantations offer hikes, waterfalls, local temples and the opportunity to sample some of Phú Quốc's speciality produce, such as pepper, fish sauce and *rượu sim* (berry liquor).

Beaches With over 150km of coastline, Phú Quốc has dozens of beaches to choose from. As a general rule, the west coast is characterised by long, sandy beaches with patches of dense development, while the east coast is more rugged and sparsely populated; the northern beaches are almost entirely in their natural state but difficult to access, and the southern end of the island tapers to a thin tail leading to the An Thới Islands, a mini archipelago of green islets. Most beaches have an area accessible to the public, but some are dominated by hotels and resorts. Note that rubbish washed up on the beaches can be an issue, especially after rough weather.

West coast Stretching from Gành Dầu in the north to An Thới in the south, this is the most intensively developed side of the island, and it's also where the longest, sandiest beaches are located. The west coast is bookended by two enormous tourist and entertainment complexes: Vingroup in the north and SunGroup in the south (see below). Ông Lang is the best all-round beach, with a handful of low-rise resorts

IF WE BUILD IT, THEY WILL COME

Two of the largest conglomerates in Vietnam have developed huge chunks of Phú Quốc, transforming parts of the island beyond recognition in less than a decade. On the northwest coast, Vingroup has turned what was once an empty, 5km beach backed by rainforest into a 24-hour entertainment complex, including the Disneyland-meets-Hogwarts VinWonders theme park, a waterpark, safari park, golf course and Grand World, featuring Venetian-style canals and gondolas. On the south coast, Sun Group has made its mark with a colossal building project, including an entire faux Italian town, the ultra-modern Kiss Bridge (Cầu Hôn), which hosts a spectacular light, sound and live performance show called Kiss of the Sea, a Romanesque cable car station and numerous ostentatious luxury resorts. Even if you're not a fan of the aesthetics (not to mention the environmental impact) of these projects, it's difficult not to be impressed by their sheer scale and audacity.

LEGEND HAS IT: THE UNIVERSITY THAT NEVER WAS

At Khem Beach's southern edge is one of Phú Quốc's more outlandish resort complexes: a decadent collection of multi-storey buildings coated in bold shades of pink, yellow and blue. 'What was once a 19th-century French university,' says the hotel website, 'has been reimagined as an eclectically themed, lavish beachfront playground by renowned resort architect Bill Bensley.'

The story goes that Bensley, a Californian, spent years looking at historical accounts of the abandoned colonial-era Université Lamarck to bring the JW Marriott Phú Quốc Emerald Bay Resort and Spa into being. He converted the dean's library – home to more than 1,500 books – into the hotel reception. He upcycled the department of anthropology to house lavish hotel rooms. The department of mycology (the study of fungi) was reincarnated as the luxurious Spa Chanterelle.

This is, of course, total fantasy. There was never a French university on Phú Quốc, and local historians and heritage enthusiasts have, with good reason, questioned Bensley's romanticised interpretation of Vietnam's colonial history.

on a sandy bay with rocky outcrops. **Vũng Bầu** is a relaxed and quiet crescent of sand backed by jungle and **Long Beach** (Bãi Trường) is 20km of palm-shaded sand lined with international resort chains.

East coast Two of the most striking beaches on the island are on the southeast coast: **Khem Beach** and **Sao Beach** both feature white sand, turquoise water and coconut palms. However, Khem Beach is now part of a large resort and residential complex, and Sao has lost some of its charm due to shabby temporary developments, rubbish and jet skis. **Cây Sao**, on the central east coast, is an up-and-coming beach with a backdrop of jungle-covered mountains and several good places to stay, eat and drink.

✷ *North coast* Stretching from Gành Dầu in the west to Thơm Beach in the east, this is the least developed coastline on the island. Parts of **Rạch Tràm**, **Rạch Vẹm** (popularly known as **Starfish Beach**) and Hàm Rồng (**Dragon Beach**) are among the most beguiling and idyllic bays on Phú Quốc. Roads reach some of the northern beaches, but visitors will need to travel here independently with their own wheels or book a tour.

An Thới Islands

Accessible by boat or cable car, these small, green islands lying off Phú Quốc's southern tip are a popular day trip. Independent travellers can take the 20-minute, 7.9km-long over-sea cable car (🕘 09.00–17.00 daily; 650,000VND return trip) to Hòn Thơm (Pineapple Island) and then visit Aquatopia (🕘 10.00–17.00 daily; 200,000VND), a huge waterpark on the island. But to access the other islands it's necessary to book a tour: **John's Tours** (see opposite) offers a variety of round-trip packages including several islands, watersports, onboard seafood lunch and cable car for the return journey. Tommie Local Tours (see opposite) organises much smaller and more personal tours of the archipelago, including secret beaches and barbecue lunches on the sand.

Dương Đông town

Located on the central west coast and with a population of over 60,000, Dương Đông is the largest settlement on the island. The town's animated streets sprawl either side of the Dương Đông River, dotted with sky-blue fishing boats as it snakes through town before emptying into the Gulf of Thailand, where there's a harbourfront park. This waterfront area is increasingly appealing, with cafés, eateries and ice cream parlours.

Dinh Cậu Shrine (Khu phố 2) The harbourfront park (Công Viên Bạch Đằng) looks out over the diminutive Dinh Cậu Shrine, perched on a rocky outcrop. Built in the 1930s by a community that relied heavily on fishing, the temple is dedicated to Thiên Hậu (page 479), divine protector of seafarers. The shrine features traditional Vietnamese architectural elements, including curved roofs, vibrant colours and a small but richly decorated area for worship.

Markets On opposite banks of the river, Dương Đông's **fish market** (Chợ Dương Đông; Trần Phú) is busiest in the early mornings, whereas the **Night Market** (Chợ Đêm; along Bạch Đằng) is packed with diners from dusk onwards.

Cao Đài Temple (40 Nguyễn Trãi) The town's backstreets are pleasant to wander around, dotted with eateries, cafés and pagodas, including a small Cao Đài Temple. The size of the temple does not reflect Phu Quoc's important role in the inception of this 20th-century religion: it was on the island that the Supreme Being visited Ngô Văn Chiêu, the founder, during a séance that shook tables in the room in 1919 (page 33).

Fish sauce factories A large fishing fleet helps supply the town's *nước mắm* (fish sauce) factories, whose distinctive aroma pervades the town. Tour operators can arrange visits: one of the most popular is **Khải Hoàn** (11 Hùng Vương; w khaihoanphuquoc.com.vn; 🕘 07.00–19.00 daily).

Other settlements and sights Other areas of interest, including small settlements, pepper farms, temples and the island's infamous prison are speckled across Phú Quốc. None of these sights needs to be booked in advance, so you can incorporate them into a self-designed itinerary of the island.

✷ ***Gành Dầu village*** At the northwestern tip of the island, this village has a lively market (Chợ Gành Dầu), a good beach with seafood restaurants and sunset bars with views of the Cambodian islands, and the ornate Nguyễn Trung Trực Temple (see opposite).

FISHERMAN'S BEST FRIEND

The Phú Quốc Ridgeback is the island's very own rare breed of dog. Excellent hunters and comfortable in the water (they even have partially webbed feet), these handsome dogs are now a coveted pet throughout Vietnam. On the east coast you sometimes see fishing families entering the water with their dogs accompanying them to forage for shellfish and crustaceans. In the sea, the dogs act just as they would on land, albeit at a much slower pace – paddling ahead of their owners, looking out for potential threats and scouting for prey. Visitors can find out more at **Thanh Nga Dog Conservation Centre** (Trung Tâm Bảo Tồn Chó Xoáy Phú Quốc Thanh Nga; Suối Mây, DT47; 🕘 07.30–17.30 daily).

NGUYỄN TRUNG TRỰC: RESISTANCE FIGHTER

Born in 1838 in the Mekong Delta, Nguyễn Trung Trực came to maturity as the French colonisation of Southern Vietnam got under way. By the time he was 20, the French had taken Saigon and began to establish the state of Cochinchina, spreading south into the delta region. Trained in fighting from an early age, Nguyễn Trung Trực joined the resistance against the French, earning his most celebrated victory in 1861 when he ambushed and sank the French ship *L'Espérance* in a Mekong canal, killing most of the crew. He then fought in Kiên Giang Province and fled to Phú Quốc, where he continued his resistance activities but was ultimately arrested on the island, detained in Saigon and beheaded in Rạch Giá in 1868. Today, Nguyễn Trung Trực is revered on Phú Quốc, particularly at two shiny temples, in Gành Dầu (Đình Thần Nguyễn Trung Trực; 🕘 dawn–dusk daily) and Cửa Cạn (Đền Thờ Nguyễn Trung Trực; 🕘 dawn–dusk daily). Both locations feature statues of him stepping forward and drawing his sword, as well as portraits on the altars and frescoes depicting his exploits.

An Thới port At the far south is this thriving settlement packed with boats and local food stalls. Behind the port, a short hike leads up to a lighthouse (Hải Đăng An Thới; 🕘 dawn–dusk daily), which offers views of the harbour and outlying islands.

Coconut Tree Prison (Nhà Tù Phú Quốc; 350 Nguyễn Văn Cừ; 🕘 07.00–17.00 daily) Other sights in the south include the prison that was used by South Vietnam to incarcerate prisoners-of-war during the American War. It is now a museum, featuring life-size mannequins of inmates undergoing brutal treatment by their captors.

Hộ Quốc Pagoda (Chùa Hộ Quốc; Dăm Beach; 🕘 24hrs) This is an elaborate complex of Buddhist temples and colossal statues overlooking a green bay on the southeast coast. A towering white statue depicts Quan Âm, Goddess of Compassion (page 293).

Phú Quốc Countryside Farm (Suối Cái; **w** pepperfarmphuquoc.com) Of all the pepper plantations in Phú Quốc, this family-run establishment might be the friendliest. Tours are informal, without a set script, but the guides are knowledgeable and happy to answer questions about the practicalities of running a farm on the island. There's also a café and restaurant.

Hiking and waterfalls Because development has been focused on the coast, inland Phú Quốc remains relatively untouched. Most of the interior is covered in dense jungle, where cool streams trickle beneath giant trees before collecting in natural pools and cascading over rocks. Some waterfalls have been turned into attractions where visitors can bathe and walk. **Suối Tranh** (🕘 07.00–18.00 daily; 30,000VND) is the most popular and can get busy in the afternoon, but visiting in the early morning or midday is very pleasant. **Suối Đá Bàn** (🕘 07.00–18.00 daily; 10,000VND) and **Suối Tiên** (🕘 07.00–18.00 daily; 20,000VND) are less developed, but suffer from litter. The further upstream you walk, the better the state of the natural environment. Phú Quốc has potential as a hiking destination, but so far only a handful of trails have opened. The steep ascent to **Tiên Sơn**

Đỉnh (w vietnamcoracle.com/trekking-to-dinh-tien-son-peak-phu-quoc-island; 2–3 hours return) is a pretty forest walk with large boulders at the top affording excellent panoramas. Other hikes are possible, but some require a guide: ask at your accommodation or tour agency (page 433).

✷ Motorbiking and cycling Almost all of Phú Quốc's roads are now paved, making every corner of the island accessible on two wheels. The east coast road between Hàm Ninh and Thơm Beach is a quiet, attractive stretch of tarmac with fishing hamlets and empty beaches. The northern roads pass through thick jungle belonging to the national park, and the spur road to Rạch Tràm leads to a long stretch of undeveloped palm-fringed beach. There are regular petrol stations. You will be able to rent bicycles and motorbikes from your accommodation.

Diving, snorkelling, sailing and fishing Most of the good coral for snorkelling and diving is off the southern coast, in the An Thới islands. Although the marine environment here is not as impressive as in other regional countries like the Philippines and Thailand, the An Thới islands are about as good as it gets in Vietnam, with the exception of the Côn Đảo islands (page 448). **Rainbow Divers** (w divevietnam.com) and **Flipper** (w flipperdiving.com) both offer trips and PADI courses. **John's Tours** (page 434) organises fun squid fishing packages, setting sail in the evening and dining from the catch onboard. For anyone wanting to try their hand at sailing, **Viet Sail** (f vietsailing) has lessons on a small catamaran.

CÔN ĐẢO

The Côn Đảo archipelago is one of the best-preserved natural environments in Vietnam. **Côn Sơn**, the largest of the 16 islands lying 80km southeast of the Mekong Delta, has a population of just 10,000 and this is where all services and amenities are based. 80% of the archipelago is a national park and much of the surrounding sea is a marine protected area, boasting the richest dive sites in the country. Inland, hiking trails weave beneath the thick jungle canopy, providing a habitat for wildlife, some of which are endemic to Côn Đảo. Despite Côn Sơn's rugged and mountainous topography, the island is easily traversed by a cliff-hugging coastal road connecting the airport in the north with the port in the south, via the agreeable town of Côn Sơn clustered around a bay at the centre. But this tropical island has a dark past: for more than a century, its remote location was exploited by the colonial French, who used it as a penal colony to incarcerate many of Vietnam's now-celebrated national heroes.

Côn Đảo therefore offers visitors both outdoor activities and historical sites. Hiking, swimming, boat trips, diving and wildlife-spotting opportunities abound. But there are also informative museums, century-old heritage buildings and temples dedicated to local legends. The island is a popular pilgrimage for domestic tourists but receives few foreign travellers. Côn Đảo's natural beauty is its major appeal, but the echo of the suffering endured here by tens of thousands of prisoners is palpable, adding another dimension.

HISTORY Located on the maritime route between Southeast Asia and China, Côn Đảo has long been strategically important for trading nations. The archipelago was on the map for Malay, Khmer and Arab traders during the first millennium CE. Contact with the West followed a familiar succession of seafaring European

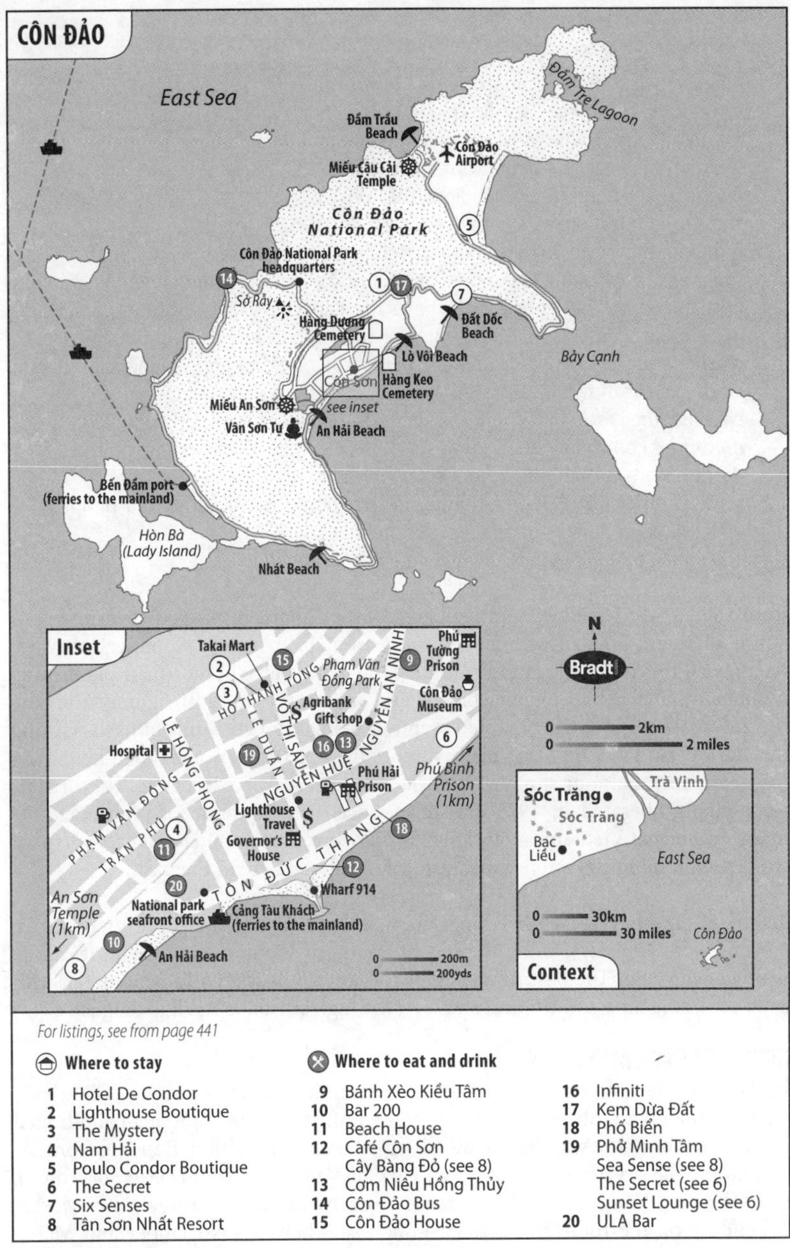

For listings, see from page 441

Where to stay

1 Hotel De Condor
2 Lighthouse Boutique
3 The Mystery
4 Nam Hải
5 Poulo Condor Boutique
6 The Secret
7 Six Senses
8 Tân Sơn Nhất Resort

Where to eat and drink

9 Bánh Xèo Kiều Tâm
10 Bar 200
11 Beach House
12 Café Côn Sơn
Cây Bàng Đỏ (see 8)
13 Cơm Niêu Hồng Thủy
14 Côn Đảo Bus
15 Côn Đảo House
16 Infiniti
17 Kem Dừa Đất
18 Phố Biển
19 Phở Minh Tâm
Sea Sense (see 8)
The Secret (see 6)
Sunset Lounge (see 6)
20 ULA Bar

colonial powers: Spanish and Portuguese mariners in the 16th century, the British East India Company in the 18th century (who set up a trading fort in 1702, but abandoned it a few years later when they were massacred by their own mercenary workforce), and the French who, having toyed with the idea of occupying the islands since the 17th century, eventually took control in 1861. This ushered in over a century of use as a penal colony, starting with the French colonial administration

RESPECT VS REVENUE

Thanks to its remote location, natural beauty and unique history, visitors and developers alike treat the Côn Đảo islands with a level of respect that's rarely found at other tourist destinations in Vietnam. But, as a new generation of Vietnamese travellers begin to see the islands as a place of leisure first and pilgrimage second, there are signs that developers' attitudes are changing too, viewing it more as a lucrative tourist destination than a sacred place of remembrance. Côn Sơn's demographics are shifting as people migrate from the mainland to start life and business in this thriving tourist enclave, and new transportation connections have the capacity to bring around 3,000 people each day – equal to a third of the island's population. Single-use plastic is rife (despite government billboards discouraging it), the island's landfill is overflowing and even ritual offerings have a detrimental impact because they're full of chemicals. Wildlife continues to flourish, including macaques commonly seen on the roadside, but they are only there because, despite signs prohibiting it, tourists continue to feed them. It remains to be seen whether Côn Đảo can accommodate more infrastructure and people while safeguarding its natural environment.

from 1862 to 1954, followed immediately by the American-backed government of South Vietnam, both of whom used the prisons to incarcerate political activists. As a result, this remote location is unique in having been 'home' to an astonishing number of Vietnam's most celebrated and important political figures from the revolutionary period, the notable exception being Hồ Chí Minh himself. During this dark period of Côn Đảo's history, more than 20,000 prisoners died here from mistreatment, malnourishment, hard labour, disease or execution. The prisons were finally liberated in 1975 and have since become a site of pilgrimage for many millions of Vietnamese. Today, Côn Đảo looks to develop its tourist potential while maintaining a reverence for those who suffered here in the past.

WHEN TO VISIT Weather in Côn Đảo is unlike anywhere else in Vietnam. In November to February, when the rest of Southern Vietnam is pleasant, it can be windy and rough. The best time to visit climatically is March to September, with calm seas, sunshine and tropical showers; the high season is April to August.

GETTING THERE AND AWAY

By sea At the time of research there were four sea routes connecting Côn Đảo with the mainland, on modern boats with comfortable seating in air-conditioned cabins, but check the websites below for up-to-date information. Ranging from 2½ to 6 hours, the sea routes operate from Hồ Chí Minh City, Trần Đề (in Sóc Trăng), Cần Thơ and Vũng Tàu. Sailings range from twice daily to three times weekly depending on the route and season. Rough seas between November and March often lead to cancellations. Book online via **Côn Đảo Express** (from Hồ Chí Minh City, Trần Đề and Vũng Tàu; **w** phuquocexpress.com), **Superdong** (from Trần Đề; **w** superdong.com.vn) and **Mai Linh Express** (from Cần Thơ; **w** taucaotocmailinh.vn). Boats arrive and depart at either **Bến Đầm port** (inconveniently located in the south of the island) or the new **Cảng Tàu Khách** pier, located on the main town's seafront. Taxis and electric buggies meet the boats and some hotels can arrange pick-up if told in advance.

By air Located at the north of Côn Sơn island, the runway at Côn Đảo Airport can only accommodate small propeller aircraft or limited-capacity jet planes. There are no international connections. At the time of research only **Vietnam Airlines** (w vietnamairlines.com; often operated by its subsidiary VASCO) was operating direct flights to Côn Đảo from Hồ Chí Minh City and Cần Thơ. Until recently there were direct flights from Hanoi, Đà Nẵng and Vinh on other domestic airlines, but they have ceased. Such is the growing demand for air travel to Côn Đảo that it's surely just a matter of time before these routes reopen. The **airport** is 13km from town. Most accommodation options can arrange complimentary airport pick-up/drop-off for their guests. If you arrive without a hotel booking, you can find a taxi outside the arrivals hall or hitch a ride on an electric buggy for a small (negotiated) fee.

GETTING AROUND Côn Sơn town's well-kept, elegant, tree-lined main streets and quiet lanes are easy to navigate on foot. The rest of the island is ideal for exploring by self-drive **motorbike** (available to rent from most hotels) or **bicycle** (harder to find but some hotels offer them for free). The well-maintained coast roads are virtually empty and the views are superb. Best arranged through your accommodation, local **taxis and hybrid electric buggies** (aimed at small groups and seating up to 12 passengers) can take you anywhere on the island. Speedboats to other islands (page 448) can be arranged at the national park's seafront office (Tôn Đức Thắng).

WHERE TO STAY *Map, page 439*

Most of the accommodation is clustered in Côn Sơn town, along the seafront boulevard (Tôn Đức Thắng) and An Hải Beach, although a couple of high-end options are located further afield on private beaches. Expect to pay 20–30% more for all standards of accommodation compared with the mainland. Booking in advance is advisable if travelling on weekends, public holidays or high season (April–August).

✷ **Hotel De Condor** Khu 2, Phan Chu Trinh; f. This small, colourful, great-value hotel features cosily decorated rooms with tiled floors, lanterns & bright bathrooms. The common areas are good for socialising & relaxing. **$**

Lighthouse Boutique Hotel 10 Hồ Thanh Tòng; f khachsanlighthouse.condao. Simple, clean rooms, attractive décor & friendly staff make this small boutique hotel on a quiet backstreet a popular budget choice for travellers. **$**

✷ **The Mystery** Lê Thanh Nghị; f The Mystery Condao Hotel. Stylishly furnished rooms with bamboo blinds, freestanding ceramic sinks, rattan cupboard doors & tiled bathroom floors, this classy boutique hotel on a backstreet in Côn Sơn town is tasteful & comfortable. **$$**

Nam Hải Hotel 5 Trần Phú; f Nam Hai Con Dao Hotel. Spotless, plain rooms with balconies in town just 2 blocks from the seafront road, Nam Hai is an excellent mini hotel. Rooms are bright, if a bit small. **$$**

Tân Sơn Nhất Resort 6 Nguyễn Đức Thuận; f cphongghoa.ad. Set in the shade of a canopy of tropical almond trees, this resort's shortcomings – no pool, & average service & b/fast – are easily forgotten due to its beachfront location. There's a new (& ugly) wing at the front offering cheaper rooms. **$$**

✷ **Poulo Condor Boutique** Bãi Vông, Cỏ Ống; w poulocondorresort.com. This luxury resort has the long arcing sands of Vông Beach all to itself. Spacious, Indochina-style villas, with architectural features echoing the French colonial-era shophouses in Côn Sơn town, are set among lush gardens & lakes in the shadow of looming, jungle-covered mountains. **$$$**

The Secret 8 Tôn Đức Thắng; w thesecretcondao.com. A modern, 196-room hotel on the elegant seafront road, The Secret offers contemporary, minimalist rooms, multiple dining & drinking options, a big swimming pool, 24hr gym & spa. The property can feel a bit sterile & impersonal. **$$$**

Six Senses Đất Dốc Beach; **w** sixsensescondao.com. 2 rows of low-rise, contemporary-looking villas constructed using traditional materials along a private sandy beach sliding into clear seas, Six Senses is one of the most exclusive resorts in Vietnam. The villas are spacious, low impact & well designed, all with ocean views & private infinity pools. Service, facilities, build quality & dining are exceptional. This all comes at a price. **$$$$**

WHERE TO EAT AND DRINK *Map, page 439*

Almost all dining options are located in and around Côn Sơn town; in particular, it's an excellent place to eat fresh seafood (*hải sản*; see below), including at the night market, **Chợ Hải Sản Đêm**. Meanwhile the **Cooked Food Market** (Chợ Ẩm Thực; Phạm Văn Đồng; 06.00–20.00 daily; **$**) is a covered area packed with dozens of stalls serving delicious and cheap classic Vietnamese dishes, such as noodle soups, rice meals, desserts and juices; it's ideal for breakfast.

Restaurants and street food

Bánh Xèo Kiều Tâm Nguyễn An Ninh; 08.00–23.00 daily. Savoury crepes with pork & shrimp filling, these Mekong-style *bánh xèo* are huge. They also serve hearty *cháo vịt* (duck rice porridge). **$**

✷ **Cơm Niêu Hồng Thủy** Tô Hiệu; 07.00–23.00 daily. This friendly, informal establishment offers hearty, home-cooked lunches & dinners, serving Southern Vietnamese specialities such as *cá kho tộ* (caramelised fish), *canh chua* (sour soup) & *bông bí xào* (stir-fried pumpkin blossom). **$**

Kem Dừa Đất Phan Chu Trinh; f Thaykemduadatcondao; 08.00–23.00 daily. The proliferation of coconut ice cream establishments on the island in the last few years is incredible, but Dừa Đất is regarded as the best. **$**

Phở Minh Tâm Trần Phú; 06.00–23.00 daily. This is a typical noodle soup house selling decent *phở* & *bò kho* (beef stew). **$**

Bar 200 4 Nguyễn Đức Thuận; f; 11.00–23.00 daily. With good-value Western food in a garden near the beach, the menu at Bar 200 features burgers, pizzas, milkshakes & some Vietnamese dishes too. There are also generously sized cocktails & a variety of beers. **$$**

✷ **Beach House** Phan Chu Trinh; f localcasualdining; 17.00–23.30 daily. An enterprising restaurant in an intimate setting with excellent food & drink, including wines & cocktails. The creative menu features fusion dishes cooked to order in a small kitchen next to the dining area. **$$**

Cây Bàng Đỏ Part of Tân Sơn Nhất Resort (page 441); 06.30–22.00 daily. This restaurant is atmospherically situated beneath large tropical almond trees on the beach. The extensive menu of Vietnamese dishes is very good, although the fresh seafood is expensive. **$$**

CÔN ĐẢO'S SPECIALITY DISHES

HẢI SẢN Lining the central street of Phạm Văn Đồng, a dozen open-fronted *quán hải sản* (seafood restaurants) serve any number of fresh fish, shellfish and crustaceans caught in the seas surrounding the island. Busy in the evenings, there's not much to choose between each restaurant but **Làng Chài**, **Cây Bàng** and **Ốc Điệp** are all good and reasonably priced. On the same street, **Chợ Hải Sản Đêm** is a night market featuring a throng of street vendors with mobile kitchens all cooking up fresh, inexpensive seafood. Some places do have English menus, but as most of the seafood is displayed in the open, pointing will suffice. As with many dining experiences in Vietnam, it's not just about the food, it's about the ambience, which is informal and lively.

KEM DỪA Another, perhaps unexpected, speciality of the island is *kem dừa* (coconut ice cream), which is a time- and labour-intensive process resulting in a silky and refreshing dessert. **Kem Dừa Đất** (see above) might be the best.

Infiniti Khu 8, Trần Phú; w infiniticondao.ezyro.com; ⌚ 10.30–14.00 & 17.30–21.30 daily. A Côn Đảo institution, this modern, minimalist restaurant-cum-coworking space wouldn't look out of place in Hồ Chí Minh City. Western-oriented, the food & drink are quite good & it attracts young travellers, but there's no natural light & it can feel stuffy. Think cappuccinos, signature cocktails & spaghetti carbonara. $$

Phố Biển 16B Tôn Đức Thắng; ⌚ 11.00–21.00 daily. Housed in a beautiful colonial villa (formerly the island doctor's residence) on the coastal road, this seafood restaurant has higher prices than the local restaurants but you're paying for the location. $$

The Secret Restaurant Part of The Secret hotel (page 441); ⌚ 07.00–11.00 & 16.00–21.30 Wed–Thu, 07.00–14.00 & 16.30–21.30 Fri–Sun. A handsomely restored heritage villa on the seafront road, this classy restaurant is a fantastic location for premium dining. Opening hours are erratic – always check & book before deciding to eat here. The menu has a strong French influence with the addition of local seafood. $$$

Bars and coffee houses

✷ **Café Côn Sơn** Tôn Đức Thắng; ⌚ 07.00–20.00 daily. This open-air café is housed in the handsome colonial-era former customs house, looking over the ocean at the centre of the seafront road. Seating is outside beneath the boughs of century-old tropical almond trees.

Côn Đảo Bus Thăng Long; ⌚ 16.00–19.30 daily. On the new & deserted west coast road, this converted minibus is set up on a ledge overlooking the ocean with great sunset views, serving fresh coconuts & juices.

Côn Đảo House Khu 7, Võ Thị Sáu; f; ⌚ 06.00–23.00 daily. A classy little bar on the backstreets of town, with a modest wine list & elegant cocktails. Good for a nightcap after dinner.

✷ **Sea Sense** 6 Nguyễn Đức Thuận; ⌚ 17.00–22.00 daily. On the beachfront outside Tan Son Nhat Resort (page 441), this pop-up beach bar serves an impressive variety of inexpensive cocktails & beer from a small, portable kiosk. Come at sunset.

Sunset Lounge Part of The Secret hotel (page 441); ⌚ 17.00–midnight daily. On the hotel's top floor, this stylish bar has sea views & an extensive drinks list. Prices are fairly high, so make sure you get here for the sunset happy hour (17.00–19.00). Entertainment is provided by table football & regular live music after dark.

ULA Bar 102 Tôn Đức Thắng; f ulabar.condao; ⌚ 08.00–22.00 daily. At the end of the seafront road, this new bar has an inventive cocktail list, including signature drinks based on the zodiac. Decent quality, but the music is far too loud.

OTHER PRACTICALITIES The **national park HQ** (w condaopark.com; ⌚ 07.00–17.00 daily) is located in the hills behind town, but there's another office on the seafront road (Tôn Đức Thắng) opposite the boat pier. Both can arrange good tours of Côn Sơn and the outlying islands, including hiking, boat trips, snorkelling and turtle nesting. Tourist information and maps are also available here, but neither are particularly high quality. **Con Dao Dive Centre** (w divecondao.com; ⌚ 07.00–20.30 daily) is the place to go for all sea-related tours, especially diving. **Lighthouse Travel** (12 Lê Duẩn; ☎ 0344 683866) is a good all-round option. In addition, most hotels can arrange tours for guests.

Côn Sơn town only has two banks with **ATMs**: VietinBank (corner of Lê Duẩn and Lê Văn Việt) and Agribank (corner of Phạm Văn Đồng and Võ Thị Sáu). It's best to rely on **cash** as only the higher-end places tend to accept cards. The **hospital** is at the corner of Phạm Văn Đồng and Lê Hồng Phong. When it comes to **shopping**, Takai Mart (corner of Hồ Thanh Tòng and Võ Thị Sáu) is as close as the island gets to a supermarket for general supplies, and for souvenirs, such as a jar of delicious *hạt bàng* (tropical almonds) from Côn Đảo's century-old trees, there's the town's gift shop (8 Nguyễn An Ninh).

WHAT TO SEE AND DO The main island of Côn Sơn is ideal for independent exploration, either on foot or on two wheels. Côn Sơn town and the island's coast roads and inland hiking trails will reveal enough of their beauty and history to keep visitors engaged for several days. Beaches, historical sites, forest trails, colonial architecture, markets and mountains can fill a week-long itinerary. To explore the outlying islands of the Côn Đảo archipelago it's necessary to join a boat tour or go on a diving trip (page 448).

✷ **Côn Sơn town** The only significant settlement in the archipelago, Côn Sơn is one of the most pedestrian-friendly towns in Vietnam, with a slow-paced charm that's best experienced by promenading the elegant seafront road (Tôn Đức Thắng), lined with century-old Malabar almond trees, in the early mornings or late afternoons, when breezes sweep in off the ocean and families play in the surf. Located on a gaping bay at the centre of the eastern coast, the town's layout and some of its crumbling colonial architecture date from the late 19th century. Besides the town's specific sights, wandering aimlessly on foot along Côn Sơn's languid, shady backstreets, peppered with an increasing number of enticing cafés, eateries and street markets, is a rewarding activity. It's difficult to reconcile the present-day, laid-back grace of this small settlement with the suffering that it was originally built to facilitate.

The town and its environs are where most of the island's major historical sites are located, the majority of which are related to Côn Sơn's period as a penal colony under the French colonial administration (1862–1954) and the US-backed government of South Vietnam (1954–75). Purchased at the Côn Đảo Museum (see below), one ticket (50,000VND) covers five sites for one day, including the museum, governor's palace and three prisons. Other interesting historical buildings that are free to visit include the old **customs house** (now Café Côn Sơn; page 443), a handsome building on the seafront where prisoners were processed on arrival; the colonial **doctor's house** (now the restaurant Phố Biển; page 443); and the little-known site of the former **French cemetery**, which is now a public park (Phạm Văn Đồng).

✷ ***Côn Đảo Museum*** (Nguyễn Huệ; 🕘 07.30–11.30 & 13.30–17.00 daily; 50,000VND all-in-one ticket) Providing historical background to the islands, this well-organised museum was relocated to a sprawling new building in 2013. The

TEENAGE HEROINE

Of all the celebrated former inmates held on the island, none is more revered than Võ Thị Sáu, a young woman filled with revolutionary fervour from an early age. Having thrown a grenade at a group of French colonial soldiers – killing one and injuring others – in her hometown near Vũng Tàu when she was just 14, Võ Thị Sáu was eventually tracked down by French authorities, arrested, sentenced and shipped to Côn Sơn. On her last night in prison, she was said to be heard singing patriotic songs that penetrated the thick walls of her cell. The next morning, on 23 January 1952, Võ Thị Sáu refused to wear a blindfold as she was led out and executed by firing squad. She was only 19. Today, her story resonates deeply with many Vietnamese, evocating a strong sense of national pride. Her grave in **Hàng Dương Cemetery** is now a site of pilgrimage for many thousands of Vietnamese, most of whom visit during the night in a moving spectacle of respect, commemoration and faith. Most Vietnamese cities have a major road named after her.

LEGEND HAS IT: LADY PHI YẾN

In 1783, Lord Nguyễn Ánh arrived on the islands with his entourage, having escaped capture by his military and political rivals, the Tây Sơn brothers. He devised a plan to broker a deal with the French for assistance in defeating his enemy, but one of his wives, Lady Phi Yến, scolded him for bringing foreign powers into a domestic war. Enraged, Nguyễn Ánh imprisoned Phi Yến in a cave on one of the islands, today called **Hòn Bà** (Lady Island).

When his enemies attacked Côn Đảo, Nguyễn Ánh fled again, this time to Phú Quốc, leaving his wife behind. Their young son, Prince Cải, pleaded with his father to free Phi Yến, but Nguyễn Ánh was furious and cast his son into the sea. The prince's body was recovered by islanders, who buried him at **Miếu Cậu**, near Đầm Trầu Beach, where he is worshipped to this day. When locals rescued Phi Yến, she was devastated by her son's death and stayed to live on the island to tend his grave. One day, she was accosted by another man, but rather than betray Nguyễn Ánh, despite his cruelty, she took her own life. Since then, Lady Phi Yến is worshipped at **An Sơn Temple** (Hoàng Phi Yến) and her death anniversary (Lễ Giỗ Bà Phi Yến) is celebrated every year on the 17th–18th of the tenth lunar month (October).

Although this story is based on certain historical figures and events, it is now generally agreed that the details are purely legend – indeed, it is even disputed whether Nguyễn Ánh ever set foot on Côn Đảo. But the power of this tale is very real, as evidenced by the thousands who continue to come to the islands each year to pray and pay their respects to Phi Yến and her son.

exhibits are labelled in Vietnamese and English and are chronologically arranged, beginning with Côn Đảo's early history, nature and geology, through to its acquisition by the French and use as a penal colony, all the way to its liberation in 1975 and modern-day developments for tourism and industry (including a model of the archipelago marked with future construction projects for 2030). There are photographs of some of the more famous of Côn Sơn's former inmates, including the likes of Phạm Văn Đồng and Tôn Đức Thắng, who became long-serving prime minister and president of Vietnam respectively.

Prisons (🕘 07.30–11.30 & 14.00–17.00 daily; 50,000VND all-in-one ticket) Closed since liberation in 1975, the prisons are preserved as a memorial to the thousands of Vietnamese political prisoners who were incarcerated in appalling conditions over more than a century of use. There are several penitentiaries in Côn Sơn town: **Phú Hải** appears unthreatening from the outside, with its colonial-era walls and turrets, but one look inside the cells – at the horrific, green, corpse-like mannequins – brings home the reality of what conditions were like here; **Phú Tường** is best known as the site of the French 'tiger cages' (*chuồng cọp Pháp*) and nearby **Phú Bình** is where the American take on tiger cages were located. These small cells with grilles in the ceilings – through which guards poked prisoners with sticks and threw lime on them to burn their skin – became the subject of wide condemnation after *Life* magazine published an article exposing conditions here on 17 July 1970, a copy of which is now an exhibit in the Côn Đảo Museum (see opposite).

Governor's House (Tôn Đức Thắng; 🕘 07.00–11.00 & 13.30–17.00 daily; 50,000VND all-in-one ticket) Serving as the residence for the island's governor, this attractive French colonial villa was constructed between 1862 and 1876. Over the 113 years that the island served as a penal colony, a total of 53 governors lived in this luxurious property, which features large, wooden-shuttered windows leading on to a broad terrace surrounded by manicured gardens. It's chilling to think that, while enjoying the elegant furniture, stylish tiled floors, ceramic vases, lamps, a billiard table and wooden bar, the governor and his guests could talk, drink and play in sight of the prison boats landing at the wharf, disembarking their prisoners and processing them at the customs house, just metres from the residence.

Spiritual loop (🕘 dawn–dusk daily, unless stated otherwise; **respectful dress** is mandatory at all sites) In the last decade, the popularity of 'spiritual tourism' on Côn Sơn has soared. Today, it's not only the prisons and revolutionary sites that draw domestic pilgrims to the island. Several other historical and semi-religious locations attract hundreds of visitors each day. These sites, along with those related to Lady Phi Yến (page 445), form a kind of 'spiritual loop' that most Vietnamese visitors follow, both to pay their respects and to pray for good personal fortune. All the following sites are walkable from Côn Sơn town except the last one, which requires a taxi or motorbike. Directly in front of the Governor's House, **Wharf 914** (Tôn Đức Thắng) is a stone pier named after the number of prisoners who died through forced labour during its construction, which began in 1873. The **former police station** (Lê Duẩn) dates from 1929 and houses an exhibition about Võ Thị Sáu (page 444), who was held in a cell here the night before her execution. **Hàng Keo Cemetery** (Nguyễn Văn Cừ) is another beautiful location that belies its macabre history: here, beneath casuarina trees on the beach, the bodies of thousands of prisoners were dumped during the first half of the 20th century. In 1997, the remains were unearthed and reburied in **Hàng Dương Cemetery** (Nguyễn An Ninh; 🕘 07.00–22.00 daily), among them Võ Thị Sáu's grave. **Vân Sơn Tự** is a Buddhist pagoda complex on a small hill just southwest of town, accessed via 200 steps with good views at the top. **Miếu An Sơn** is a small temple dedicated to the worship of Lady Phi Yến. And, in the northwest of the island, near Đầm Trầu Beach, **Miếu Cậu Cải** features statues of two horses guarding the tomb of Prince Cải, son of Phi Yến.

Around Côn Sơn Beyond town, Côn Sơn is a wild and rugged island, with a healthy and well-protected natural environment. Inland, the jungle canopy hums with wildlife and lofty mountains descend to the ocean, creating a dramatic coastline of bays, headlands and beaches. Exploring the island independently – on foot or two wheels – is richly rewarding.

✷ ***Beaches*** While Côn Sơn's beaches are more spectacularly situated than the ones you find on Phú Quốc, not all of them are archetypal tropical beaches with long arcing sands and leaning palms. The water is generally good for swimming, except during rough seas. Most beaches are free to access – except Đầm Trầu (3,000VND) and those accessed via national park trails (50,000VND) – and can be visited by motorbike, bicycle, taxi or on foot. The following is only a selection: **An Hải** is a wide, sandy beach fringed with coconut palms and casuarina trees within 5–10 minutes' walk of Côn Sơn town, but sandflies can be a problem. With rice-white sand stretching for several kilometres along gin-clear water punctuated by black rocks on the southern coast, **Nhát Beach** feels like it could be the film set for *Jurassic Park*: great for photos but very exposed during the day. **Đầm Trầu**, a wide arc of golden sand shaded by casuarina trees and flanked by rocky headlands, has recently been cleaned up and is looking better than ever. A popular activity is watching planes land on the runway which protrudes on to the beach. **Lò Vôi** is a sweep of hard-packed sand shaded by whispering casuarina trees, just north of town where the water is very shallow.

✷ ***Hiking*** Côn Sơn is a good hiking destination, with at least half a dozen well-marked trails leading through the national park, all of which can be undertaken independently, without a guide. The scenery and views are excellent and there's a high chance of seeing wildlife, especially the long-tailed macaque (*Macaca fascicularis*) and black giant squirrel (*Ratufa bicolor*). Pay the national park **entrance fee** (50,000VND) at the national park HQ or its Côn Sơn office (page 443) and pick up a (disappointing) trail map. The trailheads are pretty easy to find and the routes easy to follow, along which there are informative signs about flora and fauna. The most accessible hike for good views is the **Sở Rẫy Plantation** trail leading up and down a hill behind Côn Sơn town, with a lookout pavilion at the top offering panoramas of the east coast. The best overall hike is to Đầm Tre Lagoon, a 2-hour trek along Vông Beach and through humid jungles to an isolated circular bay, where you can hire stand-up paddleboards and snorkelling equipment.

✷ ***Motorbiking and cycling*** Scooters (150,000VND/day) are ideal for exploring the island's quiet coastal roads, and Côn Sơn is the perfect place to learn to ride, if you don't already know how. The well-maintained but empty roads give you all the space and time you need to become familiar with riding. A complete circuit of all the island's breezy roads can be ridden in a single day as a loop. The main road, following the east coast from the airport in the north to Bến Đầm port in the south, is a scenic 25km ride that can now be linked with the recently opened west coast road, connecting Bến Đầm with the national park HQ, behind Côn Sơn town. This loop provides numerous glimpses of hidden beaches and coral-rich bays at which to stop for a swim or a picnic. Note that there are only two petrol stations, both in town. Cycling is great too, but so far only a handful of bicycle rentals exist.

Other islands Some of the 15 outlying islands in the archipelago can be visited on boat tours or as part of snorkelling and diving trips. There's been very little development on these islands so far and their natural state remains pristine. Good coral, marine life and some submerged wrecks make Côn Đảo by far the best diving location in Vietnam, although it does not compare with the quality of many other Southeast Asian dive destinations.

TURTLE NESTING

From May to October, several species of endangered sea turtle lay their eggs on the islands' beaches. Even if the eggs hatch successfully, only a very small number of baby turtles will survive. The national park runs a conservation programme to protect the turtle nesting grounds and help to save as many as possible from natural threats, predators and human poachers. Early-morning trips to Bảy Cạnh island (from 1,000,000VND/person) can be arranged through the national park, where you can see the hatching sites and even help release baby turtles into the ocean. Since the conservation programme began in the mid-1990s, it is estimated that some 1.5 million baby turtles have been successfully hatched and released into the sea.

✷ ***Boat trips*** Speedboats leave from the beach next to the passenger boat pier in Côn Sơn town every morning and afternoon on half- or full-day tours arranged through the national park office, Con Dao Dive Centre (page 443), or your hotel (1,000,000–5,000,000VND). Prices are relatively high so it's best to go with a small group to share the cost. Popular itineraries include **Bảy Cạnh**, the second-largest island in the archipelago, where there's good snorkelling and a hike up to a colonial-era lighthouse with fantastic views, and **Hòn Cau**, which has a good beach and several cafés renting watersports equipment.

Diving and snorkelling The diving season lasts from March to September, when the water is generally clear and calm; November to February can be very choppy, and diving trips are usually cancelled. With 25 dive sites scattered around the archipelago, Con Dao Dive Centre (page 443; snorkelling/dive trips 1,000,000–3,600,000VND) is the go-to place for arranging a diving trip. Bamboo shark, clownfish, barracuda, parrotfish and good coral can all be seen in season and PADI courses are also available.

13

Hồ Chí Minh City

Hồ Chí Minh City, formerly and colloquially Saigon (Sài Gòn in Vietnamese), is the biggest and brashest city in Vietnam. It is a frenetic, electric and vivid place, riddled with a shambolic jumble of omnipresent, cacophonous and miasmic traffic. In the central districts, frenzied neighbourhoods swirl around glossy skyscrapers. On the outskirts, new precincts of grey residential high-rises multiply like mushroom troops.

Like other regional megalopolises, Hồ Chí Minh City does what a big city is supposed to do well. There is anonymity and opportunity here, attracting young and ambitious Vietnamese from every corner of the country, including Hanoi. The architecture of buildings such as the Museum of Fine Arts and General Sciences Library is varied and interesting, reflecting the city's defining historical eras. The museums, including the War Remnants Museum and History Museum, are reasonably well funded and well attended, and not just by tourists. The quantity and diversity of entertainment, hotels, boutiques, restaurants, bars, clubs and other urban delights eclipse everywhere else in the country.

Hồ Chí Minh City also grapples with the same set of urban challenges as other Asian economic capitals. Green space is notoriously difficult to come by, though the sylvan streets and broad pavements of the centre will offer some respite from the glass, concrete and tarmac. Air quality is predictably poor, though for reasons of geography, Hanoi is worse. Public transport is in a very sorry state of affairs: the stop-start sky train and metro system seems caught in a web of corruption scandals, though one line finally opened at the end of 2024, to much fanfare.

Despite the transforming cityscape, old Saigon still shines (and grimes) through in the historic districts. In districts 1 and 3, particularly around the Independence Palace, large, shaded avenues dominate the French grid-iron street plan. In District 5's Chợ Lớn, sometimes referred to as the world's biggest Chinatown (the superlative is debatable), atmospheric, incense-filled temples speckle the skein of streets and alleyways. Across all the central districts, street-food stalls and pavement beer bars rub shoulders with chic spas and fine international restaurants, while cafés and cocktail speakeasies are squirrelled away in decaying antique buildings.

Hồ Chí Minh City lacks the long history and heritage architecture of Hanoi. But due to its more forgiving climate, the near-endless list of entertainment opportunities and a fun-loving, open-minded and hedonistic population, many foreigners come away from Vietnam preferring this southern belle. Vietnam's demographics reflect this: despite most diplomats taking up residence in Hanoi, Hồ Chí Minh City still has twice the number of expatriates. While the city's turbulent history is not forgotten, the Vietnamese are not particularly sensitive about the name of the city: Saigon and Hồ Chí Minh City are used interchangeably in everyday conversation. You may do the same.

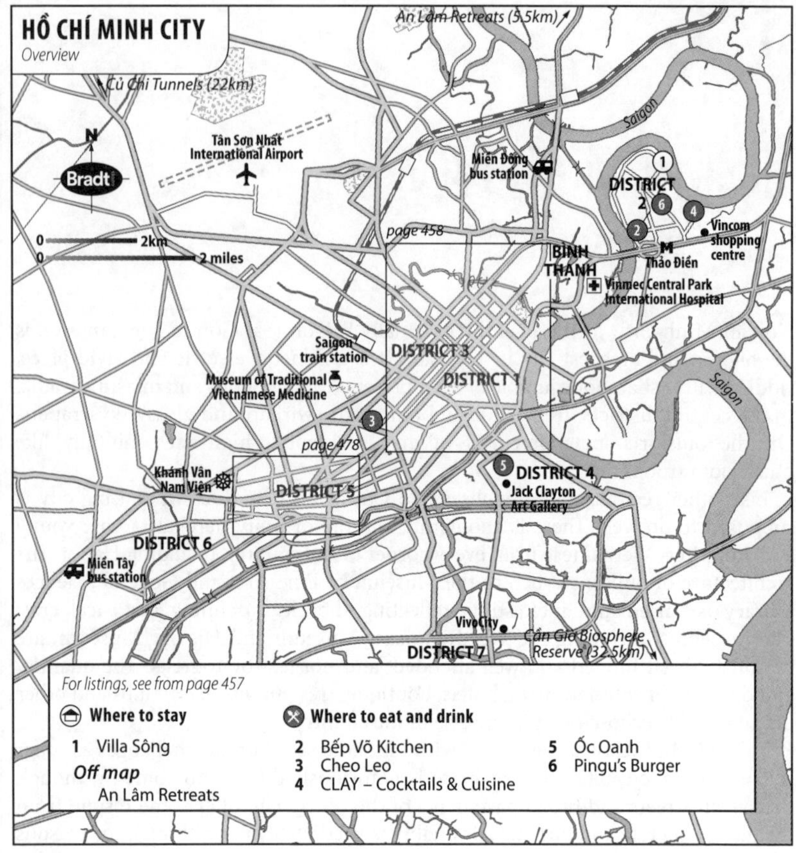

HISTORY

Originally called Prei Nokor, this area was a distant outpost of the powerful Khmer empire until the Việts gained a foothold here in the 17th century, after defeating the Cham in present-day Central Vietnam. The scholar and poet Trịnh Hoài Đức, writing in 1786, mentions another name, Đồng Nai (now a province northeast of the city), where merchant seamen docked early in the 17th century. By 1679 this small hamlet had become a military post in the prefecture of Gia Định. Strategically it was superbly positioned, surrounded on three sides by wide rivers and on the other by a huge bay. Nguyễn Ánh (later Emperor Gia Long; page 266) built a citadel here in 1790, and it was regarded as one of the most magnificent sights in the Việt nation.

SAIGON Etymologists still argue about the origin of the word Sài Gòn, the penultimate name of the city and still the name of the river that runs through it. After Minh Mạng's reign, the French, who had realised the importance of the site for future raids into Cambodia, sent in a fearsome war fleet in 1859 from Đà Nẵng, a city it failed to conquer. By 1861, France had come to dominate the surrounding provinces, and a peace treaty ceding the conquered territories to the colonists was signed in 1862 by Tự Đức. As the French territory grew, it came to be known as Cochinchina and Saigon was its capital.

From 1900 onwards came three decades of discontent, during which Vietnamese journalists opposed the colonial message that was being proclaimed with ever-increasing intensity. Riots sparked by Vietnamese bourgeoisie were commonplace during World War I and spread rapidly, inciting strikes and rebellions. Chợ Lớn, a huge ethnic Chinese enclave west of Saigon, was absorbed into the city in 1931 (for a while the city was referred to as Saigon–Chợ Lớn), which significantly increased its size. Three months after the start of World War II, an attempt was made by the Vietnamese to overthrow the French. By 1940 the Japanese had succeeded, though only temporarily. By 1945, the French were back.

On 2 September 1945, around 1.5 million people reportedly thronged to the centre of the city to welcome the Hồ Chí Minh government, sparking the First Indochina War. Years of unrest followed, during which President Diệm experienced considerable opposition from the Việt Minh, Buddhists and followers of the Hòa Hảo faith (page 34). With the French defeat in 1954, Vietnam was divided into North Vietnam and South Vietnam, with Saigon the capital of the capitalist south.

A boom period followed, buoyed by Western support of South Vietnam and an influx of skilled and industrious refugees from the north. The city became a hub of Vietnamese urban culture as music, fashion and architecture flourished, but it also developed a sleazy reputation. During the Second Indochina War, or American War, US military operations were headquartered in Saigon. Parts of the city were destroyed by fighting in the late 1960s, and until 1975 demoralised inhabitants saw their everyday lives become a struggle.

HỒ CHÍ MINH CITY On 30 April 1975, North Vietnamese (NLF) troops captured Saigon, signalling the end of the war. The NLF flag, blue and red with a distinct yellow centre, was hoisted on the Presidential Palace and tanks streamed into the city. A new era had begun. Thousands of flags bearing the slogan 'Nothing is more precious than Independence and Liberty' (which you still see across Vietnam today) waved goodbye to the old regime.

By 1976, Vietnam was reunified and Saigon had a new name: Hồ Chí Minh City. The city had experienced a sevenfold increase in size since its early colonial days, and the new communist government made efforts to bring down the population. Years of rampant inflation following reunification meant that many of the city's residents – 90% of whom (if employed) worked for the state – were still extremely poor. The city's entrepreneurial zeal lay dormant, waiting to be unleashed.

ĐỔI MỚI By 1986, the upsurge in bourgeois liberalism that followed the introduction of *đổi mới* (page 21) saw a relaxation of government regulations. Capitalism began to replace the hardline Marxist-Leninist dogma and new tax incentives brought investment from abroad. With bureaucracy much reduced, businesspeople began to realise the city's potential, not just as a place for tourists but also as a keen commercial centre.

Handicraft households increased rapidly, and by 1994 there were 14,000 scattered all over Hồ Chí Minh City and its suburbs. These became beehives of free enterprise, producing basketry, silk, rush mats, lacquerware, bamboo blinds, carpets and ceramics. Some morphed into gigantic factories and moved to the provinces surrounding Hồ Chí Minh City, particularly Bình Dương. Despite the radical changes that followed *đổi mới*, large state enterprises still existed in the city as the government refused to close them down, despite their continued losses. The economic reforms brought greater prosperity to many, but the gap between rich and poor widened – and continues to do so. This caused some discontent and a rise in tension, as strikes and increased corruption created a less favourable climate for international business.

The number of unemployed and underemployed reached an all-time high in 1995, the year the city celebrated the 20th anniversary of the war's end. Tens of thousands of soldiers who fought for South Vietnam joined their ranks; unlike their counterparts in the north, they received no golden handshake or pension and were forced to take up work as cyclo drivers, touts, newspaper salesmen and shoe-shiners. And yet the city still developed rapidly. The traffic chaos caused by greater prosperity had reached nightmare proportions. The lively city of Hồ Chí Minh was no longer the relaxed 'Pearl of the Orient' but a dynamic boom-town complete with all the problems of capitals such as Bangkok and Jakarta. However, some early big-time investors, despite socio-political infrastructure deficiencies and only mediocre legal safety nets, continued to pour in funds.

A MEGACITY EMERGES There's been an ebb and flow of investment into the city since the 1990s, powering a boom that feels far from over. Its citizens have come to grips with modern progress as the sound of drills, sledgehammers and giant bulldozers greets each new dawn. The only hiatus came in mid-2021, when the city experienced the strictest and lengthiest Covid-19 lockdown in the country. But when the city emerged from the pandemic in 2022, it was as if it never happened. Hồ Chí Minh City's district divisions continue to be revised regularly. Until recently, the city had 24 districts (12 numbered districts and 12 named districts), but in 2020 three of those districts (District 2, District 9 and Thủ Đức) were grouped into a new municipality. Today, Hồ Chí Minh City's population is approaching 10 million and the World Bank has designated it an emerging megacity.

WHEN TO VISIT

Hồ Chí Minh City is tropical, with year-round warm temperatures. The dry season runs from December to April, with the most comfortable temperatures between December and February. March and April can be uncomfortably dry, hot and polluted. The rainy season begins in May, peaks in September and lasts until November. The city floods regularly but drains fairly quickly. Rainstorms can be very intense, but they often pass quickly; typhoons are rare. Hồ Chí Minh City can be an enjoyable time to experience the build-up to Tết (January or February; page 41), but once it begins the city population shrinks significantly. Due to its sizeable Christian population (and consumerist inclinations), the city takes Christmas seriously, with temporarily gilded churches (and shopping centres).

GETTING THERE AND AWAY

BY RAIL **Saigon train station** [map, page 450] (1 Nguyễn Thông) is situated in District 3, a short Grab or taxi journey from districts 1 and 5 (see page 454 for orientation). The station is generally calmer and more relaxed than in Hanoi, with an orderly queue of taxis waiting at the front. The station offers basic amenities, including ATMs and small snack stalls, but don't expect to find quality meals here. Trains only depart northwestwards from here, towards Phan Thiết, Phan Rang, Nha Trang, Diêu Trì (for Quy Nhơn), Đà Nẵng (for Hội An) and beyond. It's possible, though perhaps not desirable, to take the train from Hồ Chí Minh City all the way to Hanoi (35hrs). For more information on how to purchase tickets and navigate the train system, see page 59.

BY BUS Hồ Chí Minh City is at the centre of a vast and often chaotic bus network that reaches every corner of the country. Many bus companies directed at tourists come and go from the Phạm Ngũ Lão neighbourhood in District 1; this is usually more convenient than the major bus stations, which are far from the city centre. Two of the largest and most important stations are **Miền Đông** (Bình Thạnh District) in the northeast and **Miền Tây** (395 Kinh Dương Vương) in the west [both on map, page 450]. In theory, the former handles buses going north and the latter handles buses going south, but in reality you can go almost anywhere from either. If you arrive at any of these stations, continuing your journey by taxi or Grab will be straightforward. It's often possible to show up at one of these major bus stations without a ticket and be on your way within an hour. A simpler and more convenient option is to book a ticket through your accommodation or one of the travel agents in District 1, many of which are in the Phạm Ngũ Lão area. They'll not only arrange your ticket but often provide shuttle pick-ups directly from your hotel or a nearby location. For advice on booking buses online and recommended websites to use, see page 60.

BY CAR AND MOTORBIKE You need the reflexes of a superhero and the patience of a saint to drive in and out of Hồ Chí Minh City, as the roads are clogged with unpredictable motorbike drivers and smog-spewing trucks. If you have a driver, they'll handle the tricky tasks of pick-up, drop-off and parking. If you're driving yourself, parking will be a challenge, so request clear instructions from your hotel.

BY AIR Hồ Chí Minh City's main gateway for both international and domestic flights is the obscenely overstretched **Tân Sơn Nhất International Airport** [map, page 450] (Tân Bình District; w vietnamairport.vn), located just 7km from the city centre. After collecting baggage, you'll find kiosks selling SIM cards with data (highly recommended), as well as ATMs and currency exchange desks. The proximity makes for a relatively quick journey into central districts, typically taking between 20 and 45 minutes by taxi depending on traffic. Taxis are readily available outside the arrivals area, and a ride to District 1 should cost around 150,000VND. It's a good idea to ensure the driver agrees to use the meter before you load your luggage. Unfortunately, the odd taxi driver may try to squeeze more money from you after you begin the journey, claiming that it's a parking fee to be paid by the passenger. One way to combat this is just to simply refuse, continue to smile and point at the meter. Grab taxis are cheaper and less scam-prone but more inconvenient as they wait in a designated parking area across from the terminals, and locating the right car can be a challenge. The bright yellow bus 109 is a clean and air-conditioned option that takes you directly into the city centre and costs 15,000VND. The bus route passes by major spots such as Bến Thành Market, Phạm Ngũ Lão and the train station. You can purchase tickets on board directly from the conductor, and they're usually helpful in advising where to disembark if you show them your accommodation's address.

GETTING TO CAMBODIA FROM HỒ CHÍ MINH CITY

Hồ Chí Minh City to Phnom Penh via the Mộc Bài border crossing [map, page 381] (Xuyên Á, Lợi Thuận, Tây Ninh Province) is one of the most popular cross-border routes, and several bus companies make the journey. Book these on Bao Lau (w baolau.com). The trip usually takes 6 hours or so, including time spent at the border, and the whole process is usually straightforward.

BY BOAT Vũng Tàu (page 382) and Côn Đảo (page 438) are the only places you can get to reliably by boat.

ORIENTATION

Many Vietnamese will tell you that Hồ Chí Minh City has 24 districts: 12 numbered and 12 named. This was true until 2020, when three of those districts (District 2, District 9 and Thủ Đức) were sequestered to form their own municipality named Thủ Đức City. The idea hasn't really taken off, at least in the way residents conceptualise their city, and this guide will orientate Hồ Chí Minh City as it was before the partition. Only four districts have traditionally been of interest to visitors: districts 1, 3, 5 and Củ Chi.

Districts 1 and 3 hold the bulk of Hồ Chí Minh City's tourist sites. This is essentially the city's French Quarter, with many broad, leafy boulevards. There are several loosely defined neighbourhoods within these central districts. Bùi Viện Street and around, known as the Phạm Ngũ Lão neighbourhood [459 C7], is the nightlife and backpacker precinct, with a lot of budget accommodation and tour agencies. Nguyễn Huệ Street [459 F6] and around is statelier, with more upmarket hotels, boutiques and restaurants. Northwest of the Independence Palace [459 D5], District 1 merges with District 3 to form a grid of handsome but busy streets. Đa Kao [458 D3], the somewhat messier northern corner of District 1, is a trendy neighbourhood bookended by a lively canal and home to galleries, cafés and cocktail bars.

Around districts 1 and 3 are various other areas of interest. Across the canal from District 1, triangular **District 4** [map, page 450], the city's smallest, is Hồ Chí Minh City's former centre of organised crime, but now a pleasant neighbourhood to get lost in, with a handful of sites and a boisterous local street-food scene. **Bình Thạnh** [map, page 450], on the other side of District 1, has fewer things to do but also makes for fun neighbourhood wanderings. **District 2** [map, page 450], particularly Thảo Điền, is where many wealthier expatriate families live and has some of the country's best international restaurants. The city's first metro line, which opened at the end of 2024, conveniently connects Bến Thành Market, a central landmark in District 1, with Thảo Điền.

District 5 [map, page 478] is the heart of Chợ Lớn, or Chinatown. In some ways, this district is to Hồ Chí Minh City what the Old Quarter is to Hanoi: the historical trading quarter of the city, with market streets and incense-scented religious buildings, but with a distinct, Chinese-influenced food scene. Chinatown goes beyond District 5, however, as virtually all of the surrounding districts hold remnants of old Chợ Lớn. District 6 lacks the temples and clan houses of District 5, but remains a fascinating area of commerce, especially in and around the monstrous Bình Tây Market. Many ethnic Chinese families live in districts 10 and 11.

Củ Chi is the location of the Củ Chi tunnels, an underground network that has long been the city's most popular day trip. Another rural district of interest is Cần Giờ, at the opposite end of the city.

GETTING AROUND

Districts 1 and 3 – those where you're likely to spend most of your time – are accessible for **pedestrians**, a legacy of French urban planning. In these gridded neighbourhoods, boulevards flank the bigger streets and the lofty trees help take the edge off the year-round heat. Most of the other districts – including District

5 – don't even have pavements, let alone boulevard sidewalks, but exploring them by foot is still nevertheless the way to go. Though Hồ Chí Minh City has a bus network, few visitors take the time to figure it out. Several metro lines (w maur.hochiminhcity.gov.vn) are under construction, but only one was operational at the time of research: Line 1. A boon for commuters, it is not especially useful for visitors except for those who are planning a trip to Thảo Điền. Until the network expands, **taxis and Grab** remain the most convenient option for getting between neighbourhoods. You can flag one down almost anywhere, and fares for rides between central neighbourhoods typically stay under 100,000VND. Always ask drivers to use the meter to avoid any surprises. Some visitors rent motorbikes to travel around the city, which is usually possible at your accommodation, but this should never be attempted by the uninitiated.

TOUR OPERATORS

Between this guidebook and the generally comprehensive information offered at museums and historical sites, an organised tour is not necessarily essential. However, there are some standout tour providers that can help you dig deeper. **Old Compass Travel** (w oldcompasstravel.com) has a limited collection of in-depth walking tours in historical neighbourhoods, which link the city's built heritage with its history. **XO Tours** (w xotours.vn) offers energetic and affordable motorbike tours of the city run by young women with excellent English. **Les Rives** (w lesrivesexperience.com) has a fleet of speedboats offering sunset cruises, as well as jaunts to the Củ Chi Tunnels (page 481) and Cần Giờ Biosphere Reserve (page 482). **Hoa Tuc** [459 F5] (74/7 Hai Bà Trưng; w hoatuc.com; 🕘 11.00–22.00 Mon–Sat) has long been known for its cooking classes. **Chôm Chôm Travel** (w chomchomtravel.com) has several kid-friendly tours in Hồ Chí Minh City. **Lacàph Coffee Experiences Space**, within the Lacàph café [459 E7] (page 462), has some excellent coffee workshops, teaching participants what goes into the famous Vietnamese brew. Like Hanoi, Hop-On Hop-Off Bus Tours (w hop-on-hop-off-bus-tours.com) have also made it to Hồ Chí Minh City. Also like Hanoi, the roads don't seem best suited to the concept, but it is nevertheless a novel way to explore the main sights, and can be a good option for those with restricted mobility. For an audio tour of central Hồ Chí Minh City, download the VoiceMap app (w voicemap.me).

WHERE TO STAY

Most visitors choose to stay in District 1. If looking for your own accommodation here, the neighbourhoods close to Nguyễn Huệ Street [459 F6] have character and are walking distance to many of the city's major sights. The dearth of green space in Hồ Chí Minh City is criminal, but there are some park-adjacent neighbourhoods that are also worth investigating when looking for somewhere to stay, namely Tao Đàn Park [459 C6] and Lê Văn Tám Park [458 C3]. Budget accommodation can be found around Bùi Viện Street [459 C8], a nightlife hub.

For those who want to be action-adjacent rather than right in the thick of it, the streets of District 3 [459 B5] are slightly quieter, particularly close to the Thị Nghè Canal. Those who want to be far from it might opt for the uninteresting but orderly streets of Thảo Điền, an expat enclave in District 2, or District 7. Districts 4 and 5 are atmospheric places to stay, but their location is far from most of the major sights and there are no hotels of note. If you'd like to stay here, look at Airbnb. While you might occasionally find better deals by walking in or booking directly through the hotel's website, the up-to-date reviews on online travel agents like Booking.com often help you get a clear sense of the accommodation available.

DISTRICTS 1 AND 3

M Village Kỳ Đồng [458 A4] 20/9 Kỳ Đồng; w mvillage.vn. Sparkling new property that is well priced due to its location in District 3, a little far from the sights. It is, however, close to the train station, as well as the Thị Nghè Canal. Many of the higher-up rooms are spacious, with big balconies. **$$**

The Rice Hotel [459 D7] 40/9 Bùi Viện; w booking.com. Decent budget hotel in an enclave of various good-value choices, with a helpful reception team & popular – if uninspiring – ground-floor restaurant. **$$**

✷ **Amanaki Saigon** [459 F7] 65 Hồ Tùng Mậu; w amanaki.vn. Tall & slender boutique hotel in the thick of the action but with quiet, comfortable rooms & a (small) rooftop pool with views. **$$$**

Hotel Continental Saigon [459 E5] 134 Đồng Khởi; w booking.com. No longer the best hotel in the city but perhaps the most storied (page 467); this is where Graham Greene penned some of *The Quiet American*. The hotel feels very dated, but there's nowhere better to absorb the character of old Saigon. **$$$**

✷ **M Village Tôn Thất Đạm** [459 E6] 131 Tôn Thất Đạm; w mvillage.vn. Chợ Cũ (page 471), an all-day street market, greets you as soon as you step out of M Village, a branch of a new hotel group with locations across the city. Rooms are modern, with floor-to-ceiling windows, & there's a rooftop pool. **$$$**

✷ **Wink Hotel Saigon Centre** [458 E3] 75 Nguyễn Bỉnh Khiêm; w wink-hotels.com. Wink's Hồ Chí Minh City location is a little far from the sights but walking distance to District 3 & Bình Thạnh. The group prides itself on tech-driven services like self-check-in & hip staff who can recommend cafés & cocktail bars nearby. Rooms are small but intelligently designed. **$$$**

Hotel Grand Saigon [459 F6] 8 Đồng Khởi; w hotelgrandsaigon.com. Another heritage hotel in a similar vein to the Continental, but perhaps a tad more modern & upmarket. There are views of the sunset over the Saigon River from the rooftop bar. **$$$$**

The Myst [459 F6] 6–8–10 Hồ Huấn Nghiệp; **w** themystdongkhoihotel.com. Central Hồ Chí Minh City's most characterful hotel is The Myst, designed by modern architecture firm A21, with plants that bulge from the façade & a lobby that has repurposed parts of a demolished shipyard. **$$$$**

ELSEWHERE IN THE CITY *Map, page 450, unless otherwise stated*

✷ **White Lotus Boutique** [458 G3] 76E/2 Phạm Viết Chánh; **w** booking.com. A little glitzy, but an extraordinarily friendly boutique hotel in Bình Thạnh (page 454), a busy corner of the city with few sights but brimming with local life. **$$**

Villa Sông 197/2 Nguyễn Văn Hưởng; **w** villasong.com. Riverside hotel all the way out in Thảo Điền, Hồ Chí Minh City's listless expatriate enclave but with many excellent food & beverage options. The rooms are classic, clean & comfortable, & there's a popular riverside terrace that catches the breeze. **$$$**

✷ **An Lâm Retreats** 21/4 Trung; **w** anlam.com. This bucolic garden hotel is actually in Bình Dương, the province next to Hồ Chí Minh City, & a 30min drive to District 1. The distance comes with clear benefits, however, as the timber villas are surrounded by trees & look over the Saigon River. **$$$$**

WHERE TO EAT AND DRINK

As a home to immigrants from across Vietnam, Hồ Chí Minh City has a rich culinary tradition, and as people from most of the world's imagined corners have settled here, its offerings have become even more diverse. You could quite easily eat a different provincial speciality every night for several months. You could then spend several more months working through all the international cuisines. European food is well represented, but there are many more restaurants from Asian countries, especially Japan and Korea: a rabbit warren of alleyways just off Lê Thánh Tôn has become known as 'Japan Town' (page 467) on account of the number of Japanese restaurants (among more nefarious establishments).

Phạm Ngũ Lão, the backpacker area, is chock-a-block with low-cost local and international restaurants. But as is often the case in Vietnam, the best-value meals are in family-owned eateries with limited menus. Do not overlook the street and streetside stalls, where staples and specialities (page 460) are fresh and delicious.

HỒ CHÍ MINH CITY *Districts 1 and 3*
For listings, see opposite

Where to stay

No.	Name	Grid
1	Amanaki Saigon	F7
2	Hotel Continental Saigon	E5
3	Hotel Grand Saigon	F6
4	M Village Kỳ Đồng	A4
5	M Village Tôn Thất Đạm	E6
6	The Myst	F6
7	The Rice	D7
8	White Lotus Boutique	G3
9	Wink Hotel Saigon Centre	E3

Where to eat and drink

No.	Name	Grid
10	Ănăn Saigon	E7
11	Bâng Khuâng	F5
12	Bún Chả Hanoi 26	F5
13	The Cocoa Project	B5
14	Cơm Chay Mai Anh	G3
15	Cơm Chiên Bé Tám	E7
16	Cơm Tấm 43	G2
17	Cục Gạch Quán	B2
18	Hồng Phát	A7
19	Ittou Ramen	F4
20	Ivoire Pastry Boutique	F5
21	Izakaya Ten	F5
22	The Joi Factory	B8
23	Katinat (Đồng Khởi)	F6
24	Kậu Ba Quán	E2
25	Lacàph	E7
26	Mom's Indian Cuisine	G2
27	Ốc Bà Cô Lóc Cóc	D4
28	Okkio	E6, F6
29	Oryz	C2
30	Phở Hòa	B3
31	Phở Miến Gà Kỳ Đồng	A4
32	Phở Minh	E6
33	Phở Phượng	F2
34	Quán Ăn Cô Liêng	B7
35	Sipply Coffee	C3
36	YUNKA	F6

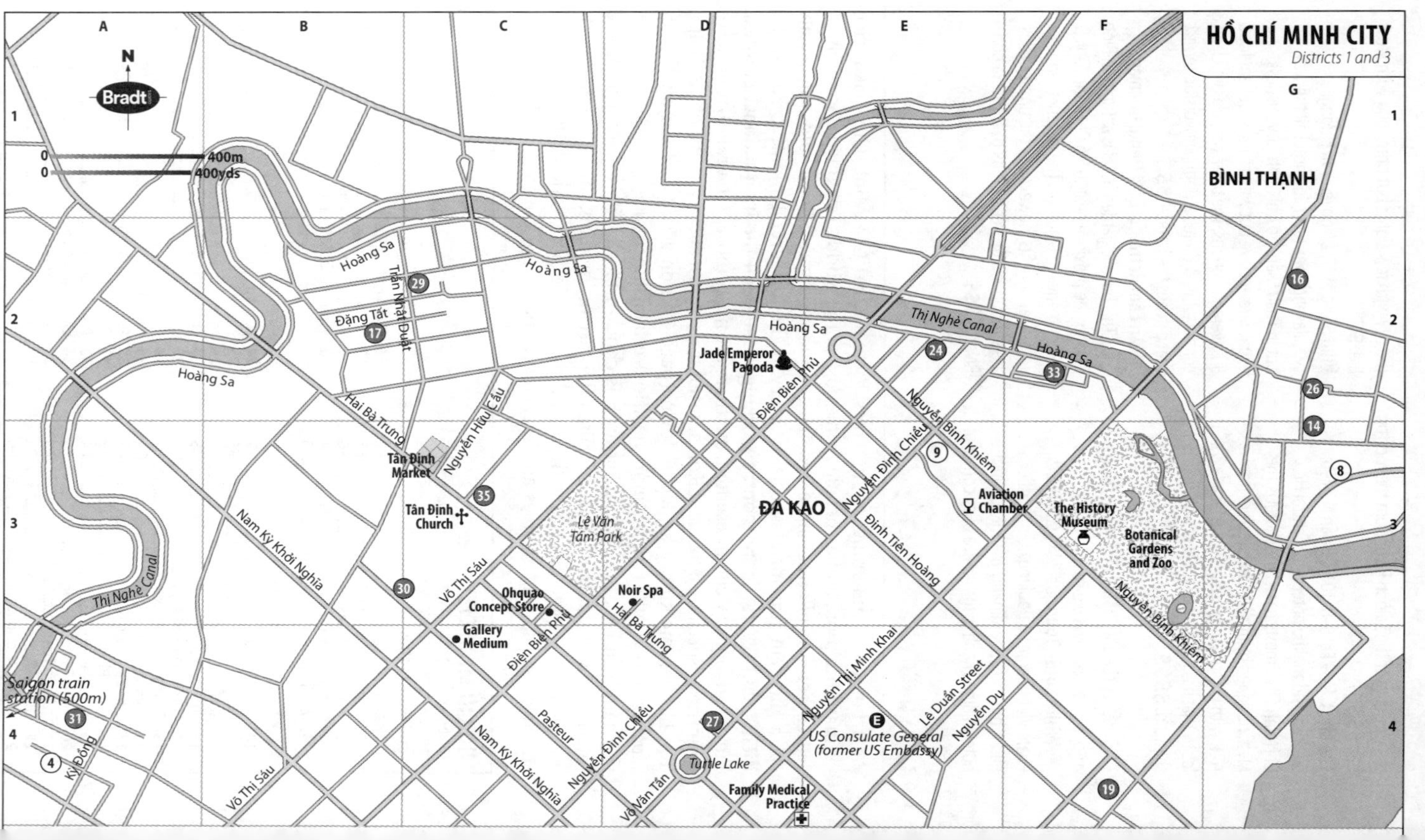
HỒ CHÍ MINH CITY
Districts 1 and 3
Bradt
N
0 400m
0 400yds
BÌNH THẠNH
ĐA KAO
Hoàng Sa
Trần Nhật Duật
Đặng Tất
Hai Bà Trưng
Nguyễn Hữu Cầu
Tân Định Market
Tân Định Church
Nam Kỳ Khởi Nghĩa
Võ Thị Sáu
Thị Nghè Canal
Saigon train station (500m)
Kỳ Đồng
Lê Văn Tám Park
Ohquao Concept Store
Gallery Medium
Điện Biên Phủ
Noir Spa
Pasteur
Nguyễn Đình Chiểu
Turtle Lake
Võ Văn Tần
Family Medical Practice
Jade Emperor Pagoda
Nguyễn Thị Minh Khai
US Consulate General (former US Embassy)
Lê Duẩn Street
Nguyễn Du
Đinh Tiên Hoàng
Nguyễn Bỉnh Khiêm
Aviation Chamber
The History Museum
Botanical Gardens and Zoo

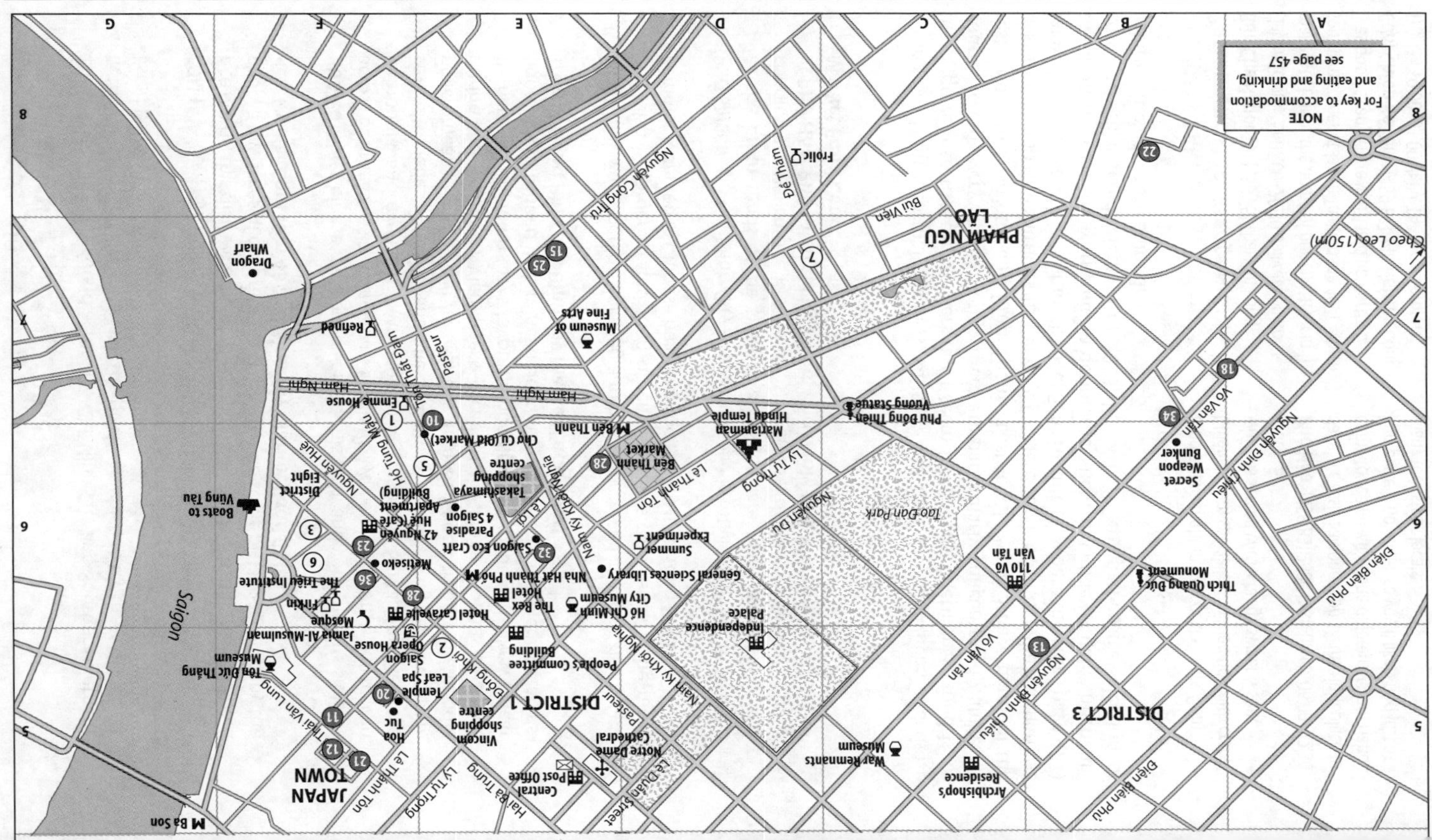

JAPAN TOWN
DISTRICT 1
DISTRICT 3
PHẠM NGŨ LÃO
Saigon
M Ba Son
Tôn Đức Thắng Museum
Thái Văn Lung
Lê Thánh Tôn
Lý Tự Trọng
Hai Bà Trưng
Lê Duẩn Street
Central Post Office
Notre Dame Cathedral
Pasteur
Nam Kỳ Khởi Nghĩa
Vincom shopping centre
Đồng Khởi
Hòa Túc
Temple Leaf Spa
Saigon Opera House
Jamia Al-Musulman Mosque
Firkin
The Triệu Institute
Boats to Vũng Tàu
District Eight
Nguyễn Huệ
Hồ Tùng Mậu
Emme House
Hàm Nghi
Tôn Thất Đạm
Refined
Dragon Wharf
Metiseko
42 Nguyễn Huệ (Café Apartment Building)
Hotel Caravelle
People's Committee Building
The Rex Hotel
Nhà Hát Thành Phố M
Saigon Eco Craft
Paradise 4 Saigon
Takashimaya shopping centre
Lê Lợi
Chợ Cũ (Old Market)
Hồ Chí Minh City Museum
General Sciences Library
Summer Experiment
Bến Thành Market
M Bến Thành
Museum of Fine Arts
Nguyễn Công Trứ
Independence Palace
Nguyễn Du
Mariamman Hindu Temple
Phù Đổng Thiên Vương Statue
Tao Đàn Park
Đề Thám
Frolic
Bùi Viện
War Remnants Museum
Archbishop's Residence
Võ Văn Tần
Nguyễn Đình Chiểu
110 Võ Văn Tần
Thích Quảng Đức Monument
Điện Biên Phủ
Secret Weapon Bunker
Cheo Leo (150m)
NOTE
For key to accommodation and eating and drinking, see page 457

HỒ CHÍ MINH CITY'S SPECIALITY DISHES

These specialities are found across Hồ Chí Minh City and Southern Vietnam, in the Mekong Delta in particular. The places at which to try these dishes are listed below.

CƠM TẤM *Cơm tấm* means broken rice, and as it's made with cheaper, stunted rice grains, this dish was one of the original peasant foods. A thin grilled pork chop, a few slices of cucumber and tomato and some pickles accompany the rice. Try it at **Cơm Tấm 43** and **Bình Tây Market Food Court**.

HỦ TIẾU The Chinese diaspora invented this dish, and you'll find its siblings across Southeast Asia: *kuai tiao* in Thailand, *kyay oh* in Myanmar, *kuyteav* in Cambodia, and even *char kway teow* in Malaysia and Singapore. There are several varieties of *hủ tiếu*, and one of the most popular is *hủ tiếu Nam Vang*, which means *Phnom Penh hủ tiếu*; this entered Saigon through Cambodia during the exodus of Vietnamese escaping the Khmer Rouge. *Hủ tiếu* is perhaps Hồ Chí Minh City's favourite noodle soup, made with chewy clear noodles and topped with minced pork, shrimp, blood cake and vegetables. Try it at **Hồng Phát** and **Bình Tây Market Food Court**.

MÌ VỊT TIỀM Egg noodles, duck leg and bok choy served in a dark, rich broth. This dish is harder to find than other specialities, and tends to be more commonly served in Chinese neighbourhoods. Try it at **Hồng Phát**.

PHỞ SAIGON Hồ Chí Minh City's version of *phở* is totally different to Hanoi's, as the broth tends to be sweeter and there are many more sides and condiments. Which one is superior is, of course, deeply controversial. Try it at **Phở Hòa**, **Phở Miến Gà Kỳ Đồng**, **Phở Minh**, **Phở Phượng** and **Bình Tây Market Food Court**.

Eating out is an informal business; suits are not necessary anywhere, and those that require men to wear trousers don't seem to last long. Vietnamese food is, of course, found everywhere, though there are particularly concentrated patches of restaurants in District 4 and Bình Thạnh. Districts 1, 2 and 3 have many of the best international restaurants in the city. Chinese food, or rather the Vietnamese take on Chinese food, is best in districts 5, 6, 10 and 11, where the Hoa (page 477) traditionally lived and worked. If in doubt, the Michelin Guide (**w** guide.michelin.com), which entered Vietnam in 2023, has a fairly comprehensive selection of eateries, including street food.

DISTRICTS 1 AND 3

Restaurants and street food

Bún Chả Hanoi 26 [459 F5] Thái Văn Lung (Japan Town); ⌚ 07.00–20.30 daily. If you don't make it to Hanoi, the home of *bún chả*, try it in the southern corner of Japan Town (page 467), which is as good as anywhere you'll find up north. **$**

Cơm Chiên Bé Tám [459 E7] 248 Nguyễn Công Trứ; ⌚ 19.00–01.00 daily. The ideal comfort food after a night in the cocktail bars, Cơm Chiên Bé Tám specialises in fried rice with crab, which is served with a tangy sweet & sour sauce. **$**

Phở Hòa [458 B3] 260C Pasteur; ⌚ 06.00–22.30 daily. A classic Saigonese *phở* & the right place to come to see how it's done differently from Hanoi. This place is no secret, so you'll likely find just as many tourists as locals. **$**

Phở Miến Gà Kỳ Đồng [458 A4] 14/5B Kỳ Đồng; 🕘 05.30–22.30 daily. Specialising in all things chicken, this cavernous eatery tucked down an alleyway serves different types of noodles, with or without broth, & a tasty chicken salad. If you're confused about the noodle types, go to the counter & point at the ones you like the look of. **$**

✷ **Phở Minh** [459 E6] 63/3 Pasteur; 🕘 06.30–10.00 daily. Classic *phở* restaurant tucked down an alleyway that seems to have been around forever (hence the retro sign), serving the southern beef version of Vietnam's national dish. They also serve sides of *pâté chaud*, a savoury French pastry, designed for dunking. **$**

Quán Ăn Cô Liêng [459 B7] 321 Võ Văn Tần; 🕘 08.30–22.00 daily. Cô Liêng is so well known for her do-it-yourself spring roll variations (beef is the best) that she now appears in the Michelin Guide. **$**

Hồng Phát [459 A7] 391 Võ Văn Tần; **w** hutieuhongphat.com; 🕘 06.30–22.30 daily. Around for more than half a century, Hồng Phát specialises in *hủ tiếu Nam Vang*, which was created by Chinese immigrants & transported to Saigon via Phnom Penh. Hồng Phát makes a fairly good claim to be the 1st place to start serving the dish. **$$**

The Joi Factory [459 B8] Alley 212/2B Nguyễn Trãi; 🕘 06.30–21.00 daily. Vegan cuisine, both Vietnamese & Western, served in a spacious villa, giving the space homely & comfortable vibes. The Vietnamese noodle dishes are good, but not quite enough for a full meal, so order some spring rolls on the side. **$$**

✷ **Phở Phượng** [458 F2] 25 Hoàng Sa; 🕘 05.30–20.30 daily. A unique take on *phở* that you won't find anywhere else in the country. They specialise in a hearty oxtail version, & the staff will demonstrate how to concoct your own dipping sauce to dunk the meat in. **$$**

✷ **Cục Gạch Quán** [458 B2] 10 Đặng Tất; **w** cucgachquan.com; 🕘 09.00–23.30 daily. Simple food done extremely well in a huge villa with multiple dining rooms spread across multiple floors. Try the stewed pork & the tofu with lemongrass & chilli. **$$$**

Ittou Ramen [458 F4] 8/8 Lê Thánh Tôn; **f** ittoulethanhton; 🕘 11.00–22.00 daily. Given its huge Japanese community, Hồ Chí Minh City must surely be one of the best places outside of Japan to get Japanese food, as demonstrated by Ittou Ramen. The standout feature here is the broth, which is so deliciously rich that they offer to water it down a little if it's too much. **$$$**

Izakaya Ten [459 F5] 8d1 Thái Văn Lung; 🕘 17.00–03.00 daily. With tightly packed tables, a cosmopolitan clientele & a huge menu of Japanese grilled goodies served late into the night, Izakaya Ten will transport you to Tokyo (& yet it's a fraction of the cost). **$$$**

Kậu Ba Quán [458 E2] 85 Hoàng Sa; 🕘 11.00–23.00 daily. This canal street has many places to *nhậu* (drink beer & eat), but Kậu Ba Quán stands out for its elevated menu crafted by something of a celebrity chef. **$$$**

Ốc Bà Cô Lóc Cóc [458 D4] Alley 28, 40A Trần Cao Vân; **f** bacoloccoc; 🕘 11.30–21.30 daily. This is the place to come for snails, a favourite of the Saigonese, with a handy picture menu that makes for easy ordering. **$$$**

✷ **Oryz** [458 C2] 51 Trần Nhật Duật; **w** oryzsaigon.com; 🕘 17.30–23.30 Tue–Sun. Singaporean chef Chris Fong fell in love with Hồ Chí Minh City & Vietnamese food before opening Oryz, which contemporises food from across Asia in a fine-dining setting. The themed tasting menus are creative & good value, considering the quality. **$$$$**

YUNKA [459 F6] Đồng Khởi; 🕘 17.00–01.00 Tue–Sun. Serving Nikkei (ie: Peruvian Japanese) cuisine to fashionable & pretty things in a converted corner building that overlooks Hồ Chí Minh City's glitziest street. The hobnobbing continues after dinner when the restaurant morphs into a bar with DJs. **$$$$**

Ănăn Saigon [459 E7] 89 Tôn Thất Đạm; **w** anansaigon.com; 🕘 17.00–23.00 Tue–Sun. The winner of Hồ Chí Minh City's first Michelin star is Vietnamese-American Peter Cuong Franklin's Ănăn Saigon, atmospherically positioned in the middle of Chợ Cũ. The tasting menus feature modern reimaginings of Vietnamese classics. **$$$$$**

Coffee houses

Bâng Khuâng [459 F5] 2nd Fl, 9 Thái Văn Lung; **f** BangKhuangCafe; 🕘 07.00–22.00 daily. Nostalgic café in an old apartment building that serves delicious Vietnamese coffee, smoothies & juices. There's also a lunch menu.

✷ **Cheo Leo** [map, page 450] 109/36 Nguyễn Thiện Thuật; **f** cheoleocafe; 🕘 06.00–18.00

daily. A classic Vietnamese café that brews the black stuff using traditional methods & serves it up in the living room, which seemingly hasn't changed in decades.

✷ **The Cocoa Project** [459 B5] 143 Nguyễn Đình Chiểu; **w** thecocoaproject.vn; ⌚ 08.00–22.00 daily. The coffee here is just OK, but the real draw is the locally produced chocolate, flavoured with local ingredients like roast cashew, dried banana, kumquat jam & *mắc khén*, a spice from Northern Vietnam.

Ivoire Pastry Boutique [459 F5] 28 Cao Bá Quát; **f** ivoirepastry; ⌚ 10.30–20.30 daily. Probably the best French patisserie in the country, the cakes & pastries can compete with the very best from Paris. Pair these expensive treats with a variety of teas & coffees in a reimagining of the tube house (page 107) by local modern architectural firm T3 Architects.

Katinat (Đồng Khởi) [459 F6] 91 Đồng Khởi; **w** katinat.vn; ⌚ all day daily. This successful Vietnamese coffee chain overtakes heritage buildings & converts them into cafés serving affordable local coffee to a mostly young clientele. The Đồng Khởi location is particularly appealing because it sits in a curved, multi-storey, colonial-era corner building.

✷ **Lacàph** [459 E7] 220 Nguyễn Công Trứ; **w** experiences.lacaph.com; ⌚ 07.30–19.30 daily. Lacàph is seeking to elevate what the world thinks about Vietnamese coffee by sourcing premium beans & crafting artisanal brews. They also organise coffee experiences (page 456).

Okkio (Lê Lợi) [459 E6] 120–122 Lê Lợi; **f** okkiocaffe; ⌚ 07.30–20.00 daily. This is a small coffee shop group that prioritises contemporary interior design & delicious coffee & cakes. Other locations to look out for are on Đồng Khởi [459 F6] & in District 2.

✷ **Sipply Coffee** [458 C3] 73 Đinh Công Tráng; **f** sipply.coffee; ⌚ 07.30–22.00 daily. Beautiful design coffee shop in a repurposed modernist house, in a tucked-away alley close to Tân Định Church. Order one of their various signature teas & coffees & get comfortable either in the front garden or on one of their thoughtfully reimagined floors.

OTHER DISTRICTS

Bình Tây Market Food Court [map, page 478] 57A Tháp Mười; ⌚ 07.00–18.00 daily. A hidden treasure trove of street-food counters inside the city's most interesting market, & one of the best places to eat in the neighbourhood. $

Cơm Chay Mai Anh [458 G3] 59 Phạm Viết Chánh; ⌚ 08.00–21.00 daily. Hồ Chí Minh City is full of vegan & vegetarian restaurants, but few are better value than Mai Anh, which has veganised most of Vietnam's most famous dishes, including *mi Quảng* & fresh spring rolls. $

✷ **Cơm Tấm 43** [458 G2] 43 Nguyễn Văn Lạc; ⌚ 06.00–noon daily. Hole-in-the-wall eatery serving broken rice, one of Hồ Chí Minh City's most famous dishes. This is the real deal, so prepare to squeeze on to tables with locals, bear the heat of the grill & pay next to nothing. $

Bếp Võ Kitchen [map, page 450] 90 Quốc Hương; ⌚ 10.00–22.00 daily. If you find yourself in District 2 looking for simple, tasty, well-priced food, this is the place to come. It's especially popular with the expats who live & work nearby. $$

Mom's Indian Cuisine [458 G2] 37 Huỳnh Tịnh Của; ⌚ 10.00–21.30 daily. An unlikely & humble South Asian restaurant that appears in what feels like a very Vietnamese neighbourhood. The food is deliciously spiced, & there's only a handful of tables. $$

Pingu's Burger [map, page 450] 26 No 2 St, Thảo Điền; **w** pingusburger.com; ⌚ 15.00–23.00 Mon–Fri, 11.00–23.00 Sat–Sun. High-quality but affordable burgers served in very casual surroundings on a leafy street in one of the more pleasant areas of Thảo Điền. $$

✷ **CLAY – Cocktails & Cuisine** [map, page 450] 18 No 6 St, Thảo Điền; **w** linktr.ee/claysaigon; ⌚ 15.00–midnight Tue–Sun. Connected with YUNKA (page 461) in District 1, CLAY is similarly hip, serving contemporary cuisine with a European lean in an airy, open-plan modern building. $$$

Cửu Long Quán [map, page 478] 76 Bùi Hữu Nghĩa; ⌚ 07.00–14.00 & 17.00–22.00 daily. Classic Chinese restaurant specialising in dim sum, though there's a huge menu of other dishes from north of the border. $$$

Ốc Oanh [map, page 450] 534 Vĩnh Khánh; ⌚ 13.00–midnight daily. Vĩnh Khánh is one of Hồ Chí Minh City's premier food streets, especially at night. These raucous open-air eateries, including Ốc Oanh, specialise in snails & seafood. If this 1 doesn't appeal, stroll up & down the street until you find a place that feels right. $$$

Vịt Quay Vĩnh Phong [map, page 478] 527 Phan Văn Trị; ⌚ 05.00–20.00 daily. *Vịt quay* is roast duck, a dish popular throughout Vietnam but originally from China. Where better to try it than in Chinatown? $$$

ENTERTAINMENT AND NIGHTLIFE

Aviation Chamber [458 E3] 12T3 Nguyễn Thị Minh Khai; f aviation.chamber; ⌚ 18.00–02.00 daily. Super friendly & low-key cocktail bar that is far enough away from the centre that it rarely gets uncomfortably busy. The smiley bartenders will personalise a drink for you if you tell them what you like.

Bùi Viện Street [459 C8] This bonkers street needs to be seen to be believed, with over a hundred bars competing for your attention with bright neon lights, obscenely loud music and skimpily dressed staff.

Emme House [459 F7] Hàm Nghi/70 Ward; ⌚ 18.00–midnight daily. Pretty little cocktail bar with views of Hồ Chí Minh City's mismatched architecture outside. The space is intimate & ideal for small groups.

✷ **Firkin** [459 F6] 20 Mạc Thị Bưởi; f firkinbar; ⌚ 18.00–01.00 daily. Timeless whisky & cocktail bar tucked away in the centre of town, you need to be looking for Firkin to find it. Book ahead as space is limited.

Frolic [459 D8] 151 Đề Thám; f FrolicBarSaigon; ⌚ 20.00–06.00 daily. One of Hồ Chí Minh City's livelier LGBTQIA+ bars, which gets packed on w/end evenings. Its clientele is typically Vietnamese & young, but the space is friendly to all.

Refined [459 F7] 14 Tôn Thất Đạm; f refinedsaigon; ⌚ 08.00–midnight daily. Refined hides away in one of Hồ Chí Minh City's most interesting buildings, a former apartment block that now hosts bars, cafés & tattoo parlours.

✷ **Summer Experiment** [459 D6] 2nd Fl, 77–79 Lý Tự Trọng; f; ⌚ 16.00–01.00 daily. Summer Experiment consistently mixes up some of the best cocktails in town, with a hand-drawn menu that draws heavily from tropical flavours. The terrace features a well-cared-for garden.

The Triệu Institute [459 F6] 10 Mạc Thị Bưởi; f; ⌚ 11.30–14.00 & 17.00–midnight daily. Both restaurant & cocktail bar, The Triệu Institute distils its own gin, which you can buy in bottles to take home. The bar & distillery is named after the fierce northern heroine (page 221).

SHOPPING

SHOPPING CENTRES Hồ Chí Minh City has a growing number of shopping centres, though still far fewer than Bangkok, Kuala Lumpur and Singapore. The most central, and earmarked for a major expansion, is Takashimaya [459 E6]

ANYTHING GOES

Hồ Chí Minh City is Vietnam's city of acceptance, which means it hosts an eccentric and evolving entertainment scene. The most popular show, which is well worth the hype, is the AO Show (w luneproduction.com), an acrobatics troupe that explores Vietnam's transition from an agrarian to an urban society through creative physical theatre in the Opera House [459 F5]. The drag scene is not as developed as in Thailand or even Cambodia, but queer and gay bars like Frolic (see above) host regular dramatic performances from local queens. Food expert Jovel Chan (w jovelchan.com) not only diligently keeps on top of Hồ Chí Minh City's food scene on her website, but also runs the monthly Saigon Supper Club, showcasing the movers and shakers in the city's dining scene. For something completely left field, see if your trip coincides with a show from Vietnam Pro Wrestling (f).

(92–94 Nam Kỳ Khởi Nghĩa; **w** online.takashimaya-vn.com; 🕘 09.30–21.30 daily). VivoCity [map, page 450] in District 7 is larger with more entertainment, including an iMax cinema. There are also several Vincom centres (35 Lê Thánh Tôn, District 1 [459 E5]; 161 Võ Nguyên Giáp, District 2 [map, page 450]) dotted around the city. Most shopping centres have cinemas, arcades, kids entertainment areas & dozens, sometimes hundreds, of shops.

MARKETS Traditional markets remain the heart and soul of commercial Hồ Chí Minh City, far outpacing shopping centres in terms of quantity and intrigue. Find them across the city, but two of particular interest are Tân Định (page 475) and Bình Tây (page 477).

OTHER SHOPS

Art, design and crafts

For a broader collection of art galleries, some with art for sale, see page 470.

District Eight [459 F6] 33 Đồng Khởi; **w** districteight.com.vn; 🕘 09.00–19.00 daily. Upmarket furniture company that has appeared in many of the world's top design magazines, District Eight delicately incorporates Vietnamese heritage into its premium quality products. Expect to pay international prices.

Gallery Medium [458 C4] 240B Pasteur; **w** gallerymedium.com; 🕘 10.00–18.00 Wed–Sun. Carefully curated art gallery with some fine pieces from established Vietnamese artists, including painting and sculpture.

Jack Clayton Art Gallery [map, page 450] 10 No 7 St, District 4; **w** jackclaytonart.com; 🕘 10.00–18.00 Thu–Sun. If exploring District 4, stop by & say hello to British illustrator & printmaker Jack, who has recreated various Vietnamese scenes in imaginative ways. He specialises in woodcut.

✷ **Ohquao Concept Store** [458 C3] Alley 58, Phạm Ngọc Thạch; **w** ohquao.com; 🕘 09.00–20.00 daily. The place to come for design-focused gifts & souvenirs that are all Saigon- or Vietnam-themed, including playing cards, T-shirts, posters & more. There's also an exhibition space upstairs.

Saigon Eco Craft [459 E6] 36 Lê Lợi; **w** saigonecocraft.com; 🕘 08.00–22.00 daily. Various souvenir items sold right in the centre of town, with a good blend of fabrics, pottery & design items.

Fashion

Metiseko [459 F6] 101 Đồng Khởi; **w** metiseko.com; 🕘 08.30–21.30 daily. Slow fashion brand that brings Vietnamese design elements into its various lines. They work with artisanal teams from across the country.

Paradise 4 Saigon [459 E6] 42 Tôn Thất Thiệp; **w** paradise4saigon.com. Modern streetwear targeting a younger crowd, Paradise 4 Saigon offers all the flair you might expect from Generation Z's creative class. Their pop-up store – in a former apartment (page 466) – operates sporadic opening hours; visit their website and contact them in advance if you're planning a visit.

Thuy Design House [459 E5] In the Hotel Continental Saigon (page 467); **w** thuydesignhouse.com; 🕘 11.00–20.00 daily. Thuy Design House specialises in *áo dài*, Vietnam's national dress, but brings in various modern elements to enhance the designs.

OTHER PRACTICALITIES

BANKS, ATMS AND MONEYCHANGERS Banks and **ATMs** are widespread, but it's always smart to use machines inside or attached to banks in case something goes wrong. Most ATMs charge a fee and typically have a withdrawal limit of 3,000,000VND (around US$120) per transaction, though you can reinsert your card for further withdrawals until you reach your home bank's limit. Banks usually offer poor exchange rates. For better rates, you can head to moneychangers and gold shops around Bến Thành Market [459 D6] or along Hàm Nghi Street [459 E7].

HEALTH For medical emergencies, dial ☎ **115** to request an ambulance. If possible, find someone who speaks Vietnamese to help convey the situation quickly and clearly to the operator.

Family Medical Practice [458 D4] Diamond Plaza, 34 Lê Duẩn; ☎ 28 3822 7848; w vietnammedicalpractice.com; ⌚ all day daily

Vinmec Central Park International Hospital [map, page 450] 208 Nguyễn Hữu Cảnh, Bình Thạnh District; ☎ 28 3622 1166; w vinmec.com; ⌚ all day daily

SAIGON CENTRAL POST OFFICE The city's main post office, Saigon Central Post Office [459 E5] (2 Công xã Paris; ⌚ 08.00–18.00 daily) is a storied historic sight (page 468), but also offers a fully functioning postal service. It's convenient for sending letters or small packages, though more complex services, like international shipping, are available through private courier services such as Vietnam Post, Viettel Post, EMS, DHL, FedEx and UPS. For more information on sending post from Vietnam, see page 73.

SPAS There are various spas offering massages in District 1, and thanks to online reviews, competition is fierce. One reliable group is **Temple Leaf Spa**, with a few locations including 74/1A Hai Bà Trưng [459 F5] (⌚ 10.00–23.30 daily). **Noir Spa** [458 D3] (178B Hai Bà Trưng; ⌚ 10.00–21.00 daily) also comes recommended.

WHAT TO SEE AND DO

This guide groups the main sights into two main areas: District 1, District 3 and around (the colonial city); and District 5 and around (Chinatown). For neighbourhood guides on other areas of the city, see page 476.

DISTRICT 1, DISTRICT 3 AND AROUND These districts form the economic and historical heart of Saigon and hold the bulk of the city's areas of interest. This cosmopolitan area encapsulates modern Vietnam, where shiny glass towers overshadow 20th-century edifices and there's a never-ending hum of street vendors, commuters, shoppers and tourists. At the heart of these districts is Nguyễn Huệ Boulevard, a wide pedestrian street that stretches from the People's Committee Building to the Saigon River and sits flanked by hotels, restaurants and luxury shops. It's a favourite for both locals and visitors, especially during evenings when families stroll along the broad walkway under the neon glow of multi-storey buildings. West of here lies Bến Thành Market, a sprawling bazaar that has been a fixture in the city since perhaps the 17th century (though the building was completed in 1914), and the backpacker Phạm Ngũ Lão neighbourhood. To the north are the gridded neighbourhoods of District 3. To the south is District 4, the city's smallest district.

A good starting point for a **walking tour** is the northern end of Nguyễn Huệ Street, at the People's Committee Building. Walk down the street with the committee building behind you before moving over to parallel Đồng Khởi Street. Then walk in the opposite direction, towards Notre Dame Cathedral, before heading to the Independence Palace, War Remnants Museum and beyond. The ordering of the sights that follow reflects this approach.

Nguyễn Huệ Street This pedestrianised walkway was originally a waterway, probably a canal to connect Gia Định Citadel with the Saigon River. The French named it Le Grand Canal, but nevertheless promptly began filling it up in the

REPURPOSED APARTMENT BUILDINGS IN HỒ CHÍ MINH CITY

Hồ Chí Minh City has the act of transforming former apartment buildings into creative hubs down to a fine art. The Café Apartment Building at 42 Nguyễn Huệ makes for a photogenic spectacle, but with so few returning customers, many of the cafés prioritise style over substance. You'll find less conspicuous – and perhaps more interesting – repurposed apartment buildings with cafés, bars, boutiques and restaurants at 14 Tôn Thất Đạm and 26 Lý Tự Trọng, both of which are nearby.

second half of the 19th century. By 1889 it was entirely filled and parroted the boulevards of Paris; in 1955 it acquired the name Nguyễn Huệ after the hero of the Tây Sơn Rebellion (page 332); and in 2015 the inner section was pedestrianised. The disappointing lack of shade makes the street more enjoyable to explore early in the morning or in the evening.

People's Committee Building [459 E5] (86 Lê Thánh Tôn; **w** vpub.hochiminhcity.gov.vn; ⌚ 07.30–11.30 & 13.00–17.00 daily) This building is a rather wacky-looking, neo-Renaissance city hall, with a bronze statue of Hồ Chí Minh in front. Once called the Hôtel de Ville, it was built in 1908 and repainted bright ochre-yellow in 1993. If you are lucky enough to visit on National Day (2 September), the city hall and the whole of Nguyễn Huệ Boulevard will be covered in red flags with yellow stars to commemorate the 1945 Declaration of Independence. Unfortunately, the general public are not allowed inside the building, which is now used as the headquarters of the Hồ Chí Minh Council People's Committee.

The Rex Hotel [459 E6] (141 Nguyễn Huệ; **w** rexhotelsaigon.com) Situated at the junction with Lê Thánh Tôn, the Rex was a favourite haunt for American officers before 1975. Formerly the Bến Thành, this was the plushest hotel in the city when Western tourists started to return to Vietnam in the 1980s. Now, despite an exorbitantly expensive face lift, it has to contend with competition from luxury giants such as the Hyatt (2 Công trường Lam Sơn) and Reverie (22–36 Nguyễn Huệ). From the dated rooftop bar one can look out over the People's Committee Building and along Nguyễn Huệ Boulevard where, during colonial times, Les Grands Magasins Charner, a posh French department store, took pride of place. In the other direction along Lê Lợi, you can make out Saigon Opera House (see opposite).

42 Nguyễn Huệ [459 F6] Also known as the Café Apartment Building, this quirky, nine-storey structure with an advent calendar façade was built in the 1960s as a residential apartment block. After reunification, the building fell into disrepair, but began to transform after pedestrianisation of the street in 2015, when entrepreneurs repurposed the old apartments into cafés, boutiques and creative spaces. Despite the prime location, the building retains a worn charm, with faded balconies and unpolished exteriors. The building has become an icon of the city and an Instagram and TikTok showpiece, and yet the city authorities claim that, one day, they'll tear it down.

Đồng Khởi Street Slender, elegant and upmarket Đồng Khởi was once known as Tự Do (Freedom) and was a sleazy hotbed of titillating temptation. Bars such as Uncle Sam's, Miami and the California throbbed with music far into the night.

During colonial times, this street, then known as Rue Catinat, was the most fashionable in Saigon; posh café bars, elegant shops and cinemas were haunts of the city's French elite. Among the most popular was the Taverne Alsacienne, which was famous throughout Indochina for its fine French wines. Nowadays, among the tedious international luxury brands, you'll still find some individual and local luxury boutiques.

Jamia Al-Musulman Mosque [459 F6] (66 Đông Du; 🕘 04.00–19.45 daily) Built during the colonial era by Indian Islamic traders, the mosque remains a vital centre for the city's Muslim community, which now includes Cham (page 343) and international worshippers. Fridays see the mosque come alive as congregants gather in the large courtyard. During Ramadan, the mosque becomes a hub of communal activity, with iftar meals shared by the faithful in the serene courtyard. At other times it is quiet, though there are usually one or two simple street cafés serving juice.

Hotel Caravelle [459 F6] (19–23 Công trường Lam Sơn; **w** caravellehotel.com) Facing the Continental and also adjoining Đồng Khởi Street is the Hotel Caravelle, which opened for business in 1959. The tenth floor housed a famous bar, a favourite spot for wartime reporters, and during the 1960s the Associated Press, NBC, CBS, *The New York Times* and *The Washington Post* based their offices here. The press escaped casualties when, on 25 August 1964, a bomb exploded in room 514, on a floor mostly used by foreign reporters. The hotel suffered damage and there were injuries, but the journalists were all out in the field. It was renamed Độc Lập (Independence) in 1975, but not before a Vietnamese tank trundled down the Rue Catinat and aimed its turret at the hotel; to this day nobody knows why it did not fire. During the filming of Graham Greene's *The Quiet American*, actors Michael Caine and Brendan Fraser stayed here.

Saigon Opera House [459 F5] (7 Công trường Lam Sơn; **w** saigonconcert.com) Completed in 1899 and designed by French architect Eugène Ferret to serve as the cultural centrepiece of colonial Saigon, its simple façade, at least compared with that of its flashy sister in Hanoi (page 105), was inspired by the Petit Palais in Paris. Designed to beguile French colonists, it showcased the finest in European operas and classical performances. After 1956, the building was repurposed as the seat of South Vietnam's National Assembly, but it returned to its theatrical roots a few years after reunification, in 1979. In 1998, the Opera House underwent extensive restoration to mark its centenary. Today, it hosts ballets, symphonies and the AO Show (page 463). Booking a show is the only way to see the interiors.

✷ ***Continental Hotel*** [459 E5] (page 456) The stately, French Continental Hotel is on the intersection with Đồng Khởi Street and Lê Thánh Tôn Street. Built in

JAPAN TOWN

Two blocks east of the Saigon Opera House and the Continental Hotel is Hồ Chí Minh City's Japan Town [459 F5], an atmospheric enclave of Japanese restaurants, massage parlours and beer bars. Competition is fierce and the food is generally good, but for specific recommendations see the map. The neighbourhood exudes seedy vibes, but is well worth exploring, day or night.

1885 by one of the grandest building syndicates in Indochina, the Société des Grands Hôtels Indochinois, this symbol of simple elegance and timeless formality reopened in 1989. The hotel's claim to fame is none other than Graham Greene, who mentions it in his novel *The Quiet American*. This old journalists' haunt was, according to war journalist Jon Swain, 'a famous veranda where correspondents, spies, speculators, traffickers, intellectuals and soldiers used to meet during the war to glean information and pick up secret reports, half false, half true or half disclosed'. Today it is a storied – but simple – place to stay.

Notre Dame Cathedral [459 E5] (1 Công xã Paris) At the north end of Đồng Khởi Street is the imposing, red-brick, twin-spired Notre Dame Cathedral, overlooking a grassed square in which a statue of the Virgin Mary stands holding an orb. The statue was the subject of intense scrutiny in 2005 when it was said that it had shed tears. The cathedral was built between 1877 and 1880 and is possibly on the site of an ancient pagoda. Mass times are a spectacle as crowds, unable to squeeze through the doors, attempt to listen to the service while perched on their parked motorbikes. At the time of research it was undergoing extensive restoration and was encased in ugly scaffolding.

Central Post Office [459 E5] (2 Công xã Paris; 🕘 07.30–17.00 daily) Facing on to Công xã Paris (Paris Square) is the Central Post Office, built in the 1880s in a French style. It is a distinguished building and notably more elegant than the People's Committee Building (page 466). The front façade has attractive cornices with the names of notable French thinkers. Note the naga – mythical snake dragons – on the rooftop corners, a distinctly Khmer motif (page 414). War buffs may remember the infamous photograph taken by Hubert van Es in 1975 on the eve of the North Vietnamese takeover of Saigon. In the photo, a helicopter perches on a narrow rooftop above a snaking line of desperate evacuees. If you face the post office and look to your right, you can still make out the rooftop. Inside the post office, the high, vaulted ceiling and fans create a cooler atmosphere in which to scribble a postcard, though the overabundance of souvenir shops is regrettable. Note the old wall-map of Cochinchina (Southern Vietnam) that has miraculously survived. The enormous portrait of Hồ Chí Minh, hanging at the end of the hall, completes the sense of grandeur.

✷ **Independence Palace** [459 D5] (Dinh Độp Lập; w dinhdoclap.gov.vn; 🕘 08.00–15.30 daily; 40,000/10,000VND adult/child; 2–3hrs including a walk around the grounds) The Independence Palace (also known as the Reunification Hall) is in a large, leafy park and southwest of Nam Kỳ Khởi Nghĩa Street. The residence of the French governor was built on this site in 1868 and was later renamed the Presidential Palace. In February 1962, a pair of planes took off to attack Việt Cộng emplacements – piloted by two of the South's finest airmen – but they turned back to bomb the Presidential Palace in a futile attempt to assassinate President Diệm. The president, who held office between 1955 and 1963, escaped with his family to the cellar (Diệm was later assassinated after a military coup; page 17), but the palace had to be demolished and was replaced with a new building by Ngô Viết Thụ, a celebrated modernist architect. One of the most memorable photographs taken during the American War was of a North Vietnamese Army tank crashing through the gates of the palace on 30 April 1975 – symbolising the end of South Vietnam and its government. The President of South Vietnam, General Dương Văn Minh, along with his entire cabinet, was arrested in the palace shortly afterwards. The hall has been preserved as it was found in 1975. In the Vice President's Guest Room, there is a lacquered painting of the Temple of Literature in Hanoi, while the Presenting of Credentials Room contains a fine 40-piece lacquer work showing diplomats presenting their credentials during the Lê Dynasty (15th century). In the basement there are operations rooms, military maps, radios and other paraphernalia. In essence, it is a 1960s-style building filled with 1960s-style official furnishings that will look stylish or kitsch depending on your design tastes. Not only was the building designed according to the principles of Chinese geomancy but the colour of the carpets – lurid mustard yellow in one room – was also chosen depending on whether it was to calm or stimulate users of the rooms. There are guided tours available upon request, but the audio guide is clear, with a lot of information.

South of Independence Palace

Hồ Chí Minh City Museum [459 E6] (65 Lý Tự Trọng; w hcmc-museum.edu.vn; 🕘 08.00–17.00 daily; 30,000VND; 1–2hrs) This museum includes a mixed bag of displays concerning the history of the city and the revolution, with a display of photographs, a few pieces of hardware (a helicopter and anti-aircraft guns) in the back compound, and some memorabilia. Other exhibits chart the development of the city and its economy. Look out for any imagery or mention of the citadel, which, if it still stood, would have been a site to behold. The building itself is historically important. Dominating a prominent intersection, the grey-white classical French-designed building was built as a museum before it became the palace for the governor of Cochinchina in 1890. After the 1945 Revolution it was used for administrative offices before returning to the French as the High Commissioner's residence in September 1945. During the American War, Ngô Đình Diệm sometimes resided here under its new name as the Southern Governor's Office; during the reign of Nguyễn Văn Thiệu (1967–75), it operated as the supreme court. A highlight of visiting the museum is delving into the downstairs war bunker, where residents and workers would escape to and hide.

General Sciences Library [459 E6] (69 Lý Tự Trọng; 🕘 07.30–19.00 Mon–Thu, 09.00–17.00 Sat–Sun) If the architecture of the Neoclassical Hồ Chí Minh City Museum is not to your liking, hop over the road to the General Sciences Library, which also occupies the bulk of a city block. Built by local architect Bùi Quang Hanh and completed in 1971, this is one of the city's most distinguished modernist buildings. With a perforated façade, plenty of trees and a moat, the building was designed to cool naturally before air conditioning was a viable option. It remains an excellent example of Vietnam's contribution to the modernist movement. The library isn't set up to receive visitors as the building is mostly used by students as a study space, but there's nothing stopping you from wandering through the front gate and enjoying the grounds.

Mariamman Hindu Temple [459 D6] (45 Trương Định) Although clearly Hindu, with a statue of Mariamman flanked by Maduraiveeran and Pechiamman, the temple is largely frequented by worshippers who wouldn't necessarily identify as such. This makes for an unusual sight of Vietnamese clasping incense sticks and prostrating themselves in front of a Hindu deity, as they would to a Buddha image.

Bến Thành Market [459 D6] (Chợ Bến Thành) A large, covered central market, Bến Thành Market sits on a busy intersection roundabout which has benefitted from a recent facelift, though there's a notable lack of trees and shade (and still no metro station). Bến Thành is well stocked with cheap clothes (think T-shirts with 'I Love Vietnam' and the like), household goods, and a wide choice of souvenirs, lacquerware, embroidery and so on, as well as some terrific sections with fresh produce. Though very touristy, the fresh food is proof that locals still use the market, even if you don't see any (they tend to go first thing in the morning). Two of the most attractive features of the market are the east and west gates, which have *cửa đông* (east gate) and *cửa tây* (west gate) written in a stylised Art Deco font. To get a more authentic sense of a busy city market, head to Bình Tây Market (page 477).

Museum of Fine Arts [459 E7] (97A Phó Đức Chính; **w** baotangmythuattphcm.com.vn; 🕘 08.00–17.00 daily; 30,000VND/free adult/child; 1hr) Housed in an atmospheric, spruced-up colonial building, this museum is a very pleasant place to escape the heat of the city and take a look at some 1920s architecture close up. The interior is wonderfully tiled, there is a photogenic courtyard to the rear, and the first chamber houses an ancient, disused iron lift. The architecture overshadows the lacklustre collection, though there are works from the 4th century right up until the contemporary era. The American War features heavily in the post-1975 work and the theme can become a little tiresome, but there is plenty of other art on offer, including some interesting Cham-era pieces. The museum has a fairly lively events schedule, which includes activities for children on the weekends. It is also plugged into the international museum community, and there are regular temporary exhibits in the other handsome buildings in the compound; check the website for details.

CONTEMPORARY ART HUBS IN HỒ CHÍ MINH CITY

It's sometimes possible to purchase pieces from the hubs below, but private ownership of the pieces is not the focus.

Galerie Quỳnh 118 Nguyễn Văn Thủ; **w** galeriequynh.com; 🕘 10.00–19.00 Tue–Sat. Prominent gallery with a long history & in a central location, with works exhibited over several floors of a narrow building. It closes sporadically so calling ahead is sensible.

Lotus Gallery Khu chế xuất, D3/12–13 Tân Thuận; **w** lotusgallery.vn; 🕘 09.00–18.00 daily. Whitewashed industrial space in District 7 that has existed in one form or another since 1991. Arriving here feels like stumbling across something special.

Nguyễn Art Foundation EMASI Nam Long, District 7 & EMASI Vạn Phúc, Thủ Đức District; **w** nguyenartfoundation.com; 🕘 changeable hours. A huge collection of contemporary art – possibly Vietnam's largest – with arresting & topical exhibitions curated by Bill Nguyễn in 2 locations outside central Hồ Chí Minh City. Both locations are in international schools and operate changeable hours. Contact the gallery a few days in advance to let them know you're coming.

Quang San Art Museum 189B/3 Nguyễn Văn Hưởng; **w** quangsanartmuseum.com.vn; 🕘 09.00–16.30 Tue–Sun. Somewhat indulgent space with a collection of contemporary art exhibited in a mansion on the riverfront in District 2.

Sàn Art 132 Bến Vân Đồn; **w** san-art.org; 🕘 11.00–18.00 Tue–Sat. Committed but occasionally disorganised hub currently located in a high-rise residential block in District 4, close to District 1.

✷ ***Chợ Cũ Market*** [459 E6] (Old Market; Tôn Thất Đạm; ⌚ 09.00–19.00 daily) An unlikely local commercial street right in the centre of the city, there has been some sort of market here for a century. Unlike Bến Thành Market, there are few tourist knick-knacks or holiday T-shirts, just locals going about their daily shop. A handful of juice stands are squeezed between the market stalls, and here you can sip on a coconut and watch the world go by.

Dragon Wharf [459 F7] (1 Nguyễn Tất Thành; **w** bennharong.vn; ⌚ 07.30–11.30 & 13.30–17.00 daily; 30 mins) Forever immortalised as the place from which Nguyễn Ái Quốc (later Hồ Chí Minh) set sail for Europe in 1911, the Dragon Wharf, now in District 4 (page 476), was an important trading harbour built by the French in 1862. The rose-pink building is clearly French in style, but note the tiled rooftop with dragons, somewhat reminiscent of a pagoda or temple, which has given the wharf its name. The museum it houses is dedicated to Hồ Chí Minh, with hundreds of photos depicting his various talents (composing, orating, fishing). Note the two altars, one to Hồ Chí Minh and a smaller one dedicated to Tôn Đức Thắng, his successor, where you may catch people praying. The building is pleasant to walk around in and the encircling breezy garden offers plenty of shade, but the exhibits are a little dry, except perhaps for Hồ Chí Minh's most ardent fans.

Tôn Đức Thắng Museum [459 F5] (5 Tôn Đức Thắng; **w** baotangtonducthang.vn; ⌚ 07.30–17.00 Mon–Fri; 1hr) Once a well-curated history museum inaugurated in 1988, the fantastically modernist Tôn Đức Thắng Museum building was demolished in 2016 and at the time of research the modern replacement had only just opened. Tôn Đức Thắng was a prominent Vietnamese revolutionary leader and the second president of North Vietnam, succeeding Hồ Chí Minh. He became the first president of the Socialist Republic of Vietnam after reunification in 1976. The museum opened on what would have been his 100th birthday (he died in 1980), and although there were exhibits focused on his life, they helped frame Vietnam's broader modern history.

North and west of Independence Palace

Turtle Lake [458 D4] (Công trường Quốc Tế) This little lake and local photography hotspot has a fascinating history. Originally the site of one of eight citadel gates and lookout towers, it was the location of a water tower during the colonial period until the 1920s, and then a war memorial for World War I victims. Students toppled this monument in the 1960s to protest the memory of French colonialism and only then did the modernist structure you see today begin to take shape. It's believed that so much effort was put into the square because Ngô Đình Diệm (page 16), president of South Vietnam and a firm believer in *phong thủy* (feng shui), needed to pin down the tail of a dragon that was writhing around and causing instability in the nation, echoing the myth of the Japanese Bridge in Hội An (page 307). The octagonal square and roundabout is a nod to the old citadel, while the concrete blossoming lotus symbolises freedom. There are various elevated cafés encircling the square from which you can look over this leafy patch of District 3.

War Remnants Museum [459 C5] (28 Võ Văn Tần, one block north of the palace; **w** baotangchungtichchientranh.vn; ⌚ 07.30–17.30 daily; 40,000VND/free adult/child; 2–3hrs) All the horrors of the American War from Vietnam's perspective, including photographs of atrocities and action, bombs, planes and more, are graphically displayed in this organised museum. In the courtyard are tanks, bombs and helicopters, while the new museum, arranged in five new sections, records man's inhumanity. The display covers the Sơn Mỹ (Mỹ Lai) Massacre on 16 March 1968 (page 324), the effects of napalm and phosphorous, and the after-effects of Agent Orange defoliation (this is particularly disturbing, with bottled malformed human foetuses). This museum has gone through some interesting name changes over the years. It began life as the Exhibition House of American and Chinese War Crimes. In 1990, 'Chinese' was dropped from the name, and in 1994 'American' was too. Since 1996 it has simply been called the War Remnants Museum. The audio guide is recommended.

✷ ***Archbishop's Residence*** [459 C5] (180 Nguyễn Đình Chiểu; **w** tgpsaigon.net; ⌚ 07.30–14.30 Mon–Sat) The gigantic Archbishop's Residence building is a photogenic chunk of colonial architecture, but perhaps more impressive is tucked away in a corner of the compound: probably Hồ Chí Minh City's oldest structure. With dark wooden walls and yin–yang tiles, the small, one-storey chapel would seem more at home in imperial Huế were it not for the Latin cross on the rooftop. Built at the end of the 18th century during the nascent Nguyễn Dynasty as a home for Bishop Pigneau de Béhaine, a French Catholic priest, the building was originally located near the Thị Nghè Canal. At some point, though it's not clear when, it was moved here and became a chapel. You can't enter the compound from the main gate on Nguyễn Đình Chiểu. Instead, go around the corner, find the gate on Trần Quốc Thảo and politely ask the security guard if you can go inside to see the small chapel.

110 Võ Văn Tần [459 C6] This compelling project, known as Ville le Voile, is rejuvenating an ornate villa, built in 1930, with the help of restoration specialists Stonewest of London, UK, and Palazzo Spinelli of Florence, Italy. The restoration process was ongoing at the time of research and the villa's life post-recovery is unclear, but it's possible to make out the details on the rooftop from the street.

Thích Quảng Đức Monument [459 B6] (185 Cách Mạng Tháng 8) In August 1963 there was a demonstration of 15,000 people at the Xá Lợi Pagoda, with speakers denouncing the Diệm regime and telling jokes about Diệm's sister-in-law, Madame Nhu, who later called monks 'hooligans in robes'. Two nights later, ARVN (South Vietnam) special forces (from Roman Catholic families) raided the pagoda, battering down the gate, wounding 30 and killing seven people. Soon afterwards Diệm declared martial law. The pagoda became a focus of discontent, with several monks committing suicide through self-immolation to protest against the Diệm regime.

The first monk to immolate himself was 66-year-old Thích Quảng Đức, from Huế, and this little green patch commemorates the event with a striking sculpture. On 11 June 1963, his companions poured petrol over him and set him alight as he sat in the lotus position. Pedestrians prostrated themselves at the sight; even a policeman threw himself to the ground in reverence. The next day, the picture of the monk in flames filled the front pages of newspapers around the world. Some 30 monks and nuns followed Thích's example in protesting against the Diệm government and US involvement in South Vietnam. Two young US protesters also followed suit, one committing suicide by self-immolation outside the Pentagon and the other next to the UN, both in November 1968. Madame Nhu, a Catholic, is reported to have said after the monks' death: 'If the Buddhists wish to have another barbecue, I will be glad to supply the gasoline and a match.'

Phù Đổng Thiên Vương Statue [459 C7] (Ngã sáu Phù Đổng) This statue was inaugurated in 1967 during a time of intense political and social change in South Vietnam, and was intended to serve as a symbol of national pride and resilience. In retrospect, the timing of the statue is especially curious: when this celebration of Phù Đổng Thiên Vương, the embodiment of resistance against foreign invaders (see below), was erected, US involvement in Vietnam was still ramping up to its peak in 1969. Phù Đổng Thiên Vương, more commonly known as Thánh Gióng, today overlooks a chaotic roundabout.

✷ ***Secret Weapon Bunker*** [459 B6] (70 Nguyễn Đình Chiểu; ⌚ 09.00–17.00 Mon–Fri) Hidden beneath an ordinary house is the oft-overlooked Secret Weapon Bunker, a key Việt Cộng armoury during the American War, used to stockpile weapons for the 1968 Tết Offensive. Disguised as a typical family home, the underground bunker remained completely undetected throughout the conflict, and it's easy to see why. Today, you can access the compact space via a trapdoor, revealing hidden compartments once filled with ammunition and

LEGEND HAS IT: A PRECOCIOUS TANTRUM OF RESISTANCE

From the moment he was born, during the semi-mythical Hùng Dynasty, there was clearly nothing ordinary about Phù Đổng Thiên Vương (Thánh Gióng). He barely grew during his infant years, and on the day he turned three, his parents bewailed their son's inability to walk or talk. Little did they know that their child was destined for greatness.

Thánh Gióng and his family were citizens of a fledgling nation that existed under constant threat of a northern invasion. As rumours of a great army amassing at the northern border mounted, King Hùng Vương (page 10) sent out a royal decree calling upon warriors to defend the land. Messengers travelled far and wide, and when they arrived in Thánh Gióng's village, the silent child finally stirred. As soon as he heard the call to arms, he spoke his first words. 'Mother,' he said. 'Summon the king's envoys. I shall drive away the invaders.'

His confounded parents called for the envoys, who arrived to witness the toddler now speaking with great authority. He instructed them to go back to the king and ask for a suit of iron armour, an iron sword and an iron horse. The messengers, awestruck, hurried back to the king. Hùng Vương sensed that the gods were at work, and he ordered his smiths to craft the metalwork requested – including a life-size iron horse.

Meanwhile, the boy devoured everything in sight, and in a matter of days, he had grown into a towering giant, his strength not matched even by a hundred men. When the iron armour, sword and horse arrived, the boy transformed into Thánh Gióng, the embodiment of divine strength.

Mounted on his iron steed (now animate), he rode into battle. Flames erupted from the horse's nostrils as Thánh Gióng struck fear into the hearts of the invading forces. With his sword, he cleaved through the enemies with ease. The invaders fled in terror but Thánh Gióng pursued them relentlessly until the northern menace was utterly vanquished. His mission complete, Thánh Gióng rode his iron horse to Sóc Mountain, just outside of present-day Hanoi, and soared into the heavens, never to be seen again. He is now considered one of the Four Immortals (page 210).

explosives. The tiny site offers a rare glimpse into wartime ingenuity and remains largely untouched.

East of the Independence Palace

Lê Duẩn Street [459 D5] North of the cathedral is Lê Duẩn Street, the former corridor of power, with Ngô Đình Diệm's Palace (now the Independence Palace) at one end, the zoo at the other and various former embassy buildings in between. A few blocks away from the Independence Palace is the former US Embassy. After diplomatic ties were resumed in 1995 the Americans lost little time in demolishing the 1960s building that held so many bad memories. The US Consulate General [458 E4] now stands on this site.

Botanical Gardens and Zoo [458 F3] (2 Nguyễn Bỉnh Khiêm; **w** saigonzoo.net; ⏲ 07.00–17.30 daily; 60,000/40,000VND adult/child) At the end of Lê Duẩn Street are the Botanical Gardens, which run alongside Nguyễn Bỉnh Khiêm Street at the point where the Thị Nghè Channel flows into the Saigon River. The gardens were established in 1864 by French botanist Jean-Baptiste Louis Pierre; by the 1970s they had a collection of nearly 2,000 species, and a particularly fine display of orchids. With the dislocations of the immediate post-war years, the gardens fell into decline, a situation from which they are still trying to recover. In the south quarter of the gardens is a depressing zoo with a rather moth-eaten collection of animals. Some may have mixed feelings about how to approach this zoo. The grounds are undeniably beautiful, with many grand mahogany trees and manicured flower gardens. But sadly one can't enjoy the grounds without paying to enter the zoo and thus contribute to the barbaric conditions suffered by the animals.

✷ ***The History Museum*** [458 F3] (Bảo Tàng Lịch Sử Việt Nam; 1 Tràng Tiền; **w** baotanglichsu.vn; ⏲ 08.00–noon & 13.30–17.00 Tue–Sun; 40,000/10,000VND adult/child; 2hrs) This museum is in an elegant building constructed in 1928 in a pagoda-esque style that is not dissimilar to the History Museum in Hanoi. Exhibit rooms are neatly arranged around a pretty but messy courtyard with a pond and some outdoor sculpture. Note that the museum has two entrances: one next to the zoo and one on Nguyễn Bỉnh Khiêm Street. Enter near the zoo as then the flow of the museum will be more coherent. It displays a wide range of artefacts from the prehistoric (300,000 years ago) and the Đông Sơn (1000BCE–1st century CE) periods before skipping the period of Chinese domination (111BCE–CE938). The museum then moves through the different dynasties fairly coherently, starting with the Lý (1009–1225) and culminating with the Nguyễn (1802–1945). Despite obvious digs at the Nguyễn, the dynasty that oversaw French colonialism, the museum houses a lovely display of art from that era. Particularly impressive are the Cham sculptures, though they sit in a room far removed from the Cham towers in Central Vietnam, and they are presented in a way that lacks any kind of narrative or historical connection to the land. Nevertheless, notable pieces include a delicately carved Devi (Goddess) dating from the 10th century; the head of Shiva, Hindu destroyer and creator, from the 8th to 9th century; and Ganesh, elephant-headed son of Shiva and Parvati, also dating from the 8th to 9th century. Other highlights include wooden stakes planted in the Bạch Đằng riverbed for repelling the warships of the Mongol Yuan in the 13th century (page 203). Remember these wooden stakes, as when you leave through the Nguyễn Bỉnh Khiêm Street entrance you can look for the huge brown mural that depicts the battle of Bạch Đằng; see if you can make out the sticks emerging from the water. Labelling throughout the museum is in English and Vietnamese. Though water puppetry originated in the north, there are morning and afternoon shows here Tuesday to Sunday. If this is of interest, confirm the time when you arrive at the museum and work around it.

Đa Kao and around

✷ ***Jade Emperor Pagoda*** [458 D2] (73 Mai Thị Lựu; 🕘 07.00–18.00 daily) This pink pagoda, built early in the 20th century, has two names in Vietnamese: Chùa Ngọc Hoàng and Phước Hải Tự. It feels far from Hồ Chí Minh City's other central sites, but hunting it out is well worth the effort, especially if you don't have time to visit the temples and pagodas in Chợ Lớn (page 476). Find it nestling behind low walls, close to the Thị Nghè Channel. The pagoda, traditionally a Buddhist place of worship, is unusual as it's dedicated to the Jade Emperor, the supreme god of the Taoists, and he sits in the main altar room draped in robes and flanked by guardians. The pagoda contains a wide range of other Buddhist deities, however, including the archangel Michael of the Buddhists, a Sakyamuni (historic) Buddha and statues of the two generals who tamed the Green Dragon and the White Tiger. An entire floor is devoted to the popular Buddhist figure Quan Âm, the Goddess of Compassion (page 293). There is a terrace connected to Quan Âm's chamber from where you can marvel at the ornate roof decorations. It's easy to spend an hour or more here as you move around the pagoda, observe local worship and try to decode the striking imagery.

Tân Định Church [458 C3] (289 Hai Bà Trưng; **w** giaoxutandinh.net; 🕘 07.30–11.30 & 14.30–18.30 daily) Inaugurated in 1876, Tân Định Church is one of Hồ Chí Minh City's oldest and most important Roman Catholic institutions. Much of the current structure, which blends Romanesque, Gothic and Renaissance styles, dates back to the 1890s. The church took on its iconic pink demeanour in 1957 after one of several refurbishments. The building proper doesn't necessarily keep to its advertised opening hours, but it's usually possible to circumnavigate it within the church grounds.

Tân Định Market [458 C3] (336 Hai Bà Trưng) This large, covered market is worth visiting for the fabric section, where stalls bulge with textiles boasting every colour and pattern imaginable. There's also an excellent street-food row that runs along Nguyễn Hữu Cầu Street, a good spot for *bánh mì*, *bún* (noodles) and juice. A few blocks south of Tân Định Market is Lê Văn Tám Park [458 C3], one of central

LEGEND HAS IT: FIRE FALLS ON SACRIFICE

After reunification in 1976, history books used in schools across the country included the remarkable story of the teenage martyr Lê Văn Tám, who, in 1946, drenched himself in petrol, lit himself alight and charged into a French-controlled petrol storage container on the Thị Nghè Canal. Many young children learned this brutal story of tremendous sacrifice and patriotism through comic-book-like drawings that depicted an ablaze Lê Văn Tám making an unlikely sprint towards a distant container. However, in 2005, Professor Phan Huy Lê discovered that while revolutionaries did destroy a petrol storage container in 1946, the kamikaze mission of Lê Văn Tám was fabricated by propagandists. The erroneous tale was swiftly removed from the curriculum as a result.

Hồ Chí Minh City's loveliest green spaces, especially at dawn and dusk, when nearby residents flock to the square for their daily dose of exercise. At the centre of the park is an ivory-white socialist Realist sculpture of the eponymous Lê Văn Tám, a semi-legendary figure (page 475).

DISTRICT 5 (CHỢ LỚN) AND AROUND An early map printed in 1815 shows Saigon linked to a huge market by a single road. This commercial area came to be known as Chợ Lớn, which means 'big market' in Vietnamese, a name it retains today. It was founded in the 18th century by Chinese immigrants, and these days Chợ Lớn could claim to be the world's largest Chinatown by both population and land area. While District 5 is the centrepiece of this huge community, the Chinese have also shaped districts 6, 8, 10 and 11. The sights listed here – by no means an exhaustive account – are organised from west to east, and to walk between and visit all the temples, pagodas, streets and markets would take the better part of a day. You'll need a taxi to visit the Museum of Traditional Vietnamese Medicine, which is between districts 1 and 5 but not walking distance from either. There are plenty of coffee pit stops

GETTING LOST

Sights are thin on the ground in many Hồ Chí Minh City districts, but some will still appeal to intrepid pedestrian explorers. Bear in mind that walking the streets of Hồ Chí Minh City is an art, and you'll be sharing the road with the traffic most of the time.

DISTRICT 4 Across the Bến Nghé Canal from District 1 is District 4, which has undergone a dramatic transformation from its days as a mafia stronghold in the 1980s. Today, this district – the smallest in the city – is a lively place, with few sights per se but many atmospheric neighbourhoods. The district's principal attraction is the Dragon Wharf (page 471), where there are views back to the skyscrapers in District 1. Interesting areas for random wandering are around Jack Clayton Art Gallery (page 464) and the 19th-century Xóm Chiếu Parish Church (92B/20 Tôn Thất Thuyết). Vĩnh Khánh Street comes alive at night with restaurants serving seafood, snails and countless crates of cold beer.

BÌNH THẠNH DISTRICT Across from the Thị Nghè Canal in Đa Kao in District 1 is Bình Thạnh District, a tightly packed neighbourhood of higgledy-piggledy market streets and residential alleyways. Aside from the very limited public green space around Landmark 81 (720A Điện Biên Phủ) – Vietnam's tallest skyscraper, which provides sweeping views of the city – atmospheric neighbourhoods include the hipster hangout around Phạm Viết Chánh Street, which has a burgeoning international food and nightlife scene.

THẢO ĐIỀN, DISTRICT 2 Thảo Điền is a rapidly growing area across the Saigon River from Bình Thạnh that has transformed into an expatriate hub. Many of those who live there barely ever leave its relatively quiet but unfinished streets. Known for its upscale boutiques and international restaurants, Thảo Điền is more about its food and beverage scene than hard-and-fast sights. Neighbourhoods suited to aimless wandering between design cafés include the streets north of Xuân Thủy Street.

THE HOA

There are perhaps as many as 1 million ethnic Chinese, or Hoa, in Vietnam, 80% living in the south of the country. Before reunification in 1975 there were even more; hundreds of thousands left due to persecution by the authorities and a lack of economic opportunities after the process of socialist transformation. Many more left in 1979 in response to China's invasion of the northern border. With the reforms of the 1980s, the authorities' view of the Chinese changed as they began to appreciate the crucial role they could continue to play in the economy. The Hoa population began to increase again when China normalised its relations with Vietnam in 1991. Today, ethnic Chinese in Vietnam can own and operate businesses and are once again allowed to join the Communist Party and the army and to enter university. The Hoa have become very much a part of the Vietnamese community. Their children often speak Chinese but attend Vietnamese-language schools. Religion, particularly the teachings of Confucius, remains important, just as it is for the Vietnamese. Festivals, especially Tết (Lunar New Year), are a time for lavish celebrations. At all times of year, the streets of District 5 are festooned with Chinese characters and chime with the sounds of Chinese pop songs and television shows. While most Hoa are in Hồ Chí Minh City, they also live in villages along the Chinese border in Northern Vietnam.

along the way. For food, try the excellent food market in Bình Tây Market or the restaurants on the map on page 478.

✷ **Bình Tây Market** [map, page 450] (57A Tháp Mười; **w** chobinhtay.gov.vn; ◷ 07.00–18.00 daily) While most tourists visit Bến Thành Market (page 469), Bình Tây Market is the more rewarding. Sandwiched between Tháp Mười and Phan Văn Khỏe streets, it is one of the most colourful and exciting markets in Vietnam, with an array of noises, smells and colours of stalls that have passed from generation to generation, creating a rich sense of history and belonging. It sprawls over a large area and is contained in what looks rather like a royal palace. Every conceivable space is used, with stalls festooned with everything from spices to flip-flops. This is also a good place to seek out a bowl of noodles in the food court at the back or grab a cup of strong iced coffee and watch the chaos unfold in front of you.

It was built in 1928 by wealthy Chinese merchant and philanthropist Quách Đàm, who financed the construction as part of his contribution to the local community. The market was designed with traditional Chinese architectural influences, featuring a distinctive pagoda-style roof, curved eaves and a central clock tower, but also incorporated elements of French colonial architecture. After its completion, Bình Tây Market became the main trading hub for goods flowing between Saigon and the Mekong Delta. During the war years, it remained an important centre of commerce and continued to thrive, even amid the political turmoil. After the reunification of Vietnam in 1975, the market expanded to serve the growing population of Hồ Chí Minh City. In 2016–18, it underwent a major renovation.

St Francis Xavier Church (25 Học Lạc; ◷ 05.00–23.00 daily) This church was finished in 1902 by bishop Jean-Marie Depierre but financed by the local Chinese Catholic community. It was designed with a blend of European Gothic and traditional Asian architectural elements, featuring a vaulted interior but

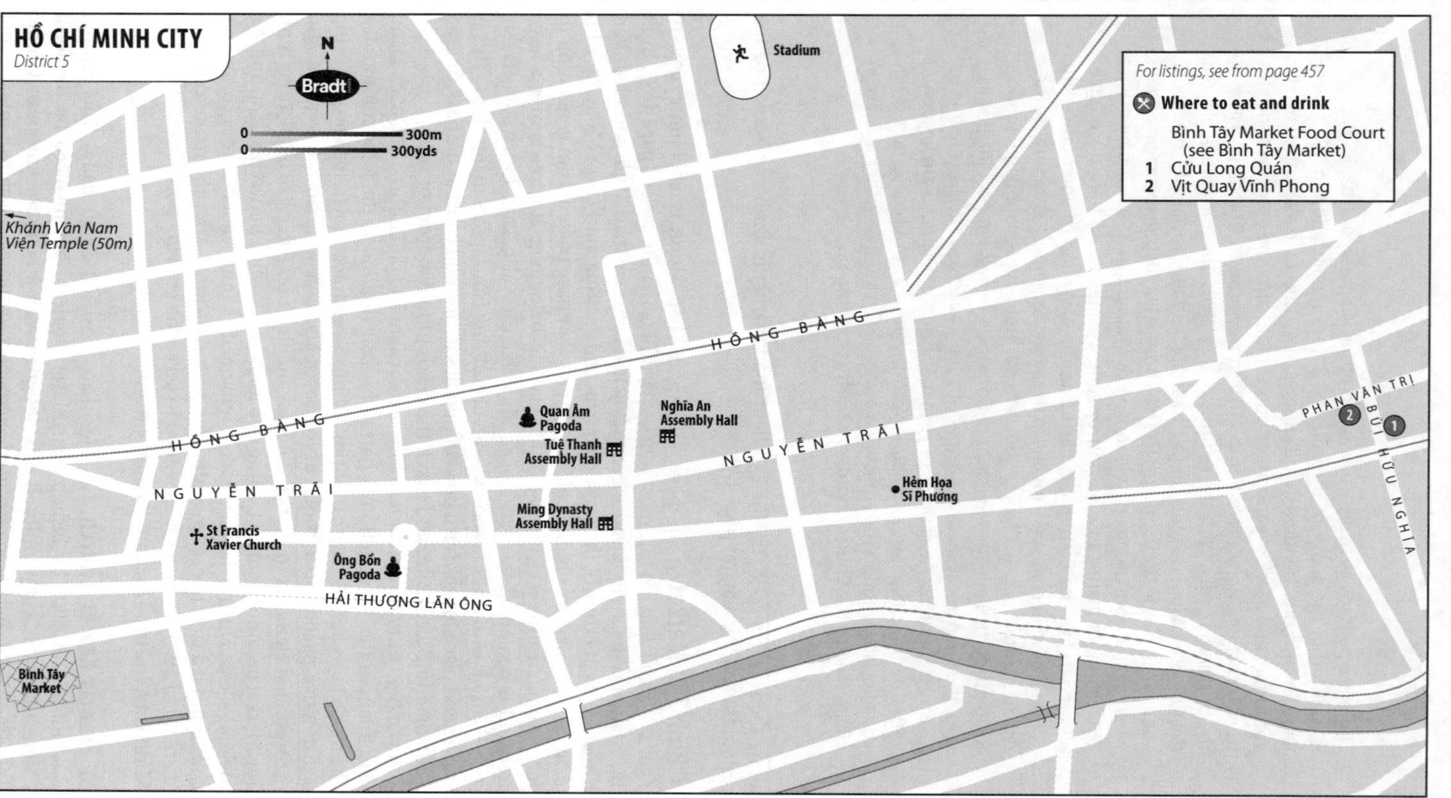
HỒ CHÍ MINH CITY
District 5
N
Bradt
0 300m
0 300yds
Khánh Vân Nam Viện Temple (50m)
Stadium
For listings, see from page 457
Where to eat and drink
Bình Tây Market Food Court (see Bình Tây Market)
1 Cửu Long Quán
2 Vịt Quay Vĩnh Phong
HỒNG BÀNG
HỒNG BÀNG
NGUYỄN TRÃI
NGUYỄN TRÃI
PHAN VĂN TRỊ
BÙI HỮU NGHĨA
Quan Âm Pagoda
Nghĩa An Assembly Hall
Tuệ Thanh Assembly Hall
Hẻm Họa Sĩ Phương
Ming Dynasty Assembly Hall
St Francis Xavier Church
Ông Bổn Pagoda
HẢI THƯỢNG LÃN ÔNG
Bình Tây Market
2
1

Chinese inscriptions. During the 1963 coup (page 17), the church gained historical significance as the refuge of President Ngô Đình Diệm and his brother Ngô Đình Nhu, both devout Catholics. After praying here, they were arrested, taken to a street corner and shot. Today there is a small plaque to show where they sat moments before the arrest.

Ông Bổn Pagoda (264 Hải Thượng Lãn Ông) This pagoda is dedicated to Ông Bổn, a deity with diverse origins, but generally believed to protect and bring prosperity. Built by Fujianese Chinese in the 18th century, the temple is designed in a traditional Chinese architectural style, with detailed wood carvings, colourful altars and red pillars leading to the main worship area. The pagoda is especially notable for its large circular porthole windows and doors and its gallery of spiritual heroes, including Quan Âm, Buddha and the Monkey King.

✷ **Quan Âm Pagoda** (12 Lão Tử) The brightly coloured Quan Âm Pagoda is thought to be one of the oldest in the city. Its roof supports four sets of impressive mosaic-encrusted figures, while inside, the main building is fronted with old gold-and-lacquer panels of guardian spirits. In front of the main altar is a white ceramic statue of Quan Âm, the Goddess of Compassion (page 293), with several more altars dedicated to Buddhist and Buddhism-adjacent deities in the back courtyard. On the other side of the street is a small courtyard with a pond and some benches.

Tuệ Thanh Assembly Hall (710 Nguyễn Trãi; 🕘 06.00–17.30 daily) Constructed in the 18th century, this assembly hall is Chinese in inspiration and is dedicated to the worship of both the Buddha and Thiên Hậu (see below), the Goddess of the Sea

LEGEND HAS IT: WITH GREAT POWER COMES GREAT RESPONSIBILITY

Thiên Hậu, a young girl from a Chinese fishing village, could sense storms before they arrived and had the remarkable power to assist her family through prayer when they were in danger. One fateful day, while her father and two brothers were out fishing, a storm suddenly struck. Thiên Hậu entered into a trance, as she always did at times of meteorological crisis, and saw the ship that carried her family in peril. She stretched out her hands to save her family, grasping her father in one hand and her brothers in the other. As she hauled them to safety, her mother shook her awake. Tragically, she lost her grip on one brother, who was swept away by the sea.

Though Thiên Hậu saved her father and one of her brothers, the loss of the other was too heavy a burden to bear. She vowed to use her powers not just to help her father and brothers, but all fishermen, and Thiên Hậu soon became widely known for her abilities. As her powers grew, she found that she could extend her protection not just to local fishermen, but to all seafarers. Thiên Hậu eventually grew so powerful that she transcended death; after she passed away in this world, she ascended to the heavens and continued to watch over the seas and rescue those in need. This became her sole purpose, and even when presented with an opportunity for marriage, she refused (see page 309 for the continuation of her story).

Thiên Hậu Thánh Mẫu is a popular deity for the Chinese diaspora in Southeast Asia, most of whom travelled by boat, and you'll find temples dedicated to her in Chinatowns across the region, including in other parts of Vietnam.

and the protector of sailors. One enormous incense urn and an incinerator can be seen through the main doors. Inside, the principal altar supports the gilded form of Thiên Hậu, with a boat to one side. Silk paintings depicting religious scenes decorate the walls. By far the most interesting part of the pagoda is the roof, which can best be seen from the small open courtyard. It must be one of the finest and most richly ornamented in Vietnam, with the high-relief frieze depicting episodes from the Legends of the Three Kingdoms, a Chinese epic. In the post-1975 era, many would-be refugees (the Boat People; page 20) prayed here for safe deliverance before casting themselves adrift on the East Sea. A number of those who survived the perilous voyage and achieved a level of success abroad sent offerings to the merciful goddess and the temple has been well maintained since. On busy days it is smoky, atmospheric and moving, with worshippers coming from across Asia and the wider world. Look up on leaving to see over the front door a picture of a boiling sea peppered with sinking boats. A benign Thiên Hậu looks down mercifully from a cloud.

Ming Dynasty Assembly Hall (Đinh Minh Hương Gia Thạnh; 380 Trần Hưng Đạo; 🕘 08.00–noon daily) The Ming Dynasty Assembly Hall was built by the Cantonese community that arrived in Saigon via Hội An in the 18th century. It was built in 1789 for the dedication and worship of the Ming Dynasty, although the building we see today dates largely from an extensive renovation carried out in the 1960s. There is some old furniture: a heavy marble-topped table and chairs that arrived in 1850 from China. It appears that the Vietnamese Emperor Gia Long used the Chinese community for cordial relations with the Chinese royal court, and one of the community, Trịnh Hoài Đức, was appointed Vietnamese ambassador to the Ming Dynasty. In the main hall there are three altars, which follow imperial tradition. The central altar is dedicated to the Ming Dynasty (royalty), the right-hand altar is dedicated to two mandarin officers (military) and the left-hand altar is dedicated to two other mandarin officers (civil).

Nghĩa An Assembly Hall (678 Nguyễn Trãi; 🕘 06.00–17.00 daily) A magnificent carved, gold-painted wooden boat hangs over the entrance to the Nghĩa An Assembly Hall. To the left, on entering the temple, is a larger-than-life representation of Quan Công's horse and groom. (Quan Công was a loyal military man who lived in China in the 3rd century.) At the main altar are three figures in glass cases: the central red-faced figure with a green cloak is Quan Công himself; to the left and right are his trusty companions, General Châu Xương (very fierce) and the mandarin Quan Bình respectively. On leaving, note the fine gold figures of guardians on the inside of the door panels.

Hẻm Họa Sĩ Phương (206 Trần Hưng Đạo) This 100-year-old alley is known for its French and Chinese architectural mix, with colourful two-storey houses lining both sides, connected by a shared balcony and narrow passageways. The alley was originally designed as tenement housing for Chinese merchants and labourers. Today, it is largely unchanged and remains an unusually photogenic residential area, but be mindful not to linger or make too much noise.

✷ **Khánh Vân Nam Viện** [map, page 450] (Nguyễn Thị Nhỏ, District 11; 🕘 06.00–17.30 daily) Built in the 1930s and renovated many times since, the temple is one of the few dedicated only to Taoism in the country. The temple's architecture features pagoda-style roofs, green eaves and bright red walls, and is fronted by a feng shui pond. The main shrine is dedicated to Lão Tử, whose ornate altar is adorned with colourful drapes and intricate carvings of dragons and phoenixes. The courtyard is shaded by mature trees and lined with bamboo. It's possible to wander around the religious building at will, but some areas are inaccessible to non-worshippers, which will be made clear in a firm but polite way by the caretakers. Note that this temple is far from the other religious buildings in this section, so you may wish to take a taxi.

Museum of Traditional Vietnamese Medicine (FITO; 41 Hoàng Dư Khương; w fitomuseum.com.vn; 🕘 08.30–17.00 daily; 180,000/90,000VND adult/child) This museum delves into Vietnam's rich history of traditional medicine. The visit starts with an uninspired 15-minute introductory video, which seeks to distinguish Vietnamese medicine from its Chinese counterpart, though it acknowledges some overlap. The museum is heavily affiliated with the FITO brand, a traditional medicine company, and the tour's promotion of their products is not subtle. Begin on the fourth floor with an impressive tree mural listing important doctors, which reportedly took two years to complete. On the fifth floor, there's a 19th-century traditional house brought from Hanoi which contains some Cham artefacts, though the lack of signage can make these hard to fully appreciate. The third floor is devoted to the tools of the trade, from herb-cutting implements to storage jars and drawers. On the second floor, you'll see equipment for boiling and weighing herbs, along with some unsettling displays like vats containing preserved animals, including a cobra clutching another snake in its mouth. Before leaving you'll be offered a cup of tea and introduced to some of FITO's products.

AROUND HỒ CHÍ MINH CITY

As well as the day trips mentioned here, other out-of-town areas of interest include Vũng Tàu (page 382) and the Mekong Delta (page 396), but both warrant at least two days. The Cao Đài Temple (page 392) in Tây Ninh used to be coupled with the Củ Chi Tunnels to form an uncomfortably long and rushed day trip because they are both in the same general direction, but due to the distance and time on the road, this itinerary has fallen out of fashion. A better option is to head to Tây Ninh on the first day, overnight in the province, and visit the Củ Chi Tunnels on the way back to the city.

✸ **CỦ CHI TUNNELS** The Củ Chi Tunnels [map, page 381] (Phú Hiệp, Củ Chi District; w diadaocuchi.com.vn; 🕘 07.00–17.00 Mon–Sat; 70,000VND per international visitor) are about 55km northwest of District 1, and although the area is rural, they are still administratively within the city limits. Dug by the Việt Minh, who began work in 1948, they were later expanded by the People's Liberation Armed Forces (PLAF, or Việt Cộng) and used for storage and refuge, and contained sleeping quarters, hospitals and schools. Between 1960 and 1970, a remarkable 200km of tunnels were built, some of which were many metres under the surface. At the height of their usage, a staggering 300,000 people were living underground. The width of the tunnel entry at ground level was 22cm by 30cm and the tunnels are now too narrow for many modern adults. A short section of the network has been especially widened to allow tourists to share the experience, but tall or large people might still find it a claustrophobic squeeze. Entering the tunnels is not a requirement, however, nor is it necessary during a visit to what is perhaps Vietnam's most interesting sight related to the American War.

Củ Chi was one of the most fervently communist of the districts around Hồ Chí Minh City and the tunnels were used as the base from which the Việt Cộng mounted the operations of the Tết Offensive in 1968. This was for all intents and purposes the endpoint of the torturous Hồ Chí Minh Trail (page 275), as much of the artillery transported south was stored here before being distributed to revolutionary cells across South Vietnam. Communist cadres were active in this area of rubber plantations even before World War II. Vann and Ramsey, two American soldiers, were to notice the difference between this area and other parts of the south in the early 1960s: 'No children laughed and shouted for gum and candy in these hamlets. Everyone, adult and child, had a cold look' (*A Bright Shining Lie*, Neil Sheehan, 1989).

When the Americans first discovered this underground base on their doorstep they would simply pump gas down the tunnel openings and then set explosives. They also pumped river water in and used German Shepherd dogs to smell out air holes. The Việt Cộng, however, smothered the holes in garlic to deter the dogs. They also used cotton from the cotton tree to stifle the smoke from cooking. Nevertheless 40,000 people were killed in the tunnels in ten years. Later, realising that the tunnels might also yield valuable intelligence, volunteer 'tunnel rats' from the South Vietnam army were sent into the earth to capture prisoners.

Củ Chi District was a free-fire zone and was assaulted using the full battery of ecological warfare. Defoliants were sprayed and 20-tonne ploughs carved up the area in the search for tunnels. Later, the tunnels were carpet-bombed, with 50,000 tonnes dropped on the area in ten years. The Việt Cộng littered the land with booby traps that are the stuff of nightmares, and some of these have been reconstructed as exhibits for visitors to gawp at.

There are two sections to visit – Bến Đình and Bến Dược – and both offer a similar experience. At Bến Đình (An Nhơn Tây), visitors are shown an antique but interesting film of the tunnels during the war, before being taken into the tunnels and seeing some of the rooms and the booby traps that the GIs encountered. There's also a firing range where you can try your hand at firing an ancient AK47. Bến Dược (Phú Mỹ Hưng, Củ Chi) has a temple in memory of the Saigonese killed; the exterior is covered in mosaic murals. It stands in front of a rather beautiful sculpture of a tear called 'Symbol of the Country's Spiritual Soul'. Near the tunnels is the Củ Chi graveyard for patriots, with 8,000 graves and a striking bas-relief of Soviet Realist images along the perimeter of the entrance.

Most visitors reach Củ Chi on a tour or charter a car. It is also possible to ride a motorbike from Hồ Chí Minh City, but the road is becoming increasingly dangerous. Though you can just turn up and jump on a tour, it's highly recommended to book an alternative tour with an expert guide in Hồ Chí Minh City through Old Compass Travel or Les Rives (page 455). The Old Compass Travel tour includes lunch in their café; the Les Rives tour beats the traffic and arrives at the Củ Chi Tunnels by speedboat.

CẦN GIỜ BIOSPHERE RESERVE At the other end of the city you'll find the Cần Giờ Biosphere Reserve, about 50km southeast of District 1. Cần Giờ is a coastal district known for its vast mangrove forests. The area was severely affected by Agent Orange during the American War and much of the mangrove forest was destroyed. However, post-war restoration efforts have led to the somewhat successful replanting of the mangroves, and today the 75,000ha reserve is recognised as a UNESCO-listed site for its diversity of plant and animal species, including saltwater crocodile (*Crocodylus porosus*), king cobras (*Ophiophagus hannah*) and spot-billed pelican (*Pelecanus philippensis*). The district has a population of around 70,000, but most of this is uninhabitable mangrove forest. Much like the Củ Chi Tunnels, it's possible to turn up at the reserve unannounced at one of the tourist zones – like Monkey Island (Long Hòa, Cần Giờ District; 35,000VND) – and see some animals. The journey there by road includes a ferry crossing from Nhà Bè District to Cần Giờ District, making it hard to believe that you're still in Vietnam's biggest city. But you'll get the most out of an experience on an organised tour from Hồ Chí Minh City. Les Rives (page 455) offers boat tours through the reserve.

Appendix 1

MENU DECODER

RICE

Cơm	steamed rice
Xôi	sticky rice
Cháo	rice porridge
Cơm rang (in the north)/*cơm chiên* (in the centre and south)	fried rice

Popular rice dishes

Cơm tấm	rice with grilled pork cutlet, a fried egg, pickles, tomato and cucumber. Popular in Saigon and the south.
Xôi xéo	sticky rice with mung bean, deep-fried shallots and various meats and vegetables. Popular in the north.
Cháo sườn	rice porridge with pork ribs. Popular in the north.
Cơm rang dưa bò	fried rice with pickles and beef. Popular in the north.
Cơm chiên hải sản	fried rice with seafood. Popular along the coast.

NOODLES Most noodles come in noodle soup form, but with *phở*, *bánh đa*, *miến* and *mì* dishes, you can sometimes ask for *trộn* ('mixed'; the word used in the north) or *khô* ('dry'; the word used in the south) to indicate that you want the broth served on the side.

Phở	flat rice noodles shaped like Italian linguine, but thinner and wider
Bún	round rice noodles shaped like Italian vermicelli
Bánh canh	thick tapioca noodles shaped like Japanese udon
Bánh đa	browned flat rice noodles shaped like Italian tagliatelle
Miến	round glass noodles
Mì	vague term to describe noodles usually (but not always) made with wheat

Popular noodle dishes

Phở bò/gà	beef/chicken noodle soup. Popular in the north and the south (less so in the centre).
Bún bò	spicy beef noodle soup originating in Huế but popular throughout the country.
Bánh canh cá lóc	tapioca noodle soup served with snakehead fish.
Bánh đa cua	browned noodle soup with crab. Popular in Hải Phòng.
Miến ngan	glass noodle soup with goose. Popular in Hanoi.
Mì tôm	instant noodles. Popular and ubiquitous.

SAVOURY CAKES (BÁNH)
Popular bánh dishes

Bánh mì	short, fat French baguettes packed with cold cuts, pickles and vegetables.
Bánh xèo	savoury rice pancake served with pork shrimp and beansprouts. Popular in the south.
Bánh Huế	refers to a handful of savoury cakes from Huế. Some wrapped in a banana leaf.
Bánh cuốn	wet rice-paper dumpling-like rolls with minced pork and mushrooms. Popular in the north.

VEGETABLES

Rau muống	water spinach	*Cải xanh*	mustard greens
Cải ngọt	choy sum	*Cà rốt*	carrot
Cải thìa	bok choy	*Khoai lang*	sweet potato leaves
Bầu	bottle gourd	*Măng*	bamboo shoots
Bí đao	winter melon	*Giá*	bean sprouts
Bí đỏ	pumpkin	*Mồng tơi*	Malabar spinach
Mướp	loofah	*Ớt*	chilli
Cà tím	aubergine	*Hành*	onion
Su su	chayote	*Tỏi*	garlic
Ngọn su su	chayote leaves	*Đạu*	tofu
Đậu bắp	okra		

HERBS

Rau mùi	coriander	*Diếp cá*	fish mint
Ngò gai	sawtooth coriander	*Bạc hà*	mint
Tía tô	perilla leaves	*Húng quế*	Thai basil

DIPPING SAUCES

Nước mắm pha	fish sauce	*Tương ớt*	chilli sauce
Nước mắm chua ngọt	sweet and sour fish sauce	*Muối tiêu chanh*	salt, pepper and lime dip
Nước mắm gừng	ginger fish sauce	*Sốt đen*	hoisin sauce
Nước tương	thick, homemade soy sauce	*Tương cà*	tomato ketchup (common for fried dishes, especially with children)
Xi dầu	thin, industrial soy sauce		
Mắm tôm	fermented shrimp paste	*Sốt ma-o-ne*	mayonnaise

MEAT

Bò	beef	*Vịt*	duck
Lợn (in the north)/ *Heo* (in the centre and south)	pork	*Cừu*	lamb
		Dê	goat
		Thỏ	rabbit
Gà	chicken	*Chim*	bird meat

FISH AND SEAFOOD

Cá	fish	*Cá ngừ*	tuna
Cá hồi	salmon	*Cá mú*	grouper

POPULAR RESTAURANT DISHES

If you find yourself in a far-flung restaurant and you're having trouble ordering, point at the names of these dishes for a varied and healthy meal. Kitchens should have the ingredients to make most of these dishes.

Đậu sốt cà chua	tofu with tomato sauce
Đậu tẩm hành	tofu with spring onions
Gà rang gừng	chicken fried with ginger
Gà xào nấm	chicken stir-fried with mushrooms
Bò xào sả ớt	beef stir-fried with lemongrass and chilli
Bò xào dứa	beef stir-fried with pineapple
Thịt kho	braised pork
Thịt luộc	boiled pork
Cá chiên	crispy fried fish
Cá kho	braised fish
Trứng tráng	omelette
Rau muống xào tỏi	water spinach stir-fried with garlic
Rau củ luộc	boiled assorted vegetables
Cơm	steamed rice
Canh chua	sour soup

Cá trích	herring	*Hàu*	oyster
Cá lóc	snakehead fish	*Ngao*	clam
Tôm	shrimp	*Nghêu*	hard-shell clam
Cua	crab	*Ốc*	snail
Ghẹ	swimming crab	*Sò*	scallop
Mực	squid	*Tôm hùm*	lobster
Bạch tuộc	octopus	*Sứa*	jellyfish

FRUIT

Xoài	mango	*Lê*	pear
Chuối	banana	*Bơ*	avocado
Dừa	coconut	*Mận*	plum
Táo	apple	*Hồng*	persimmon
Cam	orange	*Na (Mãng cầu ta)*	sugar apple
Chanh	lime	*Mãng cầu xiêm*	soursop
Quýt	tangerine	*Chôm chôm*	rambutan
Dưa hấu	watermelon	*Nhãn*	longan
Dưa lê	cantaloupe	*Vải*	lychee
Dứa (in the north)/ *Thơm* (in the centre and south)	pineapple	*Thanh long*	dragon fruit
		Đu đủ	papaya
		Dâu tây	strawberry
Mít	jackfruit	*Nho*	grape
Sầu riêng	durian	*Lựu*	pomegranate
Ổi	guava	*Bưởi*	pomelo

COOKING STYLES

Nướng	grilled	*Kho*	braised or caramelised

Rang/chiên	fried	*Xào*	stir-fried
Hấp	steamed	*Quay*	roasted
Luộc	boiled		

Appendix 2

FURTHER INFORMATION

BOOKS

Fiction

Vietnamese novels available in English

Bảo Ninh *The Sorrow of War* Secker & Warburg, 1993. Set during and after the American War, this is a harrowing, non-linear exploration of trauma and loss, offering an unflinching account of the war's enduring impact on the psyche of a soldier. The book was banned after publication in Vietnam due to its raw portrayal of the war, but this was lifted in 2006.

Dương Thu Hương *Paradise of the Blind* William Morrow Paperbacks, 2002. Critiques ideological rigidity and examines personal sacrifices in Communist-era Vietnam, illuminating the tension between loyalty to tradition and the yearning for individual freedom.

✷ Nguyễn Phan Quế Mai *The Mountains Sing* Oneworld, 2020. Spanning the 20th century, this offers a multi-generational saga of a Vietnamese family's resilience through colonialism, war and upheaval.

Nguyễn Phan Quế Mai *Dust Child* Oneworld, 2023. Examines the lives of Amerasians, exploring themes of identity, abandonment and redemption, revealing the lingering personal scars of the American War.

✷ Vũ Trọng Phụng *Dumb Luck* Ann Arbor, 2002. Set in colonial Hanoi, *Dumb Luck* is a hilarious satirical critique of Vietnam's rapid modernisation and its corrupt overlords, exposing the absurdities and contradictions of colonial rule and the erosion of traditional values.

Vietnamese short-story collections available in English

Bảo Ninh *Hanoi at Midnight* Texas Tech University Press, 2023. Poignant collection exploring the lingering effects of the American War on Vietnamese society, capturing the intersection of personal memory and collective trauma with Bảo Ninh's signature introspection.

Lê Minh Khuê *The Stars, The Earth, The River* Northwestern University Press, 1997. Spotlights the lives of women during and after the war, weaving intimate stories of courage and sacrifice amid the backdrop of a transforming country.

✷ Nguyễn Huy Thiệp *The General Retires* Oxford University Press, 1992. Seminal collection that critiques Vietnam's post-war society, blending sharp realism and biting satire to explore themes of power, morality and the complexities of familial and societal expectations. Nguyễn Huy Thiệp's liberal use of magical realism has led commentators to draw parallels with Gabriel García Márquez.

Nguyễn Quang Lập *Behind the Red Mist* Northwestern University Press, 1998. Surreal collection delving into the scars of war and its haunting legacy, blending magical realism with raw emotion to portray a Vietnam shaped by suffering and resilience.

Vietnamese poetry available in English

Hồ Xuân Hương *Spring Essence: The Poetry of Hồ Xuân Hương* Copper Canyon Press, 2000. Collection celebrating the bold and subversive voice of Hồ Xuân Hương, whose 18th-century poetry combines wit and sensuality to critique societal norms and honour female resilience.

Nguyễn Du *Truyện Kiều: The Tale of Kiều* Vintage Books, 1973. Originally published in 1820 and considered Vietnam's literary masterpiece (though, controversially, the plot was likely based on a 17th-century Chinese novel), *Truyện Kiều* is an epic poem of romance, tragedy and social critique.

Trương, Monique *The Women Carry River Water* University of Massachusetts Press, 1997. Powerful collection highlighting the strength and perseverance of Vietnamese women across generations.

Western novels set in Vietnam

Duras, Marguerite *The Lover* Flamingo, 1985 (English translation). Semi-autobiographical exploration of forbidden love, class and cultural tensions, reflecting the personal and political complexities of colonial Indochina. Perhaps best known for the 1992 film adaptation (page 491).

✷ Greene, Graham *The Quiet American* William Heinemann, 1955. Set in French Indochina, *The Quiet American* examines the naivety and hubris of American intervention through a complex love triangle, serving as a prescient allegory for the looming American War.

Le Guin, Ursula K *The Word for World is Forest* Doubleday, 1972. Not set in Vietnam, but a distant planet in the universe of Le Guin's seminal Hainish Cycle series, this is allegorical of the misguided arrogance and cruelty of the American War.

✷ Nguyễn Thanh Việt *The Sympathizer* Grove Press, 2015. Gripping tale of duality and betrayal, exploring the fractured identity of a Vietnamese double agent. Adapted as an HBO mini-series in 2024.

Vương, Ocean *On Earth We Were Briefly Gorgeous* Penguin, 2019. Set in the United States but deeply rooted in the Vietnamese diaspora, this is an epistolary novel reflecting the intergenerational trauma of the American War and its lasting scars on identity, memory and belonging. Explores queer themes throughout.

Visual books

Garel, Alexander *Modernist Architecture in Vietnam*, 2021. Comprehensive visual collection of Vietnam's unique modernist architecture from across the country.

Schenck, Mel *Southern Vietnamese Modernist Architecture*, 2020. In-depth study of the modernist movement in South Vietnam, showcasing the creative and forward-thinking designs that defined the erstwhile country's urban landscape from the 1940s to 1980s.

Trần, GB *Vietnamerica: A Family's Journey* Random House, 2010. Visually stunning graphic memoir recounting Trần's family's immigration story, weaving together personal, cultural and historical threads.

History and politics

Đặng Thùy Trâm *Last Night I Dreamed of Peace* (Đêm Qua Tôi Mơ Thấy Hòa Bình), Harmony Books 2007. Based on her wartime diaries, young female doctor Đặng Thùy Trâm offers a poignant and deeply personal account amid the horrors of the American War.

Doling, Tim *Exploring Huế* Thế Giới Publishers, 2018. Doling's huge and comprehensive guide to Huế is proof that the former imperial capital deserves more attention that it gets.

Doling, Tim *Exploring Quảng Nam* Thế Giới Publishers, 2020. Doling's in-depth guide to Quảng Nam and a major source for this guide, with walking tours for Hội An, Đà Nẵng, Mỹ Sơn and Tam Kỳ.

Doling, Tim *Exploring Saigon-Chợ Lớn – Vanishing Heritage of Hồ Chí Minh City* Thế Giới Publishers, 2019. A deep dive into Hồ Chí Minh City's history and heritage neighbourhoods, with walking tours written by resident historian Tim Doling.

Hastings, Max *Vietnam: An Epic Tragedy, 1945–1975* William Collins, 2018. Sweeping account of the American War; Hastings attempts a balanced and deeply human perspective on the conflict, valiantly capturing experiences with vivid detail.

Hayton, Bill *Vietnam: Rising Dragon* Yale University Press, 2010. Engaging and readable account of Vietnam's rapid economic and social transformation, this book examines the country's rise as a dynamic force in Southeast Asia amid persistent political constraints.

Howland, Carol *Hanoi of a Thousand Years* Mynah Bird Books, 2018. Intertwines historical milestones with personal observations, celebrating the city's enduring legacy as the cultural and political heart of Vietnam.

Scott, James C *The Art of Not Being Governed: An Anarchist History of Upland Southeast Asia* Yale University Press, 2009. Provocative exploration of the stateless highlands of Southeast Asia (Zomia), this book sheds light on how marginalised communities resisted state control, offering parallels to Vietnam's historical struggles.

Sheehan, Neil *A Bright Shining Lie* Random House, 1988. Pulitzer Prize-winning account of the American War, examining the life of Lieutenant Colonel John Paul Vann to expose the flawed strategies and moral contradictions of the American intervention. Neil Sheehan's meticulous research and vivid storytelling offer a scathing critique of US hubris.

Culture and society

Jamieson, Neil L *Understanding Vietnam* University of California Press, 1993. Comprehensive sociopolitical analysis delving into the country's history, culture and enduring spirit, providing profound insights into Vietnam's complexities and its transformation through centuries of conflict and upheaval.

Nguyễn, Luke *The Food of Vietnam* Hardie Grant, 2013. Vibrant exploration of Vietnamese cuisine that offers an immersive journey through regional dishes, cultural traditions and personal stories, celebrating the flavours and heritage of Vietnam.

Stedman, Nicholas and Fanchette, Sylvie *Discovering Craft Villages in Vietnam: Ten Itineraries Around Hanoi* French National Research Institute for Sustainable Development, 2009. Large, picture-filled book detailing the history of Hanoi's craft villages, with various do-it-yourself itineraries.

FILM AND TELEVISION

Vietnamese films

Chuyện Của Pao (Pao's Story, 2006). Attempts a heartfelt exploration of familial bonds and cultural traditions in a mountainous Hmong community, with cinematography that captures the otherworldly landscapes of Northern Vietnam.

Cyclo (1995). Paints a harrowing portrait of urban poverty in 1990s Hồ Chí Minh City. Trần Anh Hùng's masterful direction captures the chaos and despair of a young cyclo driver's descent into the criminal underworld with outstanding cinematography.

Đào, phở và piano (2024). *Peach Blossom, Phở and Piano* is a government-funded and profusely patriotic tour de force that offers insight into how today's bigwigs want the younger generations to understand the fight for independence. Though an unashamed exercise in contemporary propaganda, the film offers flashes of brilliance.

Đời Cát (Sandy Lives, 1999). Portrays the struggles of a post-war love triangle with cinematography that captures the desolate beauty of Vietnam's central coastline.

Furie (2019). Follows Veronica Ngô as Hai Phượng, a former gang member turned protective mother on a relentless quest to rescue her kidnapped daughter. The plot is absurd and implausible, and at times completely incoherent, but the film entertains, with high-octane fight sequences and emotional depth.

Go-Go Sisters (2018). Melodramatic, heartwarming, comical and nostalgic tale of friendship and reconciliation. The film alternates between past and present as estranged friends reconnect, reliving their youth in a camply styled 1970s Đà Lạt.

Hương Ga (2014). Tells the rise and fall and rise again of Vietnam's most notorious female gangster (played by Trương Ngọc Ánh). Based on true events, the film combines energetic fight sequences and high-stakes drama to explore themes of resilience and betrayal in Saigon's criminal underworld.

Inside The Yellow Cocoon Shell (2023). Directed by Phạm Thiên Ân and a masterful exploration of grief, faith, and belonging, the film's protagonist journeys through rural Vietnam, confronting loss and searching for meaning. At almost 3 hours, the film is a slog, but remains one of the most deeply reflective and artful pieces in contemporary Vietnamese art-house cinema.

Mùi Đu Đủ Xanh (The Scent of Green Papaya, 1993). Offers a meditative glimpse into 1950s Vietnam through the eyes of a young servant girl. Trần Anh Hùng's excellent direction and serene cinematography capture the subtleties of daily life in a way that is emotionally resonant.

The Rebel (2007). Showcases Vietnam's struggle for independence through fantastical martial arts choreography. *The Rebel* is by no means a great film, but Johnny Trí Nguyễn and Veronica Ngô deliver dynamic performances, balancing visceral fight sequences with heartfelt drama.

✷ *Ròm* (2019). Heartbreaking and stunningly shot, *Ròm* tells the story of a lottery-ticket hawker in an impoverished housing estate in Hồ Chí Minh City. The director grappled with the Ministry of Culture for years to allow the award-winning film to be screened to domestic audiences due to the sensitivity of the subject matter.

✷ *Song Lang* (2018). Supremely touching, with delicate queer undercurrents, *Song Lang*, set in 1980s Hồ Chí Minh City, is undoubtedly one of the best Vietnamese dramas in recent years. The story follows Linh Phụng (played by Isaac), a *cải lương* performer, and Dũng (played by Liên Bỉnh Phát), a socially alienated gangster.

Western films set in Vietnam

✷ *Apocalypse Now* (1979). Epic and generation-defining but nevertheless an appallingly one-sided depiction of the American War. Referring to the war, director Francis Ford Coppola famously said 'This film is Vietnam' – and yet there are no Vietnamese characters and the film was shot in the Philippines. A discerning and critical eye is required.

Da 5 Bloods (2020). Though it received rave reviews for its worthy portrayal of the Black American experience of the war, Spike Lee's *Da 5 Bloods* ultimately falls into the same traps of falsely portraying Vietnam as a dangerous and lawless place, with poorly rendered Vietnamese characters.

Full Metal Jacket (1987). Stanley Kubrick's cinematic take on the American War delivers stark realism and biting satire, though its shift in tone between training and combat sections creates a somewhat disjointed narrative.

✷ *Good Morning Vietnam* (1987). War comedy with an energetic performance from the late Robin Williams. Balances humour and poignancy, though its light-hearted tone sometimes overshadows the setting's deeper complexities.

Indochine (1992). *Indochine* explores love and colonial tensions against stunning Vietnamese backdrops, though its lengthy run time occasionally slows its otherwise sweeping and visually opulent narrative. Filmed in stunning Vietnamese locations, including Hạ Long Bay and Ninh Bình, the film attempts to capture the grandeur and complexity of 1930s French Indochina.

The Lover (1992). Sensual and at times steamy forbidden love drama, with stunning cinematography and an evocative performance by Jane March. The film is based on the semi-autobiographical novel by Marguerite Duras. Shot in southern Vietnam, primarily Hồ Chí Minh City, Cần Thơ and Sa Đéc.

Platoon (1986). Gritty war drama with a powerful performance by Charlie Sheen. *Platoon* captures the chaos and moral ambiguity of Vietnam, balancing visceral combat scenes with a deeply human exploration of loyalty and conflict. Written and directed by Oliver Stone, an American War veteran himself.

The Quiet American (2002). The first Hollywood blockbuster filmed in Vietnam after the war, *The Quiet American* is relaxed viewing but only captures some of the novella's genius. Michael Caine is a convincing Fowler, a weary and cantankerous British journalist.

Documentary films and series

Children of the Mist (2021). Invites a raw, intimate glimpse into the life of a Hmong girl in rural Vietnam and the practice of 'bride kidnapping.' Diễm Hà Lệ's documentary captures the tensions between tradition and modernity with unflinching honesty.

✷ *A Crack in the Mountain* (2022). Explores the discovery, rediscovery and surveying of Hang Sơn Đoòng, the world's largest cave, with breathtaking visuals and themes of environmental protection and human impact.

Last Days of Vietnam (2014). Harrowing documentary capturing the chaos and heroism of the final days of the American War, as servicemen attempted evacuations before North Vietnam's imminent arrival.

✷ *The Vietnam War* (2017). Ken Burns's ten-part series is a valiant attempt at a balanced, emotionally resonant exploration of the war's human and historical impact through a blend of archival footage and interviews with some of the theatre's most important actors.

PODCASTS

A Vietnam Podcast Prolific podcaster Niall Mackay covers a wide range of topics with an eclectic collection of guests and diligently releases a new episode every few days.

The Vietnam Weekly Podcast American journalist Mike Tatarski talks to a slew of international guests about the myriad issues facing Vietnam, from confrontations with China in the East Sea to wildlife conservation.

You Don't Know Vietnam British entrepreneur, rapper and podcaster Ian Paynton seeks to challenge preconceptions (hence the title) by interviewing Vietnamese and Vietnam-based guests who are shaping the country's future in creative ways.

WEBSITES

News

w **vietnamnews.vn** Vietnam's official (ie: government) English-language print and online newspaper, with predominantly dry but up-to-date articles and the occasional thought-provoking op-ed.

w **e.vnexpress.net** Arguably Vietnam's most compelling English-language news source, with journalists focusing on areas of interest for the international community, including foreign affairs, culture and tourism.

w **tuoitrenews.vn** One of Vietnam's more daring and critical newspapers, with reasonably comprehensive English-language coverage.

Culture

w **saigoneer.com** Vietnam's most highly respected and long-running online international newspaper, covering offbeat topics and unsung stories, with some informed guest writers and superb photo essays.

W historicvietnam.com Intermittently updated but well-researched evergreen articles on various heritage neighbourhoods and buildings in Vietnam, put together by Hồ Chí Minh City-based historian Tim Doling, who helped with the history section in *Chapter 1* (page 7).

Travel

W vietnam.travel The quality of Vietnam's official tourism website has waned in recent years, but there are still some useful and informative articles to be found deeper in the archives.

W joshuazukas.com Official website of the author of this guidebook, which acts as an online portfolio showcasing recent long-reads, itineraries, guides and books.

W vietnamcoracle.com Invaluable resource for independent travellers, with an emphasis on motorbike guides, written by Tom Divers, author of *Chapter 12*.

W jovelchan.com Honest reviews and round-ups of Vietnam's newest restaurants and bars, put together by Hồ Chí Minh City-based Singaporean Jovel Chan, a bona fide food and drink expert and keen advocate for the country's burgeoning dining scene.

W noisehanoi.com Probably the most accessible list of the kinds of gigs that are likely to appeal to the more cosmopolitan wing of Hanoi's music-loving community.

W noisesaigon.com Much like Noise Hanoi, but for the southern metropolis.

W thedotmagazine.com Crisply presented information detailing the ins and outs of Vietnam's myriad urban food scenes, put together by impassioned long-term resident David Kaye.

W fvheritage.org Hanoi-based Friends of Vietnam Heritage is run by a diligent and discerning team of volunteers who arrange events and talks, mainly in the capital.

Index

Page numbers in **bold** indicate the most important entries in a list; those in *italics* indicate maps. Alphabetisation is in English and does not account for Vietnamese letters and diacritics.

INDEX OF ADVERTISERS

THE BRADT STORY

In the beginning

It all began in 1974 on an Amazon river barge. During an 18-month trip through South America, two adventurous young backpackers – Hilary Bradt and her then husband, George – decided to write about the hiking trails they had discovered through the Andes. *Backpacking Along Ancient Ways in Peru and Bolivia* included the very first descriptions of the Inca Trail. It was the start of a colourful journey to becoming one of the best-loved travel publishers in the world; you can read the full story on our website (**bradtguides.com/ourstory**).

Getting there first

Hilary quickly gained a reputation for being a true travel pioneer, and in the 1980s she started to focus on guides to places overlooked by other publishers. The Bradt Guides list became a roll call of guidebook 'firsts'. We published the first guide to Madagascar, followed by Mauritius, Czechoslovakia and Vietnam. The 1990s saw the beginning of our extensive coverage of Africa: Tanzania, Uganda, South Africa, and Eritrea. Later, post-conflict guides became a feature: Rwanda, Mozambique, Angola, and Sierra Leone, as well as the first standalone guides to the Baltic States following the fall of the Iron Curtain, and the first post-war guides to Bosnia, Kosovo and Albania.

Comprehensive – and with a conscience

Today, we are the world's largest independently owned travel publisher, with more than 200 titles. However, our ethos remains unchanged. Hilary is still keenly involved, and **we still get there first**: two-thirds of Bradt guides have no direct competition.

But we don't just get there first. Our guides are also known for being **more comprehensive** than any other series. We avoid templates and tick-lists. Each guide is a one-of-a-kind expression of an expert author's interests, knowledge and enthusiasm for telling it how it really is.

And a commitment to wildlife, conservation and respect for local communities has always been at the heart of our books. Bradt Guides was **championing sustainable travel** before any other guidebook publisher. We even have a series dedicated to Slow Travel in the UK, award-winning books that explore the country with a passion and depth you'll find nowhere else.

Thank you!

We can only do what we do because of the support of readers like you – people who value less-obvious experiences, less-visited places and a more thoughtful approach to travel. Those who, like us, take travel seriously.

Bradt GUIDES

TRAVEL TAKEN SERIOUSLY